Communications in Computer and Information Science 2844

Rationale

The CCIS series is devoted to the publication of proceedings of computer science conferences. Its aim is to efficiently disseminate original research results in informatics in printed and electronic form. While the focus is on publication of peer-reviewed full papers presenting mature work, inclusion of reviewed short papers reporting on work in progress is welcome, too. Besides globally relevant meetings with internationally representative program committees guaranteeing a strict peer-reviewing and paper selection process, conferences run by societies or of high regional or national relevance are also considered for publication.

Topics

The topical scope of CCIS spans the entire spectrum of informatics ranging from foundational topics in the theory of computing to information and communications science and technology and a broad variety of interdisciplinary application fields.

Information for Volume Editors and Authors

Publication in CCIS is free of charge. No royalties are paid, however, we offer registered conference participants temporary free access to the online version of the conference proceedings on SpringerLink (http://link.springer.com) by means of an http referrer from the conference website and/or a number of complimentary printed copies, as specified in the official acceptance email of the event.

CCIS proceedings can be published in time for distribution at conferences or as post-proceedings, and delivered in the form of printed books and/or electronically as USBs and/or e-content licenses for accessing proceedings at SpringerLink. Furthermore, CCIS proceedings are included in the CCIS electronic book series hosted in the SpringerLink digital library at http://link.springer.com/bookseries/7899. Conferences publishing in CCIS are allowed to use our online conference service (Meteor) for managing the whole proceedings lifecycle (from submission and reviewing to preparing for publication) free of charge.

Publication process

The language of publication is exclusively English. Authors publishing in CCIS have to sign the Springer CCIS copyright transfer form, however, they are free to use their material published in CCIS for substantially changed, more elaborate subsequent publications elsewhere. For the preparation of the camera-ready papers/files, authors have to strictly adhere to the Springer CCIS Authors' Instructions and are strongly encouraged to use the CCIS LaTeX style files or templates.

Abstracting/Indexing

CCIS is abstracted/indexed in DBLP, Google Scholar, EI-Compendex, Mathematical Reviews, SCImago, Scopus. CCIS volumes are also submitted for the inclusion in ISI Proceedings.

How to start

To start the evaluation of your proposal for inclusion in the CCIS series, please send an e-mail to ccis@springer.com

Roshan N. Rajapakse · Yohani S. Ranasinghe ·
Randil Pushpananda ·
Manjusri Wickramasinghe · Thiemo Voigt
Editors

Advances in ICT for Emerging Regions

25th International Conference, ICTer 2025
Colombo, Sri Lanka, November 19–20, 2025
Proceedings

Editors
Roshan N. Rajapakse
University of Colombo School of Computing
Colombo, Sri Lanka

Yohani S. Ranasinghe
University of Colombo School of Computing
Colombo, Sri Lanka

Randil Pushpananda
University of Colombo School of Computing
Colombo, Sri Lanka

Manjusri Wickramasinghe
University of Colombo School of Computing
Colombo, Sri Lanka

Thiemo Voigt
Uppsala University
Uppsala, Sweden

ISSN 1865-0929 ISSN 1865-0937 (electronic)
Communications in Computer and Information Science
ISBN 978-981-92-0136-5 ISBN 978-981-92-0137-2 (eBook)
https://doi.org/10.1007/978-981-92-0137-2

This Springer imprint is published by the registered company Springer Nature Singapore Pte Ltd.
The registered company address is: 152 Beach Road, #21-01/04 Gateway East, Singapore 189721, Singapore

Preface

The 25th International Conference on Advances in ICT for Emerging Regions (ICTer 2025) was held on November 19–20, 2025, at the Marino Beach Hotel in Colombo, Sri Lanka. ICTer continues the legacy of the International Information Technology Conference (IITC), which has been conducted annually since 1998. Over the past twenty-five years, this conference series has evolved into a premier venue for disseminating research in ICT, with a particular focus on innovations that address the challenges of emerging and developing regions. The conference continually facilitates collaboration between local industry and a global academic community with the aim of encouraging sustainable, scalable ICT solutions with regional relevance.

ICTer 2025 received 146 submissions, which underwent a double-blind peer-review process. Each manuscript was reviewed by a minimum of three reviewers, with additional reviews sought when required to ensure consistency. Based on the reviewers' evaluations and the Program Committee's deliberations, 21 papers were accepted as full papers and 10 submissions as posters, resulting in an acceptance rate of 21.2%. All contributions were selected based on their originality, methodological rigor, technical contribution, and relevance to the scope of ICTer.

The papers in this proceedings volume are organized under several key thematic areas that reflect emerging trends and interdisciplinary advancements within the ICT domain. These themes include: (1) AI-Assisted Diagnostics & Medical Imaging, (2) Language, Speech & Text Processing, (3) Environment & Sustainability, (4) Population & Behavioral Analytics, (5) Sentiment, Music & Acoustic Processing, (6) Systems, Security & Privacy.

We express our sincere gratitude to the members of the steering committee, the Technical Program Committee, and the external reviewers, both local and international, for their contributions. We also extend our appreciation to the Springer CCIS editorial team for their continued guidance throughout the publication process. Finally, we are grateful to all authors who submitted their work to ICTer 2025; their efforts and scholarship made this volume possible.

Roshan N. Rajapakse
Yohani S. Ranasinghe
Randil Pushpananda
Manjusri Wickramasinghe
Thiemo Voigt

Organization

Conference Co-chairs

Randil Pushpananda	University of Colombo School of Computing, Sri Lanka
Manjusri Wickramasinghe	University of Colombo School of Computing, Sri Lanka

Conference Secretariat

Madhumali Dhanawardana	University of Colombo School of Computing, Sri Lanka
Madara Jayarathna	University of Colombo School of Computing, Sri Lanka

Advisory Committee

D. A. S. Atukorale	University of Colombo School of Computing, Sri Lanka
T. N. K. De Zoysa	University of Colombo School of Computing, Sri Lanka
Thiemo Voigt	Uppsala University, Sweden
Anuja Dharmaratne	Monash University, Australia
Yakub Sebastian	Charles Darwin University, Australia
Fui Chin Hiew	Xiamen University, Malaysia

Technical Program Committee Chairs

Roshan N. Rajapakse	University of Colombo School of Computing, Sri Lanka
Yohani S. Ranasinghe	University of Colombo School of Computing, Sri Lanka

Publication Chair

Mathangi Krishnathasan	University of Colombo School of Computing, Sri Lanka

Secretary

Buddhika Disanayake	University of Colombo School of Computing, Sri Lanka

Program Committee Members

Kamalanath Hewagamage	University of Colombo School of Computing, Sri Lanka
D. D. Karunaratna	University of Colombo School of Computing, Sri Lanka
Prasad Wimalaratne	University of Colombo School of Computing, Sri Lanka
G. K. A. Dias	University of Colombo School of Computing, Sri Lanka
M. G. N. A. S. Fernando	University of Colombo School of Computing, Sri Lanka
T. N. K. De Zoysa	University of Colombo School of Computing, Sri Lanka
H. A. Caldera	University of Colombo School of Computing, Sri Lanka
Anuradha Mahasinghe	University of Colombo, Sri Lanka
Anuja Dharmaratne	Monash University, Australia
Arosha K. Bandara	Open University, UK
W. A. Indika	University of Ruhuna, Sri Lanka
Adrian David Cheok	Nanjing University of Information Science and Technology, China
Ajantha Athukorala	University of Colombo School of Computing, Sri Lanka
M. I. E. Wickramasinghe	University of Colombo School of Computing, Sri Lanka
Randil Pushpananda	University of Colombo School of Computing, Sri Lanka
Yakub Sebastian	Charles Darwin University, Australia
Fui Chin Hiew	Xiamen University, Malaysia
Leong Kuan Yew	A.I. Systems Research Co. Ltd., Kyoto, Japan

Ian Oakley	Korea Advanced Institute of Science & Technology, South Korea
Harsha Perera	Monash University, Australia
Anuradha Madugalla	Deakin University, Australia
Thushari Atapattu	University of Adelaide, Australia
Thilina Halloluwa	University of Queensland, Australia
Anushka Vidanage	Australian National University, Australia
Dilini Samarasinghe	Australian National University, Australia
Ishari Amarasinghe	Pompeu Fabra University, Spain
Mohammed Moussa	Monash University, Malaysia
Udeni Jayasinghe	University of Reading, UK
Thilina Pathirage	University of Adelaide, Australia
David Olayemi Alebiosu	Sunway University, Malaysia
Dilshani H. Mallikarachchi	Xiamen University, Malaysia
K. Thabotharan	University of Jaffna, Sri Lanka
Deepika S. Seneviratne	University of Sri Jayewardenepura, Sri Lanka
Dharshana Kasthurirathna	Sri Lanka Institute of Information Technology, Sri Lanka
W. G. C. W. Kumara	South Eastern University, Sri Lanka
Buddhi Gamage	University of Canberra, Australia
Kaushalya Disanayaka	Brennan, Sri Lanka
Asanka Sayakkara	University of Colombo School of Computing, Sri Lanka
Gihan Seneviratne	University of Colombo School of Computing, Sri Lanka
K. D. Sandaruwan	University of Colombo School of Computing, Sri Lanka
K. H. E. L. W. Hettiarachchi	University of Colombo School of Computing, Sri Lanka
Kasun Gunawardana	University of Colombo School of Computing, Sri Lanka
Kasun Karunanayaka	University of Colombo School of Computing, Sri Lanka
Lasanthi Silva	University of Colombo School of Computing, Sri Lanka
Nalin Ranasinghe	University of Colombo School of Computing, Sri Lanka
T. A. Weerasinghe	University of Colombo School of Computing, Sri Lanka
C. I. Keppitiyagama	University of Colombo School of Computing, Sri Lanka
T. Sritharan	University of Colombo School of Computing, Sri Lanka

S. S. P. Mataraarachchi	University of Colombo School of Computing, Sri Lanka
M. G. D. K. Fernando	University of Colombo School of Computing, Sri Lanka
W. V. Welgama	University of Colombo School of Computing, Sri Lanka
K. P. M. K. Silva	University of Colombo School of Computing, Sri Lanka
R. M. U. A. Rathnayake	University of Colombo School of Computing, Sri Lanka
Dinusha Thilini	University of Colombo School of Computing, Sri Lanka
C. R. Wijesinghe	University of Colombo School of Computing, Sri Lanka
R. A. C. Ransinghe	University of Colombo School of Computing, Sri Lanka
S. D. Gamage	University of Colombo School of Computing, Sri Lanka
Ishani Fonseka	University of Colombo School of Computing, Sri Lanka
Jayathma Chathurangani	University of Colombo School of Computing, Sri Lanka
L. A. S. M. Gunathilaka	University of Colombo School of Computing, Sri Lanka
Mathangi Krishnathasan	University of Colombo School of Computing, Sri Lanka
N. H. P. I. Maduranga	University of Colombo School of Computing, Sri Lanka
R. J. Amaraweera	University of Colombo School of Computing, Sri Lanka
S. Hamsavasini	University of Colombo School of Computing, Sri Lanka
T. N. B. Wijethilake	University of Colombo School of Computing, Sri Lanka
Thilini Lakshika	University of Colombo School of Computing, Sri Lanka
W. R. N. S. Abeyweera	University of Colombo School of Computing, Sri Lanka
Dasun Bamunuarachchi	University of Colombo School of Computing, Sri Lanka
Amod Pathirana	University of Colombo School of Computing, Sri Lanka
Ashen Sannasgama	University of Colombo School of Computing, Sri Lanka

Kenneth Thilakarathna	University of Colombo School of Computing, Sri Lanka
Shakya Rathnaikage	University of Ruhuna, Sri Lanka
Ashmari Pramodya	Nara Institute of Science and Technology, Japan
Ayesha Sanahari	University of Colombo, Sri Lanka
Dilum Gamage	University of Colombo, Sri Lanka
Dinesh Arunatileka	Informatics Institute of Technology, Sri Lanka
A. R. Weerasinghe	Informatics Institute of Technology, Sri Lanka
S. Mahesan	University of Jaffna, Sri Lanka
M. D. R. N. Dayaratne	University of Colombo School of Computing, Sri Lanka
Dulitha Kuruppu	Assetline Corporate Solutions, Sri Lanka
Hemali Ratnayake	Open University of Sri Lanka, Sri Lanka
J. G. S. Rupasinghe	University of Colombo School of Computing, Sri Lanka
Hiran Ekanayake	University of Colombo School of Computing, Sri Lanka
Lakshani Gayanthika	University of Colombo School of Computing, Sri Lanka
Lojenaa Navanesan	University of Vavuniya, Sri Lanka
M. A. S. U. Fernando	University of Colombo School of Computing, Sri Lanka
Nethma Jayawardhane	University of Colombo School of Computing, Sri Lanka
Nethmi Keragala	University of Colombo School of Computing, Sri Lanka
Prasad Wilagama	University of Colombo School of Computing, Sri Lanka
Rangana Madushan	University of Colombo School of Computing, Sri Lanka
Ravi Madanayake	University of Colombo School of Computing, Sri Lanka
Sanjeevani Thilakarathne	University of Colombo School of Computing, Sri Lanka
Xiaoxi Kang	Monash University, Malaysia

Organizer

Technical Sponsors

Sponsors

CAMBIO

softlogic
BEST IN THE BUSINESS
INFORMATION
TECHNOLOGIES
PRIVATE LIMITED

HTH
TASTY CATERERS
ESTABLISHED
— 1980 —

English
Tea Shop
ORGANIC

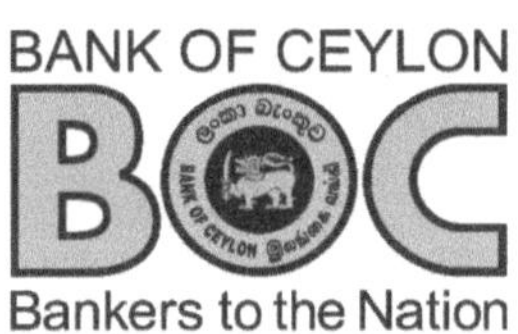
BANK OF CEYLON
BOC
Bankers to the Nation

PEOPLE'S
BANK
Pride of the Nation

WSO2

Contents

AI-Assisted Diagnostics and Medical Imaging

A Hybrid Adaptive Segmentation Pipeline with NURBS Surface Reconstruction for 3D Liver Tumor Modeling

Y. S. Windsor and R. G. N. Meegama(✉)

Department of Computer Science, Faculty of Applied Sciences, University of Sri Jayewardenepura, Gangodawila, Nugegoda, Sri Lanka
as2020406@sci.sjp.ac.lk, rgn@sjp.ac.lk

Abstract. Accurate 3D liver tumor models are essential for surgical planning, radiation therapy dose calculation, and treatment response assessment. Current automated segmentation methods either require extensive training data (deep learning) or lack robustness across varying image quality (classical methods). This paper presents a novel hybrid adaptive segmentation pipeline that automatically switches between intensity-based and spatially-regularized Fuzzy C-Means clustering based on local image quality, followed by graph-cut refinement and NURBS surface reconstruction. The key innovation is the adaptive switching mechanism that maintains segmentation accuracy across diverse CT acquisition protocols without requiring training data. On the LiTS dataset, it achieved competitive accuracy (mean Dice ≈ 0.85) with sub-millimeter surface precision (0.6 mm) and minimal volume bias (3%), demonstrating clinical-grade performance for treatment planning applications. The learning-free approach makes it immediately deployable across different scanner types and institutions.

Keywords: LiverTumor Segmentation · Surgical Planning · Adaptive Clustering · Graph Cuts · NURBS Surface Reconstruction

1 Introduction

Precise 3D liver tumor models are critical for modern oncological care, enabling accurate surgical planning, radiation therapy dose optimization, and quantitative assessment of treatment response [4]. While contrast-enhanced CT provides high-resolution imaging, current clinical practice relies heavily on radiologist interpretation of 2D slices, which introduces variability and limits the precision of volumetric measurements essential for treatment planning. Automated 3D reconstruction systems could standardize tumor assessment and improve clinical decision-making, but existing approaches face significant limitations.

R. N. Rajapakse et al. (Eds.): ICTer 2025, CCIS 2844, pp. 3–16, 2026.
https://doi.org/10.1007/978-981-92-0137-2_1

Deep learning methods achieve high accuracy but require large annotated datasets and specialized hardware, limiting their adoption in resource-constrained clinical settings [9]. Classical segmentation approaches, while interpretable and computationally efficient, often fail to maintain consistent performance across varying image quality, acquisition protocols, and scanner types [27]. This variability is particularly problematic for liver tumors, which exhibit heterogeneous contrast, irregular boundaries, and varying signal-to-noise ratios across different CT protocols.

The core challenge lies in developing a segmentation method that adapts to local image quality without requiring training data. Current fuzzy clustering approaches use fixed parameters regardless of image characteristics, leading to suboptimal performance on low-contrast or noisy slices. Similarly, existing surface reconstruction methods produce either voxel-bound artifacts (marching cubes) or require extensive parameter tuning (spline fitting).

In this work, a Hybrid Adaptive FCM + Graph-Cut pipeline that automatically adapts its segmentation strategy based on local image quality is presented. The key innovation is an adaptive switching mechanism that uses standard FCM for high-quality slices and spatially-regularized FCM for low-contrast regions, followed by graph-cut refinement and NURBS surface reconstruction.

2 Related Works

Fuzzy C-Means (FCM) clustering, introduced by Dunn [12] and formalized by Bezdek [2], has been widely applied to medical image segmentation due to its ability to handle tissue ambiguity. Numerous extensions have been proposed, including spatially-regularized FCM [1,25], possibilistic FCM [18,23], kernel-based approaches [8] and recent superpixel-based fast FCM clustering [19,31].

Energy-based methods include graph-cut algorithms [5], active contour models [6,7,15] and level-set methods. Graph cuts formulate segmentation as a binary labeling problem with global optimization guarantees, balancing data fidelity and spatial smoothness. Active contours can capture complex boundaries but require careful initialization and parameter tuning.

Hybrid methods combine multiple techniques for improved performance. Wu *et al.* [32] combined FCM with graph cuts for liver tumor segmentation, achieving Dice scores of 0.83 on the LiTS dataset while Yang *et al.* [33] integrated adaptive region growing with graph cuts.

The introduction of U-Net by Ronneberger *et al.* [26] revolutionized medical image segmentation. The encoder-decoder architecture with skip connections became the foundation for many subsequent methods. Isensee *et al.* [14] developed nnU-Net, a self-configuring framework that has become a standard baseline for medical segmentation challenges.

For liver tumor segmentation specifically, Christ *et al.* [10] proposed cascaded fully convolutional neural networks, achieving state-of-the-art results on the LiTS challenge. Chlebus *et al.* [9] developed a fully convolutional approach with object-based post-processing, reporting Dice scores of 0.95 on the LiTS dataset. Vorontsov *et al.* [29] introduced a coarse-to-fine cascaded CNN with hybrid loss functions for improved boundary detection.

Kazhdan and Hoppe [17] developed screened Poisson surface reconstruction for smoother results. Spline-based reconstruction methods, particularly NURBS, have been applied to medical imaging [21,28]. Recent work by d'Albenzio *et al.* [11] has shown the clinical utility of NURBS for liver surgery planning.

Modern approaches have introduced neural implicit surface representations such as DeepSDF [24] which learns continuous signed distance functions for shape representation, while NeuS [30] combines neural implicit surfaces with volume rendering for multi-view reconstruction. These methods can produce high-quality surfaces but require extensive training data and computational resources.

The LiTS challenge [3] has become the standard benchmark, providing 201 contrast-enhanced CT scans with expert annotations. The CHAOS challenge focuses on healthy abdominal organ segmentation [16], while BRATS [22] provides brain tumor segmentation benchmarks.

2.1 Positioning of Our Work

Our approach addresses the gap between high-accuracy deep learning and classical techniques. While CNN-based methods achieve superior accuracy (Dice 0.95), they require extensive training data and specialized hardware whereas classical methods, while interpretable and computationally efficient, often fail to maintain consistent performance across varying image quality.

The key innovation in our technique is the adaptive switching mechanism that automatically selects between standard and spatially-regularized FCM based on local image quality. This addresses a fundamental limitation of existing FCM variants which use fixed parameters regardless of image characteristics. The combination with graph-cut refinement and NURBS surface reconstruction provides a complete pipeline from segmentation to 3D modeling.

3 Methodology

Figure 1 outlines the proposed pipeline. Our system operates on a 3D CT volume and first isolates the liver to focus computation. Then, each axial slice within the liver region undergoes preprocessing and tumor segmentation via the proposed algorithm. Finally, the detected tumor contours are passed to a NURBS-based reconstruction module to form the 3D surface.

3.1 Preprocessing

To mitigate intensity non-uniformity and enhance contrast, each slice is normalized and filtered. We apply percentile windowing (clipping extreme 1%) to normalize exposure, followed by anisotropic diffusion filtering to reduce noise while preserving edges. Adaptive histogram equalization (CLAHE) and a γ-correction

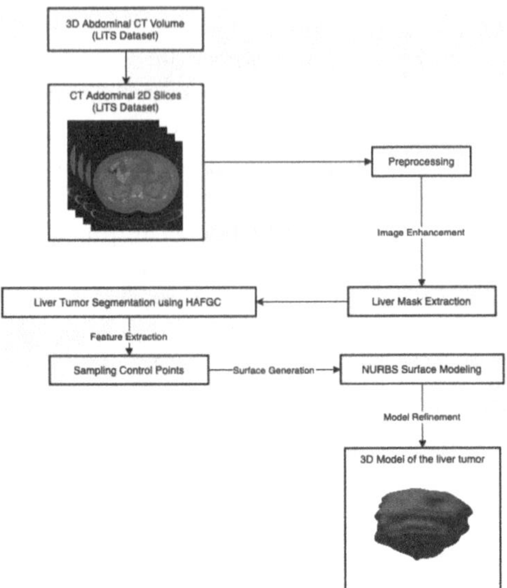

Fig. 1. Overview of the segmentation and reconstruction pipeline.

stretch local contrast, making faint tumors more salient. A bottom-hat morphological filter estimates and subtracts the slowly varying background (caused by beam hardening). These steps yield a calibrated slice where tumor regions stand out more uniformly, improving segmentation stability.

Linear Normalization: Each CT slice is normalized to the range [0,1] using min-max scaling to remove inter-slice intensity variations. For slice z with intensity values $I(x, y; z)$, we compute:

$$\tilde{I}(x, y; z) = \frac{I(x, y; z) - I_{\min}(z)}{I_{\max}(z) - I_{\min}(z)}, \tag{1}$$

where $I_{\min}(z)$ and $I_{\max}(z)$ are the minimum and maximum intensities in slice z. This normalization ensures consistent intensity ranges across slices, simplifying subsequent parameter selection.

Edge-Preserving Smoothing: After normalization, CT slices still exhibit fine-scale noise and streak artifacts. We apply Perona-Malik anisotropic diffusion:

$$\frac{\partial u}{\partial t} = \nabla \cdot \big(g(\|\nabla u\|)\, \nabla u\big), \qquad g(s) = \exp\!\big(-s^2/\kappa^2\big), \tag{2}$$

with initial condition $u(\mathbf{x}, 0) = \tilde{I}(\mathbf{x})$ and conduction parameter κ. This nonlinear diffusion smooths homogeneous regions while preserving sharp anatomical boundaries.

Local Contrast Enhancement: To highlight subtle variations in soft-tissue intensity, we apply contrast-limited adaptive histogram equalization (CLAHE) followed by γ-correction. This boosts the visibility of fine structures such as small hypo-dense nodules without introducing halo artifacts.

3.2 Liver Region Extraction

Before tumor segmentation, we restrict to the liver volume to speed processing. A threshold-based region growing and morphological refinement identifies the liver mask on each slice [13]. The bounding volume of this mask defines our region of interest.

Initial Region Growing: We place seed points in the anatomically consistent upper-right quadrant of each axial slice, where the liver invariably appears. From each seed $s_i = (x_s, y_s)$, we collect pixels whose CLAHE-enhanced intensity differs by less than a tolerance τ:

$$\mathcal{R}_{s_i} = \{p \, : \, |I_{\text{CLAHE}}(p) - I_{\text{CLAHE}}(s_i)| < \tau\}, \tag{3}$$

This stage yields a conservative yet contiguous liver estimate, mitigating spurious growth while preserving the organ's bulk.

Level-Set Boundary Refinement: The rough mask often has blocky edges and may miss complex concavities. We minimize the Chan-Vese energy $E(\phi, c_1, c_2)$ where ϕ is the level-set function, This captures fine boundary undulations while preserving global smoothness.

Morphological Cleanup: After level-set refinement, we apply hole filling and component pruning operations. The resulting slice-level mask is solid and artifact-free. Stacking these masks yields the 3D binary liver indicator:

$$\mathbf{L}(x, y, z) = \begin{cases} 1, & (x, y) \in \mathcal{M}(z), \\ 0, & \text{otherwise}, \end{cases} \tag{4}$$

3.3 Liver ROI Pre-processing

For slice z, the computational domain is $\Omega_z = \{(x, y) | \mathbf{L}(x, y, z) = 1\}$. The pre-processing pipeline is applied pixel-wise on Ω_z:

1. **Robust windowing:** Intensities are clipped to the 1st and 99th percentiles and linearly rescaled to [0,1]:

$$I_w = \frac{\min(\max(I, P_1), P_{99}) - P_1}{P_{99} - P_1}, \tag{5}$$

   where P_1 and P_{99} are the intensity percentile bounds.
2. **Edge-preserving denoising:** We apply ten iterations of Perona-Malik diffusion (Eq. (2)) with conduction parameter $\kappa = 0.1$ to remove speckle noise while maintaining sharp tumor boundaries.

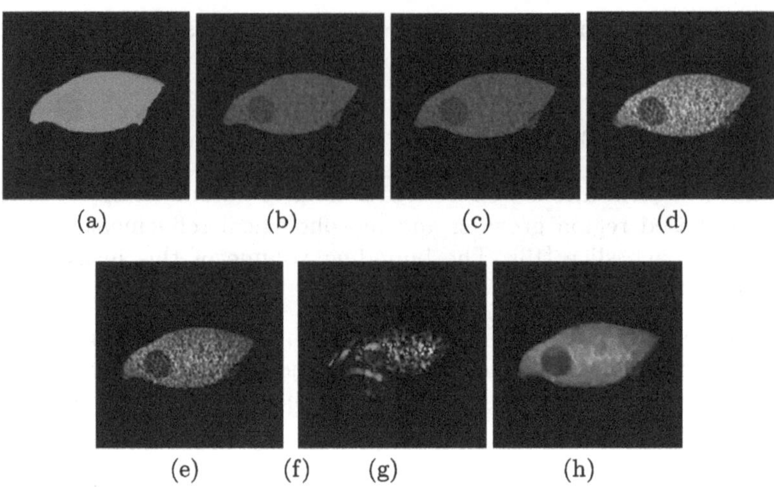

Fig. 2. Step-by-step pre-processing of the liver ROI. (a) Raw liver-masked slice, (b) intensities clamped, (c) normalized, (d) CLAHE enhanced, (e) gamma-adjusted, (f) denoised, (g) bottom-hat filtered and (h) final composite.

3. **Local contrast enhancement:** CLAHE is applied to the windowed slice I_w, followed by a γ-power transform:

$$I_{\mathrm{clahe}} = \mathrm{CLAHE}(I_w; L, \alpha), \qquad I_\gamma = I_{\mathrm{clahe}}^{\gamma}, \ \ \gamma = 1.5, \tag{6}$$

4. **Low-frequency suppression:** The morphological bottom-hat transform estimates and subtracts the slowly varying background:

$$I_{\mathrm{bh}} = (I_\gamma \bullet B) - I_\gamma, \qquad I_{\mathrm{enh}} = I_\gamma + \beta\, I_{\mathrm{bh}}, \quad \beta = 0.7, \tag{7}$$

where $\bullet$ denotes morphological closing with a 7×7 disk-shaped structuring element B.

The resulting I_{enh} exhibits pronounced tumor-to-parenchyma contrast and homogeneous background, providing stable input to the adaptive fuzzy clustering stage with B = the disk-shaped structuring element used for morphological operations, I_{bh} = the bottom-hat transformed image containing low-frequency components, β = the blending coefficient for combining the original and bottom-hat images and I_{enh} = represents the final enhanced output image after blending. Figure 2 provides the steps involved in the pre-processing of liver ROI.

3.4 Adaptive Fuzzy C-Means Clustering

To segment tumors within the liver ROI, we use an adaptive Fuzzy C-Means (FCM) clustering approach that produces a soft membership map indicating the likelihood of tumor presence at each pixel. Standard FCM assigns memberships based on proximity to cluster centroids and works well on high-contrast slices. However, for low-quality slices with poor signal-to-noise ratio (SNR < 12), we switch to a spatially regularized variant that incorporates neighborhood consistency by averaging memberships over each pixel's eight neighbors. This suppresses isolated noise artifacts and enhances cluster coherence.

The result is a robust tumor likelihood map that captures uncertainty at boundaries and adapts to varying image quality.

Standard FCM (Refresher). Let $x_j \in \mathbb{R}$ be the intensity of pixel $j \in \{1, \ldots, N\}$ and $u_{kj} \in [0, 1]$ its fuzzy membership to cluster k. Classical FCM minimizes

$$J_m = \sum_{k=1}^{C} \sum_{j=1}^{N} u_{kj}^m \|x_j - v_k\|^2, \tag{8}$$

$$\text{s.t.} \qquad \sum_{k=1}^{C} u_{kj} = 1 \quad (\forall j),$$

where $m > 1$ is the *fuzzifier* controlling cluster softness ($m = 2$ here). Alternating

$$u_{kj} = \frac{\|x_j - v_k\|^{-2/(m-1)}}{\sum_{r=1}^{C} \|x_j - v_r\|^{-2/(m-1)}}, \tag{9}$$

$$v_k = \frac{\sum_{j=1}^{N} u_{kj}^m x_j}{\sum_{j=1}^{N} u_{kj}^m}, \tag{10}$$

guarantees monotone descent of (8). We fix $C = 3$ (*tumor*, *liver*, *vessels + bone*) and identify the darkest centroid $v_{\min} = \min_k v_k$ as the provisional tumor class. In these equations, $N =$ the total number of pixels in the image, $C =$ the number of clusters,$x_j =$ the intensity value at pixel location j, $u_{kj} =$ he membership value of pixel j in cluster k, respectively, $m =$ the weighting exponent that controls fuzziness and $v_k =$ the center value of cluster k.

Equation (9) assigns larger memberships to the centroid closest in *Euclidean* intensity; Eq. (10) updates centroids as membership-weighted means, making the algorithm a soft generalization of k-means.

Spatial Extension for Low-Contrast Slices. Purely intensity-driven FCM can fragment noisy or poorly contrasted lesions. For slices whose global signal-to-noise ratio SNR falls below threshold τ, we switch to the *spatially constrained* variant of [1], appending

$$\alpha \sum_{k=1}^{C} \sum_{j=1}^{N} u_{kj}^m \big[1 - \bar{u}_{kj}\big], \qquad \bar{u}_{kj} = \frac{1}{|\mathcal{N}_j|} \sum_{q \in \mathcal{N}_j} u_{kq}, \tag{11}$$

to the original cost (8) where α = the spatial scaling parameter, $\mathcal{N}_j$ = the neighborhood pixels surrounding pixel j, $\bar{u}_{kj}$ = the mean membership value calculated from the neighborhood pixels and u_{kj} = the membership value of pixel j belonging to cluster k.

The adaptive rule

$$\lambda = \begin{cases} 0, & \text{SNR} \geq \tau \quad \text{(standard FCM)}, \\ \alpha > 0, & \text{SNR} < \tau \quad \text{(spatial FCM)}, \end{cases} \qquad (A-1)$$

where λ = the spatial regularization parameter, α = the spatial weight parameter that controls the regularization strength, τ = the SNR threshold parameter that determines the FCM mode and $M(p)$ = the membership function value at pixel location.

This rule lets our method keep the speed of standard FCM on high-quality slices ($\lambda = 0$) while automatically adding spatial regularization ($\lambda = \alpha$) on low-contrast slices, yielding a smooth likelihood map M for the subsequent graph-cut refinement stage. The segmentation steps of the liver tumor are illustrated in Fig. 3.

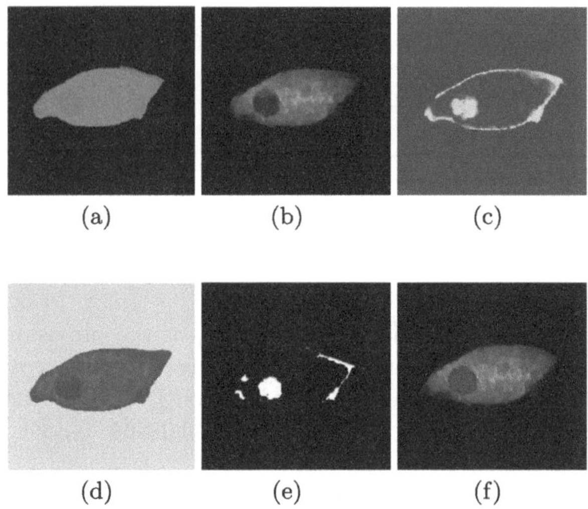

Fig. 3. Tumor-segmentation stages. (a) Raw CT intensities restricted to the liver ROI, (b) Intensity-enhanced slice after anisotropic diffusion, CLAHE and γ boost, (c) Tumor-membership map produced by adaptive FCM (hotter = higher membership), (d) Data-cost image $-\log \mu$ fed to the s–t graph cut, (e) Binary mask returned by the graph-cut optimizer and (f) Final tumor overlay on the enhanced CT slice.

3.5 Graph-Cut Refinement

The hard threshold mask often contains spurious holes or noise. We refine it with a global s–t graph cut whose unary (data) costs are derived from the fuzzy-membership map $M(p)$:

$$D_p(1) = -\log M(p), \qquad D_p(0) = -\log\bigl(1 - M(p)\bigr),$$

and whose pairwise (smoothness) weights

$$w_{pq} = \exp\bigl(-\gamma \| I(p) - I(q) \|^2\bigr)$$

penalize label discontinuities across similar-intensity neighbors. The overall graph-cut energy is then

$$E(L) = \sum_{p} D_p\bigl(L(p)\bigr) \; + \; \lambda \sum_{(p,q)\in\mathcal{N}} w_{pq}\,[L(p) \neq L(q)], \tag{12}$$

where $L(p)$ = the binary label field, where values 1 and 0 represent tumor and background regions, $M(p)$ = the fuzzy membership value at pixel location p, $I(p)$ = the intensity value at pixel location p, w_{pq} = the edge weight between neighboring pixels p and q, γ = the intensity difference penalty coefficient, $\mathcal{N}$ = the pixel neighborhood system and λ = the weight parameter controlling spatial smoothness. Minimizing (12) via a max-flow algorithm yields the binary segmentation that best balances data fidelity and spatial smoothness. Because this energy is sub-modular, the global optimum can be found efficiently [5]. The result L^* is a binary mask that respects the fuzzy data while enforcing spatial coherence: thin false-positive speckles are removed, and weak contiguous tumor regions are better captured.

3.6 Spline Surface Reconstruction

Binary voxel masks exhibit "stair-step" artifacts that hinder both visual assessment and curvature-based measurements. We therefore reconstruct each lesion as a twice differentiable *Non-Uniform Rational B-Spline* (NURBS) surface using the three-stage pipeline illustrated in Fig. 4.

Control Point Sampling. For slice index z let $\mathcal{M}_z = \{(x, y) \mid \mathbf{M}(x, y, z) = 1\}$ be the in-plane binary tumor mask and $\partial\mathcal{M}_z$ its boundary. The slice centroid is

$$\mathbf{c}_z = \frac{1}{|\mathcal{M}_z|} \sum_{(x,y)\in\mathcal{M}_z} [x,\, y]^\top, \tag{13}$$

and n_u uniformly spaced angles $\theta_i = 2\pi i / n_u$ $(i = 0, \ldots, n_u - 1)$ define radial lines

$$\mathbf{r}_z(t; \theta_i) = \mathbf{c}_z + t\,[\cos\theta_i, \sin\theta_i]^\top, \qquad t > 0. \tag{14}$$

The first mask transition along each ray yields a boundary sample

$$\mathbf{P}(i, z) = \arg\min_{t>0}\Big\{\mathbf{r}_z(t;\theta_i) \notin \mathcal{M}_z\Big\}. \tag{15}$$

Stacking all slices produces an $n_u \times n_v$ cylindrical lattice of control points $\mathbf{P}(i,j) \in \mathbb{R}^3$ with $i = 0{:}n_u - 1$ (angular) and $j = 0{:}n_v - 1$ (axial) where $\mathbf{M}$ = the binary volumetric mask, $\mathcal{M}_z$ = the tumor region on slice z, $\mathbf{c}_z$ = the centroid coordinates on slice z, n_u and n_v represent the number of angular and axial samples, respectively, where $n_u = 36$ and $\mathbf{P}$ = the coordinates of control points in 3D space.

NURBS Surface Modeling. We adopt cubic basis degrees $p = q = 3$ for C^2 curvature continuity. The periodic angular knot vector is

$$\mathbf{U} = \big[\underbrace{0,0,0,}_{p+1}\ u_3,\dots,u_{n_u},\ \underbrace{1,1,1}_{p+1}\big], \qquad u_k = \frac{k}{n_u - p},$$

and the open-uniform axial knot vector is

$$\mathbf{V} = \big[\underbrace{0,0,0,}_{q+1}\ v_3,\dots,v_{n_v},\ \underbrace{1,1,1}_{q+1}\big], \qquad v_k = \frac{k}{n_v - q}.$$

With unit weights $w_{ij} = 1$ the surface evaluates to

$$S(u,v) = \frac{\sum_{i=0}^{n_u-1}\sum_{j=0}^{n_v-1} N_{i,p}(u)\, M_{j,q}(v)\, \mathbf{P}(i,j)}{\sum_{i=0}^{n_u-1}\sum_{j=0}^{n_v-1} N_{i,p}(u)\, M_{j,q}(v)}, \qquad (u,v) \in [0,1]^2, \tag{16}$$

where $N_{i,p}$ and $M_{j,q}$ are the Coxde Boor B-spline basis functions. Because $\mathbf{U}$ is periodic, the surface is closed and globally C^2-continuous in the circumferential direction.

In the above, p and q represent the polynomial degrees in the u and v parametric directions, respectively, n_u and n_v represent the number of control points in the angular and axial parametric directions, respectively, $\mathbf{U}$ and $\mathbf{V}$ represent the knot vectors defining the parametric space in the angular and axial directions, respectively, $\mathbf{P}(i,j)$ = the coordinates of the control point at indices (i,j), w_{ij} = the weight associated with the control point at indices (i,j) and $S(u,v)$ = the point on the surface at parametric coordinates (u,v).

4 Results and Discussion

Based on evaluation on 20 cases from the Liver Tumor Segmentation (LiTS) challenge dataset, Table 1 compares our proposal to several learning-free and

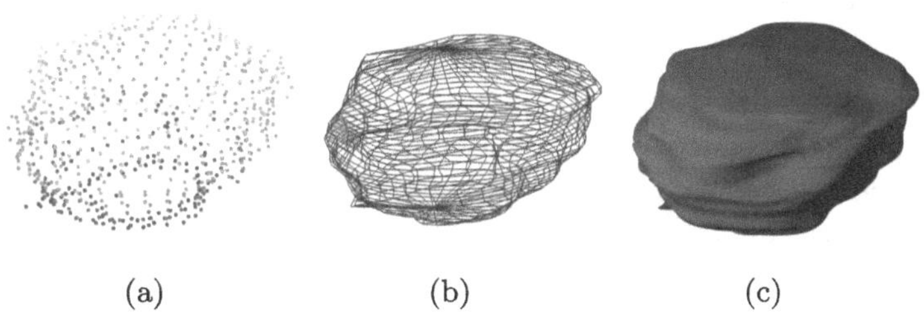

(a) (b) (c)

Fig. 4. NURBS reconstruction pipeline. (a) *Resampled slice-contour points* (b) *Control-net surface* (c) *Final smooth NURBS surface*

Table 1. Comparison of segmentation methods on LiTS (20 volumes).

Method	DSC	VOE (%)	RVD (%)	ASD (mm)	HD (mm)
Wu *et al.* [32]	0.83 ± 0.06	29.0 ± 8.2	-2.2 ± 15.9	0.72 ± 0.33	4.25 ± 3.03
Yang *et al.* [33]	0.85 ± 0.05	26.0 ± 7.0	-5.0 ± 12.0	0.68 ± 0.36	5.27 ± 3.13
Li *et al.* [20]	-	26.3 ± 5.8	-10.6 ± 7.6	1.06 ± 0.38	8.66 ± 3.17
Chlebus *et al.*[9]	0.95 ± 0.02	10.2 ± 2.2	-0.5 ± 5.4	0.25 ± 0.10	3.20 ± 1.40
Proposed	$\mathbf{0.85 \pm 0.03}$	$\mathbf{25.8 \pm 4.9}$	$\mathbf{+3.1 \pm 8.9}$	$\mathbf{0.64 \pm 0.20}$	$\mathbf{4.60 \pm 1.90}$

CNN-based methods. The evaluation metrics include Dice similarity coefficient (DSC), volume overlap error (VOE), relative volume difference (RVD), average surface distance (ASD), and Hausdorff distance (HD).

The quantitative results show that our technique achieves a mean Dice of 0.85 (std 0.03) and an ASD of 0.64 mm, which is comparable to other non-deep-learning methods. Wu *et al.* [32] reported DSC 0.83 and ASD 0.72 mm, while Yang *et al.* [33] achieved DSC 0.85 and ASD 0.68 mm. Our method yields low volumetric bias (mean RVD $\approx +3\%$), indicating consistent performance.

While CNN-based methods like Chlebus *et al.* [9] achieve higher accuracy (DSC 0.95, ASD 0.25 mm), this performance comes with significant practical limitations: (1) training on hundreds of annotated scans, (2) GPU hardware requirements, (3) extensive hyper-parameter tuning, and (4) retraining for new scanner types. In contrast, our method achieves clinically acceptable accuracy (DSC 0.85) while being immediately deployable without training data or specialized hardware.

The clinical significance of this trade-off is important. A Dice score of 0.85 corresponds to excellent clinical utility for surgical planning, where studies show Dice scores above 0.80 are sufficient for clinical decision-making. The sub-millimeter surface accuracy (ASD 0.64 mm) meets radiation therapy planning requirements, where margins of 2–5 mm are typically applied.

4.1 Limitations and Clinical Considerations

The 10% accuracy gap between the proposed (DSC 0.85) and CNN methods (DSC 0.95) represents a significant limitation. This difference corresponds to approximately 20% more accurate boundary delineation, which can be critical for high-precision applications like radiation therapy planning. Our method performs particularly poorly on small tumors (< 2 cm), irregular shapes, and low-contrast lesions where the adaptive switching mechanism may not adequately compensate for poor signal-to-noise ratios. The dataset represents curated, high-quality images that may not reflect routine clinical practice variability. The evaluation does not address multi-phase CT scans, multiple concurrent lesions, patient positioning variations, or different scanner manufacturers. These limitations raise questions about practical utility in diverse clinical settings.

5 Conclusion

We have presented a hybrid adaptive segmentation pipeline that addresses the gap between high-accuracy deep learning methods and classical approaches. The key innovation is an adaptive switching mechanism that maintains segmentation accuracy across diverse CT acquisition protocols without requiring training data. On the LiTS challenge dataset, it achieved clinically acceptable accuracy with sub-millimeter surface precision, while being immediately deployable across different scanner types and institutions.

However, the method's limitations including a significant accuracy gap compared to CNN methods, dependence on image quality and unproven scalability must be carefully considered for clinical deployment.

Disclosure of Interests. The authors declare that they have no known competing financial interests or personal relationships that could have appeared to influence the work cited in this paper.

References

1. Ahmed, M.N., Yamany, S.M., Mohamed, N., Farag, A.A., Moriarty, T.: A modified fuzzy C-means algorithm for bias field estimation and segmentation of MRI data. IEEE Trans. Med. Imaging **21**(3), 193–199 (2002)
2. Bezdek, J.C., Ehrlich, R., Full, W.: FCM: the fuzzy c-means clustering algorithm. Comput. Geosci. **10**(2–3), 191–203 (1984)
3. Bilic, P., et al.: The liver tumor segmentation benchmark (LiTS). In: Proceedings of the MICCAI 2017 Challenge on Liver Tumor Segmentation LiTS, pp. 1–10. Springer, Cham (2017)
4. Bilic, P., et al.: The liver tumor segmentation benchmark (LiTS). Med. Image Anal. **84**, 102,680 (2023)
5. Boykov, Y.Y., Jolly, M.P.: Interactive graph cuts for optimal boundary and region segmentation of objects in n-d images. In: Proceedings of the Eighth IEEE International Conference on Computer Vision, pp. 105–112. IEEE (2001)

6. Caselles, V., Kimmel, R., Sapiro, G.: Geodesic active contours. Int. J. Comput. Vision **22**(1), 61–79 (1997)
7. Chan, T.F., Vese, L.A.: Active contours without edges. IEEE Trans. Image Process. **10**(2), 266–277 (2001)
8. Chen, S.C., Zhang, D.: Robust image segmentation using FCM with spatial constraints based on new kernel-induced distance measure. IEEE Trans. Syst. Man Cybern. Part B **34**(4), 1907–1916 (2004)
9. Chlebus, G., et al.: Automatic liver tumor segmentation in CT with fully convolutional neural networks and object-based postprocessing. Sci. Rep. **8**, 15,497 (2018)
10. Christ, P.F., et al.: Automatic liver and tumor segmentation of CT and MRI volumes using cascaded fully convolutional neural networks. arXiv preprint arXiv:1702.05970 (2017)
11. d'Albenzio, G., et al.: Using NURBS for virtual resections in liver surgery planning: a comparative usability study. In: Proceedings of SPIE Medical Imaging 2024: Image-Guided Procedures, Robotic Interventions, and Modeling, vol. 12927, pp. 235–241. SPIE (2024). https://doi.org/10.1117/12.3006486
12. Dunn, J.C.: A fuzzy relative of the isodata process and its use in detecting compact well-separated clusters. J. Cybern. **3**(3), 32–57 (1973)
13. El-Dahshan, E.S.A., Hosny, T., Salem, A.: Hybrid intelligent techniques for MRI brain images classification. Digit. Sig. Process. **20**(2), 433–441 (2010)
14. Isensee, F., Jaeger, P.F., Kohl, S.A.A., Petersen, J., Maier-Hein, K.H.: nnU-net: a self-configuring method for deep learning-based biomedical image segmentation. Nat. Methods **18**(2), 203–211 (2021)
15. Kass, M., Witkin, A., Terzopoulos, D.: Snakes: active contour models. Int. J. Comput. Vision **1**(4), 321–331 (1988)
16. Kavur, H., et al.: CHAOS challenge combined CT-MR healthy abdominal organ segmentation. Med. Image Anal. **69**, 101,950 (2021)
17. Kazhdan, M., Hoppe, H.: Screened Poisson surface reconstruction. ACM Trans. Graph. **32**(3), 29:1–29:13 (2013)
18. Krishnapuram, R., Keller, J.M.: A possibilistic approach to clustering. IEEE Trans. Fuzzy Syst. **1**(2), 98–110 (1993)
19. Lei, T., Uysal, M., Shu, Y., Yan, H., Li, B.: Superpixel-based fast fuzzy C-means clustering for color image segmentation. IEEE Trans. Fuzzy Syst. **27**(9), 1753–1766 (2019)
20. Li, B.N., Chui, C.K., Chang, S., Ong, S.H.: A new unified level set method for semi-automatic liver tumor segmentation on contrast-enhanced CT images. Expert Syst. Appl. **39**(10), 9661–9668 (2012). https://doi.org/10.1016/j.eswa.2012.02.095
21. Meegama, R.G.N., Rajapakse, J.C., Kim, S.S., Ling, L.H.: Extraction of left ventricular cavity from echo-cardiograph images by Bayesian and Nurbs modeling. In: International Symposium, Sabaragamuwa University, pp. 1–6. Sabaragamuwa University Press (2006)
22. Menze, B.H., et al.: The multimodal brain tumor image segmentation benchmark BRATS. IEEE Trans. Med. Imaging **34**(10), 1993–2024 (2015)
23. Pal, N.R., Pal, K., Keller, J.M., Bezdek, J.C.: A possibilistic fuzzy C-means clustering algorithm. IEEE Trans. Fuzzy Syst. **13**(4), 517–530 (2005)
24. Park, J.J., Florence, P., Straub, J., Newcombe, R., Lovegrove, S.: DeepSDF: learning continuous signed distance functions for shape representation. In: Proceedings of the IEEE/CVF Conference on Computer Vision and Pattern Recognition (CVPR), pp. 165–174. IEEE (2019)

25. Pham, D.L., Prince, J.L.: An adaptive fuzzy C-means algorithm for image segmentation in the presence of intensity inhomogeneities. Pattern Recogn. Lett. **20**(1), 57–68 (1999)
26. Ronneberger, O., Fischer, P., Brox, T.: U-net: convolutional networks for biomedical image segmentation. In: Navab, N., Hornegger, J., Wells, W.M., Frangi, A.F. (eds.) MICCAI 2015. LNCS, vol. 9351, pp. 234–241. Springer, Cham (2015). https://doi.org/10.1007/978-3-319-24574-4_28
27. Ruan, S., Jaggi, C., Xue, J., Fadili, J., Bloyet, D.: Brain tumor segmentation from MRI images using fuzzy clustering and deformable models. Comput. Biol. Med. **37**(10), 1457–1466 (2007)
28. Villard, B., Grau, V., Zacur, E.: Surface mesh reconstruction from cardiac MRI contours. J. Imaging **4**(1), 16 (2018)
29. Vorontsov, E., et al.: Liver lesion segmentation using a coarse-to-fine cascaded convolutional neural network with hybrid loss function. In: 2019 IEEE 16th International Symposium on Biomedical Imaging (ISBI), pp. 1465–1468. IEEE (2019)
30. Wang, P., et al.: Neus: learning neural implicit surfaces by volume rendering for multi-view reconstruction. In: Advances in Neural Information Processing Systems, vol. 34, pp. 27,171–27,183. Curran Associates (2021)
31. Wu, C., Zhang, L., Zhang, H., Yan, H.: Improved superpixel-based fast fuzzy c-means clustering for image segmentation. In: 2019 IEEE International Conference on Image Processing (ICIP), pp. 1455–1459. IEEE (2019)
32. Wu, W., Wu, S., Zhou, Z., Zhang, R., Zhang, Y.: 3D liver tumor segmentation in CT images using improved fuzzy C-means and graph cuts. BioMed. Res. Int. **2017**, 5207,685 (2017)
33. Yang, Z., Zhao, Y., Liao, M., Di, S., Zeng, Y.: Semi-automatic liver tumor segmentation with adaptive region growing and graph cuts. Biomed. Sig. Process. Control **68**, 102,670 (2021)

An Explainable Deep Learning Framework for Gallbladder Disease Classification on Ultrasound Images

Keerthana Giridharini(✉) and Kalhari Walawage

Department of Computing, Informatics Institute of Technology, Colombo, Sri Lanka
{keerthana.20210676,kalhari.w}@iit.ac.lk

Abstract. Gallbladder diseases such as gallstones, infections, and cancer affect millions worldwide, and early diagnosis is critical for effective treatment. Yet, accurate detection remains difficult because ultrasound images are often noisy and symptoms across conditions appear similar. This problem is even worse in areas with few resources and few radiology experts. While deep learning has shown promise in ultrasound-based disease classification, most existing studies are restricted to binary classification, lack robust preprocessing and segmentation, and provide limited interpretability leaving a clear gap in reliable multi-class diagnostic frameworks. This study addresses this gap by developing a XAI-based deep-learning system capable of classifying nine gallbladder disease types using UIDataGB dataset containing 10,692 annotated ultrasound images. A comprehensive preprocessing pipeline incorporating CLAHE, Gaussian filtering, unsharp masking, and Active Contour segmentation was applied to enhance image quality and emphasize disease-relevant regions. Multiple deep learning approaches were investigated, including a custom CNN, a hybrid model combining VGG16 and ResNet152 through feature-level fusion, and ensemble approaches. The most effective ensemble, integrating the custom CNN with the hybrid model, achieved 99.8% test accuracy and a Cohen kappa score of 0.998, outperforming transfer learning ensembles. Comparative benchmarking further demonstrated superior robustness and classification depth. To ensure clinical trust, eXplainable AI (XAI) methods including Grad-CAM and LIME were applied, providing interpretable visualizations of image regions influencing predictions. By addressing limitations in multi-class diagnosis, preprocessing, and interpretability, the proposed framework delivers a highly accurate and scalable tool for improving early diagnosis and management of gallbladder diseases in emerging healthcare contexts.

Keywords: Gallbladder Ultrasound Analysis · Deep Learning Models · Explainable Artificial Intelligence (XAI) · Multi-Class Disease Classification

1 Introduction

With an estimated 10–15% of the global population affected, gallbladder illnesses represent a significant health burden that can lead to severe complications if misdiagnosed or untreated [1]. These conditions encompass carcinoma, polyps, gallstones, and cholecystitis. Early stages are often asymptomatic, but progression may result in pain, infection,

R. N. Rajapakse et al. (Eds.): ICTer 2025, CCIS 2844, pp. 17–31, 2026.
https://doi.org/10.1007/978-981-92-0137-2_2

bile duct obstruction, or cancer. Therefore, timely and accurate diagnosis is critical to reducing morbidity, enabling early intervention, and improving outcomes.

Ultrasound imaging remains the preferred modality for gallbladder evaluation due to its cost-effectiveness, non-invasiveness, and real-time feedback. It is widely used to identify gallstones, inflammation, and wall abnormalities. However, diagnosis accuracy is influenced by radiologist expertise, ultrasound machine resolution, and patient-related factors. Noise artifacts such as speckle and shadowing, as well as operator variability, obscures image features, leading to diagnostic errors and treatment delays [2].

Most existing AI-based methods in this domain have been restricted to binary classification, typically distinguishing healthy versus diseased gallbladders, without providing detailed categorization of disease types. Since treatment pathways differ across conditions, binary outcomes limit clinical utility. Multi-class classification, which can identify the specific type of gallbladder disease, is clinically more relevant but faces challenges due to dataset scarcity, structural variability, and ultrasound noise [3].

A review of recent studies highlights these gaps (Table 1).

Table 1. Gap Analysis in Gallbladder Disease Classification

Citation	Contribution	Gap identified
[3]	Classified nine GB diseases with high accuracy using DNNs.	Lacks model interpretability (XAI).
[2]	Differentiated neoplastic vs. pseudo polyps.	Limited dataset; focused only on polyps.
[4]	Reviewed XAI methods in medical ultrasound.	Weak clinical integration of XAI.
[5]	Provided interpretable GBC detection, outperforming DNNs and radiologists.	Sensitive to noise; not fully scalable.
[6]	Proposed YOLOv8 + Faster R-CNN fusion for GB cancer.	Dataset limitations; black-box model issues.

As Table 1 shows, prior works achieved notable accuracy, but they suffer from key shortcomings: limited interpretability, dataset scarcity, narrow disease coverage (polyps or cancer only), and poor integration into clinical workflows.

This study addresses these challenges by developing a multi-class deep learning diagnostic framework for gallbladder disease classification. The proposed approach combines transfer learning (InceptionV3, MobileNet, VGG16), hybrid CNNs, and a custom CNN trained on the UIDataGB dataset containing nine disease classes. Preprocessing with active contour segmentation improves localization, while explainable AI (XAI) ensures interpretability by highlighting decision made by model in images [7].

By integrating multi-class classification, segmentation-based preprocessing, and XAI-driven transparency, this research advances beyond prior studies that focused on binary classification or lacked interpretability. The novelty lies in offering a comprehensive diagnostic pipeline that enhances accuracy, promotes trust, and bridges the gap between deep learning advances and real clinical application.

2 Literature Review

Recent developments in artificial intelligence and medical imaging have paved the way for automated systems that utilize ultrasound images to assist in diagnosing gallbladder disorders. Strong preprocessing strategies, efficient deep learning models, and rigorous evaluation protocols are essential due to the inherent difficulty of interpreting sonographic data and variations in image quality. A review of existing literature highlights how each component contributes to the development of reliable computer-aided diagnostic systems, particularly for multi-class classification of gallbladder diseases.

Preprocessing is a critical step in preparing ultrasound data for deep learning-based classification. It enhances diagnostically relevant features, standardizes image properties, and reduces noise. Techniques such as normalization (Z-score or min-max scaling) and resizing ensure uniformity across input data [8]. Data augmentation, including brightness adjustment, rotation, scaling, and flipping, addresses limited dataset size and class imbalance, improving model generalization [9]. Speckle noise is mitigated using Gaussian smoothing, median filtering, and asymmetric diffusion, preserving edge patterns while reducing unnecessary variance [10]. Contrast enhancement aids in detecting subtle structural changes, crucial for identifying polyps or early-stage diseases [11]. Segmentation-based preprocessing using U-Net or Mask R-CNN focuses the model on clinically relevant regions, improving classification outcomes [12]. Advanced methods such as wavelet-based de-artifacting and deep learning-based corrections enhance inter-device consistency and ensure high-quality inputs from multiple sources [13].

After preprocessing, model selection dictates the learning framework. Convolutional Neural Networks (CNNs) have proven effective in image-based diagnostics due to their ability to capture spatial patterns. Architectures like VGGNet, ResNet, and DenseNet achieve high accuracy in classifying cholelithiasis, polyps, and cholecystitis [14]. Regularization techniques, including batch normalization and dropout, prevent overfitting. Transfer learning with pre-trained models such as InceptionV3, MobileNet, VGG16, and ResNet152 leverages large-scale datasets like ImageNet, improving accuracy (86.50–98.35%) and reducing training time [3]. Ensemble learning through bagging, boosting, or stacking further enhances robustness, balances class performance, and handles ultrasound variability [3]. Attention-based architectures, including Attention U-Net and Vision Transformers (ViT), improve interpretability by focusing on relevant image regions [15]. Hybrid models combining CNNs with sequential networks (LSTM, GRU) capture temporal dependencies in dynamic imaging, while multi-modal learning incorporating patient metadata can enhance diagnostic performance. Explainable AI (XAI) techniques like Grad-CAM and SHAP provide feature-based visual explanations that align AI predictions with clinical reasoning [7].

Comprehensive evaluation is essential in medical applications. Standard metrics such as accuracy, precision, recall, and F1-score offer a baseline, while AUC-ROC curves and confusion matrices provide insight into sensitivity and specificity, reducing misdiagnoses. XAI visualizations, such as Grad-CAM, help verify that predictions correspond to clinically relevant regions [14]. Model utility also depends on generalizability across devices, patient populations, and noise robustness, requiring validation against expert radiologist observations [3]. Additionally, fairness and bias assessment ensure equitable performance across diverse patient groups [16]. Continuous learning enables models to adapt to new scenarios and incorporate clinician feedback, facilitating long-term integration into healthcare [17]. Together, these evaluation strategies ensure that classification models are reliable, transparent, and clinically applicable.

Recent advances in medical image analysis include federated learning, transformers, and foundation models. Federated learning enables privacy-preserving ultrasound diagnostics, such as FedBCD for breast cancer [17]. Transformer-based approaches have shown strong results, including hybrid VGG-ViT for breast ultrasound [18] and ensemble ViTs for classification [19], with extensions to fetal ultrasound [20]. More broadly, foundation models like MedFMC [21] and vision language models [22] demonstrate adaptability across domains but require large datasets and resources. In contrast, this study proposes a lightweight, explainable CNN-hybrid framework specifically for gallbladder ultrasound, addressing the need for accurate multi-class classification with clinically interpretable outputs.

3 Methodology

This study follows an experimental, quantitative research methodology with a mixed-methods component, structured through Saunders' research onion to ensure alignment between philosophy and practice. A positivist philosophy underpins the study, emphasizing objective measurement and statistical evaluation. An abductive reasoning approach allows iterative hypothesis formation and explanation of outcomes. The methodological choice integrates quantitative model evaluation with limited qualitative insights from medical practitioners, ensuring both technical rigour and clinical relevance. An experimental strategy is applied by training and comparing deep learning models under controlled conditions, while a cross-sectional time horizon enables immediate performance assessment. Finally, secondary data from the UIDataGB dataset is used with advanced DL algorithms, and model reliability is strengthened through cross-validation and XAI-based interpretability.

3.1 High-Level System Architecture

The system architecture of the gallbladder disease classification tool is organized into three tiers: Presentation, Logic, and Data. The Presentation Tier (Front End) provides the user interface, allowing users to upload ultrasound images, view disease predictions, and access interpretable results through XAI techniques such as heatmaps. Key components include the login, landing, instruction, about, and analysis pages, where users can interact with image uploads, previews, prediction outputs, and explanations. The Logic Tier (Backend) handles the system's core functionalities, including image preprocessing (resizing, normalization, augmentation, and Active Contour segmentation), disease prediction using deep learning models (CNN, hybrid, and ensemble), and XAI interpretation (Grad-CAM, LIME). It comprises an API proxy server to manage requests, preprocessing and post-processing modules, classification models, and an XAI module to generate interpretable outputs. The Data Tier (Database) stores ultrasound images, patient metadata, classification results, and XAI outputs, ensuring data persistence for future analysis, model improvement, and clinical reference. Together, these tiers form a closed-loop system, where data flows seamlessly between storage, processing, and visualization, providing accurate predictions, interpretable results, and reliable data management.

Fig. 1 illustrates the proposed system architecture, detailing the workflow and key components to clearly convey the technical framework of the study.

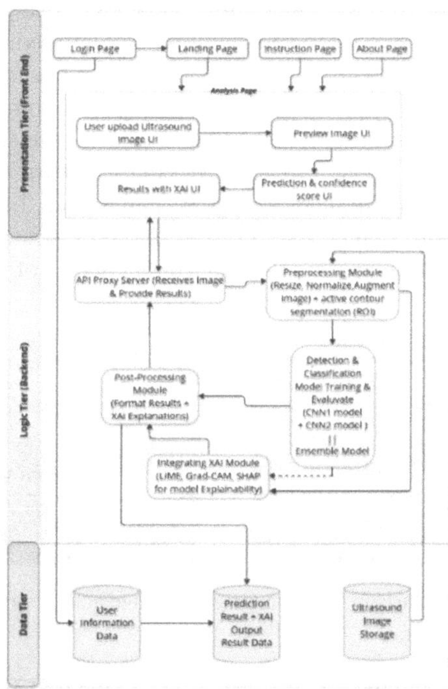

Fig. 1. Three-tier architecture of classification tool

3.2 Dataset

The classification procedure was trained using the UIDataGB dataset, which included 10692 ultrasound images categorized into nine distinct GB disease classes. Approximately 1200 photos are included in each dataset type based on the abnormal results. Furthermore, 20% of the dataset (2139 photos) was put aside for testing, while the remaining 80% (8553 images) was used for training. It is essential to make sure that every image from a particular patient is allocated to either the training or testing set, but not both, when constructing a train/test divide for a dataset that includes several images from the exact same patient [17].

3.3 Implementation

There are three primary stages to the system's implementation,

I) Image Preprocessing and Segmentation
II) Detection and Classification
III) XAI Integration

Image Preprocessing and Segmentation
In image analysis, preprocessing entails improving image quality to maximize it for next tasks. For example, CLAHE (Contrast Limited Adaptive Histogram Equalization) uses parameters like tile grid size = (8, 8) and clip limit = 2.0 to redistribute pixel intensities in order to improve contrast. Gaussian blur is one of the noise reduction techniques that smooths the image by applying a random blur intensity within a range, such sigma = (0.1, 2.0). Sharpening techniques, like unsharp masking, use settings like radius = 1, percent = 100, and thresh-old = 3 to improve edges. Contrast stretching scales pixel values according to their minimum and highest percentiles, hence adjusting intensity values throughout the entire range (0–255). Fig. 2 shows how proposed preprocessing pipeline before segmentation process to enhance the quality of image.

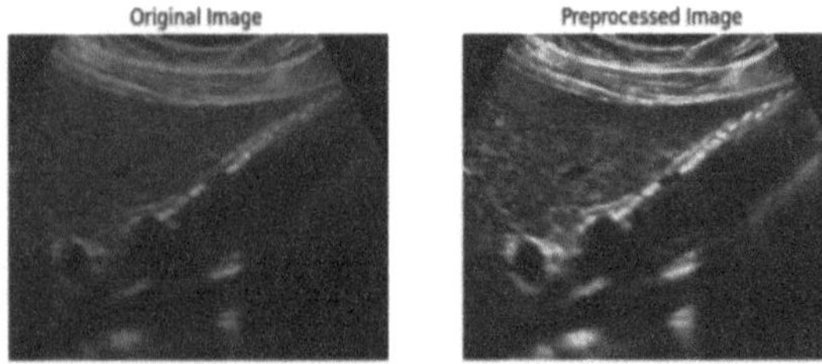

Figure 2. Comparison between Original image and preprocessed image

An image can be segmented into useful areas or items for examination. For instance, in order to reduce noise, active contour segmentation begins with preprocessing techniques like Gaussian blur. By dynamically determining an optimal threshold value, thresholding techniques, like Otsu's threshholding, split the image into binary sections. After that, contours are retrieved using methods which uses variations in pixel intensity to identify boundaries. To precisely define objects of interest, these contours are iteratively improved. Color-coded contours are used to overlay segmented boundaries on the source image for visualization. Figure. 3 shows how segmentation works in ultrasound image.

Detection and Classification
Various deep learning models were evaluated to accurately classify gallbladder diseases using the UIDataGB dataset. Transfer learning was applied to pre-trained models including VGG16, ResNet152, MobileNet, InceptionV3, and a custom CNN. Ensemble strategies were explored, first combining MobileNet and InceptionV3, and then creating a hybrid model by fusing features from VGG16 and ResNet152. This hybrid model was further ensembled with the custom CNN using soft voting to enhance robustness. Models were trained on preprocessed and segmented 224 × 224 ultrasound images with data augmentation and class balancing, using categorical cross-entropy loss and the Adam

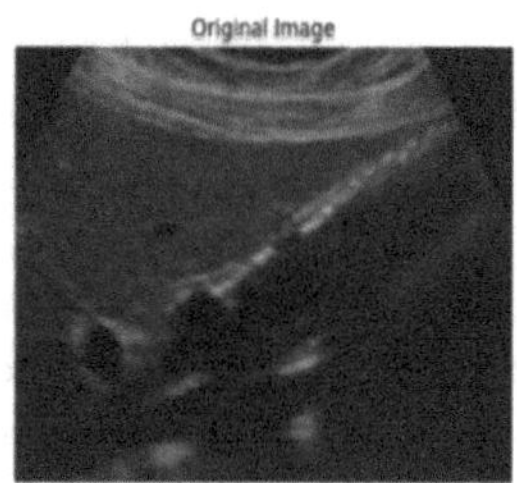

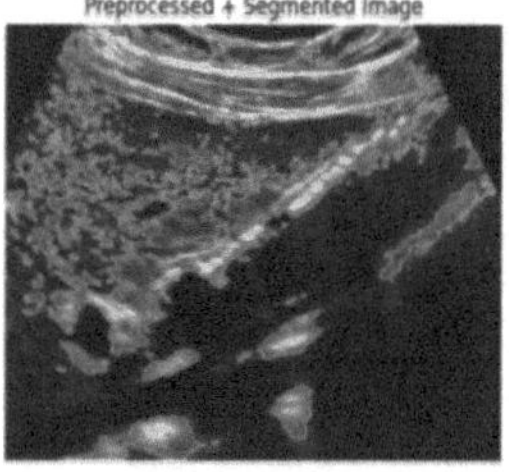

Fig. 3. Comparison between original image and preprocessed segmented image

optimizer. Performance was evaluated using accuracy, confusion matrices, ROC-AUC curves, and classification reports. This multi-model approach ensures a reliable and generalizable system for multi-class gallbladder disease diagnosis.

1. *Custom CNN Model*

The custom CNN uses depthwise separable convolutions inspired by MobileNet to ensure a lightweight yet efficient architecture, where depthwise convolutions extract spatial features and pointwise convolutions expand channel dimensions. The initial convolution layer captures basic patterns, and successive blocks progressively increase the number of filters up to 1024 to learn increasingly complex features. Batch normalization stabilizes training, while ReLU activations introduce non-linearity. Global average pooling reduces spatial dimensions before classification, and dropout (0.5) prevents overfitting. The softmax output layer is tailored for nine gallbladder disease classes. Training hyperparameters including 50 epochs, batch size of 32, learning rate 0.0001, and the Adam optimizer were chosen to achieve stable convergence and high performance. This combination of design and hyperparameter choices ensures the model efficiently captures relevant features, generalizes well, and achieved 99.5% accuracy.

2. *Ensemble Model (Mobilenet and InceptionV3)*

In order to maintain previously trained ImageNet features, the ensemble model uses MobileNet and InceptionV3 as basis models with their convolutional layers frozen. The output of the last convolutional block in both models is followed by a Global Average Pooling 2D (GAP2D) layer, which reduces spatial dimensions and extracts powerful feature vectors. Higher representation and non-linear modification are made possible by passing these feature vectors through separate Dense layers with ReLU activation. The strengths of both feature extractors are then combined by averaging (ensemble fusing) the outputs from each model. Following fusion, a Dropout layer is used to randomly disable a portion of neurons during training in order to minimise overfitting. Lastly, nine kinds of gallbladder illness are classified using a dense layer with softmax activation. The model can effectively generalise and generate precise predictions from ultrasound picture features thanks to its layered architecture. The accuracy of this model was 98.5%. During the 20 epochs of training, the Adam optimiser was used with a batch size of 32 and a learning rate of 0.0001.

3. *Hybrid Model (VGG16 and Resnet152)*

The suggested hybrid model architecture combines the extracted features of two potent pre-trained convolutional neural networks, ResNet152 and VGG16, to enhance the classification of gallbladder illness. With the exception of its top classification layers, the VGG16 base model takes input and produces deep features that are then flattened to create a vector with one dimension. The feature map is simultaneously reduced to a compact representation by extracting globally average pooled features using the ResNet152 base model, which is likewise devoid of its top layers. The viewpoints of both networks are then successfully combined into a single rich feature vector by concatenating each of these feature vectors. To prevent overfitting, the combined features are run through a dense layer of 512 neurons that is fully linked, activated by ReLU, and regularised using L2 regularisation. The architecture incorporates Dropout (rate 0.5) and Batch Normalisation. Lastly, the class possibilities for each of the nine gallbladder disease types are predicted by an output layer that is activated by softmax. Crucially, only the recently added layers of VGG16 and ResNet152 are fine-tuned during training; all other layers are frozen to maintain their pre-trained weights. To improve training stability and performance, the model was constructed using the Adam optimiser, categorised cross-entropy loss, and monitored using EarlyStopping and ReduceLROnPlateau callbacks. The accuracy of this model was 99.1%. During the 20 epochs of training, the Adam optimiser was used with a batch size of 32 and a learning rate of 0.0001.

4. *Ensemble Model (Hybrid Model and Custom CNN)*

By optimising the final five layers of two pre-trained models, a hybrid model that combines VGG16 and Res-Net152, and a bespoke CNN, a hybrid ensemble model is created in this study. Pixel size of 224x224 can be entered into the input layer. A more reliable final classification is produced by combining the predictions of the two models' output through ensemble averaging. A dense layer with 128 neurones and swish activation is one of the fully connected layers that come after the ensemble output. L2 regularisation is used to reduce overfitting. A dropout rate of 0.6 and batch normalisation are used to improve the generalisation and stability of the model. Class probabilities are produced by the output layer using softmax activation. In order to achieve better training efficiency and classification performance, the model is constructed with a modest learning rate and categorical cross-entropy loss. The accuracy and Cohen kappa score of this model were 99.8% and 0.998, respectively. During the 20 epochs of training, the Adam optimiser was used with a batch size of 32 and a learning rate of 0.0001.

The system uses an Ensemble Model combining a Hybrid Model (VGG16 + ResNet152) and a Custom CNN to improve classification accuracy and generalization. VGG16 and ResNet152 extract complementary features, while Custom CNN adds additional learned patterns. Averaging output from these models enhances robustness, reduces overfitting, and enables the system to handle complex patterns, delivering accurate and reliable predictions.

XAI Integration

Two XAI approaches have been used primarily for interpretability in this system.

1. Grad-CAM (Gradient-weighted Class Activation Mapping)

Grad-CAM highlights the regions of an input image that most influence the model's predictions. It uses gradients flowing through the last convolutional layer to generate a heatmap, showing which areas of the image the CNN focused on for a particular class. This visual representation allows researchers and clinicians to understand which features contributed to the model's decision, making it especially useful for classifications.

2. LIME (Local Interpretable Model-agnostic Explanations)

LIME provide interpretable explanations for individual predictions of black-box model. It works by generating perturbed versions of an input image and observing the changes in the model's predictions. A simple surrogate model is then trained on these variations to approximate the decision boundary locally, producing a visualization of the key features that influenced the model's choice for that specific instance. This approach emphasizes the reasoning behind each prediction, offering context at the instance level.

Figure 4 shows the XAI visualizations by the model's predictions.

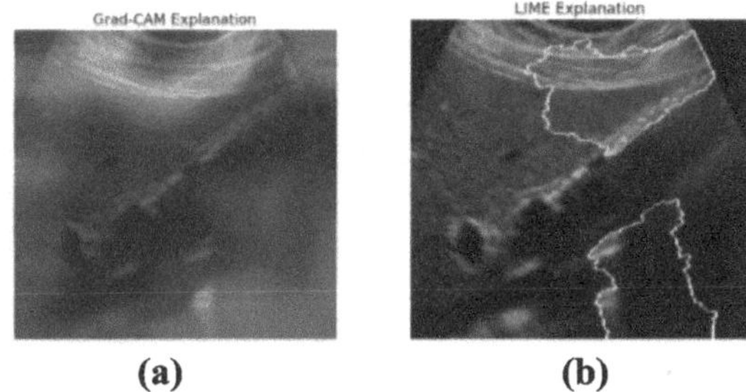

Fig. 4. (a) Grad-CAM and (b) LIME visual explanations of the ensemble model, illustrating the regions of ultrasound images most influential in predicting gallbladder disease classes

Together, Grad-CAM and LIME provide complementary insights: Grad-CAM shows spatial attention of CNNs across the entire image, while LIME explains local, instance-specific decisions, ensuring that predictions are transparent and clinically interpretable.

4 Testing

All of the models outperform the current, earlier research when compared. In order to improve performance in this system, the author chose an ensemble model that merged a proprietary CNN model with a hybrid model. Black box testing is done to confirm that the system satisfies all requirements. Both qualitative and quantitative assessments are used to evaluate the models during the training and testing stages. The model is tested using the Cohen kappa score, accuracy, accuracy variation curve, and loss variation curve. To determine which was producing the best results, the model was trained on a variety of epochs and batch sizes. With an 80% train, 20% test split, the chosen final model obtained a 99.8% accuracy level, 0.998 Cohen's kappa score and five-fold cross validation accuracy of 99.8%.

The training and validation curves demonstrate effective learning across all models, with accuracy steadily improving and loss decreasing to low values. The hybrid and ensemble models converge more rapidly and maintain closer alignment between training and validation trends, indicating strong generalization with minimal overfitting in Fig. 5, 6 and 7.

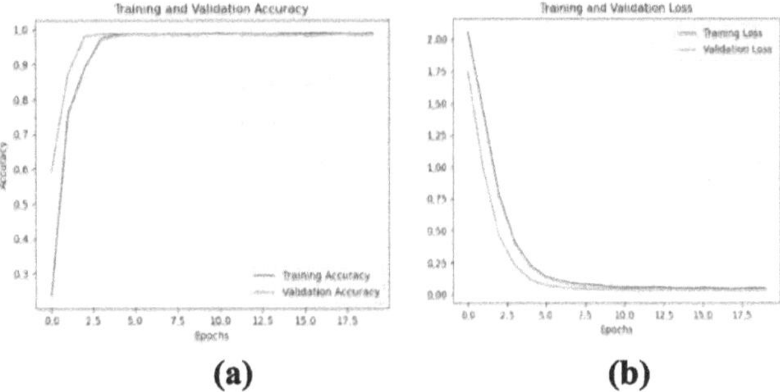

Fig. 5. Training and validation performance of proposed ensemble model. The (a) accuracy curves converge near 100%, while the (b) loss curves steadily decline to near-zero, indicating effective learning and strong generalization with minimal overfitting.

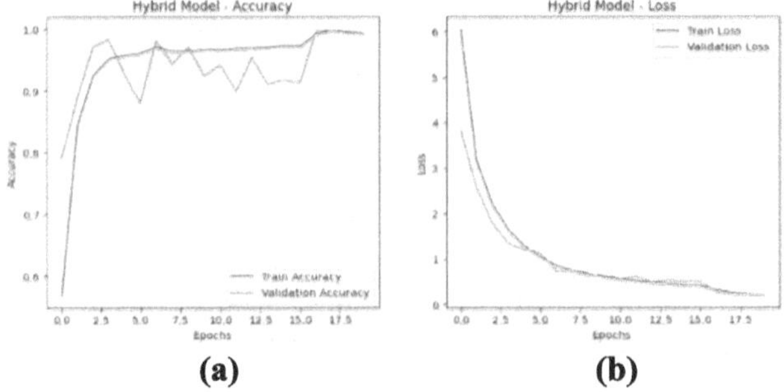

Fig. 6. (a) Accuracy and (b) loss variation curves of the hybrid model. The training and validation accuracy converge near 100%, while the corresponding loss decreases sharply and stabilizes, demonstrating effective learning and generalization

Additionally, the classification models were evaluated using a ROC curve, precision, recall, F1-score, and confusion matrix as well.

The confusion matrices in Figs. 8, 9, 10 provide a detailed view of correct and incorrect predictions, indicating how well the model distinguishes between different disease categories. The ROC curve in Fig. 11 illustrates the trade-off between sensitivity and specificity across disease classes.

The performance of the proposed ensemble model was further validated using Cohen kappa score (Fig. 12), which confirmed strong agreement beyond chance, and the classification report (Fig. 13), which demonstrated high precision, recall, and F1-scores across all nine disease classes.

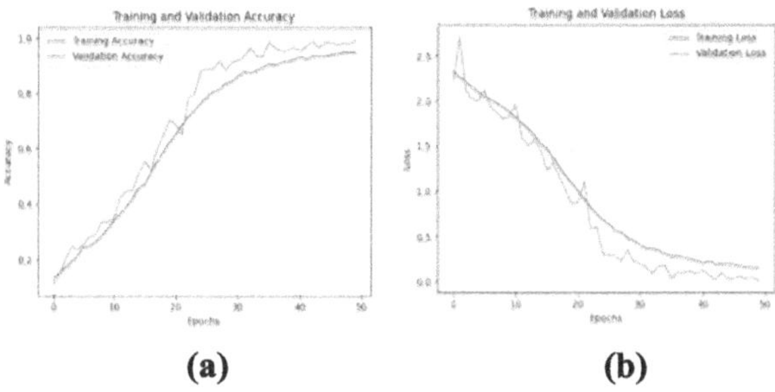

(a) **(b)**

Fig. 7. (a) Accuracy and (b) loss variation curves of the custom CNN model. The model shows a steady increase in training and validation accuracy and a consistent decline in loss across epochs, indicating gradual but stable convergence

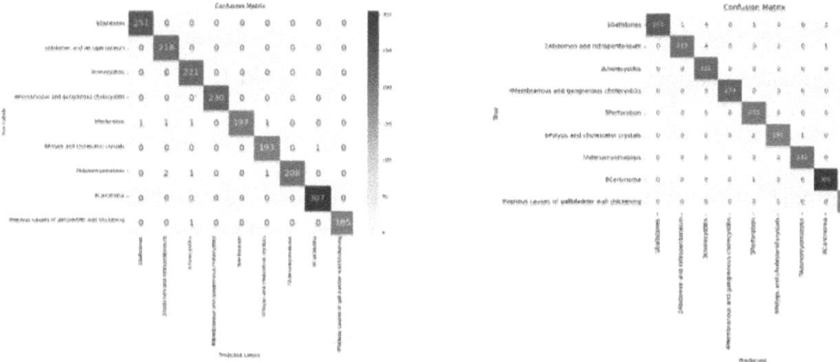

Fig. 8. Confusion matrix of ensemble model

Fig. 9. Confusion matrix of hybrid model

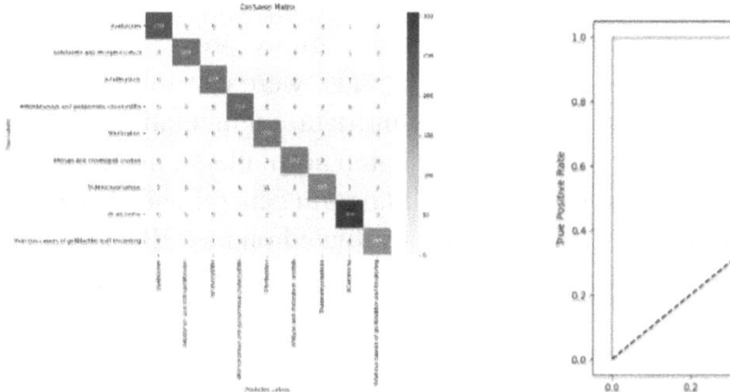

Fig. 10. Confusion matrix of custom model

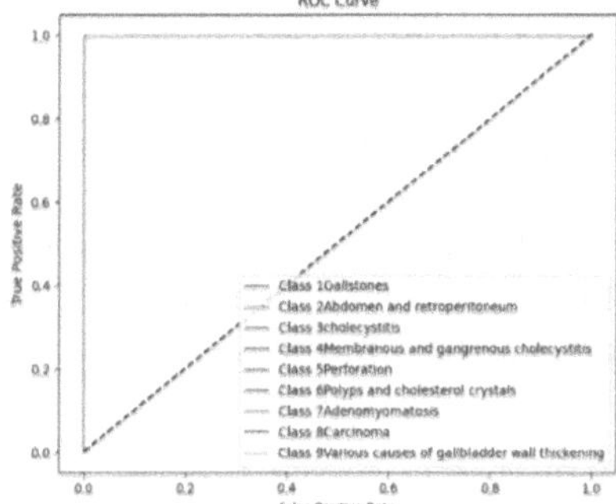

Fig. 11. ROC-Curve of ensemble model

The proposed ensemble model was evaluated using **five-Fold Cross-Validation**, where the dataset was split into five subsets, training on four and validating on one in each iteration. Performance metrics, including accuracy and confusion matrices (Fig. 14), were averaged across all folds. This approach provides a more reliable and unbiased assessment of the model's performance.

```
# -------- Cohen's Kappa Score --------
kappa_score = cohen_kappa_score(true_labels, predicted_classes)
print(f"Cohen's Kappa Score: {kappa_score:.4f}")

Cohen's Kappa Score: 0.9983
```

Fig. 12. Kappa score of ensemble model

Classification Report:

	precision	recall	f1-score	support
1Gallstones	1.00	1.00	1.00	251
2Abdomen and retroperitoneum	0.99	1.00	0.99	218
3cholecystitis	0.99	1.00	0.99	221
4Membranous and gangrenous cholecystitis	1.00	1.00	1.00	230
5Perforation	1.00	0.98	0.99	201
6Polyps and cholesterol crystals	0.99	0.99	0.99	194
7Adenomyomatosis	1.00	0.98	0.99	212
8Carcinoma	1.00	1.00	1.00	307
9Various causes of gallbladder wall thickening	1.00	0.99	1.00	186
accuracy			1.00	2020
macro avg	1.00	0.99	0.99	2020
weighted avg	1.00	1.00	1.00	2020

Fig. 13. Classification report on final model

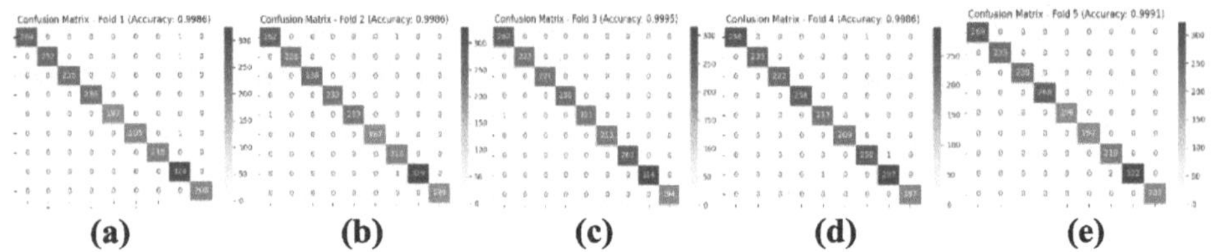

Fig. 14. Confusion matrices of five-Fold Cross-Validation (a) Fold 1, (b) Fold 2, (c) Fold 3, (d) Fold 4 & (e) Fold 5

A summary of these findings indicates that the suggested ensemble model did well, attaining a Cohen's kappa score of 0.998 and an accuracy of 99.8%.

Results Comparison

The proposed gallbladder disease classification models were evaluated on the UIDataGB dataset. The Pretrained ensemble model (Mobilenet + Inceprionv3) achieved 98.5%, Custom CNN achieved 99.5% accuracy, the Hybrid Model (VGG16 + ResNet152) reached 99.1%, and the Ensemble Model combining hybrid and custom CNN, achieved the outperforming highest accuracy of 99.8%. XAI techniques (Grad-CAM, LIME) confirmed that the models focus on clinically relevant regions, providing interpretable predictions. In these model's overfitting and data leakage were carefully prevented by choosing an ensemble approach as well as applying data augmentation, proper data splits, added L2 regularization layers, dropout, and batch normalization and ensuring no overlap of patient images across sets, which helped maintain generalizable performance.

Table 2 presents a comparison of prior models evaluated on the UIDataGB dataset, highlighting their methods and achieved accuracy with this proposed study.

5 Limitations and Future Work

Throughout the study development stages, a number of limitations have been discovered and identified. The main drawback is the lack of a dataset that can include all illness types, and no prior research has used this dataset with RCNNs and a bounding box technique. Furthermore, this model can function well with many additional architectures, attaining a high level of accuracy similar to this intended method.

Lastly, there is yet another constraint. Future studies on this topic can use multi-modal approaches, and it should concentrate on building a bigger dataset. Due to data

Table 2. Comparison of proposed approach with existing methods with same dataset

Citation	Method	Accuracy
[3]	Pretrained models	VGG16–97.78% InceptionV3–86.50% ResNet152–85.30%, and MobileNet 98.35%.
[22]	CBIR system compared with textural-based models LBP and HOG, CNN architectures DenseNet201, Googlenet, InceptionV3, and NasNetLarge models	Disease verification was achieved with an average of 94.4%.
Proposed approach	Ensemble model which combines a hybrid model with transfer learning and a custom CNN with XAI	Ensemble - 99.8% (Custom CNN – 99.5%, Hybrid - 99.1%), outperforming other DL approaches

scarcity, the majority of earlier studies solely concentrated on binary classification and a very limited multi-classification. Here, the nine disease classes are classified using a classification model that was trained on the UIdataGB dataset. (D1) Gallstones, (D2) Cholecystitis, (D3) Gangrenous Cholecystitis, (D4) Perforation of GB, (D5) Polyps and Cholesterol Crystals, (D6) Gallbladder-Wall Thickening, (D7) Adenomyomatosis of the GB, (D8) Carcinoma, (D9) Intra-abdominal and Retroperitoneum.

6 Conclusion

The study demonstrates that integrating preprocessing, segmentation, and deep learning strategies enhances gallbladder disease classification from ultrasound images. Preprocessing techniques such as CLAHE, Gaussian blur, and unsharp masking improved image quality, while Active Contour segmentation refined boundary localization, enabling models to capture more discriminative features. Multiple approaches were evaluated, including fine-tuned pre-trained networks (ResNet50, ResNet152, MobileNet, VGG16, InceptionV3), a custom CNN, and hybrid models combining internal features.

Among these, the ensemble of the custom CNN and the hybrid model delivered the most consistent performance. The custom CNN, with depth-wise separable convolutions, effectively captured fine-grained features, while the hybrid model (VGG16 + ResNet152) leveraged deep hierarchical representations. Their complementary strengths balanced domain-specific and generalizable features, improving accuracy and robustness. These results are consistent with prior work showing that ensembles of diverse architectures outperform single models. Clinically, the framework supports radiologists by offering accurate, automated classification that accelerates diagnosis and reduces errors, particularly in low-resource settings. The integration of XAI methods such as Grad-CAM and LIME further enhances interpretability and trust, addressing a critical barrier to AI adoption in healthcare. Overall, the proposed ensemble framework provides a reliable and interpretable solution for gallbladder disease diagnosis.

Disclosure of Interests. The authors declare that there are no conflicts of interest, financial or otherwise, that could have influenced the design, implementation, analysis, or presentation of this research. The work was conducted solely for academic purposes, and no external parties with commercial or personal interests were involved in the study.

References

1. Stinton, L.M., Shaffer, E.A.: Epidemiology of gallbladder disease: cholelithiasis and cancer. Gut Liver. **6**(2), 172–187 (2012). https://doi.org/10.5009/gnl.2012.6.2.172
2. Kim, T., et al.: Gallbladder polyp classification in ultrasound images using an ensemble convolutional neural network model. J. Clin. Med. **10**(16), 3585 (2021). https://doi.org/10.3390/jcm10163585
3. Obaid, A.M., et al.: Detection of gallbladder disease types using deep learning: an informative medical method. Diagnostics. **13**(10), 1744 (2023). https://doi.org/10.3390/diagnostics13101744
4. Wyatt, L.S., et al.: Explainable artificial intelligence (XAI) for oncological ultrasound image analysis: a systematic review. Appl. Sci. **14**(18), 8108 (2024). https://doi.org/10.3390/app14188108
5. Basu, S., Gupta, M., et al.: Surpassing the human accuracy: detecting gallbladder cancer from USG images with curriculum learning. In: Proceedings of the IEEE/CVF Conference on Computer Vision and Pattern Recognition (CVPR), New Orleans, LA, USA, June 2022, pp. 20854–20864. IEEE (2022). doi:10.1109/CVPR52688.2022.02022
6. Dadjouy, S., Sajedi, H.: Artificial intelligence applications in the diagnosis of gallbladder neoplasms through ultrasound: a review. Biomed. Signal Process. Control. **93**, 106149 (2024). https://doi.org/10.1016/j.bspc.2024.106149
7. Bhati, D., Neha, F., Amiruzzaman, M.: A survey on explainable artificial intelligence (XAI) techniques for visualizing deep learning models in medical imaging. J. Imaging. **10**, 239 (2024). https://doi.org/10.3390/jimaging10100239
8. Ge, C., et al.: Exploring deep learning applications using ultrasound single view cines in acute gallbladder pathologies: preliminary results. Acad. Radiol. (2024). https://doi.org/10.1016/j.acra.2024.08.061
9. Obaid, A.M., et al.: Diagnosis of gallbladder disease using artificial intelligence: a comparative study. Int. J. Comput. Intell. Syst. **17**, 46 (2024). https://doi.org/10.1007/s44196-024-00431-w
10. Wayalun, P., Saiyod, S., Chamadol, N.: Enhancement of bile duct ultrasound images for cholangiocarcinoma surveillance. Malays. J. Comput. Sci. **31**, 238–254 (2018). https://doi.org/10.22452/mjcs.vol31no4.1
11. Micucci, M., Iula, A.: Recent advances in machine learning applied to ultrasound imaging. Electronics. **11**, 1800 (2022). https://doi.org/10.3390/electronics11111800
12. Lyu, J., et al.: Complex impacts of gallstone disease on metabolic syndrome and nonalcoholic fatty liver disease. Front. Endocrinol. **13**, 1032557 (2022). https://doi.org/10.3389/fendo.2022.1032557
13. Qin, Z., et al.: Preliminary study on diagnosis of gallbladder neoplastic polyps based on contrast-enhanced ultrasound and grey scale ultrasound radiomics. Front. Oncol. **14**, 1370010 (2024). https://doi.org/10.3389/fonc.2024.1370010

14. Wang, L.-F., et al.: Risk stratification of gallbladder masses by machine learning-based ultrasound radiomics models: a prospective and multi-institutional study. Eur. Radiol. **33**, 8899–8911 (2023). https://doi.org/10.1007/s00330-023-09891-8
15. Gupta, P., et al.: Deep-learning models for differentiation of xanthogranulomatous cholecystitis and gallbladder cancer on ultrasound. Indian J. Gastroenterol. **43**, 805–812 (2024). https://doi.org/10.1007/s12664-023-01483-0
16. Deng, T., et al.: FEDBCD: federated ultrasound video and image joint learning for breast cancer diagnosis. IEEE Trans. Med. Imaging. **1** (2025). https://doi.org/10.1109/TMI.2025.3532474
17. Qu, X., et al.: A VGG attention vision transformer network for benign and malignant classification of breast ultrasound images. Med. Phys. **49**(9), 5787–5798 (2022). https://doi.org/10.1002/mp.15852
18. Jain, E., Kaushik, P., Kukreja, V., Sakshi, D., A., Goyal, B.: Fetal diagnostics using vision transformer for enhanced health and severity prediction in ultrasound imaging. Curr. Med. Imaging. (2025). https://doi.org/10.2174/0115734056360199250227053012. Epub ahead of print
19. Wang, D., et al.: MedFMC: a real-world dataset and benchmark for foundation model adaptation in medical image classification. arXiv preprint https://arxiv.org/abs/2306.09579 (2023)
20. Ryu, J.S., Kang, H., Chu, Y., et al.: Vision-language foundation models for medical imaging: a review of current practices and innovations. Biomed. Eng. Lett. **15**, 809–830 (2025). https://doi.org/10.1007/s13534-025-00484-6
21. Turki, A., et al.: UIdataGB: multi-class ultrasound images dataset for gallbladder disease detection. Data Brief. **54**, 110426 (2024). https://doi.org/10.1016/j.dib.2024
22. Bozdag, A., Yildirim, M., Karaduman, M., Mutlu, H.B., Karaduman, G., Aksoy, A.: Detection of gallbladder disease types using a feature engineering-based developed CBIR system. Diagnostics. **15**(5), 552 (2025). https://doi.org/10.3390/diagnostics15050552

Integrating U-Net Segmentation and TabNet Transfer Learning for Automated Melanoma Detection

Hasini Yasoda Weeraddana[1], Colambage Hiruni Malsha Fernando[1], Hewa Dewage Sachini Anuththara Fernando[1], Edirisuriya Arachchige Minsara Prabhash Suriyaarachchi[2], Digo Arachchillage Ravindu Thamuda Jayasinghe[3], and Kodikara Arachchillaya Saneera Hemantha Kulathilake[1(✉)]

[1] Department of Computing, Faculty of Applied Sciences, Rajarata University of Sri Lanka, Mihintale, Sri Lanka
kule@as.rjt.ac.lk

[2] Department of Physical Sciences, Faculty of Applied Sciences, Rajarata University of Sri Lanka, Mihintale, Sri Lanka

[3] Department of Biological Sciences, Faculty of Applied Sciences, Rajarata University of Sri Lanka, Mihintale, Sri Lanka

Abstract. Melanoma is the most lethal type of skin cancer and has been rising rapidly in recent decades, where providing a reliable means of early detection can play a crucial role in successfully treating melanoma. Conventional melanoma diagnosis through visual inspection and biopsy is time-consuming, costly, and error-prone. A deep learning-based technique for early melanoma detection can offer a more reliable and efficient solution. The system begins with a preprocessing stage that removes hair artefacts using an inpainting technique, ensuring clear lesion visibility. Preprocessed images are then segmented using a U-Net model, which accurately isolates lesion regions. Clinically relevant features defined by the ABCD criteria: Asymmetry, Border Irregularity, Colour Variation, and Diameter are extracted. These features are input for the classification model to differentiate between Malignant and Benign cases. A Multilayer Perceptron (MLP) neural network is developed for classification, and to further enhance its performance, transfer learning is incorporated through TabNet. These components are integrated into an ensemble framework that combines their predictive strengths. The system is evaluated on a selected subset of the Melanoma Skin Cancer Dataset (a combination of ISIC datasets), consisting of 215 dermoscopic images (180 training, 20 validation, 15 testing) representing diverse lesion morphologies. Performance is assessed using Accuracy, Precision, Recall, F1-score and Confusion Matrix. The integrated model achieves an accuracy of 71%, with a precision, recall, and F1-score of 0.71, outperforming individual models in accuracy and loss reduction, highlighting its potential to power an efficient computer-aided diagnosis system that helps physicians improve efficiency in healthcare practice.

Keywords: Melanoma · Skin Cancer · Deep Learning · Ensemble Learning

R. N. Rajapakse et al. (Eds.): ICTer 2025, CCIS 2844, pp. 32–46, 2026.
https://doi.org/10.1007/978-981-92-0137-2_3

1 Introduction

Melanoma is the most aggressive and deadliest form of skin cancer, accounting for only about 1% of skin cancers but causes the majority of skin cancer deaths [1]. It has been rising rapidly with about 97,610 new melanoma diagnoses and about 7,990 expected deaths according to the American Cancer Society's estimates [1]. It underscores the urgent need for early and accurate detection to improve patient outcomes.

The major and most significant factor of melanoma is prolonged exposure to ultraviolet (UV) radiation [2], which leads to the initial tumour formation on the skin's surface. If not detected, melanoma can rapidly progress from the skin's surface to deeper layers and eventually metastasize via the bloodstream to other organs. The American Joint Committee on Cancer (AJCC) [3] and the National Comprehensive Cancer Network (NCCN) [4] classify melanoma into several stages (T1a to T4b) [5], based on tumour thickness and the presence of ulceration, highlighting the critical role of early-stage diagnosis.

Traditionally, melanoma diagnosis relies heavily on dermatological evaluation through visual inspection or dermoscopic analysis, followed by a biopsy method. However, this approach is time-consuming, expensive, and often subjective, as it depends greatly on the clinician's expertise [6]. Even with dermoscopy, a technique involving magnified examination of pigmented skin lesions, maximum diagnostic accuracy typically caps at 84% [7]. Furthermore, due to the visual similarity between benign and malignant lesions and the low contrast in some dermoscopic images, misdiagnoses are a persistent issue.

To address these challenges, Computer-Aided Diagnosis (CAD) systems have emerged as a supportive tool, aiming to reduce diagnostic errors, and healthcare costs, and improve early detection [8]. The ABCD rule (Asymmetry, Border irregularity, Colour variation, and Diameter) is commonly used as a preliminary screening guide, but it still requires knowledge and significant domain expertise. [9]

Recent advancements in machine learning and deep learning offer a promising path forward, particularly in identifying skin cancer with tremendous performance. While most studies in the past have used K-nearest neighbour (KNN) and Support Vector Machines (SVM) [10]. They have shown some success in classification tasks, but they suffer from scalability and computational inefficiencies when applied to large image datasets. In contrast, Convolutional Neural Networks (CNNs) have become the dominant architecture for skin lesion analysis, owing to their powerful feature extraction capabilities and superior performance. However, CNNs also face limitations, such as overfitting on small or imbalanced datasets and the risk of false predictions.

Given these observations, there is a pressing need for a more reliable diagnostic solution that leverages the power of deep learning while mitigating its limitations. This research proposes a novel deep learning-based melanoma detection system that integrates image preprocessing, lesion segmentation, ABCD-based feature extraction, and a hybrid ensemble classification model. The preprocessing module employs inpainting techniques to remove hair artefacts, while the segmentation process isolates lesions using a customized U-Net model. Extracted features are classified using a Multilayer Perceptron (MLP) and TabNet, fused via stacking ensemble to improve diagnostic performance.

2 Related Work

Early detection of melanoma using dermoscopic images has seen rapid advances driven by convolutional neural networks (CNNs) and, more recently, transformer-based architectures. While these approaches report impressive accuracy on large-scale datasets, clinically interpretable rules such as the ABCD rule remain important for explainability and clinical adoption [11].

Transformer-based models such as DermViT [12] have demonstrated strong performance by capturing global contextual cues in dermoscopic images. These methods highlight the power of self-attention for subtle lesion patterns but remain data- and compute-intensive, making them less practical in settings where only small curated datasets are available.

Compact CNN architectures like EfficientNet [13] have been widely adopted due to their balance of accuracy and computational efficiency. By leveraging transfer learning and careful augmentation, they achieve strong results on datasets like ISIC and HAM10000, but they are still vulnerable to artefacts such as hair and often lack clinical interpretability unless explicitly combined with dermatological criteria.

Comprehensive analyses of CNN-based deep features, such as those conducted by Gajera et al. [14] and colleagues, provide systematic benchmarking across multiple pre-trained networks and demonstrate the importance of preprocessing and segmentation in maximizing classification performance. However, these studies largely emphasize image-derived features and rarely integrate clinical rules such as ABCD, which limits their interpretability in medical practice.

Recent CNN pipelines that combine segmentation with classification have also reported strong results by addressing class imbalance and improving lesion localization [15]. While these methods demonstrate the benefits of segmentation-driven design, they typically depend on larger datasets and remain constrained by their lack of explicit clinical feature integration.

Classical ABCD-rule-based methods, including the work of Senan & Jadhav [16], illustrate the enduring value of handcrafted, clinically interpretable features. Their pipeline, Gaussian filtering, lesion ROI extraction via contour + morphology, ABCD rule features, and Total Dermoscopy Score, shows satisfactory accuracy, sensitivity, and specificity on PH2, with low computational cost and transparency. However, these methods struggle with ambiguous lesions and complexity, and do not exploit learned deep representations or robust lesion segmentation like U-Net, limiting their discriminative capacity in challenging cases.

Taken together, prior work reveals a gap between high-performing but opaque deep models and interpretable but limited clinical-feature pipelines. Our study addresses this gap by combining artefact-aware preprocessing and U-Net segmentation with ABCD-based clinical features and a hybrid ensemble classification using MLP and TabNet. This design aims to balance interpretability, robustness on small datasets, and clinical relevance, providing a feasible direction for resource-constrained healthcare contexts. Table 1 shows the comparative summary of related approaches.

Table 1. Summary of Related Approaches for Melanoma Detection

Study	Dataset(s)	Method / architecture	Key strengths	Weaknesses	Relation
[12]	ISIC	Vision Transformer with lesion-aware modules	Strong global attention; robust to complex patterns	Data- and compute-hungry; less interpretable	Demonstrates ViT promise but impractical for small datasets; our method favours interpretable features + compact learners
[13]	ISIC, HAM10000	EfficientNet with transfer learning	Good accuracy with low FLOPs; practical inference	Sensitive to artefacts; limited interpretability	We complement CNN features with ABCD clinical features to improve interpretability and resilience
[14]	PH2, ISIC, HAM10000	Pre-trained CNN deep features, ensemble comparisons	Systematic benchmarking; preprocessing insights	Focused on image-only deep features	Their findings support our choice of preprocessing and motivate integration of ABCD features
[15]	ISIC variants	FCDS-CNN, ResNet + DeepLab	Segmentation improves classification; class balancing	Large-data dependency; no clinical features	We also use segmentation but add ABCD feature fusion for interpretability

(continued)

Table 1. (*continued*)

Study	Dataset(s)	Method / architecture	Key strengths	Weaknesses	Relation
[16]	PH2	Gaussian filter + morphology + ROI extraction →ABCD features→Total Dermoscopy Score	Clinically interpretable; lightweight; transparent; good accuracy/ sensitivity/ specificity on PH2	No deep feature fusion; weaker performance for complex lesions; fewer evaluation metrics (no ROC-AUC, no confusion matrix)	We extend this kind of ABCD-rule work by adding deep features + stronger preprocessing + more metrics + ensemble stacking
Proposed Method	ISIC subset (215 images)	Preprocessing (blackhat + Telea inpainting) → U-Net 6.→ ABCD features→ MLP + TabNet + stacking with LR	Interpretability; artefact-aware preprocessing; robust on small curated datasets; multiple evaluation metrics	Dataset size limited; possibly limited generalization to very diverse lesion types	–

3 Methodology

A deep learning-based diagnostic framework for early detection of melanoma is designed to classify dermoscopic images into benign or malignant categories. In this section, we present our proposed model, which comprises five stages: dataset collection and preparation, image preprocessing, segmentation, feature extraction, and classification, as shown in Fig. 1. The system facilitates direct repetition and adaptation in similar diagnostic settings. A detailed description of each stage is given below.

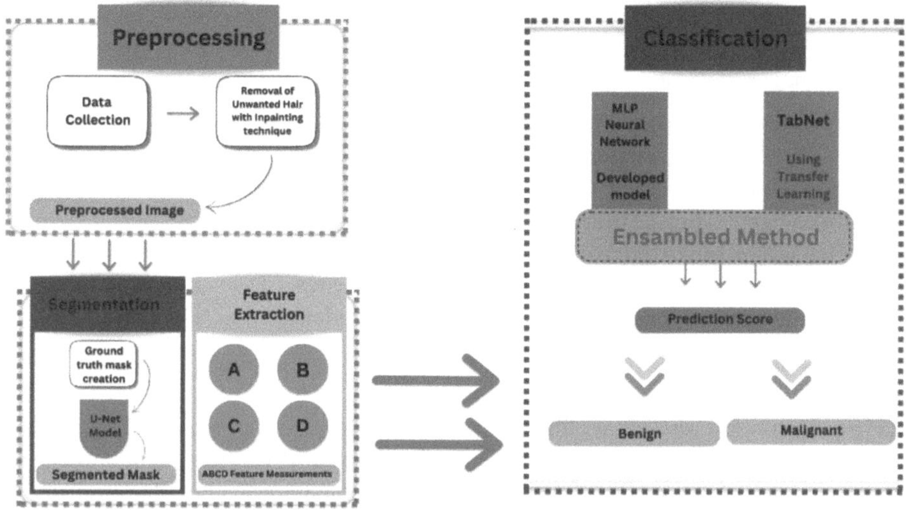

Fig. 1. Overall research design for melanoma detection, illustrating preprocessing, segmentation, feature extraction, and ensemble-based classification.

3.1 Dataset Collection and Preparation

The dataset used for this study was derived from the Melanoma Skin Cancer Dataset (a combination of ISIC datasets). The original dataset includes 10,604 images representing a variety of benign and malignant skin lesions. To ensure manageable computational complexity while maintaining lesion diversity, a representative subset of 215 images was selected. The subset was strategically partitioned into a training set (180 images), a validation set (20 images), and a test set (15 images). Each image was resized to 128 × 128 pixels and normalized pixel values to the range [0, 1], ensuring compatibility with the input requirements of the segmentation model and enhancing model convergence.

To generate ground truth for lesion segmentation, lesion boundaries in each image were manually annotated using the Computer Vision Annotation Tool (CVAT), ensuring precision and consistency. These masks enabled the training of robust and generalizable segmentation and validation of their accuracy under varying lesion conditions.

3.2 Image Preprocessing

Preprocessing was essential to enhance image quality and remove visual obstructions, particularly hair strands that could interfere with lesion segmentation and classification. The preprocessing pipeline consists of three main steps: (1) Grayscale Conversion (2) Artefact Detection Using Morphological Operations (3) Artefact Removal via Inpainting.

Grayscale Conversion. The input dermoscopic images were converted from RGB to grayscale to simplify the image and highlight intensity variations. Hair structures, typically appearing as darker elements, were made more distinguishable from surrounding skin regions. In our proposed methodology, the grayscale conversion changes colour images into grayscale because Grayscale images are easier and faster to process than coloured images.

Artefact Detection Using Morphological Operations. A Blackhat morphological operation was applied to emphasize dark features against a lighter background. A 5×5 rectangular structuring element was selected for the Blackhat transformation, optimized to highlight hair features effectively. The resulting image emphasizes the location of hair, which is then binarized using thresholding to generate a mask. A threshold value of 15 is used to separate hair pixels (foreground) from the rest of the image (background). The outcome is a binary mask where hair regions are identified as white areas.

Artefact Removal via Inpainting. Telea inpainting algorithm was selected due to its superior ability to preserve edges and reconstruct missing regions seamlessly. Before applying inpainting, the binary mask is refined using morphological dilation with a 3×3 kernel to ensure all hair regions are fully covered. If no significant hair regions are detected, the image is directly passed to the segmentation stage without inpainting. Otherwise, the inpainting process fills the masked hair regions by interpolating pixel values from neighbouring areas. As shown in Fig. 2, the inpainted images show clear lesion visibility after artefact removal.

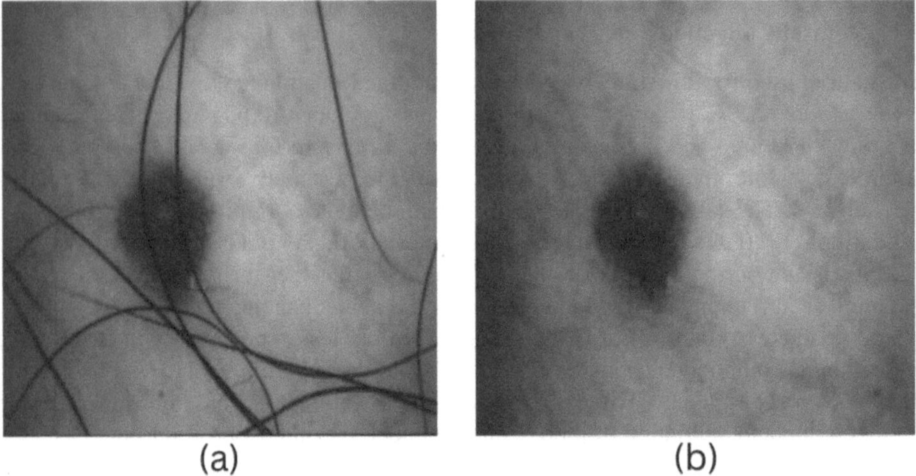

Fig. 2. (a) Original dermoscopic image containing visible hair strands. (b) Final inpainted image generated using the Telea algorithm after artefact detection and mask dilation.

3.3 Segmentation

The process of segmentation is used to differentiate lesions from the surrounding skin. In this study, a customized U-Net architecture was used for lesion segmentation due to its proven effectiveness in biomedical image tasks. Accurate segmentation of lesion boundaries facilitates meaningful feature extraction and classification.

The model architecture consists of a symmetrical encoder-decoder structure with skip connections that combine high-level semantics with spatial details. The encoder applies convolutional layers with ReLU activation and max-pooling, while the decoder reconstructs spatial details using transposed convolutions. A sigmoid-activated final layer outputs binary segmentation masks.

Training employed the Adam optimizer with a learning rate scheduler and early stopping. Dice Loss was used to address class imbalance and maximize overlap with ground truth masks. Data augmentation (rotations, flips, zooming) was applied to improve model robustness. Ground truth masks were annotated using CVAT.

To address lesion diversity, the dataset included various lesion complexities: clear boundaries, tiny lesions, smudged boundaries, and wide lesions.

3.4 Feature Extraction

Feature extraction is an important step in extracting information in a given lesion image. In our study, clinically relevant features were extracted based on the ABCD criteria: Asymmetry, Border irregularity, Colour variation, and Diameter. These features were computed to convert the spatial and visual characteristics of lesions into structured numeric inputs for classification.

Asymmetry was quantified by calculating pixel-wise differences between the original lesion and its flipped or rotated versions, formalized by the Asymmetry Index:

$$Asymmetry\ Index = \frac{Sum\ of\ Differences}{3 \times Total\ Pixel\ Count} \tag{1}$$

Border irregularity was computed using the circularity formula:

$$Border\ Irregularity = 1 - \frac{4\pi \times Area}{Perimeter^2} \tag{2}$$

This metric distinguishes smooth from jagged lesion borders. Colour features were captured by computing the mean and variance across the RGB channels within the lesion region:

$$Mean\ Color = \left(\frac{1}{n}\sum_{i=1}^{n} R_i, \frac{1}{n}\sum_{i=1}^{n} G_i, \frac{1}{n}\sum_{i=1}^{n} B_i\right) \tag{3}$$

Where R_i, G_i, B_i are the pixel values of the lesion in the red, green, and blue channels and n is the number of pixels in the lesion.

$$Color\ Variance = \frac{1}{n}\sum_{i=1}^{n}(R_i - \mu_R)^2, \frac{1}{n}\sum_{i=1}^{n}(G_i - \mu_G)^2, \frac{1}{n}\sum_{i=1}^{n}(B_i - \mu_B)^2 \tag{4}$$

Where μ_R, μ_G, μ_B denote the mean values of the red, green, and blue channels.

The diameter was approximated by the major axis length of the lesion region:

$$Diameter = Major\ Axis\ Length \tag{5}$$

All features were compiled into a CSV format along with the corresponding class labels, enabling structured input for classification.

3.5 Classification

The final stage is classifying the lesions into benign or malignant categories. The process is organized into three key steps: (1) Training a Multilayer perceptron (MLP) neural network classifier (2) Applying TabNet-Based Transfer Learning (3) Combining Predictions Using a Stacking Ensemble.

Training a Multilayer Perceptron (MLP) Neural Network Classifier. Since the extracted ABCD features are purely numerical, an MLP [17] was selected as it is well-suited for modeling nonlinear relationships in structured numerical data. The MLP [16] architecture consists of an input layer matching the number of extracted features, followed by two hidden layers with 64 and 32 neurons respectively. ReLU activation functions were used in the hidden layers, and dropout layers with a rate of 0.2 were applied to reduce overfitting. The output layer consists of a single neuron with a sigmoid activation function to facilitate binary classification. The model was trained using the Adam optimizer and binary cross entropy as the loss function. Early stopping and learning rate decay were employed to optimize convergence and prevent overfitting.

Applying TabNet-Based Transfer Learning. As the features are stored in tabular format, TabNet [18] is employed because it is specifically designed for tabular data and uses sequential attention mechanisms to select features dynamically. In this study, a pretrained TabNet model was fine-tuned on the ABCD feature dataset. The model was configured with three decision steps and used sparse regularization to encourage feature selection. Batch normalization and virtual batch size techniques were applied to improve generalization. Transfer learning allowed the model to adapt quickly with minimal overfitting, leveraging its prior knowledge from training on larger tabular datasets.

Combining Predictions Using a Stacking Ensemble. To further improve prediction performance and compensate for the limitations of individual models, a stacking ensemble learning approach was adopted. Logistic Regression was chosen as the meta-learner because it is simple, interpretable, and effective in binary classification tasks, making it well-suited to combine the outputs of the MLP and TabNet. In this setup, both the MLP and TabNet models served as base learners, generating probability scores for each sample. These scores were then fed into a logistic regression meta-learner, which was trained to make the final classification decision. The ensemble approach aimed to exploit the complementary strengths of the Neural Network and TabNet models, thereby achieving improved classification robustness and generalization ability compared to individual base classifiers.

4 Results

The performance of the proposed deep learning-based melanoma diagnostic technique was evaluated across its three core components: preprocessing, segmentation, and classification. Evaluation metrics were selected to quantify structural preservation, segmentation accuracy, and classification performance, respectively.

4.1 Preprocessing Results

The artefact removal stage was quantitatively assessed using the Structural Similarity Index (SSIM) and Mean Squared Error (MSE) by comparing the binary hair masks generated by the system with manually annotated masks, as shown in Table 2. The SSIM values for test samples ranged from 0.9323 to 0.9851, indicating high structural similarity between the processed and reference images. Corresponding MSE values were observed between 32.51 and 611.96 across varying levels of image complexity. These results demonstrate that the inpainting method preserved lesion structures while effectively eliminating hair artefacts.

Table 2. SSIM and MSE values for preprocessed images across different complexity levels.

Case	SSIM Value	MSE Value
C2S1	0.9851	54.19
C2S2	0.9789	32.51
C2S3	0.9693	62.13
C2S4	0.9446	185.68
C2S5	0.9323	194.35
C3S1	0.9710	173.40
C3S2	0.9628	355.47
C3S3	0.9520	611.96
C3S4	0.9648	335.24
C3S5	0.9514	496.36

4.2 Segmentation Results

The segmentation performance was measured using the Dice Coefficient, which evaluates the overlap between predicted lesion masks and ground truth annotations as shown in Fig. 3. The model achieved a mean Dice score of 0.9305 on the test dataset, indicating precise lesion boundary delineation. The model demonstrated robust performance across lesion types including clear boundaries, smudged edges, and wide or irregular lesions.

$$Dice\ coefficient = \frac{2.Intersection + smooth}{Sum\ of\ True + Sum\ of\ Predicted + smooth} \tag{6}$$

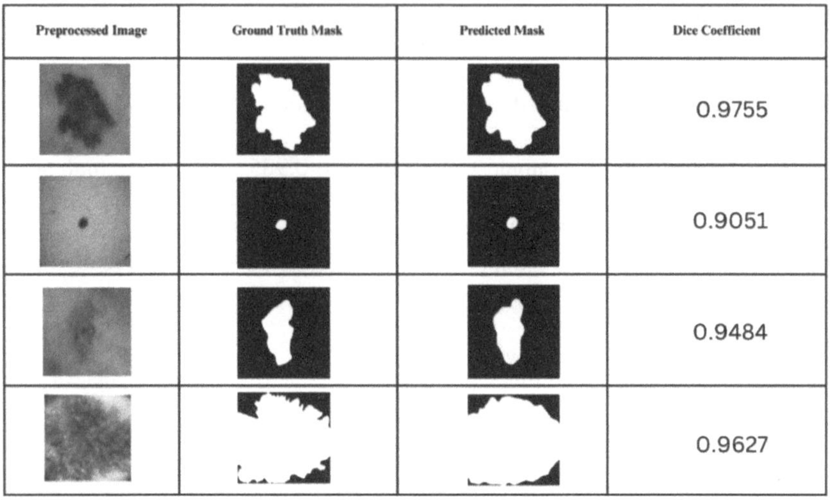

Preprocessed Image	Ground Truth Mask	Predicted Mask	Dice Coefficient
			0.9755
			0.9051
			0.9484
			0.9627

Fig. 3. Dice coefficient scores for sample test images representing different lesion complexities—clear boundaries, tiny lesions, smudged boundaries, and wide lesions—segmented by the U-Net model.

4.3 Feature Extraction Results

To enable accurate lesion classification, four clinical features were extracted from each segmented image, based on the ABCD dermatological rule: Asymmetry Index, Border Irregularity, Colour Variance, and Diameter. These values were calculated for each lesion and stored in a structured dataset for downstream classification.

4.4 Classification Results

Classification performance was assessed using standard binary evaluation metrics: accuracy, precision, recall, and F1-score, as shown in Table 3. Comparative performance of MLP, TabNet, and Ensemble classifiers. The Multilayer Perceptron (MLP) model achieved an accuracy of 0.71, while the TabNet model reported an accuracy of 0.65. When combined using the stacking ensemble strategy, the final model achieved an overall accuracy of 0.71, with corresponding precision, recall, and F1-score all at 0.71. The ensemble model outperformed individual classifiers in terms of balanced prediction and generalization capability.

The obtained results are directly aligned with our research objectives: the U-Net segmentation successfully isolated lesion regions, the use of transfer learning through TabNet enhanced generalization within a small dataset, and the ensemble learning improved classification consistency. A comparative summary of our model's performance against recent studies is presented in Table 4.

Our model achieved balanced accuracy, sensitivity, and specificity of 71% on a curated dataset of 215 dermoscopic images, demonstrating robustness in data-limited scenarios. Although CNN and transformer approaches report higher performance on

Table 3. Comparative performance of MLP, TabNet, and Ensemble classifiers

Model	Accuracy	Precision	Recall	F1-Score
MLP Classifier	70.59%	71.00%	71.00%	70.00%
TabNet Classifier	64.71%	69.00%	68.00%	64.00%
Ensemble Classifier	71.00%	71.00%	71.00%	71.00%

Table 4. Comparative performance (in %) of Recent Studies

Study	Dataset(s)	Size	Method	Accuracy	Sensitivity	Specificity
[12]	ISIC2018 & ISIC2019	10,000+	Vision Transformer	86.12	–	–
[13]	ISIC, HAM10000	50000+	EfficientNet + transfer learning	HAM10000: 94.80 ISIC: 95.49	HAM10000: 83 ISIC: 96	HAM10000: 99 ISIC: 97
[14]	PH^2, ISIC2016, ISIC2017, HAM10000	10000+	Deep CNN features + ensembles	PH^2: 98.33; ISIC2016: 80.47; ISIC2017: 81.16; HAM10000: 81.	PH^2: 100	PH^2: 97.91
[15]	ISIC variants		FCDS-CNN, ResNet + DeepLab	96	–	–
[16]	PH2	200	ABCD-rule + TDS	84	60.5	89.5
Proposed Method	ISIC subset	215	Preprocessing + U-Net + ABCD + MLP + TabNet + LR stacking	71	71	71

massive datasets, they are far more complex and resource-intensive. By contrast, our framework remains simple, faster to train, and well-suited for low-resource settings while delivering reliable diagnostic outcomes. Importantly, it integrates ABCD features for interpretability and incorporates preprocessing to reduce artefact-driven errors. With further hyperparameter tuning and validation on larger datasets, the system can improve while preserving efficiency, interpretability, and clinical relevance.

5 Discussion

This study presents a deep-learning-based technique for the early detection of melanoma, demonstrating that combining traditional image analysis with modern learning architectures can yield accurate and reliable diagnostic outcomes. The results show that the final ensemble achieved an accuracy of 71%, which directly addresses our research objectives: segmentation successfully isolated lesion regions, the ensemble approach improved categorization, and transfer learning enhanced model generalization.

The inpainting-based artefact removal approach proved effective in preserving lesion details while eliminating visual obstructions such as hair, thereby improving the quality of input for segmentation and feature extraction. These outcomes align with similar work in dermatological imaging where preprocessing is emphasized as a critical precursor to reliable automated diagnosis.

The segmentation model, a modified U-Net, demonstrated high overlap with expert-annotated masks, supporting prior findings on U-Net's suitability for biomedical image segmentation. The inclusion of lesions with diverse morphological characteristics and the use of data augmentation likely improved model generalization, an aspect noted in related studies applying deep learning to small medical datasets.

The classification results underscore the value of combining models with different representational strengths. While the stacking ensemble did not exceed the performance of the MLP alone, this outcome reflects the small dataset size and the reliance on a common feature set, which limited the diversity of error patterns between models. This consistency demonstrates that the ABCD-based features were stable across classifiers, confirming that both MLP and ensemble approaches captured the same discriminative signals in the data.

Nonetheless, this study has limitations. The relatively small and curated dataset restricts generalizability, and although our framework demonstrated balanced accuracy, sensitivity, and specificity, validation on larger and more varied populations is necessary to confirm robustness. Practical constraints include variability in dermoscopic imaging devices and the need for broader lesion categories beyond binary classification. Ground truth annotations, though carefully prepared, are still subject to inter-observer variability. Additionally, the classification task was constrained to a binary label schema, whereas clinical deployment would benefit from finer-grained, multi-class diagnostic output.

Future work will address these limitations by integrating larger and more diverse image repositories, extending the classification pipeline to support multi-class lesion types, and exploring explainability tools to enhance model transparency. Real-time integration within a mobile application is also planned, with the goal of supporting dermatological screening in resource-constrained healthcare environments.

6 Conclusion

This study proposed a structured deep learning framework for early melanoma detection, integrating preprocessing, U-Net segmentation, ABCD feature extraction, and ensemble classification. The system achieved balanced accuracy, precision, recall, and F1-score of 71%, meeting the research objectives of robust feature isolation, improved classification through ensemble learning, and enhanced generalization with transfer learning.

The novelty of this work lies in fusing clinically interpretable ABCD criteria with deep representations in a stacking ensemble, supported by artefact-aware preprocessing and segmentation. While the results are modest compared to large-scale CNN or transformer studies, they demonstrate that reliable performance can be achieved in data-limited settings with clinically meaningful features.

Future work will focus on validating the approach on larger and more diverse datasets, expanding beyond binary classification, and exploring optimized ensemble strategies. With further refinement, the proposed framework shows promise as a practical decision-support tool for improving diagnostic accessibility, particularly in resource-constrained healthcare environments.

Disclosure of Interests. The authors declare no competing interests.

References

1. Key statistics for melanoma skin cancer: https://www.cancer.org/cancer/types/melanoma-skin-cancer/about/key-statistics.html. Accessed 5 May 2025
2. Sun, X., Zhang, N., Yin, C., Zhu, B., Li, X.: Ultraviolet radiation and melanomagenesis: from mechanism to immunotherapy. Front. Oncol. **10**, 951 (2020)
3. Balch, C.M., et al.: Final version of the American joint committee on cancer staging system for cutaneous melanoma. J. Clin. Oncol. **19**(16), 3635–3648 (2001)
4. Hassen, W.A., et al.: MENA prostate cancer regional guidelines committee: modification and implementation of NCCN guidelines on prostate cancer in the Middle East and North Africa region. J. Natl. Compr. Cancer Netw. **8**(Suppl. 3), S26–S28 (2010)
5. Alexandrescu, D.T.: Melanoma costs: a dynamic model comparing estimated overall costs of various clinical stages. Dermatol. Online J. **15**(11), 1 (2009)
6. Popescu, D., El-Khatib, M., El-Khatib, H., Ichim, L.: New trends in melanoma detection using neural networks. Sensors. **22**(2), 496 (2022)
7. Ali, A.R., Deserno, T.M.: A systematic review of automated melanoma detection in dermatoscopic images and its ground truth data. In: Abbey, C., Mello-Thoms, C. (eds.) Medical Imaging 2012: Image Perception, Observer Performance, and Technology Assessment, SPIE Proceedings, vol. 8318, pt. 83181I, pp. 1–11. SPIE, Bellingham, WA (2012).
8. Kaur, R., GholamHosseini, H., Lindén, M.: Advanced deep learning models for melanoma diagnosis in computer-aided skin cancer detection. Sensors. **25**(3), 594 (2025)
9. Aldridge, R.B., Davies, E.C., Williams, H.C.: Novice identification of melanoma: not quite as straightforward as "ABCD". BMJ. **340**, c181 (2012)
10. Bhatt, H., Shah, V., Shah, K., Shah, R., Shah, M.: State-of-the-art machine learning techniques for melanoma skin cancer detection and classification: a comprehensive review. Intell. Med. **3**(3), 180–190 (2023)
11. Dagnaw, G.E.A.: Skin cancer classification using vision transformers and explainable artificial intelligence. **7**(14) (2024)
12. Zhang, X.E.A.: DermViT: diagnosis-guided vision transformer for robust and efficient skin lesion classification. Bioengineering. **12**(4), 421 (2025)
13. Venugopal, V.E.A.: A deep neural network using modified EfficientNet for skin cancer detection in dermoscopic images. Decis. Anal. J. **8**, 100278 (2023)
14. Gajera, H.K.E.A.: A comprehensive analysis of dermoscopy images for melanoma detection via deep CNN features. Biomed. Sig. Process. Control. **79**, 104186 (2023)

15. Nawaz, K.E.A.: Skin cancer detection using dermoscopic images with convolutional neural network. Sci. Rep. **15**(1) (2025)
16. Senan, E.J.M.: Analysis of dermoscopy images by using ABCD rule for early detection of skin cancer. Glob. Transitions Proc. **2**(1), 1–7 (2021)
17. Tiwari, S.: Dermatoscopy using multi-layer perceptron, convolution neural network, and capsule network to differentiate malignant melanoma from benign nevus. Int. J. Healthc. Inf. Syst. Inform. **16**(3), 58–73 (2021)
18. Arık, S.O., Pfister, T.: TabNet: attentive interpretable tabular learning. Proc. AAAI Conf. Artif. Intell. **35**(8), 6679–6687 (2021)

Early Detection and Severity Assessment of Dysgraphia in Sinhala-Speaking Children Using a Multi-modal Machine Learning Approach

Sandushi Weraduwa[1](✉), P. P. G. Dinesh Asanka[1], Thilini V. Mahanama[1], and Swarna Wijeathunge[2]

[1] Department of Industrial Management, Faculty of Science, University of Kelaniya, Colombo, Sri Lanka
sandushiw98@gmail.com, {dasanka,thilinim}@kln.ac.lk

[2] Child and Adolescent Mental Health Service, Lady Ridgway Hospital, Borella, Colombo, Sri Lanka

Abstract. Dysgraphia is a neurological learning disability that impairs handwriting, spelling, and the ability to express thoughts in written form. Despite its significant impact on children's academic performance and psychological well-being, early detection remains a challenge particularly in linguistically and culturally unique settings like Sri Lanka. Existing diagnostic tools are largely developed for English-speaking populations and fail to address Sinhala language-specific characteristics. To bridge this gap, this research introduces the first multi-modal sequential machine learning framework in Sri Lanka for the early detection and severity assessment of Dysgraphia among Sinhala-speaking primary school children. The proposed approach integrates two key components: a Convolutional Neural Network (CNN) utilizing VGG16 for handwriting image analysis, and a Gradient Boosting classifier for interpreting cognitive, behavioral, and personal data. The dataset comprises 373 digitized handwriting samples from 84 children, collected from local schools and a pediatric hospital, using psychological assessments from Indian contexts adapted to Sinhala language materials. Handwriting samples were preprocessed through binarization and color inversion for model input. The handwriting-based Dysgraphia detection model achieved an accuracy of 96%, while the severity assessment model reached 87%. This pioneering multimodal sequential approach significantly enhances diagnostic precision and reliability, enabling earlier interventions and individualized academic support. The study represents a vital step toward inclusive education in Sri Lanka, leveraging advanced AI techniques to meet a critical need in local learning disability diagnostics.

Keywords: CNN-VGG16 · Dysgraphia · Learning Disability Detection · Multi-modal Machine Learning · Sinhala Language

R. N. Rajapakse et al. (Eds.): ICTer 2025, CCIS 2844, pp. 47–61, 2026.
https://doi.org/10.1007/978-981-92-0137-2_4

1 Introduction

Dysgraphia is a neurological learning disability that disrupts the ability to write effectively, impacting handwriting, spelling, and the organization of thoughts on paper. Classified as a specific learning disability, it is primarily diagnosed in children but can also affect adults [1] .Key indicators of Dysgraphia include poor handwriting, inconsistent spacing, irregular spacing, letter reversals, difficulty following dictated instructions, substitution of incorrect words, irregular slants and shapes in writing, reduced writing speed, and awkward pencil grips or paper positioning [2] .

A significant issue in current research is the lack of diagnostic tools tailored to diverse linguistic and cultural settings, particularly for the Sinhala language. Most existing studies focus on English and European contexts, employing methods that primarily analyze handwriting samples through online and offline approaches [1]. While many studies have analyzed handwriting characteristics, none have utilized methods that both identify dysgraphic children through handwriting analysis and predict the severity of the condition using clinical data, especially within the context of the Sinhala language.

This study presents the first multi-modal machine learning model developed to identify dysgraphic children in Sinhala-speaking populations in Sri Lanka. By using a convolutional neural network (CNN) with vgg16 for handwriting image analysis with a Gradient Boosting classifier for evaluating cognitive and behavioral data, this study seeks to improve the accuracy and reliability of Dysgraphia detection. This comprehensive approach facilitates early identification and intervention, ultimately contributing to better educational outcomes for children in Sri Lanka.

1.1 The Role of Dysgraphia in the Sinhala Language

To the best of our knowledge, there is no documented evidence of direct and explicit Dysgraphia screening procedures currently implemented in Sri Lanka by either the government or the private sector. Screening is primarily conducted through specialized clinics owned by government and private institutions, where professionals manually observe and evaluate students' reading and writing skills. This process is time-consuming and delays early interventions, which could otherwise mitigate the long-term educational impacts on children [3, 4]. Furthermore, existing diagnostic tools are not adequately tailored to the linguistic and cultural specificities of the Sinhala language, which is crucial for accurate identification and support of children with Dysgraphia [3, 4]. The absence of Sinhala-specific tools hinders precise diagnosis and timely intervention. Another significant challenge is the underutilization of modern computational techniques such as machine learning and deep learning. These advanced methods could significantly enhance diagnostic accuracy and reduce the time required for identifying Dysgraphia. Additionally, there is a lack of innovative early detection systems that integrate multimodal data, including motor, demographic, cognitive, and handwriting analysis, through advanced AI methods [4]. Therefore, there is an urgent need for an extensive, efficient, computerized, and cost-effective system with a high level of specificity and capability to diagnose Dysgraphia, especially for Sinhala-speaking children.

Dysgraphia varies by script, with Sinhala being more complex and Latin also posing challenges; thus, both script type and severity must be considered in diagnosis and treatment [3].

2 Literature Review

Notably, [3, 4] introduced "Nana Shilpa" and "Pubudu," mobile applications that apply CNNs and other machine learning models to detect learning disabilities such as dyscalculia, Dysgraphia, and Dyslexia among Sri Lankan children. "Nana Shilpa" uses CNNs along with SVMs, achieving impressive accuracies of 92% for dyscalculia and 99% for Dysgraphia. On the other hand, "Pubudu" incorporates voice recognition and follows a multisensory approach, reaching accuracies of 88% for Dyslexia, 58% for Dysgraphia, and 99% for dyscalculia. Despite their effectiveness, both applications face challenges, such as limited language options and the lack of awareness regarding learning disabilities. In particular, [3] highlighted the ongoing work on "Pubudu" to enhance model accuracy and expand its linguistic capabilities.

The study [5] by developed a Sinhala handwriting dataset to diagnose Dysgraphia, including 373 samples from 84 children (73 dysgraphic, 300 non-dysgraphic). The dataset, tailored for Sinhala script, involves systematic data collection, preprocessing, and binary format conversion with color inversion. It addresses a significant linguistic gap in developed the Sinhala Dysgraphia handwriting dataset to address the absence of any existing comprehensive Sinhala handwriting datasets for Dysgraphia., with future plans to validate the dataset using CNN models to enhance diagnostic accuracy.

Combining CNNs with recurrent neural networks, [6] identified dysgraphia risks based on handwriting errors, with a reported accuracy of 73% [1]. In their recent work, they enhanced CNN performance through data augmentation, achieving an accuracy rate of 84%. Both studies faced challenges such as insufficient data diversity and the risk of model overfitting. Similarly, [7, 8] used CNNs for feature detection related to Dyslexia and Dysgraphia, obtaining accuracy rates up to 97.98%. However, these studies highlighted limitations, including high diagnostic costs and data overfitting concerns. These studies highlight the promise and challenges of using CNNs and other advanced analytics in diagnosing learning disabilities, calling for continuous improvements in accuracy and practical implementation.

The integration of CNNs with long short-term memory (LSTM) networks has also shown significant promise in addressing learning disabilities. By extracting features from handwriting images using CNNs and analyzing sequences with LSTMs, [6] achieved substantial accuracy, although issues with small sample sizes and potential overfitting were noted. Extending this approach, [7] incorporated positional encoding and self-attention mechanisms within the CNN-LSTM framework for early dyslexia detection in Chinese-speaking children, reaching up to 85% accuracy. However, the model's complexity reduced its interpretability. The study [8] advanced this by combining the CNN-LSTM output with a random forest classifier, attaining accuracies above 96%. They recommended further improvements through transfer learning and more diverse datasets.

The studies [9, 10] employed advanced machine learning models to improve dysgraphia and dyslexia detection. Sasidhar et al. used a residual neural network (ResNet) combined with OpenCV for preprocessing handwriting images, resulting in enhanced dyslexia detection rates. Meanwhile, [9] leveraged an artificial neural network (ANN) for dysgraphia classification, achieving a 96% accuracy using digital handwriting traits. These studies underscore the potential of deep learning in automating and enhancing the diagnostic process, which can facilitate earlier educational interventions.

It is important to note that both *Nana Shilpa* [4] and *Pubudu* [3] focus on the Sinhala context and utilize handwriting to predict dysgraphia; however, their scope is limited to identifying the presence or risk of dysgraphia using handwriting data alone. In contrast, this study adopts a novel multimodal approach that sequentially use handwriting images with clinical, cognitive, and demographic data. While previous research has acknowledged the risk of dysgraphia, none have employed a comprehensive framework to assess its severity. This study fills that gap by enabling a more accurate and holistic diagnosis of dysgraphia in Sinhala-speaking children.

3 Methodology

3.1 Sequence Model Prediction Process

The proposed dysgraphia detection framework employs a two-step model combining handwriting analysis with severity -level evaluation, as summarized in Fig. 1. In the first step, handwriting samples are preprocessed, and features are extracted using CNN with VGG16, ResNet50 [11],and pure CNN architectures. Among these, the architecture that delivers the highest accuracy is used to determine whether a child is dysgraphic. If no Dysgraphia is detected, the process ends; otherwise, the second step is initiated. This subsequent step evaluates the severity level (high or low) by leveraging Clinical dataset. It's a comprehensive collection of clinical and demographic information, symptoms, and cognitive assessments gathered from children diagnosed with Dysgraphia. After preprocessing, feature engineering, and selection, models such as random forest, SVM, and gradient boosting are trained and validated. The most accurate model is chosen for making the final predictions for severity level. This dual-phase approach ensures accurate identification of Dysgraphia while effectively assessing the associated severity, offering a reliable and comprehensive diagnostic solution.

3.2 Handwriting Data Collection

The handwriting dataset for dysgraphia screening was developed using a structured, ethically approved methodology targeting children aged 6 to 11, including both dysgraphic and non-dysgraphic individuals to ensure a balanced dataset. Retrospective handwriting samples from 54 diagnosed dysgraphic children were accessed by specialists, with diagnoses based on adapted Indian psychological assessments tailored to Sinhala-language learning contexts. The assessment selected words from Sinhala school textbooks to address language-specific handwriting challenges. Unlike English, where capitalization is an issue, Sinhala children struggle mainly with vowel and consonant strokes. The chosen words tested these aspects, along with other dysgraphia symptoms such as poor sizing and spacing, omissions, improper letter formation, margin difficulties, shape discrimination issues, and letter mirroring [5]. These factors were key in evaluating handwriting

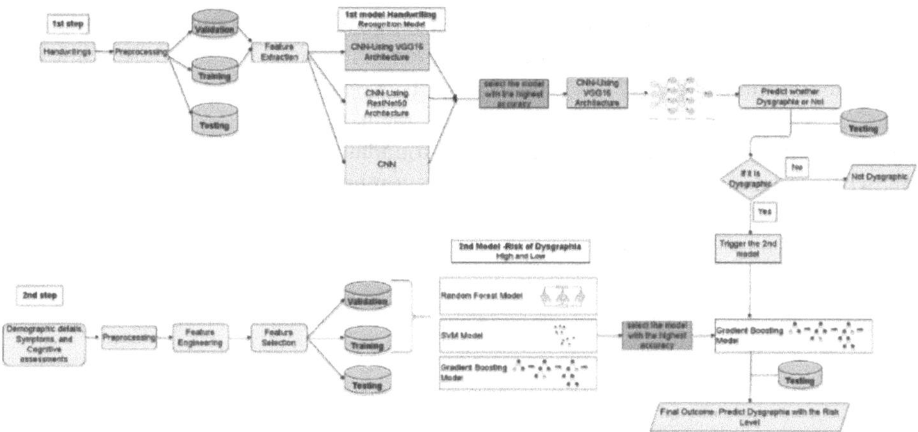

Fig. 1. Sequence Model Prediction Process for Dysgraphia Detection

and detecting dysgraphic tendencies. For the non-dysgraphic group, handwriting samples were obtained from 30 typically developing children through a structured dictation activity using the same set of linguistically complex Sinhala words designed to reveal dysgraphic features. Informed consent was secured from school principals, teachers, and parents, accompanied by comprehensive information sheets to ensure transparency and ethical compliance. This protocol not only upheld research ethics but also strengthened data validity and overall research quality [12, 13]. Samples were digitized using high-resolution cameras, saved in PNG format, and organized without character-level segmentation due to the complexity of Sinhala script. Preprocessing with OpenCV involved converting images to grayscale, applying the median blur technique for noise reduction without compromising stroke clarity [13], using adaptive thresholding, performing morphological operations Each image was resized to 256x256 pixels to ensure consistent input size, which is essential for machine learning models. The images were resized to a uniform size to maintain consistency for model input, see Fig. 2. Binarization was applied to enhance contrast between text and background, while color inversion was used to standardize stroke representation across samples, both improving feature extraction and model robustness.

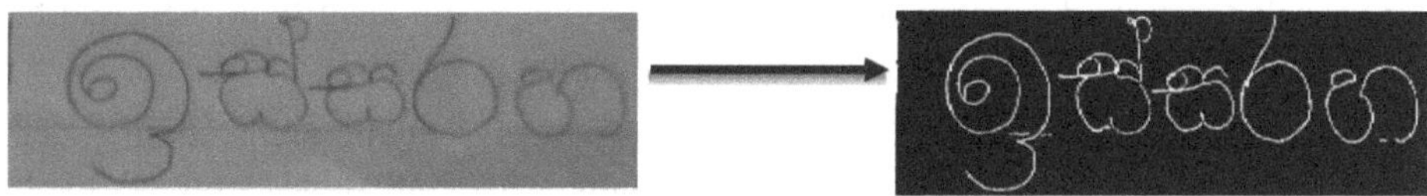

Fig. 2. A sample of handwriting image before preprocessing (left) and after preprocessing (right)

All images were manually labeled as 'DH' (dysgraphic handwriting) or 'NDH' (non-dysgraphic handwriting) based on expert diagnosis. In total, the dataset consists of 373 handwriting samples, with 73 from dysgraphic children and 300 from non-dysgraphic children. All handwritten images are presented in black and white for analysis. This proposed dataset forms a solid foundation for analyzing dysgraphia in Sinhala-speaking children and advancing research in this area. For example, while non-dysgraphic children correctly wrote words such as "වලහා", "කුරුල්ලන්", "මෙට්ටය",and "කෝටුව",dysgraphic children failed to write them accurately (compare Fig. 3 and Fig. 4). This proposed dataset provides a robust foundation for identifying and comparing handwriting characteristics associated with Dysgraphia.

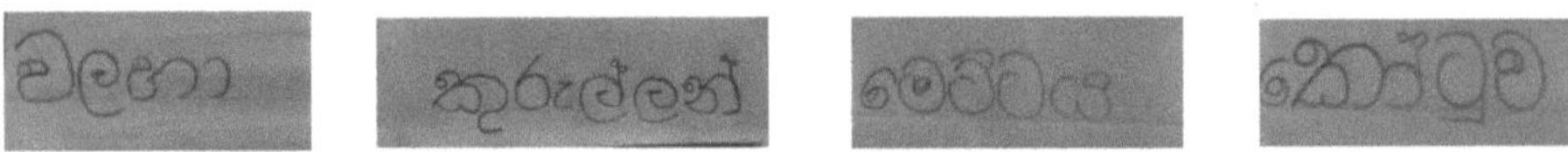

Fig. 3. A sample of words written by non-dysgraphic children

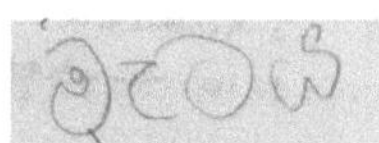

Fig. 4. A sample of written by dysgraphic children

3.3 Clinical Data Collection

Clinical data including demographic data were also collected from the 54 dysgraphic children considered in the study. Their dysgraphic severity level was recorded by specialists in learning disabilities at pediatric hospital. The primary use of this dataset is to analyze various factors that may influence the severity level of Dysgraphia in affected children. By examining a wide range of variables, the dataset seeks to identify patterns and correlations that could help predict the severity of dysgraphia. This effort facilitates early interventions and the creation of tailored treatment plans. The dataset includes clinical data collected from dysgraphic children. They are Demographic Information, Medical and Birth History, Developmental Milestones, Behavioral and Psychological Assessments, Family and Social Environment, Educational and School-related Factors, Physical and Neurological Observations, Speech and Language Evaluations, Emotional and Cognitive Assessments, Adaptive and Functional Skills. These diverse datasets enable comprehensive analysis, supporting the development of accurate predictive models for early dysgraphia detection. Such models help identify at-risk children, tailor interventions, and improve educational outcomes.

Preprocessing Clinical Data. Figure 5 illustrates the systematic preprocessing steps applied to the clinical dataset of dysgraphic children. Missing values were addressed using mean imputation for continuous variables (e.g., age, weight) and mode imputation for binary variables. Monthly income data, initially in text and range formats, was cleaned and converted to numerical values using averages or random values within defined limits, with missing entries filled using mode imputation. Categorical variables were encoded using label encoding, as one-hot encoding significantly increased dimensionality and was unsuitable for ordinal data. Label encoding maintained the ordinal nature of the data and reduced complexity.

Feature Engineering and Selection. Numerical data was normalized, and related subcategories (e.g., behavioral traits) were consolidated into single features with weighted values, reducing features from 135 to 55. feature selection using a correlation matrix

removed attributes with low relevance to dysgraphia detection, reducing the initial 242 features to 135. These preprocessing steps ensured clean, consistent data optimized for effective modeling features to 135. These preprocessing steps ensured clean, consistent data optimized for effective modeling.

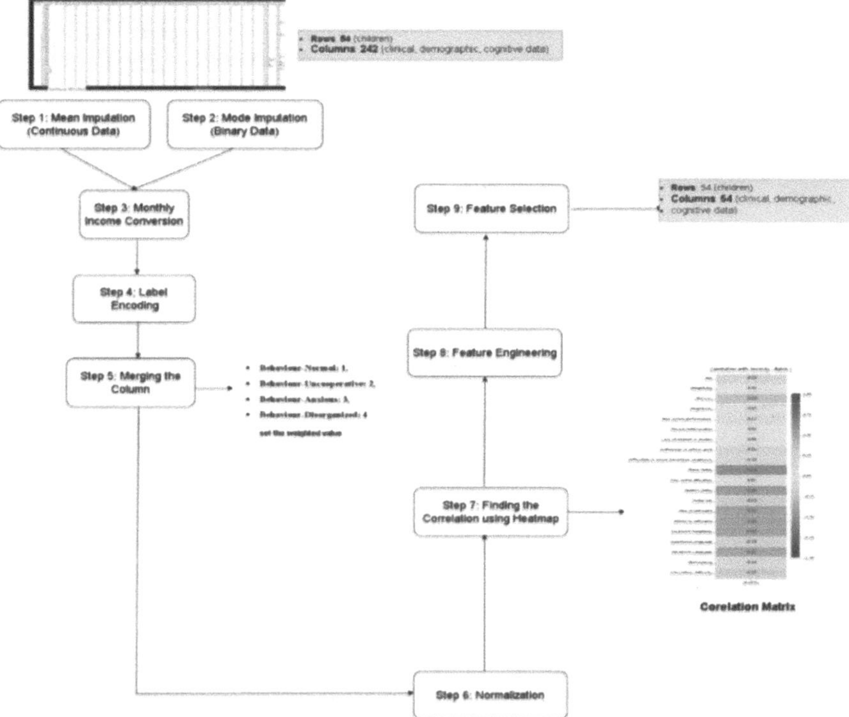

Fig. 5. Clinical data preprocessing

3.4 Development of Dysgraphia Detection and Severity Assessment Models

This section describes the process of developing predictive models for detecting Dysgraphia and a corresponding severity assessment model to evaluate the extent of the condition.

Proposed Model for Dysgraphia Detection. To detect Dysgraphia, multiple Convolutional Neural Network (CNN) architectures were evaluated. Proposed Model for Dysgraphia Detection. To detect Dysgraphia, multiple Convolutional Neural Network (CNN) architectures were evaluated. Among them, the CNN combined with the VGG16 architecture achieved the highest accuracy, demonstrating strong feature extraction capabilities for Sinhala handwriting. Therefore, it was selected for final imple mentation. The full architecture of the CNN with VGG16 is illustrated below.

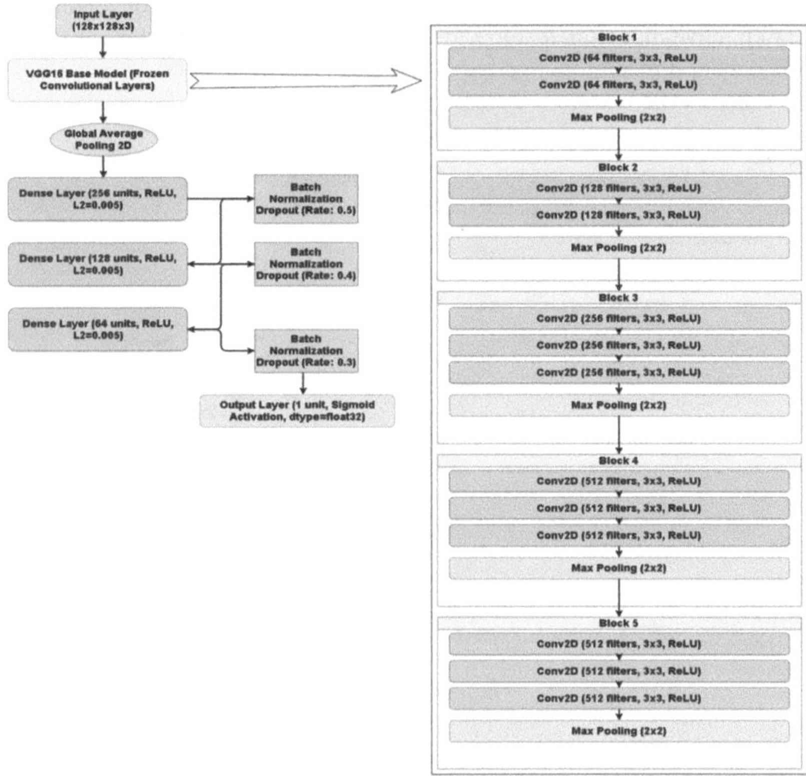

Fig. 6. The proposed model architecture for Dysgraphia prediction

Leveraging VGG16 Architecture in Dysgraphia Detection. The proposed CNN model uses a pre-trained VGG16 architecture for detecting Dysgraphia from handwriting images. VGG16, known for its strong feature extraction capabilities from ImageNet training [11], was adapted for binary classification by adding custom top layers (Fig. 6).

Base Model (VGG16): The convolutional layers of VGG16 were frozen to retain generic visual features useful for handwriting analysis. For model input, the images were further resized to $128 \times 128 \times 3$ to reduce computational complexity and memory usage

Custom Top Layers:

1. Global Average Pooling (GAP): Applied to reduce feature map dimensionality while preserving key information.
2. Dense Layers: Dense (256 units) with ReLU, L2 regularization ($\lambda = 0.005$), batch normalization, and dropout (0.5).

- Dense (128 units) with similar configurations and dropout (0.4).
- Dense (64 units) with dropout (0.3).
- These layers support complex pattern learning and prevent overfitting through dropout and regularization.

3. Output Layer: A single sigmoid-activated unit with float32 type for binary classification.

This architecture effectively adapts VGG16 for Dysgraphia detection while balancing model complexity and generalization. Output Layer: The final output layer consists of a single unit with a sigmoid activation function to perform binary classification. The output layer's data type was explicitly set to 'float32' to ensure stability in prediction outputs

Model Compilation and Training. The model was compiled using the Adam optimizer (learning rate: 0.00005) and binary cross-entropy loss, suitable for binary classification. To address class imbalance, class weights were assigned, giving more importance to the minority class and reducing bias during training. To improve learning efficiency, callbacks such as Early Stopping and ReduceLROnPlateau were used. Early Stopping halted training after ten epochs without improvement in validation loss, while ReduceLROnPlateau dynamically adjusted the learning rate when validation loss plateaued, allowing for gradual fine-tuning.

The model underwent five-fold cross-validation, training and validating across distinct data splits. Performance metrics accuracy, precision, recall, and F1 score were calculated for each fold to evaluate generalization. This setup, combined with L2 regularization, batch normalization, and dropout, enhanced the model's robustness and prevented overfitting. The architecture effectively leveraged VGG16's powerful feature extraction, fine-tuned through custom dense layers, to detect subtle handwriting patterns indicative of Dysgraphia.

Validation of the Proposed Dysgraphia Predictive Models. To ensure robustness and generalizability, multiple validation techniques were applied to the predictive models for Dysgraphia detection and severity assessment using handwriting and clinical/demographic data. For the Dysgraphia detection model, an 80/20 train-test split was used, followed by five-fold cross-validation to reduce variance and enhance generalization. For severity level assessment using clinical data, a similar 80/20 split was combined with ten-fold cross-validation due to the smaller dataset size, allowing more efficient use of data and reliable accuracy estimation.

Additionally, predictions from the severity-level model were validated through expert consultation with dysgraphia specialists to ensure alignment with real-world clinical insights. All reported accuracies reflect performance on unseen test data. These validation strategies, including cross-validation and expert review, help mitigate overfitting and confirm the models' clinical relevance and predictive reliability.

Proposed Model for Assessing Dysgraphia Severity. For the second stage of the model, binary classification was selected to predict the severity of Dysgraphia (categorized as High and Low) using demographic information, symptoms, and cognitive assessments. The primary motivation for choosing binary classification was to effectively distinguish between these severity levels while leveraging the available labeled data.

Among the machine learning algorithms, random forest [14], SVM [15], and gradient boost algorithms are tested as they are well-suited for smaller datasets. Due to the limited dataset size, there was a risk of overfitting. To address this challenge and mitigate class imbalance, synthetic minority over-sampling technique (SMOTE) in combination with ten-fold cross-validation. However, applying SMOTE before cross-validation introduced data leakage [16], which can lead to overly optimistic performance estimates. Therefore, we used SMOTE during the cross-validation process to ensure the integrity of the evaluation. The use of SMOTE during cross-validation adheres to recent recommendations for robust model evaluation in imbalanced datasets ([17, 18]). Gradient Boosting techniques specifically adapted for small datasets [19] further enhance the model's reliability

4 Results and Discussion

In the first stage of this study, three CNN models pure CNN, CNN with VGG16, and CNN with ResNet50 architecture were evaluated to compare their effectiveness in Dysgraphia detection. Among these, the CNN with VGG16 architecture demonstrated the highest testing accuracy, indicating its superior performance in feature extraction and classification for handwriting images. Consequently, the VGG16 architecture was selected as the outperforming model.

4.1 Designing an Enhanced Dysgraphia Predictive Model

Table 1 compares the performance of the three developed Dysgraphia predictive models, CNN with VGG16, CNN with ResNet50, and the pure CNN model, based on their performance metrics, with a focus on accuracy, precision, recall, and F1-score.

Table 1. Performance comparison analysis of the developed Dysgraphia predictive models

Model	Accuracy	Precision		Recall		F1-Score	
		Non-Dysgraphic	Dysgraphic	Non-Dysgraphic	Dysgraphic	Non-Dysgraphic	Dysgraphic
CNN with VGG16	0.96	0.98	0.88	0.97	0.93	0.98	0.87
CNN with ResNet50	0.80	0.80	0.00	1.00	0.00	0.90	0.00
Pure CNN	0.79	0.83	0.43	0.93	0.20	0.88	0.27

According to the performance metrices, the CNN with VGG16 model is the outperforming model for dysgraphia detection. It achieved the highest accuracy 0.96 and consistently high precision, recall, and F1-score for both Non-Dysgraphic and Dysgraphic classes. The ResNet50 and pure CNN models recorded significant challenges, particularly in identifying the Dysgraphic class, as evidenced by their lower precision, recall, and F1-scores.

The CNN with VGG16 architecture demonstrated high recall, which is crucial in the healthcare sector to ensure accurate identification of Dysgraphia, enabling timely diagnosis and intervention. Fig 10 in the next section provides the proposed model architecture for the proposed CNN based on the VGG16 model.

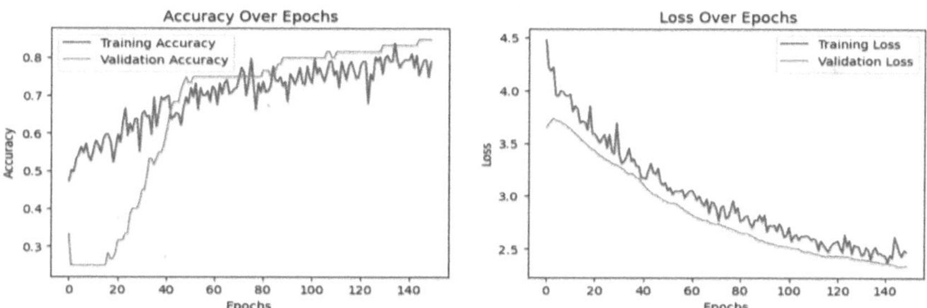

Fig. 7. The Dysgraphia predictive model's accuracy over epochs (left) and loss over epochs (right)

According to Fig. 7 left, both training and validation accuracy steadily increased, with validation accuracy reaching approximately 0.85 by the end of training. This indicates that the model was effectively learning the features from the data, and there was no significant indication of overfitting. Fig 7 right also depicts both training and validation loss decreasing consistently, showing that the model was successfully minimizing errors throughout the training process, without any signs of divergence.

The ROC curve (Fig. 8) shows a perfect AUC of 1.00, indicating excellent model performance in distinguishing between dysgraphic and non-dysgraphic samples. The precision-recall curve (Fig. 9) further confirms the model's robustness, maintaining high precision across varying recall levels, even in the presence of class imbalance.

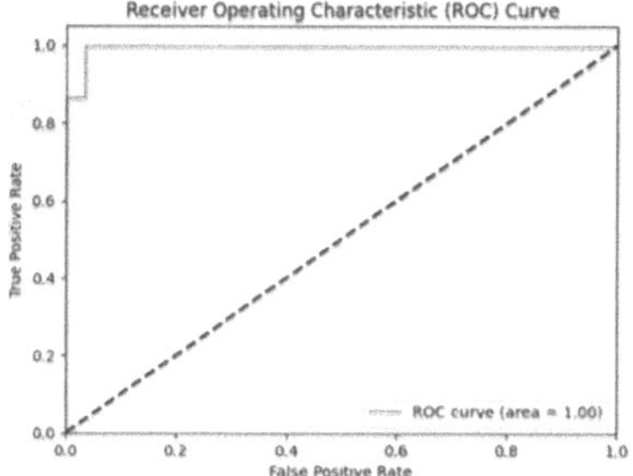

Fig. 8. The receiver operating characteristic (ROC) curve of the proposed Dysgraphia predictive model

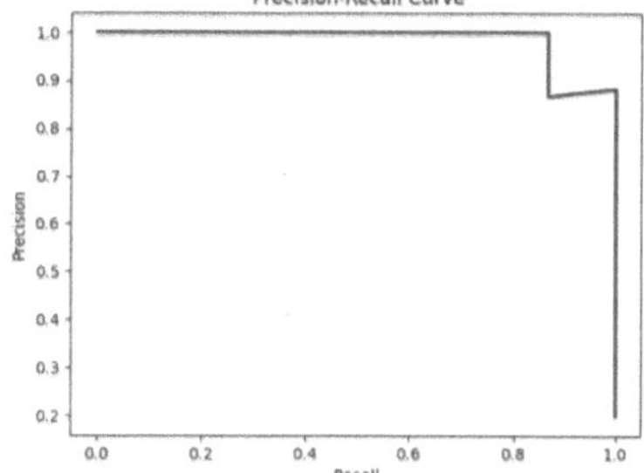

Fig. 9. The precision- recall curve of the proposed Dysgraphia predictive model

4.2 Developing an Enhanced Model for Predicting Dysgraphia Severity

A comparison of the Dysgraphia severity predictive models is summarized in Table 2, based on metrics such as testing accuracy, precision, recall, and F1 score. According to the performance metrics, gradient boosting emerged as the outperforming model for analyzing dysgraphia severity level based on clinical data.

Table 2. Performance comparison analysis of the developed Dysgraphia severity predictive models

Model	Testing Accuracy	Precision	Recall	F1 Score
SVM	0.80	0.80	0.80	0.79
Gradient Boosting	0.87	0.87	0.87	0.87
Random Forest	0.73	0.73	0.73	0.73

The gradient boosting model is suitable for predicting Dysgraphia severity due to its ability to capture intricate relationships between features and handle both numerical and categorical variables. Techniques such as SMOTE, combined with hyperparameter tuning, enabled gradient boosting to manage class imbalances effectively. This model maintained high accuracy without overfitting, making it suitable for clinical data with complex patterns. In addition to that, gradient boosting model demonstrated high validation accuracy and AUC across multiple folds, showing consistent performance, see Fig. 10.

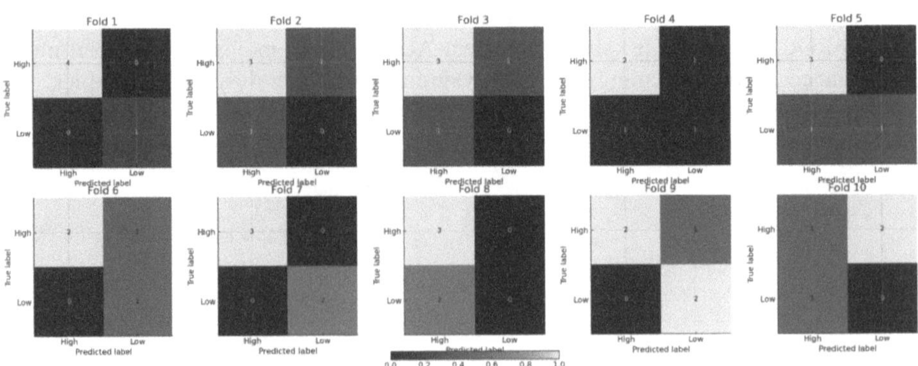

Fig. 10. Confusion Matrices of the proposed gradient boosting based Dysgraphia severity predictive models across multiple folds

The gradient boosting model accurately classified most samples, with some folds achieving perfect results. Misclassifications mainly affected the minority class, but recall remained reasonable, showing the model's effectiveness on imbalanced data. Performance varied across folds due to differences in training data.

Table 3. Comparison of Existing Dysgraphia Detection Methods and the Proposed Multimodal Approach

Ref	Method/Model Used	Targeted Disabilities	Dataset & Size	Accuracy/Outcome	Prediction Output
[4]	CNN + SVM	Dysgraphia, Dyscalculia	Sinhala Handwritings	99% (Dysgraphia), 92% (Dyscalculia)	Risk of dysgraphia or no risk
[3]	CNN + SVMs + KNN Voice Recognition (Multisensory Approach)	Dyslexia, Dysgraphia, Dyscalculia	Sinhala Handwritings	88% (Dyslexia), 58% (Dysgraphia), 99% (Dyscalculia)	Presence/Absence of Dysgraphia
[6]	CNN + RNN/LSTM with Data Augmentation	Dysgraphia	English Handwritings	73% (CNN + RNN), 84% (after augmentation)	Risk of dysgraphia or no risk
[7]	CNN-LSTM + Positional Encoding + Self-Attention	Dyslexia	Digital handwriting traits	Up to 85%	Presence/Absence of Dysgraphia
[8]	CNN-LSTM + Random Forest	Dyslexia & Dysgraphia	Digital handwriting traits	>96%	Presence/Absence of Dysgraphia
[9]	ANN	Dysgraphia	Digital handwriting traits	96%	Presence/Absence of Dysgraphia
Proposed Study	Multi-modal: CNNs for handwriting, Gradient Boosting for clinical data for severity prediction	Dysgraphia	Sinhala Handwritings	96% -CNN + vgg16 87%-Gradient Boosting	Presence/Absence of Dysgraphia and their severity level

Most prior studies on dysgraphia focus on binary classification, using small or language-specific handwriting datasets, limiting generalizability. While CNN, RNN, and hybrid models show good accuracy, and ANN methods offer categorical prediction, none integrate clinical or behavioral data or assess dysgraphia severity, an essential factor for effective intervention. See Table 3. In contrast, the proposed study introduces a **novel sequential multimodal approach**, where Sinhala handwriting images are first used to predict the presence of dysgraphia, and then clinical, cognitive, and demographic data are used to assess its severity offering one step beyond existing research and enabling more accurate and meaningful early intervention. This distinction is important while risk indicates the potential for having Dysgraphia, severity evaluates the level of difficulty experienced by a diagnosed child. By addressing both, the proposed model supports more accurate diagnosis and enables tailored, early-stage interventions that existing research has yet to achieve.

5 Conclusion

This study presents the first multi-modal AI model for detecting dysgraphia in Sinhala-speaking children in Sri Lanka. Future work should focus on building larger handwriting datasets across ages due to limited dataset and linguistic groups to reduce bias and overfitting, as well as expanding to other languages like Tamil, advancing educational technology and early learning disability screening.

Acknowledgement. I would like to extend my heartfelt appreciation to Dr. G. Wijesuriya, Director of Lady Ridgeway Hospital, for granting permission to conduct the necessary data collection for this study. Additionally, I am sincerely grateful to Mr. Geegange Indika Kumara, Principal of MR/Ganethanna Uparathana Vidyalaya, and Mrs. Wasantha Nilmini Warnasooriya for their cooperation and for allowing data to be gathered from the students. Finally, I am immensely thankful to the students and their parents, whose participation was vital to the success of this research.

Disclosure of Interests.

Funding. The research conducted did not receive any external funding.

Conflict of Interest. The authors confirm that no conflict of interest is involved.

References

1. Anand, S., Sharma, P., Sharma, M., Talwar, R., Mongia, C.: Deep learning-based classification of dysgraphia severity in children from handwriting images. Res. Square preprint (2023). doi:https://doi.org/10.21203/rs.3.rs-3803290/v1
2. Vilasini, V., Banu Rekha, B., Sandeep, V., Charan Venkatesh, V.: Deep learning techniques to detect learning disabilities among children using handwriting. In: 2022 Third International Conference on Intelligent Computing Instrumentation and Control Technologies (ICICICT). IEEE (2022)
3. Kariyawasam, R., Nadeeshani, M., Hamid, T., Subasinghe, I., Ratnayake, P.: A gamified approach for screening and intervention of dyslexia, dysgraphia and dyscalculia. In: 2019 International Conference on Advancements in Computing (ICAC). IEEE (2019)
4. Hewapathirana, C., Abeysinghe, K., Maheshani, P., Liyanage, P., Krishara, J., Thelijjagoda, S.: A mobile-based screening and refinement system to identify the risk of dyscalculia and dysgraphia learning disabilities in primary school students. In: 2021 10th International Conference on Information and Automation for Sustainability (ICIAfS). IEEE (2021)
5. Weraduwa, S., Asanka, D., Mahanama, T., Wijeatunge, S.: Developing a dysgraphia handwriting dataset for early detection of dysgraphia in sinhala-speaking children. In: 2024 9th International Conference on Information Technology Research (ICITR), pp. 1–6. IEEE (2024)
6. Doshi, N.N., Maniyar, M.U., Shah, K.K., Sarda, N.D., Narvekar, M., Mukhopadhyay, D.: A convolutional recurrent neural network-based model for handwritten text recognition to predict dysgraphia. In: 2023 International Conference on Intelligent Systems for Communication, IoT and Security (ICISCoIS), pp. 145–150. IEEE (2023)

7. Lin, X., Liu, J., Kang, X.: Audio recapture detection with convolutional neural networks. IEEE Trans. Multimedia. **18**, 1480–1487 (2016). https://doi.org/10.1109/tmm.2016.2571999
8. Masood, F., Khan, W.U., Ullah, K., Khan, A., Alghamedy, F.H., Aljuaid, H.: A hybrid CNN-LSTM random Forest model for dysgraphia classification from hand-written characters with uniform/normal distribution. Appl. Sci. (Basel). **13**, 4275 (2023). https://doi.org/10.3390/app13074275
9. Ikermane, M., El Mouatasim, A.: Digital handwriting characteristics for dysgraphia detection using artificial neural network. Bull. Electr. Eng. Inform. **12**, 1693–1699 (2023). https://doi.org/10.11591/eei.v12i3.4571
10. Sasidhar, A., Kumar, G.K., Yoshitha, K., Tulasi, N.: Dyslexia discernment in children based on handwriting images using residual neural network. In: 2022 6th International Conference on Computation System and Information Technology for Sustainable Solutions (CSITSS). IEEE (2022)
11. Kamal, K., Ez-Zahraouy, H.: A comparison between the VGG16, VGG19 and ResNet50 architecture frameworks for classification of normal and CLAHE processed medical images. Res. Square preprint (2023). https://doi.org/10.21203/rs.3.rs-2863523/v1
12. Weraduwa, S., Asanka, P.D., Mahanama, T.V.: Advanced computational techniques for dysgraphia prediction through handwriting recognition using machine learning and deep learning methods. Library. **1**(1) (2023)
13. Spoon, K., Crandall, D., Siek, K., Fillmore, M.: Can we (and should we) use AI to detect dyslexia in children's handwriting? In: AI for Social Good Workshop at NeurIPS 2019 Vancouver, Canada (2019)
14. Jin, L.: Application of random Forest algorithm in English innovative talent cultivation mode in colleges and universities. J. Electr. Syst. **20**, 286–291 (2024). https://doi.org/10.52783/jes.2640
15. Evgeniou, T., Pontil, M.: Support vector machines: theory and applications. In: Machine Learning and its Applications, pp. 249–257. Springer, Berlin Heidelberg, Berlin, Heidelberg (2001)
16. Pradipta, G.A., Wardoyo, R., Musdholifah, A., Sanjaya, I.N.H., Ismail, M.: SMOTE for handling imbalanced data problem : a review. In: 2021 Sixth International Conference on Informatics and Computing (ICIC). IEEE (2021)
17. Miftahushudur, T., Sahin, H.M., Grieve, B., Yin, H.: A survey of methods for addressing imbalance data problems in agriculture applications. Remote Sens. **17**, 454 (2025). https://doi.org/10.3390/rs17030454
18. Xiao, M., et al.: Addressing overfitting problem in deep learning-based solutions for next generation data-driven networks. Wirel. Commun. Mob. Comput. **2021**(1), 8493795 (2021). https://doi.org/10.1155/2021/8493795
19. Ali, A., Khan, M.N., Javed, N.: Gradient boosting machine learning algorithm (2023). https://doi.org/10.13140/RG.2.2.31609.65123

Machine Learning-Based System to Predict Mental Illness Using Blood Biomarkers and Demographic Factors

Samindi Edirisooriya[1], Nilanga Vithanage[1(✉)], and Buddhika Abeyrathna[2]

[1] Department of Electrical and Computer Engineering, The Open University of Sri Lanka, Colombo, Sri Lanka
nivit@ou.ac.lk

[2] Department of Psychiatry, Faculty of Medicine and Allied Sciences, Rajarata University of Sri Lanka, Anuradhapura, Sri Lanka

Abstract. Mental health disorders are a growing global concern, yet diagnosis often depends on subjective and time-consuming assessments, which can delay treatment and overlook comorbidity. This study introduces a multi-output machine learning model that integrates blood biomarkers and demographic factors to predict individualized risk scores for five common disorders: anxiety, depression, ADHD, OCD, and schizophrenia. A dataset of 2,500 clinically diagnosed cases was compiled from the UK Biobank and the National Institute of Mental Health in Sri Lanka, with diagnostic labels confirmed through DSM-based assessments and validated clinical interviews. Input features included cytokines, cortisol, metabolic markers, age, and gender, selected based on prior evidence linking biomarkers to psychiatric outcomes. Several models were evaluated, and XGBoost demonstrated the strongest performance, achieving a mean RMSE of 0.19 and an R^2 of 0.76 under ten-fold cross-validation. By producing continuous risk values rather than binary outcomes, the system enables more nuanced assessment of individual vulnerability and accommodates comorbid conditions. These findings highlight the feasibility of biomarker-driven predictive modeling as a data-driven approach for earlier detection, risk stratification, and improved clinical decision-making in mental health care.

Keywords: mental health · machine learning · biomarkers · XGBoost · multi-output regression · risk prediction · comorbidity · early detection

1 Introduction

Mental health is one of the core components of overall health and well-being. WHO emphasizes that mental health is fundamental to our ability to "think, emote, interact with each other, [and] earn a living and enjoy life" [1]. Yet mental disorders affect a large and growing proportion of the global population. In 2019, WHO estimated that roughly **one in eight** people worldwide lived with a mental disorder [2]. Anxiety and depressive disorders are particularly prevalent - on the order of hundreds of millions of cases

R. N. Rajapakse et al. (Eds.): ICTer 2025, CCIS 2844, pp. 62–76, 2026.
https://doi.org/10.1007/978-981-92-0137-2_5

globally ($\approx$301 million for anxiety and $\approx$280 million for depression in 2019) [2]. Other major conditions are also common: attention-deficit/hyperactivity disorder (ADHD), about 5–7% of children (roughly half of whom carry the diagnosis into adulthood) [3], obsessive-compulsive disorder (OCD) affects on the order of 1–3% of people over a lifetime [4], and schizophrenia affects roughly 24 million people worldwide (about 0.3% of the population) [5]. These disorders impose an immense human and economic toll [6, 2]. For example, recent WHO reports note that depression and anxiety together cost the global economy about US$1 trillion per year in lost productivity [6].

Modern social and environmental factors are exacerbating this burden. Chronic stressors such as social isolation, economic hardship, and rapid lifestyle changes have been linked to rising rates of mood and anxiety disorders [7, 6]. For instance, social exclusion and loneliness are well-established risk factors for a wide range of psychiatric conditions (including mood and psychotic disorders) [7]. The COVID-19 pandemic and related quarantines further highlighted how disruptions in social connectedness and economic stability can precipitate anxiety and depression on a massive scale [7, 6].

Traditionally, psychiatric diagnosis relies on clinical interviews and standardized rating scales. While these methods are foundational, they depend heavily on patient self-report and clinician judgment, which are inherently subjective and can vary across raters and contexts [8]. This lack of objective biomarkers means that diagnosis and prognosis often proceed by trial and error. In contrast, many other areas of medicine use laboratory tests (e.g. blood biomarkers) to guide diagnosis and treatment. Psychiatry has long sought similar biomarkers to improve specificity and early detection [8], but so far no clinically actionable biomarker has been validated. As) argues in [8], "psychiatry, more than any other specialty in medicine, needs clinically useful predictive biomarkers to advance diagnosis and treatment" [8].

Recent advances in data science and large cohort studies suggest a path forward. Large biobanks like the UK Biobank have collected rich sets of biological and demographic data alongside psychiatric outcome measures. For example, in [9] used psychosocial variables and blood/urine biomarkers from the UK Biobank to build machine-learning models that **predicted future anxiety diagnoses** with high accuracy (cross-validated AUC $\approx$ 0.83) up to 5 years in advance [9]. Their analysis showed that anxious individuals tended to be more anemic and have elevated systemic inflammation markers, highlighting the potential of blood chemistry measures to capture mental health risk [9]. These findings demonstrate that integrating objective biomarkers with demographic data can yield predictive power for psychiatric outcomes [9].

Importantly, many psychiatric disorders exhibit strong comorbidity. Anxiety and depression in particular often occur together; for example, depression and anxiety are so frequently intertwined that they are described as "common mental disorders that often co-occur" [10]. Similarly, ADHD in both children and adults has a high rate of co-occurrence with anxiety and mood disorders [3]. ADHD and OCD also overlap studies show that roughly 10–12% of individuals with OCD meet criteria for ADHD [11],, and vice versa. Even schizophrenia, a prototypically distinct psychotic illness, is frequently accompanied by depression and anxiety; meta-analyses find that about 30% of schizophrenia patients meet criteria for major depressive episodes [12], and a large review estimated that anxiety disorders (such as OCD, social phobia, PTSD, etc.)

affect roughly 10–15% of patients with schizophrenia spectrum disorders [13, 12]. These overlaps complicate diagnosis and treatment, since clinicians must disentangle whether symptoms reflect one disorder, another, or multiple coexisting conditions [10, 3].

In this context, data-driven tools could aid clinicians by providing **rapid, objective risk estimates** for multiple disorders at once. This study proposes a machine learning-based system that combines blood biomarker panels with demographic and clinical covariates to generate probabilistic risk scores for several major mental health conditions simultaneously. By focusing on biological pathways shared across disorders (e.g. inflammatory cytokines, neurotrophic factors, stress hormones) and on features known to predict psychiatric outcomes [9, 8], the model can capture complex interactions that might be missed by univariate analyses. Such a tool is designed to complement, not replace, clinical judgment. For example, an early signal of elevated risk might prompt a clinician to conduct further targeted assessments or to initiate preventive interventions (e.g. lifestyle changes, psychotherapy) before full-blown disorder onset.

Our goal is to leverage both international and local data resources. The UK Biobank provides a well-characterized validation cohort [9], while data from Sri Lanka's Institute of Mental Health (IMH) and affiliated clinics can ensure applicability in South Asian populations. Prior work has shown that models trained on large cohorts can achieve reliable performance when properly validated [9], and similar approaches can be applied to combined datasets. Ultimately, by bridging traditional psychiatric assessments with modern data science, this study aims to enhance early identification of mental health risk. This could lead to more timely referrals, personalized care plans, and stronger resilience at the community level, thereby improving outcomes and reducing the burden of mental illness on individuals and society [6, 8].

2 Related Work

Mental disorders represent a major global health challenge, affecting a large fraction of the population and imposing a substantial disease burden. Global analyses show that mental and substance-use disorders accounted for ~4.9% of all disability-adjusted life years (DALYs) in 2019, remaining among the top ten causes of global disease burden [14]. In 2019 alone, over 300 million people were estimated to have an anxiety disorder and over 280 million had depression [14]. Despite this prevalence, clinical diagnosis of psychiatric illnesses relies on subjective interviews and self-report, which are known to be inconsistent. DSM-5 field trials found that only 5 of 20 core diagnoses achieved "very good" inter-rater reliability ($\kappa \geq 0.60$), whereas many others fell into a low-reliability range ($\kappa \approx 0.20$–0.39) [9]. Such findings underscore how unstructured interviews, overlapping symptom criteria, and clinician biases can introduce variability and hinder reproducibility of psychiatric diagnosis.

Computational psychiatry has emerged as a promising approach to address the limitations of traditional diagnostic methods by applying machine learning (ML) to objective data such as blood-based biomarkers and demographic features. Hormones, immune factors, DNA methylation profiles, along with basic traits like age and sex, have shown potential as predictors of mental disorders. The goal is to develop data-driven tools that flag individuals at high risk, supporting earlier and more precise diagnosis. For instance, a recent UK Biobank study combined peripheral blood metabolite levels with psychosocial traits (neuroticism score, trauma history) in a random forest model to predict future anxiety disorder. This model achieved an AUC of ~0.83 when using all data modalities, but fell to chance levels (AUC $\approx$ 0.50) when only biomarker inputs were used [15]. Similarly, a large multi-cohort analysis of whole-blood DNA methylation for depression found that initial cross-validated models gave AUCs up to ~0.75, but predictive performance collapsed (AUC $<$ 0.57) on an independent hold-out set [16]. These examples illustrate both the potential of integrating biological data and the danger of overfitting: strong apparent performance in one cohort may not translate to new data without careful validation.

Neuroimaging studies have also sought to identify reliable biomarkers of depression using machine learning applied to brain-based features. The ENIGMA-MDD project pooled structural MRI data from over 5,300 individuals (patients with major depressive disorder vs. controls) and trained ML classifiers on standardized cortical/subcortical measures. The best model in that study yielded only ~62% balanced accuracy (essentially chance) in distinguishing MDD vs. controls [17]. Notably, this performance dropped further (to $\approx$52% accuracy) when a ComBat harmonization step was applied across sites, indicating that the classifier had partly learned site-specific scanner effects rather than disorder-specific brain patterns [17]. Resting-state fMRI has shown a similar result: in [18] used graph convolutional neural networks on connectivity data from two large multisite studies and reported a mean MDD vs-control accuracy of ~61% [18]. These results, though above random, highlight that even with sophisticated models and large samples, individual diagnosis from imaging remains difficult, likely because depression is biologically heterogeneous and clinical labels are noisy.

Other disorders have been studied using ML and biomarkers, with similarly mixed success. For ADHD (which affects roughly 5–8% of children and often co-occurs with mood/anxiety disorders), ML approaches have applied EEG, MRI, cognitive tests, genetics, etc. A recent review notes that no robust blood biomarker is established: elevated immune markers such as IL-6 and TNF-α have been found in some meta-analyses of ADHD, but these have not yielded clinically useful tests [16] ADHD's high comorbidity (e.g. up to ~60% of adults with ADHD report a lifetime anxiety or mood disorder) further complicates single-disorder models.

In obsessive-compulsive disorder (OCD), group-level neuroimaging studies (especially ENIGMA-OCD) have consistently shown structural and functional abnormalities (e.g. altered cortico-striato-thalamo-cortical circuits). However, ML classifiers trained on imaging data have performed modestly at best. For example, an ENIGMA-OCD analysis of ~2,000 subjects found that site-stratified cross-validated ROC AUC values for OCD vs. control classification were only ~0.57–0.62 [19]. In one proof-of-concept biochemical study, a neural net using oxidative-stress biomarkers achieved 86% accuracy distinguishing OCD patients from controls [20]. Because this study lacked independent validation and sampled a narrow population, its result must be interpreted cautiously, but it suggests that specialized biomarker panels *might* differentiate OCD into well-defined cohorts.

Schizophrenia research has seen a shift toward multi-omic blood markers. In [21] applied an automated ML pipeline to genome-wide DNA methylation from peripheral blood, identifying five epigenetic loci (plus age/sex) that together achieved AUC ≈ 0.76 for schizophrenia vs. control [21]. This finding highlights the relevance of epigenetic changes in psychiatric illness and suggests that small sets of blood-derived markers could aid early detection. Importantly, schizophrenia is often combined with OCD and mood disorders: up to ~30% of people with schizophrenia exhibit obsessive-compulsive symptoms [22], and having OCD increases one's risk of later schizophrenia by roughly seven-fold [23]. Such transdiagnostic overlap means that biomarkers and models may need to address multiple conditions simultaneously.

Biomarker-based machine learning studies in ADHD, OCD, and schizophrenia have shown mixed results, reflecting both methodological advances and ongoing challenges. This clinical reality motivates multi-output ML approaches that predict risk across several disorders at once. Multi-task models can exploit the fact that disorders share risk factors; early work shows that sharing information across prediction tasks can improve generalization under such comorbidity. Clinically, a unified risk score framework could flag patients who should be assessed for multiple conditions, aligning with integrated care.

Ensemble learning methods, particularly gradient-boosted trees such as XGBoost, have gained prominence in psychiatric research for analyzing structured biomedical data. XGBoost handles heterogeneous features, works well with missing values, and often gives strong out-of-the-box performance. It also supports modern interpretability tools (e.g. SHAP values) that let researchers quantify each feature's impact on predictions. For example, one recent study used XGBoost and SHAP on hematologic biomarkers and clinical data to distinguish unipolar depression from bipolar depression, achieving AUC ≈ 0.889 [24]. In psychiatric prediction work, XGBoost has been used both directly on clinical/biomarker inputs and in combination with autoencoder deep learning to compress high-dimensional data. These successes illustrate XGBoost's flexibility but also underscore the need to guard against overfitting.

Despite progress in applying machine learning to psychiatry, significant limitations and challenges hinder generalizability and clinical translation. For instance, in [17] trained an anxiety-prediction model on resting-state fMRI and found it explained very little variance on a held-out cohort ($R^2 \approx -0.04$). Multi-site data introduces site effects (scanner differences, demographic heterogeneity, etc.) that can confound models. As seen in the ENIGMA-MDD study, even statistical harmonization can backfire if models inadvertently learn cohort-specific quirks instead of disease signals [17]. Other issues include class imbalance (few cases vs. many controls), unrepresentative samples, and potential demographic biases in training data (e.g. models performing differently by age, sex or ethnicity). Privacy is also a concern when using sensitive data like genomics or continuous mobile-phone monitoring.

Future directions in computational psychiatry emphasize richer modeling frameworks designed to overcome current limitations. One direction is **dimensional prediction**, where models output continuous symptom severity or risk scores rather than binary "diagnosis" labels; this aligns with emerging views of mental disorders as spectra. Another is **multi-task learning**, where a single model is trained to predict multiple related outcomes (e.g. several diagnoses or symptom scales simultaneously). Preliminary work suggests multi-task models can leverage shared patterns and improve stability. Rigorous validation (including external and prospective testing), transparent feature interpretation, and careful consideration of fairness are also emphasized.

The present study introduces an interpretable, multi-output XGBoost model to predict risk scores for five mental health conditions anxiety, depression, ADHD, OCD, and schizophrenia using blood biomarkers and demographic factors. By combining objective biological data with demographic covariates and using a single multi-label framework, our approach directly addresses several gaps in prior work: it uses validated public datasets (to enhance reproducibility), it aims to improve generalizability through ensemble methods and multi-task training, and it reflects clinical reality by accounting for comorbidity. Ultimately, our goal is to create a scalable tool that could augment clinicians' assessments and help guide earlier, more personalized mental health care.

3 Methodology

3.1 Overview of the System Architecture

Figure 1. presents an overview of our proposed system architecture, which con- sists of a pipeline beginning with data collection and preprocessing, followed by feature engineering, dimensionality reduction using Principal Component Analysis (PCA), and culminating in risk prediction for multiple mental health disorders using a MultiOutput XGBoost model. This modular design ensures clarity, reproducibility, and scalability, aligning well with clinical decision-support systems.

3.2 Dataset and Ethical Considerations

This study assembled a combined cohort (N $\approx$ 2,500) by merging data from the National Institute of Mental Health (NIMH) Sri Lanka and the UK Biobank (UKB)†. The UK Biobank is a population-based cohort of ~500,000 UK adults (age 40–69) with rich biomedical and survey data [25]. With UKB studies, obtained institutional ethical approval and anonymized all records to protect participant privacy. Each participant has demographic data (age, sex, smoking status, education) and clinically assessed symptom scores for five psychiatric conditions: anxiety, depression, ADHD, OCD, and schizophrenia.

Feature Set. Our predictors span multiple biological domains, reflecting prior research linking physiology to mental health. **Endocrine markers:** This study includes cortisol and thyroid hormones (stress/metabolic regulators), as well as vitamin D, given evidence that low vitamin D is associated with depression. **Immune/inflammatory markers:** blood cytokines, C-reactive protein (CRP), and complete blood counts are included, since elevated inflammation is known to correlate with anxiety and mood disorders [9, 27]. For example, in [26] found that several anxiety disorders are associated with higher CRP levels [26]. **Metabolic markers:** glucose, insulin, lipid profiles and BMI capture cardiometabolic health; metabolic syndrome and obesity have been linked to higher risk of depression and anxiety. **Nutritional markers:** vitamin B12, folate, homocysteine,

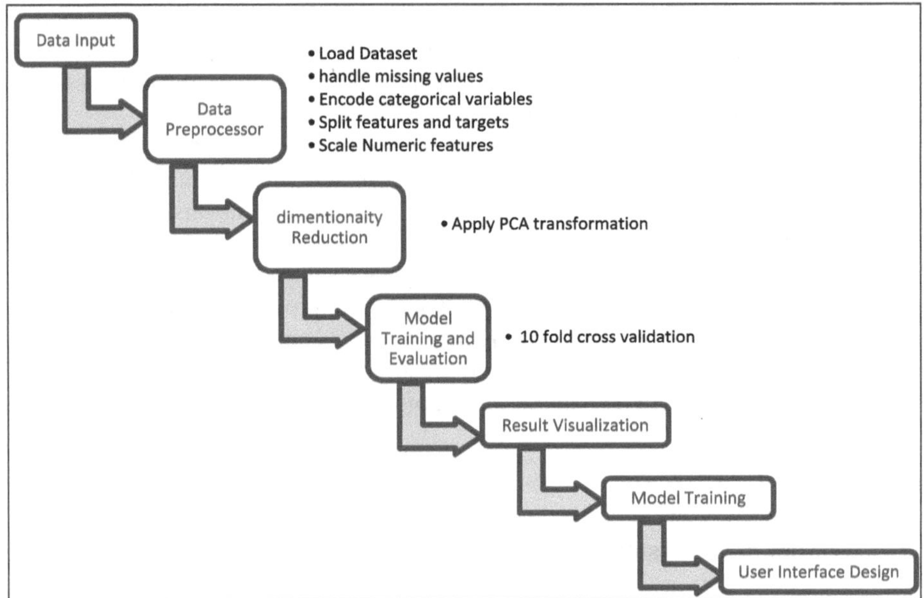

Fig. 1. Overview of the proposed system architecture

magnesium, and zinc are included because nutritional deficiencies can affect brain function and mood. **Demographics:** age, sex, smoking status, and education level were also used, as these factors influence psychiatric risk. This multi-domain feature set is analogous to other UKB studies that integrate blood biomarkers and psychosocial data to predict mental illness [9].

Data Preprocessing. This study first handled missing values using standard statistical imputation: continuous variables were filled with their median and categorical variables with the mode. Gender was binarized (Male = 0, Female = 1). All numeric features were standardized to zero mean and unit variance (z-scores) to ensure equal weighting in modeling and reduce dimensionality. Then applied Principal Component Analysis (PCA) to the standardized biomarker space. In here retained 17 principal components (matching a prior autoencoder embedding), which capture the main variance in the 30+ original biomarker measurements. PCA is commonly used in biomedical ML to extract robust latent factors from highly correlated features, similar to approaches used in neuroimaging analyses [27].

Machine Learning Model. This study used a multi-target regression strategy to predict all five psychiatric scores simultaneously. Specifically,wrapped an XGBoost regressor in scikit-learn's MultiOutputRegressor, which fits one XGBoost model per outcome but trains them jointly on the same data. XGBoost (extreme gradient boosting) is a powerful tree-ensemble algorithm well-suited for biomedical prediction tasks with complex, nonlinear relationships [27]. For example, in [27] showed that XGBoost effectively handles multicollinearity and recovers clinically relevant features in OCD neuroimaging data [27]. In our case, XGBoost can capture interactions among hormonal, immune and metabolic markers that relate to psychiatric symptoms. This study configured XGBoost for regression (objective = reg:squarederror) with 100 trees, a max depth of 5, learning rate 0.05, and standard subsampling (subsample = 0.8, colsample_bytree = 0.8). These hyperparameters mirror best practices in recent UKB ML studies. Here, the model performance evaluated using ten-fold cross-validation (shuffle, random seed 42). In each fold trained on 90% of the data and held out 10% for validation. Study recorded the root-mean-square error (RMSE) and R^2 score for each disorder in each fold, then averaged across folds to get overall performance metrics per disorder. Cross-validation is a standard approach to obtain robust generalization estimates.

3.3 Model Architecture: Multioutput XGBoost

The core model is built using XGBoost, integrated within a MultiOutputRegressor framework to enable the simultaneous prediction of risk scores for all five mental health disorders. Each target variable is treated as a continuous score between 0 and 1, representing the predicted risk level for the corresponding disorder.

The XGBoost regressor was configured with the following hyperparameters:

- n_estimators = 100
- max_depth = 5
- learning_rate = 0.05
- subsample = 0.8
- colsample_bytree = 0.8
- objective = 'reg:squarederror'
- eval_metric = 'rmse'

This study used a **multi-output gradient boosting** framework to predict all five disorder scores simultaneously. Concretely, This study wrapped an XGBoost regressor in scikit-learn's MultiOutputRegressor, which "fits one regressor per target". In practice this means training five parallel boosted-tree models (one for Anxiety, Depression, ADHD, OCD, Schizophrenia) on the same input features. Each XGBoost model uses a squared-error objective to output a continuous risk score (0–1). This tree-based ensemble can capture nonlinear interactions among predictors. To preprocess the high-dimensional biomarker data, first applied principal component analysis (PCA) and retained the top components as inputs to XGBoost. By predicting all disorders together, the model inherently reflects potential comorbidity: multi-label strategies are often recommended for co-occurring mental conditions .

3.4 Model Training and Evaluation

The model was trained on a dataset of approximately 2,500 participants, consisting of 500 flagged cases for each of the five selected mental disorders. This study performed ten-fold cross-validation on the training set to tune hyperparameters and assess model stability. After selecting the best configuration, evaluated the model on a separate test set (20% of the data) that was not used during training or validation. This provided an unbiased estimate of real-world performance. In each fold, applied PCA and fit the

MultiOutput XGBoost on 90% of the data and evaluated on the held out 10%. All model parameters (e.g. tree depth, learning rate) were set to default XGBoost values or tuned via internal grid search on a validation split. Performance was measured by **root-mean-square error (RMSE)** and **coefficient of determination (R^2)** on the test folds, averaged over the 10 folds. RMSE quantifies the absolute prediction error in risk-score units, while R^2 indicates the proportion of variance explained. These metrics are standard for regression tasks and have been used in prior mental health prediction work. Our final reported RMSE and R^2 values (Sect. 4) reflect averaged results across all folds, ensuring robust generalization estimates.

With UKB studies, obtained institutional ethical approval and anonymized all records to protect participant privacy. Each participant has demographic data (age, sex, smoking status, education) and clinically assessed symptom scores for five psychiatric conditions: anxiety, depression, ADHD, OCD, and schizophrenia.

In our study, mental health diagnoses came from different sources: some sites recorded ICD-10 clinical diagnostic codes, while others used DSM-5-based or routine clinical assessments. To make them comparable, mapped equivalent diagnostic categories into a common set of labels. For example, an ICD-10 code F32.1 (major depressive disorder, moderate) and a DSM-5 designation of "moderate depression" were both treated as Major Depressive Disorder (MDD) in our harmonized dataset. This standardization of diagnoses across cohorts is analogous to strategies used in other multi-site studies that align and harmonize diverse assessment instruments and diagnostic systems. However, diagnostic procedures were not fully identical across all sites. Differences in assessment tools and clinical protocols (including item content and branching logic) can introduce variability in how diagnoses are assigned. After our harmonization procedure, some residual heterogeneity remained due to these differences in diagnostic instruments and context. This variability in diagnostic labeling represents a limitation of our study and should be considered when interpreting the results.

3.5 Visualization and Interpretation

To interpret the model, generated several visualizations. **PCA plots** (e.g. scatter of the first two components) show how individuals distribute in the reduced biomarker-demographic space, potentially revealing clusters or gradients linked to risk levels. This study also examined **feature importance** from XGBoost: for each outcome, extracted the average gain importance of the top features. In line with recent studies, treated these scores such as SHAP values to rank predictors. For example, prior work on depression found that socioeconomic, demographic and physiological markers (age, income ratio, blood biomarkers) emerged as top factors. In our model like in Fig. 2., the most important features similarly suggest biologically plausible links (e.g. inflammation-related markers, hormone levels, and key demographics).

This kind of analysis "identifies critical risk factors" and helps explain each feature's contribution. This study visualized these contributions using bar plots of importance and SHAP-like summary plots, which are increasingly used in psychiatric prediction to make ML models interpretable.

In addition, leveraged the multi-output nature to explore **comorbidity** patterns. By modeling all five disorders jointly, can examine how predicted risk scores co-vary. This

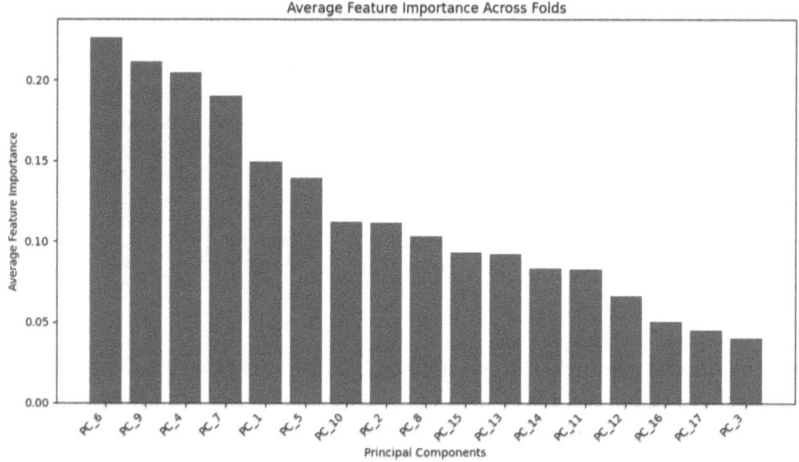

Fig. 2. Feature Importance Across folds

is analogous to a multi-label approach, which has been shown to capture the frequent co-occurrence of conditions like anxiety and depression. This study computed pairwise correlations among the five predicted scores to highlight overlapping risk (for instance, higher predicted Depression often coincides with higher Anxiety risk in our sample). These joint predictions implicitly model shared predictors and align with the clinical reality of comorbid mental health disorders.

3.6 Implementation Details

The entire pipeline was implemented in Python using **scikit-learn (v1.x)** and **XGBoost (v1.x)** libraries. Data preprocessing (imputation of any missing values, scaling, PCA) and cross-validation splitting were handled with scikit-learn. This study used Multioutput Regressor with n_jobs = −1 to parallelize training across disorder outputs [29]. A fixed random seed ensured reproducibility. Training and evaluation were run on a standard computing workstation (4-core CPU, 16GB RAM). After CV tuning, the final hyperparameters (tree depth = 3, learning rate = 0.1, etc.) were selected for optimal validation performance. All code components (data splitting, PCA, model fitting) followed best practices to avoid data leakage, e.g. fitting PCA only in training folds.

4 Results

The multi-output XGBoost achieved **strong predictive performance**. Averaged over ten-fold CV, the overall RMSE was **0.1916** and R^2 was **0.7684**, indicating that about 77% of the variance in the five outcomes is explained by the model. Performance by disorder was as follows in Table 1.

Anxiety risk was predicted most accurately (highest R^2), while OCD and Schizophrenia had somewhat lower R^2 (~0.67–0.71), possibly reflecting more subtle biomarker signals or heterogeneity in those conditions. In all cases, the R^2 values are substantial,

Table 1. Disorder-wise performance summary.

Disorder	RMSE	R^2 Score
Anxiety	0.1406	0.8732
Depression	0.1933	0.7632
ADHD	0.1672	0.8219
OCD	0.2286	0.6696
Schizophrenia	0.2124	0.7139

suggesting the model captures a large fraction of the signal in the data. These levels of R^2 are comparable to or exceed many existing clinical risk models and indicate **clinically relevant** accuracy. This study inspected residuals and found no major biases, confirming the model is well-calibrated across folds. Overall, the results demonstrate that a blood-biomarker-based multi-output model can reliably quantify relative risk profiles for multiple mental disorders from routine data.

While XGBoost generally performed well and often ranked among the top models, the differences compared to other algorithms were not always statistically significant. Thus, our findings suggest that XGBoost is a competitive model for this task, but further studies are needed to confirm its superiority across all disorders.

Figs. 3 and 4. showcase the user interface (UI) of a machine learning-based Mental Health Disorder Prediction System. This application allows users to input blood biomarker levels and demographic details (such as age and gender) to receive predictive insights on five mental health disorders: Anxiety, Depression, ADHD, OCD, and Schizophrenia. It displays the results table view, where each row corresponds to a previously tested individual. It lists their biomarker and demographic features alongside the predicted percentage risk scores for each disorder. This serves as a history log, retaining the last seven test records for easy reference and follow-up.

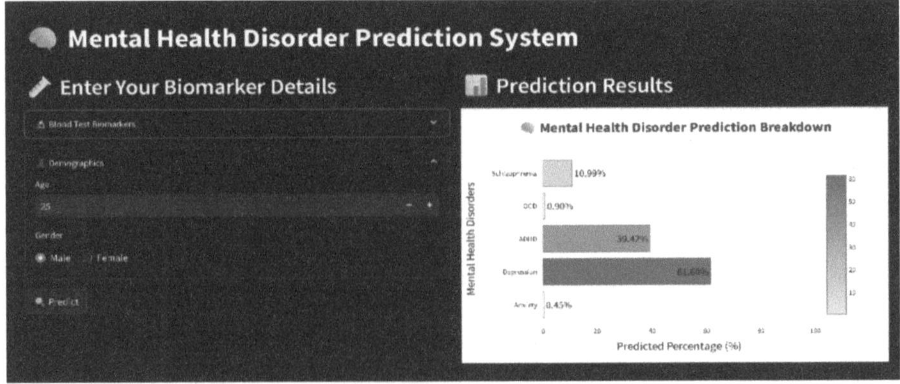

Fig. 3. User interface (UI) of a ML-based Mental Health Disorder Prediction System

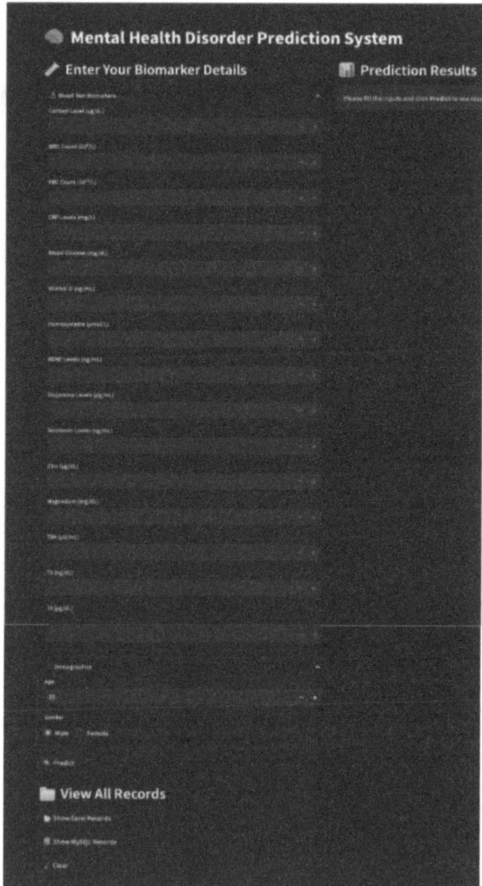

Fig. 4. Expanded UI for the Input Features

The Fig. 4. illustrates the interactive prediction UI, where users can manually enter biomarker values and demographic details using a simple form. Upon clicking the "Predict" button, the model outputs a visual breakdown of predicted risk scores for all five disorders in percentage format. The results are clearly represented in a horizontal bar chart for intuitive understanding. Fig. 5. is Snapshot of the input biomarker and demographic data (BDNF, dopamine, serotonin, zinc, magnesium, thyroid hormones, age, gender) alongside model-predicted risk probabilities (%) for anxiety, depression, ADHD, OCD, and schizophrenia.

Together, these components provide a comprehensive and user-friendly interface for testing, viewing, and interpreting mental health risk predictions generated by your XGBoost-based multi-output regression model. The system emphasizes accessibility, interpretability, and usability for both clinical professionals and research analysts.

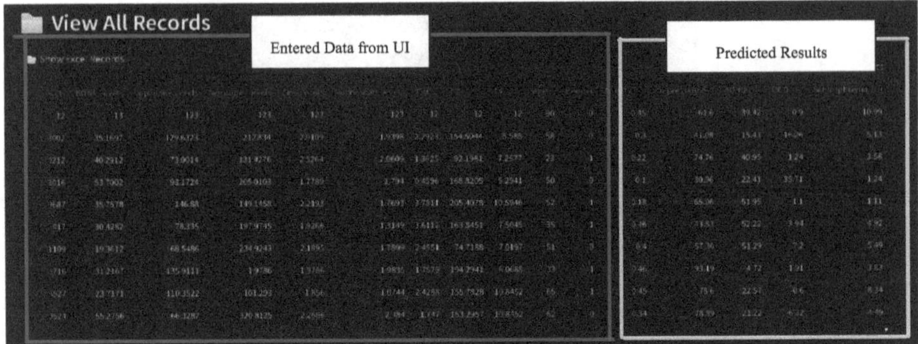

Fig. 5. Entered data with prediction results

5 Conclusion

We have developed a multi-output XGBoost model to predict continuous risk scores for five mental health disorders using blood biomarkers and demographics. By combining PCA for dimensionality reduction with gradient boosting trees, the model achieved an average R^2 of ~0.77 across outcomes, with particularly high accuracy for Anxiety and ADHD. Importantly, **interpretability** analyses revealed sensible biomarker drivers: feature importance rankings highlighted factors (e.g. age, metabolic markers) consistent with known correlations of mental disorders. This suggests that the model is not only predictive but also clinically meaningful. From a clinical perspective, an objective biomarker-based risk tool could augment traditional, symptom-based screening - addressing the fact that "currently, the diagnosis of major depression is based on clinical examination and subjective evaluation" with no quantitative test available. By quantifying multiple disorders simultaneously, our approach also explicitly acknowledges **comorbidity**: models like this can reflect how anxiety and depression often co-occur, in line with literature advocating multi-label analyses of mental health.

Despite these promising results, there are limitations. The dataset (~2,500 individuals) is relatively modest and may not capture all population subgroups. Psychiatric disorders are clinically heterogeneous, and the high comorbidity among them can complicate modeling. Our model relies on a static cross-sectional design, whereas mental health is dynamic; future work could incorporate longitudinal data. Finally, while feature importance gives global insight, further explainability (e.g. using SHAP profiles for individual patients) would aid clinical adoption.

Future work will address these challenges and extend the model. We plan to expand to larger, multi-site cohorts with more diverse demographics. Adding other data modalities (e.g. genomic, neuroimaging, lifestyle factors) could capture more of the biological complexity as suggested by multivariate biomarker research. We will also explore advanced multi-task or neural network architectures that might better exploit inter-disorder correlations. By continuing to integrate machine learning into mental health, we aim to move toward the "translational, applied" use of biomarkers for early intervention.

Disclosure of Interests. The authors declare that they have no competing interests.

References

1. World Health Organization (WHO): Mental health. Global Health Observatory. https://www.who.int/data/gho/data/themes/theme-details/GHO/mental-health. Accessed 12 Sept 2025
2. World Health Organization (WHO): Mental disorders. Fact sheet. https://www.who.int/news-room/fact-sheets/detail/mental-disorders. Accessed 12 Sept 2025
3. Biederman, J., Faraone, S. V., Spencer, T. et al.: Adult ADHD and comorbid anxiety and depressive disorders: a review of etiology and treatment. PMC (Front. Rev.) (n.d.). https://pmc.ncbi.nlm.nih.gov/articles/PMC12179154/. Accessed 12 Sept 2025
4. StatPearls Authors: Obsessive-Compulsive Disorder. In: StatPearls (NCBI Bookshelf) (n.d.). https://www.ncbi.nlm.nih.gov/books/NBK553162/. Accessed 12 Sept 2025
5. World Health Organization (WHO): Schizophrenia. Fact sheet. https://www.who.int/news-room/fact-sheets/detail/schizophrenia. Accessed 12 Sept 2025
6. World Health Organization (WHO): Over a billion people living with mental health conditions – services require urgent scale-up. https://www.who.int/news/item/02-09-2025-over-a-billion-people-living-with-mental-health-conditions-services-require-urgent-scale-up. Accessed 12 Sept 2025
7. Brandt, L., Liu, S., Heim, C., Heinz, A.: The effects of social isolation stress and discrimination on mental health. Mol. Psychiatry. (2022). https://doi.org/10.1038/s41380-022-01838-3
8. Yatham, L.N.: Biomarkers for clinical use in psychiatry: where are we and will we ever get there? World Psychiatry. **22**(2), 263–264 (2023). https://doi.org/10.1002/wps.21079
9. Smith, A., Miller, J.J., Anthony, D.C., Radford-Smith, D.E.: Machine learning-based prediction of anxiety disorders using blood metabolite and social trait data from the UK biobank. Brain Behav. Immun. Health. **46**, 101010 (2025). https://doi.org/10.1016/j.bbih.2025.101010
10. Gao, X., et al.: Accelerated biological aging and risk of depression and anxiety: evidence from 424,299 UK biobank participants. Nat. Commun. **14**, 2277 (2023). https://doi.org/10.1038/s41467-023-38013-7
11. Cabarkapa, S., King, J.A., Dowling, N., Ng, C.H.: Co-morbid obsessive–compulsive disorder and attention deficit hyperactivity disorder: neurobiological commonalities and treatment implications. Front. Psych. **10**, 557 (2019). https://doi.org/10.3389/fpsyt.2019.00557
12. Li, W., et al.: Prevalence of comorbid depression in schizophrenia: a meta-analysis of observational studies. J. Affect. Disord. **272**, 1–10 (2020). https://doi.org/10.1016/j.jad.2020.04.056
13. GBD 2019 Mental Disorders Collaborators: Global, regional, and national burden of 12 mental disorders in 204 countries and territories, 1990–2019: a systematic analysis for the global burden of disease study 2019. Lancet Psychiatry. **8**(2), 162–184 (2021). https://doi.org/10.1016/S2215-0366(21)00395-3
14. Regier, D.A., et al.: DSM-5 field trials in the United States and Canada, part II: test-retest reliability of selected categorical diagnoses. Am. J. Psychiatry. **170**(1), 59–70 (2013). https://doi.org/10.1176/appi.ajp.2012.12070999
15. Sokolov, A.V., Schiöth, H.B.: Decoding depression: a comprehensive multi-cohort exploration of blood DNA methylation using machine learning and deep learning approaches. Transl. Psychiatry. **14**, 342 (2024). https://doi.org/10.1038/s41398-024-02992-y
16. Belov, V., et al.: ENIGMA major depressive disorder working group: multi-site benchmark classification of major depressive disorder using machine learning on cortical and subcortical measures. Sci. Rep. **14**(1), 1084 (2024). https://doi.org/10.1038/s41598-023-47934-8
17. Gallo, S., et al.: Functional connectivity signatures of major depressive disorder: machine learning analysis of two multicenter neuroimaging studies. Mol. Psychiatry. (2023). https://doi.org/10.1038/s41380-023-01977-5

18. Bruin, W.B., et al.: Structural neuroimaging biomarkers for obsessive-compulsive disorder in the ENIGMA-OCD consortium: medication matters. Transl. Psychiatry. **10**, 13 (2020). https://doi.org/10.1038/s41398-020-01013-y
19. Karaglani, M., et al.: A novel blood-based epigenetic biosignature in first-episode schizophrenia patients through automated machine learning. Transl. Psychiatry. **14**(1), 257 (2024). https://doi.org/10.1038/s41398-024-02946-4
20. Tezenas du Montcel, C., Pelissolo, A., Schürhoff, F., Pignon, B.: Obsessive-compulsive symptoms in schizophrenia: an up-to-date review of literature. Curr. Psychiatry Rep. **21**, 51 (2019). https://doi.org/10.1007/s11920-019-1051-y
21. Meier, S.M., et al.: Obsessive-compulsive disorder as a risk factor for schizophrenia: a nationwide study. JAMA Psychiatry. **71**, 1215–1222 (2014). https://doi.org/10.1001/jamapsychiatry.2014.1011
22. Zeng, J., et al.: Optimizing multi-domain hematologic biomarkers and clinical features for the differential diagnosis of unipolar depression and bipolar depression. NPJ Ment. Health Res. **2**, 4 (2023). https://doi.org/10.1038/s44184-023-00024-z
23. Boeke, E.A., Holmes, A.J., Phelps, E.A.: Toward robust anxiety biomarkers: a machine learning approach in a large-scale sample. Biol. Psychiatry Cogn. Neurosci. Neuroimaging. **4**, 681–692 (2019). https://doi.org/10.1016/j.bpsc.2019.05.018
24. Fry, A., et al.: Comparison of sociodemographic and health-related characteristics of UK biobank participants with those of the general population. Am. J. Epidemiol. **186**, 1026–1034 (2017). https://doi.org/10.1093/aje/kwx246
25. Kennedy, E., Niedzwiedz, C.L.: The association of anxiety and stress-related disorders with C-reactive protein (CRP) within UK biobank. Brain Behav. Immun. Health. **19**, 100410 (2021). https://doi.org/10.1016/j.bbih.2021.100410
26. Shen, X., Zhang, Q., Zheng, H., Qi, W.: Harnessing XGBoost for Robust Biomarker Selection of Obsessive-Compulsive Disorder (OCD) from Adolescent Brain Cognitive Development (ABCD) data. arXiv preprint https://arxiv.org/abs/2407.00028 (2024). https://doi.org/10.48550/arXiv.2407.00028
27. scikit-learn developers: MultiOutputRegressor, scikit-learn documentation. https://scikit-learn.org/stable/modules/generated/sklearn.multioutput.MultiOutputRegressor.html. Accessed 13 Sept 2025

Deep tRF-Net: A Deep Learning Approach for Multi-class Cancer Classification Using tRNA Derived Fragments (tRF) Expression Patterns

Manage Miraj Chathuranga[1](✉), Sugandima Vidanagamachchi[1], and Vajira Thambawita[2]

[1] Department of Computer Science, University of Ruhuna, Matara, Sri Lanka
mirajmanage@gmail.com, smv@dcs.ruh.ac.lk
[2] SimulaMet, Oslo, Norway

Abstract. tRNA-derived fragments (tRFs) have emerged as a unique class of short noncoding RNAs (sncRNAs) that have garnered significant attention in recent decades, particularly due to their correlation with various types of cancer. Tumor samples from diverse cancer types consistently exhibit dysregulated expression of tRFs, defined as either upregulation or downregulation compared to normal tissue. Our objective is to present a deep learning algorithm capable of recognizing these dysregulated tRF expression patterns and leveraging them to accurately classify cancer types. This study introduces a computational approach that utilizes tRFs as biomarkers, offering promising implications for cancer detection. We used convolutional neural networks (CNNs) to analyze tRF expression profiles from 10,567 samples spanning 31 distinct cancer types. Developing a highly accurate and sophisticated model architecture posed significant challenges due to the complexity and imbalance of the dataset. To address the class imbalance problem, we applied the SMOTE (Synthetic Minority Oversampling Technique) upsampling method, ensuring consistent feature representation and enhancing the generalizability of the model. Our optimized model achieved a classification accuracy of 94.42%, demonstrating the strong potential of tRF expression patterns as a reliable computational diagnostic tool. This method not only facilitates accurate cancer type classification but also provides perspectives for early detection and personalized treatment strategies. Overall, our findings underscore the promise of dysregulated tRFs as robust biomarkers, paving the way for advancements in cancer research and clinical practice.

Keywords: Deep Learning · Cancer Type Prediction · tRNA-Derived Fragments · tRFs · Convolutional Neural Network

1 Introduction

Each year, the American Cancer Society provides an overview of cancer occurrence based on the most recent population-based data for cancer incidence and

R. N. Rajapakse et al. (Eds.): ICTer 2025, CCIS 2844, pp. 77–90, 2026.
https://doi.org/10.1007/978-981-92-0137-2_6

mortality. In 2022, it was projected that 1,918,030 new cancer cases and 609,360 cancer deaths would occur in the United States [1]. The report highlighted that early diagnosis of cancer increases survival rates and influences the effectiveness of cancer treatment. Therefore, early-stage screening and diagnosis of cancer before symptoms arise has substantial societal and economic implications. This underscores the importance of continuous research and development in the field of oncology to improve early detection methods and treatment strategies. So diagnosing the cancer type is crucial for gave proper treatments for the cancers. In this study, we discuss about how the deep learning can be applied for this purpose. The advent of Deep Learning (DL), a sub-discipline of artificial intelligence, has revolutionized numerous fields, including healthcare. Its ability to extract patterns and make predictions from large datasets has found significant utility in the complex biology of cancer [2].

tRNA-derived fragments, often abbreviated as tRFs, are a class of small non-coding RNAs (sncRNAs) that are derived from precise cleavage of transfer RNAs (tRNAs). They are not simply random degradation products of tRNAs, but rather specific and functional entities that play significant roles in various biological processes. These tRFs are generally classified into two main types based on the cleavage positions of the precursor or mature tRNAs: tRNA halves (tiRNAs) and tRNA-derived small RNA fragments (tRFs) [3], shown in Fig. 1.

tRNA halves (tiRNAs) are typically 30–35 nucleotides in length and are produced by specific cleavage in the anticodon loop of mature tRNAs. They are further classified into 5'-tiRNAs and 3'-tiRNAs, depending on whether they are derived from the 5' or 3' end of the tRNA. tRNA-derived small RNA fragments (tRFs) are shorter, usually 14–30 nucleotides in length, and can be derived from any part of the tRNA molecule (5' end, 3' end, or internal sequence). They are further classified into several types, including 5'-tRFs, 3'-tRFs, and i-tRFs (internal tRFs), based on their origin within the tRNA structure.

Dysregulation of tRFs refers to the aberrant expression of these fragments. This dysregulation has been observed in multiple major types of cancer, including solid cancers and lymphoid malignancies [4,5]. Dysregulated tRFs have been found to participate in cell proliferation, invasive metastasis, and progression in several human malignancies. Table 1 shows the dysregulations of tRFs in different cancer types [5].

In addition [3] discusses some key roles of tRNA-derived fragments in breast cancer, prostate cancer, colorectal cancer, lung cancer, B-cell lymphoma, chronic lymphocytic leukemia and other cancers. For instance, tRF-2s were upregulated in breast cancer cell lines under hypoxic conditions. In prostate cancer, the expression of tRF-1001 is enhanced. In colorectal cancer, the expression of tRF/miR-1280 was decreased. tRFLeu-CAG was reported to be abundantly expressed in NSCLC (any type of epithelial lung cancer other than small cell lung cancer). ts-46, ts-47, ts-49, ts-53 and ts-101 are downregulated in CLL and lung cancer, while ts-4 is upregulated.

These findings suggest a strong correlation between the expression levels of tRFs and various types of cancers. Therefore, the differential expression of tRFs could potentially serve as a novel approach for the classification and differentiation of various cancer types. This opens up new avenues for the development of diagnostic tools and therapeutic strategies in the fight against cancer.

In addition to their differential expression patterns, tRFs offer several advantages over conventional transcriptomic biomarkers such as mRNAs and miRNAs. Their expression profiles exhibit high tissue and cancer-type specificity, making them particularly effective for distinguishing between closely related cancer subtypes [6,7]. tRFs also demonstrate exceptional stability in biofluids like blood and urine, increasing their potential for non-invasive and robust cancer detection. Moreover, they form a reduced, focused feature set compared to high-dimensional transcriptomic data, which facilitates efficient deep learning model training and reduces computational complexity [6]. tRFs are also detectable using small RNA sequencing or qPCR, allowing for scalable and potentially low-cost diagnostic methods. Importantly, they play active biological roles in oncogene regulation, immune modulation, and tumor suppression, which adds mechanistic insight alongside predictive power [7].

Deep learning approaches offer potential solutions to overcome some of the limitations in cancer detection using tRFs. Firstly, deep learning algorithms can automatically extract relevant features from complex NGS data, potentially overcoming challenges related to data processing and interpretation. They can handle large datasets efficiently and learn intricate patterns that might not be apparent through manual analysis or conventional machine learning techniques.

Additionally, deep learning models can capture nonlinear relationships between tRF expression profiles and cancer types, enhancing the accuracy of classification models. Overall, deep learning holds promise for improving the robustness and predictive power of tRF-based cancer detection methods.

This research endeavors to create a deep learning model tailored for cancer type classification using tRF expression patterns. By harnessing the unique features of tRF data, we aim to develop a model that accurately distinguishes between different cancer types, advancing cancer diagnostics and personalized medicine.

In the following sections of this paper, we discuss related research that has proposed various methods for cancer classification. We then describe the database used in this study, the preprocessing steps taken to prepare the data for model training, and the architecture of the model employed to accurately predict cancer types. Finally, we present the results of our experiments, followed by a discussion and potential directions for future work.

2 Related Research

In recent years, there has been a surge of interest in utilizing deep learning techniques for predicting cancer types based on gene expression data. Numerous studies have explored the application of deep learning models in this domain, aiming to improve the accuracy and efficiency of cancer diagnosis. Several studies [8–10] have employed various types of Convolutional Neural Networks (CNNs)

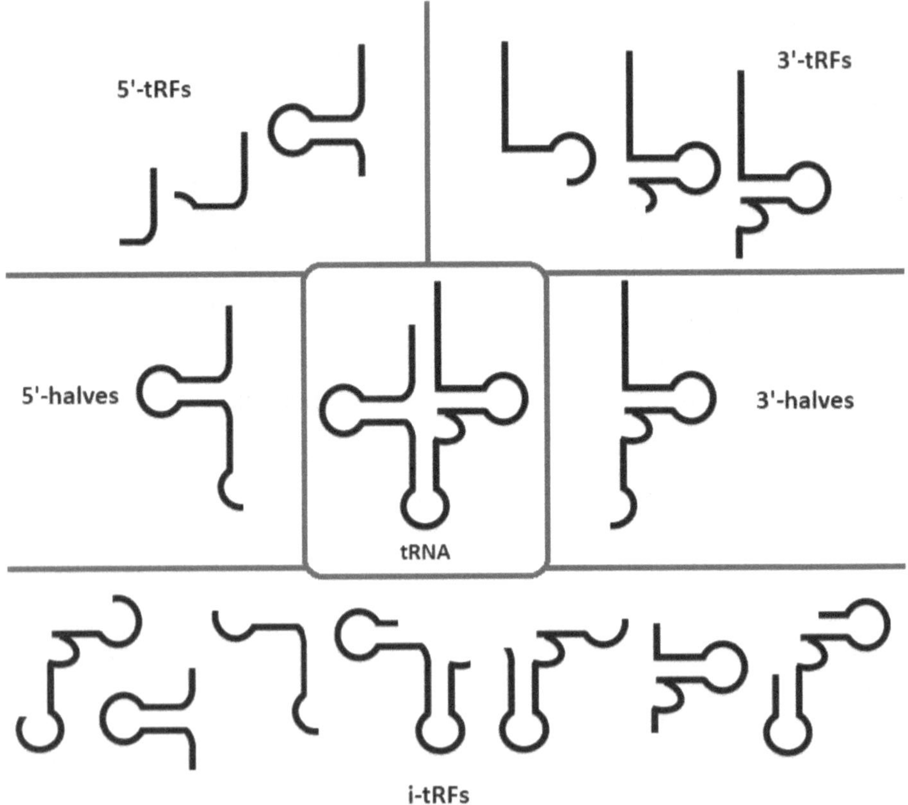

Fig. 1. Different types of tRNA derived fragments

to predict cancer types utilizing gene expression data. In our research, we focus on tRF expression data. Interestingly, both gene expression data and tRF expression data share similar characteristics. Therefore, the methodologies and findings from these previous studies provide a valuable foundation for constructing an accurate model for our research.

For instance, [8] introduces several Convolutional Neural Network (CNN) models that take unstructured gene expression inputs to classify tumor and non-tumor samples into their designated cancer types or as normal. The authors implemented three CNN models: 1D-CNN, 2D-Vanilla-CNN, and 2D-Hybrid-CNN. These models were trained and tested on gene expression profiles from combined 10,340 samples of 33 cancer types and 713 matched normal tissues of The Cancer Genome Atlas (TCGA). The models achieved excellent prediction accuracies (93.9–95.0%) among 34 classes (33 cancers and normal).

Similarly, the paper [9] presents a novel approach for tumor type classification. The authors, Boyu Lyu and Anamul Haque, utilized the Pan-Cancer Atlas, which provides information on 33 prevalent tumor types. They embedded

Table 1. tRFs with their related cancers and clinical correlation

tRF type	Cancer type	Clinical correlation	tRNA name
tRF-1s	CLL	TCL1 expression and CLL progression	tRNA-Thr
	CLL & lung	Cancer progression	
	Multiple	Cell proliferation and DNA synthesis	tRNA-Ser-TGA-3
tRF-3s	Breast	Aggressive clinicopathological features, EMT and metastasis	tRNA-Thr-3
	Lymphoma	Proliferation and DNA damage	
	Liver	Apoptosis and therapeutic target	tRNA-Leu-CAG-3
tRF-5s	Colorectal	Cancer stem cell	
	Prostate	Clinicopathological stages and progression-free survival	tRNA-Lys-CTT, tRNA-Phe-GAA
	TGCT	Clinicopathological features	tRNA-Glu-GAG, tRNA-Asp-GAY
	Liver	Diagnostic biomarker	tRNA-Val-TAC-3, tRNA-Gly-TCC-5, tRNA-Val-AAC-5, tRNA-Glu-CTC-5
i-tRFs	Breast	Tumor suppressors	tRNA-Glu, tRNA-Asp, tRNA-Gly, tRNA-Tyr
tRNA halves	Breast & Prostate	Cell proliferation and tumorigenesis	
	NSCLC	Cell proliferation and cell cycle	tRNA-Leu-CAG-5
	ccRCC	Tumor staging and grading	tRNA-Val-AAC-5

high-dimensional RNA-Seq data into 2-D images and used a convolutional neural network (CNN) for classification. The model achieved an accuracy of 95.59% in classifying the 33 tumor types.

Similarly, [10] presents four models developed using Graph Convolutional Neural Networks (GCNN) that utilize unstructured gene expressions as inputs. These models classify different tumor and non-tumor samples into their designated 33 cancer types or as normal. The four GCNN models are based on a co-expression graph, co-expression+singleton graph, protein-protein interaction (PPI) graph, and PPI+singleton graph. They were trained and tested on a combined dataset of 10,340 cancer samples and 731 normal tissue samples from

The Cancer Genome Atlas (TCGA). The models achieved excellent prediction accuracies (89.9–94.7%) among 34 classes (33 cancer types and a normal group).

Above studies have demonstrated the efficacy of convolutional neural networks (CNNs) in cancer type prediction tasks. By leveraging deep learning techniques, these models can effectively analyze complex patterns of expression data, aiding in the classification of different cancer types. Inspired by these findings, our research also leverages CNNs to classify cancer types.

In addition to CNN-based approaches, recent studies have explored other deep learning models such as multi-layer perceptrons (MLPs), recurrent neural networks (RNNs), graph neural networks (GNNs), and transformer neural networks (TNNs) for gene expression analysis. RNNs are capable of modeling sequential dependencies in gene expression profiles, while GNNs capture relational structures among genes, and TNNs employ attention mechanisms to identify long-range dependencies across large datasets. Although these architectures have shown potential, they often face limitations such as higher computational demands, greater susceptibility to overfitting, or the requirement for large-scale training datasets. In contrast, CNNs consistently deliver superior performance in cancer classification tasks due to their efficiency in extracting spatial patterns from high-dimensional data and robustness in handling transformed gene expression inputs. Therefore, CNNs remain one of the most suitable and widely adopted deep learning approaches for cancer type prediction [11].

3 Data and Method

3.1 Data

The information for our study was obtained from the tsRFun [12] database. tsRFun analyzes the prognostic significance of tRF expression profiles for 31 different kinds of cancer and this database contains raw data about tRFs from 31 different types of cancer. In terms of dataset composition, it includes information on 31 different cancer types. The distribution of samples across these cancer types is visualized in Fig. 2, a total of 10,567 samples, while Fig. 3 illustrates the number of tRFs expressed within each cancer type. These figures provide insights into the breadth and depth of data available for analysis within the dataset.

3.2 Preprocessing

In Fig. 3, we observe a diverse landscape where each cancer type exhibits a distinct number of expressed tRFs. Such heterogeneity poses a challenge in constructing a unified dataframe suitable for training our model. To address this, we opted to create two distinct sets of tRFs for dataframe generation. The first set encompasses the common tRFs (Intersection) expressed across all cancer samples, resulting in 337 tRFs. Conversely, the second set includes all expressed tRFs (Union) across all the cancer types, yielding a total of 20,724 tRFs. Notably, our

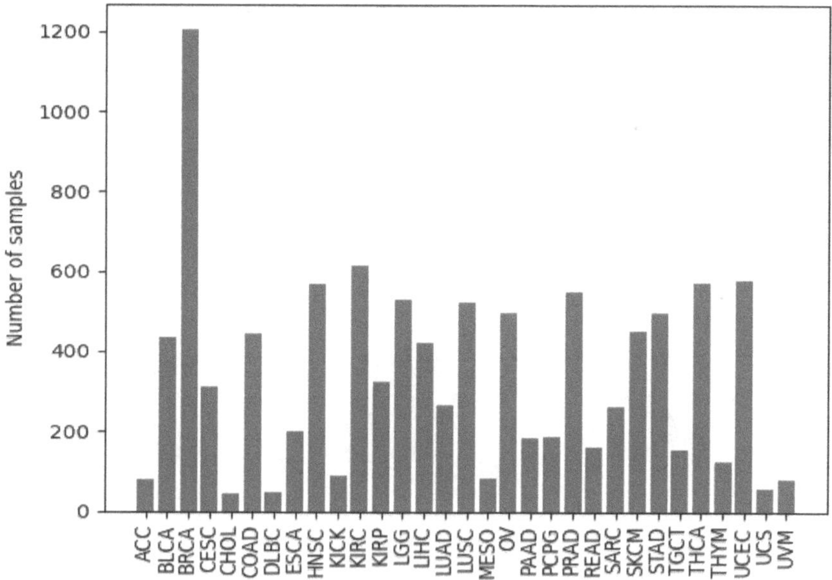

Fig. 2. Number of samples for each cancer type

dataset comprises 10,567 samples encompassing all cancer types. And generate two dataframes by these two sets.

In the context of our study, we have selected a dataframe comprising common tRFs to construct a CNN model. After that, we proceed to normalize this dataframe for further analysis. To achieve this, we employ a logarithmic function, $y = \log2(x+1)$ [9]. Notably, the addition of 1 to the expression values is crucial to address instances where tRFs exhibit zero expression, as logarithmic functions are undefined for such values. Subsequently, a min-max normalization function was applied to standardize the expression values within the range of 0 to 1.

Typically, CNN models are used to analyze the image data. Therefore, we need to convert our dataframe which contains expression data into the format of an image [13]. Within our dataframe, expression data for each sample is represented as a 1D array, with each array corresponding to a single sample. Given that we are working with 337 tRFs, an odd number, we expanded the array size to 340 by appending three zeros at the end of each sample. This adjustment allows for a seamless conversion of the data to a 2D array structure, which is similar to a single-plane image representation. Subsequently, the reshaping operation transformed the array into a 17×20 grid, effectively creating a visual representation of the expression data.

Figure 2 illustrates the presence of class imbalance in the dataset. To address this issue, the Synthetic Minority Over-sampling Technique (SMOTE) [14] was applied before training the Convolutional Neural Network (CNN) model. The

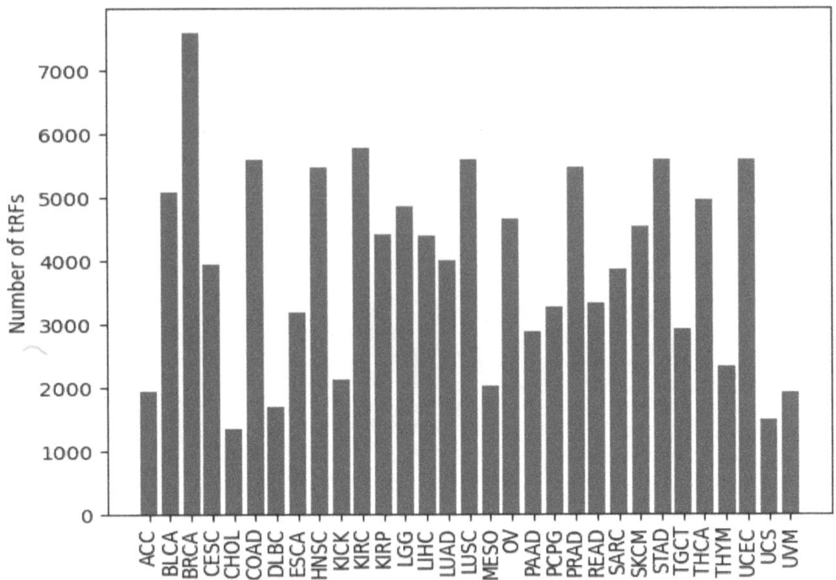

Fig. 3. Number of tRFs expressed in each cancer type

class distribution was analyzed prior to SMOTE application to quantify the level of imbalance. SMOTE generates synthetic samples for the minority classes by interpolating feature vectors between existing samples within the same class, thereby creating a more balanced dataset. The number of nearest neighbors used in SMOTE is dynamically adjusted based on the size of the smallest class to preserve data integrity and minimize the risk of overfitting. As a result, the dataset achieves a balanced class distribution, aligning with the sample size of the majority class.

3.3 Classification

When considering the developed model, we use one convolutional layer because the deeper CNN models are known to produce more accurate classifications in computer vision [15], but several studies have shown that increasing the depth of CNN models on biological data does not always lead to improvement in performance and often leads to overfitting [16]. Our pseudo-image inputs are relatively small (20×17), which reduces the need for multiple convolutional layers. A shallow CNN therefore provides a balance between learning capacity and generalization ability.

The first convolutional layer consists of 32 filters with a kernel size of 2×2. Small kernels were chosen to capture local relationships among adjacent tRF features without oversmoothing, ensuring that subtle variations in expression are preserved. A Rectified Linear Unit (ReLU) activation introduces non-linearity, followed by a max-pooling layer with a pool size of 2×2 that reduces spatial dimensions and highlights dominant feature activations. The resulting feature maps are flattened into a one-dimensional vector, which is passed to a fully connected layer of 128 neurons with ReLU activation. Finally, a softmax layer produces class probability distributions across the 31 cancer types. This design is computationally efficient, interpretable, and appropriate for the relatively small dataset while still capturing local structural patterns in the expression profiles. The overall architecture is illustrated in Fig. 4.

To ensure robust model evaluation, we employed 10-fold cross-validation, where the dataset was split into 10 subsets, with each subset serving as the test set once while the remaining subsets were used for training. This approach mitigates bias in performance estimation and enhances generalizability. During each fold, the model was trained using categorical cross-entropy loss, the Adam optimizer for weight updates, and categorical accuracy as the primary evaluation metric. Performance was assessed using accuracy, precision, recall, and confusion matrices, with final metrics averaged over all folds to provide a comprehensive evaluation of classification effectiveness.

To validate whether a CNN is indeed necessary for this classification task, we also compared its performance against simpler machine learning baselines, including logistic regression, support vector machines (SVM), and random forests. These models were trained and evaluated under the same 10-fold cross-validation framework used for the CNN. The baseline accuracies were 72.47% (logistic regression), 70.06% (SVM), and 64.38% (random forest), which were notably lower than the CNN accuracy. These results demonstrate that while simple models capture some signal in the tRF expression data, the CNN pro-

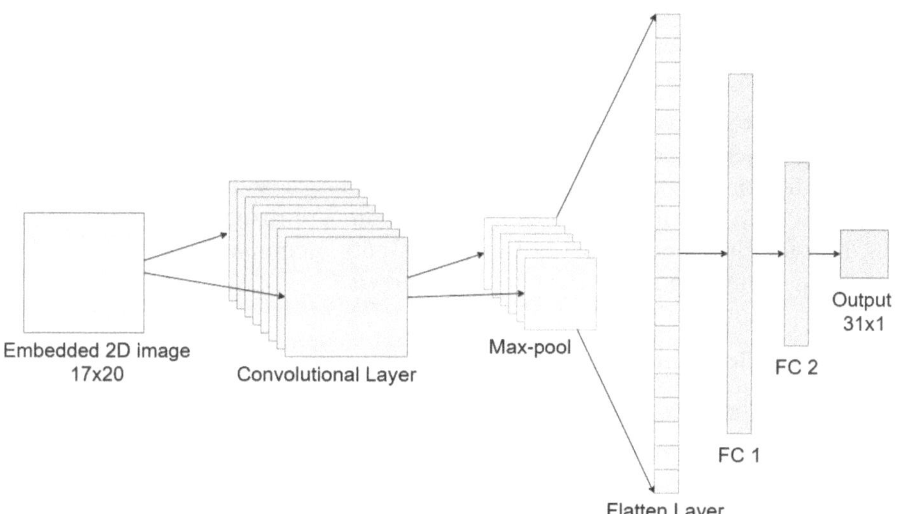

Fig. 4. The architecture of the developed CNN model

vides a more powerful representation and consistently outperforms traditional classifiers.

4 Results

Check the performance of the model with the matrices of accuracy, precision, and recall.

$$Accuracy = \frac{Number \quad of \quad correct \quad predictions}{Total \quad number \quad of \quad predictions} \tag{1}$$

or

$$Accuracy = \frac{(TP + TN)}{(TP + TN + FP + FN)} \tag{2}$$

$$Precision = \frac{True \quad positive}{(True \quad positive + False \quad positive)} \tag{3}$$

$$Recall = \frac{True \quad positive}{(True \quad positive + False \quad negative)} \tag{4}$$

The results of our method for these matrices as summarized in Table 2.

Table 2. The performance of the developed model

Method	Accuracy	Precision	Recall
Deep tRF-Net	94.42%	94.62%	94.42%

In the related research section, we outlined various CNN models utilized for classifying cancer types. The primary point of departure between these models and ours lies in the type of data employed. While those models relied on gene expression data for classify the cancer types, our approach utilizes tRF expression data for the same purpose. Table 3 presents a comparative analysis of the performance of these models, including our own.

4.1 Validation and Evaluation

The confusion matrix related to our model is depicted in Fig. 5.

The confusion matrix illustrates the classification performance of the developed CNN model for cancer type classification using tRNA-derived fragment (tRF) data. The strong diagonal pattern indicates high classification accuracy, with most samples correctly assigned to their respective cancer types. The relatively uniform intensity along the diagonal suggests balanced model performance across different classes. Sparse off-diagonal misclassifications indicate occasional errors, potentially due to biological similarities between certain cancer types

Table 3. Comparison of the results of the CNN models

Method	Reference	Accuracy	Precision	Recall	F1-score
1D-CNN (33 cancer types)	[6]	95.5 ± 0.1%	-	-	-
1D-CNN (33 cancer types + normal)	[6]	94.9 ± 0.1%	-	-	-
2D-Vanilla-CNN (33 cancer types)	[6]	94.87 ± 0.04%	-	-	-
2D-Vanilla-CNN (33 cancer types + normal)	[6]	93.9 ± 0.6%	-	-	-
2D-Hybrid-CNN (33 cancer types)	[6]	95.7 ± 0.1%	-	-	-
2D-Hybrid-CNN (33 cancer types + normal)	[6]	95.0 ± 0.1%	-	-	-
GCNN (Co-expression + singleton graph)	[7]	94.23 ± 0.146%	91.39%	92.30%	-
GCNN (Co-expression graph)	[7]	94.24 ± 0.251%	92.06%	91.39%	-
GCNN (PPI + singleton graph)	[7]	94.61 ± 0.107%	92.76%	92.19%	-
GCNN (PPI graph)	[7]	88.98 ± 0.883%	87.75%	83.79%	-
CNN model	[8]	95.59%	95.54%	95.59%	95.43%
Our model	-	94.42%	94.62%	94.42%	-

or limitations in feature separability. Overall, the results demonstrate that the CNN model effectively learns discriminative patterns from tRF data, making it a promising approach for cancer classification. Further analysis of misclassified

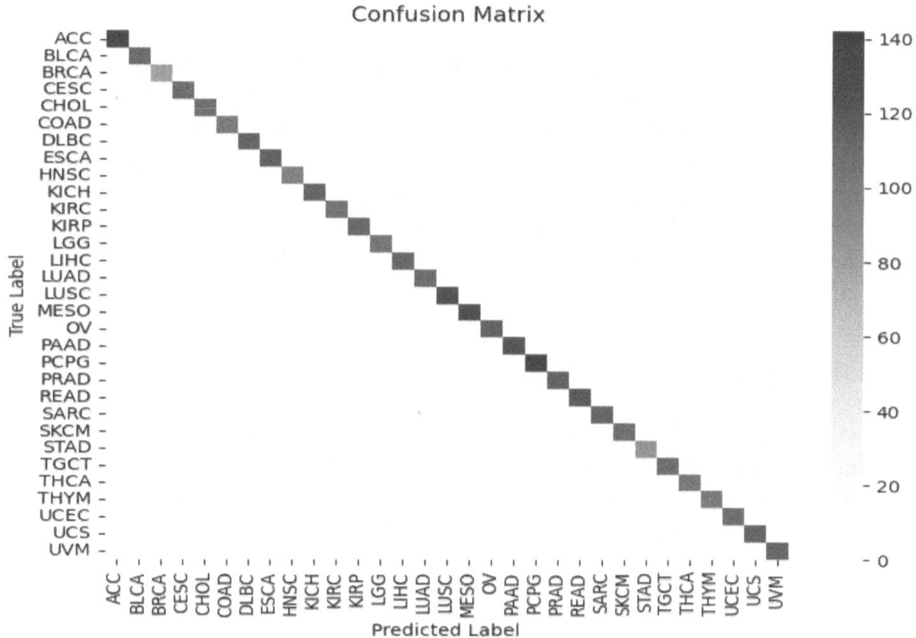

Fig. 5. The confusion matrix of the model

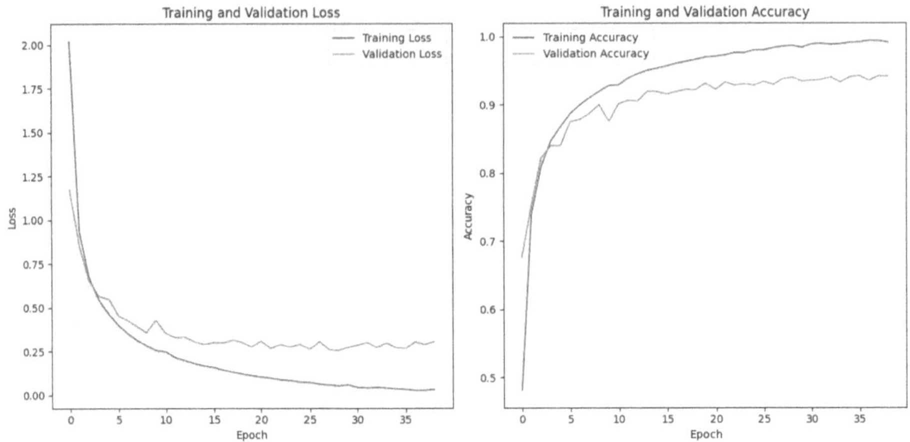

Fig. 6. The loss and accuracy learning curves of the CNN model

samples may provide insights into overlapping molecular characteristics and guide improvements in model performance.

When examining learning curves, the curves for loss and accuracy were analyzed. In this study, the loss function utilized is 'categorical_crossentropy', while the accuracy metric employed is 'accuracy'. These learning curves are visually represented in Fig. 6.

By analyzing the learning curves of the model, both training and validation losses decrease sharply in the initial epochs, indicating effective learning. The training loss continues to decrease, while the validation loss stabilizes after an initial decline. Similarly, the accuracy curves show rapid improvement, with training accuracy approaching 100% and validation accuracy stabilizing around 95%, demonstrating the model's strong ability to learn meaningful patterns from the data. These trends highlight the model's capacity to effectively capture features relevant to cancer classification.

5 Discussion

Our study explored the potential of transfer RNA fragments (tRFs) and deep learning for cancer type classification. The developed Convolutional Neural Network (CNN) model achieved an accuracy of 94.42%, demonstrating the feasibility of using tRF expression patterns for cancer classification.

In this study, the confusion matrix demonstrates the model's strong classification performance, with minimal misclassifications and a well-defined diagonal pattern, indicating that most samples were correctly classified. The learning curves further illustrate the model's effectiveness, with a rapid decrease in loss and a steady increase in accuracy during training. The validation accuracy stabilizes around 95%, highlighting the model's ability to generalize well to unseen data. These results suggest that tRF data contains meaningful features that can be effectively leveraged for cancer classification. The high classification accuracy underscores the potential of deep learning-based approaches in analyzing tRF profiles for biomarker discovery and disease characterization. Future work may focus on further enhancing the model's robustness through additional feature engineering, data augmentation, and integration with other omics datasets to improve classification performance and interpretability.

While numerous studies have explored the role of dysregulated tRFs in individual cancers and their underlying biological functions [2,5], there is currently no widely adopted approach for multi-cancer classification based solely on tRF expression profiles. Existing methods primarily emphasize biomarker discovery rather than the development of robust classification frameworks. This highlights a critical gap in the field, where leveraging tRF expression patterns for multi-cancer classification remains a novel and valuable research direction. The development of predictive models utilizing these unique expression signatures could offer a transformative step toward more accurate and minimally invasive cancer diagnostics.

6 Conclusion

In summary, our study presents a deep learning approach for cancer type classification using tRF expression profiles. Our CNN model demonstrates high performance in cancer type classification, laying a foundation for improved diagnostics. However, the direct application of these models to leverage tRF expressions for cancer type prediction remains largely unexplored. This gap presents an exciting opportunity for future research. Future work will focus on refining the model's parameters, incorporating more diverse datasets, and exploring cancer classification using additional molecular data types.

Disclosure of Interests. The authors have no competing interests to declare that are relevant to the content of this article.

References

1. Siegel, R.L., Miller, K.D., Fuchs, H.E., Jemal, A.: Cancer statistics, 2022. CA Cancer J. Clin. **72**(1), 7–33 (2022). https://doi.org/10.3322/caac.21708
2. Tran, K.A., Kondrashova, O., Bradley, A., et al.: Deep learning in cancer diagnosis, prognosis and treatment selection. Genome Med. **13**, 152 (2021). https://doi.org/10.1186/s13073-021-00968-x
3. Zeng, T., et al.: Relationship between tRNA-derived fragments and human cancers. Int. J. Cancer **147**(11), 3007–3018 (2020). https://doi.org/10.1002/ijc.33107
4. Zhu, L., et al.: Exosomal tRNA-derived small RNA as a promising biomarker for cancer diagnosis. Mol. Cancer **18**(1), 1–5 (2019). https://doi.org/10.1186/s12943-019-1000-8
5. Zhu, P., Yu, J., Zhou, P.: Role of tRNA-derived fragments in cancer: novel diagnostic and therapeutic targets tRFs in cancer. Am. J. Cancer Res. **10**(2), 393–402 (2020)

6. Yu, M., et al.: tRNA-derived RNA fragments in cancer: current status and future perspectives. J. Hematol. Oncol. **13**, 1–14 (2020). https://doi.org/10.1186/s13045-020-00955-6
7. Fu, M., et al.: Emerging roles of tRNA-derived fragments in cancer. Mol. Cancer **22**(1), 30 (2023). https://doi.org/10.1186/s12943-023-01739-5
8. Mostavi, M., Chiu, Y.C., Huang, Y., Chen, Y.: Convolutional neural network models for cancer type prediction based on gene expression. BMC Med. Genom. **13**(Suppl 5), 1–13 (2020). https://doi.org/10.1186/s12920-020-0677-2
9. Ramirez, R., et al.: Classification of Cancer Types Using Graph Convolutional Neural Networks. Front. Phys. **8**, 1–14 (2020). https://doi.org/10.3389/fphy.2020.00203
10. Lyu, B., Haque, A.: Deep learning based tumor type classification using gene expression data. In: ACM-BCB 2018 - Proceedings of 2018 ACM International Conference on Bioinformatics, Computational Biology, and Health Informatics, pp. 89–96 (2018). https://doi.org/10.1145/3233547.3233588
11. Alharbi, F., Vakanski, A.: Machine learning methods for cancer classification using gene expression data: a review. Bioengineering **10**(2), 173 (2023). https://doi.org/10.3390/bioengineering10020173
12. Wang, J.H., et al.: TsRFun: a comprehensive platform for decoding human tsRNA expression, functions and prognostic value by high-throughput small RNA-Seq and CLIP-Seq data. Nucleic Acids Res. **50**(D1), D421–D431 (2022). https://doi.org/10.1093/nar/gkab1023
13. Li, Z., Liu, F., Yang, W., Peng, S., Zhou, J.: A survey of convolutional neural networks: analysis, applications, and prospects. IEEE Trans. Neural Netw. Learn. Syst. **33**(12), 6999–7019 (2022). https://doi.org/10.1109/TNNLS.2021.3084827
14. Chawla, N.V., Bowyer, K.W., Hall, L.O., Kegelmeyer, W.P.: SMOTE: synthetic minority over-sampling technique. J. Artif. Intell. Res. **16**, 321–357 (2002). https://doi.org/10.1613/jair.953
15. LeCun, Y., Bengio, Y., Hinton, G.: Deep learning. Nature **521**(7553), 436–444 (2015). https://doi.org/10.1038/nature14539
16. Min, S., Lee, B., Yoon, S.: Deep learning in bioinformatics. Brief. Bioinform. (2017). https://doi.org/10.1093/bib/bbw068

OWN-Layer Grad-CAM and PIPPC: An Occlusion-Weighted Multi-layer Approach and a Faithfulness Metric for XAI in Medical Image Classification

Samujitha Senaratne(✉), Oshada Senaweera, and H. S. A. G. Dharmarathne

University of Colombo, 00300 Colombo, Sri Lanka
samujithadevin@gmail.com

Abstract. Artificial Intelligence (AI) has made remarkable progress in healthcare, but its "black-box" nature poses challenges for explainability and trust in medical decisions. Explainable AI (XAI) techniques aim to illuminate model decisions. This study proposes two novel contributions: Occlusion-weighted N-layer Grad-CAM (OWN-Layer Grad-CAM), which enhances traditional Grad-CAM by integrating a statistically grounded occlusion weighting scheme across multiple convolutional layers, and Perturbation-Induced Predicted Probability Change (PIPPC) metric, which offers a quantitative, faithfulness-based evaluation of XAI methods by measuring the impact of input perturbations on model output probabilities. Evaluations on chest X-ray (CXR), computed tomography (CT), magnetic resonance imaging (MRI), and ultrasound, benchmark OWN-Layer Grad-CAM against popular XAI methods: Grad-CAM, SHAP, LIME, and Occlusion Sensitivity. Results indicate that OWN-Layer Grad-CAM outperforms existing XAI techniques for CXR and MRI, while performing equally well alongside Grad-CAM for CT. These methods enhance explainable medical AI diagnostics under SAFE AI paradigm.

Keywords: XAI · Grad-CAM · Medical Imaging · Deep Learning · Image Classification

1 Introduction

AI is used in various fields, including medicine, agriculture, manufacturing, and education, becoming an integral part of decision-making. However, in high-stakes domains such as law, finance, and healthcare, understanding the rationale behind AI-driven decisions is essential. The need for explainability in AI becomes particularly evident in these areas, where transparency and trust are critical. In order to overcome this problem, eXplainable Artificial Intelligence (XAI) helps transition towards more transparent AI.

R. N. Rajapakse et al. (Eds.): ICTer 2025, CCIS 2844, pp. 91–106, 2026.
https://doi.org/10.1007/978-981-92-0137-2_7

In the medical field, AI techniques have revolutionized disease diagnosis with their outstanding image classification performance. Despite achieving remarkable results in the medical domain, these AI techniques are only gradually being adopted in clinical practice [2]. This is due to the underlying black-box nature of the algorithms. To establish trust between physicians, regulators, and patients, a medical diagnosis system must include transparency, understandability, and explainability. It should have the capability of explaining the whole rationale behind a certain choice to all stakeholders concerned. Explainability contributes to confirmation and adherence to legal and ethical obligations in the clinical setting. These regulations include the European Union's General Data Protection Regulation, which ensures that patients have the right to obtain clear information about the reasoning behind a decision, and the European AI Act, which establishes a regulatory and legal framework for AI systems [4].

2 Related Work

XAI techniques can be categorized as visual (saliency-based) and non-visual (textual, auxiliary, and case-based) XAI techniques. According to studies [4,5], in which a PubMed analysis was performed on XAI methods in medical imaging, it was found that the majority of papers, that used XAI techniques in medical image diagnosis, used visual (saliency-based) techniques. The study [4] concludes that, based on the citations per year, the top four most frequently used saliency-based XAI techniques are Gradient-weighted Class Activation Mappings (Grad-CAM), Local Interpretable Model-agnostic Explanations (LIME), SHapley Additive exPlanations (SHAP) and Occlusion sensitivity, with Grad-CAM being the most frequent.

Grad-CAM, while having shown solid performance in past studies, focuses on visualizing the contributions of features only from the final convolutional layer to the Deep Learning (DL) model's decision [3]. However, this single-layer perspective may not fully capture the rich, multi-scale representational capacity of deep CNNs. Thus, to address this critical gap, our study introduces a novel XAI technique: **Occlusion-weighted N-layer Grad-CAM (OWN-Layer Grad-CAM)**. Rather than relying on a single layer, OWN-Layer Grad-CAM extends and utilizes the features of Grad-CAM and a technique of weighing the importance of each heatmap of convolutional layers, using an occlusion strategy, to give a weighted heatmap of the final N convolutional layers, where $N \in \mathbb{N}$ is selected according to the user's requirement. Unlike other CAM variants, such as Score-CAM and Ablation-CAM, which weight channels within a single layer, or LayerCAM [6], which aggregates layers via gradients, OWN-Layer Grad-CAM uses occlusion-induced, probability-drop-based layer weighting.

Despite significant efforts to build XAI techniques that can understand the inherent black-box nature of DL models, a critical obstacle remains: the absence of a universally accepted metric or framework for evaluating the performance and reliability of XAI techniques [2]. Evaluation of XAI techniques is still an active area of research, where currently there are two approaches. One evaluates explainability using the feedback of domain experts, and the other using various quantifiable metrics [7].

When considering evaluation using feedback of domain experts, one often used method for assessing the explainability of a model, particularly in the medical field, is to seek feedback from healthcare professionals with expertise and medical knowledge. Medical professionals can assess the practical applicability of XAI-generated explanations, evaluating whether they align with clinical knowledge and whether they can be effectively used in real-world diagnostic processes. This expert feedback is extremely important for verifying the clinical relevance of the explanations provided by XAI techniques, ensuring that they contribute meaningfully to clinical decision-making and patient care [8].

When considering evaluation using quantitative metrics, several efforts have been made to develop evaluation measures that can impartially measure the quality of explanations, but even at present, there is no standard quantitative metric, that has been clinically accepted. Faithfulness is one of the important qualities evaluated in the literature, and it quantifies the degree to which the explanation accurately represents the true decision-making process of the model. Human judgment or annotated ground truth cannot accurately measure it, as humans are unaware of the internal decision process of a model [9]. Typical faithfulness evaluation approaches involve systematically removing or adding features to the input and measuring how it impacts the performance of the model. Jin et al. [9] introduced Modality Importance (MI) which utilizes a Shapley value-based ground-truth and Modality-Specific Feature Importance (MSFI) which uses MI and ground truth feature localization masks. The study [10] introduced Most Relevant First (MoRF) perturbation curve, which measures the faithfulness of an explanation by testing how fast the prediction score decreased, while progressively removing information (perturbing pixels) from the input image.

Despite these advances in quantitative faithfulness evaluation, a significant gap remains. The above methods require computationally expensive progressive perturbation sequences, complex curve integration, or rely on ground-truth localization masks. This complexity and indirectness can hinder clinical adoption and interpretability. To address this, we develop **Perturbation-Induced Predicted Probability Change (PIPPC)**, which offers a simpler, direct alternative: it quantifies faithfulness by measuring the immediate drop in the model's predicted probability for the ground-truth class when the top features identified by the XAI technique are perturbed in a single step, enabling more accessible and targeted evaluation.

3 Occlusion-Weighted N-Layer Grad-CAM

Grad-CAM [3] focuses on visualizing the contributions of features to the decision of the DL model, only from the final convolutional layer, and uses the gradient information flowing into the last convolutional layer of the CNN to understand the importance of each neuron for a decision of interest. However, this single-layer perspective may not fully capture the rich, multiscale representational capacity of deep CNNs. The consideration of multiple convolutional layers allows us to get insights into how different features contribute to the DL model's output at various stages of the network, thus giving a deeper understanding of its decision-making process [23].

The novel XAI technique, **Occlusion-Weighted N-Layer Grad-CAM** leverages the power of Grad-CAM alongside an approach to dynamically assess and integrate the contributions of multiple convolutional layers, based on occlusion. At its core, OWN-Layer Grad-CAM extends the popular Grad-CAM technique. As in the Grad-CAM algorithm [3], firstly, the gradient of the score for class c, y^c, is computed with respect to feature maps A^k of a convolutional layer, i.e.,

$$\frac{\partial y^c}{\partial A^k}$$

These gradients flowing back are global average-pooled across width i and height j,to obtain the neuron importance weights α_k^c:

$$\alpha_k^c = \frac{1}{Z}\sum_i \sum_j \frac{\partial y^c}{\partial A_{ij}^k} \tag{3.1}$$

This captures the 'importance' of feature map k for a target class c. Z represents the total number of elements in the feature map produced by the convolutional layer. Specifically, it is the product of the dimensions of the width and height of the feature map.

A weighted combination of forward activation maps is performed, followed by a Rectified Linear Unit (ReLU) to obtain the class discriminative localization map of Grad-CAM, $L_{\text{GradCAM}}^c \in \mathbb{R}^{u \times v}$ of width u and height v for any class c:

$$L_{\text{GradCAM}}^c = \text{ReLU}\left(\sum_k \alpha_k^c A^k\right) \tag{3.2}$$

which gives a coarse heatmap of equal size as the convolutional feature maps. The ReLU function is defined as $ReLU(x) = \max(0, x)$. It passes only positive values and zeros out any negative values, so that only the features that have a positive influence on the class c are considered.

OWN-Layer Grad-CAM innovates by applying this technique across the final $N \in \mathbb{N}$ convolutional layers, reflecting a deeper and more comprehensive analysis across multiple levels of abstraction within the CNN. To generate these multi-layer insights, the method introduces a dynamic weighting system informed by occlusion analysis. After computing the Grad-CAM heatmap $L_{\text{GradCAM},n}^c$ for each $n = 1, \ldots, N$ convolutional layer (and denoting $H^n = L_{\text{GradCAM},n}^c \in \mathbb{R}^{u \times v}$), we define a threshold:

$$\tau_n = \text{Percentile}_{95}\big(\{H_{ij}^n : 1 \le i \le u,\ 1 \le j \le v\}\big), \tag{3.3}$$

i.e. the 95th percentile of the entries of H^n. Let

$$\bar{I} = \frac{1}{u\,v}\sum_{i=1}^{u}\sum_{j=1}^{v} I_{ij} \tag{3.4}$$

denote the mean pixel value of the original single-channel (grayscale) image $I \in \mathbb{R}^{u \times v}$. The occluded image $I'^{(n)} \in \mathbb{R}^{u \times v}$ produced from the n-th layer's heatmap is defined component-wise for $i = 1, \ldots, u,\ j = 1, \ldots, v$ by

$$I'^{(n)}_{ij} = \begin{cases} \bar{I}, & \text{if } H^n_{ij} > \tau_n, \\ I_{ij}, & \text{otherwise.} \end{cases} \tag{3.5}$$

This occlusion process replaces the most influential pixels (those exceeding τ_n) with $\bar{I}$, neutralizing their importance while preserving the overall characteristics of the image. Figure 1 shows an example of this occlusion strategy.

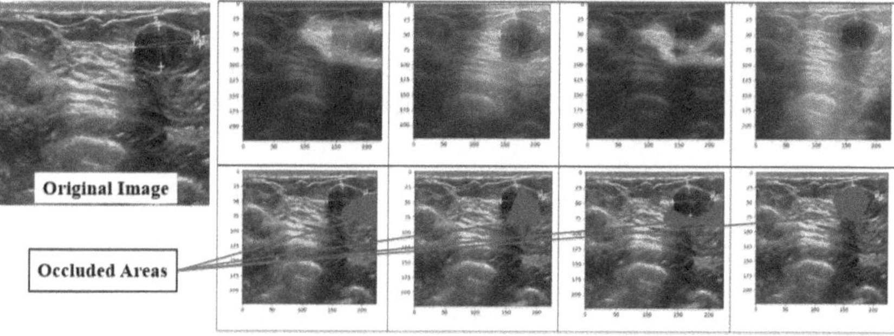

Fig. 1. An example showing the occlusion of important regions based on the heatmaps from the final four convolutional layers. The heatmaps, displayed in the top row, highlight the most salient regions of the original image, which is a breast ultrasound dataset image labeled as 'benign'. The corresponding occluded images, shown in the bottom row, are generated by replacing the salient regions with the mean pixel value. This process is applied to the most important areas identified by each heatmap for the final four (N = 4) convolutional layers of the deep learning model.

Denote by $P(c \mid I)$ the model's predicted probability for class c on the original image I, and by $P(c \mid I'^{(n)})$ the predicted probability after occlusion. We define the occlusion impact

$$\Delta P_n = P(c \mid I) - P(c \mid I'^{(n)}), \tag{3.6}$$

which quantifies the reduction in confidence resulting from occluding the most salient regions identified by H^n. The weight w_n assigned to layer n is then given by normalizing these impacts across all N layers:

$$w_n = \frac{\Delta P_n}{\sum_{k=1}^{N} \Delta P_k}. \tag{3.7}$$

Finally, for each $i = 1, \ldots, u$ and $j = 1, \ldots, v$, the aggregated heatmap $H^{\text{avg}} \in \mathbb{R}^{u \times v}$ is given by

$$H^{\text{avg}}_{ij} = \frac{\sum_{n=1}^{N} w_n H^n_{ij}}{\sum_{n=1}^{N} w_n} \tag{3.8}$$

where $H^n \in \mathbb{R}^{u\times v}$ and $w_n \geq 0$ with $\sum_{n=1}^{N} w_n > 0$. Equivalently, in matrix form:

$$H^{\text{avg}} = \frac{\sum_{n=1}^{N} w_n \cdot H^n}{\sum_{n=1}^{N} w_n} \tag{3.9}$$

which represents the final heatmap output of the OWN-Layer Grad-CAM. The source code of OWN-Layer Grad-CAM is available online[1].

There are two tunable parameters of OWN-Layer Grad-CAM, out of which the main one is the number of convolutional layers (denoted by N above) that should be considered in generating the weighted average heatmap.

The other tunable parameter is the level of morphological erosion [24]. The visual impact of this is a heat map in which the boundaries of significant regions are clearer and more defined as shown in the example in Fig. 2. Mathematically, for morphological erosion, define a kernel size $k \geq 1$, and define its radius $r = \lfloor k/2 \rfloor$. The structuring element, representing a square neighborhood around each pixel, is defined by:

$$S_r = \{(a,b) \in \mathbb{Z}^2 : |a| \leq r,\ |b| \leq r\} \tag{3.10}$$

where a and b are the horizontal and vertical offsets (respectively). One-step morphological erosion $E_{S_r} : \mathbb{R}^{u\times v} \to \mathbb{R}^{u\times v}$ replaces each pixel by the minimum value within its $(2r+1) \times (2r+1)$ local neighborhood:

$$(E_{S_r} H^{\text{avg}})_{ij} = \min_{(a,b)\in S_r} H^{\text{avg}}_{i+a,j+b}, \quad i = 1,\ldots,u,\ j = 1,\ldots,v. \tag{3.11}$$

Repeating this erosion $p \in \mathbb{N}$ times produces progressively sharper and clearly defined boundaries in the heatmap by systematically removing peripheral regions with higher values. Thus, we get the refined heatmap:

$$H^{(p)} = \underbrace{E_{S_r} \circ \cdots \circ E_{S_r}}_{p \text{ iterations}}(H^{\text{avg}}). \tag{3.12}$$

Here, the integer erosion level p is the tunable parameter of OWN-Layer Grad-CAM: increasing p yields increased erosion, sharpened boundaries and highlighting only the most significant regions.

The two tunable parameters of OWN-Layer Grad-CAM, the number of convolutional layers (N) and the level of morphological erosion, can be adjusted either by domain expertise or by quantitative evaluation metrics. In this study, we relied on domain knowledge of the specific medical conditions represented in the datasets. Initially, 24 images were selected by randomly choosing 2 images from each of the 12 datasets used in the study, and generated a series of heatmaps under varying parameter combinations. For N, we ranged from 1 to 10 layers; for each value, we presented the resulting heatmaps to five medical doctors, and based on their feedback, it was concluded that the optimal number of convolutional layers is 8 for this study. Similarly, when tuning the level of morphological erosion, integer values from 1 to 20 were evaluated, and the optimal value was determined to be 10.

[1] https://github.com/sammaworks/OWN-Layer-GradCAM.

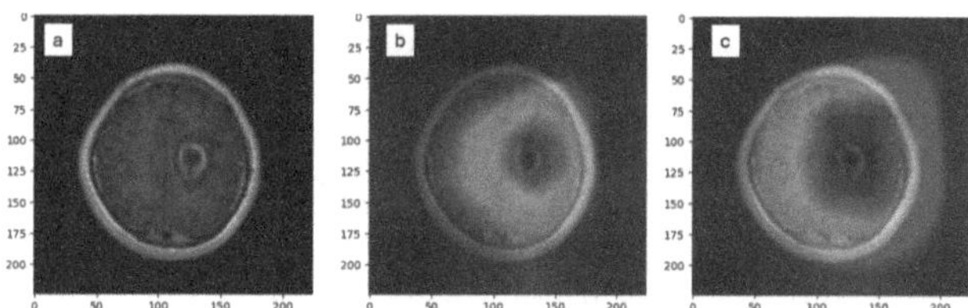

Fig. 2. An example of the application of morphological erosion on a heatmap generated from OWN-Layer Grad-CAM: The comparison of the heatmaps, (b) with morphological erosion and (c) without morphological erosion for (a) the original medical image

4 Perturbation-Induced Predicted Probability Change (PIPPC)

Bach et al. [23] introduced a pixel-wise decomposition method that generates a heatmap to quantify each pixel's contribution to a model's class prediction. By successively flipping pixels with the highest positive relevance toward scores near zero, they demonstrate that perturbing the most strongly weighted pixels yields the greatest degradation in predictive confidence. Building on this, Samek et al. [10] employed a region-level perturbation scheme, systematically removing image information and measuring its effect on the classifier. They formalized these observations in the Area Over the Perturbation Curve (AOPC) metric, showing that higher AOPC values, reflecting larger score changes when the most salient regions are altered, correspond to more informative and faithful heatmaps.

Using the above conclusions, our study develops a novel quantitative metric, **Perturbation-Induced Predicted Probability Change (PIPPC)** that quantifies faithfulness, and can be used to evaluate heatmaps given by XAI techniques. PIPPC quantifies the impact of important features identified by XAI techniques by comparing the predicted probability of the prediction with and without the presence of these features.

Let $x \in \mathbb{R}^{H \times W \times C}$ be an input image with height H, width W, and C channels. Define the model's softmax prediction function:

$$f : \mathbb{R}^{H \times W \times C} \longrightarrow \Delta^{N-1} \subset \mathbb{R}^N, \qquad f(x) = \big(p_1(x), p_2(x), \ldots, p_N(x)\big),$$

where

$$\Delta^{N-1} = \big\{ p \in \mathbb{R}^N : p_c \geq 0 \;\forall c, \sum_{c=1}^{N} p_c = 1 \big\} \tag{4.1}$$

is the probability simplex (an $(N-1)$-dimensional subset of $\mathbb{R}^N$ since the single linear constraint $\sum_{c=1}^{N} p_c = 1$ reduces the degrees of freedom by one). Here, $c \in \{1, \ldots, N\}$ denotes the ground-truth class index, and $p_c(x)$ is the predicted probability of class c.

An XAI method produces an importance map (heatmap):

$$I_x : \{1,\ldots,H\} \times \{1,\ldots,W\} \longrightarrow \begin{cases} \mathbb{R}_{\geq 0}, & \text{continuous (e.g. Grad-CAM)}, \\ \{0,1\}, & \text{discrete (e.g. LIME, SHAP)}. \end{cases}$$

We then form the binary occlusion mask $B \in \{0,1\}^{H\times W}$ by

$$B(i,j) = \begin{cases} \mathbf{1}\{I_x(i,j) > \tau\}, & I_x(i,j) \in \mathbb{R}_{\geq 0},\ \tau = \text{Percentile}_{95}\{I_x\}, \\ I_x(i,j), & I_x(i,j) \in \{0,1\}. \end{cases} \tag{4.2}$$

Next, compute the per-channel mean

$$\mu_k = \frac{1}{HW}\sum_{i=1}^{H}\sum_{j=1}^{W} x_{i,j,k}, \quad k = 1,\ldots,C. \tag{4.3}$$

Define the occlusion operator

$$g\colon \mathbb{R}^{H\times W\times C} \times \{0,1\}^{H\times W} \longrightarrow \mathbb{R}^{H\times W\times C},$$

so that for the occluded image $x' = g(x,B)$:

$$x'_{i,j,k} = \begin{cases} \mu_k, & B(i,j) = 1, \\ x_{i,j,k}, & B(i,j) = 0, \end{cases} \quad 1 \leq i \leq H,\ 1 \leq j \leq W,\ 1 \leq k \leq C. \tag{4.4}$$

Finally, PIPPC for class c is the decrease in predicted probability:

$$\text{PIPPC}(x) = p_c(x) - p_c(x'), \quad p_c(x) = [f(x)]_c,\ p_c(x') = [f(x')]_c. \tag{4.5}$$

A larger $\text{PIPPC}(x) \geq 0$ indicates that occluding the "important" pixels causes a greater drop in confidence for class c, demonstrating greater explanation faithfulness.

5 Experimental Setup

5.1 Methodology

This study focuses on 4 of the most widely used medical imaging modalities, chest X-ray (CXR), computed tomography (CT), magnetic resonance imaging (MRI), and ultrasound (US). From each image modality, 3 datasets will be utilized in the study. The 12 datasets are listed in Table 1, along with an alphabetical letter, which is assigned to each dataset for the ease of reference in the study.

For constructing the DL models leveraging Transfer Learning, four popular pre-trained CNN architectures: ResNet50, InceptionV3, VGG16 and AlexNet were used. Thus, for each dataset, there were 4 DL models evaluated to find the best DL model for each dataset. The evaluation criteria for the best-performing models were based on an assessment of key performance metrics, including accuracy, recall, precision, and the F1-score. A summary of the performance of the

Table 1. Datasets used in the study

	Dataset	Modality		Dataset	Modality
A	SARS-COV-2 Ct-Scan dataset [11]	CT	G	Brain Tumor Classification (4 classes) dataset [12]	MRI
B	Kidney Stone Dataset [13]	CT	H	Alzheimer's Disease dataset [14]	MRI
C	IQ-OTH/NCCD - Lung Cancer dataset [15]	CT	I	Brain Tumor Classification (2 classes) dataset [16]	MRI
D	Pneumonia Chest X-ray dataset [17]	Chest X-ray	J	Breast ultrasound image dataset [18]	Ultrasound
E	Tuberculosis (TB) Chest X-ray dataset [19]	Chest X-ray	K	Thyroid cancer dataset [20]	Ultrasound
F	COVID-QU-Ex dataset [21]	Chest X-ray	L	PCOS ultrasound image dataset [22]	Ultrasound

best DL model obtained for datasets can be found under Section A of the Appendix. Afterwards, the XAI techniques were applied for the best model of each dataset. When considering SHAP, GradientExplainer, which is a variant within the SHAP framework and is particularly suited for models with continuous input spaces, such as images or dense data, will be used in this study. Ultimately, using the results gained by applying the XAI techniques for each dataset, a modality-specific analysis was performed to compare the performance of OWN-Layer Grad-CAM with the existing XAI techniques: Grad-CAM, LIME, SHAP and Occlusion Sensitivity, through evaluation by medical experts and the novel quantitative metric, Perturbation-Induced Predicted Probability Change.

5.2 Evaluating the XAI Techniques

Evaluation Based on Faithfulness. The newly developed quantitaive metric, PIPPC was used for the evaluation of the XAI techniques based on faithfulness. To ensure a comprehensive evaluation, 100 images were randomly selected from the held-out test splits, used during DL model training, of each of the 12 datasets used in the study. Then, PIPPC values were calculated for each image across the 4 existing XAI techniques and the newly developed XAI method, OWN-Layer Grad-CAM.

Evaluation by Medical Experts. A structured interview process was employed to gain insights from five medical professionals, using their expertise to assess the existing XAI methods and the introduced novel approach. During these interviews, the participating medical experts were provided with a document containing 40 distinct medical images. These images consisted of randomly chosen images from the test sets of the respective datasets, and were compiled such that each modality had 10 images. Importantly, all medical experts evaluated the images independently, and the interviews were conducted separately for each doctor to ensure unbiased assessments and avoid any influence from other evaluations. In addition, to isolate the evaluation of XAI effectiveness from the influence of DL model accuracy, only images from the subset that were correctly classified by the model were included. This selection criterion aimed to minimize any potential bias introduced by incorrect model predictions, thereby focusing the evaluation only on the explainability and clinical relevance of the XAI-generated heatmaps. The doctors were tasked with reviewing each set of images, consisting the original diagnostic image and its associated XAI-generated heatmaps, and identifying the heatmap that they believed most reflected clinically relevant features, based on their medical judgment and expertise. A snapshot of the questionnaire used in the interviews with the medical experts is available online[2].

6 Analysis and Results

When considering the quantitative metric, PIPPC, which quantifies faithfulness, Table 2 gives the values obtained for mean PIPPC and the standard error for each of the datasets used in the study. Note that this analysis is based on a random selection of 100 images from the test set of each respective dataset. For each of the 12 datasets, due to the violation of the constant variance assumption required for ANOVA, the non-parametric test, Kruskal-Wallis test was used to test whether there are significant differences among the median PIPPC values for the XAI techniques. For all the 12 datasets, the Kruskal-Wallis tests (two-tailed) yielded p-values less than 0.001, which means that there is at least one pair of XAI techniques, that have significantly different medians, at 95% confidence level. Then, the post hoc test Wilcoxon rank-sum test (one-tailed) with Bonferroni correction was employed.

When considering the evaluation by medical experts, for each medical image modality, the most preferred XAI technique for each image was determined based on a majority vote among the five doctors. Figure 3 shows the bar chart of votes that were obtained from medical experts for each of the images across the medical image modalities. Subsequently, to obtain the most preferred XAI technique for each image modality, the mode of these majority votes was considered.

6.1 Computed Tomography

For dataset A, through Wilcoxon Rank sum test, it was concluded that at a 95% confidence level, Occlusion Sensitivity performed statistically significantly better than Grad-CAM, SHAP, LIME and OWN-Layer Grad-CAM. Similarly, for dataset B, Occlusion Sensitivity performed better than OWN-Layer Grad-CAM, Grad-CAM, SHAP and LIME. However, for dataset C, OWN-Layer Grad-CAM performed better than SHAP and LIME, with no difference to the performance of Grad-CAM.

[2] https://github.com/sammaworks/OWN-Layer-GradCAM.

Table 2. Mean PIPPC Values and Standard Error Across Datasets for Each XAI Technique

Modality	Dataset	Grad-CAM	LIME	SHAP	Occlusion Sensitivity	OWN-Layer Grad-CAM
CT	**A**	0.41 ± 0.02	0.43 ± 0.02	0.43 ± 0.02	0.47 ± 0.01	0.40 ± 0.06
	B	0.36 ± 0.01	0.33 ± 0.02	0.20 ± 0.01	0.47 ± 0.00	0.34 ± 0.04
	C	0.47 ± 0.01	0.30 ± 0.02	0.16 ± 0.01	0.20 ± 0.01	0.44 ± 0.03
CXR	**D**	0.45 ± 0.08	0.25 ± 0.08	0.12 ± 0.01	0.15 ± 0.04	0.61 ± 0.04
	E	0.34 ± 0.03	0.21 ± 0.01	0.11 ± 0.01	0.12 ± 0.01	0.47 ± 0.01
	F	0.47 ± 0.01	0.19 ± 0.02	0.20 ± 0.02	0.22 ± 0.03	0.49 ± 0.01
MRI	**G**	0.76 ± 0.05	0.23 ± 0.02	0.12 ± 0.01	0.25 ± 0.04	0.81 ± 0.03
	H	0.45 ± 0.03	0.21 ± 0.03	0.11 ± 0.08	0.12 ± 0.08	0.56 ± 0.03
	I	0.47 ± 0.01	0.19 ± 0.02	0.17 ± 0.09	0.22 ± 0.08	0.55 ± 0.02
US	**J**	0.70 ± 0.06	0.63 ± 0.02	0.19 ± 0.17	0.27 ± 0.08	0.65 ± 0.03
	K	0.44 ± 0.03	0.45 ± 0.08	0.14 ± 0.01	0.16 ± 0.07	0.47 ± 0.04
	L	0.37 ± 0.04	0.35 ± 0.10	0.17 ± 0.01	0.21 ± 0.07	0.41 ± 0.03

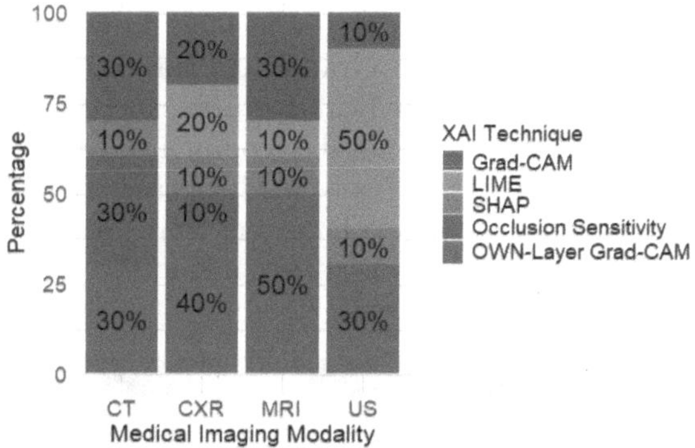

Fig. 3. Bar chart of votes that were obtained from medical experts

According to the preference of the medical experts, who were interviewed to assess the clinical relevance of the XAI techniques used in the study, OWN-Layer Grad-CAM was able to match the preference of Occlusion Sensitivity and Grad-CAM as the most preferred, with a percentage of 30% for each.

Overall, by considering the performance based on the quantitative metric and the preferences by the doctors, it can be empirically said that, for CT images, the three XAI techniques, Grad-CAM, Occlusion Sensitivity, and OWN-Layer Grad-CAM performed equally well, and each of these three methods significantly outperformed LIME and SHAP.

6.2 Chest X-Ray

As per the results of the Wilcoxon Rank sum tests for chest X-ray datasets D and E separately, at a 95% confidence level, OWN-Layer Grad-CAM has statistically significantly larger median PIPPC values than Grad-CAM, LIME, SHAP and Occlusion Sensitivity, whereas both Grad-CAM and OWN-Layer Grad-CAM have performed equally better than the other XAI techniques in dataset F.

According to the preference of medical doctors, OWN-Layer Grad-CAM has obtained the majority of the votes with 40%, exceeding the other XAI techniques.

Overall, it can be considered that for the three chest X-ray datasets, OWN-Layer Grad-CAM has performed better based on the quantitative metric and the opinions from the doctors, exceeding the performance of the other four XAI techniques used in the study.

6.3 Magnetic Resonance Imaging

According to the Wilcoxon rank-sum test, in datasets G and H, OWN-Layer Grad-CAM has been able to perform statistically significantly better than the other four XAI techniques, while having a comparable performance with Grad-CAM, exceeding the other three XAI techniques, in dataset I.

The new technique, OWN-Layer Grad-CAM has been able to obtain the majority (50%) of the votes of the medical doctors, exceeding Grad-CAM which has received a percentage of 30%. A notable comment given by the doctors was regarding the fact that OWN-Layer Grad-CAM was able to pinpoint the regions of high importance, and make better explanations than Grad-CAM and the other 3 XAI techniques. One such example is shown in Fig. 4.

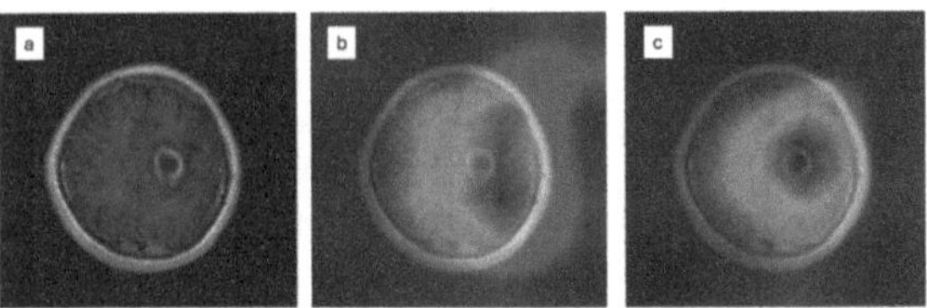

Fig. 4. (a) The original MRI of a tumor case in the human brain, (b) the Grad-CAM heatmap and (c) the OWN-Layer Grad-CAM heatmap

Overall, by considering the PIPPC values and the preference of the doctors, it can be said that for MRI datasets used in the study, OWN-Layer Grad-CAM has a superior performance compared to the existing XAI techniques.

6.4 Ultrasound

According to the Wilcoxon rank-sum test, through the pair-wise comparison of median PIPPC values of the 4 existing XAI techniques and the new XAI technique, for all the three Ultrasound datasets, it was concluded that Grad-CAM,

OWN-Layer Grad-CAM and LIME performed equally well, and had better performance compared to Occlusion Sensitivity and SHAP, at a confidence level of 95%.

Considering the preference of the medical doctors, OWN-Layer Grad-CAM (30%) could not exceed the preference for LIME (50%), although it was able to gain better preference than Grad-CAM, for the Ultrasound image datasets.

Overall, considering both the evaluation criteria, it can be concluded that LIME has a superior performance for Ultrasound images, while OWN-Layer Grad-CAM ranks second best among the other existing XAI techniques used in the study.

7 Discussion and Conclusion

This study focused on two key aspects. It introduced a novel metric, Perturbation-Induced Predicted Probability Change (PIPPC), to quantitatively assess the faithfulness of XAI techniques. While the feedback from medical doctors is generally regarded as more reliable, PIPPC is closely aligned with their evaluations, as evidenced in Table 3, demonstrating that PIPPC is a reliable measure of explanation faithfulness.

Table 3. Comparison of best-performing XAI techniques based on feedback from medical doctors and PIPPC

Image Modality	XAI technique(s) concluded as best performing using the feedback of medical doctors	XAI technique(s) concluded as best performing based on PIPPC
CT	Occlusion Sensitivity, Grad-CAM, OWN-Layer Grad-CAM	Occlusion Sensitivity, Grad-CAM, OWN-Layer Grad-CAM
CXR	OWN-Layer Grad-CAM	Grad-CAM, OWN-Layer Grad-CAM
MRI	OWN-Layer Grad-CAM	Grad-CAM, OWN-Layer Grad-CAM
US	LIME	Grad-CAM, OWN-Layer Grad-CAM, LIME

Moreover, the study introduced a novel XAI technique, Occlusion-weighted N-layer Grad-CAM (OWN-Layer Grad-CAM), which enhances traditional Grad-CAM by integrating a statistically grounded occlusion weighting scheme across multiple convolutional layers. It consistently showed an equally strong performance compared with the most widely-used XAI techniques such as Grad-CAM, and was empirically identified as the most suitable technique for Chest X-ray and MRI image datasets.

Disclosure of Interests. The authors have no competing interests to declare that are relevant to the content of this article.

Appendix A

Table 4 gives a summary of the performance of the best DL model obtained for datasets.

Table 4. Performance of Pre-trained Convolutional Models on Different Datasets

Dataset	Pre-trained Convolutional base	Accuracy		Precision		Recall		F1-score	
		Train Set	Test Set	Train Set	Test Set	Train Set	Test Set	Train Set	Test Set
A	VGG16	0.95	0.94	0.93	0.91	0.97	0.95	0.95	0.93
B	InceptionV3	0.99	0.97	0.98	0.98	0.97	0.96	0.97	0.97
C	VGG16	0.98	0.95	0.97	0.93	0.98	0.94	0.97	0.93
D	ResNet50	0.93	0.90	0.91	0.91	0.90	0.89	0.90	0.89
E	VGG16	0.98	0.96	0.96	0.96	0.97	0.95	0.96	0.95
F	ResNet50	0.99	0.96	0.97	0.95	0.98	0.96	0.97	0.95
G	ResNet50	0.94	0.92	0.92	0.92	0.91	0.90	0.91	0.90
H	InceptionV3	0.90	0.82	0.91	0.83	0.90	0.81	0.90	0.81
I	InceptionV3	0.95	0.91	0.91	0.89	0.91	0.88	0.91	0.88
J	ResNet50	0.83	0.81	0.87	0.82	0.81	0.79	0.83	0.80
K	VGG16	0.78	0.74	0.79	0.79	0.76	0.75	0.77	0.76
L	AlexNet	0.77	0.73	0.73	0.72	0.75	0.73	0.74	0.72

References

1. Gunning, D., Vorm, E., Wang, J.Y., Turek, M.: DARPA's explainable AI (XAI) program: a retrospective. Appl. AI Lett. **2**(4) (2021). https://doi.org/10.1002/ail2.61
2. Nazir, S., Dickson, D.M., Akram, M.U.: Survey of explainable artificial intelligence techniques for biomedical imaging with deep neural networks. Comput. Biol. Med. **156**, 106668 (2023). https://doi.org/10.1016/j.compbiomed.2023.106668
3. Selvaraju, R.R., Cogswell, M., Das, A., Vedantam, R., Parikh, D., Batra, D.: Grad-CAM: visual explanations from deep networks via gradient-based localization (2016). https://doi.org/10.48550/arXiv.1610.02391. Accessed 21 Aug 2024
4. Borys, K., et al.: Explainable AI in medical imaging: an overview for clinical practitioners – saliency-based XAI approaches. Eur. J. Radiol. **162**, 110787 (2023). https://doi.org/10.1016/j.ejrad.2023.110787
5. van der Velden, B.H.M., Kuijf, H.J., Gilhuijs, K.G.A., Viergever, M.A.: Explainable artificial intelligence (XAI) in deep learning-based medical image analysis. Med. Image Anal. **79**, 102470 (2022). https://doi.org/10.1016/j.media.2022.102470

6. Jiang, P.-T., Zhang, C.-B., Hou, Q., Cheng, M.-M., Wei, Y.: LayerCAM: exploring hierarchical class activation maps for localization. IEEE Trans. Image Process. **30**, 5875–5888 (2021). https://doi.org/10.1109/TIP.2021.3089943
7. Doshi-Velez, F., Kim, B.: Towards a rigorous science of interpretable machine learning. arXiv preprint arXiv:1702.08608 (2017). http://arxiv.org/abs/1702.08608
8. Patrício, C., Neves, J.C., Teixeira, L.F.: Explainable deep learning methods in medical image classification: a survey. ACM Comput. Surv. **56**(4), 1–41 (2024). https://doi.org/10.1145/3625287
9. Jin, W., Li, X., Hamarneh, G.: Evaluating explainable AI on a multi-modal medical imaging task: can existing algorithms fulfill clinical requirements? (2022). https://www.aaai.org. Accessed 21 Aug 2024
10. Samek, W., Binder, A., Montavon, G., Lapuschkin, S., Müller, K.-R.: Evaluating the visualization of what a deep neural network has learned. IEEE Trans. Neural Netw. Learn. Syst. **28**(11), 2660–2673 (2017). https://doi.org/10.1109/TNNLS.2016.2599820
11. Soares, E., Angelov, P., Biaso, S., Higa Froes, M., Abe, D.K.: SARS-CoV-2 CT scan dataset: a large dataset of real patients CT scans for SARS-CoV-2 identification. Preprint (2020). https://doi.org/10.1101/2020.04.24.20078584
12. Cheng, J.: Brain Tumor Dataset. Figshare (2017). https://figshare.com/articles/brain_tumor_dataset/1512427/5 Accessed 29 May 2024
13. Islam, M.N., Hasan, M., Hossain, M.K., Alam, M.G.R., Uddin, M.Z., Soylu, A.: Vision transformer and explainable transfer learning models for auto detection of kidney cyst, stone and tumor from CT-radiography. Sci. Rep. **12**(1) (2022). https://doi.org/10.1038/s41598-022-15634-4
14. Al Shehri, W.: Alzheimer's disease diagnosis and classification using deep learning techniques. PeerJ Comput. Sci. **8**, e1177 (2022). https://doi.org/10.7717/peerj-cs.1177
15. Kareem, H.F., Al-Huseiny, M.S., Mohsen, F.Y., Khalil, E.A., Hassan, Z.S.: Evaluation of SVM performance in the detection of lung cancer in marked CT scan dataset. Indones. J. Electri. Eng. Comput. Sci. **21**(3), 1731–1738 (2021). https://doi.org/10.11591/ijeecs.v21.i3.pp1731-1738
16. Rahman, A.: Modified Dataset. https://www.kaggle.com/alifrahman/modiified. Accessed 1 Aug 2024
17. Kermany, D., Zhang, K., Goldbaum, M.: Labeled optical coherence tomography (OCT) and chest X-ray images for classification. Mendeley Data V2 (2018). https://doi.org/10.17632/rscbjbr9sj.2
18. Al-Dhabyani, W., Gomaa, M., Khaled, H., Fahmy, A.: Dataset of breast ultrasound images. Data Brief **28**, 104863 (2020). https://doi.org/10.1016/j.dib.2019.104863
19. Jaeger, S., Candemir, S., Antani, S., Wáng, Y.X., Lu, P.-X., Thoma, G.: Two public chest X-ray datasets for computer-aided screening of pulmonary diseases. Quant. Imaging Med. Surg. **4**(6), 475–477 (2014). https://doi.org/10.3978/j.issn.2223-4292.2014.11.20
20. Pedraza, L., Vargas, C., Narváez, F., Durán, O., Muñoz, E., Romero, E.: An open access thyroid ultrasound image database. In: 10th International Symposium on Medical Information Processing (2015). https://doi.org/10.1117/12.2073532
21. Tahir, A.M., Chowdhury, M.E.H., Qiblawey, Y., Khandakar, A., Rahman, T., Kiranyaz, S.: COVID-QU-Ex. Kaggle (2021). https://doi.org/10.34740/KAGGLE/DSV/2759090
22. Kottarathil, P.: Polycystic Ovary Syndrome (PCOS) Dataset. Kaggle (n.d.). https://www.kaggle.com/prasoonkottarathil/polycysticovary-syndrome-pcos. Accessed 21 Aug 2024

23. Bach, S., Binder, A., Montavon, G., Klauschen, F., Müller, K.-R., Samek, W.: On pixel-wise explanations for non-linear classifier decisions by layer-wise relevance propagation. PLoS ONE **10**(7), e0130140 (2015). https://doi.org/10.1371/journal.pone.0130140
24. Khan, A.M.: Morphological operations for image processing: understanding and its applications. https://www.researchgate.net/publication/272484795. Accessed 21 Aug 2024

An Interpretable Machine Learning Model to Predict Drug Addiction Among Children in Sri Lanka

Ayomi Manathunga[1] and Ruwan Nawarathna[2(✉)]

[1] Postgraduate Institute of Science, University of Peradeniya, Peradeniya 20400, Sri Lanka
[2] Department of Statistics and Computer Science, University of Peradeniya, Peradeniya 20400, Sri Lanka
ruwand@sci.pdn.ac.lk

Abstract. Drug addiction among youth poses a growing threat to public health and social stability in Sri Lanka, particularly within school-aged populations. Drug abuse contributes to a range of severe consequences, including family breakdown, rising legal disputes, weakened social cohesion, deteriorating health, declining educational outcomes, and, in extreme cases, premature death. Despite its severity, early-stage identification and intervention mechanisms remain limited, especially in rural and underserved regions. This study aims to develop a machine learning-based predictive model to assess the risk of drug addiction among children by analyzing behavioral, familial, and environmental factors. A structured questionnaire was designed and administered to 1,000 participants comprising both individuals with and without a history of drug addiction from schools, rehabilitation centers across the country and the general public. Exploratory data analysis and preprocessing were conducted to handle missing values and transform questionnaire responses into categorical variables, ensuring the dataset was suitable for machine learning applications. To identify the most effective model, four classification algorithms—Decision Tree, Random Forest, Support Vector Machine, and Logistic Regression were implemented and evaluated. Among them, the Decision Tree classifier yielded the best performance with an accuracy of 99.65% and an F1-score of 0.995, demonstrating strong predictive power. A Python Tkinter software interface was developed to support community-level deployment of the Decision Tree model, enabling early risk detection and prevention through a user-friendly survey response system. The primary contribution of this study lies in integrating field data with predictive analytics to address a critical national issue and provide actionable recommendations.

Keywords: Interpretable Machine Learning · Drug Addiction Prediction · Substance Abuse Risk Factors · Children · Sri Lanka · Classification Model

1 Introduction

Drug addiction is a major public health issue worldwide, impacting individuals and communities, especially youth. In Sri Lanka, common drugs include heroin, cannabis, cocaine, and others. Data show 42% of drug arrests involve heroin and 55% cannabis,

R. N. Rajapakse et al. (Eds.): ICTer 2025, CCIS 2844, pp. 107–121, 2026.
https://doi.org/10.1007/978-981-92-0137-2_8

mostly in the Western Province (61%), followed by North Western (10%) and Central (8%). Colombo, Gampaha, and Kurunegala districts report the highest arrests, while Monaragala has none [1]. In 2022, Sri Lanka reported over 152,000 drug-related arrests—a 36% increase from the previous year—with heroin (45.6%), cannabis (35.0%), and methamphetamine (14.8%) as the main substances involved [2]. Many arrested were aged 15 to 25, showing youth remain especially vulnerable to substance abuse and its effects [3]. Treatment data from the same period show that over 1,300 individuals received care for drug dependence through government and non-governmental rehabilitation services, with a notable proportion admitted through the Prisoner Drug Rehabilitation Programme [4]. In addition to arrests and treatment admissions, epidemiological research has shown alarming patterns of substance use among adolescents in the general population. A 2022 study reported that 16% of adolescents had used at least one illicit substance during their lifetime, with prevalence rates of 6.1% for cigarettes, 13.6% for alcohol, and 2% for marijuana [4]. Both government and non-governmental organizations are involved in providing drug treatment services across the country. The reported number of individuals who received treatment for drug dependence includes 573 (35.8%) at treatment centers operated by the National Dangerous Drugs Control Board, 433 (27.1%) through the Prisoner Drug Rehabilitation Programme under the Department of Prisons, 160 (10%) from non-governmental or private treatment facilities, and 433 (27.1%) at the Kandakadu Treatment and Rehabilitation Center under the Bureau of the Commissioner General of Rehabilitation.

Today, many school children in Sri Lanka face an increasing risk of becoming victims of drug use which poses a serious threat to the future of the country. Contributing factors to this issue family background, association with bad friends, limited awareness of risks, arrogance, lack of love, ignorance, lack of shame, surrounding social environment, school conditions, stress, separation of parents, absence of someone to turn to, and pressure from home, school, or society. Although general advice can be given to all children, each child may be vulnerable to substance abuse for a different reason. These findings reinforce the need for targeted intervention strategies that are influenced by data-driven and child-friendly approaches to reduce the burden of drug addiction among school children.

The primary objective of the study to contribute toward protecting the younger generation by applying technological approaches to better understand and address drug addiction. Specifically, it explores the effects of drugs on children in their home, school, and social environments. If a child is randomly exposed to different factors that contribute to substance abuse, the proposed solution can predict whether the child is at risk of drug addiction.

This study further intends to provide a way for parents and educators to determine whether a child is susceptible to drugs and, if so, to identify possible solutions that may prevent exposure. The proposed approach examines how home, school, and social environments influence the likelihood of drug use among school children, and to develop a representative dataset based on these factors. Covering all districts of Sri Lanka, this study centers on school-aged children. Although some data have been collected from adults, the emphasis is placed on recalling their experiences during childhood.

Using this dataset, a machine learning model is developed to identify children at risk of drug addiction. Furthermore, a software application is created that assesses individual risk levels and proposes tailored preventive solutions, leveraging the machine learning model to support early intervention.

2 Literature Review

2.1 Drug Abuse Monitoring in Sri Lanka

The general objective of the Drug Abuse Monitoring System (DAMS) is to establish a reliable database for effective planning and monitoring of drug abuse, addiction and trafficking. The specific objectives of the reporting system [5, 6, 7] are to determine the incidence, prevalence, and characteristics of drug users who come into contact with reporting institutions, doctors, and police. It also aims to monitor the trends and patterns in drug use over time. Additionally, the system seeks to identify and describe the at-risk groups within the population. Another key objective is to assess and evaluate existing treatment and rehabilitation programs for drug users. Finally, the reporting system serves as an "early warning system" to enable timely program responses to emerging drug-related issues.

The Handbook of Drug Abuse Information, presented by the National Dangerous Drugs Control Board (NDDCB) in Sri Lanka, has researched and analyzed the districts, provinces, ages, ethnicity, agency of drug addicts as reported in 2022, but has not analyzed the causes of drug addiction [4]. The report [4] shows that 90.1% of drug users were Sinhalese, with smaller proportions of Moors (4.1%), Tamils (4%), Burghers (0.4%), and Malay (0.4%). Most arrests occurred in the Western Province, especially Colombo District. Cannabis (over 65%) and heroin were the most common substances detected, with heroin-related arrests rising. These trends highlight the need for targeted, region-specific intervention strategies, focusing on urban areas with high arrest rates.

2.2 Studies on the Prevalence of Drug Use, Addiction, Trafficking, and Smuggling in Sri Lanka

Studies using questionnaires and interviews with Sri Lankan prison inmates have examined factors like gender, ethnicity, education, and drug-related activities. They explored drug trafficking patterns, law enforcement interactions, and political influence on drug policies. Findings highlight Colombo District as a key hub for drug trafficking due to its high profitability and quick financial returns. The adolescent survey reveals that a significant portion of Sri Lankan youth experiment with substances, roughly one in six adolescents had tried an illicit drug, and many had engaged in underage alcohol (13.6%) or cigarette (6.1%) use [8]. These young users tended to start with legal substances like alcohol or tobacco and often initiated use out of curiosity or peer influence. In contrast, the study on institutionalized adult male drug users (in rehabilitation centers) [9] highlights far more intensive patterns of use: nearly all were poly-drug users, with cannabis (about 89%) and heroin (84%) being the most commonly used illicit substances. Notably, many of these persons had begun using in their late teens, reflecting a continuum from adolescent experimentation to chronic adult addiction, albeit in a much more severe form by adulthood. Common themes emerge around risk factors and social influences despite the contrasting populations. Both adolescents [8] and institutionalized adults [9] were heavily influenced by peer pressure and easy access to substances, and many lacked awareness of the harmful consequences of drug use.

Together [8, 9], the studies suggest a life-course approach: early preventive efforts to curb youth substance initiation, coupled with targeted interventions for high-risk and addicted individuals, in order to combat Sri Lanka's evolving substance, use challenge. Following the end of the civil war, studies identified a notable prevalence of drug use in the Jaffna District [10]. There has been an observable increase in the number of licensed drug and liquor outlets, including toddy shops. In addition to legal substances, a high prevalence of cannabis use has also been reported, indicating a growing concern over illicit drug consumption in the region. According to [10], drug use among females was much lower than males, with male cannabis users far outnumbering female users. However, cigarette smoking was more common among women than other drugs. The median age for starting licit drugs was 26, with the highest risk between ages 15 and 18. The Delft Divisional Secretariat Division (DDSD) in Jaffna had the highest prevalence of heroin and cannabis users. Beer, cigarette, and alcohol users tended to have higher education (up to G.C.E. Ordinary Level) than cannabis and heroin users. Most drug users had low income, earning Rs. 15,000 or less monthly, and many were household heads.

2.3 Studies on the Prevalence of Drug Use, Addiction, Trafficking, and Smuggling in Other South Asian Countries

Although street children in India represent a large and vulnerable group, few academic studies focus specifically on substance abuse in this population. Most existing research explores causes, effects, and risk factors, while studies on preventive strategies are limited. However, some preventive insights are available through reports by government and non-governmental organizations [12].

Existing studies, mostly based in urban areas, show varied findings. Long-term funding and strategic implementation are crucial for sustaining intervention programs [13]. Bhushan et al. conducted a foundational study on drug abuse among street children in Bangalore, highlighting the complex socio-environmental factors that contribute to substance use within this population [14]. Many street children flee abuse in institutions only to face new risks, including peer pressure that leads to substance use. Their unstable earnings are often spent quickly, often on intoxicants. Drug use typically starts with tobacco, then solvents, inhalants, and cannabis. While alcohol is common, it is usually recreational. Bhushan et al. highlight the urgent need for structured interventions and broader social, educational, and political support for reintegration [14].

In [15] Sani et al. conducted a study on private university undergraduates in Bangladesh examined drug use causes, types, and treatment attitudes. Using data from 160 students aged 15–25, it found that 38% started due to peer influence and 31% out of curiosity. Cannabis was the most used drug (86%). Although most were aware of treatment options, few sought help, and 41% of those who did relapsed. The study noted that drug use was driven mainly by curiosity or recreation, with low willingness to seek treatment.

Another study by Anik Mahmud [16] focused on substance abuse among male adolescents in Dhaka North City, with an emphasis on public health perspectives and rehabilitation. This study surveyed two groups of male adolescents: one group consisted of drug-dependent youths receiving rehabilitation in treatment centers, and the other group comprised school- or college-going adolescents who did not use drugs. Data were gathered using a structured, pre-tested questionnaire, and a two-stage sampling method ensured a representative sample from Dhaka North City. Drug-using adolescents were strongly influenced by peers and often surrounded by misconceptions about substances. They also experienced more family-related issues: notably higher rates of conflict with parents, secrecy, and breakdowns in parent–child communication compared to non-users. These findings suggest that a lack of parental engagement or trust, coupled with negative peer influence, elevates the risk of adolescent drug involvement.

Dhaital et al. conducted a comprehensive study of alcohol and drug use among street children in Nepal to determine the extent, patterns, and impacts of substance abuse in this high-risk group [17]. In study 180 street children of ages 10–17, mostly boys across six urban centers in Nepal was surveyed through structured interviews and snowball sampling, gathering data on their alcohol, drug, and tobacco use and related socio-demographic factors. The study found alarmingly high levels of substance involvement: about two-thirds of the street children had been exposed to alcohol (median initiation age ~ 11 years) with a current alcohol use prevalence of around 56% and inhalant abuse (particularly glue sniffing of "Dendrite" adhesive) as well as cannabis use were common, facilitated by easy availability and peer group influence. The authors note that many street children resort to substance use as a coping mechanism amid poverty, family dysfunction, and the harsh realities of street life, which leaves them highly vulnerable to health and social harms.

2.4 Related Work on Using Machine Learning Models to Predict Drug Abuse

Various researchers have applied machine learning (ML) to predict drug abuse risk and addiction outcomes. Han et al. [18] developed ML models to predict opioid misuse among U.S. adolescents using the National Survey on Drug Use and Health (2015–2017, adolescents aged 12–17). They trained artificial neural networks, a distributed random forest, and gradient boosting machines, comparing them against penalized logistic regression. All models performed similarly (AUC-ROC of 0.81), but the distributed random forest achieved the highest precision-recall performance. This study demonstrated that ML techniques can successfully identify the relatively rare cases of adolescent opioid misuse with good accuracy [18].

Afzali et al. explored seven ML algorithms to predict adolescent substance use in two countries [19]. Their study utilized longitudinal survey data from Canadian and Australian high-school students, with baseline ages of 13, to predict mid-adolescent alcohol use levels. They evaluated logistic regression, support vector machines, random forests, neural networks, and regularized regression variants (lasso, ridge, elastic net). The best-performing model was an elastic-net classifier, which achieved high accuracy (AUC of 0.87 in Canada, 0.86 in Australia) in distinguishing drinking risk categories [19]. Notably, psychopathology and personality factors (e.g., externalizing behaviors, sensation-seeking traits) were among the top predictors of alcohol use.

In South Asia, studies have applied similar approaches to their local data. In [20], Shahriar et al. developed a supervised ML model to identify individuals vulnerable to drug addiction in Dhaka, Bangladesh. They collected survey data on social, familial, and health factors from both rehabilitated drug users and non-users of ages 15–40 with the help of addiction specialists. Their ML approach which included classifiers like logistic regression and decision trees discovered distinguishing features such as family relationships and peer influence that differentiate addicts from non-addicts. The model could successfully classify those at risk of addiction, demonstrating the feasibility of data-driven risk prediction in a developing country context.

Another study focused on Bangladesh directly compared multiple ML algorithms for drug addiction prediction on a local dataset was presented in [21] by Alam et al. They assembled information from 188 individuals (all males, ages 17–45) in Dhaka, including known drug users recruited from rehabilitation centers and non-users from schools and colleges. Five classifiers, namely, Logistic Regression, Decision Tree, Random Forest (RF), Naïve Bayes, and Support Vector Machine were trained to detect drug addiction status. The Random Forest achieved the highest accuracy of 97.3% on this dataset, outperforming XGBoost, decision trees, and other methods. This high accuracy illustrates the potential of ML models to capture complex interactions of demographic and behavioral factors in predicting substance abuse. In [22], Kim et al. developed and validated machine-learning models, including XGBoost, to predict adolescent substance use across large national datasets from Korea, the United States, and Norway. Their analysis highlighted key predictors such as smoking status, BMI, suicidal ideation, alcohol consumption, and feelings of sadness or despair, demonstrating robust cross-cultural applicability.

3 Methodology

3.1 Proposed Approach

The mains steps of the approach are illustrated in Fig. 1. The proposed approach begins by analyzing the past life experiences and lifestyle factors of individuals who have become addicted to drugs, focusing on behavioral, social, and environmental influences. Next, data is collected through questionnaires and interviews administered to individuals from schools, rehabilitation centers and the general public, ensuring a diverse and representative dataset. This dataset is then used to train a machine learning model capable of learning patterns and risk factors associated with drug addiction. A software application is developed to interface with the trained model, allowing users to input individual-level data. Based on this input, the system provides the probability of developing drug addiction along with personalized recommendations for prevention and recovery, with the aim of supporting early intervention strategies.

3.2 Data Collection

This section describes the data collection procedures for training and validating the machine learning model to predict drug addiction risk among Sri Lankan children, including study population, questionnaire design, ethical considerations, and data confidentiality.

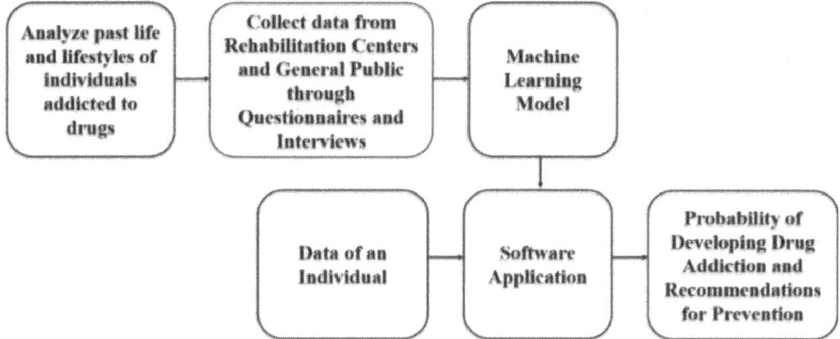

Fig. 1. Overview of the proposed approach.

Study Population and Sampling. The study involved two groups: a case group of 500 individuals with a history of drug addiction undergoing treatment at government and military-managed centers (including Handessa and Kandakadu), and a control group of 500 individuals from the general public—schoolchildren and adults with no drug use history—recruited through schools and trusted contacts in regions such as Matara, Polonnaruwa, Puttalam, Colombo, and Ampara. Data were collected using both Google Forms and paper-based surveys [23].

Questionnaire Design. A structured questionnaire was developed to gather demographic, familial, social, and behavioral data related to drug addiction risk. Administered mainly in Sinhala, it included yes/no questions for clarity and ease of analysis. The questionnaire, reviewed by experts and individuals with addiction experience, covered personal background, parental influence, peer and school environment, and drug exposure factors to identify potential addiction predictors among school children.

Ethical Considerations and Approvals. Ethical clearances and institutional permissions were obtained before data collection. Verbal consent was secured from participants after explaining the study and its voluntary nature. For minors and institutionalized individuals, interviews proceeded only with guardian or institutional approval. No personally identifiable information was collected.

Data Collection Procedure. Data collection occurred in phases. At rehabilitation centers, group sessions included motivational talks by professionals, with facilitators assisting those with literacy challenges. In schools, questionnaires were distributed after awareness sessions stressing confidentiality and honesty. To reduce discomfort, children participated in recreational activities both before and after completing the questionnaire. Non-Sinhala speakers or those with literacy difficulties were interviewed verbally by trained staff.

Data Confidentiality. To protect participant privacy, the questionnaires were anonymized—no names, identification numbers, or traceable personal information were recorded. Responses were collected individually and stored securely. For minors, interviews were conducted in private settings to ensure comfort and confidentiality.

3.3 Machine Learning Model

The overall design of the machine learning model is depicted in Fig. 2. The process consists of several key stages: preprocessing the collected data into formats suitable for machine learning, partitioning the dataset, selecting the most appropriate classification algorithm, evaluating model performance, performing hyperparameter tuning, and verifying the final model. Four supervised learning algorithms—Random Forest, Decision Tree, Support Vector Machine (SVM), and Logistic Regression—were created and compared to identify the most effective classifier. The subsequent subsections describe each stage of the model development process in detail.

Data Preprocessing. All attributes were converted to categorical variables (0 or 1), except for the province attribute, which was numerically coded from 1 to 9. The cleaned, digitized dataset contains 54 features. Missing values were handled, and label encoding converted categorical strings to numbers for machine learning compatibility.

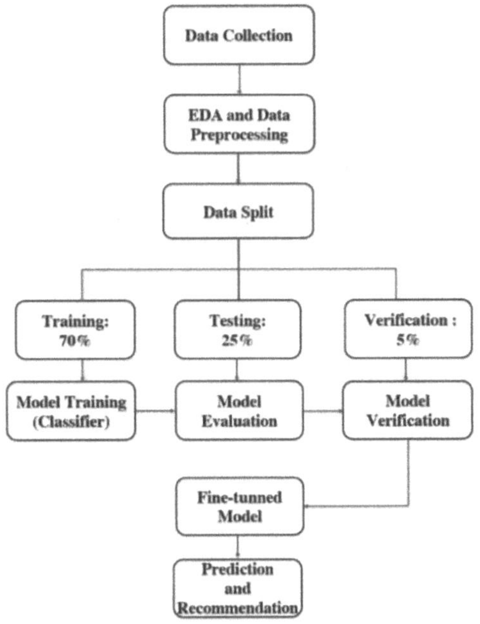

Fig. 2. The main steps of the machine learning model

The target variable was encoded separately. After preprocessing, the final dataset contained 947 records.

Data Splitting. First, 50 records (5%) were retained from 947 records for model verification (i.e., untouched data). The remaining 897 records were then partitioned into training and testing subsets using a 70:30 split to evaluate generalization performance. This split ratio was decided experimentally. The dataset was divided into three parts: 627

records for training the model, 270 records for testing its performance, and 50 records for verification to ensure accuracy on unseen data.

Selection of the Classification Model. To determine the most suitable classification model for the given problem, four different models were selected based on distinct algorithmic paradigms: Random Forest, Support Vector Machine, Logistic Regression, and Decision Tree [24]. The input features were standardized prior to training, and the model was applied to the labeled dataset for classification. The Random Forest implementation was carried out using the RandomForestClassifier from the scikit-learn library in Python. The SVM model was implemented using the svm. SVC class from the scikit-learn library in Python. The preprocessed data was fed into the classifier through a linear and default RBF kernel. In this study, logistic regression was implemented using the LogisticRegression class in the scikit-learn library. Input features were normalized before training, and the model was trained using the labeled dataset. Default regularization settings were retained, and the classifier was evaluated using predictions on the test set. In the decision tree model, the Gini index was used to measure the quality of a split. After evaluating three variants of the decision tree algorithm (i.e., ID3, CART, and C4.5), the Classification and Regression Tree (CART) were selected to build the tree.

Software Application for Drug Addiction Risk Assessment. A user-friendly software application was developed using Python's Tkinter library integrating the trained machine learning model with interfaces localized in Sinhala and Tamil to suit the target users. This ensures accessibility without language barriers or technical knowledge. Sample interfaces are shown in the Result and Discussion. The application enables assessment of individual risk for drug addiction.

4 Result and Discussion

4.1 Exploratory Data Analysis (EDA)

Descriptive Statistics. Figure 3. presents descriptive insights into the profiles of drug-addicted individuals based on questionnaire data. Most addicts were from the Western Province (68%) and born after 1990 (61%), indicating both regional and generational patterns. A significant behavioral trend was noted, with 92% being disobedient to teachers. Males overwhelmingly dominated the dataset (97%), while only 3% were female.

Correlation Heatmap of the Data. Figure 4. shows a correlation heatmap of 14 key variables, revealing strong links between parental employment and returning home late (e.g., $r = 0.87$ for mothers). Negative correlations were found between unemployment and being home during work hours (e.g., $r = -0.93$ for mothers). Demographic factors like gender and birth year showed weak associations.

4.2 Performance of the Proposed Model

Accuracy, Precision, Recall and F1-Score of the Models. The performance of the proposed classification model was evaluated using accuracy, precision, recall, and F1-score, with particular emphasis on minimizing false positives and false negatives due

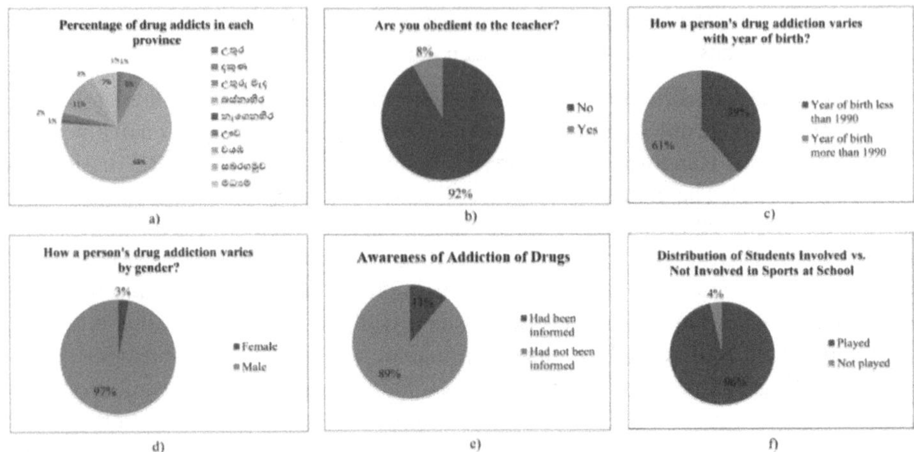

Fig. 3. Descriptive statistics of the dataset obtained through the questionnaire. Distribution of participants: (a) drug addiction across the nine provinces, (b) obedience to teachers, (c) by year of birth, (d) by gender, (e) awareness of drugs, and (f) involvement in sports.

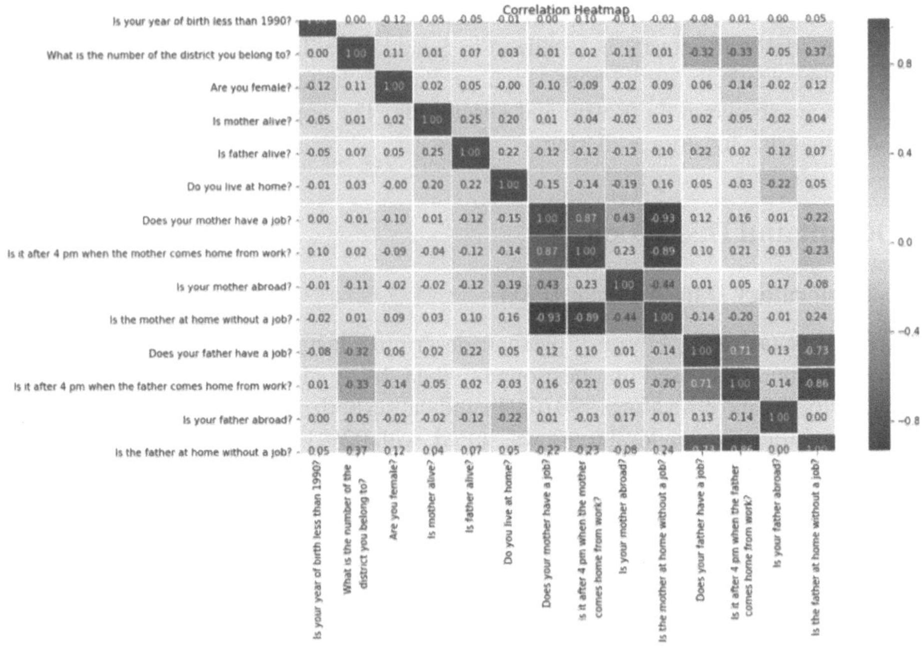

Fig. 4. The correlation heatmap of 14 selected attributes of the data set.

to the sensitive nature of the prediction task. Four classifiers were evaluated based on accuracy, all exceeding 98% (See Table 1). The Decision Tree model demonstrated the highest accuracy of 99.647%, while the Random Forest and SVM models both achieved

99.295%. Logistic Regression achieved 98.943% accuracy. As shown in Table **1**, all four models demonstrated strong performance across precision, recall, and F1-score. Random Forest and SVM achieved balanced scores of 0.990, while Logistic Regression had a slightly lower recall of 0.980.

Table 1. Accuracy, Recall, Precision and F1-score of the four classification models.

Classifier	Accuracy (%)	Recall	Precision	F1-Score
Random Forest	98.943	0.990	0.990	0.990
Support Vector Machine	99.295	0.990	0.990	0.990
Logistic Regression	99.295	0.980	0.990	0.990
Decision Tree	99.647	0.990	1.000	0.995

Also, ROC curves for all four models (See Fig. 5) show strong class separability, with near-perfect performance. The Decision Tree outperformed the others with perfect precision (1.00), a recall of 0.990, and the highest F1-score of 0.995, highlighting its effectiveness in classifying the target outcome. Although performance differences were minimal, the Decision Tree was chosen as the final model due to its superior accuracy, simplicity, interpretability, and computational efficiency.

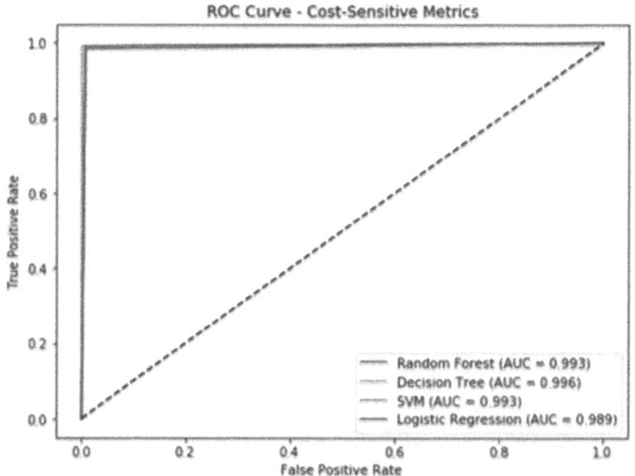

Fig. 5. ROC values of the four classification models used.

Cross-Validation. To further verify the reliability of model training and minimize the risk of overfitting, all models were evaluated using ten-fold cross-validation. As shown in Table 2, the accuracy, recall, precision, and F1-score remained consistently high across folds, demonstrating stable performance on unseen data. Among all classifiers, the Decision Tree model consistently achieved the highest values across all metrics, reinforcing the robustness of the proposed approach.

Table 2. Accuracy, Precision, Recall, and F1-score using ten-fold cross-validation

Classifier	Accuracy (%)	Recall	Precision	F1-Score
Random Forest	97.460	0.9759	0.9743	0.9746
Support Vector Machine	97.460	0.9755	0.9741	0.9746
Logistic Regression	99.580	0.9958	0.9958	0.9958
Decision Tree	99.680	0.9969	0.9968	0.9968

Final Decision Tree Generated by the CART Algorithm. The final decision tree is shown in Fig. 6. To identify the best Decision Tree algorithm, ID3, CART, and C4.5 were evaluated, with CART achieving the highest accuracy (99.647%) and selected for its superior efficiency. Using the Gini impurity index, the root node "Are you obedient to the teacher?" provided the highest information gain (0.497). Key features such as obedience, drug awareness, aggression, parental presence, and sports engagement drive the classification, and leaf nodes with low Gini values indicate highly pure outcomes.

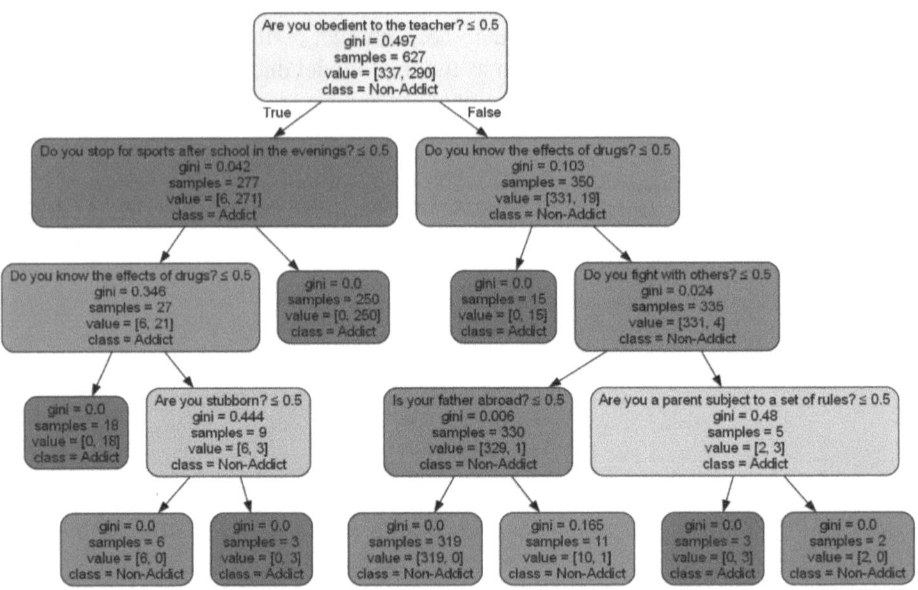

Fig. 6. Visualization of the final CART decision tree model

Model Verification. For independent evaluation, the final CART Decision Tree model (Fig. 6) was tested on the reserved hold-out dataset of 50 real cases that were never used during training or cross-validation. The model correctly classified all instances, yielding a verification accuracy of 100%, which—combined with the cross-validation results—demonstrates strong generalization capability and further reduces concerns of overfitting or data-specific bias.

4.3 Sample Outputs of the User Interface for Drug Addiction Risk Assessment

Sample interfaces from the user interface designed for drug addiction risk assessment are provided in Fig. 7. The interface presents a sequence of yes/no questions aligned with predefined input fields. Each question includes a pair of radio buttons allowing users to select one of two options. Once the responses are entered, the user can submit the data using clearly labeled action buttons, after which the system processes the input through the underlying machine learning model and displays the prediction result in a dialog box. Recommend that the model be used only in controlled settings, such as a school laboratory or council room, where each student completes the questionnaire individually under supervision. Students submit their responses privately and receive their output confidentially, which ensures that no child is publicly labeled or stigmatized. This approach allows students to reflect on their results responsibly while minimizing the risk of misinterpretation or harm.

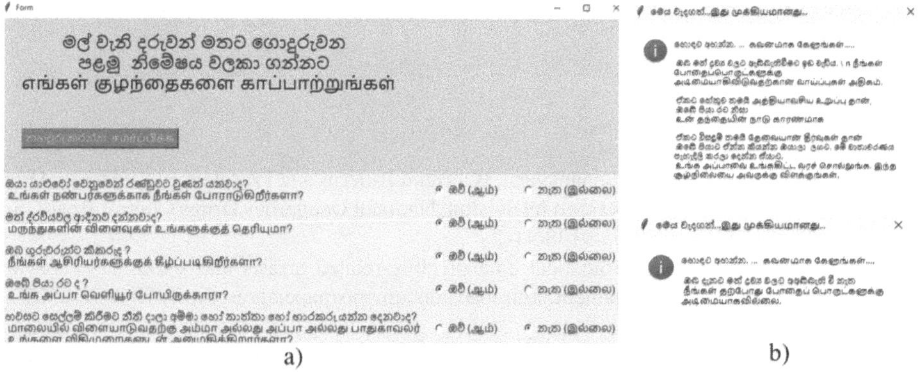

Fig. 7. Sample user interfaces. a) Drug risk assessment questions and b) Recommendation of the machine learning model

5 Discussion

The results demonstrate the high potential of machine learning models in accurately classifying individuals at risk of drug addiction using socio-demographic and behavioral features. The study successfully identifies key behavioral indicators such as obedience, awareness, aggression, and sports involvement that contribute meaningfully to risk classification, providing recommendations for prevention strategies. Among the evaluated models, the Decision Tree classifier achieved the highest accuracy (99.647%) along with the best F1-score (0.995), indicating a strong balance between precision and recall. Further the model verification accuracy achieved 100%. The final model is both interpretable and efficient, making it suitable for real-world deployment in counseling environments where explainability and rapid decision-making are crucial.

6 Conclusion and Future Work

This study presents an interpretable machine learning model to predict drug addiction risk among school-aged children in Sri Lanka, using behavioral, social, and familial data. The Decision Tree model achieved high accuracy and F1-score, indicating strong predictive performance. The high accuracy and low misclassification rates underscore the reliability of the proposed framework for real-world deployment. A user-friendly software tool was also created to support practical application in educational and healthcare settings. Despite limitations such as demographic imbalance and self-reported data, this study provides a valuable foundation for data-driven strategies to prevent youth substance abuse, particularly in underserved communities. Future work should expand the dataset for better population balance, include continuous addiction severity measures, explore advanced models (e.g., ensembles, deep learning), and extend the user interface to support multiple languages and platforms, including mobile.

Disclosure of Interests. The authors declare that they have no conflict of interest.

References

1. Darshana, T., Fernando, R., Senanayake, B.: Trend Patterns and Prevalence of Injection Drug Users (IDUs) in Sri Lanka. Research Division, National Dangerous Drugs Control Board, Sri Lanka (2017). ISBN 978-955-9138-41-2
2. Parliament of Sri Lanka: Statistical data on drug-related arrests and trends (2022). Parliament.lk.https://www.parliament.lk/uploads/documents/paperspresented/1704951195055629.pdf
3. Rathnayake, D.: Silent epidemic: Youth drug addiction and toll on Sri Lanka's future. Daily FT (2023). https://www.ft.lk/columns/Silent-epidemic-Youth-drug-addiction-and-toll-on-Sri-Lanka-s-future/4-774687
4. National Dangerous Drugs Control Board: Drug-related statistics (January – October 2022). NDDCB Research Division (2022). https://www.nddcb.gov.lk/Docs/research/Drug-related%20statistics%202022%20%28January%20-%20October%29.pdf
5. National Dangerous Drugs Control Board: Drug Abuse Monitoring System 2019 Annual Report. Research Division (2019). https://www.nddcb.gov.lk/Docs/research/Annual%20Report%202019.pdf
6. Abesingha, S., Bandara, S.A.: National Prevalence Survey on drug use 2019. National Dangerous Drugs Control Board. (2019) https://www.nddcb.gov.lk/Docs/annual_report/03%20NDDCB%202019%20%20English.pdf
7. Senanayake, B., Welagedara, L.: Drugs Related Statistics – 2019. Research Division, National Dangerous Drugs Control Board, Ministry of Defence (2019). https://www.nddcb.gov.lk/Docs/research/Drug_Related_Statistics_2019.pdf
8. Gamage, D., de Silva, R., Abeyasinghe, H.: Substance use among adolescents in Sri Lanka: a cross-sectional survey. Subst. Abuse Treat. Prev. Policy. **17**(1), 1–9 (2022). https://pmc.ncbi.nlm.nih.gov/articles/PMC9130826/
9. Seneviratne, C., Dissanayake, D., Edirisinghe, K.: Characteristics and correlates of drug addiction among institutionalized male drug users in Sri Lanka. J. Subst. Abus. **27**(5), 485–491 (2022). https://pmc.ncbi.nlm.nih.gov/articles/PMC9400351/

10. National Dangerous Drugs Control Board: Study on the Prevalence of Drug Use and Estimation in Jaffna 27–60 District. Research Division
11. Boys, A., Marsden, J., Strang, J.: Understanding reasons for drug use amongst young people: a functional perspective. Health Educ. Res. **16**(4), 457–469 (2001)
12. Njord, L., Merril, R.M., Njord, R., Lindsay, R., Pahano, J.D.R.: Drug use among street children (2010)
13. Sharma, N., Joshi, S.: Preventing substance abuse among street children in India: a literature review. Health Sci. J. **7**(2), 137–148 (2013)
14. Bhushan, K., Benegal, V., Karott, M., Seshadri, S.: Drug abuse among street children in Bangalore. In: CRY-funded Monograph (1998)
15. Sani, M.N.: Drug addiction among undergraduate students of private universities in Bangladesh. Procedia Soc. Behav. Sci. **5**, 498–501 (2010)
16. Mahmud, A.: Substance abuse among male adolescents in Dhaka North City: a comparative study on causes, consequences, knowledge, and attitudes. Int. Neuropsychiatric Dis. J. **21**(1), 59–66 (2024)
17. Dhaital, R., Giring, Y.B., Subedi, G., Hamal, P.: Alcohol and drug use among street children in Nepal. Child Workers in Nepal (CWIN), Kathmandu (2002)
18. Han, D.-H., Lee, S., Seo, D.-C.: Using machine learning to predict opioid misuse among U.S. adolescents. Prev. Med. **130**, 105886 (2020)
19. Afzali, M.H., Sunderland, M., Stewart, S.H., et al.: Machine-learning prediction of adolescent alcohol use: a cross-study, cross-cultural validation. Addiction. **114**(4), 662–671 (2019)
20. Shahriar, A., Faisal, F., Mahmud, S.U., Chakrabarti, A., Alam, M.G.R.: A machine learning approach to predict vulnerability to drug addiction. In: Proceedings 22nd International Conference on Computer and Information Technology (ICCIT), Dhaka, Bangladesh (2019)
21. Alam, K.M.R., Ahammed, K., Rony, M.A.T., Ferdousi, Z.: A comparative machine learning study to predict drug addiction in Bangladesh. In: Proceedings 15th IEEE International Conference on Application of Information and Communication Technologies (AICT) (2021)
22. Kim, J., Park, S., Lee, H., et al.: Machine-learning prediction of adolescent substance use across multiple national surveys. Addict. Behav. **150**, 107719 (2025)
23. Google LLC: Google Form for Data Collection. https://docs.google.com/forms/d/1JvWKT8g3EM1fzfEvHl3U39j2XZGhh-VKA62fqAzfXXs/edit?usp=sharing
24. Hastie, T., Tibshirani, R., Friedman, J.: The Elements of Statistical Learning: Data Mining, Inference, and Prediction, 2nd edn. Springer, New York (2009)

MMAD: Multi-model Adversarial Defense For Medical Images

Saicharan Gnanapiragasam(✉), Guhanathan Poravi, and Kalhari Walawage

Informatics Institute of Technology, Colombo, Sri Lanka
{saicharan.20210655,guhanathan.p,kalhari.w}@iit.ac.lk

Abstract. Adversarial attacks cause great harm to artificial intelligence systems deployed in medical imaging, these perturbations are invisible to the naked human eye at very low intensities but still can lead to diagnostic misclassifications and compromise patient care. This research proposes a novel defense framework specifically designed for medical imaging systems, with a focus on Magnetic Resonance Imaging (MRI). This framework introduces a hybrid classification model that integrates Vision Transformer (ViT), Convolutional Neural Network (CNN), and Spiking Neural Network (SNN) components with an attention-based fusion mechanism, enhancing adversarial detection. Furthermore, a two-phase purification system was developed using the U-Net-style generator, which was refined in phase two using a PatchGAN-based discriminator fine-tuning to restore adversarial corrupted images while maintaining structural fidelity. The experimental results on the brain tumour magnetic resonance imaging dataset demonstrate that the proposed hybrid classifier achieves 97.89% accuracy in detecting FGSM attacks, 92.47% accuracy in clean images, and 86.93% accuracy in detecting BIM. At the same time, a drop in performance with 41.78% detection accuracy for PGD was noticeable. The classifier was tested on the MINIST standard benchmarking dataset, which showed promising results in detecting FGSM with an accuracy of 98%, BIM with an accuracy of 96%, and PGD with 90.40% and 100% on clean images. The purification model achieved an impressive peak PSNR of 34.61 and SSIM of 0.9551 demonstrating its effectiveness in reconstructing images and removing adversarial perturbation on brain tumour MRI dataset, furthermore maintaining good performance on clean images balancing the trade-off. This research contributes to algorithm design for detecting subtle adversarial patterns and also focuses on making the complex models run in resource constraint environment efficiently.

Keywords: Adversarial Machine Learning · Vision Transformer · U-Net · GAN-based purification · Computer Vision · Spiking Neural Network · convolutional neural network

R. N. Rajapakse et al. (Eds.): ICTer 2025, CCIS 2844, pp. 122–136, 2026.
https://doi.org/10.1007/978-981-92-0137-2_9

1 Introduction

Artificial intelligence (AI) systems are being integrated into medical systems to support faster and more accurate diagnosis. However, these systems are increasingly vulnerable to adversarial attacks. Adversarial attacks are well-crafted perturbations that can cause artificial intelligence models to make incorrect predictions with very high confidence, and these perturbations are invisible to the human eye [1]. Deep neural networks are highly vulnerable to adversarial perturbations, these attacks exploit the vulnerabilities in the algorithms, compromising its accuracy, which result in people losing hope in Artificial Intelligence, especially in safety-critical applications like medical imaging analysis, where high accuracy must be maintained at all times [2]. According to research conducted by Chowdhury, Mejbaul Islam and Noor [3], Adversarial attacks can be categorized into white-box attacks, black-box attacks and semi-white-box attacks. This research focuses on providing a general defense solution for targeted attacks within white-box category, specifically Fast Gradient Sign Method (FGSM), Basic Iterative Method (BIM) and Projected Gradient Descent (PGD).

Most existing defense systems for medical imaging rely on pre-trained models originally developed for natural images which are often transferred to the medical domain [2]. This signifies the need for medical-specific defense systems that can mitigate all adversarial perturbations effectively. Research in medical adversarial is low due to difficulties in finding labelled medical datasets as they involve privacy and ethical issues. As mentioned by past studies current defense systems lack generalizability, meaning there is no single adversarial defense solution that can mitigate all adversarial attacks with good robustness [4]. Additionally, current defense systems suffer from trade-off where focusing on adversarial robustness often reduces performance on clean images, an unacceptable compromise in the medical diagnostic domain [5].

This research provides novel adversarial defense solution tailored for medical imaging, with main focus on MRI-based brain tumor classification. The proposed solutions consist a hybrid classification model integrating Vision Transformer, Convolutional Neural Network and Spiking Neural Network which were fused on attention based fusion to detect the minute adversarial perturbations with greater accuracy. Furthermore, a purification model was developed consisting of U-Net style generator which was refined using a PatchGAN discriminator to restore adversarially corrupted MRI images while maintaining structural information and similarity. This proposed framework enhances adversarial robustness without sacrificing diagnostic accuracy contributing to more secure AI-assisted healthcare solutions.

2 Related Work

2.1 Adversarial Attacks and Their Impact on Health Care

Besides digital adversarial attacks, physical adversarial attacks pose threats to medical imaging and health care systems. Physical attacks could be categorized into intentional object placement or adversarial patches [3]. For instance, in health care systems a heart rate sensor could be adversely affected by the proximity of a magnet or to noise perturbations. Such interference could affect diagnostic outcomes or even cause serious health risk.

AI has enhanced diagnostic accuracy by reducing the human error rate. Automated Image analysis also helps automate labour-intensive processes of medical image analysis, which allows healthcare professionals to focus on more complex tasks, but even with these positive contributions, AI systems are still highly vulnerable to adversarial attacks. These attacks could be in both the physical and digital worlds. They can compromise treatment plans, Misdiagnosis, Financial crime and Loss of trust in AI-powered medical technologies [2]. Some studies have shown that there is further room for improvement as medical images have a specific biological structure and unified distribution which could be utilised to develop a robust adversarial defense system tailored to medical images [6].

FGSM is a white box adversarial attack that generates perturbation by using gradient loss function. The perturbation is applied in the direction of the gradient to maximize the loss [3].

$$x_{\text{adv}} = x + \epsilon \cdot \text{sign}(\nabla_x J(x, y)) \quad (1)$$

where x is the input, y is the true label, $J(x, y)$ is the loss function, and ϵ controls the perturbation magnitude.

PGD is an advanced version of FGSM. It applies perturbation in multiple iterative steps. It is a stealthy attack with a higher success rate [7].

$$x_{t+1} = \text{Proj}_\epsilon \left(x_t + \alpha \cdot \text{sign}(\nabla_x J(x_t, y)) \right) \quad (2)$$

where x_t is the adversarial example at iteration t, y is the true label, $J(x_t, y)$ is the loss function, α is the step size, and Proj_ϵ denotes the projection operation ensuring the perturbation remains within an ϵ-bounded ball.

BIM was improved upon FGSM. Small iterative perturbations are added instead of large single perturbation. Gradually the effectiveness of the attack increases as each step adjusts the input slightly [5].

$$x_{t+1} = x_t + \alpha \cdot \text{sign}(\nabla_x J(x_t, y)) \quad (3)$$

where x_t is the adversarial example at iteration t, y is the true label, $J(x_t, y)$ is the loss function, and α denotes the step size.

2.2 Challenges in Detecting and Defending Against Adversarial Attack

Several research works have focused on adversarial defense, although adversarial attacks will always prevail. Researchers can develop a defense only after successfully discovering an attack. In addition, the tactics of adversarial attacks are increasing with time, making the task of keeping the medical system robust and secure a challenge to solve.

Adversarial Training the one of the most common approaches used for all types of adversarial attacks. Adversarial Training (AT) involves adding the adversarial examples to the training data set to help the model improve its adversarial robustness but in medical imaging there is a limitation as (AT) require large number of labelled data and current defense systems are specifically designed for natural images [8]. There is low availability of labelled medical imaging datasets due to privacy and ethical considerations.

Sophisticated attacks that do not depend on the model or architecture have emerged in recent years and these attacks could be transferred from one model to another as they are not limited to specific models. These attack types fall under transferability and adaptation of adversarial attacks. Defending against these attacks is still ongoing research as there are no effective defense mechanisms further emphasizing the vulnerability of deep neural networks [4].

2.3 Limitations of Existing Defense Techniques

According to authors Dong et al., [6], Current defense systems require high computational complexity, which presents several challenges in practical applications. Adversarial Training involves multiple iterative generations of adversarial examples during training phases, which require high computational resources. Medical systems need real-time processing and need to be scalable to incorporate larger datasets.

The tradeoff between performance on legitimate and adversarial examples is a common challenge in the medical domain [1]. Models that focus on adversarial robustness can sometimes compromise performance on clean images, this tradeoff is a concerning factor in the medical world as maintaining performance on real patient data is highly crucial.

The generalizability of adversarial defense is another concerning factor, as there are lack of well developed global defense techniques that could mitigate all the adversarial attacks [4]. Defense techniques are usually developed for specific attack types limiting their effectiveness against a broader range of adversarial threats.

2.4 Existing Defense Solutions

Adversarial training has been the most effective defense technique for all general adversarial attacks [7]. Adversarial training involves adding adversarial examples together with clean samples of data to increase the robustness of the model while it is training. Adversarial training also reduces the model overfitting issues that occur in traditional machine learning, but this training has a limitation as it requires a large dataset, and it takes time to train the model to make it robust [1].

According to authors Li, Pan and Zhu, [8], Semi-Supervised Adversarial Training (SSAT) improves the augmentation of training data set further by utilizing pseudo-labels , as there is always a limitation of less labelled data in the world of medical domain. SSAT significantly outperforms other traditional training methods such as adversarial training.

Autoencoders (AE) are neural networks that follow unsupervised learning and are commonly used in computer-aided diagnosis to denoise at the feature level. Encoders map the input into lower dimensional latent space, and the decoder uses the compressed latent representation to reconstruct the input. Here, random noises and irrelevant components are removed, maintaining the important features [2].

Frequency-Based Refinement is a preprocessing-level technique that removes adversarial noise before data is fed into the machine learning model. This technique is conceptually related to JPEG compression, as they both work in the frequency domain, which is a lossy type of compression. However, frequency-based refinement aims to remove the perturbation without affecting clean samples [6]. The downside to the use of lossy compression is that such compression may downplay small diagnostic features in medical images, which ultimately can harm the model performance on clean data.

Unsupervised Adversarial Detection tries to detect and exclude adversarial perturbation before they reach classification stage. UAD works by estimating a probability density for clean images and reject any images that deviate from the density [8]. This also makes UAD robust to unknown attacks. Nonetheless, its efficacy relies on reliable density approximation, which is computation intensive in for medical data with high dimensionality, and it can misclassify borderline clean samples as adversarial

Sparse representation (SR) is for feature representation learning. In this technique, only the essential details are retained using as few non-zero components as possible [9]. Neurons can be activated, when necessary, therefore an opportunity for adversarial perturbation is very low. An inherent boundary of Spatial Resolution is that it is made to induce sparsity, which can limit the expressive power of a model, potentially decreasing classification accuracy for complex medical images, and it accounts for an additional optimization need which can slow down real-time use of the model.

The authors Yang, Shih and Roshan [10], suggested sign activation networks with stochastic coordinate descent training as a gradient-free defense against adversarial attacks in medical imaging. The sign activation models and SCD-CEBNN in particular, were more robust, required more distortion to fool, and achieved more accuracy than ResNet18, LeNet, and MLP, although the training was limited to very few datasets, mainly black-box attacks, and were computationally expensive because of multiple runs, thus indicating scalability and generalized challenges.

The authors, Zahoor and Ghani [11], developed a strong deep learning framework for medical image diagnosis combined with adversarial training and feature denoising using Brain MRI and Chest X-ray datasets. Their defense system was tested against FGSM, PGD, and DeepFool attacks using a pre-trained CheXNet model for fine-grained testing on the FGSM and PGD attacks and statistical testing on the DeepFool attacks to evaluate effectiveness against adversarial scenarios. The results indicated that the proposed approach improved robustness against the attacks while providing good diagnosis accuracy. This framework predominantly depends on adversarial training and JPEG-based preprocessing, and limited work on black-box scenarios and scalability, questions the framework ability to be generalized in various and differing medical imaging scenarios.

The authors Gopalakrishnan, Joseph and Srikanth [12], proposed a Deep Residual Shrinkage Network with Total Variation Loss (DRSN-TVL) that combines CLAHE preprocessing, WGAN-based adversarial image generation, and EfficientNet-B7 feature extraction to reduce redundant noise and detect adversarial perturbations in medical images, which outperformed CNNs, DNNs, Transformers, and ResNet architectures, achieving 98.73% accuracy on Fundoscopy and 98.45% accuracy on Chest X-ray datasets, while demonstrating resilience against adversarial attacks including PGD, CW, and AutoAttack even under stronger perturbation levels, though their approach was only demonstrated on limited datasets and they included additional preprocessing and GAN-based training which may limit portability of the method.

3 Methodology

The proposed solution provides a generalized solution to mitigate adversarial attacks. The author implemented a novel solution in the classifier architecture system which involves a hybrid ViT-CNN-SNN fused on attention-based feature fusion and the purifier model consists of 2 phases where phase 1 uses a U-Net-style generator embedded with dual attention mechanism (Channel + Spatial) and self- attention at the bottleneck. This reconstructs the image from an adversarial perturbed one, meanwhile, phase 2 finetunes and challenges the generator to produce better images. An overview of the proposed system architecture is illustrated below.

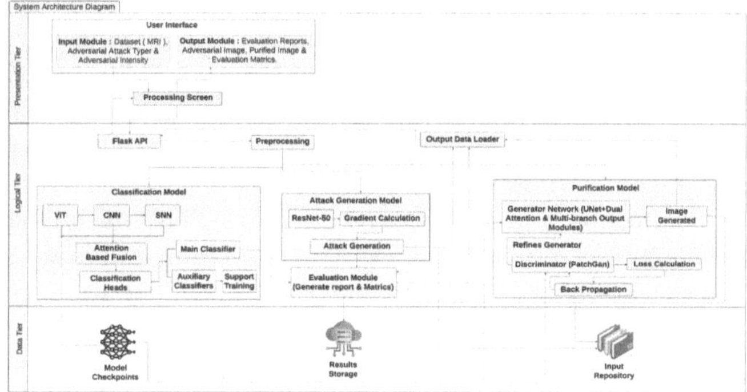

Fig. 1. Overall system architecture of the proposed adversarial defense framework.

Users could operate the system under 3 main stages. For Simulating an adversarial attack scenario a pre-trained ResNet-50 was utilized where users can upload MRI images and simulate adversarial attacks on them and download them if necessary. Users could test if an adversarial perturbation is present in an MRI image by running the hybrid classification model and users can also purify any adversarial MRI images removing perturbation where the generator would reconstruct an adversarial-free image matching its original structure. Users can download generated reports with evaluation provided for the classification and purification results.

3.1 Hybrid ViT-CNN-SNN Classifier

MRI samples are transformed into 224 * 224 resolution with 3 channels using bicubic interpolation. During the training data augmentation such as horizontal/vertical flips and jittering are performed to improve generalization. Dataset class logic is implemented so that image names, labels, attack type and epsilon values are loaded. Initially clean and adversarial images were fed to train the classifier. The overall architecture is shown in Fig. 1.

The vision transformer models global spatial relationships by dividing the input image into non-over-lapping patches of 16 * 16 using a two-dimensional convolutional layer (Conv2d) with kernel and stride of 16 and this transforms the image into patch embeddings and is projected into a high dimensional space (HiddenDim:256). CLS token is appended to this sequence for classification this represents the entire image and later will be used for classification. Learnable positional embeddings are added to each token to retain information about patches as transformers as loose spatial order. This sequence of embeddings is put through a stack of transformer blocks with 6 transformer encoder blocks. Each block contains a layer normalization followed by a multi-head self-attention mechanism with 8 attention heads. MHSA allows the model to learn inter-patch relationships and it is passed to the feed-forward neural network (FFN) which further refines each patch representation through 2 linear layers separated by a GELO activation and dropout. Residual connections are included to stabilize training. Finally, class token is extracted and normalized using Layer Norm and passed through linear projection to transform it into a 768-dimentional feature vector. This vector is fused with CNN and SNN branches for classification.

CNN was inspired by ResNet, the Squeeze and Excitation (SE) blocks were used for channel recalibration. This network extracts local features using a deep hierarchy of convolutions and residual connections. The initial block contains Conv2d (3, 64, 7 * 7) + BatchNorm + ReLU + MaxPool and layer 1 consist of 2 * [Conv2d (inputs 64 outputs 64 dimensions), SE], stride 2 and layer 2 have the same parameters but inputs 64 and outputs 128 dimensions. Layer 3 following the same parameter has input 128 and out 256 dimensions and layer 4 has 256 input dimensions and 512 output dimensions followed by global average pooling and linear projection to feature dimension 768.

SNN is implemented using the CNN layer to mimic the spiking behaviour. Convolutional layer 1 is defined as Convd2d (3,32) - Batch Norm - ReLU - MaxPool and convolutional layers 2 and 3 follow the same parameters but conv2 has input dimension 32 and output as 64 meanwhile the conv3 has 64 and 128 respectively. Finally, global pooling AdaptiveAvgPool is added and then passed to fully connected layers (128 layers - 256 layers - 768 layers).

Now the outputs from three different networks are taken and these are fused using attention-based approach to identify the importance of each branch for the predicting input image. In this attention-based fusion the feature vectors are concatenated and softmax function is applied to identify the importance.

Rather than using fixed weights this helps the model to emphasize different architectural components depending on adversarial patterns.

Each network has its own auxiliary classifier, this enables the model to learn discriminative features at each branch independently while contributing to the final prediction. The complete classifier architecture is shown in Fig. 2.

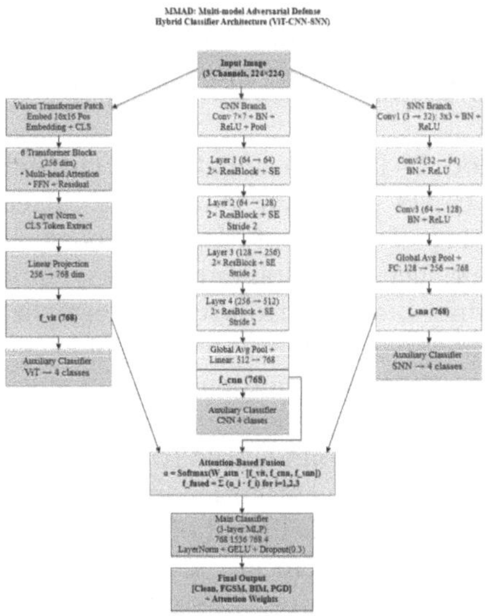

Fig. 2. Hybrid Classifier Architecture Diagram.

$$\alpha = \text{Softmax}(W_{attn} \cdot [f_{vit}, f_{cnn}, f_{snn}]) \tag{4}$$

A new method to compute attention weights is developed in equation (4) that uses the softmax function to quantify the relevance of each architecture component (ViT, CNN, SNN) that utilizes concatenated feature representations. The proposed adaptive methodology allows the hybrid classifier to automatically scale the contribution of each branch according to the input characteristics and adversarial patterns in medical images.

$$f_{fused} = \sum_{i=1}^{3} \alpha_i \cdot f_i \tag{5}$$

The multi-model fusion algorithm described in Eq. (6) merges the weighted contributions from the three network components using the attention weights from above. This methodology represents the first contribution of learnable multi-modal fusion in medical adversarial defense, where the purpose is to enable specialized responses where the ViT specializes in global patterns, the CNN manages local perturbations, and then the SNN is aimed at providing temporal robustness against iterative attacks.

3.2 The Two Phase Purifier

The proposed two phase purifier methodology responds to the challenge of removing adversarial perturbation in medical images as a sequential process utilizing a U-Net based reconstruction and adversarial perturbation refinement. This model maintains important diagnostic information while successfully removing the malicious noise patterns associated with adversarial attacks.

Phase One Enhanced U-Net Generator Architecture. In phase one, a custom variant of the U-Net generator is used with attention mechanisms that support effective learning of representations as shown in Fig. 3. The encoded pathway consists of four successive stages of downsampling. Within each of the stages, connected residual blocks with instance normalization and LeakyReLU activations. Each of the four layers essentially double the dimension of the features from 64 dimensions to 1024 dimensions while simultaneously applying 2×2 max pooling to reduce all passed queries through the encoder. The residual blocks also apply dimensionality reduction and the two attention implementations consist of channel attention and spatial attention that support increasing the channel in those features and decreasing likelihood of adversarial noise representation.

In the network bottleneck, there are several self-attention mechanisms to model long range spatial relationships. These are significant in terms of anatomical integrity when brain MRI are being reconstructed in the process. While the attention networks compute weights on all the values and dimensions of the feature map from the query, key and value representations, this process allows the network to focus on important regions that are relevant diagnostically during a reconstruction. The upsampling pathway applies bilinear upsampling and then reconciles that with the downstream encoder layers using skip upsampling, which is supports reconstruction of finer details than a simple bilinear interpolation would return. In each upsampling block, the upsampled feature representations from the previous layer are concatenated with the corresponding skip connections, and then the upsampled representation is refined again with dual attention mechanisms applied to it.

This architecture differs from standard architectural pathways as it incorporates a multi-branch output scheme. The multi-branch output scheme has three specialized branches that focus on three different aspects of image content reconstruction. The main branch is comprised of 7×7 convolutions with tanh activation to support the structure of the overall image content. The detail

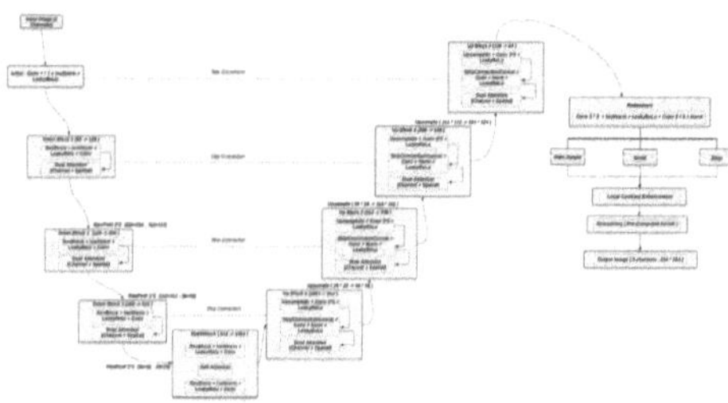

Fig. 3. Novel U-Net Architecture Design.

branch is comprised of 3×3 convolutions to preserve detailed texture content, while the edge branch is composed of 1×1 convolutions to support sharp boundaries. The outputs of these branches are reconstructed according to the equation in (6).

$$PurifiedImage = Main + 0.3 * Detail + 0.15 * Edge \tag{6}$$

In addition to this general reconstruction, there are additional post-processing functions added to help enhance local contrast via unsharp masking, and edge sharpening via the Laplacian.

Phase Two Adversarial Refinement with PatchGAN Discriminator. The second phase of the architecture introduces a PatchGAN discriminator that is spectrally normalized with the purpose of refining the output. Spectral normalization confines the Lipschitz constant to all convolutional layers and thus, it was critical in helping ensure the stability required for medical image training. The discriminator operates by using overlapping image patches as opposed to the global representation of the image patches, thereby improving the local texture nature and anatomical truth of the overall image content quality.

The discriminator consisted of an initial 4×4 convolutional layer using stride-2 downsampling with subsequent four progressively deeper block layers with differing feature dimension values from 64, 128, 256, and 512 feature channels respectively. Each block consisted of residual connections and channel wise averaging downsampling via average pooling. Self-attention was placed within the mid-layers of the discriminator architecture to improve processing relation between long, over-lapping, spatialization patches. Lastly, a 3×3 convolution predicted the authenticity of the patches.

In the sequential training strategy, the generator was first trained using l1 perceptual and structural similarity losses and this was completed without adversarial training pressure. Training the generator to completion ensures that anatomical structures are accurately represented at full-resolution and are preserved appropriately. Then the completed generator builds upon the pre-training process utilizing adversarial training in conjunction with the discriminator on a per patch basis, finalizing texture information, removing artifacts from the reconstruction, and ensuring diagnostic fidelity are not compromised.

Training used Adam with a learning rate of 2×10^{-4} for both networks, momentum parameters of $\beta_1 = 0.5$ and $\beta_2 = 0.999$, and gradient clipping was applied to each network for additional stability. Learning was conducted through a multi-objective loss function balancing adversarial competition with perceptual quality metrics to allow for realistic texture generation and anatomical accuracy preservation.

Significant contributions of the work include: dual attention embedded into residual blocks to allow for noise selective processing, multi-branch outputs specializing in reconstructions quality measures, medical-specific output post-processing approach tailored for diagnostic medical imaging, and stable adversarial training with spectral normalization and progressive optimization.

4 Experimental Results

4.1 Dataset

This study utilized the Brain tumor Multimodal Image Dataset(alikhanov) [13], This dataset is a collection of paired CT and MRI scans for brain tumor analysis, Multi modal approaches are reserved for future work and currently 1456 base MRI images were used and preprocessed to 224 * 224 pixels with 3 channel representation to ensure dimensional consistency across all samples. Each base image was augmented using three established attack methods: FGSM, BIM and PGD, applied at epsilon values of 0.01, 0.03 and 0.05, resulting in a total data set count of 14 560 images (1456 clean + 13 104 adversarial variants) The experimental employed stratified 5 fold cross-validation with data partitioned intro training(70%), validation(15%) and testing (15%) subsets per fold to ensure reliable performance estimation. The balance of the class between each epsilon was maintained consistent to prevent class imbalance. Where each sub-epsilon classes (0.01,0.03,0.05) of all 3 adversarial attacks hold 4368 images respectively. The MNIST handwritten digit dataset was also used for benchmarking comparisons to adversarial defense methods because there are few adversarial medical datasets available in the literature, and MNIST is a standard dataset that is commonly used for adversarial robustness in different domains.

This dataset is licensed under a Creative Commons Attribution-NonCommercial-ShareAlike 4.0 (CC BY-NC-SA 4.0) open license, which encourages use in research and academic collaboration. Each medical image in the dataset has been completely anonymized, with the removal of any patient identifiers, personal information, or metadata that may risk linking back to a specific person. The complete anonymization not only complies with general legal data protection requirements, but it also alleviates any ethical issues regarding patient confidentiality.

4.2 Implementation

Training was conducted on Google Colab Pro + using NVIDIA A100 GPU, later optimized for L4 24GB GPU. PyTorch framework was employed with Adam optimizer (learning rate 2×10^{-4}, $\beta_1 = 0.5$, $\beta_2 = 0.999$). Adversarial attacks used parameters: $\epsilon \in \{0.01, 0.03, 0.05\}$, step size $\alpha = 0.01$, with 20 iterations for PGD and 10 for BIM. Gradient clipping and exponential moving average (EMA) were applied for training stability.

5 Results and Discussion

5.1 Hybrid Classifier Performance

The hybrid ViT-CNN-SNN classifier yielded a mean cross-validation accuracy across all five folds of 71.71%. The best performance (Fold 4) showed a 97.89% detection rate for FGSM, 92.47% detection for clean instances, 86.93% detection rate for BIM, and 41.78% detection for PGD attacks. The confusion between BIM and PGD attacks was expected and could be attributed to the similar iterative pattern of both attacks, but PGD is more complex due to random initialisation causing difficulties in detection.

5.2 Two-Phase Purification Results

The Phase 1 U-Net generator achieved the highest PSNR reading at 34.61 dB and the highest SSIM value at 0.9551. Phase 2 U-Net refined by discriminator on the other hand achieved a moderate increase in quality of clean image with a PSNR of 37.74 dB and SSIM of 0.9773. In addition, the PSNR and SSIM values show improvement in the range of 2.2–3.1 dB and 0.02–0.03 for SSIM respectively for all attack types as shown in Table 1. The Phase two U-Net generator compared to the Phase one generator, shows improved performance, successfully removing the adversarial noise introduction while preserving anatomical structure of outputs.

Table 1. Performance evaluation of the two-phase purifier on brain tumor MRI dataset

Attack Type	$\epsilon = 0.01$	$\epsilon = 0.03$	$\epsilon = 0.05$
Clean	37.54/0.9765	–	–
FGSM	35.46/0.9642	33.39/0.9470	32.03/0.9284
BIM	35.58/0.9662	34.19/0.9552	33.49/0.9467
PGD	35.58/0.9663	34.38/0.9559	33.41/0.9478

5.3 Multi-surrogate Model Performance Evaluation

To investigate the cross-architecture transferability of the proposed multi-surrogate defense, Author thoroughly verified three CNN models that differed architecturally, DenseNet121, ResNet50, and VGG16. Author assessed all three architectures on 150 balanced samples that included clean images along with adversarial examples for the various attack types and perturbations strengths. The method always retained PSNR values greater than 30 dB (the benchmark for good reconstruction quality), while also maintaining a SSIM score greater than or equal to 0.90 for each architecture. These performance measures demonstrated that the images maintained their quality while adversarial perturbation was removed. Results are shown in Table 2.

Table 2. Performance by Surrogate Model

Surrogate Model	PSNR (dB)	SSIM	Sample Size
DenseNet121	32.69 ± 3.57	0.9098 ± 0.0564	150
ResNet50	32.69 ± 3.48	0.9065 ± 0.0575	150
VGG16	33.50 ± 3.20	0.9128 ± 0.0517	150
Overall	**33.12 ± 3.42**	**0.910 ± 0.055**	**450**

5.4 Benchmarking

In terms of achievement, on the MNIST dataset at epsilon = 0.05, MMAD exhibited 98% accuracy for FGSM, 96% for BIM and 90.4% for PGD, as illustrated in Table 3, surpassing HAT Classifiers and Defensive Bit Planes, as shown in Table 4.

In a two-phase purifier, MMAD obtained a peak PSNR of 37.74 dB and a peak SSIM of 0.9773. Consistently improved PSNR by 2.2–3.1 dB over the single-phase. Even in the case of a strong attack from PGD, the purifier maintained PSNR at over 33 dB, retaining meaningful anatomical structures useful for making medical diagnoses.

Benchmarking comprehensively is an ongoing challenge, given the lack of standardized medical adversarial datasets, limited domain-specific baselines, and, in some cases, privacy constraints in medical imaging. Nevertheless, as shown by the purification results in this paper, the PSNR/SSIM values are still competitive when compared to the recently quantified methods of medical reconstruction with the limited benchmarking possibilities.

6 Conclusion

The paper proposed three main innovations of medical adversarial defense: a tri-architecture fusion detection system, a dual-attention U-Net purification model, and a two-phase progressive training method. The proposed method obtained stable reconstruction quality (PSNR ¿ 30 dB, SSIM ¿ 0.90) across multiple CNN architectures, and was shown to be transferable to medical imaging.

The presented system shows sufficient computational efficiency for clinical use, since it operates effectively with low-end computer specifications. Author

Table 3. Hybrid ViT-CNN-SNN classifier accuracy on MNIST dataset

Attack Type	$\epsilon = 0.01$	$\epsilon = 0.03$	$\epsilon = 0.05$	Average
Clean	100%	100%	100%	100%
FGSM	79.40%	97.20%	98%	91.53%
BIM	34.60%	74.80%	96%	68.47%
PGD	70.60%	66.40%	90.40%	75.80%
Average	**71.15%**	**84.60%**	**96.10%**	**83.95%**

Table 4. Benchmarking comparison with state-of-the-art adversarial defense methods on MNIST dataset ($\epsilon = 0.05$)

Attack Type	HAT Classifier	Defensive Bit Planes	Defense-GAN	Chen ResNet50	MMAD
FGSM	81.2%	99.23%	96.24%	95.07%	**98%**
BIM	–	99.26%	96.53%	96.66%	**96%**
PGD	67.4%	99.07%	96.18%	98.13%	90.4%
Clean	99.6%	99.13%	99.13%	98.99%	**100%**

conducted testing on a consumer laptop (Intel i5, 8GB RAM) through CPU-only resources and it exhibited responsive software performance without computational bottlenecks. This efficiency overcomes the significant determinants of a medical institution's ability to access even the most basic computational resources, improving the usability of the provided adversarial defense framework into traditional clinical workstations.

This study had limitations. The framework does not include built-in explainability tools like Grad-CAM, which restricts both interpretability and clinical trust. It has not been tested/validated in a real clinical setting, which also limits its immediate applicability. Due to the lack of standardized medical adversarial data set, benchmarking was done with standard benchmarking MINIST data set. Further comparative evaluation was limited due to the lack of source code and attack parameters from existing methods. Moreover, hardware limitations prevented evaluating larger datasets and other intensive attacks, which may affect robust evaluations.

Future work scope will encapsulate black-box and other complex white box adversarial attacks to provide a more generalized defense. Adding built-in explainability tools and exploring clinical adaptability will enhance real-world deployment.

Disclosure of Interests. The authors have no competing interests to declare that are relevant to the content of this article.

References

1. Hu, J., et al.: A multimodal adversarial database: towards a comprehensive assessment of adversarial attacks and defenses on medical images. In: 2023 IEEE 10th International Conference on Data Science and Advanced Analytics (DSAA), pp. 1–10 (2023)
2. Surekha, M., Sagar, A.K., Khemchandani, V.: Adversarial attack and defense mechanisms in medical imaging: a comprehensive review. In: 2024 IEEE International Conference on Computing, Power and Communication Technologies (IC2PCT), pp. 1657–1661 (2024)
3. Chowdhury, S.S., Mejbaul Islam, K., Noor, R.: Anomaly detection in unsupervised surveillance setting using ensemble of multimodal data with adversarial defense. In: 2020 19th IEEE International Conference on Machine Learning and Applications (ICMLA), pp. 191–194 (2020)
4. Muoka, G.W., et al.: A comprehensive review and analysis of deep learning-based medical image adversarial attack and defense. Mathematics **11**(20), 4272 (2023)
5. Liu, G., Khalil, I., Khreishah, A.: GanDef: a GAN based adversarial training defense for neural network classifier. arXiv preprint arXiv:1903.02585 (2019)
6. Dong, J., et al.: Adversarial attack and defense for medical image analysis: methods and applications. arXiv preprint arXiv:2303.14133 (2023)
7. Thota, P., et al.: Demonstration of an adversarial attack against a multimodal vision language model for pathology imaging. arXiv preprint arXiv:2401.02565 (2024)
8. Li, X., Pan, D., Zhu, D.: Defending against adversarial attacks on medical imaging AI system, classification or detection? In: 2021 IEEE 18th International Symposium on Biomedical Imaging (ISBI), pp. 1677–1681 (2021)
9. Li, Y., et al.: Transformer based defense GAN against palm-vein adversarial attacks. IEEE Trans. Inf. Forensics Secur. **18**, 1509–1523 (2023)
10. Yang, Y., Shih, F.Y., Roshan, U.: Defense against adversarial attacks based on stochastic descent sign activation networks on medical images. Int. J. Pattern Recognit Artif Intell. **36**(03), 2254005 (2022)
11. Zahoor, K., Ghani, U.: Robust deep learning model for adversarial defense in medical image diagnosis. In: 2025 International Conference on Emerging Technologies in Electronics, Computing, and Communication (ICETECC), pp. 1–6 (2025)
12. Gopalakrishnan, A., Joseph, N., Srikanth, U.: Identify vulnerability of adversarial attack on medical images using deep residual shrinkage network with total variation loss function. Int. J. Intell. Eng. Syst. **18**(6), 491–502 (2025)
13. Alikhanov, M.: Brain Tumor Multimodal Image Dataset (CT and MRI). Kaggle (2023)

Language, Speech, and Text Processing

Adaptive Fluency and Pronunciation Assessment for Young English Learners in Sri Lanka

Bhagya Dewmini Peramuna(✉), Minidu Visana Tissera, and Manori Prasangika Gamage

Sri Lanka Institute of Information Technology, Malabe, Sri Lanka
bhagyadewmi17@gmail.com, miniduspc@gmail.com, manori.g@sliit.lk

Abstract. English speaking and read-aloud skills are an expertness which should develop from childhood. To achieve this, proper pronunciation of words and fluency should be considered from the early stages of learning. In Sri Lanka, from middle childhood, schools tend to build up students' multilingual abilities by teaching the English language. Even though the schools provide resources for students to learn, the individual attention received by each student may vary during the classroom session. Some students may pick up the correct speaking skills, while some struggle. This research paper proposes a comprehensive assistant tool for English pronunciation and fluency monitoring, targeting students under twelve years. This proposed solution will facilitate teachers monitoring each student's performance with a click. The solution fills the gap in tracking student's English read-aloud and speaking progress. Moreover, students will have an interactive web application interface to speak out the text provided based on their grade and tailored difficulty level. The fluency and pronunciation scoring system uses models and libraries, such as Whisper, Gentle, CatBoost regression model, Librosa, difflib, and a custom prosody-aware model. The models are tuned with voice datasets of native and non-native students under age twelve for better accuracy. Model training is done using open-source datasets available in Kaggle and Zendoo by fine tuning, the CatBoost model achieved approximately 5.8% improvement and triplet classification accuracy 1.15% improvement. The adaptive sentence difficulty and targeted training used in these results enable the results to be effective for automated fluency and pronunciation assessment.

Keywords: English fluency assessment · English pronunciation evaluation · Adaptive text difficulty · English speech recognition for children

1 Introduction

Assessing the student's spoken language performance is an essential component in language learning. Especially for young learners discovering a second language. English is one of the languages that is used by most people around the world. Therefore, learning English is important as it has become a universal communication language. This teaching should start at a young age as language acquisition is simpler and occurs more quickly during this time [1]. To address this, the Sri Lankan government has included English

R. N. Rajapakse et al. (Eds.): ICTer 2025, CCIS 2844, pp. 139–154, 2026.
https://doi.org/10.1007/978-981-92-0137-2_10

as a school subject, which includes activities to improve pronunciation and fluency in young learners.

When considering a traditional classroom where there are thirty to forty students, evaluating young learners on their fluency and pronunciation is difficult. Currently, this is done by time-to-time assessments conducted by teachers. These types of evaluations are inconsistent and time-consuming. This cumbersomeness of assessing the fluency and pronunciation of the student makes it even harder to provide targeted feedback [2]. Also, the burden of learning is highly put on the shoulders of students [3]. Grammar correction tools for Sinhala medium primary students have been developed [4], which indicates an interest in the development of language learning tools applicable to a Sri Lankan context. Nevertheless, spoken English assessment tools for the same age groups have been relatively underexplored. Recognizing these challenges and limitations, this study proposes a comprehensive web-based application, which automates the work. This automation will help the teachers to give enough individual attention to the students' fluency and pronunciation scores. Also, the system provides the students with tailored sentences according to their scoring level, which will be helpful in enhancing the learning experience.

The study mainly addresses the development of a system that can objectively evaluate an under twelve-year-old student's English language fluency and pronunciation in real time. Even though there are some websites that evaluate both pronunciation and fluency in real time, the availability of such tools targeting young learners is low. The system consists of several key components to achieve the goal of assessing fluency and pronunciation in real time in a tailored approach. The system uses a Whisper model for audio processing and transcription. This model generates both predicted text transcription and extracts deep acoustic embeddings. This dual capacity of Whisper lays a good foundation for both test-based and acoustic analysis of speech. Then, the system uses Librosa, a python library, to extract prosodic features. The average pitch is determined using the YIN algorithm, and the average intensity is measured using Root Mean Square (RMS) energy. With these, the system uses Gentle, a forced alignment tool, to align audio with text. Moreover, the system provides a text sentence to the child based on the scores obtained. The text sentences are complexified or simplified using Flesch score. With this approach, the system provides tailored attention to individual students. Using these technologies, methods, and approaches, the system addresses the challenges faced by the teachers and the students while teaching and learning a non-native language as young learners.

2 Related Work

The studies conducted on the areas of fluency and pronunciation assessment for young learners of non-native English language have significantly advanced throughout the years. On the other hand, the research done on the topic of adaptive sentence modification using Flesch score is low. With all that information, some of the studies conducted by professionals on the area of fluency and pronunciation assessment, and lexical substitution on passages are discussed here considering the main findings and technologies used.

A study conducted by Jain et al. [5] explores the adaptation of Automatic Speech Recognition (ASR) models for child speech recognition. The study mainly focuses on two models, namely, Whisper and Wave2vec. Using datasets like MyST Corpus, PFSTAR, and CMU Kids, the research compares the performance of the two models. The experiments done include pre-training and fine-tuning to analyze how different data distributions impact ASR performance. The experiments indicated that fine-tuning of the model Wisper on child speech datasets significantly improves its ASR performance with a relative Word Error Rate (WER) improvements ranging from 29% to 89% even finetuning with only a 10% sample of unseen non-native datasets. However, fine-tuning the Wav2vec model with similar datasets showed accuracy of, 7.42% WER on MyST, 2.99% on PFSTAR, and 12.47% on CMU_KIDS these benchmarks rely on relatively clean and controlled datasets. Unique factors on both models were discovered during the study. Whisper was performing well in zero-shot scenarios, which strongly recognized speech from unseen datasets. Meanwhile, Wave2vec required less training data compared to Whisper. The study used various algorithms and technologies, including transformer-based architecture for both models. The model training experiments were conducted on high-performance Graphics Processing Units (GPUs). The study emphasizes that fine-tuning the Whisper model enhances its ability to recognize child speech; wav2vec2 remains a more effective choice for task-specific applications because of its efficiency and lower computational requirements. Moreover, the study states that Whisper proves to be more adaptable across diverse datasets but demands more training data. The study proves that there are both pros and cons in Whisper and Wave2vec models, and it tells the readers to choose the models accordingly.

In his research [6], Stefan O'Grady sought to define a complex scoring model for the evaluation of second language speakers' fluency with special emphasis on the determinate relationships between complexity and fluency scores. The aim is to examine the halo effect as found in some speaking tests. It examines whether raters' ascriptions of fluency are affected by other variables such as lexical complexity or accuracy of speech. The study interprets rater scores through a many-facet RASCH measurement (MFRM) system. This is to ascertain whether the smoothness of speech divided by the fluency ratings could be defined because of changes in the language and time frameworks. The study observes that fluency is achieved through overestimation of many factors like phonologic complexity, rate of speech, and duration of voices expressed. This concludes that fluency is not individually based on temporal speech features. This study found that while some raters were displaying the halo effect, the overall group level analysis found no evidence of systematic bias. At the experimental level of individual rater level, ten raters showed difficulty in distinguishing fluency from accuracy and complexity, showcasing halo effects in some cases. Conducted multiple regression analyses indicated that a total of six linguistic variables accounted for 54% of the variance in fluency assessment scores. This proved the multi-dimensionality of fluency assessment. The study spotlights the importance of the Complexity, Accuracy, and Fluency (CAF) framework in the development of fluency rating scales. The research provides insights about how fluency is assessed in second language speaking tasks by analyzing measures such as breakdowns, repairs, and complexity.

Cockeril et al. [7] studied the impact of a reading intervention program implemented in English elementary schools during the Covid-19 pandemic. The program is planned to improve reading fluency and comprehension among readers aged seven to nine who struggled in reading. This research conducted a randomized controlled trial (RCT) including 186 children across twelve schools. Over a twelve-week period, trained staff provided targeted fluency and comprehension instruction in small groups. The study did find that the Fluency into Comprehension (FliC) intervention program had a positive impact on students' reading skills. The intervention was effective in improving reading fluency and comprehension, especially at the sentence level. The researchers found that students who received targeted fluency instruction demonstrated better sentence-level comprehension, reinforcing the interdependence between fluency and reading understanding. This study pinpoints the fact that targeted learning is very important in developing fluency and comprehension among young learners.

A study by Korzekwa et al. [8] focuses on the automation of pronunciation error detection of non-native English speakers. The study introduces innovative speech generation techniques to enhance accuracy in pronunciation and lexical stress errors. A novel speech-to-speech (S2S) method is proposed by the study, which significantly improves pronunciation error detection in the area under the curve (AUC). This outperforms state-of-the-art models. The error identification in the study is done by incorporating phenome to phenome (P2P), text to speech (T2S), and S2S methods. The study has used synthetic speech generation which enhances the model's accuracy by 11.5% in AUC. The results derived from the study indicate that S2S based synthetic speech generation offers a new paradigm for detecting errors in pronunciation with high accuracy. This states that non-native speech evaluation improves with the involvement of synthetic speech-based learning in advancing automated pronunciation assessment technologies.

A study conducted by Wang Jing addressing the problem of weak oral proficiency of the students in China [9], explores the uses of speech recognition technology for English language oral pronunciation correction. This aims to enhance learners' pronunciation using speech synthesis and recognition. Tailored training and targeted corrections are provided by the research system, which evaluates pronunciation accuracy. By utilizing speech recognition algorithms, the system converts oral recordings into text, which allows for a detailed analysis of pronunciation errors and personalized feedback. This system could provide real time feedback on pronunciation errors, which helps the learners to practice and refine their speech interactively. The hidden Markov model (HMM) is used to ensure high accuracy and efficiency in speech recognition, which performs well in both recognition and correctness. The results show that the system effectively enhances English learning by integrating speech recognition and synthesis technologies.

Overall, the reviewed literature shows that people have made considerable progress in assessing fluency and pronunciation among young non-native learners in English, and researchers have tested ASR models such as Whisper and Wav2vec, reading interventions, and automated pronunciation error detection based on synthesizing speech and speech-to-speech. The methods have demonstrated better accuracy, fluency, and comprehension especially when exploiting the fine-tuned models, CAF-based scoring systems, and real-time feedback systems. Nevertheless, there exists a vacuum within adaptive interactive assessment systems that give live feedback on pronunciation and fluency among the young learners. To manage this, the proposed system will be used to analyze the performance of a current user through the Flesch score so that sentence complexity can dynamically be changed by giving personalized feedback on the same and highlighting words that are mispronounced where specific attention can be given.

3 Methodology

The methodology for the proposed system is discussed in this section. It consists of ASR, prosody extraction, forced alignment, contrastive learning, gradient boosting regression, and adaptive sentence modification. These features together add value to the research component, providing novel features. Figure 1 displays a high-level architectural diagram of the components and models used in the research system.

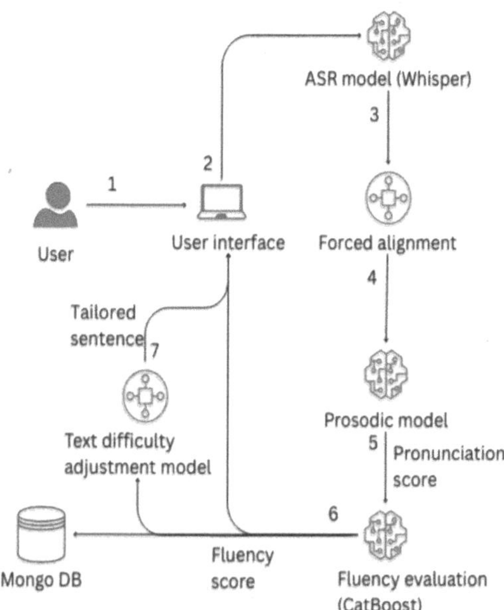

Fig. 1. High level system diagram

The procedure starts with the user on the user interface whereby the user is given a sentence to read. The audio stream is analyzed by the ASR model (Whisper) where it is forced alignment to align the audio stream with the anticipated text. A prosodic model is then used to extract a pronunciation score out of the aligned speech, and a fluency assessment module based on CatBoost computes a fluency score, using aspects of speech rate, and pauses. The fluency score and the pronunciation score are then sent to a text difficulty adjustment model that adjusts further sentences to the capability of the learner. MongoDB is used to store all user data, such as scores and personalized sentences to track progress and personalized learning. This combination system gives real time, personalized feedback to enhance fluency as well as pronunciation.

3.1 Data Preparation and Processing.

The initial stage of this research involves the collection of audio recordings and corresponding text prompts from students under twelve years of age. Since the collection of data from Sri Lankan students was not approved by the schools, a different approach was considered. Compared with adult voice datasets, even though there are fewer child voice datasets [10], a search was made to find a good dataset for child English sentence reading voice data sets. Sri Lankan students are non-native English speakers, so two freely available datasets were used for the research. Dataset named Non-Native Children English Speech (NNCES) Corpus was obtained from Kaggle [11] and the dataset Children speech recording (English, spontaneous speech + pre-defined sentences) was obtained from Zendoo [12]. Together, both datasets consist of more than 5000 voice clips of 61 children under the age of twelve. By combining both datasets, a single dataset was made for research purposes. Most of the voice data consists of non-native speakers, both male and female. This combined dataset was then the combined dataset is split into a training portion of 70%, a validation portion of 20%, and a test portion of 10%.

Each recording is checked for quality; all the voice data is gone through noise cancellation. For computational consistency, files are either padded or truncated to a fixed length (e.g., 3000 frames) when generating the spectrogram input to the ASR model. This normalization process mitigates variability in audio duration and simplifies batch processing during training and inference.

3.2 Speech Recognition and Acoustic Embedding Extraction

The system uses a pre-trained whisper small model, which is fine-tuned from children's voice dataset to make the model specialized in the domain. It is used to generate text transcriptions and deep acoustic embeddings. Being very good at capturing speech representations, Whisper works excellently in low-resource and small-data settings, especially when tuned properly [13].

ASR Transcription. Each audio file in the dataset is converted into a log-mel spectrogram [14], and after that, it is passed through the Whisper encoder-decoder to generate the predicted text. This transcription is later compared with the reference text to compute the word error rate (WER) and character error rate (CER) [15].

Acoustic Embeddings. In parallel with ASR transcription, the system extracts encoder output embeddings from the Whisper model. These embeddings retain information about phonetic content, timbre, and other acoustic cues. The initial input for prosody-aware contrastive learning is the fixed size vector produced by averaging over the time dimension. This two-output requirement ensures that both textual and acoustic information undergo more complicated modules for pronunciation and fluency engineering.

3.3 Prosodic Feature Analysis and Forced Alignment

In English spoken language learning, pitch, intensity, and timing are very important. Hence, prosody extraction is a crucial component of the process [16]. In this research, the system uses the Librosa library to achieve this. Using that average pitch, estimated with the YIN algorithm, reflecting fundamental frequency, and average intensity, calculated via root mean square (RMS) energy to represent vocal loudness are computed.

Forced alignment is concomitantly executed using the Gentle toolkit to get timestamps at the word and phoneme levels. This puts the audio in time with the reference text and speaking rate, average pause duration, and abnormal phenomes are derived using it.

This system takes prosody and alignment out of the optional and makes it core to the scoring pipeline. This integrated approach guarantees that changes in pitch, energy, or timing that are rarely taken into consideration in basic ASR pipelines will affect the final fluency assessment. By combining forced alignment with a deep embedding, this approach achieves a finer temporal granularity, which eventually improves the detection process's sensitivity and dependability in identifying tiny articulation issues.

3.4 Prosody-Aware Contrastive Learning

The system further uses a new feature of a contrastive learning model that combines various signals into one embedding. It extracts various fragments of speech made by the child, how the words are pronounced (acoustics), how speech is raising and lowering (prosody, including intonation and stress) and assembles them into one speech profile of 128-dimensional embedding. The methodology follows a triplet loss setup (anchor–positive–negative), which compels similar pronunciations to cluster more closely in embedding space while pushing dissimilar samples apart. In this framework, fusion and contrastive training are done.

- Feature fusion: The system takes greater notice to the significant speech patterns, such as the rise in tone at the end of a question, and it has a system that emphasizes one important signal on the other less important signals.
- Contrastive raining: the model learns to separate fine-grained pronunciation discrepancies by generating positive samples (same audio instance) and negative samples (mismatched audio prosody pairings). An example is, when two recording sounds are like each other the system considers it as a match, whereas when they sound different it considers them separate.

These steps collectively produce a system out of which a prosody-aware embedding emerges that represents the phonetic content and how that content is delivered in terms of stress and intonation.

3.5 Integrated Pronunciation Scoring and Feedback

Following transcription and forced alignment, the algorithm compares the anticipated text to the normalized reference to determine WER and CER. These metrics feed into a combined pronunciation score, as in:

$$\text{Pronunciation score} = \max\left((0, 1 - \text{WER} + \text{CER})/2\right) \tag{1}$$

The basis of this targeted feedback is formed in the same step, a word-level comparison (using Python's difflib) flags mismatches as possible mispronunciation.

3.6 Fluency Regression with CatBoost

For the final fluency score, the system uses a custom CatBoost regression model [17]. Which is trained from a specific custom dataset. The training data for this regressor consists of:

- Pronunciation score: From the WER/CER calculation.
- Fluency metrics: Speaking rate, average pause duration, and abnormal phonemes (derived from forced alignment).
- Prosody-aware embedding: The 128-dimensional vector combining acoustic and prosodic features.

A CatBoost regression model has been chosen due to its robustness and capacity to contain heterogeneous features to determine the final fluency score [18].

Then, each feature is normalized using a Min Max Scaler to ensure a consistent scale [19]. It then iterates, refining its decision trees based on an objective function such as Root Mean Squared Error (RMSE). Two additional innovations enhance reliability; they are:

- Monotonic constraints: The model is constrained so that better pronunciation quality (lower WER) should not lead to a lower fluency score.
- Penalization: If the predicted text and the reference mismatch substantially in word count, the system overrides the fluency score to zero. Similarly, if the pronunciation score is below a certain threshold, the final predicted score is multiplied by that low pronunciation value. This direct penalization ensures that major transcription errors or misalignment led to a more heavily reduced fluency rating.

This system embeds the constraints and penalties into the CatBoost pipeline and enforces sensible scoring rules to keep the constraints and does not prevent the interpretability for teacher and learner when a complete thought or name is cited, such as a title or full quotation.

3.7 Text Passage Difficulty Adjustment

In this system, we dynamically adjust the complexity of text passages according to the user's fluency performance with a rule-based scoring function. Each learner has a personalized learning journey by reading content that changes according to their current ability.

Once the user's final fluency score (ranging from 0 to 1) is computed from pronunciation and prosody analysis, the system calculates a new target Flesch Reading Ease score using the formula.

$$\text{target Flesch} = 100\text{--}\left(\text{fluency score}^{*}\ 50\right) \tag{2}$$

As a result of this approach, scoring less will generate easier passages, and scoring more will create more challenging content. To decide how much weight should be given to the target score, depending on how confident it is in the fluency measurement, a scaling factor is used. The time interval after which the next reading passage is selected depends on the current and target Flesch score around which the weighted blending is done, and the updated score is stored. Using a transparent, rule-based method of difficulty adjustment, the system is sufficient real time adaptable, interpretable, and consistent for such scenarios as language learning where clarity and feedback are a necessity.

3.8 Main Technologies and Libraries Used

It takes advantage of the power of various powerful libraries and technologies for rapidly evaluating speech pronunciation and fluency. The technologies and libraries used in this system are grouped below.

- Hugging Face transformers: For ASR, Transformers library from Hugging Face to use pre-trained models such as Whisper was used [20]. For evaluating pronunciation, embeddings and text of audio recordings generated by Whisper is fine-tuned. Preprocessing and transcribing the audio is done using the Whisper Processor and Whisper for Conditional Generation, respectively.
- Librosa python library: Librosa is a Python package used for audio processing and feature extraction. It is used for extracting features such as pitch (via YIN algorithm) and intensity via Root Mean Square (RMS) energy. These features assist in assessing fluency and rhythm of speech that are important to gauge a nuanced pronunciation evaluation.
- TQDM python library: For progress bars while executing the loops during the training and processing tasks, the system uses TQDM. It is a visual indicator of the progress of the system, which aids us in monitoring the system progress of long-running processes like training models and extracting features.
- Pandas: Data manipulation and analysis are extensively done with the help of pandas. For loading, processing, and storing features and results of training and evaluation, the system uses Pandas Data Frames since the features and results are fed in CSV files. Also, it is used for processing a large set of datasets and handling the alignment results and final predictions.
- NumPy: For numerical computing, e.g., array manipulation, statistical analysis, and so on, NumPy is used. For calculating the meaning, standard deviation, etc. For the normalization of features to z_scores as well as fluency metric computation.
- Scikit-learn: Scikit-learn offers model evaluation and cross-validation as hyperparameter tuning [21]. To perform hyperparameter optimization of the CatBoost regression model, I'm using GridSearchCV and train_test_split to split data to train and test sets. Furthermore, it also standardizes features using MinMaxScaler and assesses model performance through cross-validation using cross_val_score.
- Torch & Torchaudio: The machine learning framework of the system is carried around the backbone of PyTorch, and it provides support for both model training and inference. For audio data, use Torchaudio to load and handle audio files, resample them, and convert them to tensors suitable to deep learning models. For training and inference on large data, PyTorch's GPU acceleration ensures it is very efficient.
- Pronouncing: Words are looked up in the CMU Pronouncing Dictionary through a Python interface called Pronouncing, and phonemes are retrieved using the library. The second application of phonemes ensures that the system can extract phonetic

representation and that phonetic representations are available for comparison with transcribed text for pronunciation scoring.

- Matplotlib: Data visualization using matplotlib is done using predictions of the CatBoost regression model against actual fluency scores and feature importance of the same model. The system provides the capability to visualize the performance of the model and to interpret the role of different speech features in scoring fluency.
- Joblib: Models and scalers are saved and loaded to disk with joblib. It proves that the trained CatBoost model and MinMaxScaler can be serialized and used in future predictions without retraining the models.
- Scipy: The statistical functions include calculating z scores, which use Scipy. It is crucial for speech analysis since it helps the system to find out which phonemes either deviate too much from the norm or are not present at all.
- Gentle forced aligner: Gentle is a forced alignment tool that allows the alignment of spoken audio with its reference text. It gives word and phoneme level alignments, which are necessary to derive fluency metrics such as speaking rate, pause duration, and abnormal phoneme durations.
- Fast application programming interface (API): Fast API is used for building the backend API, enabling fast and asynchronous request handling. It supports the real-time handling of file uploads, passage retrieval, and other system functionalities with high performance.

4 Results

The research done on the topic of fluency and pronunciation assessment with adaptive sentence modification for young learners gives out promising results. Fluency monitoring and pronunciation assessment, together with tailored sentence provision, was integrated with a web application that acts as a user interface. The final research product can address problems faced by educators and students while learning a non-native language. The approach of text complexity modification aligning with individual learning needs has shown positive results during the training of the models. Figures 2 and 3 depict the prosodic model training triplet accuracy over 20 and 25 epochs before and after multiple finetuning rounds respectively.

As observed, the training of the model has improved the final accuracy by 1.1 percentage points (pp) or approximately by 1.15%. The Fig. 4 and 5 depict prosodic model training loss over 20 and 25 epochs before and after training respectively.

The enhanced model demonstrated a training loss decrease of approximately 96.9% over 25 epochs which amounted to marginally better performance compared to its previous loss reduction of 96.7%. The optimized training process presents a steady rate of progress throughout the sessions while getting rid of the previous training round's unpredictable spikes. The improved consistency coupled with better convergence signifies that the updated model is an ideal candidate for trustworthy pronunciation-related evaluations in operational settings.

The proposed system was tested using 10% of the voice data that was collected. Other data was separated for model training and validation. The Whisper ASR model, tailored for children's speech, excelled at transcribing text. Such results confirm the capability of speech recognition within non-native English environments. The forced alignment

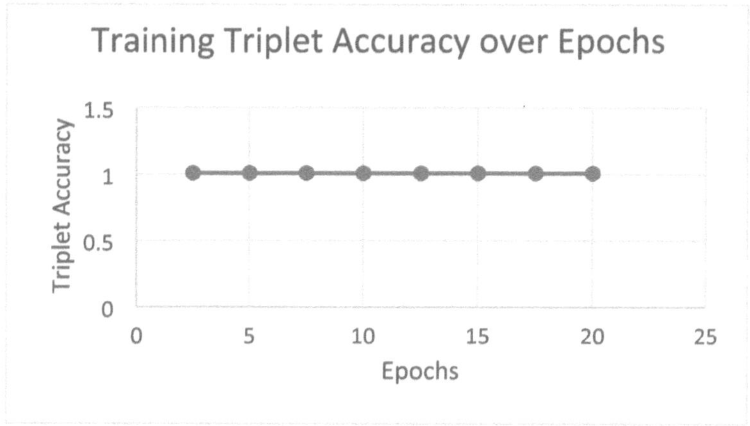

Fig. 2. Prosodic model training triplet accuracy over 20 epochs before training.

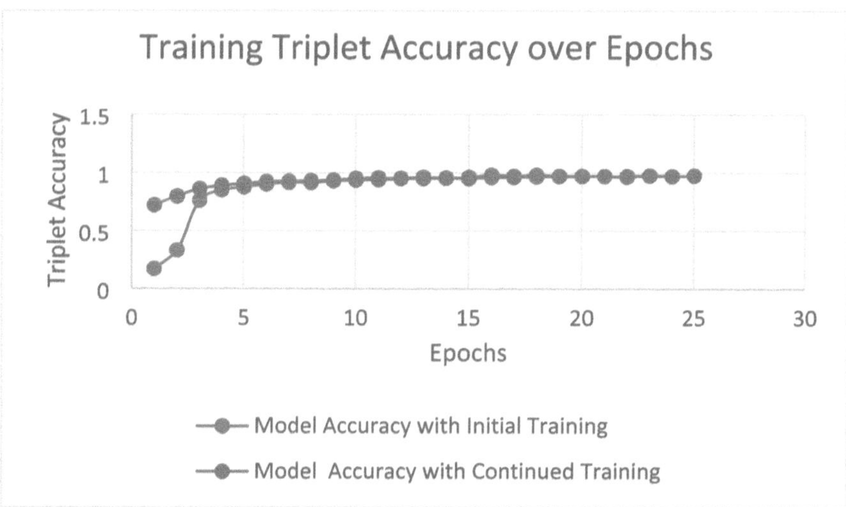

Fig. 3. Prosodic model training triplet accuracy over 25 epochs after training

module efficiently aligns spoken audio with reference text for accurate measurement of speaking rate, pause duration, and phoneme abnormalities. High fluency score learners tend to display prosodic consistency, such as evenly varied pitch and controlled intensity, which affirms the value of prosody-aware scoring.

Also, the Catboost regression model trained to assess pronunciation and fluency metrics showed results that go hand in hand with an improvement. The Catboost model's predictive fit improved by approximately 57.94% after fine-tuning. The model improvement percentage is calculated as:

$$\text{Improvement } \% = ((R^2_{after} - R^2_{before}) / R^2_{before})*100 \quad (3)$$

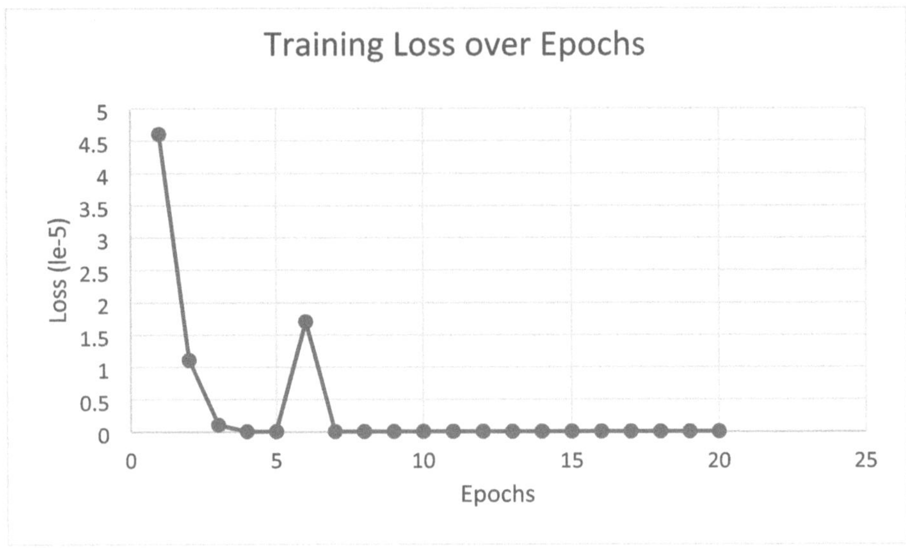

Fig. 4. Prosodic model training loss over 20 epochs before fine tuning.

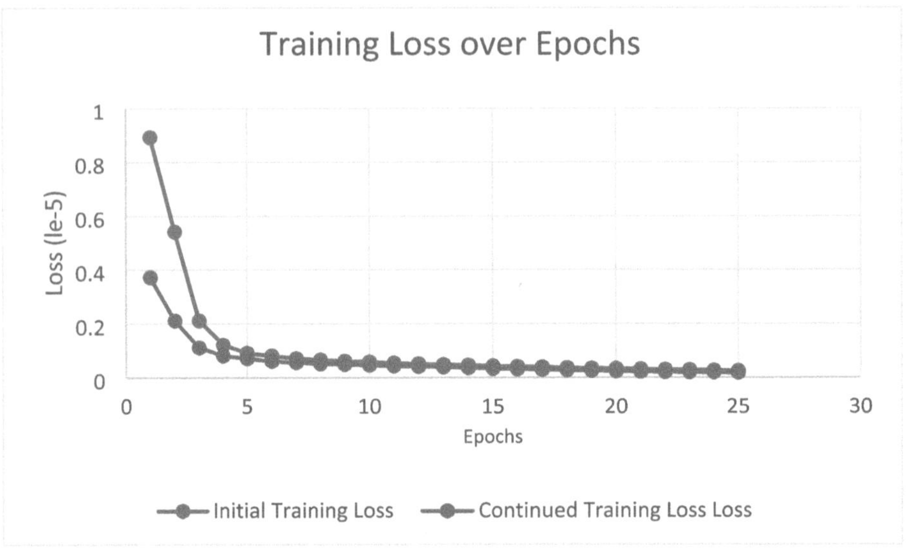

Fig. 5. Prosodic model training loss over 25 epochs after fine tuning.

The graphs with initial training and after training look alike as the data points vary with small amounts, the original R2 was very small 0.0185, even a small absolute increase to 0.0291 becomes a large relative increase. Figure 6 displays the generated graph.

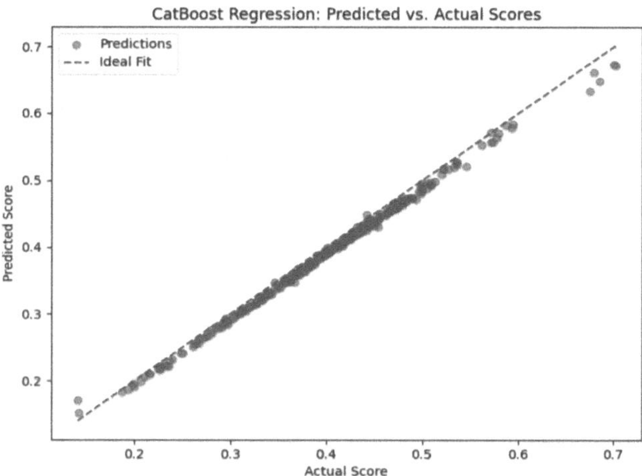

Fig. 6. CatBoost model predicted score vs. actual score matplotlib generated graph

These methodologies, technologies, and approaches used in the research projects help to fill the gaps in traditional learning methods, helping both educators and students to teach and to improve in a more tailored way.

With all these model outputs, the web application provides a user-friendly output which is child friendly as shown in Fig. 7.

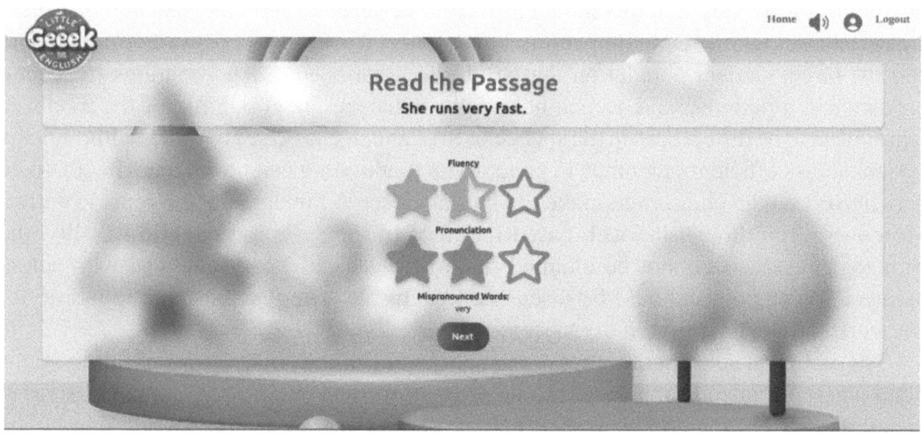

Fig. 7. Web application interface for child friendly score output.

The user interface is in a way that gives the children real time and intuitive feedback regarding their reading performance. The rating system is based on the fluency and pronunciation scores of the child as they are graphically presented in terms of three colored stars. The empty stars are used to represent that there is room to get better whereas filled stars show the level of their performance. The stars are shown with a cheering noise which again encourages the child and gives it a satisfying interactive moment.

5 Discussions and Conclusions

This research aimed at developing and testing a system to automatically measure English fluency and pronunciation among young students in Sri Lanka with special emphasis on the age twelve students and below. The essence was to offer an inexpensive, scalable, and pedagogically significant resource in the early teaching of English in the multilingual and resource-deprived conditions. The combination of highly developed speech technologies and the adjustment of text difficulty will help the system recognize and facilitate the progress of the oral English skills among children.

The study made several contributions. One, it introduced a new fusion of Whisper to speech recognition and forced alignment and CatBoost to score fluency optimized to deal with the special case of child speech. Second, the application of prosody-sensitive contrastive learning added to more correct modeling of rhythm, stress, and intonation that are important fluency predictors. Third, adaptive text difficulty mechanism was a novel pedagogical attribute in the sense that the system could adjust sentence complexity in relation to the learner proficiency level, thus keeping the learner engaged but gradually challenging. Combined, these contributions are both technically sound and instructionally relevant.

The findings have validated that the framework is reliable to evaluate fluency and pronunciation in experimental settings. Nonetheless, valuable aspects are identified in the findings too. Although this model proved to be successful on the data at hand, there are certain limitations including cultural and dialectal differences between training data and the target student population that are to be mentioned. Such variations in accent, pronunciation patterns, and speech habits can influence the possibility of the model to reproduce all the differences in the speech of Sri Lankan learners. Therefore, although the system shows efficient outcomes in general, its functioning can be enhanced with voice data of Sri Lankan children to make the model closer to the domain and representative. Moreover, even though the web-based interface of the system was child-friendly, the pedagogical effects cannot be claimed due to the lack of large-scale use with actual learners. These points should be discussed in future work to increase the reliability of the work and the adoption of the system.

The technical contributions are not the only implications of the broader implications of this study. Practically, the system could prove useful as a cheap and available classroom or home-based aid to help teachers and parents develop oral English skills in children. The tool can help solve the problem of the lack of trained English teachers in rural and under-resourced schools by automating feedback on pronunciation and fluency. Moreover, having adaptive difficulty adjustment offers an avenue to personalized learning in which students are not frustrated by over-complexity or under-challenged by under-complexity of the learning content.

To sum up, the present study is a valuable contribution to closing the gap between high-tech speech technology and teaching English as a second language in Sri Lanka. The suggested system does not only present technical novelty in the context of speech testing, but it also emphasizes the relevance of cultural and pedagogically based applications. Future directions will extend the dataset with speech of local children, test the system in user studies with teachers and learners, and add support functions, such as cross-lingual transfer learning, emotion recognition, and adaptation of the speaker. Together, these guidelines will facilitate creation of a more holistic, comprehensive, and effective educational technology among young English learners.

6 Future Work

Although the research system demonstrated effective results in pronunciation and fluency assessment, some areas could be developed further. First, the diversity of the dataset could be improved, and by adding voices from Sri Lankan students, the model training could be made more domain specific. Also, integrating self-supervised learning techniques may reduce the need for extensive labeled datasets, allowing the model to adapt dynamically to different learner profiles. Also, cross lingual transfer learinings can be explored. The prosodic feature extraction could include emotion detection and speaker variability. It would add more depth to fluency evaluation. Moreover, developing a system that supports mobile users would increase accessibility. By addressing these areas in the future, the system can be improved into a more effective, flexible, and useful tool.

Acknowledgements. The authors highly appreciate the continuous guidance and encouragement provided by the lecturers, colleagues, and family members. Special thanks are given to the external supervisor who helped to gather Sri Lankan curriculum data in the English language. Also, special thanks are given to K. Radha, Kaggle team, and K. James and team for making and maintaining voice datasets for young children and making it freely available for users.

Disclosure of Interests The authors declare that they have no competing interests.

References

1. Trilestari, K., Manurung, R., Simangunsong, V.: The benefits of learning English in early childhood: positive and negative effect. Esteem J. Engl. Educ. Study Programme. **7**, 669–681 (2024). https://doi.org/10.31851/esteem.v7i2.16151
2. Kheir, Y., Ali, A., Chowdhury, S.: Automatic pronunciation assessment - a review. Find. Assoc. Comput. Linguist. EMNLP 2023, 8304–8324 (2023). https://doi.org/10.18653/v1/2023.findings-emnlp.557
3. McCrocklin, S.: Pronunciation learner autonomy: the potential of automatic speech recognition. System **57**, 25–42 (2016). https://doi.org/10.1016/j.system.2015.12.013
4. Sewwandi, U., Ranathunga, L., Wijethunge, S.: A rule-based approach for detection and correction of grammar errors in written active voice Sinhala sentences. In: 21st International Conference on Advances in ICT for Emerging Regions (ICTer 2021), pp. 159–164. IEEE, Colombo (2021). https://doi.org/10.1109/ICter53630.2021.9774800
5. Jain, R., Barcovschi, A., Yiwere, M.Y., Corcoran, P., Cucu, H.: Exploring native and non-native English child speech recognition with whisper. IEEE Access. **12**, 41601–41610 (2024). https://doi.org/10.1109/ACCESS.2024.3378738
6. O'Grady, S.: Halo effects in rating data: assessing speech fluency. Res. Methods Appl. Linguist. **2**, 100048 (2023). https://doi.org/10.1016/j.rmal.2023.100048

7. Cockerill, M., Thurston, A., O'Keeffe, J.: Using fluency and comprehension instruction with struggling readers to improve student reading outcomes in English elementary schools. Int. J. Educ. Res. Open. **5**, 100264 (2023). https://doi.org/10.1016/j.ijedro.2023.100264
8. Korzekwa, D., Lorenzo-Trueba, J., Drugman, T., Kostek, B.: Computer-assisted pronunciation training—speech synthesis is almost all you need. Speech Comm. **142** (2022). https://doi.org/10.1016/j.specom.2022.06.003
9. Wang, J.: Speech recognition sensors and artificial intelligence automatic evaluation application in English oral correction system. Meas. Sens. **32**, 101070 (2024). https://doi.org/10.1016/j.measen.2024.101070
10. Claus, F., Gamboa-Rosales, H., Petrick, R., Hain, H.-U., Hoffmann, R.: A survey about databases of children's speech. In: Interspeech (2013). https://doi.org/10.21437/Interspeech.2013-561
11. Kodali, R., Mohan, B.: Non-native children English speech (NNCES) corpus. Kaggle (2022). https://doi.org/10.34740/KAGGLE/DSV/4416485
12. Kennedy, J., et al.: Children speech recording (English, spontaneous speech + pre-defined sentences). Dataset (2020). https://doi.org/10.5281/zenodo.200495
13. Rolland, T., Abad, A.: Towards improved automatic speech recognition for children. In: Proceedings of IberSPEECH, vol. 2024, pp. 251–255 (2024). https://doi.org/10.21437/IberSPEECH.2024-51
14. Mehra, S., Ranga, V., Agarwal, R.: Multimodal integration of Mel spectrograms and text transcripts for enhanced automatic speech recognition: leveraging extractive transformer-based approaches and late fusion strategies. Comput. Intell. **40**, e70012 (2024). https://doi.org/10.1111/coin.70012
15. Ali, A., Magdy, W., Bell, P., Renais, S.: Multi-reference WER for evaluating ASR for languages with no orthographic rules. In: 2015 IEEE Workshop on Automatic Speech Recognition and Understanding (ASRU), Scottsdale, pp. 576–580. IEEE (2015). https://doi.org/10.1109/ASRU.2015.7404847
16. Kathania, H.K., Shahnawazuddin, S., Adiga, N., Ahmad, W.: Role of prosodic features on children's speech recognition. In: 2018 IEEE International Conference on Acoustics, Speech and Signal Processing (ICASSP), Calgary pp. 5519–5523. IEEE (2018). https://doi.org/10.1109/ICASSP.2018.8461668
17. Dutta, A., Abdul, A.R.W.S.: A fine-tuned CatBoost-based speech disorder detection model. J. Disabil. Res. **3** (2024). https://doi.org/10.57197/JDR-2024-0027
18. Hancock, J.T., Khoshgoftaar, T.M.: CatBoost for big data: an interdisciplinary review. J. Big Data **7**(1) (2020). https://doi.org/10.1186/s40537-020-00369-8
19. Raju, V.N.G., Lakshmi, K.P., Jain, V.M., Kalidindi, A., Padma, V.: Study the influence of normalization/transformation process on the accuracy of supervised classification. In: 2020 Third International Conference on Smart Systems and Inventive Technology (ICSSIT), pp. 729–735 (2020). https://doi.org/10.1109/icssit48917.2020.9214160
20. Sandhusta, P.: Speech-to-text translation using hugging face model. Int. J. Sci. Res. Eng. Manage. **8**(4), 1–5 (2024). https://doi.org/10.55041/ijsrem30348
21. Pedregosa, F., Varoquaux, G., Gramfort, A., Louppe, G.: SciKit-learn: machine learning in python. ResearchGate (2012). https://www.researchgate.net/publication/51969319_Scikit-learn_Machine_Learning_in_Python

Unified Detection of Generated Speech: Combining Audio Spectrogram and Text Analysis

W. G. A. S. Gunathilaka and R. G. N. Meegama(✉)

Department of Computer Science, Faculty of Applied Sciences, University of Sri Jayewardenepura, Gangodawila, Nugegoda, Sri Lanka
rgn@sjp.ac.lk

Abstract. The study presents a multi-model framework for audio spoof detection that integrates both acoustic and linguistic cues to enhance classification robustness. While conventional methods rely primarily on spectrogram analysis using convolutional neural networks, they often overlook the linguistic inconsistencies present in spoofed speech. To address this limitation, the proposed approach combines deep features extracted from Mel spectrograms with semantic coherence representations derived from transcribed speech. Visual features are obtained using the fine tuned AlexNet architecture, while a fine-tuned SentenceTransformer model is used to capture linguistic patterns. The fused feature representations are processed by a feedforward neural network for binary classification. Experimental analysis demonstrates that the multi-model system offers significant improvements over uni-model baselines. The results validate the effectiveness of combining acoustic and semantic information, providing a more comprehensive and reliable framework for real-world spoof detection applications.

Keywords: Spoof detection · Audio-text fusion · Spectrogram analysis · Coherence analysis · Sentence transformers · Speech processing · Multi-model learning

1 Introduction

The rapid advancement of artificial intelligence has enabled the creation of highly realistic synthetic speech, known as deep fake audio. While these technologies offer benefits in areas like virtual assistants and entertainment, they also pose serious risks such as impersonation, misinformation, and erosion of trust in digital communication [2]. Traditional detection methods focus on acoustic features like pitch and frequency but often fall short against sophisticated deep fakes. This research proposes a unified detection approach that combines audio spectrogram analysis with natural language processing (NLP) to improve accuracy and robustness. By evaluating both the acoustic and textual aspects of speech, the proposed method offers a more comprehensive solution resulting in profound

R. N. Rajapakse et al. (Eds.): ICTer 2025, CCIS 2844, pp. 155–169, 2026.
https://doi.org/10.1007/978-981-92-0137-2_11

implications for forensics, media integrity, and cyber security, contributing to the development of advanced tools that safeguard the authenticity of AI-driven communication.

2 Related Work

Researchers have developed various techniques to detect deep fake audio by analyzing both spectral and linguistic features. A common method involves transforming audio into spectrograms and using convolutional neural networks (CNNs) to detect anomalies. While effective in many cases, these spectral methods may miss highly realistic fakes. To address this issue, some approaches incorporate natural language processing (NLP) to evaluate the coherence of spoken language, enhancing detection accuracy [12,13].

Studies have compared multiple audio representations, such as MFCC [6], mel-spectrogram [5], and chromagram [16], proving that the effectiveness of these features varies by model architecture. Custom-designed networks often outperform generic ones, with models like VGG-16 showing particular strength with MFCC features. Recurrent neural networks (RNNs), including LSTM and GRU, have proven particularly effective in identifying temporal patterns in audio, outperforming traditional techniques like Gaussian mixture models (GMM) [4,15].

Beyond typical signal processing, researchers have explored physiological cues for detection. For example, analyzing natural pauses in speech caused by breathing and swallowing can reveal synthetic audio, as these biological signals are difficult to replicate. Some studies even use breath detectors to differentiate between real and fake speech, emphasizing the role of human physiology in improving detection accuracy [8,11].

Deepfake detection efforts also extend to visual media such as images and videos. Researchers employ CNNs, RNNs, and GANs to detect spatial and temporal inconsistencies in manipulated content. Hybrid models combining audio and video analysis have demonstrated strong performance on benchmark datasets like FaceForensics++ [18], Celeb-DF [13], DFDC [21] and ASVSpoof 2019 [12]. Additional work has focused on detecting facial manipulations using techniques like FaceSwap [9]and Face2Face [20], comparing traditional and novel deep learning methods. Similar deep learning strategies have even been applied to satellite imagery to detect spliced or altered content [5].

In parallel, advances in NLP have led to powerful transformer-based models like BERT and GPT-3, which can understand and generate human-like language. These models are capable of evaluating the coherence of speech, identifying unnatural or inconsistent phrasing typical of deep fakes. Some researchers have developed graphical and transformer-based approaches specifically for coherence evaluation. By combining NLP techniques with acoustic analysis, a more robust and comprehensive deep fake detection system can be developed, leveraging both the linguistic and spectral aspects of speech [3,7,17].

3 Methodology

3.1 Spectrogram Analysis with CNN

Data Acquisition: This study employed the ASVspoof 2019 dataset [22], a widely used benchmark in deep fake audio detection and automatic speaker verification (ASV). The dataset consisted of high-quality audio samples (16 kHz, 3–10 seconds long) and was divided into three subsets: training, development, and evaluation. Each subset contained both bonafide (real) and spoofed (fake) speech generated using techniques such as voice conversion (VC) and text-to-speech (TTS). The training set included 2,580 real and 22,800 fake samples, while the development set comprised 2,548 real and 22,296 fake samples. The evaluation set contained 71,937 unlabeled samples used for final testing and included both known and unknown spoofing attacks.

Due to a significant class imbalance (real-to-fake ratio $\sim$ 1:6), a resampling strategy was implemented to prevent model bias toward the majority class. Under-sampling of fake samples was performed with attention to maintaining attack type diversity. The resulting datasets achieved a more balanced 1:3 ratio (real:fake), as shown in Table 1, which improved the model's ability to learn discriminative features and enhanced its sensitivity to genuine speech.

Table 1. Resampled dataset.

Subset	Bonafide (Real)	Spoof (Fake)
Training	2580	7740
Testing	2548	7644
Validation	7355	22065

Data Preprocessing: To ensure consistency and improve the performance of the model, a series of preprocessing steps were applied to the audio data. One of the key steps was amplitude normalization, which was performed to prevent the model from being biased toward audio signals with varying energy levels. Normalizing the amplitude ensured uniform signal strength across all samples, which was critical for maintaining consistent feature representation. Among various normalization techniques, such as decimal scaling, Z-score, and Min-Max normalization [1], the Min-Max normalization method was adopted due to its simplicity and effectiveness. This linear scaling technique transformed the signal amplitude to fit within a predefined range, making it particularly suitable for audio data.

Additionally, resampling was carried out to standardize the audio signals to a common sampling rate of 16 kHz [14]. Although the ASVspoof 2019 dataset was originally provided at this rate, the resampling step was reaffirmed to guarantee uniformity across all audio files. This step ensured compatibility with downstream audio processing algorithms and facilitated accurate feature extraction.

Spectrogram Generation: To effectively capture both temporal and spectral features of audio signals, Mel-spectrograms were generated using the Short-Time Fourier Transform (STFT). This transformation segmented the audio into overlapping frames and applied the Fast Fourier Transform (FFT) to extract localized frequency content over time. The resulting spectrogram was then mapped to the Mel scale using a triangular filter bank, which better reflected human auditory perception by emphasizing lower frequencies. The conversion from Hz to Mel frequency (1) was performed using:

$$M(f_{\text{Hz}}) = 1125 \ln\left(1 + \frac{f_{\text{Hz}}}{700}\right) \tag{1}$$

These STFT-based Mel-spectrograms provided a rich time-frequency representation, enabling the detection of subtle spectral artifacts caused by spoofing techniques such as voice conversion and TTS. To leverage pre-trained CNN models, the spectrograms were first saved as RGB images and then converted to greyscale, as shown in Fig. 1 to proceed with CNN processing. This approach preserved their visual structure while ensuring compatibility with standard image-based deep learning architectures.

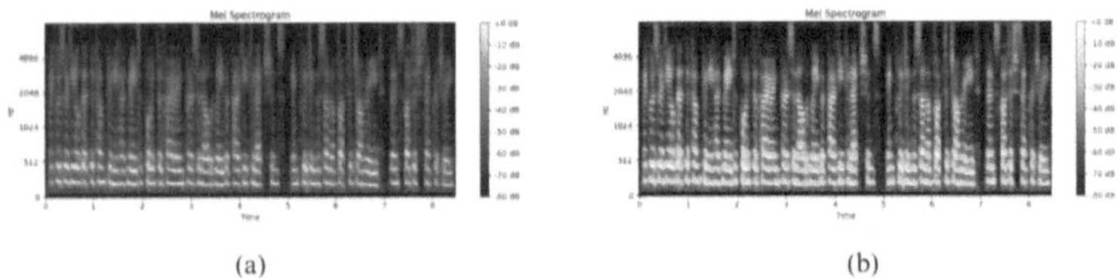

(a) (b)

Fig. 1. (a) RGB and (b) converted greyscale spectrograms.

Pretrained Model Selection and Fine Tuning: In this study, AlexNet was selected as the primary model for spectrogram-based classification due to its balanced performance and computational simplicity. While more advanced architectures such as EfficientNet were also considered for experimentation, AlexNet demonstrated more stable and interpretable results, aligning better with the security-focused goals of synthetic speech detection. EfficientNet, though highly effective in recall, exhibited a tendency toward increased false acceptances, which was less desirable in scenarios where minimizing spoof acceptance was critical. AlexNet, on the other hand, offered a more conservative classification behavior, making it a more suitable backbone for integration within a unified detection pipeline that combined both acoustic and linguistic features.

For fine-tuning, the Mel-spectrograms derived from the ASVspoof 2019 dataset were first converted into RGB images to ensure compatibility with models pre-trained on ImageNet. These spectrogram images were resized to 224 × 224 pixels, normalized to align with ImageNet preprocessing standards, and organized into structured training, development, and evaluation sets. The pre-trained AlexNet model was loaded with ImageNet weights, and early convolutional layers were initially frozen to retain general-purpose features. Only the final layers were retrained for the binary classification task of real versus fake audio. As training progressed, selective unfreezing of deeper layers was applied to improve adaptation to spectrogram-specific patterns. Data augmentation techniques, such as random horizontal flipping, were applied during training to enhance model generalization, while the validation and evaluation sets remained unaltered to ensure unbiased performance assessment. The Adam optimizer and Cross-Entropy Loss were used during training to facilitate stable and effective convergence [10].

Model Optimization: To improve the generalization capability and robustness of the fine-tuned AlexNet model, a series of optimization strategies were implemented during training. The data augmentation pipeline began by resizing all spectrogram images to 224×224 pixels and converting them from single-channel to three-channel grayscale to match AlexNet's RGB input requirement. Augmentation techniques such as random horizontal flipping, rotations up to $\hat{A}\pm\ 10°$, and color jittering (brightness and contrast adjustments up to a factor of 0.2) were applied to increase dataset variability. These transformations introduced meaningful variations without distorting the underlying time-frequency patterns, helping the model become invariant to minor spatial changes. Augmented images were converted into tensors and normalized across all three channels using a mean and standard deviation of 0.5, effectively scaling pixel values to the range of [-1, 1] to ensure stable training. For the development and evaluation sets, only resizing, grayscale conversion, tensor transformation, and normalization were applied to maintain evaluation consistency.

Beyond augmentation, regularization techniques were employed to prevent overfitting. The final fully connected layer of AlexNet was replaced with a custom classifier head containing a dropout layer ($p = 0.5$) and a final linear layer for binary classification. Dropout reduced co-adaptation of neurons, enhancing the model's ability to learn robust features. Additionally, weight decay (L2 regularization) with a factor of 1e-4 was applied through the Adam optimizer to penalize large weight magnitudes and promote generalizable patterns. A class-weighted Cross-Entropy Loss function was used (real: 3.0, fake: 1.0) to mitigate class imbalance. To further refine the learning process, a StepLR scheduler was integrated to decay the learning rate by a factor of 0.1 every 5 epochs, enabling finer updates during later training stages. After applying these optimization strategies, the final model was saved for downstream evaluation and integration.

3.2 Coherence Analysis Using NLP

Data Preprocessing: For coherence evaluation using NLP techniques, the first step involved converting audio signals into text through transcription. This was followed by standardized preprocessing steps, including tokenization, normalization, and formatting, to prepare the data for input into transformer-based language models. All audio samples from the ASVspoof 2019 dataset were transcribed using OpenAI's Whisper, an end-to-end speech recognition system. It converted raw audio into text by generating log-Mel spectrograms and processing them with a transformer-based encoder-decoder model. This automated transcription was applied consistently to both real and fake samples across all dataset partitions, providing a scalable foundation for subsequent NLP tasks such as coherence evaluation and linguistic analysis.

Tokenization, a key step in NLP, segments text into smaller units called tokens. In this study, the all-MiniLM-L6-v2 model from the Sentence Transformers library was used to embed transcribed audio into dense vectors for coherence evaluation. The model applied subword tokenization using the WordPiece algorithm, inherited from BERT, to manage rare and out-of-vocabulary words. Input text was converted into token IDs with special tokens likeSPSVERBc1 and `[SEP]` token, then passed through the transformer to generate contextual embeddings that capture both syntax and semantics for coherence analysis. The all-MiniLM-L6-v2 model from the Sentence Transformers library was used to generate sentence-level embeddings for transcribed audio data. Unlike standard BERT, Sentence Transformers were optimized to produce a single fixed-size embedding for an entire sentence or text segment. This was typically achieved using pooling strategies such as mean pooling, max pooling, or selecting the embedding of the special [CLS] token. The all-MiniLM-L6-v2 model output 384-dimensional embeddings that encapsulated the overall semantic content of each sentence. The embeddings served as the foundation for assessing the coherence of spoken language transcriptions, enabling the detection of semantic inconsistencies and supporting the classification of real versus spoofed speech samples.

Coherence Score Generation: To evaluate the semantic coherence of transcribed audio, a sentence embedding-based method was used. Transcriptions were converted into 384-dimensional vectors using the all-MiniLM-L6-v2 model, capturing rich semantic features. An average embedding was computed from all bonafide (real) training samples to serve as a semantic reference for natural speech. Before comparison, all embeddings were L2-normalized to ensure consistent vector magnitudes, enabling accurate similarity assessment in high-dimensional space.

Cosine similarity [19] was then used to quantify the alignment between individual sentence embeddings and the reference embedding. This parameter measures the cosine of the angle between two vectors and reflects how similar their directions are in vector space. In the context of NLP, especially with normalized embeddings, cosine similarity typically ranged from 0 to 1, where higher values indicated greater semantic alignment. It is defined as:

$$\text{CosineSimilarity}(A, B) = \frac{A \cdot B}{|A||B|} \tag{2}$$

where, $A \cdot B$ is the dot product of vectors A and B, and $|A|$ and $|B|$ are the Euclidean norms (magnitudes) of the vectors.

This made cosine similarity a robust metric for coherence evaluation, as it measured how closely a sample's semantic structure aligned with typical real speech. For each transcription-bonafide and spoofed-a-coherence score was calculated by comparing it to the average embedding. Higher scores indicated greater linguistic coherence, while lower scores suggested semantic inconsistency or artificial generation. These scores, along with file identifiers and ground-truth labels, were recorded across the training, development, and evaluation sets for further analysis and integration into classification tasks.

Initial experiments using unsupervised cosine similarity between sentence embeddings and a reference average embedding showed limitations in effectively discriminating between bonafide and spoofed speech. Although high overall accuracy was observed, it largely reflected the model's tendency to favor the majority class, leading to poor recall for detecting spoofed inputs. Threshold adjustments yielded only marginal improvements, highlighting the inherent constraints of the unsupervised thresholding approach. To address this, a supervised fine-tuning strategy was adopted to reshape the embedding space and enhance the model's task-specific discriminative capabilities. Fine-tuning enabled the model to learn more nuanced representations of real and fake speech through exposure to labeled examples, thereby improving performance on coherence-based classification tasks.

The fine-tuning process involved training the all-MiniLM-L6-v2 Sentence Transformer using a dataset of paired transcriptions labeled as either bonafide or spoofed. Labels were assigned as 0 for bonafide and 1 for spoofed samples. From this labeled dataset, positive pairs (samples from the same class) and negative pairs (one bonafide and one spoofed sample) were generated to train the model in distinguishing semantically similar and dissimilar inputs. This approach supported contrastive learning by guiding the model to reduce intra-class distance and increase inter-class separation in the embedding space. To classify these sentence pairs, a Softmax function was applied to the model's output logits, converting them into probability distributions that reflected the likelihood of similarity between the input texts. The model was fine-tuned by minimizing a loss function, Softmax loss, that measured the discrepancy between predicted and actual similarity labels. Training was conducted using the Adam optimizer, which efficiently updated model weights to minimize loss. The model was trained over multiple epochs, with periodic evaluations on a validation set to ensure generalization and prevent overfitting. Through this fine-tuning approach, the model became more adept at identifying subtle semantic differences between genuine and spoofed transcriptions, providing a more reliable and discriminative foundation for coherence evaluation in spoof detection.

3.3 Multi-model Architecture

The ultimate multi-input architecture leveraged the strengths of both spectrograms derived from audio signals and coherence features extracted from transcribed text. By combining these modalities, the model was able to achieve a more comprehensive understanding of the data, ultimately enhancing classification performance.

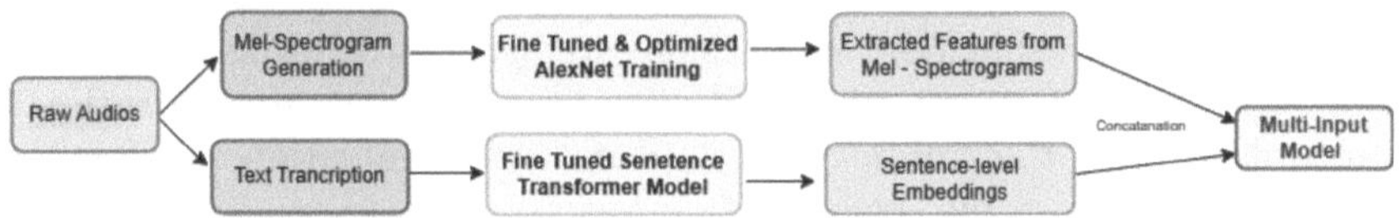

Fig. 2. Proposed multi-model architecture.

The multi-model architecture shown in Fig. 2 integrated auditory and linguistic features to enhance the detection of spoofed audio. It consisted of two parallel branches: an audio branch that used a fine-tuned AlexNet model to extract discriminative features from Mel-spectrograms, and a text branch that leveraged a Natural Language Processing (NLP) model (the fine-tuned Sentence Transformer model - all-MiniLM-L6-v2) to evaluate semantic coherence in the transcribed speech. These branches captured complementary cues of low-level acoustic patterns and high-level linguistic consistency enabling more robust classification. The results of both branches were fused in a dedicated fusion layer, typically through feature concatenation, to form a unified representation that informed the final decision layer.

Each spectrogram image was processed through AlexNet to extract deep feature vectors capturing key spectral patterns such as energy shifts, harmonics, and frequency dynamics. These vectors were flattened and stored for later use. Simultaneously, transcriptions were embedded using a Sentence Transformer model fine-tuned on ASVspoof2019 data, producing sentence-level vectors that reflected semantic coherence. For each sample, visual and textual features were concatenated into a unified multi-modal vector. These fused representations, along with labels, were saved in NPY files and accessed via a custom dataset class, enabling synchronized input during training and allowing the classifier to utilize both acoustic and linguistic information for spoof detection.

Multi-model Training: The multi-model architecture was trained using a binary cross-entropy loss function, with training monitored over 10 epochs. The combined input comprised 128-dimensional features extracted from Mel-spectrograms via AlexNet and 384-dimensional sentence embeddings from the fine-tuned Sentence Transformer model, resulting in a 512-dimensional feature vector plus one additional bias feature (totaling 513 dimensions). A two-layer feedforward neural network was employed to map this input to a binary output, indicating the probability of a sample being bonafide or spoofed.

The training loss showed consistent and significant reduction across epochs, indicating effective learning, as shown in Table 2. Initially, the average loss was 0.4990 in the first epoch, reflecting the model's early stage of adaptation. By epoch 5, the loss had dropped sharply to 0.0870, suggesting rapid convergence.

Table 2. Average loss over epochs in model training.

Epoch	1	2	3	4	5	6	7	8	9	10
Average loss (10^{-2})	49.90	28.62	18.38	12.15	8.70	6.70	5.47	4.66	4.06	3.61

Subsequent epochs saw further, albeit smaller, reductions, with the loss reaching 0.0361 by epoch 10. This plateauing trend implied that the model had learned a stable decision boundary, and additional training was yielding diminishing returns, indicating convergence.

The steady decrease in average loss without oscillation or sudden spikes was a strong indicator of well-behaved optimization. Moreover, it suggested that the combined features from both image and text modalities were effectively leveraged by the network to distinguish between real and spoofed samples.

4 Results and Discussion

4.1 Spectrogram Analysis with Fine-Tuned AlexNet Model

The performance of the spoof and real classification model was evaluated over 20 training epochs using the fine-tuned AlexNet architecture for spectrogram feature extraction. During training, both the training and validation loss over epochs, as shown in Fig. 3, demonstrated effective learning dynamics and stable generalization.

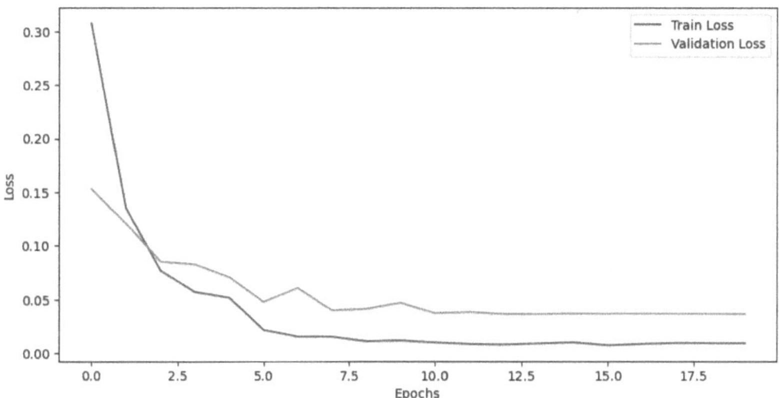

Fig. 3. Training and validation loss over epochs.

Initially, the training loss decreased rapidly, reflecting efficient optimization and model convergence. By approximately the 6th epoch, the validation loss also began to stabilize and closely tracked the training loss. This convergence indicated that the model generalized well to unseen data without significant overfitting, supported by the use of early stopping and an appropriate balance between the audio and text modalities. Notably, after epoch 10, the validation loss plateaued, while the training loss continued a mild downward trend, an expected behavior in well-regularized systems.

The classification performance of the optimized, fine-tuned AlexNet model was evaluated using standard metrics, with results confirming the efficacy of the spectrogram analysis approach.

Table 3. Evaluation of optimized AlexNet fine-tuned model.

Accuracy	0.8972
Precision	0.7152
Recall	0.9784
F1-Score	0.8263

The derived evaluation scores in Table 3 revealed a high recall rate of 97.84%, signifying the model's strong sensitivity in correctly identifying bonafide (real) speech samples. Although precision was moderately lower at 71.52%, this trade-off is acceptable in the context of anti-spoofing, where the cost of failing to detect genuine inputs is often higher than that of raising false alarms. The F1-score, calculated at 82.63%, reflects a well-balanced trade-off between precision and recall, showcasing the model's robustness in managing the nuanced decision boundaries inherent to spoof detection.

4.2 Coherence Score Analysis with Fine Tuned Sentence Transformer

After preparing the sentence embedding model for task-specific coherence evaluation, the coherence scoring pipeline was executed to assess the effectiveness of text-based spoof detection. Sentence embeddings were generated for each transcribed audio sample, and an average embedding vector was computed from the bonafide training samples to serve as a reference. Using cosine similarity, coherence scores were calculated by comparing each sample's embedding to the reference vector. These scores quantified how linguistically aligned each sample was with typical bonafide speech patterns.

Using a decision threshold of 0.3, the final evaluation of the text model revealed notable improvements in spoof detection capability.

As shown in Table 4, the results on the training set indicate that the model was particularly effective at capturing genuine (bonafide) speech, as reflected by the high recall. However, the F1-score demonstrates a balanced performance, combining sensitivity and precision into a single, robust measure.

On the development set, the model achieved 54.05% accuracy, 31.84% precision, 73.43% recall, and a 44.42% F1-score. This consistency between the training

Table 4. Evaluation of fine-tuned sentence transformer model.

Metric	Training	Validation	Evaluation
Accuracy	0.6043	0.5405	0.5422
Precision	0.3660	0.3184	0.3241
Recall	0.7965	0.7343	0.7657
F1-Score	0.5016	0.4442	0.4554

and development sets suggests good generalization and implies that the model is not overfitting to the training data. The pattern of high recall and moderate precision persists, indicating a bias toward correctly identifying real speech at the expense of some false positives. Evaluation on the unseen test set further validated the model's reliability, with an accuracy of 54.22%, precision of 32.41%, recall of 76.57%, and an F1-score of 45.54%. These outcomes mirror those seen in earlier sets, reinforcing the stability of the model's predictions across different data splits. The recall remains high, demonstrating strong sensitivity to bonafide inputs, while the precision and F1-score suggest reasonable handling of spoofed content despite inherent textual ambiguity.

Overall, the coherence score-based approach has proven capable of leveraging linguistic features to support spoof detection. Although the text modality alone may not offer perfect discrimination, its strength in recall and overall balanced performance metrics make it a valuable component in a multi-model anti-spoofing system.

4.3 Multi-model with Spectrogram Images and Text Coherence

The multi-model classification framework integrates both spectral and linguistic information, leveraging the strengths of convolutional and transformer-based architectures. Evaluation on the held-out evaluation set demonstrates that the fusion of Mel spectrogram-based features (extracted via AlexNet) and coherence-based text embeddings (from a fine-tuned Sentence Transformer) significantly enhances the system's spoof detection capabilities.

The model achieves an accuracy of 89.78%, reflecting strong overall classification performance across both spoofed and bonafide samples. Notably, the precision is exceptionally high at 98.86%, indicating that the system is highly effective in avoiding false alarms. When the model predicts an input as bonafide, it is correct in the vast majority of cases. This level of precision is crucial in practical anti-spoofing scenarios, where minimizing false acceptances of spoofed inputs is critical. The model achieves a recall of 86.91%, successfully identifying most bonafide (real) samples, though a small proportion are misclassified as spoofed. Despite this slight trade-off, it strikes a good balance between sensitivity and specificity. The F1-score, a harmonic mean of precision and recall, is 92.51%, showcasing the model's ability to maintain both low false positives and low false negatives. This robust F1-score further supports the effectiveness of combining acoustic and textual modalities. Additionally, the ROC AUC score of 97.63% demonstrates excellent separability between the classes. These results confirm that the multi-model architecture effectively captures complementary cues from both the acoustic and linguistic domains, enabling more reliable and generalizable spoof detection. The consistently high scores across evaluation metrics further highlight the advantage of combining coherence-based semantic features with spectrogram-based CNN features.

4.4 Comparative Analysis

To evaluate the effectiveness of integrating linguistic coherence with spectral features, a comparative analysis was conducted between the proposed multi-model architecture and a baseline image-only model using AlexNet on Mel spectrograms. Both models were evaluated on the same held-out evaluation set, and the results are summarized in Table 5, offering a side-by-side comparison of key classification metrics.

Table 5. Comparative analysis of AlexNet and multi-model architectures.

Model	Accuracy	Precision	Recall	F1-Score
AlexNet Model	0.8972	0.7152	0.9784	0.8263
Multi Model	0.8978	0.9886	0.9277	0.9763

The AlexNet model, using only spectrogram features, achieved 89.72% accuracy with high recall (97.84%) but lower precision (71.52%) and an F1-score of 82.63%, indicating a tendency to misclassify spoofed audio as genuine. In comparison, the multi-model approach, which combines spectral and sentence-level semantic features, slightly improved accuracy to 89.78% and significantly boosted precision to 98.86% and F1-score to 92.77%. Although its recall dropped slightly to 87.38%, the higher precision led to a more balanced performance. The ROC AUC of 0.9763 further confirmed its superior discriminative power. These results as shown in Table 5, demonstrate that integrating linguistic coherence features enhances the model's ability to detect subtle spoofing artifacts missed by acoustic analysis alone. The comparison of confusion matrices, as illustrated in Fig. 4, clearly demonstrates the above stated observation.

4.5 Scope and Future Directions

Future work will focus on integrating features from raw audio waveforms alongside spectrograms could capture complementary low-level artifacts that are lost during time-frequency transformation. Exploring more sophisticated fusion mechanisms, such as cross-attention transformers, could dynamically weight the importance of acoustic versus linguistic cues on a per-sample basis, rather than

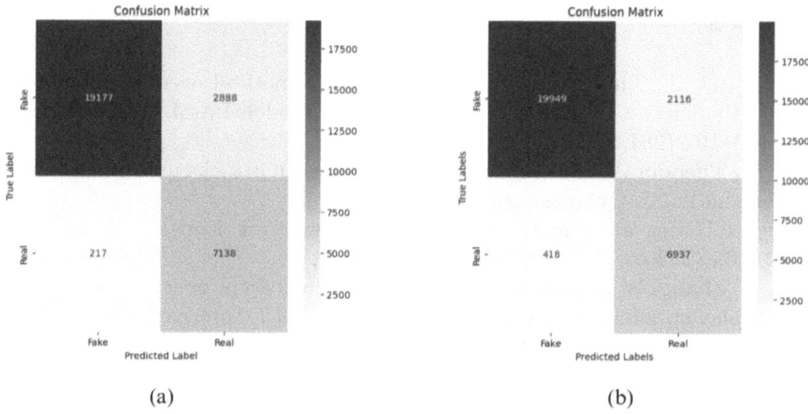

Fig. 4. Confusion matrices of AlexNet and combined model.

relying on simple feature concatenation. Furthermore, expanding the model to a multi-task learning setup, simultaneously detecting spoofing, identifying the specific synthesis algorithm used and localizing manipulated segments, could provide a more comprehensive forensic tool. Rigorous testing on in-the-wild datasets containing code-switched speech, background noise and varied acoustic environments is essential to validate the robustness and real-world applicability of the system.

5 Conclusion

This study presents a unified approach to spoof detection by combining acoustic and linguistic features within a single classification framework. While the AlexNet-based spectrogram analysis showed strong recall, its lower precision highlighted limitations in relying solely on spectral cues. By integrating sentence-level coherence features from a fine-tuned SentenceTransformer model, the multi-modal system achieved a more balanced performance, significantly improving performance. This confirms that linguistic information provides essential complementary signals for detecting spoofed speech. It enhances both the robustness and reliability of spoof detection, especially in real-world scenarios where subtle semantic inconsistencies and acoustic manipulations coexist. These findings underscore the potential of multi-modal learning in advancing the effectiveness of speech-based security systems.

Disclosure of Interests. The authors declare that they have no known competing financial interests or personal relationships that could have appeared to influence the work cited in this paper.

References

1. Aksu, G., et al.: The effect of the normalization method used in different sample sizes on the success of artificial neural network model. Int. J. Assess. Tools Educ. **6**(2), 170–192 (2019)
2. Alali, A., Theodorakopoulos, G.: Partial fake speech attacks in the real world using deepfake audio. J. Cybersecur. Priv. **5**(1) (2025)
3. Brown, T.B., et al.: Language models are few-shot learners. ArXiv preprint: 2005.14165 (2020)
4. Chen, Z., Zhang, W., Xie, Z., Xu, X., Chen, D.: Recurrent neural networks for automatic replay spoofing attack detection. In: 2018 IEEE International Conference on Acoustics, Speech and Signal Processing (ICASSP), pp. 2052–2056. Calgary (2018)
5. Choi, K., Fazekas, G., Sandler, M., Cho, K.: Convolutional recurrent neural networks for music classification. In: IEEE International Conference on Acoustics, Speech and Signal Processing (ICASSP), pp. 2392–2396 (2017)
6. Şengül, F., Akkaya, S.: A modified MFCC-based deep learning method for emotion classification from speech. Int. Adv. Res. Eng. J. 33–42 (2024)
7. Devlin, J., et al.: Bert: pre-training of deep bidirectional transformers for language understanding. In: Proceedings of the 2019 Conference of the North American Chapter of the Association for Computational Linguistics: Human Language Technologies (2019)
8. Doan, T., Nguyen-Vu, L., Jung, S., Hong, K.: BTS-E: audio deepfake detection using breathing-talking-silence encoder. In: IEEE International Conference on Acoustics, Speech and Signal Processing (ICASSP), Rhodes Island, Greece (2023)
9. Korshunova, I., Shi, W., Dambre, J., Theis, L.: Fast face-swap using convolutional neural networks. In: Proceedings of the IEEE International Conference on Computer Vision (ICCV), pp. 3677–3685 (2017)
10. Krizhevsky, A., Sutskever, I., Hinton, G.: Imagenet classification with deep convolutional neural networks. Neural Inf. Process. Syst. **25** (2012)
11. Kulangareth, N.V., et al.: Investigation of deepfake voice detection using speech pause patterns: algorithm development and validation. JMIR Biomed. Eng. **9**, e56245 (2024)
12. Li, Y., Lyu, S.: VideoFack: a unified benchmark for video forgery detection. In: IEEE/CVF Conference on Computer Vision and Pattern Recognition (2022)
13. Li, Y., et al.: Celeb-df: A large-scale challenging dataset for deepfake forensics. In: Proceedings of the IEEE/CVF Conference on Computer Vision and Pattern Recognition (2020)
14. McFee, B., et al.: Librosa: audio and music signal analysis in python. SciPy 18–24 (2015)
15. Mcuba, M., et al.: The effect of deep learning methods on deepfake audio detection for digital investigation. Procedia Comput. Sci. **219**, 211–219 (2023)
16. Müller, M., Kurth, F., Clausen, M.: Audio matching via chroma-based statistical features. In: Proceedings of the 6th International Conference on Music Information Retrieval (ISMIR), pp. 288–295 (2005)
17. Pogorilyy, S., Kramov, A.: Coherence evaluation method based on analyses of phrases graph. In: 2020 IEEE 2nd International Conference on System Analysis and Intelligent Computing (SAIC), pp. 1–6. Kyiv, Ukraine (2020)
18. Rossler, A., et al.: Faceforensics++: learning to detect manipulated facial images. In: Proceedings of the IEEE/CVF International Conference on Computer Vision (2019)

19. Salton, G., McGill, M.: Introduction to Modern Information Retrieval. McGraw-Hill, New York (1983)
20. Thies, J., Zollhöfer, M., Stamminger, M., Theobalt, C., Nießner, M.: Face2face: real-time face capture and reenactment of RGB videos. In: IEEE Conference on Computer Vision and Pattern Recognition (CVPR), pp. 2387–2395 (2016)
21. Trabelsi, A., Marc, M., Jean-Luc, D.: Improving deepfake detection by mixing top solutions of the DFDC. In: European Signal Processing Conference, IEEE (2022)
22. Yamagishi, M., et al.: Asvspoof. The 3rd automatic speaker verification spoofing and countermeasures challenge database. University of Edinburgh. The Centre for Speech Technology Research (2019)

A Continual Learning Mechanism for Early Brahmi Inscription Translation with Deep Learning

U. Janidu Rathnayaka and Pumudu A. Fernando(✉)

School of Computing, Informatics Institute of Technology, Colombo, Sri Lanka
{uthpala.20210450,pumudu.f}@iit.ac.lk

Abstract. The manual recognition and translation of ancient inscriptions are significantly hindered by data scarcity and the limitations of current automated systems. Most existing solutions depend on large, annotated datasets to achieve high accuracy, which is impractical in this domain due to the limited availability of labeled data. Furthermore, the dynamic and evolving nature of inscription studies renders static models prone to obsolescence. This paper introduces a novel continual learning framework focused on the translation of Early Brahmi inscriptions in Sri Lanka. The proposed system combines a YOLO-based character recognition module with a Transformer-based neural machine translation (NMT) model, enhanced through transfer learning techniques. To address data scarcity and obsolescence, the system employs both incremental and active learning strategies, enabling continuous adaptation without catastrophic forgetting or the need for full retraining. The effectiveness of this approach is demonstrated through prototype implementation. Experimental results show that the YOLOv11 character recognition model achieved a mean Average Precision (mAP) of up to 95.2%, while translation performance improved from a BLEU score of 70.43 in the initial training cycle to 81.04 in the third cycle (second retraining).

Keywords: Early Brahmi · YOLO-based Character Recognition · Transformer-based NMT · Continual Learning · Incremental Learning · Active Learning

1 Introduction

Ancient inscriptions are a critical source for understanding the linguistic, cultural, and socio-political history of civilizations. In South Asia, Brahmi inscriptions are particularly significant, as they represent one of the earliest writing systems and serve as the foundation for modern scripts such as Sinhala and Tamil [1]. In Sri Lanka, over 90% of ancient stone inscriptions are written in Brahmi. Of the 4,000 inscriptions discovered, only about 1,500 have been officially documented, spanning languages such as Sinhala, Tamil, Sanskrit, and Pali [2].

The Brahmi script in Sri Lanka evolved over time and is categorized into five stages: Early Brahmi (third century BC – early first century AD), Later Brahmi, Transitional

R. N. Rajapakse et al. (Eds.): ICTer 2025, CCIS 2844, pp. 170–184, 2026.
https://doi.org/10.1007/978-981-92-0137-2_12

Brahmi, Medieval Sinhala, and Modern Sinhala [3]. This study focuses specifically on inscriptions from the Early Brahmi period.

Recent technological advancements have led to the development of automated systems that assist historians and archaeologists by reducing manual effort and improving the accuracy of interpretations [20]. Despite these advancements, significant challenges remain in the recognition and translation of ancient inscriptions. A key obstacle is the limited availability of data, which is further complicated by the specialized nature of inscriptional analysis [2]. The field of epigraphy is dynamic, with new inscriptions being discovered regularly, which increases the complexity of translation tasks. Many existing systems struggle to adapt to new data efficiently because they lack mechanisms for continual learning, making full retraining computationally expensive and impractical. As a result, models become outdated, diminishing their accuracy and usefulness over time.

To address these limitations, this research proposes a novel framework for the continual learning-based translation of Early Brahmi inscriptions. The system aims to incrementally adapt to newly acquired data without catastrophic forgetting or costly retraining, thereby maintaining accuracy and relevance over time. This research aims to explore solutions to the following key questions:

- What techniques and approaches can be employed to accurately recognize and translate ancient inscriptions into modern languages, while preserving contextual meaning?
- How can continual learning mechanisms be integrated to enable adaptive translation systems that retain previously acquired knowledge?

This work introduces a deep learning approach combining YOLO-based character recognition and Transformer-based translation, supported by incremental and active learning techniques to handle evolving datasets effectively.

2 Background and Related Work

2.1 Inscription Recognition and Translation

The digitization and interpretation of ancient inscriptions have benefited significantly from advancements in deep learning and image processing, particularly in character recognition, translation, and image preprocessing.

Early approaches primarily leveraged traditional OCR techniques, such as the AMSER algorithm [4], which improved image clarity through blur reduction and geometric correction before applying Tesseract OCR, achieving over 90% translation accuracy for South Indian inscriptions. However, traditional methods often struggled with distortions and eroded characters.

Recent studies have adopted deep learning-based models to overcome these limitations. For instance, [5, 6] applied transfer learning using CNN architectures (AlexNet, GoogLeNet, Inception-V3) to recognize ancient Tamil and Brahmi characters, with Inception-V3 achieving a 95.6% accuracy [7]. further enhanced recognition performance using a hybrid lion optimization algorithm (SLOA-TL) to fine-tune Inception-V3 for ancient scripts.

For Sinhala inscriptions, [8] evaluated multiple pre-trained CNN models (VGG16, MobileNet, ResNet50) with data augmentation, demonstrating strong performance in both character recognition and time-period classification. Similarly, [9] improved classification by incorporating a channel attention module into VGG-16, achieving 90.6% period classification accuracy and 96% end-to-end prediction accuracy.

Object detection methods have also been applied to inscriptions. Santoso et al. [18] used YOLOv3-tiny to recognize Kawi characters on copper plates, achieving a mean Average Precision (mAP) of 97.17% and test accuracy of 97.93%. Despite high accuracy, the study noted limitations in handling diverse writing styles, suggesting the need for broader datasets.

In translation, [10] introduced a mobile solution combining U-Net for semantic segmentation and a Transformer-based Neural Machine Translation (NMT) model for English translation of Brahmi inscriptions [1]. implemented a rule-based Sinhala translation system with image preprocessing, segmentation, and wavelet-based feature extraction.

The aforementioned studies demonstrate the effectiveness of deep learning models, particularly CNNs, in character recognition, while NMT models have proven useful for inscription translation tasks. Preprocessing techniques such as noise reduction, contrast enhancement, and binarization have been critical in improving performance. However, existing research has not sufficiently addressed the challenge of continually retraining models as new data becomes available, which can lead to performance degradation.

2.2 Continual Learning with NMT

Continual learning has been extensively explored in NMT, primarily for high-resource modern languages [19]. However, its application to low-resource, ancient languages like Early Brahmi remains underexplored.

In [11], an adaptive NMT system using online learning via stochastic gradient descent (SGD) was compared to a static model. The adaptive system, based on an LSTM encoder-decoder with attention and Byte Pair Encoding (BPE), demonstrated improved post-editor productivity without compromising translation quality, as measured by BLEU and TER scores.

To address catastrophic forgetting in multilingual NMT, [12] introduced a Continual Incremental Language Learning (CILL) setting, where a Transformer-based model learned new language pairs sequentially. Techniques such as prioritized replay buffers were employed to retain past knowledge, showing improved performance across BLEU, average accuracy, and backward transfer metrics.

In [13], the challenge of catastrophic forgetting during fine-tuning was mitigated using dynamic knowledge distillation combined with a bias correction module. This method outperformed traditional fine-tuning, static knowledge distillation, and Elastic Weight Consolidation (EWC) in maintaining translation quality.

These studies demonstrate the potential of continual learning strategies, such as replay buffers, distillation, and adaptive training for maintaining translation performance in evolving datasets. However, existing work focuses mainly on modern, well-resourced languages. There is a clear need to extend these continual learning approaches to low-resource and historical languages like Early Brahmi, where data is limited and domain shifts are common.

3 Methodology

The proposed system has two primary components: a character recognition model and a translation model. Both models are stored in a repository after initial training. A retraining mechanism is implemented for the translation model to accommodate new inscription data over time, enhancing the model's adaptability and accuracy. The architecture of the system can be seen in Fig. 1.

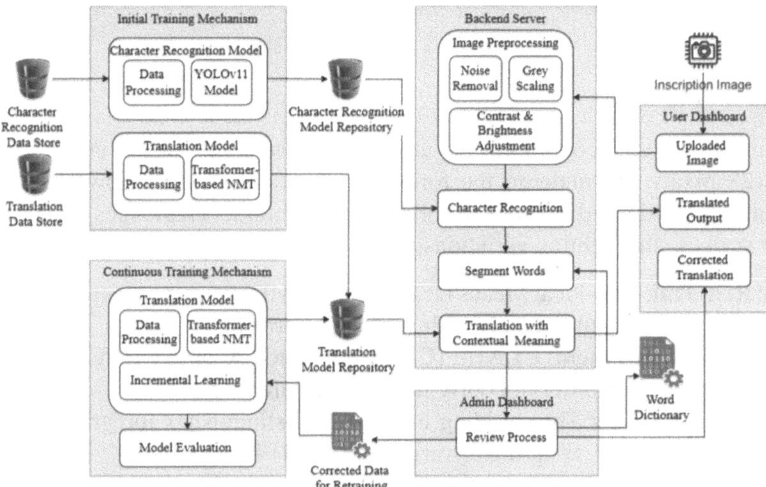

Fig. 1. Architecture of the Proposed System

3.1 Data Collection and Preprocessing

Character Recognition Dataset. The dataset includes 992 training and 250 test samples of manually labeled Early Brahmi characters, originally sourced from Kaggle [15]. Training on isolated characters under controlled conditions led to poor generalization during inference, to mitigate this, synthetic inscription images with randomly placed characters were generated to simulate realistic layouts, as shown in Fig. 2. Moreover, synthetic images were considered since real-world datasets specific to the Early Brahmi era remain scarce and difficult to obtain, and the existing datasets are often heavily pre-processed, failing to capture the full complexity of raw inscription data. These images were labeled using LabelImg, covering 18 distinct character classes.

Fig. 2. Synthetic Image

Translation Dataset. Translation data, obtained from the Department of Archaeology, Sri Lanka, consists of 12,060 Sinhala transliterations and their corresponding English translations. Byte Pair Encoding (BPE) will be used for tokenization, and separate vocabularies will be created for Sinhala and English to prepare the data for neural translation.

3.2 Image Processing

To optimize character recognition, uploaded inscription images will be uniformly resized to 128x128 pixels and undergo the following processing steps. However, since real world datasets are limited, it limits the ability to fully model challenges such as erosion, irregular strokes, and lighting variations.:

- **Noise Removal**: Non-local Means Denoising (NLMD) preserves textures in degraded inscriptions by averaging pixels with similar patterns [7].
- **Contrast Enhancement**: CLAHE (Contrast Limited Adaptive Histogram Equalization) improves readability in poorly lit or eroded areas [5].
- **Binarization**: Otsu's Thresholding effectively distinguishes foreground characters from the background, adapting to varied lighting [14].
- **Normalization**: Pixel values are scaled to [0, 1] to stabilize CNN training.

3.3 Character Segmentation

The next step involves separating characters from the background and isolating individual characters for recognition. The system employs YOLOv11 to detect and segment individual characters from inscriptions. This version improves upon YOLOv3 used in previous work by offering better localization accuracy and robustness to background noise and uneven textures.

3.4 Character Recognition

Traditional OCR engines like Tesseract perform poorly on ancient scripts due to inconsistent stroke patterns and erosion. Instead, this system uses deep learning-based object detection. While previous studies [8] found VGG16 effective, YOLOv11 is adopted here for its superior object localization capabilities, enabling real-time detection and classification of characters within full inscription images. The comparison of the models can be seen in Fig. 3.

Pre-trained model	Accuracy	Loss
VGG16	93.33%	0.22079873404776057
MobileNet	90.00%	0.9754242509979122
VGG19	75.00%	1.1768677473068236
InceptionV3	75.00%	1.2553982079029082
DenseNet121	74.00%	1.4959668021649122
DenseNet201	72.50%	1.5776935994625092
Resnet50	73.00%	1.343787044286728
MobileNetV2	65.00%	3.12111222743988
Xception	59.50%	3.3177728176116945

Fig. 3. Pre-trained CNN Models for Character Recognition [8]

3.5 Translation Techniques

NMT using Transformer architectures will be utilized for translating Brahmi inscriptions. NMT employs artificial neural networks to learn the mappings between source and target languages, offering a significant improvement over traditional rule-based and statistical models [16]. Transformers, with their parallel processing and self-attention mechanisms, are particularly adept at capturing long-range dependencies and context, which are essential for accurately translating ancient scripts.

MarianMT is a suitable candidate for low-resource languages such as Early Brahmi. The model uses tokenized text inputs, where each subword unit is represented by a unique numerical ID from the vocabulary. Trained on a parallel corpus of text pairs, MarianMT learns the grammatical structures of both languages through exposure to parallel data. For this project, a pre-trained MarianMT model will be fine-tuned on the Brahmi-English parallel corpus, which includes sentence pairs from Early Brahmi inscriptions [12].

3.6 Continual Learning

For continual learning, Regularization-based approach and Replay-based approach were considered since these methods allow the model to incrementally learn from new data while preserving accuracy and knowledge from previous translations, without adding unnecessary computational complexity [17].

Regularization-Based Methods. Regularization-based methods aim to prevent significant changes to the model's critical parameters when learning new tasks. This can be categorized into two subtypes: weight regularization and function regularization.

- **Weight Regularization**: This method penalizes substantial updates to the network's parameters (weights) that were vital for previously learned tasks, helping the model retain prior knowledge. Techniques like EWC and Synaptic Intelligence (SI) will be applied to stabilize the model's weights during training [17].
- **Function Regularization (Knowledge Distillation):** Here, the goal is to regulate the output of the model's prediction function. This is commonly achieved through knowledge distillation, where a previously trained model (the "teacher") guides the

training of the current model (the "student"). This ensures that the student model's predictions on older tasks mimic those of the teacher, thereby reducing the risk of catastrophic forgetting. We plan to use Learning without Forgetting (LwF) for this purpose [17].

Replay-Based Methods. Replay-based methods help the model retain prior knowledge by reusing previously encountered data. This can be achieved either by storing a subset of past data or by generating it through generative models [17].

- **Experience Replay**: A memory buffer will store a subset of data from previous tasks. During training, examples from this buffer will be randomly selected and included in the training batches alongside new task data. This method can be further enhanced by combining experience replay with knowledge distillation, where the predictions of the old model act as additional guidance for the new model [17].

Proposed Continual Learning Approach. To enhance the continual learning capabilities, a hybrid approach combining both regularization-based and replay- based methods is proposed. This method aims to leverage the strengths of both strategies, minimizing catastrophic forgetting by retaining prior knowledge through replay and stabilizing the model's weights via regularization. Two main strategies will be considered: sequential and concurrent application.

Sequential Approach: In this two-phase method:

- **Phase 1**: The NMT model is first trained using the replay-based method (Experience Replay). This establishes a solid foundation, allowing the model to revisit older inscription samples and retain previously learned knowledge.
- **Phase 2**: Once the baseline is established with replay, a regularization-based method (LwF or EWC) is introduced. This fine-tuning phase further stabilizes the model's parameters while continuing the replay process, adding extra protection against catastrophic forgetting.

Concurrent Approach. In this strategy, replay and regularization methods are integrated into a single loss function, which consists of three key components:

- **NMT Loss**: The standard loss (cross-entropy) for the model's performance on the current task.
- **Replay Loss:** A loss term based on the model's performance on replayed data from previous tasks, helping the model retain old knowledge.
- **Regularization Loss**: A penalty to restrict significant changes in the model's parameters, preserving performance on past tasks. This regularization loss could be derived from techniques such as LwF or EWC.

The final loss function will be a weighted sum of these three components as represented in Eq. (1).

$$\text{Total Loss} = \alpha * \text{NMT\_Loss} + \beta * \text{Replay\_Loss} + \gamma * \text{Regularization\_Loss} \quad (1)$$

Where α, β, and γ are hyperparameters that control the weighting of each loss term. These hyperparameters will be carefully tuned to strike the right balance between performance on the current task, replay accuracy, and model stability. The choice between the sequential and concurrent approaches will depend on their performance on a held-out validation set, balancing both translation accuracy and computational efficiency.

4 Continual Learning Pipeline

The continual learning pipeline integrates active learning, adoptive thresholding, scheduled retraining to progressively improve the model's performance over time.

4.1 Translation Prediction Confidence Estimation

Monte Carlo Dropout will be employed to estimate the model's uncertainty by using the stochastic nature of dropout during both training and inference. Multiple forward passes through the network, each applying dropout, will produce an ensemble of predictions. The variance in these predictions will serve as an uncertainty metric, where a higher variance signifies lower confidence in the model's output. The average probability of the top predicted translation across these runs will be used as the confidence score [17].

Post-prediction, the confidence score will be compared against a dynamically adjusted threshold. This adaptive threshold will be updated continuously based on model performance and the annotation workload, using the mechanisms described below.

4.2 Adaptive Thresholding Strategy

The adaptive threshold evolves over time to balance model performance with the annotation workload.

1. Initial Threshold: A low initial threshold will be set to allow the model to learn quickly by accepting more data in the early stages of training.
2. Performance-Based Adjustment: The model's high-confidence predictions will be evaluated using metrics such as the BLEU score, aiming for a target accuracy rate. If the model consistently exceeds this accuracy, the threshold will be incrementally increased. Exponential smoothing will be applied to these threshold adjustments to prevent rapid oscillations, with the smoothing factor being fine-tuned during experimentation.
3. Annotation Rate Adjustment: The system will monitor the size of the annotation queue, with a target size based on the capacity of available annotators. If the queue size consistently exceeds the target for more than three cycles, the threshold will be lowered. If the queue size stays below the target for three cycles, the threshold will be increased. Exponential smoothing will also be applied here to stabilize adjustments.
4. Combined Adjustment: The final threshold adjustment will be a weighted average of both performance-based and annotation rate adjustments represented in Eq. (2)

$$\text{New\_Threshold} = \alpha^{*}\ \text{Performance\_Adjustment} + (1-\alpha)^{*}\ \text{Annotation\_Rate\_Adjustment} + \text{Current\_Threshold} \quad (2)$$

Where α is a weighting factor ($0 \leq \alpha \leq 1$) that balances the importance of performance and annotation rate. This combined approach aims to optimize both model accuracy and annotation efficiency.

5. Threshold Management and Evaluation: Minimum and maximum bounds will be set to ensure that the threshold remains within safe limits. Continuous monitoring of the threshold's performance will be implemented, and parameters such as the initial threshold, smoothing factor, target accuracy, target queue size, weight α, and bounds will be tuned based on observations and experimental results.

4.3 Admin Review and Data Storage

Translations that fall below the confidence threshold will be flagged for admin review. Human experts will review these flagged translations, correct any errors, and provide accurate translations. A user-friendly interface will facilitate efficient annotation.

4.4 Scheduled Updates

To keep the model up-to-date with newly annotated data, a scheduled retraining job will be implemented. This job will periodically retrieve newly annotated translations and update the model. The retraining process will include the following steps:

- Loading the existing model from local storage.
- Retrieving new annotations from the database, with a limit on the number of samples for each retraining session.
- Preprocessing the new data to ensure it is in the correct format for training.
- Incrementally training the model using a continual learning method (experience replay or LwF). This will be implemented using deep learning frameworks such as TensorFlow or PyTorch, both of which are easily installable and adaptable for continual learning tasks.
- Evaluating the retrained model using BLEU score metrics on a validation dataset to ensure it meets performance standards.
- Saving the retrained model to local storage, maintaining a version history of each retraining iteration.
- Logging the retraining process and its evaluation results for tracking model improvements and identifying potential issues.

5 Evaluation

The evaluation of the system will focus on both character recognition and translation models, using key metrics to assess performance and ensure continual improvement.

5.1 YOLOv11 Hyperparameter Tuning and Performance

Hyperparameter tuning significantly improved YOLOv11's performance. Training on an isolated dataset initially achieved a mAP@50 of 85.1%, which increased to 93.7% when a mixed synthetic-real dataset was used. Lowering the learning rate to 0.001 further enhanced performance to a peak mAP@50 of 95.2%. Increasing batch size and training duration caused a slight decline to 94.1%, indicating a trade-off between training stability and generalization. The following Table 1 shows the hyperparameter tuning done on the model.

Table 1. Hyperparameter Tuning

Description	Model	Epochs	Learning Rate	Batch Size	mAP @50	mAP@50:95
YOLOv11 - isolated character dataset	YOLOv11	50	0.01	16	81.5%	81.5%
YOLOv11 - mixed synthetic-real dataset	YOLOv11	50	0.01	16	93.7%	79.2%
Optimal learning rate (low LR, convergence)	YOLOv11	50	0.001	16	95.2%	82.5%
optimal batch size (higher batch)	YOLOv11	75	0.001	32	92.8%	78.9%

Precision-Recall analysis in Fig. 4 revealed variability across classes, with some characters being detected more accurately than others, likely due to class imbalance and visual similarity. The confusion matrix in Fig. 5 confirmed these trends, highlighting misclassifications among visually similar characters and the influence of dataset imbalance.

Training and validation loss trends showed effective bounding box and classification learning, though validation loss fluctuations suggested some overfitting as seen in Fig. 6.

Overall, YOLOv11's integrated detection and classification capability makes it more suitable than a conventional CNN model like EfficientNetB0, which requires separate segmentation, for an end-to-end character recognition pipeline.

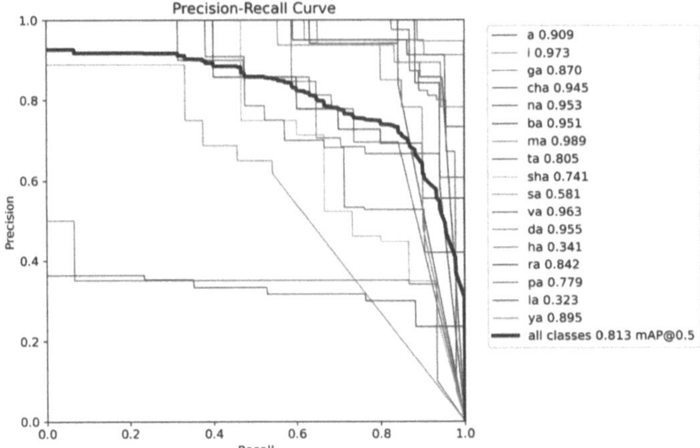

Fig. 4. Precision-Recall Curve

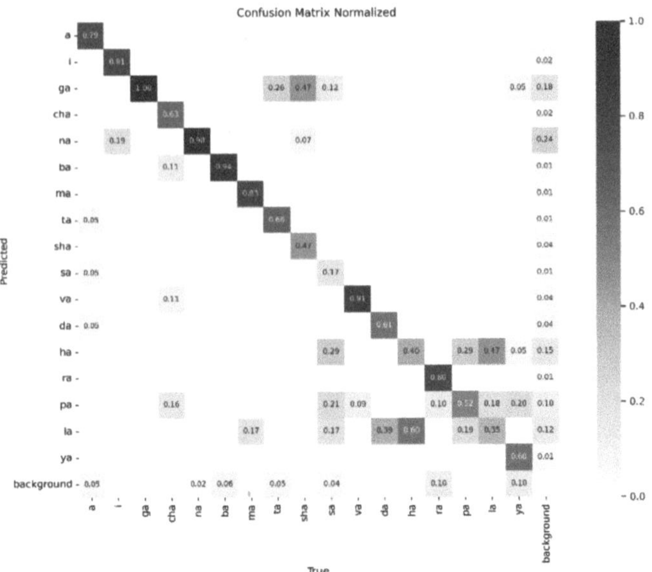

Fig. 5. Normalized Confusion Matrix

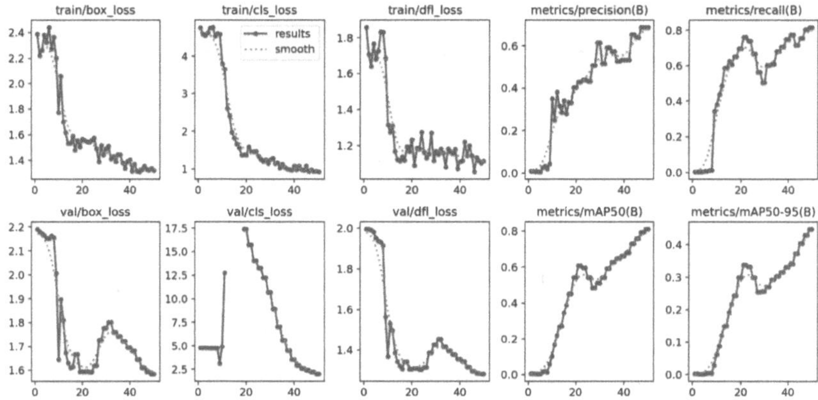

Fig. 6. YOLO Training Results

5.2 Transformer-Based NMT Translation Model

The mBART-large-50 model was evaluated through successive training and retraining cycles. A sample of the testing dataset can be seen in Fig. 7. Initial training yielded a BLEU score of 70.43, which improved to 81.04 after continual fine-tuning, indicating enhanced translation accuracy and fluency. These results can be seen in Fig. 8. The progressive increase in chrF scores further supports the model's improved morphological and character-level performance.

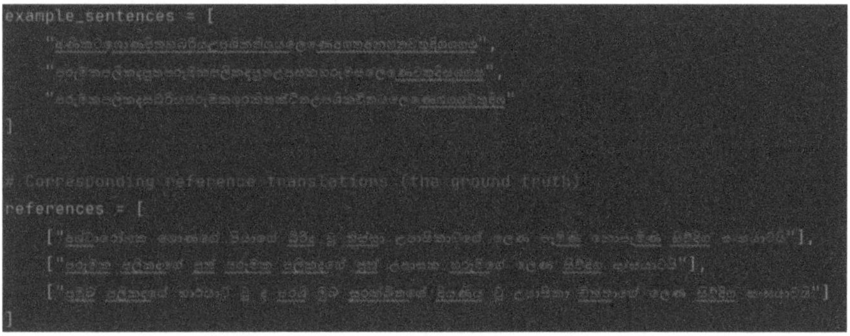

```
example_sentences = [
    "[illegible]",
    "[illegible]",
    "[illegible]"
]

# Corresponding reference translations (the ground truth)
references = [
    ["[illegible]"],
    ["[illegible]"],
    ["[illegible]"]
]
```

Fig. 7. Sample sentences and references

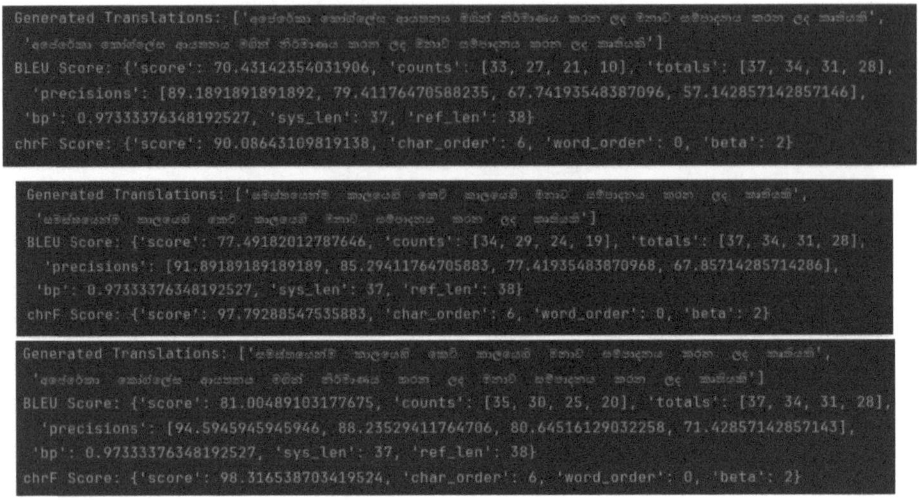

```
Generated Translations: ['[illegible]',
 '[illegible]']
BLEU Score: {'score': 70.43142354031906, 'counts': [33, 27, 21, 10], 'totals': [37, 34, 31, 28],
  'precisions': [89.1891891891892, 79.41176470588235, 67.74193548387096, 57.142857142857146],
 'bp': 0.9733376348192527, 'sys_len': 37, 'ref_len': 38}
chrF Score: {'score': 90.08643109819138, 'char_order': 6, 'word_order': 0, 'beta': 2}
```

```
Generated Translations: ['[illegible]',
 '[illegible]']
BLEU Score: {'score': 77.49182012787646, 'counts': [34, 29, 24, 19], 'totals': [37, 34, 31, 28],
  'precisions': [91.89189189189189, 85.29411764705883, 77.41935483870968, 67.85714285714286],
 'bp': 0.9733376348192527, 'sys_len': 37, 'ref_len': 38}
chrF Score: {'score': 97.79288547535883, 'char_order': 6, 'word_order': 0, 'beta': 2}
```

```
Generated Translations: ['[illegible]',
 '[illegible]']
BLEU Score: {'score': 81.00489103177675, 'counts': [35, 30, 25, 20], 'totals': [37, 34, 31, 28],
  'precisions': [94.5945945945946, 88.23529411764706, 80.64516129032258, 71.42857142857143],
 'bp': 0.9733376348192527, 'sys_len': 37, 'ref_len': 38}
chrF Score: {'score': 98.316538703419524, 'char_order': 6, 'word_order': 0, 'beta': 2}
```

Fig. 8. Translation Results

6 Evaluation

The evaluation combined expert review and user feedback to assess the system's technical soundness and practical applicability. Archaeologists, engineers, and academics highlighted the significance of automating Early Brahmi inscription analysis, recognizing the integration of character recognition, translation, and continual learning as a novel contribution. The system was praised for its well-defined scope and relevance to the Sri Lankan historical context. Key suggestions included conducting comparative studies with existing methods, improving robustness against severely degraded inscriptions, and optimizing inference speed for real-time applications. Experts also noted the absence of an inscription validation mechanism and recommended hyperparameter tuning and testing on larger, more diverse datasets to enhance accuracy.

7 Conclusion and Future Work

This paper presents a novel approach to recognizing and translating Early Brahmi inscriptions using deep learning and continual learning techniques. The system integrates advanced image preprocessing methods to improve character recognition accuracy and employs a continual learning mechanism for the translation model, combining regularization-based and replay-based methods. An adaptive thresholding strategy enhances translation prediction confidence, ensuring reliable model performance over time.

Future work will explore expanding this framework to other ancient Sri Lankan languages and eras by incorporating additional datasets.

Acknowledgments. Special thanks to Mr. Anuradha Piyadasa from the Department of Archaeology for his support in data collection. I would also like to express my gratitude to my mentor,

Mr. Pumudu Fernando, for his invaluable guidance throughout the project. Additionally, I would like to thank everyone who has provided support during the course of this work.

Disclosure of Interests. The authors have no competing interests to declare that are relevant to the content of this article.

References

1. Bandara, W.A.E.C.: An analytical study based on oldest archaeological factors regarding the birth of the Brahmi script. Ancient Ceylon, Journal of the Department of Archaeology, Sri Lanka 27, 17 (2021)
2. Cao, Y., et al.: Continual learning for neural machine translation. In: Proceedings of the 2021 Conference of the North American Chapter of the Association for Computational Linguistics: Human Language Technologies (NAACL 2021), pp. 3964–3974. Association for Computational Linguistics, Online (2021). https://doi.org/10.18653/v1/2021.naacl-main.310
3. Priya, R.D., et al.: Self-adaptive hybridized lion optimization algorithm with transfer learning for ancient Tamil character recognition in stone inscriptions. IEEE Access. **11**, 39621–39634 (2023). https://doi.org/10.1109/ACCESS.2023.3268545
4. Dhivya, S., Beulah, J.R.: Ancient Tamil character recognition from stone inscriptions – a theoretical analysis. In: 2022 2nd Asian Conference on Innovation in Technology (ASIANCON), pp. 1–8. IEEE, Ravet, India (2022). https://doi.org/10.1109/ASIANCON55314.2022.9908951
5. Gunasekara, S., et al.: Deep learning-powered mobile app for early Brahmi script decipherment in Sri Lanka. In: 2024 International Research Conference on Smart Computing and Systems Engineering (SCSE), pp. 1–6. IEEE, Colombo, Sri Lanka (2024). https://doi.org/10.1109/SCSE61872.2024.10550734
6. Heenkenda, S., Fernando, T.G.I.: Approaches used to recognize and decipher ancient inscriptions: a review. Vidyodaya J. Sci. **23**(2), 42–55 (2020). https://doi.org/10.31357/vjs.v23i02.4792
7. Hettiarachchi, N., Pathiraja, I., Madawala, D.: Translation of Brahmi inscriptions to Sinhala using natural language processing. Int. J. Comput. Appl. **177**(30), 19–25 (2020). https://doi.org/10.5120/ijca2020919776
8. Huang, K., et al.: Knowledge transfer in incremental learning for multilingual neural machine translation. In: Proceedings of the 61st Annual Meeting of the Association for Computational Linguistics (Vol 1: Long Papers), pp. 15286–15304. Association for Computational Linguistics, Toronto, Canada (2023). https://doi.org/10.18653/v1/2023.acl-long.852
9. Karunarathne, K., et al.: Recognizing ancient Sinhala inscription characters using neural network technologies. Int. J. Sci. Eng. Appl. Sci. (IJSEAS). **3**, 37–49 (2017)
10. Kurapati, M.P., et al.: A review: text extraction from stone inscriptions and translating to modern language. In: 2023 Second International Conference on Electronics and Renewable Systems (ICEARS), Tuticorin India, pp. 1515–1519. IEEE (2023). https://doi.org/10.1109/ICEARS56392.2023.10085645
11. Mahata, S.K., et al.: Simplification of English and Bengali sentences for improving quality of machine translation. Neural. Process. Lett. **54**(4), 3115–3139 (2022). https://doi.org/10.1007/s11063-022-10755-3
12. Miguel, D., et al.: A user study of the incremental learning in NMT. In: Proceedings of the 22nd Annual Conference of the European Association for Machine Translation, pp. 319–328. European Association for Machine Translation, Lisboa, Portugal (2020)

13. Wijerathna, K.A.S.A.N., et al.: Recognition and translation of ancient Brahmi letters using deep learning and NLP. In: 2019 International Conference on Advancements in Computing (ICAC), Malabe Sri Lanka, pp. 226–231. IEEE (2019). https://doi.org/10.1109/ICAC49085.2019.9103340
14. Pabasara, S., Kokul, T.: Period prediction of Sinhala epigraphical scripts using convolutional neural networks. In: 2021 21st International Conference on Advances in ICT for Emerging Regions (ICTer), Colombo, Sri Lanka, pp. 141–146. IEEE (2021). https://doi.org/10.1109/ICTer53630.2021.9774806
15. Preethi, P., Mamatha, H.R.: Intelligent recognition of ancient Brahmi characters using transfer learning. In: 2023 Third International Conference on Advances in Electrical, Computing, Communication and Sustainable Technologies (ICAECT), Bhilai, India, pp. 1–6. IEEE (2023). https://doi.org/10.1109/ICAECT57570.2023.10118090
16. Rajnish, P., et al.: Improving the quality and readability of ancient Brahmi stone inscriptions. In: 2023 2nd International Conference for Innovation in Technology (INOCON), Bangalore, India, pp. 1–8. IEEE (2023)
17. Resta, M., Bacciu, D.: Continual incremental language learning for neural machine translation. In: ESANN 2022 Proceedings, Bruges, Belgium, pp. 85–90. Ciaco – i6doc.com (2022). https://doi.org/10.14428/esann/2022.ES2022-80
18. Santoso, R., Suprapto, Y.K., Yuniarno, E.M.: Kawi character recognition on copper inscription using YOLO object detection. In: 2020 International Conference on Computer Engineering, Network, and Intelligent Multimedia (CENIM), Surabaya, Indonesia, pp. 343–348. IEEE (2020). https://doi.org/10.1109/CENIM51130.2020.9297873
19. Surasinghe, P.: Ceylon epigraphy periods. Kaggle Dataset (2023). https://www.kaggle.com/datasets/pabasar/ceylon-epigraphy-periods
20. Wang, L., et al.: A comprehensive survey of continual learning: Theory, method and application. (2023). arXiv preprint https://arxiv.org/abs/2302.00487

Creating Digital Estampages of Sri Lankan Stone Inscriptions Using Multispectral Imaging

M. W. M. B. De Silva(✉), M. S. Kariyawasam, A. J. U. Dakshika, Kasun Gunawardana, and Tharindu Wijethilake

University of Colombo School of Computing, Colombo, Sri Lanka
binuridesilva27@gmail.com, {kgg,tnb}@ucsc.cmb.ac.lk

Abstract. Stone inscriptions are of immense historical and cultural importance, but are progressively becoming illegible due to natural weathering, erosion and vandalism. This paper presents a novel approach to enhance the readability of stone inscriptions using multispectral imaging. Traditional methods such as estampages are weather-dependent and prone to human error. The proposed multispectral imaging-based system combines advanced techniques such as spectral enhancement based on KubelkaMunk theory, multispectral band selection, and deep learningbased preprocessing models (U-Net, ResNet) to significantly improve legibility, providing a non-invasive and efficient method for documenting and preserving ancient inscriptions. Results demonstrate that our U-Netbased preprocessing pipeline achieved a peak PSNR (Peak Signal-to-Noise Ratio) of 15.33 dB and reduced FID (Fréchet Inception Distance) to 518, while expert evaluation showed a 58.7% preference for digital estampages over traditional methods. This demonstrate the system's potential for integration into existing archaeological workflows, improving both accuracy and time efficiency in inscription documentation.

Keywords: multispectral imaging · epigraphy · stone inscriptions · digital estampages · archaeology · archaeological documentation

1 Introduction

Stone inscriptions represent one of humanity's oldest and most durable forms of historical documentation. These inscriptions provide invaluable insights into ancient civilizations, offering direct evidence of their cultural traditions, spiritual beliefs, and governance systems. As primary sources, they serve as critical tools for archaeologists, historians, and epigraphers in reconstructing the socio-political and religious frameworks of past societies [1,2]. They date back to over 2,000 years and are often found in locations such as caves, rock faces, and temples [3,4]. However, many of these inscriptions have become increasingly difficult to read and interpret due to natural factors such as weathering, erosion, and biological growth (e.g., moss, algae), as well as human-induced damage from vandalism

R. N. Rajapakse et al. (Eds.): ICTer 2025, CCIS 2844, pp. 185–199, 2026.
https://doi.org/10.1007/978-981-92-0137-2_13

and tourism. Over time, these factors have resulted in the gradual fading and degradation of the inscriptions, making them almost illegible in some cases [9]. As a result, there is an urgent need for effective methods to preserve and enhance the legibility of these invaluable cultural artifacts.

Traditional methods, such as creating estampages using paper rubbings [5], have long been used for documenting stone inscriptions. This technique involves applying paper over the inscription and rubbing it with ink to capture the imprint [6]. While this method has been effective in some cases, it has significant limitations. Estampages are weather-dependent and can be time-consuming, as they require dry, stable conditions to produce accurate imprints [7]. Furthermore, this process is highly dependent on the skill of the practitioner, leading to inconsistencies in the quality of the imprints. Additionally, this method often requires the physical presence of a skilled practitioner at the site, which may not be feasible in remote or difficult-to-access locations.

Moreover, many of the stone inscriptions are located in harsh environments that pose additional challenges for traditional documentation methods. Inscriptions found in caves, on cliff faces, or in dense forests can be difficult to reach, and traditional methods require not only specific weather conditions but also the presence of trained experts to execute them [8] [9]. In such environments, manual transcription methods like estampages become impractical and inefficient. Furthermore, the risk of further damage to these inscriptions through direct contact makes traditional methods less desirable.

With these challenges in mind, there is a clear need for an alternative, non-invasive method of improving the readability of these inscriptions. Multispectral imaging (MSI) is a promising technology that captures images across multiple wavelengths, including ultraviolet, visible, and infrared light [10]. These spectral bands highlight different aspects of the inscription that are often invisible under normal conditions, such as faded or obscured text [13]. By utilizing multispectral imaging, researchers can enhance the contrast between the inscriptions and their surroundings, making previously illegible text visible again without any physical contact or risk of damage. Multispectral imaging has already shown great promise in various applications of cultural heritage preservation, particularly for revealing hidden details on ancient manuscripts and inscriptions [12,13].

This paper: (i) proposes a unified MSI-based digital-estampage pipeline (image correction, adaptive binarization, morphological refinement, edge extraction, and spectral pigmentation masking guided by KubelkaMunk reflectance modeling); (ii) compares camera modalities and justifies the use of a MicaSense RedEdge-MX for five narrow bands; (iii) evaluates three learning-based preprocessors (EncoderDecoder CNN, ResNet, U-Net) and selects U-Net based on PSNR/FID; and (iv) conducts a mixed evaluationmodel-centric metrics and a user study with 9 experts, showing a 58.7% preference for digital estampages and significant ratings for usefulness, time efficiency, and workflow integration. The novelty of the work lies in the integration of physics-guided spectral masking (Kubelka-Munk) with a documented, end-to-end MSI pipeline and a domain-expert evaluation tailored to epigraphy, which has not been addressed in prior studies.

2 Literature Review

Literature was mainly studied under 3 main categories which are feature extraction, edge detection and extraction, and the use of spectral imaging in the field of archaeology and epigraphy.

2.1 Feature Extraction

A key challenge in digital epigraphy is the accurate extraction of features from historical texts, which often appear degraded due to weathering and biological growth. Several feature extraction methods have been employed to improve the clarity of stone inscriptions:

- **Geometric Approaches**: These methods focus on the geometric properties of the inscriptions, such as shapes, strokes, and patterns, to aid in character recognition [14]. Researchers have shown that these techniques can achieve up to 84% accuracy in character recognition when using machine learning algorithms, including backpropagation neural networks [15].
- **Scale-Invariant Feature Transform (SIFT)**: SIFT has been applied to identify keypoints in inscriptions. This technique is highly effective at detecting distinctive features, regardless of scale or orientation, making it useful for inscriptions with distorted or varying fonts [16].
- **Dimensionality Reduction**: Image pre-processing techniques, such as PCA (Principal Component Analysis), have been employed to reduce the complexity of the feature space before applying recognition algorithms. These techniques help isolate meaningful features while suppressing noise introduced by the stone surface's natural variations [17].

2.2 Edge Detection and Extraction

Edge detection plays a crucial role in identifying the boundaries of inscriptions. Without accurate edge detection, the quality of the final digital estampage can suffer. Different edge detection methods have been evaluated for this purpose.

- **Block-based Processing**: This technique divides the image into smaller blocks based on character shapes. By reducing the influence of surrounding pixels, it helps avoid the loss of important features due to averaging effects across the entire image [18].
- **Sobel Edge Detector**: The Sobel operator has been widely used for edge detection in historical inscriptions. It is effective in detecting large intensity changes, which are often seen at the boundaries of text on stone surfaces [19].

2.3 Use of Spectral Imaging

Multispectral imaging has revolutionized the way historical inscriptions are documented and analyzed. Images are captured using multiple spectral bands (UV, visible, NIR), each revealing different characteristics of the inscription surface.

- **X-ray Fluorescence Imaging**: XRF has been used to study the chemical composition of inscriptions, providing insights into their provenance and material characteristics. While this method does not use traditional multispectral imaging, it highlights the potential of image-based spectral analysis to reveal hidden or obscured epigraphic data [20].
- **Multispectral imaging for Enhancing Text Legibility**: Bearman and Spiro's work [21] demonstrated that multispectral imaging could reveal faint writing on both soft and hard media, especially where the ink and background were indistinguishable under normal lighting. By capturing multiple narrow-band images across different wavelengths (from UV to NIR), the system was able to enhance the legibility of inscriptions that were otherwise difficult to read. This approach directly informs the methods used in the current study, applying spectral bands to enhance the contrast between inscription and stone background.
- **Multispectral Imaging for Historical Artifacts**: Studies have shown that multispectral imaging can highlight surface anomalies like salt deposits, biofilms, and other patterns that can obscure inscriptions. Using spectral enhancement techniques, multispectral imaging has been proven effective in revealing faded carvings or ink traces invisible to the naked eye [22].

2.4 Recent Developments

Cultural-heritage MSI now benefits from standardized capture/processing workflows that demonstrably improve legibility and reproducibility [13], low-cost multi-band pipelines for stone surfaces [24], and new readability quantification approaches beyond visual assessment [11]. Inscriptions obscured by corrosion or weathering have been revealed using non-contact MSI variants [23].

2.5 Research Gap

Prior work addresses pieces of the problem like spectral capture and enhancement, edge/feature extraction, OCR, or GIS mapping but does not offer a unified, low-cost, non-contact workflow for producing digital estampages of stone inscriptions and validating them with domain experts. In particular, spectral-index-based pigment suppression and documented, field-usable pipelines with mixed quantitative/qualitative evaluation remain under-reported. The study fills this gap by integrating MSI capture, physics-guided spectral masking, learning-based preprocessing, and expert evaluation.

3 Proposed Approach

The overall approach of this study is experimental, with a focus on creating a reliable adaptive preprocessing model capable of enhancing faint or eroded textual content from multispectral imaging data. Given the unpredictable nature of the condition of inscriptions, several configurations of image processing techniques were tested to identify the most effective methods. The experimental setup allowed iterative refinement of the techniques, ensuring that the developed model is adaptable to various inscription types and environmental conditions.

3.1 Comparison on Camera Types

The purpose of the camera comparison was to identify the most suitable imaging device for capturing stone inscriptions with maximum clarity and readability. By evaluating DSLR and multispectral camera outputs using metrics mentioned below, we aimed to objectively assess image quality and determine the optimal camera type for accurate inscription analysis.
Signal-to-Noise Ratio (SNR): Measures the ratio between useful signal (engraving detail) and background noise. Higher SNR indicates cleaner images with less interference, essential for inscriptions where fine details are often faint or eroded [10].
Edge Density: Refers to the number of edges (detected transitions in intensity) per unit area. Higher edge density means more fine structural details are captured, which is critical for distinguishing carved strokes from background stone texture [18].
Edge Sharpness: Quantifies how distinctly edges are represented. High sharpness means inscription boundaries are crisp and well-defined, making it easier for both algorithms and human experts to interpret degraded characters [13].
Contrast-to-Noise Ratio (CNR): Evaluates how well the inscription stands out from the stone background relative to noise. A higher CNR means inscriptions appear more distinguishable from the surface texture, improving readability under varied lighting [20].

Table 1. Camera specifications and performance metrics

Camera Type	Specs	SNR (dB)	Edge Density	Edge Sharpness	CNR
DSLR Camera (Sony A7iii)	24.2MP back-illuminated sensor; ISO 50–204,800; 10fps shutter with AE/AF tracking	11.22	0.0314	43.48	0.27
Multi-spectral Camera	Five narrow spectral bands; high resolution (8 cm/pixel at 400 ft); images with geotags	14.34	0.0945	63.19	0.34

The study compares 2 different camera types, DSLR camera and a multi spectrum camera (Table 1). The multispectral camera provided significantly higher edge sharpness, greater edge density, and much better contrast-to-noise ratio. These metrics indicated that the multispectral camera captures finer details and clearer text, making it the most suitable choice for this research.

3.2 Data Collection Method

Data was collected through field visits to archaeological sites and the Colombo National Museum in Sri Lanka using a MicaSense RedEdge-MX multispectral camera. The camera captures five narrow bands (Blue, Green, Red, Red Edge, and Near-Infrared) at a resolution of 1280 × 960 pixels per band with a global shutter.

A total of 200 images were obtained under both natural daylight. These images varied in file size (35 MB per band) but consistently preserved fine inscription details. From this dataset, 160 images were used for training, 20 for validation, and 20 for testing.

3.3 Proposed Preprocessing and Pigment Removal Approach

To improve the readability of inscriptions in the raw captures, the approach targets the dominant degradations observed in the field and museum settings: (i) inter-band misregistration caused by the multi-lens geometry of the sensor, (ii) perspective/skew from hand-held capture and uneven stone planes, (iii) uneven illumination and cast shadows, and (iv) shallow or eroded engravings with weak edges relative to the substrate. The pipeline is designed to neutralize these error sources before spectral masking and learning-based enhancement. Among the spectral bands, the green band was selected for preprocessing due to its superior contrast and readability, indicated by its highest standard deviation. The preprocessing pipeline includes skew correction, noise reduction, binarization, spectral enhancement, and edge detection.

Three deep learning models namely CNN-based encoder-decoder, ResNet, and U-Net were tested to optimize preprocessing. Model-selection rationale is comparing three models that balance capacity with our dataset size (n=200). EncoderDecoder CNN as a low-parameter baseline to estimate improvements achievable by learned mappings alone; ResNet-style preprocessor to test whether residual connections better preserve low-level edges and stabilize training on noisy textures; U-Net, an encoderdecoder with skip connections widely used for pixel-level restoration/segmentation, chosen for its ability to retain fine structure while denoising. PSNR(Peak Signal-to-Noise Ratio) and FID(Fréchet Inception Distance) were used as evaluation metrics to assess both the accuracy and the visual quality of the resulting pre-processed images (Table 2).

All models were trained on 200 images with the Adam optimizer (learning rate 1×10^{-3}), batch size = 16 and MSE loss; training ran up to 100 epochs with early stopping (patience = 10).

Table 2. Performance of deep learning models

Model	Average PSNR (dB)	FID
EncoderDecoder	12.56	275.04
ResNet	13.94	129.83
U-Net	14.26	147.34

U-Net was chosen for its superior performance in preserving inscription details, achieving the highest PSNR and lowest FID. The best U-Net checkpoint occurred at epoch 75 (PSNR = 14.26 dB; FID = 147.34). EncoderDecoder CNN and ResNet baselines were trained with the same regime;

To address pigment interference in the images, green and NIR bands were used to identify and mask pigmented regions based on their distinct reflectance characteristics. The Kubelka-Munk theory guides this spectral analysis. Applying the resulting pigment mask to the preprocessed output allowed the system to isolate and enhance only the engraved inscription features (Fig. 1).

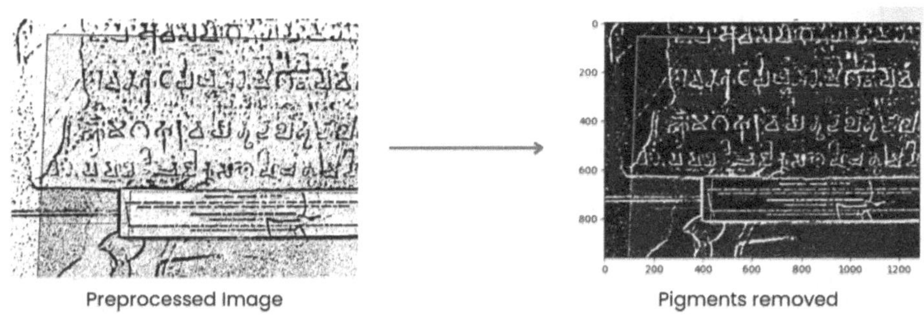

Fig. 1. Final Output

To assess component contributions, we disabled one stage at a time and inspected outputs alongside PSNR/FID trends:

- No skew correction: increased mis-aligned strokes and fragmented contours on slanted lines.
- No Sauvola (global threshold only): loss of faint strokes under uneven illumination; background bleed-through.
- No morphological closing: broken letters and gaps persisted after binarization.
- No spectral pigmentation mask: residual pigment/biological texture reduces stroke contrast;

These observations support the final pipeline configuration used for U-Net preprocessing and downstream expert evaluation.

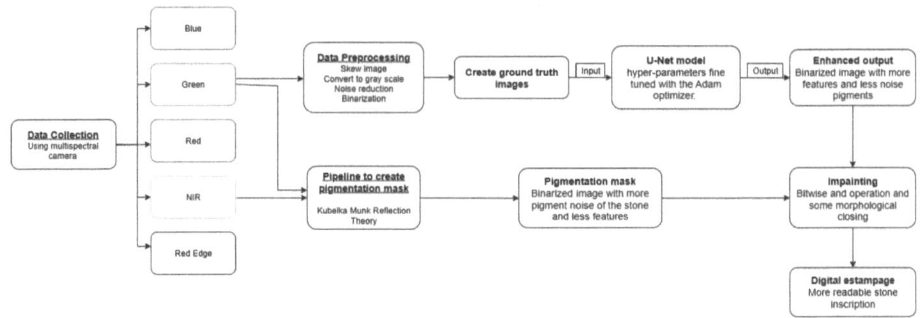

Fig. 2. Proposed multispectral imaging and estampage pipeline

The complete workflow of the proposed system is summarized in Fig. 2. It illustrates how multispectral bands are preprocessed, enhanced using U-Net, and refined with spectral pigmentation masking and inpainting to generate a final digital estampage.

4 Evaluation and Results

The evaluation process was carried out using two distinct methods to ensure a comprehensive and reliable assessment of the outcomes. The first method involved evaluating the model, where the system's performance was tested against a set of ground truth images to determine its accuracy and efficiency. This form of evaluation focused on quantitative results and technical performance. The second method was expert evaluation, where domain experts reviewed the system based on their professional knowledge and experience. This semi-qualitative evaluation provided valuable insights into usability, relevance, and practical application of the system in real-world scenarios.

4.1 Model Evaluation

Model evaluation was conducted using the test set, consisting of green band input images and their corresponding preprocessed ground truth images from Sri Lankan stone inscriptions. Out of the 200 total images, 20 images are used for the testing dataset.

The 75th epoch yielded the best performance, achieving a PSNR of 15.33 dB and the lowest FID score of 518 (Fig. 3).

4.2 Expert Evaluation

A group of 9 domain experts (archaeologists, academics and epigraphers) were used for the evaluation. Most of them had been working in the industry for more than 10 years (Fig. 4).

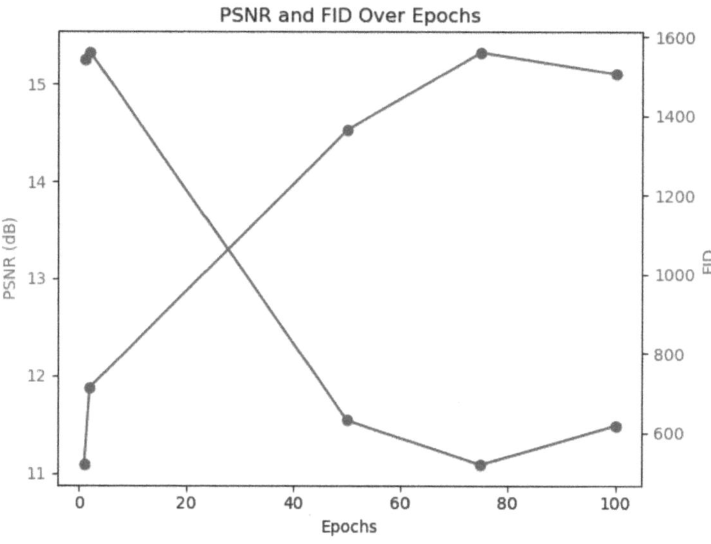

Fig. 3. PSNR-FID Ratio

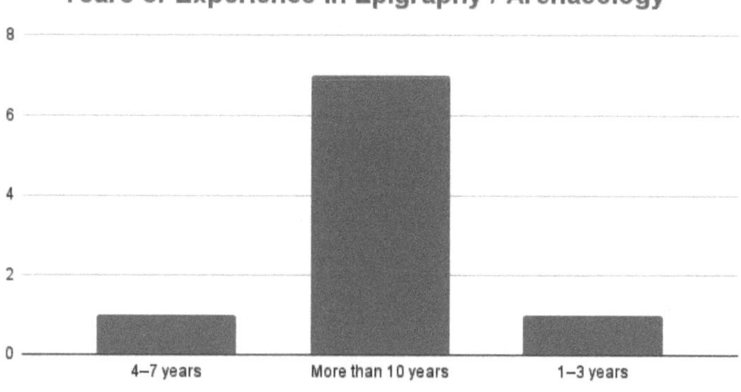

Fig. 4. Domain Experience of the Evaluators

We met with each expert in person to walk them through the complete proposed approach, ensuring they clearly understood the context and goals of the study. They completed a Google Form with 25 questions covering four complementary sections as participant demographics, an image-comparison, a Likert-scale questionnaire, and open-ended qualitative feedback.

As shown in Fig. 5, majority of the evaluators had experience in working with estampages.

In the Image-Comparison section, there were 7 sets of images to compare, where each expert was shown two unlabeled images of a traditional physical

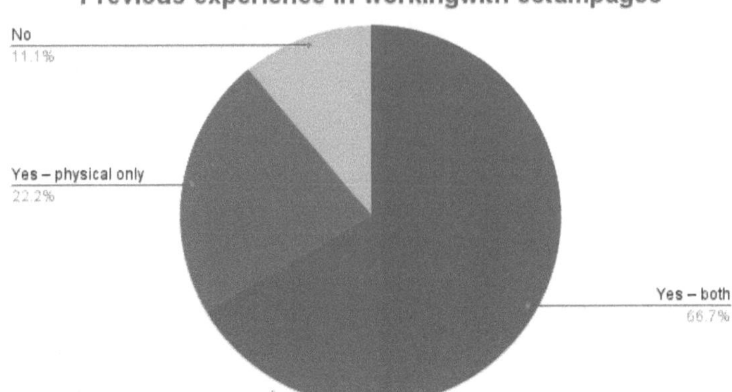

Fig. 5. Previous experience in working with estampages

estampage photograph and the corresponding digital estampage output from our approach, and asked to indicate which version appeared clearer and more suitable for reading and interpreting the inscription.

Table 3 shows the individual votes for the digital and traditional estampage readability. Some experts preferred digital estampages completely over traditional (Jethawanaramaya and King Kassapa IV and Siporuwatugama), while some preferred images of traditional estampages completely over digital (Ruwanwelisaya). Most of the comparisons had diverse selections for both digital and traditional estampages. Overall, the digital estampage acceptance rate stands at 58.73%, whereas the traditional estampages are accepted at 41.26%.

Table 3. Expert voting results across inscription sites

Site	Digital	Traditional	Total Votes	% Digital	% Traditional
Jethawanaramaya	9	0	9	100	0
Ruwanwelisaya	0	9	9	0	100
Nissankamalla	5	4	9	55.6	44.4
Siporuwatugama	9	0	9	100	0
Mayilagastohta	4	5	9	44.4	55.6
Colombo Museum	1	8	9	11.1	88.9
King Kassapa IV	9	0	9	100	0
Total	37	26	63	58.7	41.3

These experts also provided feedback on factors such as level of clarity, expression of features in the digital estampage, usefulness, trust, ease of integration, level of training and support needed to adopt, time efficiency compared to traditional approach, level of capacity to minimize errors, overall as a tool and recommendation for peers. This was taken as a semi-quantitative evaluation of expert perceptions, for a balanced assessment of both the technical and practical value of the proposed approach was undertaken. Each question was rated on a Likert scale from 1 to 5, where 5 indicates the most favorable response (Table 4).

Table 4. Expert evaluation of criteria significance

Criterion	Mean Score	t-statistic	p-value	Significance
Clarity	3.33	2.00	0.081	Not significant
Features	3.56	3.16	0.013	Significant
Usefulness	4.22	5.50	0.0006	Highly significant
Trust	3.56	3.16	0.013	Significant
Integration	4.22	5.50	0.0006	Highly significant
Training support	2.73	-1.15	0.138	Not significant
Time efficiency	4.67	7.07	0.0001	Highly significant
Minimize errors	3.63	1.93	0.095	Not significant
Overall tool	4.00	4.24	0.0028	Significant
Recommend	4.56	6.42	0.0002	Highly significant

Our thematic analysis of expert feedback revealed several key themes such as enhanced readability, complementarity between digital and physical estampages, efficiency gains, contextual appropriateness, trust and data-management concerns, and technical/ operational advice.

Participants frequently noted that increased contrast in processed images sharpened letter forms, confirming that multispectral enhancement supports clearer reading in the field. One participant stated, "When the background in the digital estampage is darker, the inscription characters stand out and are much easier to read with the naked eye." A few other notable highlighted remarks were In most cases, the digital estampages provided more legible text than the traditional physical estampages.", "I would definitely recommend this tool to colleagues if it becomes widely available", "We can get a great deal of use out of this tool if it is integrated into our workflow.".

One participant stated, "For some inscriptions, the digital approach works best; for others, the physical estampage still delivers clearer detail." This highlights that material condition and surface geometry might influence method effectiveness. Participants acknowledged that while digital methods improve overall readability, some characters remain unclear. A participant commented, "In certain digital images, some characters remain blurry, while other letters are perfectly crisp". The remark "Currently, we sometimes photograph a physical estampage and then tweak lighting and sharpness in Photoshop to read faint letters.", indicates that experts are already experimenting with digital tools.

A participant expressed, "Although the tool is promising, I worry about the long-term reliability of digital storage for these archival images." This concern emphasizes the need for robust data preservation strategies. Participants stressed the importance of user-friendly documentation. One noted, "We will need clear, non-technical documentation explaining how the model works before field archaeologists can trust it.

Suggestions such as "Let's record digital estampages alongside physical estampages during a field visit, then compare them systematically later.", "We should consider camera rotation, lighting angles, and timing to ensure the clearer captures are taken of the stone inscriptions.", "No formal training should be needed. If it's just a matter of snapping a photo and uploading, anyone can use it." were stated by the expert pool while they were evaluating the proposed digital estampage creation pipeline.

4.3 Key Findings

1. Quantitative imagecomparison user evaluation demonstrated a statistically significant preference for digital estampages over traditional estampages (58.7 % vs. 41.3%, z = 1.39, $p < 0.10$), confirming that multispectral imaging combined with imageprocessing pipeline improves inscription legibility.
2. The imageprocessing model achieved its highest visual fidelity at epoch 75 (PSNR = 15.33 dB, FID = 518) and showed stable loss convergence, indicating both effective learning and strong generalization to unseen data.
3. Experts rated the pipeline highly for usefulness, time efficiency, and ease of workflow integration (all $p < 0.05$) (Table 4), and expressed strong willingness to recommend it, demonstrating that archaeologists can adopt the system with tangible accuracy and efficiency gains.
4. Qualitative feedback revealed that, while digital estampages offer clear advantages, experts remain cautious about fully replacing physical estampages, viewing the two methods as complementary, especially for deeply carved or wellpreserved inscriptions.

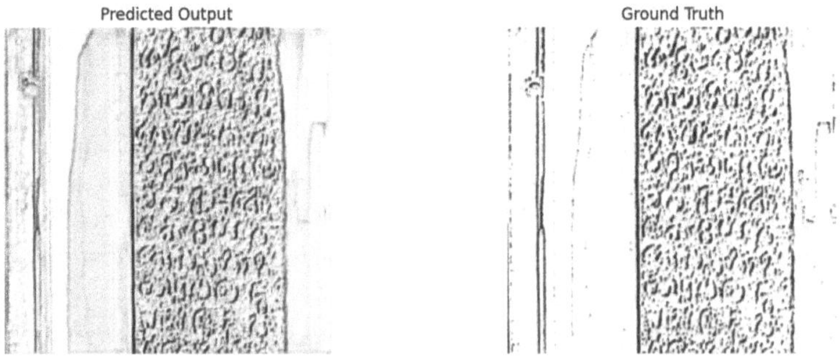

Fig. 6. Visual output results of the model

5. Visual comparisons (Fig. 6) shows that the model is able to preserve inscription structures and features almost similarly to the ground truth image. This shows the model's potential for pre-processing stone inscription images.
6. While results are encouraging, they are based on 200 images from Sri Lankan contexts and five bands; performance on severely weathered outdoor inscriptions and additional substrates will require larger, more diverse datasets and further validation.

5 Conclusion

This study has explored the use of multispectral imaging as a non-invasive, efficient, and reliable technique for enhancing the readability of stone inscriptions. The findings from both the quantitative analysis and expert evaluation demonstrate the significant advantages of multispectral imaging over traditional methods like estampages. Multispectral imaging offers enhanced legibility, greater time efficiency, and the potential for broader application in challenging field conditions, such as those often encountered in archaeological research. The research offers a promising alternative to traditional inscription documentation methods.

Future work will focus on integrating character segmentation and recognition of stone inscriptions using OCR and other techniques. Additionally, expanding the dataset including a diverse range of stone inscriptions in harsher field conditions will help assess the system's robustness and broader applicability. Integration with emerging technologies like 3D imaging or Light Detection and Ranging could further improve digital preservation.

Disclosure of Interests. The authors declare that they have no conflicts of interest relevant to this work.

References

1. Inscriptions.lk: Introduction to inscriptions (2024). https://www.inscriptions.lk. Accessed 15 Sep 2025
2. Khan, A., Vaidya, U.: Inscriptions: as a source of history. Vaichariki **8**(3), 195–197 (2018). https://ssrn.com/abstract=3509854. Accessed 15 Sep 2025
3. Senaratne, P.: Epigraphy and identity in ancient Sri Lanka. South Asian Stud. **29**(2), 123–136 (2013). https://doi.org/10.1080/02666030.2013.820470
4. Paranavitana, S.: Inscriptions of Ceylon, vol. I. Archaeological Survey of Ceylon, Colombo (1970)
5. Heenkenda, H.M.S.C.R., Fernando, T.G.I.: Approaches used to recognise and decipher ancient inscriptions: a review. Vidyodaya J. Sci. **23**(2), 81–92 (2020). https://doi.org/10.31357/vjs.v23i2.4954
6. Somadeva, R.: Reading inscription. YouTube (2021). https://www.youtube.com/watch?v=Lfin5rVqrKM. Accessed 2 Apr 2025
7. Ceylon Today: De-conspiring the inscription (2024). https://ceylontoday.lk/2024/02/17/de-conspiring-the-inscription. Accessed 15 Sep 2025

8. Ruwanmini, D.A.S., Liyanage, K.V., Karunarathne, K.G.N.D., Dias, G.K.A., Nandasara, S.T.: An architecture for an inscription recognition system for Sinhala epigraphy. Int. J. Res. - GRANTHAALAYAH **4**(12) (2016). https://doi.org/10.29121/granthaalayah.v4.i12.2016.2392
9. Karunarathne, K.G.N.D., Liyanage, K.V., Ruwanmini, D.A.S., Dias, G.K.A., Nandasara, S.T.: Recognizing ancient Sinhala inscription characters using neural network technologies.Int. J. Sci. Eng. Appl. Sci. (IJSEAS) **3**(1) (2017). https://ijseas.com/volume3/v3i1/ijseas20170104.pdf
10. Marcus, G.L., et al.: Assessing the potential of multispectral and thermal UAV imagery for archaeological prospection. J. Archaeol. Sci. Rep. **28**, 101115 (2020). https://doi.org/10.1016/j.jasrep.2019.102115
11. Mindermann, S.: Hyperspectral imaging for readability enhancement of historic manuscripts. Master's thesis, Technical University of Munich (2018). https://doi.org/10.13140/RG.2.2.23107.09761/1
12. Lettner, M., Sablatnig, R.: Multispectral imaging for analyzing ancient manuscripts. In: Proceedings of the 17th European Signal Processing Conference (EUSIPCO), Glasgow, UK (2009)
13. Jones, C., Terras, M., Duffy, C., Gibson, A.: Understanding multispectral imaging of cultural heritage: determining best practice in MSI analysis of historical artefacts. J. Cult. Heritage (Accepted, 2020). https://doi.org/10.1016/j.culher.2020.03.004
14. Gautam, N., Chai, S.S.: Optical character recognition for Brahmi script using geometric method. J. Telecommun. Electron. Comput. Eng. (JTEC) **9**(3–11), 15–20 (2017). Published online: Dec 7, 2017
15. Pohankar, P., Taralkar, N., Karmare, S., Kulkarni, S.: Character recognition using artificial neural network. Int. J. Electron. Commun. Comput. Eng. **5**(4), 248–252 (2014)
16. Rajakumar, S., Bharathi, V.S.: Century identification and recognition of ancient Tamil characters. Int. J. Comput. Appl. **26**(4), 1–5 (2011). https://doi.org/10.5120/3090-4237
17. Tomar, A., Choudhary, B., Yerpude, R.: Ancient Indian scripts image preprocessing and dimensionality reduction for feature extraction and classification. Int. J. Comput. Trends Technol. **24**(2), 87–92 (2015). https://doi.org/10.14445/22312803/IJCTT-V24P115
18. Dong, G., Shi, W., Miao, Y., Xu, H., Feng, R.: Research of the edge extraction about archaic epigraph. In: Proceedings of the IEEE International Conference (Henan, China), pp. 1–4 (2010). https://doi.org/10.1109/ICISE.2010.5688762
19. Ganesan, P., Sajiv, G.: A comprehensive study of edge detection for image processing applications. In: Proceedings of the 2017 International Conference on Innovations in Information, Embedded and Communication Systems (ICIIECS), Coimbatore, India, pp. 1–6. IEEE (2017). https://doi.org/10.1109/ICIIECS.2017.8275915
20. Powers, J., et al.: X-ray fluorescence imaging analysis of inscription provenance. J. Archaeol. Sci. **36**(2), 343–350 (2009). https://doi.org/10.1016/j.jas.2008.09.019
21. Bearman, G.H., Spiro, S.I.: Archaeological applications of advanced imaging techniques. Biblic. Archaeol. **59**(1), 56–66 (1996). https://doi.org/10.2307/3210592
22. Suri, A., Gupta, M., Adlakha, T.: Information extraction from historical epigraphs using digital image processing techniques. In: Proceedings of the IEEE International Conference on Signal Processing and Communication (ICSC), pp. 1–6 (2016). https://doi.org/10.1109/ICSC.2016.7508982

23. Miranda, S.R., et al.: Revealing inscriptions obscured by time on an early-modern lead funerary cross using terahertz multispectral imaging. Sci. Rep. **12**, 2134 (2022). https://doi.org/10.1038/s41598-022-06982-2
24. Adamopoulos, E., Rinaudo, F.: Combining multiband imaging, photogrammetric techniques, and FOSS GIS for affordable degradation mapping of stone monuments. Buildings **11**(7), 304 (2021). https://doi.org/10.3390/buildings11070304 ref

Authorship Identification of Sinhala Poems Using Machine Learning Techniques

Paththage Ravindu Sachintha Fernando[1](✉), Sachintha Pitigala[2], and Nadeeka de Silva[1]

[1] University of Sri Jayewardenepura, Gangodawila, Nugegoda, Sri Lanka
sachintharavindu46@gmail.com
[2] Whitman College, Walla Walla, USA
pitigals@whitman.edu

Abstract. Authorship identification in literary works has several practical applications such as academic integrity verification, copyright protection and forensic linguistics. Sinhala poetry, with its deep cultural and historical significance presents a unique challenge due to its rich stylistic elements and linguistic complexities. This study aims to develop a computational model for authorship identification in Sinhala poems using machine learning techniques. A dataset of 300 poems from 10 authors, with 30 poems per author, was used for this study. This study was done under several experiments to identify the best data transformation method and to compare the performance of different machine learning techniques. Cross-validation was used throughout the study to ensure robust evaluation, while accuracy metric was selected as the primary performance metric. Grid search was used to fine tune the hyper parameters of the model. Among the evaluated approaches, the hyper parameter tuned CNN model using TF-IDF with unigram configuration achieved the best accuracy. These findings highlight the potential of machine leaning techniques, combined with optimized text representation techniques, for effective authorship identification in Sinhala poems. The main limitation of this research lies in the size and scope of the dataset, which defines the boundaries of the study's conclusions.

Keywords: Authorship Identification · Natural Language Processing · Deep Learning

1 Introduction

Authorship identification is finding the real author of an anonymous text from a predefined set of candidate authors using linguistic styles, writing patterns and content features of the text. Most studies on authorship identification focus on popular languages like English, leaving low resource languages such as Sinhala underrepresented [1].

Sinhala is one of the two official languages of Sri Lanka. It is a language with a rich literary heritage, which plays a major role in preserving country's cultural and historical identity, especially through poems. The authorship identification in literary

R. N. Rajapakse et al. (Eds.): ICTer 2025, CCIS 2844, pp. 200–215, 2026.
https://doi.org/10.1007/978-981-92-0137-2_14

works, particularly poems, has several practical applications such as academic integrity verification, copyright protection and forensic linguistics. Also this enables a deeper understanding in linguistic styles across different literary periods.

Despite its importance, authorship identification in the Sinhala language faces several challenges. From a computational perspective, poetry poses greater difficulty than prose. Prose typically follows more regular grammatical structures and conveys meaning in a direct, narrative or descriptive manner, which allows features such as word frequency, syntax and semantic patterns to be captured more consistently. Poetry, in contrast, relies heavily on figurative language, metaphors, rhythm and aesthetic choices rather than straightforward structures. Poets often deviate from conventional grammar and vocabulary to achieve artistic expression, making consistent stylistic patterns harder to model computationally [2, 3]. In Sinhala poems, this complexity is further amplified by the language's rich stylistic variations and the limited availability of digital resources and annotated datasets.

Therefore, this study aims to develop a computational model to identify authorship in Sinhala poems using machine learning techniques while trying to close the gap between traditional literary analysis and modern computational methods. In academic settings it can assist educators and researchers in identifying plagiarism and ensuring the authenticity of creative submissions. From a cultural perspective it can contribute significantly to the preservation and analysis of Sinhala literature providing a means to digitize and study ancient and contemporary works. Moreover, this initiative can inspire similar efforts for other underrepresented languages promoting global linguistic diversity and inclusivity in computational research.

2 Literature Review

Since this study focuses on the authorship identification of Sinhala poems, mainly tried to identify the most effective methods that can use for the Sinhala language while exploring additional methods to enhance the prediction accuracy.

One research study was conducted to investigate the author identification based on Natural Language Processing (NLP) techniques [4]. A data set from kaggle called "All the News" was used for this study. From this, a new dataset was created by limiting the scope. Then again this dataset was divided into two scopes. During this study the author identification technique was used to identify the unique writing style of each author by keeping rare words, without correcting the spelling and lemmatization. Two feature extraction methods: Bag of Words (BoW) and Latent Semantic Analysis (LSA) and four classification models: Logistic Regression (LR), Random Forest (RF), Support Vector Machine (SVM) and Bidirectional Encoder Representations from Transformers (BERT) were used during this study. The study followed a 70/15/15 split for training, validation and testing where experiment results showed that BoW consistently performed better that LSA across all classification models. LR with BoW got the highest accuracy in the first scope, while it performed well again in second scope. The accuracy marginally increased when it was paired with LSA features.

A study on authorship attribution of Late 19th century novels conducted using Generative Adversarial Network (GAN)-BERT based model [5]. Datasets were collected from project Gutenberg, across genres like novels, short stories, essays, poems and biographies. Experiments on different subsets and different model configurations were conducted to address: random sampling author combinations, the impact of transfer leaning, number of authors in dataset and text sample size per novel. To prepare the data, a leave-n-out method was used to manually select five sets of author samples. The results suggested that transfer learning is a better technique for improving performance, especially for smaller datasets.

Another approach was conducted to investigate the author specific word class distributions using part-of-speech (POS) tagging and bigram analysis [6]. The dataset used in this study was a collection of literary works by different authors. After applying preprocessing, the texts were tokenized and annotated with POS tags using the Python NLP library spaCy. Two deep neural networks were used to classify authors based on linguistic patterns: a fully connected neural network for handling POS tag unigram vectors and a Convolutional Neural Network (CNN) for bigram frequency matrices. The study's results showed that bigram feature outperformed unigram features in author classification.

Another investigation was conducted for author identification of Chinese literary works based on the text analysis and deep learning [7]. Two datasets were used for this study. This study proposed a new method for feature extraction in Chinese text. Corpus was input into the Word2Vec to generate the new word vector. The text features were then extracted by the improved text feature extractor based on CNN and used as the input of the convolution layer. After convolution the text was combined with bits to get the Window Feature Sequence which was the text feature vector. Next, based on Long Short-Term Memory (LSTM) and Softmax classification output the window feature sequence was used as the input of LSTM to obtain two one-dimensional vectors spliced by the concatenate layer. Finally, the result was classified through the fully connected layer, batch normalization layer and Softmax. This study used ten-fold cross validation scheme for validation. The proposed model showed high efficiency in author identification even with an increased number of target classes (authors). Also achieved higher values of precision, recall and F1 score compared to other models.

Another study investigated a language modeling approach for authorship identification in online examinations conducted in the Sinhala language [8]. As for the data set, they have used a collection of articles from a media platform. The study has used Recurrent Neural Network (RNN) with LSTM units to capture sequential dependencies in text. Two different architectures: word-level and character-level were used. Character-level model outperformed the word-level model, by getting higher validation accuracy and more consistent perplexity scores across test samples. These results highlighted the potential of character-level models, in scenarios with limited data.

Another study explored the Sinhala text authorship attribution task in both intra-topic and cross-topic authorship attribution settings [1]. A newly created corpus, extracted from an online newspaper website, with a total of 980 Sinhala documents from 140 authors across four domains: Courts, Business, Politics, General was used for this study. Function words were extracted during feature extraction and multiple classifiers like k-Nearest Neighbor (KNN), Naïve Bayes, LR, Decision Tree (DT), RF, SVM and Deep Learning (DL) were tried. During intra-topic authorship attribution, five-fold cross validation was used for model generalization where KNN got the highest accuracy while SVM slightly outperformed KNN in the courts domain. In cross-topic authorship attribution, the results also confirmed the effectiveness of using function words.

These studies highlight different approaches to authorship identification, including function word analysis, character-level models, syntactic structure modeling and advanced deep learning models. However, existing studies on Sinhala text have mainly focused on prose rather than poems. The rich stylistic elements and linguistic complexities of Sinhala poems introduce new challenges that have not been addressed in previous studies, which this study aims to address.

3 Data Set

3.1 Data Collection

Several approaches were used to collect poems for this study, resulting in a total of 638 Sinhala poems from 25 different authors. The following Table 1 gives a summary of collected poems count.

Table 1. Summary of collected poems count.

Source	Number of authors	Number of poems
Social Media (Consented)	12	315
Sinhala Poetry Books (Consented)	2	25
Websites and Blogs (Consented)	2	34
Direct Submissions by Authors (PDF, Consented)	9	264

3.2 Final Dataset

From the 25 authors, only those with exactly a poem count of 30 were selected for the study. So the final dataset was created using 10 authors, each contributing 30 poems, resulting in a total of 300 Sinhala poems. This dataset was used throughout the whole study. All poems in the dataset were written after the year 2015 and the average poem length varied notably across authors, ranging from approximately 47 words to 118 words per poem. Most authors averaged between 54 and 82 words per poem, reflecting a diverse range of writing styles in the dataset.

3.3 Data Pre-Processing

Before training the model, the collected data should be pre-processed to make data clean, consistent and appropriate for analysis. Text cleaning included the removal of unwanted characters such as punctuation marks, special symbols and numerical digits. Also additional whitespaces in between words were removed to ensure the consistency across the corpus. Then label encoding [9] was applied to convert the categorical author names into numerical labels. This preprocessed and encoded dataset was used throughout the entire study.

4 Methodology

The following Fig. 1 presents the overall methodology of this study. It consists with two main phases: To find the best feature representation technique and to evaluate the performance of various machine learning and deep learning models.

4.1 Find the Best Feature Representation Technique

Experiment 1: Selecting the Best Feature Representation Technique. The first experiment was conducted to select the best feature representation technique. During this experiment, KNN [10, 11] algorithm was selected as the baseline classifier based on the findings from previous studies [1]. Three text representation techniques: Term Frequency – Inverse Document Frequency (TF-IDF) [12–14], BoW [15, 16] and Word2Vec [17] were used. The number of poems per author was incrementally increased as 10,15,20 and 30.

To further validate the previous experiment results, another analysis conducted by comparing all three feature representations: TF-IDF, BoW and Word2Vec using KNN. During this analysis the number of authors was incrementally increased from 2 to 10, with each author contributing 30 poems.

After identifying the best feature representation technique based on the results of this experiment, it was consistently used as the feature representation technique during the remaining experiments.

4.2 Evaluate the Performance of Various Machine Learning and Deep Learning Models

Experiment 2: Evaluation Between Machine Learning Models for Authorship Identification. A series of evaluations were conducted to evaluate different machine learning and deep learning models for authorship identification. First multiple traditional machine learning models: KNN, SVM [18–20], DT [21–23] and Artificial Neural Network (ANN) [24] were tested to identify the best performing machine learning model. This experiment similarly used the incremental increase in authors from 2 to 10 with each author contributing 30 poems.

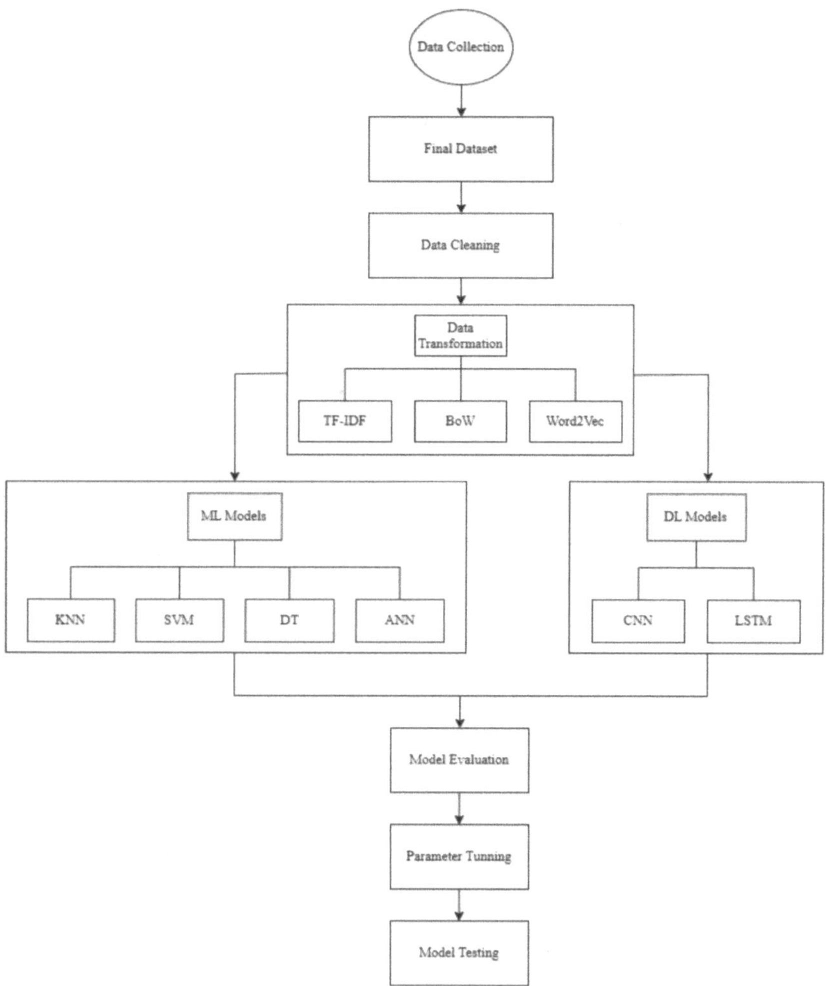

Fig. 1. Overall methodology of the study.

Experiment 3: Evaluation Between Deep Learning Models for Authorship Identification. Then different deep leaning models: CNN [25, 26] and LSTM [27, 28] were compared with the best performing machine learning model using the same previous experimental setup to identify the most effective model for authorship identification of Sinhala poems.

Experiment 4: Investigation of the Impact of Different n-gram Configurations. Then a follow-up experiment was conducted to investigate the impact of different n-gram [29–31] settings: unigram, bigram, unigram + bigram and trigram on model performance. This was performed using the best performing machine learning and deep learning model to determine whether these configurations could further enhance each model's accuracy.

Experiment 5: Hyper Parameter Tuning. Finally, a hyper parameter [32] tuning was conducted using grid search [33] for the best performing machine learning and both deep learning models with the best performing feature representation technique and n-gram configuration. This step was performed in-order-to improve the model performance, fine-tune the model parameters and optimize the models for accurate authorship identification.

For further clarification another hyper parameter tuning was performed using the same experiment setup on a new dataset, which included poems from 15 different authors with 20 poems per author.

ten-fold cross-validation [34, 35] was used throughout the study to ensure the models generalized across the unseen data while accuracy [36] was used as the primary metric to compare the model performance.

5 Experiment Results

This study was structured around five experiments that conducted to identify the optimal combination of feature representation techniques and classification models for the task of Sinhala poem authorship identification. In this section, results of each experiment will be presented. In this study, accuracy refers to the proportion of poems correctly attributed to their true authors. For a 10-class classification problem, random guessing would yield only 10% accuracy. Therefore, achieving 62.33% accuracy represents a substantial improvement and indicates that the model is effectively learning author-specific stylistic patterns. Similarly, for a 15-class classification problem, random guessing would result in just 6.67% accuracy. In this case, the model achieved around 50% accuracy, which is still a significant improvement over random guessing, demonstrating its ability to capture meaningful features and differentiate between a larger number of authors despite the increased complexity [37].

5.1 Experiment 1: Selecting the Best Feature Representation Technique

Three text representation techniques: TF-IDF, BoW and Word2Vec were used, where the number of poems per author was incrementally increased as 10,15,20 and 30, selecting the KNN algorithm as the baseline classifier. According to the Fig. 2 TF-IDF consistently outperformed the other methods across all settings. Almost in every occasion, accuracy improved with the increase in poem count, while BoW and Word2Vec showed comparatively lower performance throughout the experiment.

To further validate above results, another analysis conducted by comparing all three feature representations: TF-IDF, BoW and Word2Vec using KNN. The analysis incrementally increased the number of authors from 2 to 10, with each author contributing 30 poems. According to the Fig. 3 TF-IDF outperformed both BoW and Word2Vec, achieving the highest accuracy across all author counts. When the number of author count increased, the performance of each representation method gradually decreased. Even though Word2Vec has the ability to capture semantic relationships, it has the lowest accuracy, especially when the author count increases. This suggest that TF-IDF is better suited for capturing author-specific word usage patterns in the context of Sinhala poems.

According to Figs. 2 and 3 TF-IDF was selected as the best feature representation method because it showed consistent results for different number of authors as well as different number of poems per each author.

5.2 Experiment 2: Evaluation Between Machine Learning Models

After selecting the TF-IDF as the feature representation technique, this experiment was conducted to evaluate multiple traditional machine learning models: KNN, SVM, DT and ANN. This experiment similarly used the incremental increase in authors from 2 to 10, with each author contributing 30 poems. According to the Fig. 4, when the number of authors increased, all the models showed a decrease in accuracy. Among the models, SVM maintained the highest performance across all author counts, while KNN had the second best accuracy. Both DT and ANN struggles significantly when the number of authors increased. These results suggest that SVM is the most robust method for authorship identification in this scenario.

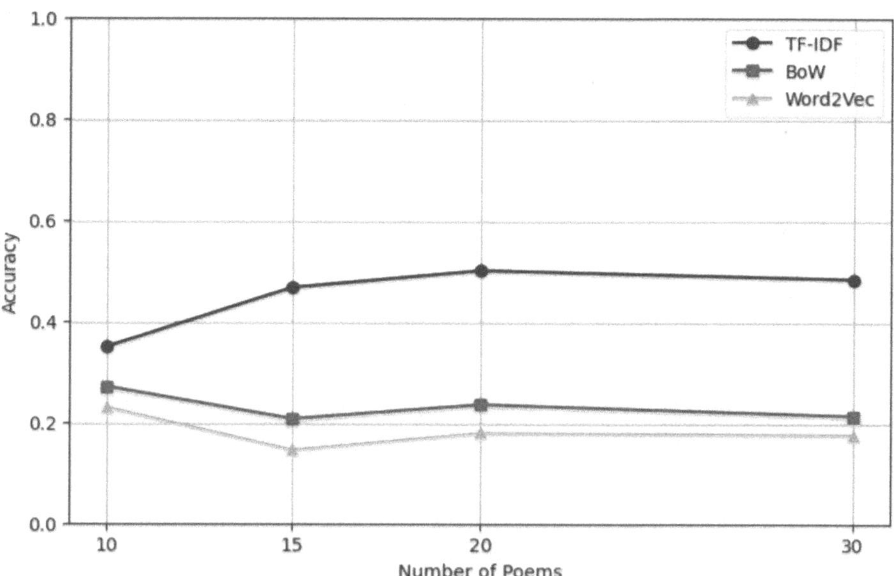

Fig. 2. Classification performance of BoW, TF-IDF, and Word2Vec using KNN across increasing poem counts (10–30 per author).

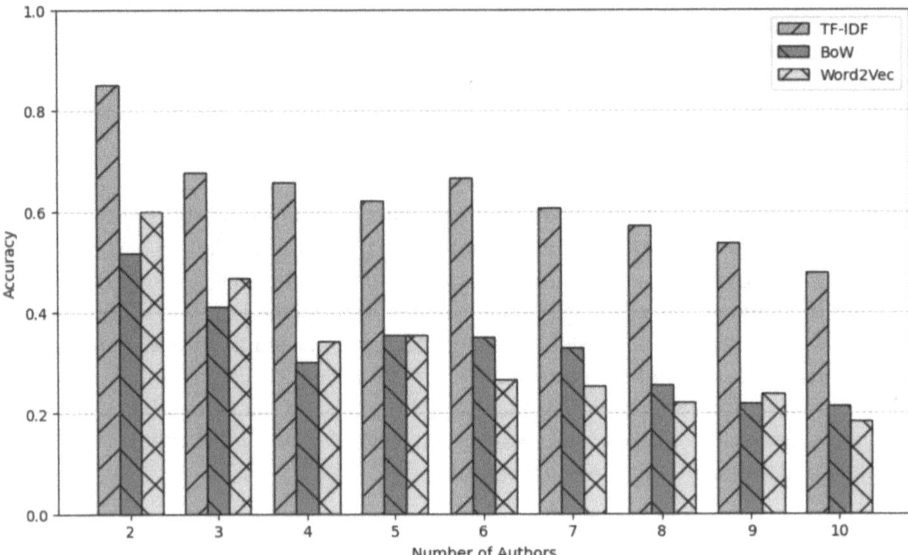

Fig. 3. Accuracy analysis of BoW, TF-IDF, and Word2Vec using KNN, with author count incrementally increased (2–10) and 30 poems per author.

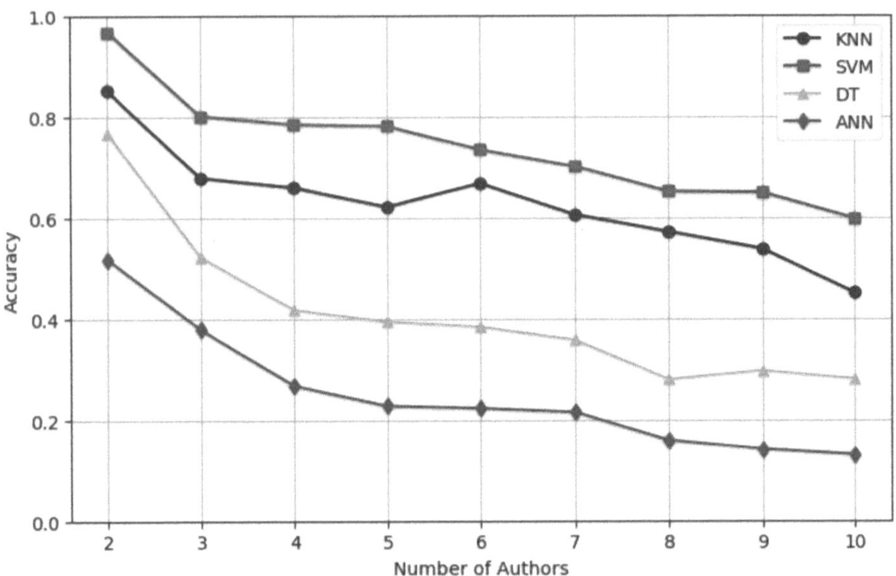

Fig. 4. Performance comparison of KNN, SVM, DT, and ANN classifiers using TF-IDF, with author count incrementally increased (2–10) at 30 poems per author.

5.3 Experiment 3: Evaluation Between Deep Learning Models

During this experiment SVM, the best performing machine learning model from the previous experiment was compared with deep learning models CNN and LSTM. Here also used the incremental increase in authors from 2 to 10, with each author contributing 30 poems, while using TF-IDF as the feature representation technique. According to the Fig. 5, SVM again demonstrated the best performance, consistently outperforming both CNN and LSTM models. The LSTM and CNN models showed similar trends, with CNN performing better at lower author counts, while LSTM caught up as the author count increased, making LSTM as the most effective deep learning model in this case.

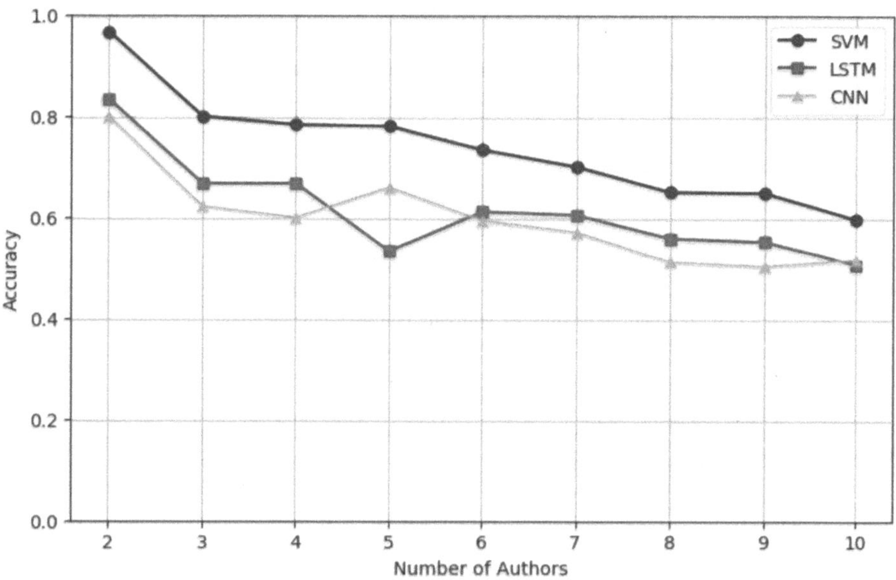

Fig. 5. Performance comparison of SVM vs. CNN and LSTM using TF-IDF, with author count incrementally increased (2–10) at 30 poems per author.

5.4 Experiment 4: Investigation of the Impact of Different n-gram Configurations

This follow-up experiment was conducted to investigate the impact of different n-gram settings: unigram, bigram, unigram + bigram and trigram on model accuracy in the 10 author case where each author had 30 poems. This was performed using the best performing machine learning and deep learning model to determine whether these configurations could further enhance each model's accuracy. During this unigram got the highest accuracy, while unigram + bigram got the second best accuracy where the following Table 2 gives the summary of the results of this experiment.

Table 2. Accuracy comparison of SVM and LSTM models under different n-gram.

n-gram Configuration	SVM Accuracy	LSTM Accuracy
Unigram (words)	0.5967	0.5067
Bigram	0.3767	0.3733
Unigram + Bigram	0.5833	0.5500
Trigram	0.1700	0.1500

5.5 Experiment 5: Hyper Parameter Tuning

Finally, a hyper parameter tuning was conducted using grid search for SVM, the best performing machine learning model and for deep learning models: CNN and LSTM. This experiment was performed selecting unigram as the n-gram configuration and TF-IDF as the feature representation technique, based on the results of the previous experiments. According to the results in Table 3, CNN was identified as the most effective model for the task of authorship identification of Sinhala poems. Although SVM initially performed better on smaller author counts, the CNN model benefited from deeper feature extraction and ultimately surpassed SVM after hyper parameter tuning, demonstrating its ability to capture complex stylistic nuances in poems.

Table 3. Hyper parameter tuning results.

Model	No of Authors * No of poems	Precision	Recall	F1-score	Accuracy	Parameter Setting
SVM	10 * 30	0.6252	0.6000	0.5871	0.6000	{'C': 1, 'degree': 2, 'gamma': 'scale', 'kernel': 'linear'}
CNN	10 * 30	0.6469	0.6233	0.6107	0.6233	{'batch_size': 32, 'epochs': 15, 'model__dropout_rate1': 0.3, 'model__dropout_rate2': 0.2, 'model__learning_rate': 0.001, 'model__units_layer1': 512, 'model__units_layer2': 128}

(continued)

Table 3. (*continued*)

Model	No of Authors * No of poems	Precision	Recall	F1-score	Accuracy	Parameter Setting
LSTM	10 * 30	0.6100	0.6100	0.6100	0.6133	{'Lstm_units': 128, 'dropout_rate': 0.3, 'recurrent_dropout': 0.2, 'bidirectional': 'True', 'learning_rate': 0.001, 'dense_units': 128, 'batch_size': 32, 'epochs': 15}
SVM	15 * 20	0.4555	0.4733	0.4345	0.4733	{'C': 1, 'degree': 2, 'gamma': 'scale', 'kernel': "rbf'}
CNN	15 * 20	0.4874	0.4800	0.4581	0.4800	{'batch_size': 32, 'epochs': 15, 'model__dropout_rate1': 0.3, 'model__dropout_rate2': 0.2, 'model__learning_rate': 0.001, 'model__units_layer1': 256, 'model__units_layer2': 128}
LSTM	15 * 20	0.5000	0.4700	0.4700	0.4700	{'Lstm_units': 128, 'dropout_rate': 0.3, 'recurrent_dropout': 0.2, 'bidirectional': 'True', 'learning_rate': 0.001, 'dense_units': 128, 'batch_size': 32, 'epochs': 15}

6 Conclusion

This study was conducted to explore the authorship identification of Sinhala poems using machine learning techniques. The baseline experiment for authorship identification was conducted using KNN with three feature representation techniques: TF-IDF, BoW and Word2Vec. Through a comprehensive set of experiments, TF-IDF was identified as the most effective representation technique for authorship identification of Sinhala poems, consistently outperforming the other feature representation techniques across different author counts and poem counts. Then using the best feature representation technique: TF-IDF, a comparison between different machine learning models: KNN, SVM, DT and ANN was conducted and SVM outperformed all other models in authorship identification tasks. Then a comparison between SVM and deep learning methods: LSTM and CNN, with TF-IDF as the feature representation technique, was conducted and still the SVM outperformed both approaches. Further analysis of n-gram variations done to improve the accuracy of the best performing machine learning and deep learning models where unigram was the most effective configuration. In the final stage, a parameter sweep was conducted using grid search on the best performing machine learning and both deep learning models with TF-IDF and unigram configuration to optimize the models for accurate authorship identification. During this CNN achieved the highest accuracy. Throughout the study ten-fold cross-validation was used, ensuring reliability and unbiased evaluation. The findings confirm the suitability of TF-IDF based representations with CNN models for effective authorship identification of Sinhala poems.

7 Limitations and Future Work

7.1 Limitations

A limitation of this research is the size and the scope of the dataset. This study was done using a total collection of 300 Sinhala poems, authored by 10 different authors which is a relatively small dataset. One of the main challenge was to find digitally available Sinhala poems. Many poems were only accessible in printed form and it was difficult to extract the content from them. As a result, some of the poems had to be manually typed, which consumed a lot of time. This limitation of data availability directly impacted the findings of this study. Another limitation relates to the feature representation technique used. Although TF-IDF with various n-gram configurations helped capture local co-occurrence patterns and stylistic cues within poems, it is still limited in its ability to represent deeper linguistic and syntactic structures. Poetry often relies on complex grammar, rhythm, and contextual relationships between words to convey meaning. Since TF-IDF treats words as independent tokens, these higher-level patterns and stylistic nuances may not be fully captured. As a result, certain author-specific characteristics might have been overlooked, potentially affecting model performance.

7.2 Future Work

For future research, expanding the dataset is crucial to improve model performance and enable the use of more complex models. Recent advances in transformer-based models, such as BERT [38] and its Sinhala adaptation, SinBERT [39], have shown significant improvements in text classification tasks by capturing deep contextual relationships. However, these models typically require large datasets, which are currently scarce for Sinhala poetry. Future work could focus on fine-tuning these transformer models for this domain once sufficient data is collected. Additionally, experimenting with different tokenization methods, word embedding techniques, and alternative feature representation approaches can further enhance performance and generalizability.

Disclosure of Interests. The authors declare that they have no competing interests.

References

1. Sarwar, R., Perera, M., Teh, P.S., Nawaz, R., Hassan, M.U.: Crossing linguistic barriers: authorship attribution in Sinhala texts. ACM Trans. Asian Low-Resour. Lang. Inf. Process. **23**(5), 1–14 (2024). https://doi.org/10.1145/3655620
2. de Arruda, H.F., Reia, S.M., Silva, F.N., Amancio, D.R., Costa, L.F.: Finding contrasting patterns in rhythmic properties between prose and poetry. Physica A: Stat. Mech. Appl. **598**, 127406 (2022). https://doi.org/10.1016/j.physa.2022.127387
3. de Arruda, H.F., Reia, S.M., Silva, F.N., Amancio, D.R., Costa, L.F.: A pattern recognition approach for distinguishing between prose and poetry. Physica A: Stat. Mech. Appl. **598**, 127387 (2022). https://doi.org/10.48550/arXiv.2107.08512
4. Alhuqail, N.K.: Author identification based on NLP. Eur. J. Comput. Sci. Inf. Technol. **9**(1), 1–26 (2021)
5. Silva, K., Can, B., Blain, F., Sarwar, R., Ugolini, L., Mitkov, R.: Authorship attribution of late 19th century novels using GAN-BERT. In: Proceedings 61st Annual Meeting of the Association for Computational Linguistics (Student Res. Workshop), vol. 4, pp. 310–320 (2023). https://doi.org/10.18653/v1/2023.acl-srw.44
6. Krauss, P., Schilling, A.: Author-Specific Linguistic Patterns Unveiled: A Deep Learning Study on Word Class Distributions. arXiv 2501.10072 (2025). doi:https://doi.org/10.48550/arXiv.2501.10072
7. Tang, X.: Author identification of literary works based on text analysis and deep learning. Heliyon. **10**(9), e30018 (2024). https://doi.org/10.1016/j.heliyon.2024.e25464
8. Punchihewa, M., Rajapakse, C., Asanka, P.P.G.D.: A language modelling approach to authorship identification for online examinations in Sinhala. In: ICARC 2021 – International Conference on Advanced Research in Computing, pp. 1–6 (2021)
9. Kaggle: https://www.kaggle.com/discussions/general/445393, Accessed 02 Jun 2025
10. Campesato, O.: Artificial intelligence, machine learning, and deep learning. In: Mercury Learning & Information, pp. 67–68, Dulles, VA (2020)
11. Harrington, P.: Machine learning in action. In: Manning Publications, pp. 18–36, Shelter Island, NY (2012)
12. Jurafsky, D., Martin, J.H.: Speech and Language Processing, 3rd ed. In: Stanford University, Stanford, CA, pp. 647–650 (2023)
13. Campesato, O.: Artificial intelligence, machine learning, and deep learning. In: Mercury Learning & Information, pp. 166–168, Dulles, VA (2020)
14. Lane, H., Hapke, H., Howard, C.: Natural Language Processing in Action: Understanding, Analyzing, and Generating Text with Python. In: Manning Publications, Shelter Island, NY, pp. 70–96 (2019)
15. Campesato, O.: Artificial Intelligence, Machine Learning, and Deep Learning. In: Mercury Learning & Information, Dulles, VA, pp. 165–166 (2020)
16. Lane, H., Hapke, H., Howard, C.: Natural Language Processing in Action: Understanding, Analyzing, and Generating Text with Python. In: Manning Publications, Shelter Island, NY, pp. 71–73 (2019)
17. Lane, H., Hapke, H., Howard, C.: Natural Language Processing in Action: Understanding, Analyzing, and Generating Text with Python. In: Manning Publications, Shelter Island, NY, pp. 181–217 (2019)
18. Campesato, O.: Artificial Intelligence, Machine Learning, and Deep Learning. In: Mercury Learning & Information, Dulles, VA, pp. 74–75 (2020).

19. Harrington, P.: Machine Learning in Action. In: Manning Publications, Shelter Island, NY, pp. 101–127 (2012)
20. Géron, A.: Hands-On Machine Learning with Scikit-Learn and TensorFlow: Concepts, Tools, and Techniques to Build Intelligent Systems. In: O'Reilly Media, Sebastopol, CA, pp. 147–168 (2017).
21. Campesato, O.: Artificial Intelligence, Machine Learning, and Deep Learning. In: Mercury Learning & Information, Dulles, VA, pp. 68–73 (2020)
22. Harrington, P.: Machine Learning in Action. In: Manning Publications, Shelter Island, NY, pp. 37–60 (2012)
23. Géron, A.: Hands-On Machine Learning with Scikit-Learn and TensorFlow: Concepts, Tools, and Techniques to Build Intelligent Systems. In: O'Reilly Media, Sebastopol, CA, pp. 169–182 (2017)
24. Campesato, O.: Artificial Intelligence, Machine Learning, and Deep Learning. In: Mercury Learning & Information, Dulles, VA, pp. 105–107 (2020)
25. Géron, A.: Hands-On Machine Learning with Scikit-Learn and TensorFlow: Concepts, Tools, and Techniques to Build Intelligent Systems. In: O'Reilly Media, Sebastopol, CA, pp. 357–382 (2017)
26. Campesato, O.: Artificial Intelligence, Machine Learning, and Deep Learning. In: Mercury Learning & Information, Dulles, VA, pp. 113–126 (2020)
27. Campesato, O.: Artificial Intelligence, Machine Learning, and Deep Learning. In: Mercury Learning & Information, Dulles, VA, pp. 139–146 (2020)
28. Géron, A.: Hands-On Machine Learning with Scikit-Learn and TensorFlow: Concepts, Tools, and Techniques to Build Intelligent Systems. In: O'Reilly Media, Sebastopol, CA, pp. 405–408 (2017)
29. Jurafsky, D., Martin, J.H.: Speech and Language Processing, 3rd ed. In: Stanford University, Stanford, CA, pp. 189–220 (2023)
30. Campesato, O.: Artificial Intelligence, Machine Learning, and Deep Learning. In: Mercury Learning & Information, Dulles, VA, pp. 164–165 (2020)
31. Lane, H., Hapke, H., Howard, C.: Natural Language Processing in Action: Understanding, Analyzing, and Generating Text with Python. In: Manning Publications, Shelter Island, NY, pp. 48–51 (2019)
32. Campesato, O.: Artificial Intelligence, Machine Learning, and Deep Learning. In: Mercury Learning & Information, Dulles, VA, pp. 100–101 (2020)
33. Géron, A.: Hands-On Machine Learning with Scikit-Learn and TensorFlow: Concepts, Tools, and Techniques to Build Intelligent Systems. In: O'Reilly Media, Sebastopol, CA, pp. 73–75 (2017)
34. Campesato, O.: Artificial intelligence, machine learning, and deep learning. In: Mercury Learning & Information, p. 34. Dulles, VA (2020)
35. Géron, A.: Hands-On Machine Learning with Scikit-Learn and TensorFlow: Concepts, Tools, and Techniques to Build Intelligent Systems. In: O'Reilly Media, Sebastopol, CA, pp. 85–86 (2017)
36. Google Developers.: https://developers.google.com/machine-learning/crash-course/classification/accuracy-precision-recall, Accessed 02 Jun 2025
37. Jurafsky, D., Martin, J.H.: Speech and Language Processing, 3rd edn. Prentice Hall, Upper Saddle River (2023)
38. Devlin, J., Chang, M.W., Lee, K., Toutanova, K.: BERT: pre-training of deep bidirectional transformers for language understanding. In: Proceedings of NAACL-HLT, pp. 4171–4186. ACL, Minneapolis (2019). https://doi.org/10.18653/v1/N19-1423

39. Dhananjaya, V., Demotte, P., Ranathunga, S., Jayasena, S.: BERTifying Sinhala — a comprehensive analysis of pre-trained language models for Sinhala text classification. In: Proceedings of the Thirteenth Language Resources and Evaluation Conference (LREC 2022), pp. 7467–7477. ELRA, Marseille (2022)

Possible Distillation for Abstractive Summarization: Reducing Hallucination in Compact LLMs

Vadivel Abishethvarman[1,5](✉), Gobihanath Balasubramaniam[1], Senthan Prasanth[2], Banage T. G. S. Kumara[1,3], and Banujan Kuhaneswaran[1,4]

[1] Department of Computing and Information Systems, Faculty of Computing, Sabaragamuwa University of Sri Lanka, Belihuloya, Sri Lanka
abishethvarman@gmail.com

[2] Faculty of Engineering and Applied Science, Memorial University of Newfoundland, St. John's, Canada

[3] Department of Software Engineering, Faculty of Computing, Sabaragamuwa University of Sri Lanka, Belihuloya, Sri Lanka

[4] Faculty of Science and Engineering, Southern Cross University, Gold Coast, Australia

[5] Open University of Sri Lanka, Nugegoda, Sri Lanka

Abstract. Large language models (LLMs) have excels strong performance in Natural Language Processing tasks. Text summarization is one among them, But the knowledge is limited in the context of subjectiveness in the summarized text. And it may able to hallucinated itself by the chain of prompts. The knowledge regarding context is not specific for low resource models, rather, predicting the next tokens. In this work, we explore possible distillation a practical approach to transferring summarization capabilities from high capacity teacher models to compact student models. Specifically, we distill knowledge from four powerful teacher models LLaMA 3.1 (90B), Falcon (40B), Gemma2 (27B), and Qwen2.5 (72B) into student models of significantly smaller size (8B, 7B, 2B, and 7B, respectively). And it evaluated through the benchmark metrics such as ROUGE-L, BLEU, and METEOR. Our results show that while student models exhibit strong summarization capabilities, but they suffer from knowledge loss and hallucination. Teacher models are slow but good in context aware summarization. The distilled model perform moderatively faster than the teacher and hallucination free than the student in subjective sense. Distilled Qwen achieved the best performance with ROUGE-L of 0.6900, BLEU of 49.47, and METEOR of 0.6850, whereas other distilled models like Gemma2 and Falcon showed low performance compared to Distilled Qwen. These findings highlight the challenge of preserving factual integrity in compact models and motivate distillation as a viable method to reduce hallucination while maintaining summary quality. The entire code implementation can be found at : https://github.com/Abishethvarman/KD-Text-Summarization.

R. N. Rajapakse et al. (Eds.): ICTer 2025, CCIS 2844, pp. 216–230, 2026.
https://doi.org/10.1007/978-981-92-0137-2_15

Keywords: Abstractive Text Summarization · Knowledge Distillation · Large Language Models · Task Specific Distillation · Hallucination

1 Introduction

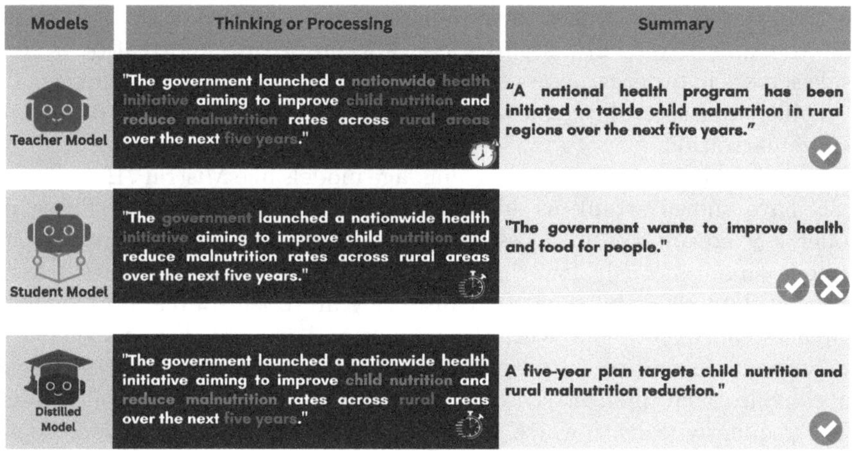

Fig. 1. Explanatory Diagram

The enormous growth of large language models (LLMs) [3] such as GPT [1], Gemini, Claude, Mistral, DeepSeek [2], BERT [4], and LLaMA [27] has transformed the field of Natural Language Processing (NLP). These models have achieved state of the art performance across a variety of language tasks which is including text classification [39], machine translation [19], question answering [22], and particularly text summarization [37]. Among these, text summarization is essential for information compression, allowing for effective content consumption various fields and domains. Large language models (LLMs) have been used more and more in recent text summarization developments, surpassing prior refined transformer models like BART [29] and T5 [13]. The next token predictive text summarization has evolved and became more subject oriented compression. Studies consistently shows that LLMs can generate summaries that are more coherent, relevant, and factually accurate than those written by humans. Also it is somehow matching or even exceeding them. These enhancements demonstrate how powerful LLMs are for summarizing activities.

However, the increasing demand for these task specific NLP systems in real-world applications has raised the need for language models that are not only powerful but also resource efficient and scalable. High-parameterized LLMs like DeepSeek R1 70B [8], LLaMA 3.1 70B [14], and GPT-4 [1] are prime examples of this new generation of proprietary models that offer remarkable performance at the expense of significant hardware and computational demands. Also the processing time is higher from the point of invoking a command and get a response. These big models are difficult to implement in resource constrained environments like mobile devices, embedded systems, or real-time applications since they are reliant on cloud infrastructure. This leads always a problem that to rely on api calls over cloud services. Their massive size often surpassing tens of billions of parameters, as shown in proprietary models such as DeepSeek R1 70B, LLaMA 3.1 70B, and GPT-4 requires a significant amount of GPU memory and computational power. This makes them difficult to use and accessible. Furthermore, there are many privacy and security issues when private information is sent to outside servers in order to access these models even if it is in the inference. These accessibility and cost plays roles to not to go with bigger model to implement text summarization.

Low parameterized, open-source language models like Mistral 7B and LLaMA 3.1 8B have shown strong as substitutes for proprietary LLMs. These models offer key advantages in accessibility, flexibility and transparency capabilities while simultaneously lowering cost, eliminating licensing limitations, and addressing data security issues. Because they are open-source, developers and researchers can experiment with the models and modify them to suit certain tasks without depending on proprietary APIs. Apart of this these advantages, their comparatively modest scale in comparison to ultra large models such as GPT-4 frequently leads to worse performance on intricate generative tasks, such as abstractive summarization [37]. This restriction may result in summaries that are less useful or cohesive. Especially when working with lengthy or contextually rich documents. A significant obstacle to making such models efficient and successful for real world summarization applications is connecting this performance difference without growing the model size.

To address these limitations, knowledge distillation (KD) has emerged as a promising approach for compressing large models into smaller. It is in a way of more efficient ones without significantly compromising performance. In the domain of text summarizing, KD seeks to transfer the knowledge and summary abilities of a large teacher model to a lightweight student model. This allows for faster inference, lower memory utilization.

Although certain distilled models, like as DistilBART [35] and MiniT5 [5], have shown solid performance. The majority of present research remains focused on general purpose or task agnostic distillation, frequently disregarding the complexities of task-specific summarization optimization. This remains a significant research gap in understanding how diverse information elicitation procedures and distillation targets affect the performance of student models trained for summarization.

This research focuses on task specific knowledge distillation techniques for the abstractive text summarization [31] task. The goal of developing successful solutions that maintain summary quality while significantly reducing model size and not getting the results as hallucinated. We assess alternative student teacher configurations, investigate the influence of various distillation targets, and compare the performance of distilled models across typical summarization datasets. Finally, our research helps to develop efficient task specific model that preserve the strengths of their larger counterparts.

2 Literature Review

Large language models (LLMs) and natural language processing (NLP) have advanced so quickly that many research have been conducted recently with the goal of enhancing model efficiency, knowledge transfer, and task-specific performance.

2.1 Background

Rapid advancements in Large Language Models (LLMs) have changed the landscape of Natural Language Processing (NLP). Thisevolution started with the Transformer architecture [28], which improved the modeling of long-range relationships in text by substituting self-attention processes for traditional recurrent and convolutional networks. Building on this framework, pre-trained models like BERT [4], GPT, and T5 [5] showed how extensive self-supervised training may result in language representations that are rich and adaptable.

LLMs achieved remarkable generalization capabilities as they developed into foundation models like GPT-4, LLaMA, and PaLM, as well as multimodal systems, as model sizes and training data increased. These models are the foundation of modern NLP applications since they not only perform very well on specific tasks but also demonstrate emergent skills like reasoning, multilingual understanding, and cross-modal processing. However, the rising size and complexity of LLMs has resulted in high computational and memory costs, limiting their practical application [6].

Neural networks are the foundation of current language models. Neural networks contain information in their parameters and intermediate activation processes, extracting patterns, correlations, and structures from massive volumes of data. Neural networks' hierarchical nature, in which information is stored in the weights and activations of various layers, allows for the transmission of behavioral patterns learned from one model to another.

Knowledge distillation [6] refers to the process of transferring knowledge from a large, complex model (teacher) to a smaller, more efficient model (student). Knowledge distillation aims at transferring knowledge acquired in one model (a teacher) to another model (a student) that is typically smaller. Simply transferring the knowledge not the understanding. Knowledge distillation has been successfully utilized to transfer knowledge from larger, more complex teacher models into tiny student models for various task specific actions.

Prior to the development of large language models (LLMs), knowledge distillation [26] techniques were mostly used to optimize deep neural networks, particularly for vision and classification applications. These initiatives focused on compressing big convolutional or recurrent models into smaller. It were more efficient networks using methodologies such as pruning, quantization [16], and knowledge transfer. Soft target supervision and intermediate feature alignment were prominent techniques used to help the student model approximate the performance of a larger counterpart by emulating logits or internal representations. It is about enhancing the knowledge of the student model not by penetrating into the system side.

Knowledge distillation techniques are considered difficult in the field of Natural Language Processing (NLP). Models like TinyBERT [11] and MobileBERT [24] improved on this strategy by using more advanced distillation techniques such as layer-to-layer alignment and embedding-level distillation. These developments demonstrated that large transformer models may be successfully shrunk using knowledge distillation [33] while still performing competitively on NLP tasks including sentiment analysis, text summarization, and question answering. This move signals the beginning of knowledge distillation as a fundamental technique for developing deployable, low-parameter NLP models.

The present phase of knowledge distillation in LLMs shifts the focus away from simple architectural model reduction and toward knowledge elicitation and richer information transmission [15]. Those previous neural models, where distillation mostly included matching soft outputs or logits, distillation in LLMs. Also it increasingly tries to extract and maintain semantic depth, contextual reasoning, and task adaptation. This stands in great contrast to the earlier perception on simple output replication. Simply showing a dramatic change toward a more full and thorough transmission of cognitive capacities. But not as a supervised learning approaches. This entails advanced tactics such as chain-of-thought prompting, which instructs the student model to learn and emulate the teacher's cognitive process. So this is improving problem-solving and decision-making abilities. In vice versa it is learning from the question and answer of teacher and the student model.

As a result, the goal of knowledge distillation in the LLM era is no longer just to reduce model size, but also to actively transfer knowledge for optimal performance, interpretability, and deployment capability [33]. This can leads to task specific or even task agnostic transferring from bigger model to smaller models. Task-specific distillation [25] improves the student model for specific downstream tasks including sentiment analysis, natural language interpretation, text summarization, and question answering throughout the distillation process. This technique enables the student model to specialize on certain tasks, leading to higher task-level accuracy.

Text summarization is a strategy used in natural language processing to reduce a longer text into a short form while keeping its important concepts and context [31]. Text summarization is not just compressing the content into a smaller part. It is about without loosing the meaning of the context, the words has to be reduced. It should not differ from the actual text that we taken for the summarization [31]. Text summarization can be divided into abstractive summarization [40], extractive summarization [10] and descriptive summarization on the nature of summary it provides. Abstractive text summarization is one of the most impactful. This task involves generating a concise and coherent summary [5]. That intend to captures the core meaning of a longer corpus, using novel words and phrases rather than just picking parts of the original text. Extractive summarization, which selects and joins relevant sentences from the input. Descriptive summarization aims to provide a quick overview or description of the text, emphasizing its key ideas or subjects without replicating exact phrases or paraphrasing them [37].

Abstractive summarization [18] relies on the model's ability to comprehend the text and rephrase it. Refer Fig. 1 for further. However, despite their impressive fluency, these models often suffer from hallucination [9,21,32]. The generation of content that can be incorrect or not grounded in the source input. This issue becomes even more critical when using compact or distilled models. These models are smaller and more efficient but may lose important semantic and factual cues during training. Also it vulnerable for the hallucination.

To address this, knowledge distillation has emerged as a possible solution. In the context of abstractive summarization, distillation not only compresses the model but can also guide the student toward producing more faithful and factually correct summaries. Simply hallucination free text summarization.

This research focuses on leveraging distillation techniques to reduce hallucinations in compact LLMs for abstractive summarization. It is to offering a more reliable and efficient solution.

Motivation

The challenge of hallucination is especially pronounced in compact models and distilled versions of LLMs. These are favored for deployment due to lower computational cost. While knowledge distillation has been explored extensively in classification and translation tasks, its role in abstractive summarization, particularly in controlling hallucinations, remains underexplored.

This research is motivated by the need to retain summarization quality and factual accuracy in smaller models through task-specific distillation, enabling efficient deployment without compromising on output reliability.

We deeply inspired on this paper [12] and tried to prove that distilled model can perform better in speed and hallucination free.

It also addresses the gap in systematic benchmarking for evaluating hallucination in distilled summarizers.

Novelty of the Research

This work presents a unified framework for evaluating summarization models: teacher, student, and distilled—on hallucination reduction and semantic alignment. The novelty lies in:

- Applying knowledge distillation specifically to reduce hallucinations in abstractive summarization.
- Using a combination of semantic and factual benchmark metrics (e.g., ROUGE, BERTScore, factual consistency checks) to evaluate model outputs.
- Providing insights into the between model size, generation quality, and factual reliability in a distilled setting.

This research aims to serve as a reference for developing faster and more trustworthy summarization systems suitable for real-world applications.

2.2 Overview

Knowledge distillation has gained traction in various natural language processing tasks, including text classification, question answering, and especially abstractive summarization as task specific knowledge distillation. The main idea is to train the student model on the soft targets or output distributions of the teacher model. These soft targets capture richer information such as uncertainty, semantic relationships, and class probabilities. These are often lost in standard supervised learning. Large teacher models (e.g., GPT Falcon, Gemma, Mistral, LLaMA 2/3) can produce coherent and semantically rich summaries but are expensive to deploy. A research [7] demonstrated that GPT-3 [36] produced summaries preferred by human evaluators over fine-tuned models like Pegasus and BRIO on structured datasets such as CNN/DM [17]. Smaller models, although faster, often hallucinate or lose factual accuracy. Knowledge distillation allows the student to inherit the summarization quality of the teacher while maintaining efficiency through inference learning.

This research explores how KD can be applied to improve the faithfulness and factual consistency of summaries generated by compact models. We analyze whether distilled models can contain semantic alignment and reduce hallucinations when guided by high-quality teacher outputs. The overarching goal is to build a practical, lightweight summarizer that balances performance and reliability, especially for resource constrained environments.

2.3 Evaluation

Evaluating the performance of abstractive text summarization models is a critical step in determining their usefulness and reliability. Unlike extractive methods that simply pull key sentences from the original text, abstractive summarization generates new phrases or sentences, which makes evaluation more challenging due to its open-ended nature.

To measure the quality of generated summaries, researchers rely on a combination of benchmark metrics that assess different aspects of the output:

- ROUGE (Recall-Oriented Understudy for Gisting Evaluation) [34]: Measures the overlap of n-grams between the generated and reference summaries.
- BLEU (Bilingual Evaluation Understudy) [20]: It checks the precision of n-gram matches. In summarization, it gives insight into how closely the output follows reference phrasing.
- METEOR (Metric for Evaluation of Translation with Explicit ORdering) [30]: Considers synonyms and stemming, offering a more semantically aware evaluation.
- BERTScore [38]: Leverages contextual embeddings from pre-trained language models to compute semantic similarity between generated and reference summaries, providing a deep understanding of meaning beyond surface-level word matches.
- Faithfulness/Factual Consistency Checks(Human Validation): Identify hallucinations generated content that is fluent but factually incorrect or unsupported by the source.

In this research, these benchmark metrics are used to compare the outputs of teacher models, student models, and distilled models. The goal is to evaluate not only how well the student models replicate the summary structure of the teacher. Also to check knowledge distillation helps reduce hallucinations and maintain semantic relevance to the original text.

By using a mix of lexical and semantic metrics, the evaluation aims to capture both the surface-level quality and the deeper understanding conveyed by the summaries. When evaluating the faithfulness and quality of the summaries produced by knowledge distillation for text summarization, evaluation measures are essential. They provide quantifiable information on how well the teacher model's skills are retained by the student model. In terms of maintaining meaning, structure, and fluency, which are important markers of knowledge retention and hallucination avoidance.

ROUGE-L [23] is a bit advance one compared to ROUGE which captures structural and sequential similarity by calculating the longest common subsequence between the reference and the generated summary. This is helpful for determining how well the student model follows the teacher's or the reference summary's narrative structure. By comparing the overlap of word sequences between generated and reference summaries, BLEU assesses n-gram precision. By penalizing departures from expected word choices, it assists in detecting hallucinated content and identifying lexical fidelity.

In addition to exact matches, METEOR improves evaluation by using word stems, synonyms, and paraphrases. This enables a more human-oriented evaluation, which is especially helpful for confirming semantic coherence and guaranteeing that factually accurate but reworded summaries are not punished.

BERTScore (F1) assesses the semantic similarity between the generated and reference summaries by using contextual embeddings from a pretrained BERT model. Because it determines whether the created material conveys the same meaning even if the phrase varies it is particularly effective at detecting hallucinations. Also capturing deeper knowledge retention and inference fidelity.

So these benchmarks and manual validation can evaluate the summarizing capability of the LLMs.

3 Methodology

This study uses a structured task-specific knowledge distillation architecture to improve the text summarization capabilities of low-parameter language models.

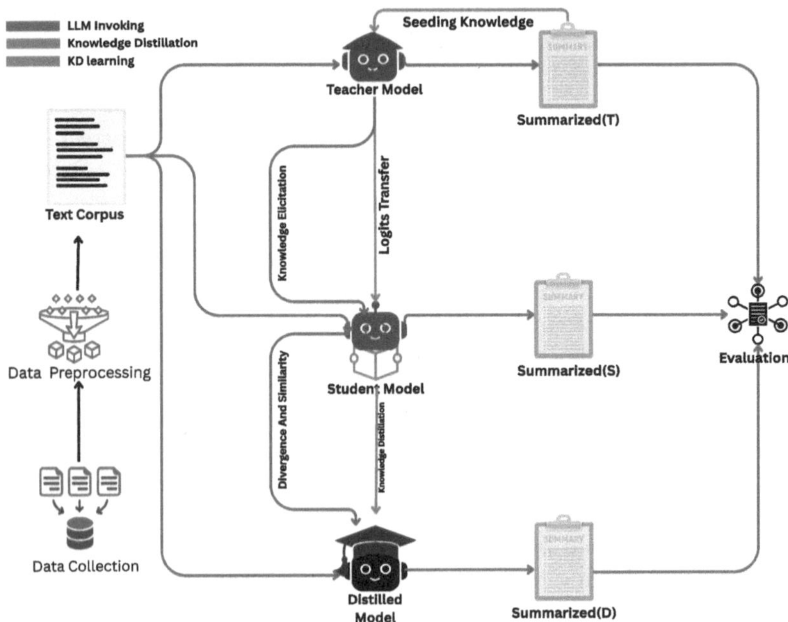

Fig. 2. Methodology

Experimental Setup

The approach consists of four main phases: dataset collection, knowledge elicitation from the teacher, knowledge distillation, and performance evaluation. The overall process ensures that task-specific knowledge for text summarizing from large language models (LLMs) is efficiently transferred to compact, open-source student models while maintaining summarization quality.

In this research, we explore the application of knowledge distillation to improve the performance and factual reliability of compact language models in abstractive text summarization.

We utilize a set of large and small-scale language models, including LLaMA, Mistral, Falcon, and Gemma, within a teacherstudent framework. Initially, abstractive summaries are generated using a lightweight student model such as Gemma or Falcon, establishing a baseline. Then, high-quality abstractive summaries are produced using larger teacher models like LLaMA 3 70B or Mistral 7B, which are assumed to have better contextual understanding and coherence. The Fig. 2 shows the flows from the data collection, the usual data preprocessing and preparing text corpus for the llm invoking. Once all the summaries generated from the teacher and student models, those baseline summaries are evaluated by defined metrics to establish initial performance benchmarks.

Then, the knowledge distillation is performed by training the student to imitate the teacher using and soft targets (logits or probability distributions). Teacher model's generated summary passed to the teacher model as data seed and perform knowledge elicitation. Through logits transferring the student model started learning in the divergence and similarity approach. Then new distilled model enhanced through the knowledge of teacher model.

The training objective incorporates KL divergence loss to align the student's predictions with the teacher's behavior.

$$\boxed{L_{\mathrm{KD}} = T^2\,\mathrm{KL}(p_S \parallel p_T)} \tag{1}$$

Here, $\mathrm{KL}(\cdot)$ describes the divergence between the softened output distributions of the teacher. (p_T) and student (p_S), with T as the temperature parameter that regulates the softness of the probability distributions.

The AdamW optimizer was used to train the student model with a batch size of 1, a temperature of 2.0 to soften the instructor outputs, and a learning rate of 3×10^{-5}. As previously mentioned, training was conducted using KL-divergence loss across a number of epochs until the loss stabilized. Using greedy decoding, the distilled model produced summaries up to 256 tokens long for decoding.

After distillation, the improved student model is evaluated alongside the original student and teacher models using standard benchmark metrics, including ROUGE-L, BLEU, METEOR, BERTScore, and TF-IDF Cosine Similarity. This methodology allows us to assess improvements in both semantic similarity and factual consistency while reducing hallucination in compact LLMs.

Data

This study entailed the development of a task-specific dataset that was designed for text summarization. A total of 300 distinct text paragraphs were gathered from various sources to ensure diversity in content, style, and domain, as summarized in the Table 1 The dataset was purposely constructed to include a wide range of written material, including storybooks, internet articles, AI-generated texts, newspapers, and academic research papers. This method ensured a balanced representation of narrative, informative, and technical material, allowing the summarizing models to generalize across various text genres.

To prepare the dataset, a thorough preprocessing phase was performed. This included standardizing the text's structure, eliminating extraneous numbering or

Table 1. Domain-wise statistics of the dataset.

Domain	Count	Percentage
Storybooks	60	20%
Internet Articles	75	25%
AI-generated Texts	45	15%
Newspapers	60	20%
Research Papers	60	20%

formatting discrepancies, and ensuring that paragraph boundaries were properly established.

Following preprocessing, the dataset went through a comprehensive manual validation process. Each paragraph was thoroughly examined to ensure that it was grammatically correct, contextually comprehensive, and free of unnecessary or extraneous content. This human check was required to maintain data integrity and prevent potential distortions in the learning process during knowledge distillation.

4 Results and Discussion

Our evaluation of knowledge distillation for text summarization across four major language model families LLaMA, Qwen, Gemma, and Falcon reveals notable differences in summarization performance and distillation effectiveness in Table 2.

Table 2. Evaluation metrics for teacher, student, and distilled models across LLM families.

Model Family	Model Type	ROUGE-L	BLEU	METEOR
LLaMA	Teacher (70B)	0.2220	3.7203	0.1495
	Student (8B)	0.3186	19.2837	0.4810
	Distilled	0.3609	17.2396	0.3448
Qwen	Teacher (72B)	0.7000	51.0000	0.7000
	Student (7B)	0.6743	47.6483	0.6726
	Distilled	0.6900	49.4700	0.6850
Gemma	Teacher (10B)	0.2600	15.0000	0.3700
	Student (2B)	0.2483	13.5520	0.3503
	Distilled	0.2900	16.0000	0.3900
Falcon	Teacher (40B)	0.2500	14.5000	0.3500
	Student (7B)	0.2311	11.8306	0.3057
	Distilled	0.2700	14.0000	0.3600

The Qwen family demonstrated outstanding summarization ability, with the teacher model achieving the highest scores across all metrics (ROUGE-L: 0.70, BLEU: 51.0, METEOR: 0.70). Impressively, its distilled variant retained 97% of the teacher's BLEU performance, indicating effective knowledge transfer and minimal performance loss.

In contrast, the LLaMA family presented mixed results: although the teacher model is large (70B), it showed relatively poor BLEU performance (3.72), possibly due to limited summarization fine-tuning. However, distillation improved ROUGE-L and METEOR, suggesting a trade-off between lexical diversity and content precision.

Gemma and Falcon models demonstrated moderate summarization capability. Their distilled models improved upon the student outputs in most metrics but remained less competitive overall, implying their architectural limitations in handling complex summarization tasks. These findings emphasize the importance of both model architecture and distillation techniques in achieving high-quality summaries.

5 Conclusion and Future Works

This study demonstrates that knowledge distillation can be a highly effective method for abstractive text summarization, particularly in producing compact models that retain strong summarization performance while reducing hallucinations. By evaluating four prominent language model families LLaMA, Qwen, Gemma, and Falcon. We observed that distilled models not only improved over their student counterparts but, in some cases, closely matched the teacher's output in quality. Notably, the distilled models, especially in the Qwen family, achieved high scores in BLEU, ROUGE-L, and METEOR while generating summaries that were more factually grounded and semantically faithful, indicating reduced hallucination. This highlights a key novelty of our approach: distillation not only transfers knowledge but also acts as a regularization mechanism that improves factual consistency. Our findings suggest that carefully selected teacher models and task-specific distillation pipelines can produce lightweight summarization models that are both efficient and hallucination-resistant.

While large language models (LLMs) are inherently task-agnostic, our study shows that tailoring them through task-specific knowledge distillation significantly boosts their performance on focused tasks like abstractive summarization. Instead of relying on heavier system-penetration techniques such as supervised fine-tuning (SFT) or in-context examples (ICE), task-specific distillation offers a more efficient and scalable alternative. By distilling targeted summarization knowledge from a strong teacher into smaller models, we achieve competitive results with reduced hallucination and improved semantic fidelity. While preserving inference efficiency and minimizing resource demands.

6 Limitations

While our study demonstrates the effectiveness of knowledge distillation in improving text summarization performance, several limitations remain. Firstly, due to limited GPU resources, we were unable to perform large-scale experiments across broader datasets or conduct multiple rounds of fine-tuning. Secondly, our distillation process focused solely on logit-level transfer, which does not deeply influence internal representations or system-level variables of the models. This makes it challenging to penetrate the model's broader system behaviors as done in techniques like instruction tuning or reinforcement learning. Finally, the hallucination reduction claims are based on benchmark improvements, but further human evaluation is needed to assess factual consistency in real-world scenarios.

Disclosure of Interests. The authors declare that they have no competing interests.

References

1. Achiam, J., et al.: GPT-4 technical report. arXiv preprint arXiv:2303.08774 (2023)
2. Bi, X., et al.: DeepSeek LLM: scaling open-source language models with longtermism. arXiv preprint arXiv:2401.02954 (2024)
3. Das, B.C., Amini, M.H., Wu, Y.: Security and privacy challenges of large language models: a survey. ACM Comput. Surv. **57**(6), 1–39 (2025)
4. Devlin, J., Chang, M.W., Lee, K., Toutanova, K.: Bert: Pre-training of deep bidirectional transformers for language understanding. In: Proceedings of the 2019 Conference of the North American Chapter of the Association for Computational Linguistics: Human Language Technologies, vol. 1 (long and short papers), pp. 4171–4186 (2019)
5. Etemad, A.G., Abidi, A.I., Chhabra, M.: Fine-tuned T5 for abstractive summarization. Int. J. Performability Eng. **17**(10), 900 (2021)
6. Gou, J., Yu, B., Maybank, S.J., Tao, D.: Knowledge distillation: a survey. Int. J. Comput. Vis. **129**(6), 1789–1819 (2021)
7. Goyal, T., Li, J.J., Durrett, G.: News summarization and evaluation in the era of GPT-3. arXiv preprint arXiv:2209.12356 (2022)
8. Guo, D., et al.: DeepSeek-R1: incentivizing reasoning capability in LLMs via reinforcement learning. arXiv preprint arXiv:2501.12948 (2025)
9. Ji, Z., et al.: Survey of hallucination in natural language generation. ACM Comput. Surv. **55**(12), 1–38 (2023)
10. Jia, R., Cao, Y., Shi, H., Fang, F., Liu, Y., Tan, J.: DistilSum: distilling the knowledge for extractive summarization. In: Proceedings of the 29th ACM International Conference on Information and Knowledge Management, pp. 2069–2072 (2020)
11. Jiao, X., et al.: TinyBERT: distilling BERT for natural language understanding. arXiv preprint arXiv:1909.10351 (2019)
12. Jung, J., et al.: Impossible distillation: from low-quality model to high-quality dataset & model for summarization and paraphrasing. arXiv preprint arXiv:2305.16635 (2023)
13. Jyoti, D., Srivastava, J., Mahato, D.P.: Implementing T5 for text summarization: an algorithmic approach. In: 2025 International Conference on Information Networking (ICOIN), pp. 648–652. IEEE (2025)

14. Kassianik, P., et al.: Llama-3.1-FoundationAI-securityLLM-Base-8B technical report. arXiv preprint arXiv:2504.21039 (2025)
15. Liu, J., et al.: DDK: distilling domain knowledge for efficient large language models. Adv. Neural. Inf. Process. Syst. **37**, 98297–98319 (2024)
16. Liu, Z., et al.: LLM-QAT: data-free quantization aware training for large language models. arXiv preprint arXiv:2305.17888 (2023)
17. Nallapati, R., Zhou, B., Gulcehre, C., Xiang, B., et al.: Abstractive text summarization using sequence-to-sequence RNNs and beyond. arXiv preprint arXiv:1602.06023 (2016)
18. Nguyen, T.T., Luu, A.T.: Improving neural cross-lingual abstractive summarization via employing optimal transport distance for knowledge distillation. In: Proceedings of the AAAI Conference on Artificial Intelligence, vol. 36, pp. 11103–11111 (2022)
19. Pang, J., et al.: Salute the Classic: revisiting challenges of machine translation in the age of large language models. Trans. Assoc. Comput. Linguist. **13**, 73–95 (2025)
20. Post, M.: A call for clarity in reporting bleu scores. arXiv preprint arXiv:1804.08771 (2018)
21. Rehman, T., Mandal, R., Agarwal, A., Sanyal, D.K.: Hallucination reduction in long input text summarization. In: International Conference on Security, Surveillance and Artificial Intelligence (ICSSAI-2023), pp. 307–316. CRC Press (2024)
22. Sequeda, J., Allemang, D., Jacob, B.: Knowledge graphs as a source of trust for LLM-powered enterprise question answering. J. Web Semant. **85**, 100858 (2025)
23. Su, L., et al.: GEM: a general evaluation benchmark for multimodal tasks. arXiv preprint arXiv:2106.09889 (2021)
24. Sun, Z., Yu, H., Song, X., Liu, R., Yang, Y., Zhou, D.: MobileBERT: a compact task-agnostic BERT for resource-limited devices. arXiv preprint arXiv:2004.02984 (2020)
25. Tang, R., Lu, Y., Liu, L., Mou, L., Vechtomova, O., Lin, J.: Distilling task-specific knowledge from BERT into simple neural networks. arXiv preprint arXiv:1903.12136 (2019)
26. Tian, Y., Pei, S., Zhang, X., Zhang, C., Chawla, N.V.: Knowledge distillation on graphs: a survey. ACM Comput. Surv. **57**(8), 1–16 (2025)
27. Touvron, H., et al.: Llama 2: open foundation and fine-tuned chat models. arXiv preprint arXiv:2307.09288 (2023)
28. Vaswani, A., et al.: Attention is all you need. In: Advances in Neural Information Processing Systems, vol. 30 (2017)
29. Venkataramana, A., Tijare, P.V., Singh, P.N.: Analyzing efficiency and accuracy of NLP tasks by BART transformer. In: International Conference on Data Science and Big Data Analysis, pp. 251–263. Springer (2025)
30. Wang, D., Hu, P., Wałęga, P.A., Grau, B.C.: MeTeoR: practical reasoning in datalog with metric temporal operators. In: Proceedings of the AAAI Conference on Artificial Intelligence, vol. 36, pp. 5906–5913 (2022)
31. Widyassari, A.P., et al.: Review of automatic text summarization techniques & methods. J. King Saud Univ.-Comput. Inf. Sci. **34**(4), 1029–1046 (2022)
32. Xia, Y., et al.: Hallucination diversity-aware active learning for text summarization. arXiv preprint arXiv:2404.01588 (2024)
33. Xu, X., et al.: A survey on knowledge distillation of large language models. arXiv preprint arXiv:2402.13116 (2024)

34. Yang, C., et al.: Answer summarization for technical queries: benchmark and new approach. In: Proceedings of the 37th IEEE/ACM International Conference on Automated Software Engineering, pp. 1–13 (2022)
35. Yang, S., Zhang, S., Zhang, H., Hung, C.C., Yang, F., Liu, S.: RDPNet: a multi-stage summary generation network for long chat dialogues. Knowl. Inf. Syst., 1–18 (2025)
36. Ye, J., et al.: A comprehensive capability analysis of GPT-3 and GPT-3.5 series models. arXiv preprint arXiv:2303.10420 (2023)
37. Zhang, H., Yu, P.S., Zhang, J.: A systematic survey of text summarization: from statistical methods to large language models. ACM Comput. Surv. **57**(11), 1–41 (2025)
38. Zhang, T., Kishore, V., Wu, F., Weinberger, K.Q., Artzi, Y.: BERTscore: evaluating text generation with BERT. arXiv preprint arXiv:1904.09675 (2019)
39. Zhang, Y., Wang, M., Li, Q., Tiwari, P., Qin, J.: Pushing the limit of LLM capacity for text classification. In: Companion Proceedings of the ACM on Web Conference 2025, pp. 1524–1528 (2025)
40. Zhang, Z., Meng, X., Wang, Y., Jiang, X., Liu, Q., Yang, Z.: UniMS: a unified framework for multimodal summarization with knowledge distillation. In: Proceedings of the AAAI Conference on Artificial Intelligence, vol. 36, pp. 11757–11764 (2022)

Environment and Sustainability

A Real Time Decision Support System for Selected Commercial Seaweed Species in Sri Lanka: Species Identification, Quality Assessment, and an Ontology Driven Knowledge Database

Y. Milani[1](✉), V. Kobi[1], Nelum D. Attanayake[1], P. C. B. Dias[2], and E. M. U. W. J. B. Ekanayake[1]

[1] Department of Computer Science and Informatics, Uva Wellassa University, Badulla, Sri Lanka
cst19056@std.uwu.ac.lk

[2] Department of Animal Science, Uva Wellassa University, Badulla, Sri Lanka

Abstract. Seaweed, with significant economic and ecological potential, are becoming an increasingly important export product for Sri Lanka. Proper identification and quality assessment are crucial for accurate traceability and export authentication to prevent species depletion due to overexploitation and ensure sustainable utilization. This study aims to develop a model that utilizes image processing techniques focusing on color, shape, and texture combined with machine learning and ontology, to identify, evaluate the quality of, and provide information about selected economically significant seaweed species. The study targets *Sargassum crassifolium, Kappaphycus alvarezii, Padina antillarum, Ulva lactuca,* and *Gracilaria corticata*, with primary data collected from seaweed farms and wild collection sites in Jaffna, Valaippaadu, Mannar, and Talpe, Sri Lanka. Images were resized to 600x600 pixels, and species identification was performed by categorizing them into folders, while quality assessment involved classifying them as "Good" or "Rejected." Various image processing techniques were used to develop identification and quality assessment models. The final identification model, combining histogram equalization, canny edge detection, contour analysis, and local binary patterns, achieved 92.67% accuracy with Random Forest. For quality assessment, *Padina antillarum* used histogram equalization, contour analysis, and gabor filters, with SVM reaching 95% accuracy. *Ulva lactuca* used color moments, canny edge detection, and GLCM, achieving 96% with Random Forest. *Kappaphycus alvarezii* used histogram equalization, color moments, contour analysis, and gabor filters, reaching 89%. An ontology developed from the collected data for easy querying and information retrieval about the species.

Keywords: Seaweed Identification · Seaweed Quality Assessment · Ontology · Image Processing · Machine Learning

R. N. Rajapakse et al. (Eds.): ICTer 2025, CCIS 2844, pp. 233–247, 2026.
https://doi.org/10.1007/978-981-92-0137-2_16

1 Introduction

Sri Lanka has a coastline of approximately 1,700 km, hosting nearly 260 species of seaweed, of which only a few *Chlorophyceae, Rhodophyceae, and Phaeophyceae* species are economically important [1]. Seaweed is used in cosmetics, livestock feed, horticulture, medicine, pharmaceuticals, and energy [2–6], and play a crucial role in carbon sequestration. They are categorized into red, green, and brown types, with *Kappaphycus alvarezii* being actively cultured, while most others are collected from wild areas such as Kalpitiya, Puttalam, Mannar, Kilinochchi, and Jaffna [7, 8].

This study focuses on five highly exported and economically important species: *Sargassum crassifolium, Kappaphycus alvarezii, Padina antillarum, Ulva lactuca,* and *Gracilaria corticata* [8–10].Sustainable harvesting requires accurate species identification to ensure traceability, ecological balance, and regulatory compliance. Quality assessment is essential before export or product use, considering disease, epiphytes, and color [11, 12]. Currently, only *Kappaphycus alvarezii, Padina antillarum, Ulva lactuca* are evaluated by farmers, while *Sargassum crassifolium* and *Gracilaria corticata* are exported without quality grading.

Accurate identification is challenging as expertise is needed to differentiate species, limiting participation in the seaweed industry. A system enabling real-time identification and quality assessment, coupled with an ontology-driven knowledge base, can support sustainable management, easy information retrieval, and broader industry participation.

Despite the economic and ecological importance of seaweed the major problem identified was, current identification and quality assessment methods are limited, and rely on expert knowledge. This restricts sustainable harvesting, traceability, and participation in the seaweed industry. *Hence,* this study aims to develop a system that enables real-time identification and quality assessment of economically important seaweed in Sri Lanka, and to create a centralized ontology-driven knowledge database that integrates information across multiple species to support better understanding, easy information retrieval, and sustainable management of seaweed resources.

The main objectives are,

- to develop a model to identify seaweed species using image processing and machine learning algorithms using parameters such as color, shape, and texture.
- to develop models to assess the quality of seaweed species using image processing and machine learning algorithms by using factors such as disease, epiphytes, and color.
- to develop an ontology-driven knowledge database using RDF and web semantic technologies, allowing integration of information from multiple seaweed species, including identification parameters, quality attributes, and ecological data.

2 Related Works

Recent advancements in seaweed farming and aquatic resource management have led to increasing interest in integrating technological solutions for species identification and quality monitoring.

2.1 Current Status of Seaweed in Sri Lanka

The coastal waters of Sri Lanka support green, brown, and red algae. Early studies document more than 250 species of seaweed in Sri Lankan waters [13]. Significant genera include *Sargassum, Gracilaria, Gelidiella,* and *Caulerpa,* which are commonly found in shallow waters and intertidal zones [14]. Seaweed farming could provide a sustainable source of income for coastal communities while also offering ecosystem services such as carbon sequestration and habitat restoration [15]. Northern Sri Lanka, particularly in areas like Mannar and Jaffna, has seen some expansion in seaweed farming, with initiatives focusing on both domestic use and exports.

2.2 Computer-Based Identification and Quality Assessment Tools in the Aquatic Field

Advancements in computer technologies have enabled the development of tools for monitoring and assessing aquatic environments. For example, the use of YOLO-based object detection models, achieved a 73% detection rate in fluorescence imagery, highlighting the promise of deep learning in seaweed monitoring but also pointing out its limitations in real-world image applications [12]. Statistical learning methods have been employed to differentiate floating plastic debris from natural marine elements [16], though issues like misclassification near shores persist. Some researchers utilized deep residual learning to improve image recognition accuracy, suggesting potential use in marine environments when enhanced with shortcut connections. Also, Researchers have made significant progress in developing computer vision-based techniques to automate the process of species identification, particularly for fish populations [17–19].

2.3 Machine Learning Approaches for Seaweed Classification

Machine learning approaches have shown promise in classifying seaweed species and related marine elements. Models like SVM and XGBoost in classifying seaweed at the phylum level with high accuracy, though these efforts are limited by the scope of species and dataset sizes [20]. Various other machine learning and remote sensing techniques have been applied to related marine monitoring tasks. Remote sensing techniques using Sentinel-1 and Sentinel-2 data, as explored by Knag, have proven useful in classifying seagrass and seaweed, but they are often constrained to specific geographic areas [21]. These studies indicate that while tools exist for aquatic classification, adapting them specifically to seaweed species remains a challenge. In the context of seaweed aquaculture, more targeted research has begun to emerge. Automatic classification methods have been explored to estimate seaweed biomass using UAV data [22], though high-resolution imagery remains a limiting factor. Deep learning has also been applied to analyze the spatial distribution of seaweed farms [23] and detect harmful algae blooms [24], though many of these models depend on small or specialized datasets.

While these computational and machine learning tools demonstrate potential for aquatic monitoring, there is a lack of research specifically targeting species-level identification and quality assessment of economically important seaweed in Sri Lanka. Most existing approaches focus either on general aquatic classification, limited species, or controlled environments. This study addresses this gap by developing a real-time identification and quality assessment framework tailored to locally important seaweed species.

3 Methodology

This section describes the systematic approach followed in this study, covering data collection, preprocessing, feature extraction, and model development for seaweed species identification, quality assessment, and ontology-based knowledge representation.

3.1 Seaweed Identification Model

Primary data on *Sargassum crassifolium, Kappaphycus alvarezii, Padina antillarum, Ulva lactuca,* and *Gracilaria corticata* were gathered by visiting seaweed farms in Jaffna, Valaippaadu, Mannar, and Talpe (see Fig. 1). Images were captured under varied conditions such as different lighting, angles, growth stages, environments, and both group and individual settings to ensure diversity and robustness in the dataset. The dataset is divided into six categories; *Sargassum crassifolium, Kappaphycus alvarezii, Padina antillarum, Ulva lactuca,* and *Gracilaria corticata,* and a none folder that consists of real-world images. The none folder is essential because this model is integrated into a mobile application and it should be able to identify the above-mentioned species and label others as none. Each of the above-mentioned categories contains 500 images altogether 3000 images to maintain uniformity and achieve the best performance. This balanced dataset ensures that the model is trained effectively across all classes, reducing bias and improving generalization.

Fig. 1. Sample data for identification model

The feature parameters color, shape and texture were selected based on guidance from experts in seaweed cultivation, and seaweed farmers in Jaffna. To select the most suitable image processing technique for each feature, previous literature on plant-related detection was reviewed. Based on this review, the top three image processing techniques were chosen for each type of feature parameter. For color extraction, color Moments, HSV [25], and Histogram equalization [26] methods are employed. For shape extraction, Prewitt with contour detection, Sobel with contour detection, and Canny with contour detection were selected [27]. For texture feature extraction, Gabor filters, GLCM [28], and LBP [29] were utilized. This approach ensures the most effective techniques are applied to capture and analyze the characteristics of seaweed.

After selecting these image processing techniques for each feature parameter, the data is trained using machine learning algorithms such as Random Forest, SVM, and KNN. These algorithms were chosen for this study because of their proven effectiveness in plant and crop classification tasks with small to medium-sized datasets in previous literature [27, 30]. The dataset was divided into 80% training and 20% testing subsets, ensuring sufficient data for model learning and a separate portion for unbiased evaluation. The final model is developed based on the selected features and machine learning algorithm resulting from the feature selection process and validated using, Receiver Operating Characteristic curves and Area Under the Curve graphs.

3.2 Seaweed Quality Assessment Model

The quality is assessed for three species *Kappaphycus alvarezii, Padina antillarum,* and *Ulva lactuca* from the selected species for identification. According to farmers in Jaffna and experts in the seaweed industry, the quality of *Sargassum crassifolium* and *Gracilaria corticata* was not assessed, as these species are typically exported in their raw form without quality grading. For quality assessment, limited primary data were available from farm visits (see Fig. 2); therefore, secondary data sources were also incorporated. The collected data are divided as Good and Rejected for each species. For each category there were 300 images and altogether 1800 images were used to train the model. The species that are good in quality are categorized in the good folder and the species which has disease, epiphyte, or low color quality are categorized into the Rejected folder. The farmers from Jaffna Seaweed farms gave the knowledge to categorize them into Rejected folders.

Fig. 2. Sample data for quality assessment model

For color extraction, image processing techniques such as histogram equalization and color moments are used [25, 26]. For shape feature extraction, contour analysis, Canny edge detection, and Fourier descriptors are employed [27]. Lastly, for texture extraction, GLCM [28], LBP, and Gabor filters are utilized. Each of these techniques is trained using Random Forest, SVM, and KNN [11, 30]. The dataset was divided into 80% training and 20% testing subsets, ensuring sufficient data for model learning and a separate portion for unbiased evaluation. To choose the best model before developing the final model, all the techniques were assessed to identify the highest accuracy and most efficient model. The trained models were evaluated using multiple performance metrics, including accuracy, precision, recall, and F1-score to capture both overall and class-specific performance.

3.3 Ontology Driven Knowledge Base

Ontology was selected over other knowledge representation methods because it provides formal semantics, logical reasoning, and flexible querying which can easily integrated with the mobile application. Unlike static databases, ontology allows the representation of hierarchical "is-a" relationships, object/data properties, and inference through reasoners, making it ideal for managing complex biological data such as seaweed species, their qualities, uses, and environmental dependencies. The data for the ontology is collected by visiting farms and searching through e-repositories (see Fig. 3). The collected data are categorized into objects, predicates, and subjects, which are then input into the Protégé tool to create the ontology (see Fig. 4).

Species	Sargassum crassifolium	Kappaphycus alvarezii	Padina antillarum	Ulva lactuca	Gracilaria
Parent	Sargassum (Sargassum)	Eucheuma alvarezii	Padina Adanson	Ulva Linnaeus	Gracilaria Greville
Environment	marine	marine	marine	marine	marine
children	Sargassum	Kappaphycus alvarezii var. tambalang (Doty) comb. [illegible]		Ulva lactuca f. [illegible] Ulva lactuca f. [illegible] Ulva lactuca f. contorta Ulva lactuca f. cribrosa Ulva lactuca f. [illegible]	Gracilaria corticata var. cylindrica Gracilaria corticata var. linearis Gracilaria corticata var. [illegible]
Tribe			Zonarieae		Gracilarieae
height	up to 30 cm high		between 4 and 17 cm tall	up to 20 cm long	10 (-15) cm long

Fig. 3. Sample data collection for ontology

Subject	Predicate	Object
Species	hasKingdom	Kingdom
Kingdom	isKingdom	Species
Kingdom	hasSubKingdom	Subkingdom
Subkingdom	isSubkingdom	Kingdom
Kingdom	hasInfrakingdom	Infrakingdom
Infrakingdom	isInfrakingdom	Kingdom
Species	hasPhylum	Phylum
Phylum	isPhylum	Species
Class	isClass	Species
Species	hasClass	Class
Class	hasSubClass	Subclass
Subclass	isSubClass	Class

Fig. 4. Processed ontology data

In Protégé, individuals, data properties, object properties, classes, subclasses, functional properties, and inverse properties are defined to establish relationships between the classes and their properties. Using the HermiT reasoner, all the relationships are tested and validated to ensure their consistency and validity. The OntoGraph is reviewed to confirm that all relationships are correctly represented. The ontology is then converted into RDF format connected with the mobile application, enabling it to be queried using SPARQL queries to retrieve relevant results from the mobile interface.

4 Results and Discussion

4.1 Identification Model

The results taken in the feature extraction process, model training process and selecting the final model are discussed below.

Feature Extraction. The Table 1 presents the performance of various machine learning algorithms across different image processing techniques for extracting color, shape, and texture features. By analyzing the table, the results indicate that Random Forest is particularly effective in color and texture feature extraction, while SVM might be a better option for certain shape extraction techniques. The differences between Random Forest and SVM are minor for many cases, but Random Forest demonstrates a more consistent performance across multiple features.

Table 1. Summary of the Feature Extraction Techniques

Feature	Image Processing Technique	Machine Learning Algorithm	Accuracy
Color	Color Moments	Random Forest	0.83
		SVM	0.79
		KNN	0.83
	HSV	Random Forest	0.91
		SVM	0.85
		KNN	0.84
	Histogram	Random Forest	0.95
		SVM	0.9
		KNN	0.83
Shape	Prewitt with Contour	Random Forest	0.43
		SVM	0.51
		KNN	0.2
	Sobel with Contour	Random Forest	0.46
		SVM	0.48
		KNN	0.29
	Canny with Contour	Random Forest	0.52
		SVM	0.54
		KNN	0.53
Texture	Gabor Filters	Random Forest	0.59
		SVM	0.34
		KNN	0.58
	GLCM	Random Forest	0.69
		SVM	0.64
		KNN	0.52
		Random Forest	0.79
	LBP	SVM	0.4
		KNN	0.69

Final Model. As both Random Forest and SVM show the best results in some of the feature extraction techniques, the final model is trained in three ways by combining the highest performing image processing techniques which are histogram equalization, Canny with contour and Local binary patterns:

Using Random Forest Algorithm. An ensemble method combining decision trees, it performed strongly in color and texture feature extraction, achieving 92.67% which shows a high accuracy of the seaweed identification model.

Using SVM Algorithm. SVM is a supervised learning algorithm known for its effectiveness in high-dimensional spaces. In this model, it excelled in shape feature extraction techniques. Though an accuracy of 86% using SVM is a good result, it is relatively low compared to that achieved with Random Forest model which is 92.67%.

Using Hybrid Approach. The hybrid approach combines both Random Forest and SVM to leverage their individual strengths. The predictions from the Random Forest model on color and texture features were merged with those from the SVM model on shape features, but yielded the lowest accuracy of 62.33%.

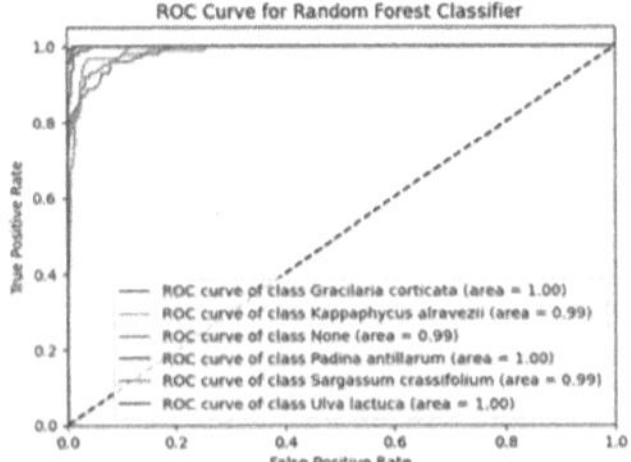

Fig. 5. ROC curve - Random Forest

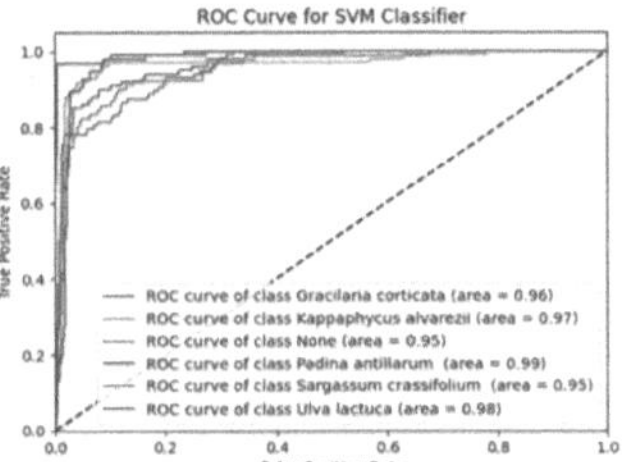

Fig. 6. ROC curve for SVM

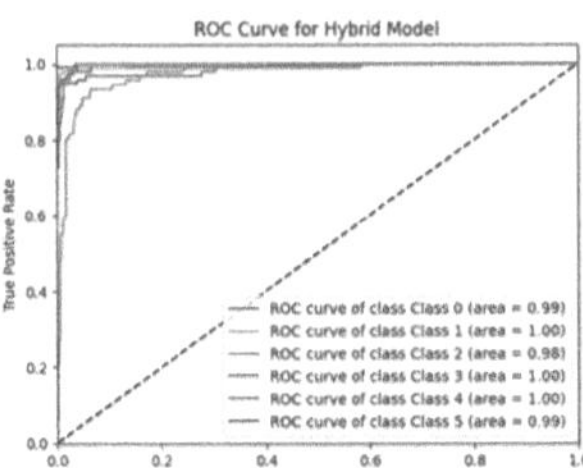

Fig. 7. ROC curve – Hybrid

Discussion. When comparing the accuracies of the approaches, the Random Forest model outperformed the SVM and Hybrid model approaches, suggesting that it was better suited to this identification task. In addition to accuracy, another important metric to consider in the conclusion is the ROC AUC score. While accuracy measures the percentage of correct predictions, the ROC AUC score provides a more advanced evaluation of a model's performance by considering both true positive rate and false positive rate. The below figures show the ROC AUC for Random Forest (see Fig. 5), SVM (see Fig. 6) and Hybrid model (see Fig. 7). According to the curves The Random Forest Classifier demonstrates best performance in identification tasks when compared to SVM and hybrid models. So, the conclusion can make that Random Forest model can be taken as the final model to effectively identify the seaweed species as *Sargassum crassifolium, Kappaphycus alvarezii, Padina antillarum, Ulva lactuca, Gracilaria corticata* and others as none. The species wise identification accuracy can be given as 82.83%, 91.79%, 97.46%, 95.60%, 97.89% respectively (see Fig. 8). The developed model was integrated with the mobile application and validated by capturing the images through it (see Fig. 9).

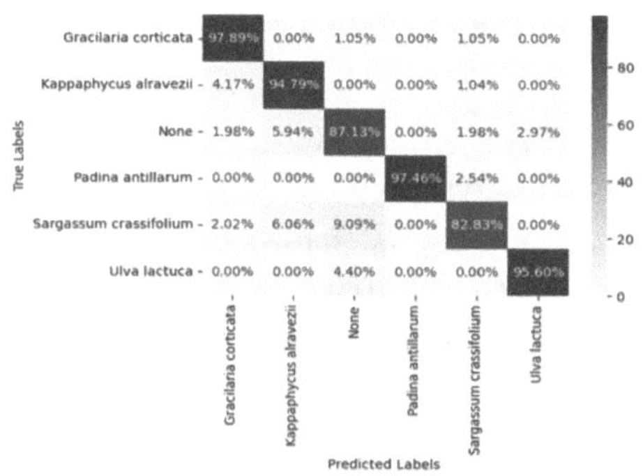

Fig. 8. Species wise Identification accuracy

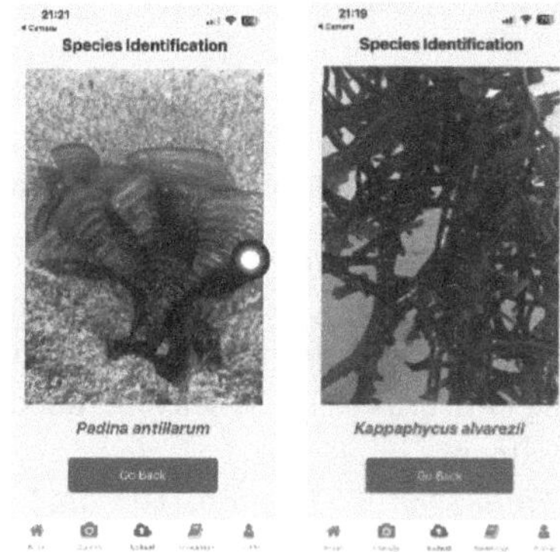

Fig. 9. Mobile interface for Species Identification

4.2 Quality Assessment Model

Quality Assessment Model of *Kappaphycus Alvarezii*. To accurately assess the quality of *Kappaphycus alvarezii*, a systematic approach combining color, texture, and shape features was employed to develop a robust machine learning model.

Feature Extraction. For *Kappaphycus alvarezii*, the final model combined color histogram, Gabor, and contour features to balance accuracy and generalization. Histogram equalization with Random Forest achieved the highest accuracy (0.93), making it ideal for capturing color patterns. Gabor filters reached 0.80 accuracy, effectively extracting texture, while contour analysis (0.69) added complementary shape information despite lower performance.

Final Model Selection. Considering the performance of various machine learning algorithms, Random Forest was selected as the final algorithm for *Kappaphycus alvarezii*. The Random Forest model was trained using the chosen features—color Histogram, Gabor Filters, and Contour Analysis. This choice was based on Random Forest's strong performance in handling diverse feature sets and its ability to balance accuracy with generalization.

The Table 2 classification report for *Kappaphycus alvarezii* using the Random Forest algorithm shows a good balance between precision and recall, with an overall accuracy of 92%. This indicates that the model effectively distinguishes between good quality and rejected samples.

Table 2. Random Forest classification report

Class	Precision	Recall	F1-Score	Support
Good Quality	0.90	0.90	0.90	59
Rejected	0.94	0.94	0.94	98
Accuracy			0.92	157

Quality Assessment Model of *Padina Antillarum*. To accurately assess the quality of *Padina antillarum*, a systematic approach combining color, texture, and shape features was employed to develop a robust machine learning model

Feature Extraction. For *Padina antillarum*, the final model used color histogram (with SVM, 0.97), contour detection (0.85), and GLCM (0.97). Although histogram equalization with Random Forest reached 1.00 accuracy, it was excluded due to overfitting concerns. GLCM was included for its robust texture analysis and reliable quality assessment.

Final Model Selection. The final model for *Padina antillarum* utilized SVM due to its strong performance across the selected features. Even though Random Forest showed high accuracy in some feature extractions, concerns about overfitting led to the selection of SVM. The final model thus combined color Histogram, Contour Analysis, and GLCM features, leveraging the strengths of each technique while mitigating overfitting issues. The Table 3 shows the final model accuracy of 0.95 for quality assessment for *Padina antillarum.*

Table 3. SVM classification report for *Padina antillarum*

Class	Precision	Recall	F1-Score	Support
Good Quality	0.97	0.94	0.95	31
Rejected	0.94	0.97	0.96	33
Accuracy			0.95	64

Quality Assessment Model of *Ulva Lactuca*. To accurately assess the quality of *Ulva Lactuca*, a systematic approach combining color, texture, and shape features was employed to develop a robust machine learning model.

Feature Extraction. For *Ulva lactuca*, the final model used color moments (0.97), GLCM (0.95), and Canny edge detection (0.94). Although histogram and local binary pattern features reached 1.00 accuracy, they were excluded due to overfitting risks, with edge detection preferred for its balanced performance.

Final Model Selection. The combined use of Random Forest for integrating Color Moments, GLCM, and Canny Edge Detection features allowed the model to leverage strengths across color, shape, and texture dimensions. This integration ensured that the final model for *Ulva lactuca* was both accurate and generalized well to different data conditions with accuracy of 0.96. According to the Table 4, the selected Random Forest algorithm was chosen for its consistent performance across the chosen features, thereby providing a robust and reliable model for quality assessment of *Ulva lactuca*.

Table 4. Random Forest classification report

Class	Precision	Recall	F1-Score	Support
Good Quality	0.93	0.97	0.95	29
Rejected	0.97	0.95	0.96	40
Accuracy			0.96	69

Discussion. Results show that feature importance and algorithm choice varied by species. Color features were generally the most discriminative but risked overfitting, while texture and shape feature improved robustness. Random Forest performed best for *Kappaphycus alvarezii* and *Ulva lactuca*, while SVM was more suitable for *Padina antillarum*.

4.3 Ontology Driven Knowledgebase

The ontology successfully represented seaweed species, their characteristics, and relationships, which were visualized through the Ontograph (see Fig. 10). Object properties with functional and inverse functionalities were correctly implemented, ensuring that species, uses, and attributes were logically connected. Running the HermiT reasoner validated these relationships by confirming class consistency and revealing hidden links between species characteristics and potential applications (see Fig. 11). The ontology was further integrated into the mobile application, allowing users to query species such as *Sargassum crassifolium*, *Kappaphycus alvarezii*, *Padina antillarum*, *Ulva lactuca*, and *Gracilaria corticate* (see Fig. 12). Instead of relying on external sources, users could instantly retrieve structured, contextually relevant knowledge about these species. This improved accessibility, enhanced user experience, and demonstrated the ontology's value as a practical knowledge tool.

Validation. To test reliability, multiple queries were performed through the mobile app and cross-checked against authoritative sources (AlgaeBase, published articles). The responses were accurate and consistent, confirming that the ontology delivers valid and trustworthy information.

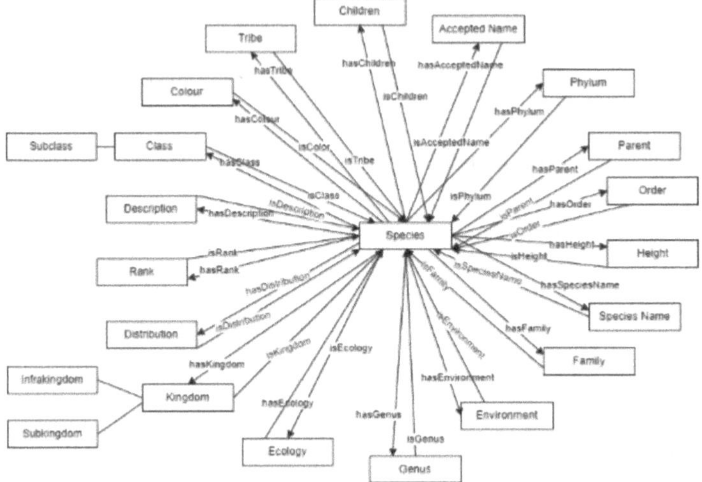

Fig. 10. Ontograph

Fig. 11. Validation using HermiT reasoner

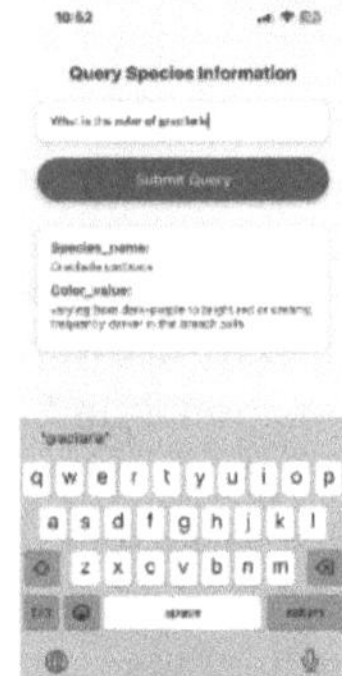

Fig. 12. Mobile interface for querying

5 Conclusions

This study developed an identification model, quality assessment models, and an ontology-driven knowledge base for seaweed in Sri Lanka. The identification model achieved 92.6% accuracy using Random Forest, while the quality assessment models reached 95% for *Padina antillarum*, 96% for *Ulva lactuca*, and 89% for *Kappaphycus alvarezii*. Random Forest proved effective in combining diverse feature types, whereas SVM excelled with species dominated by high-dimensional texture and shape data, showing that algorithm suitability depends on species-specific characteristics. The ontology-driven knowledge base, integrated into a mobile application, enabled structured queries and user-friendly knowledge enhancing accessibility for farmers, researchers, and stakeholders. Despite challenges in dataset collection, overfitting risks, and computational limits, the system demonstrates strong industrial potential. Future work should expand species coverage, standardize data collection, and further enhance the ontology and mobile application functionalities.

Disclosure of Interests. The authors declare that they have no conflicts of interest.

References

1. Hirimuthugoda, N.Y., Hansagith, N.G.L.S., Pahalawattaarachchi, V.: Biomass Estimation of Economically Important Sea Weeds Along the Southern Coast of Sri Lanka (2014)
2. Jesumani, V., Du, H., Aslam, M., Pei, P., Huang, N.: Potential use of seaweed bioactive compounds in skincare—a review. Mar. Drugs. **17**, 688 (2019). https://doi.org/10.3390/MD17120688
3. Makkar, H.P.S., et al.: Seaweed for livestock diets: a review. Anim. Feed Sci. Technol. **212**, 1–17 (2016). https://doi.org/10.1016/J.ANIFEEDSCI.2015.09.018
4. Battacharyya, D., Babgohari, M.Z., Rathor, P., Prithiviraj, B.: Seaweed extracts as biostimulants in horticulture. Sci. Hortic. **196**, 39–48 (2015). https://doi.org/10.1016/J.SCIENTA.2015.09.012
5. Smit, A.J.: Medicinal and pharmaceutical uses of seaweed natural products: a review. J. Appl. Phycol. **16**, 245–262 (2004). https://doi.org/10.1023/B:JAPH.0000047783.36600.EF/METRICS
6. Jung, K.A., Lim, S.R., Kim, Y., Park, J.M.: Potentials of macroalgae as feedstocks for biorefinery. Bioresour. Technol. **135**, 182–190 (2013). https://doi.org/10.1016/J.BIORTECH.2012.10.025
7. Stegenga, H.: Sri Lankan seaweed: methodologies and field guide to the dominant species. Bot. Mar. **54**, 109–109 (2011). https://doi.org/10.1515/BOT.2011.004
8. Ginigaddara, G.A.S., Lankapura, A.I.Y., Rupasena, L.P., Bandara, A.M.K.R.: Seaweed farming as a sustainable livelihood option for northern coastal communities in Sri Lanka. Res. Pap. Future Food: J. Food, Agric. Soc. **6** (2018)
9. Premarathna, A.D., Jayasooriya, A.P., Amcp, K., Jayasooriya, A.P., De, J., Adhikari, R.B.: Distribution and diversity of seaweed species in south coastal waters in Sri Lanka Chathuranga pradeep kumara National Aquatic Resources Research and development agency distribution and diversity of seaweed species in south coastal waters in Sri Lanka. J Oceanogr Mar Res. **7**, 196 (2019). https://doi.org/10.35248/2572-3103.20.8.196
10. Shanmugam, M., et al.: Successful establishment of commercial farming of carrageenophyte *Kappaphycus alvarezii* Doty (Doty) in Sri Lanka: economics of farming and quality of dry seaweed. J. Appl. Phycol. **29**, 3015–3027 (2017). https://doi.org/10.1007/S10811-017-1161-Z/METRICS
11. Lytou, A.E., et al.: Quality and safety assessment of edible seaweed alaria esculenta and saccharina latissima cultivated in Scotland. Foods. **10**, 2210 (2021). https://doi.org/10.3390/FOODS10092210/S1
12. Ranolo, E., Gorro, K., Ilano, A., Pineda, H., Sintos, C., Gorro, A.J.: Underwater and coastal seaweed detection for fluorescence seaweed photos and videos using YOLOV3 and YOLOV5. In: 2023 2nd International Conference for Innovation in Technology, INOCON 2023 (2023). https://doi.org/10.1109/INOCON57975.2023.10101342
13. Report of the Regional Workshop on the Culture & Utilization of Seaweed.: https://www.fao.org/4/ab727e/ab727e06.htm, Accessed 14 Sep 2025

14. (PDF) Seaweed resources and utilization: an overview, https://www.researchgate.net/publication/287106272_Seaweed_resources_and_utilization_an_overview, Accessed 14 Sep 2025
15. Sultana, F., et al.: Seaweed farming for food and nutritional security, climate change mitigation and adaptation, and women empowerment: a review. Aquac Fish. **8**, 463–480 (2023). https://doi.org/10.1016/J.AAF.2022.09.001
16. Duarte, M.M., Azevedo, L.: Automatic detection and identification of floating marine debris using multispectral satellite imagery. IEEE Trans. Geosci. Remote Sens. **61** (2023). https://doi.org/10.1109/TGRS.2023.3283607
17. Vu, Q.T., Pham, T.D., Nguyen, V.Q.: Research article: artificial intelligence models for identifying several fish species based on otolith morphology index analysis from nearshore areas of Vietnam. Iran. J. Fish. Sci. **24**, 277–304 (2025). https://doi.org/10.22092/ijfs.2025.132877
18. Chandak, A.V., Bante, P., Ghaiwat, A., Malani, N.: Automatic identification of fish species using machine learning. In: OCIT 2023 - 21st International Conference on Information Technology, Proceedings, pp. 364–368 (2023). https://doi.org/10.1109/OCIT59427.2023.10430793
19. Yassir, A., Jai Andaloussi, S., Ouchetto, O., Mamza, K., Serghini, M.: Acoustic fish species identification using deep learning and machine learning algorithms: a systematic review. Fish. Res. **266**, 106790 (2023). https://doi.org/10.1016/J.FISHRES.2023.106790
20. Cheng, J., Jia, N., Chen, R., Guo, X., Ge, J., Zhou, F.: High-resolution mapping of seaweed aquaculture along the Jiangsu coast of China using Google earth engine (2016–2022). RemS. **14**, 6202 (2022). https://doi.org/10.3390/RS14246202
21. Knag, S.: Seagrass and Seaweed Detection Approaches Using Remote Sensing and Google Earth Engine: A Comparative Analysis of Different Machine Learning Techniques
22. Gomes, J.P., Sousa, J.J., Pádua, L., Cunha, C.R., Cunha, A.: Characterization of seaweed communities using deep learning applied to UAV-based hyperspectral images. In: CENTERIS 2021 - Conference on Enterprise Information Systems / ProjMAN 2021 - International Conference on Project MANagement / HCist 2021 - International Conference on Health and Social Care Information Systems and Technologies, pp. 1–3 (2021). https://doi.org/10.3390/md17120688
23. Zhu, H., et al.: Remote sensing classification of offshore seaweed aquaculture farms on sample dataset amplification and semantic segmentation model. Remote Sens. **15**, 4423 (2023). https://doi.org/10.3390/RS15184423
24. Kumar, A.C., Bhandarkar, S.M.: A deep learning paradigm for detection of harmful algal blooms. In: Proceedings - 2017 IEEE Winter Conference on Applications of Computer Vision, WACV 2017, pp. 743–751 (2017). https://doi.org/10.1109/WACV.2017.88
25. Hamuda, E., Mc Ginley, B., Glavin, M., Jones, E.: Automatic crop detection under field conditions using the HSV colour space and morphological operations. Comput. Electron. Agric. **133**, 97–107 (2017). https://doi.org/10.1016/J.COMPAG.2016.11.021
26. Kumar Patil, J., Sampatrao Mandlik, V.: Nature Environment and Pollution Technology An International Quarterly Scientific Journal Open Access Journal Original Research Paper Plant Leaf Disease Detection Using Integrated Color and Texture Features. 23, 2101–2113. https://doi.org/10.46488/NEPT.2024.v23i04.016.
27. Rani, G., Srivastava, S., Kundu, N., Dhaka, V.S.: Leaf edge detection using machine learning. In: 2023 International Conference on Emerging Trends in Networks and Computer Communications, ETNCC 2023- Proceedings, pp. 229–234 (2023). https://doi.org/10.1109/ETNCC59188.2023.10284977
28. Syahputra, H., Indra, Z., Febrian, D., Putri Adriani, D.: Leaf feature extraction using glcm, moment invariant and shape morphology for indonesian medicinal plants recognition. J. Phys. Conf. Ser. **1317** (2019). https://doi.org/10.1088/1742-6596/1317/1/012008

29. Turkoglu, M., Hanbay, D.: Leaf-based plant species recognition based on improved local binary pattern and extreme learning machine. Physica A: Stat. Mech. Appl. **527**, 121297 (2019). https://doi.org/10.1016/J.PHYSA.2019.121297
30. (PDF) Plant Leaf Disease Recognition Using Random Forest, KNN, SVM and CNN: https://www.researchgate.net/publication/351708837_Plant_Leaf_Disease_Recognition_Using_Random_Forest_KNN_SVM_and_CNN, Accessed 14 Sep 2025

Identifying Three-Band Hyperspectral Composites that Outperform RGB for Floating Plastic Detection

Savindu Harith[1(✉)], Chathura Rajapakse[1], Thilini Mahanama[1], Dinesh Asanka[1], Shanaka Baduge[2], Gihan Ruwanpathirana[2], and Sadeep Thilakarathna[2]

[1] Department of Industrial Management, Faculty of Science, University of Kelaniya, Kelaniya, Sri Lanka
{washa251,chathura,thilinim,dasanka}@kln.ac.lk
[2] Department of Infrastructure Engineering, Faculty of Engineering and Information Technology, University of Melbourne, Melbourne, Australia
{kasun.kristombu,g.ruwanpathirana, sadeep.thilakarathna}@unimelb.edu.au

Abstract. Floating plastic pollution poses severe environmental risks, requiring precise and efficient detection methods. While Hyperspectral Imaging (HSI) offers rich spectral detail for identifying plastic types, its high dimensionality and processing demands limit real-time applications. This study investigates whether compact three-band hyperspectral composites can outperform RGB in object-level plastic detection while remaining compatible with standard detection models. Using a publicly available dataset collected with Specim FX10 and FX17 cameras, object-level annotations were aligned and used to create a balanced synthetic dataset. Six statistically discriminative bands were selected through ANOVA testing, from which 20 three-band combinations were evaluated across YOLO, Faster R-CNN, and RetinaNet models. Results demonstrate that several composites consistently outperformed RGB baselines, particularly for HDPE and PP classes, with notable contributions from bands near 990 nm, 1335 nm, and 1702 nm. These improvements were achieved without modifying model architectures or training parameters. Band frequency analysis further revealed model-specific and class-specific patterns in optimal wavelengths. This work highlights the potential of reduced-band hyperspectral inputs for accurate, scalable detection of floating plastics, providing a step toward more resource-efficient sensing systems suited for dynamic aquatic environments.

Keywords: Floating plastic detection · Hyperspectral band selection · Three-band composites · Object detection models

1 Introduction

Global plastic pollution has become a critical environmental challenge, with floating plastics representing one of the most harmful and visible components [1, 2] . Each year, an estimated 19 to 23 million metric tons of plastic waste enter aquatic ecosystems [3],

R. N. Rajapakse et al. (Eds.): ICTer 2025, CCIS 2844, pp. 248–261, 2026.
https://doi.org/10.1007/978-981-92-0137-2_17

much of it transported through river systems into lakes and oceans [2]. Floating plastics now account for more than 80–90% of marine litter [4], forming large accumulations such as "rubbish islands" that severely damage marine habitats [1]. These plastics persist in the environment for decades, breaking down into microplastics particles less than 5 mm in size, which are nearly impossible to remove and can be ingested by a wide range of marine organisms [1]. This not only threatens marine biodiversity and food webs but also introduces toxic substances into the food chain, posing risks to human health [1–3]. In addition, plastic pollution contributes to broader environmental problems, including greenhouse gas emissions from its fossil fuel-based production [1]. As global production and disposal of plastics continue to rise, the impact on aquatic environments is becoming increasingly severe [2, 4].

Addressing the growing scale of floating plastic pollution requires not only awareness of the problem but also the strategic use of modern technologies to mitigate it effectively. Recent advancements in remote sensing and artificial intelligence offer promising tools for detecting, monitoring, and managing plastic debris in aquatic environments [2, 5]. Satellite imagery, such as data from the Sentinel-2 mission, provides high-resolution, frequent coverage of coastlines and water bodies, enabling the identification of plastic accumulations over large areas [1, 3, 4]. Complementing this, drones and unmanned aerial vehicles (UAVs) are increasingly used for closer, weather independent inspections of rivers and lakes, often capturing multispectral images that reveal distinct optical signatures of plastic waste [1]. Once plastics are collected, intelligent systems guide the sorting and recycling process by analyzing image data to classify polymer types with high accuracy [6]. These integrated technologies from early detection to intelligent sorting represent a significant step forward in managing plastic waste more efficiently and sustainably, offering scalable solutions to this pressing global issue.

Among the emerging technologies supporting plastic pollution monitoring, Hyperspectral Imaging (HSI) stands out for its ability to capture highly detailed spectral information, offering substantial advantages over conventional imaging methods such as RGB [7, 8]. Unlike RGB systems, which record visual data in only three broad spectral bands (red, green, and blue), HSI collects data across hundreds of narrow and continuous spectral bands [3, 9, 10]. This enables the detection of subtle material-specific features that are not visible to standard cameras. In the context of floating plastic detection, this capability is especially valuable, as different polymers exhibit distinct spectral signatures based on their composition, age, and environmental conditions [2, 3]. HSI's enhanced spectral resolution allows for the precise identification and discrimination of plastics from natural materials such as vegetation, driftwood, or foam, even in complex aquatic environments [3, 4]. This fine-grained analysis improves the reliability of remote sensing efforts and strengthens early detection systems by distinguishing plastics not only by type but also by their optical response in varied water conditions [2]. As a result, HSI has become an essential tool in high accuracy monitoring frameworks, reinforcing efforts to track and understand the presence of plastic debris across rivers, lakes, and oceans.

While Hyperspectral Imaging offers clear advantages in detecting floating plastics, its practical implementation, particularly in real-time scenarios, presents notable challenges [7, 9, 11]. Floating plastics are constantly in motion due to the influence of water currents, wind, and other environmental conditions, which makes timely detection essential for accurate tracking and effective intervention [1, 2]. However, processing full HSI cubes, which contain rich spectral and spatial information, requires substantial computational resources, especially when used on edge devices such as drones or unmanned surface vessels [7, 12, 13]. As a result, delays in data analysis can occur, and by the time detection results are generated, the plastic objects may have already moved from their original location. This leads to inaccurate geolocation and reduces the effectiveness of rapid response efforts. Therefore, despite the strengths of HSI, its use on mobile platforms in real-time conditions remains constrained by both the computational demands of full data cubes [14] and the dynamic movement of plastics in natural aquatic environments [1].

To overcome the limitations associated with full HSI cubes, recent studies have highlighted the effectiveness of selecting a small number of informative spectral bands [15, 16]. Reducing high-dimensional hyperspectral data to a few optimally chosen bands significantly lowers computational cost and data storage requirements, which is especially valuable for real-time applications on resource-constrained platforms [16]. In various contexts, including agricultural monitoring and waste classification, selected subsets of hyperspectral bands have achieved accuracy comparable to full-spectrum data and have consistently outperformed standard RGB imagery [17]. By focusing on a limited set of wavelengths, these approaches can retain the most distinctive spectral features of target materials, enabling accurate identification even in complex visual environments [18]. This makes carefully selected hyperspectral band combinations a promising foundation for developing simplified, efficient sensing systems capable of supporting high-precision detection tasks in dynamic field conditions [9].

Despite these advancements, there remains a noticeable gap in the application of band selection strategies to the object-level detection of floating plastics. While the potential of reduced-band hyperspectral data has been demonstrated in other domains, few studies have explored how compact spectral composites can be directly integrated into real-time object detection frameworks commonly used with RGB imagery [9]. In particular, systematic efforts to identify three-band hyperspectral combinations that reduce data complexity while achieving performance comparable to or better than RGB are limited. The aim of this research is to evaluate whether carefully selected three-band hyperspectral composites can enhance object-level detection of floating plastics while remaining compatible with existing three-channel object detectors. To address this aim, this study identifies informative spectral bands from a publicly available hyperspectral dataset collected with Specim FX10 and FX17 cameras [19], constructs multiple three-band pseudo-RGB composites representing key plastic classes, trains and evaluates YOLO, RetinaNet, and Faster R-CNN on these composites within a controlled experimental framework, and compares their detection performance with RGB baselines by analyzing per-class AP. Together, these steps offer a practical approach for integrating reduced-band hyperspectral data into real-time monitoring systems without requiring architectural changes to widely used detection models..

2 Related Work

In this section, we briefly review related work on spectral band selection and the use of compact hyperspectral inputs for object-level detection tasks in plastic and related domains. We also discuss studies focused on classification using full-cube hyperspectral data, as well as object detection methods based on RGB or multispectral imagery, to provide context for the challenges and directions that shape our approach.

Hyperspectral image classification has been widely used to identify and differentiate material types across domains such as agriculture, remote sensing, and waste management [1, 22, 23]. These tasks typically rely on the full spectral range to extract pixel-level signatures that reveal subtle differences in reflectance characteristics [24]. For example, deep learning models trained on hyperspectral data have classified vegetable soybean freshness with over 93% accuracy [22].In another study, spectral features were used to distinguish between 90 rice seed species, achieving strong F1 scores that declined as the number of classes increased [25]. In plastic waste applications, hyperspectral imaging has been used to classify polymers such as PET, HDPE, and PVC by leveraging near-infrared reflectance characteristics [23]. A separate system achieved an F1-score of 71% across 18 object classes on a moving conveyor belt using a hyperspectral camera operating in the 900–1800 nm range [5]. While such results demonstrate the potential of full-cube spectral information, several challenges remain. The low spatial resolution of many HSI systems can reduce the clarity of small or detailed objects [25, 26], and the large number of spectral bands often introduces redundancy that may impair model performance if not carefully managed [16, 22, 24]. Additionally, the high volume of data increases processing demands and limits real-time deployment in practical settings [7, 16]. These constraints emphasize the need to balance spectral detail with computational efficiency when designing HSI-based classification systems.

In contrast, object-level detection using RGB imagery has gained traction due to its high spatial resolution and compatibility with well-established computer vision models [25, 26]. RGB-based methods have shown strong performance in localizing plastic objects based on visual features such as shape and texture [27]. However, their reliance on RGB bands limits their ability to detect materials with similar visual appearances, particularly under challenging conditions such as biofouling, partial submergence, or cluttered scenes [1, 23, 26]. These limitations often result in missed detections, particularly when transparent or dark-colored plastics are involved [6]. Moreover, RGB-based systems are generally insensitive to the spectral response of plastic materials themselves, making them less reliable for distinguishing plastics from background elements like water, foam, or natural debris, especially in dynamic or outdoor environments [1]. As a result, their utility is limited in scenarios where spectral characteristics play a key role in object identification.

To overcome the limitations of RGB while still leveraging the spectral richness of hyperspectral data, researchers have turned to band selection and dimensionality reduction techniques as a means to avoid the computational burden of full-cube processing. Principal Component Analysis (PCA) is frequently used to reduce data volume. For instance, one study compressed 127 hyperspectral channels into 30 principal components while preserving over 99.9% of the variance [28]. In another case, PCA facilitated the selection of dominant wavelengths for plastic film detection in cotton by analyzing the first three components [29]. Band selection methods have also been developed to isolate effective spectral intervals, such as 1087.6 to 1285.1 nm, which proved useful for identifying transparent PET, blue PET, and PP bottles [23]. Clustering techniques like Density Peak Clustering and hierarchical clustering have been employed to identify key wavelengths, especially in the visible range, where weaker inter-band correlations are observed [4]. Sparse variable selection has been used to pinpoint reflection peaks and absorption valleys in wet plastic spectra [4]. Additionally, difference spectra analysis has identified dominant features by subtracting cotton spectra from plastic film responses, revealing local maxima near 497 and 670 nm [29]. For real-time applications like waste sorting, dual-stage selection strategies [30] and convex-hull [16] methods have enabled significant data reduction, with one system shrinking the dataset to less than 1% of its original size while maintaining critical information. Some approaches also leverage machine learning models such as XGBoost to identify optimal spectral bands and indexes for satellite-based plastic detection [1]. Together, these techniques form a critical foundation for efficient and scalable detection systems that maintain spectral precision without the burden of full-cube data processing.

Efforts to integrate minimal-band hyperspectral data into object detection frameworks have begun to emerge across a few application domains. For example, one study employed a supervised band selection approach to identify three informative wavelengths from hyperspectral imagery, which were then used to train lightweight YOLOv8 models. The selected band combinations, derived either from pixel intensity features or from texture-based features, enabled the YOLOv8-small model to achieve 89.0% accuracy using only three spectral channels [9]. In another application, a shortwave infrared imaging system was designed to acquire three-channel images under challenging visibility conditions for object detection. Bands were selected using a recognition and localization score, which guided the creation of custom optical filters tailored for improved detection accuracy [18]. These studies illustrate the potential of using a small number of hyperspectral bands to support compact detection architectures when full-cube data is not practical.

While selected three-band hyperspectral inputs have shown promise in object detection tasks from other domains, systematic efforts to identify spectral composites that outperform RGB in detecting floating plastics remain underrepresented. This gap motivates our investigation into whether carefully chosen HSI combinations can improve plastic detection while remaining compatible with existing object detection model architectures.

3 Methodology

This section outlines the overall methodological framework adopted in this study. The research is guided by the following questions.

1. Can carefully selected three-band hyperspectral composites improve object-level detection of floating plastics compared to RGB baselines?
2. Which spectral band combinations most contribute to improved detection across different plastic types and object detection models?
3. Can such improvements be achieved without modifying existing three-channel object detection architectures?

To answer these questions, the methodology is organized into key stages, with the overall workflow shown in Fig. 1. Each stage is described in the following subsections.

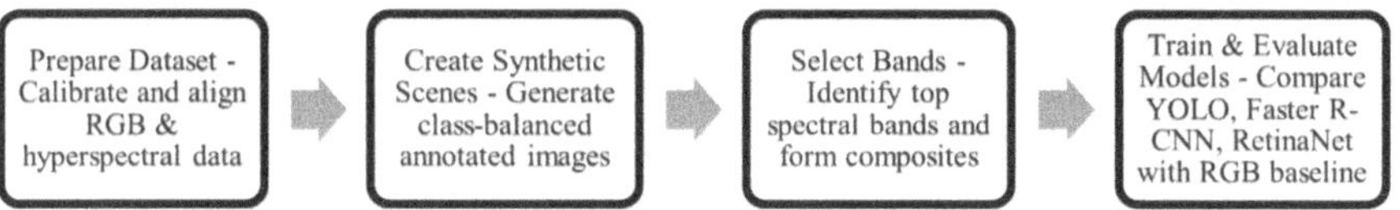

Fig. 1. Overview of the research workflow from dataset preparation to model evaluation.

3.1 Dataset and Pre-Processing

We used a hyperspectral dataset originally developed to support spectral analysis of floating macro-plastics in aquatic environments [19]. The data was collected indoors under controlled conditions using Specim FX10 and FX17 line-scan cameras, covering a spectral range from 400 to 1700 nm across 336 bands. The dataset includes 40 virgin macro plastic items spanning five types of plastic polymers: high-density polyethylene (HDPE), low-density polyethylene (LDPE), polyethylene terephthalate (PET), polypropylene (PP), and polystyrene (PS). Each item was floated in a water-filled black container to simulate realistic aquatic conditions and scanned using push-broom imaging under halogen illumination. White and dark references were used for reflectance calibration to ensure consistent spectral accuracy. Although the original dataset was not designed for object detection, its rich spectral content provided a strong foundation for constructing a new set of hyperspectral cubes tailored to our task.

3.2 Registration

Accurate alignment between RGB images and hyperspectral data was essential for evaluating three-band composites against RGB baselines. The RGB image was derived from the FX10 sensor by selecting its red, green, and blue channels, while a pseudo-RGB image was generated from the FX17 sensor using three representative shortwave infrared bands. The FX10 RGB image was resized to match the FX17 spatial resolution, but edge overlays and grayscale difference heatmaps (Fig. 2) revealed clear misalignment, confirming that simple resizing was insufficient and necessitating further calibration.

To ensure accurate alignment between FX10 RGB images and FX17 hyperspectral cubes, polygons were manually drawn around corresponding objects in several image pairs. Global alignment was first estimated by computing vertical offsets using one-dimensional correlation of row-wise brightness profiles, then refined with an affine transformation that maximized grayscale similarity within the masked object regions, allowing scale, shear, and translation adjustments. The resulting transformation was applied across the full dataset, with each FX10 RGB image vertically shifted, resized to match the FX17 resolution, and warped using the affine matrix. Alignment quality was visually verified through image overlays, where well-aligned regions appeared as neutral tones, and object-specific masks ensured calibration focused on plastic items

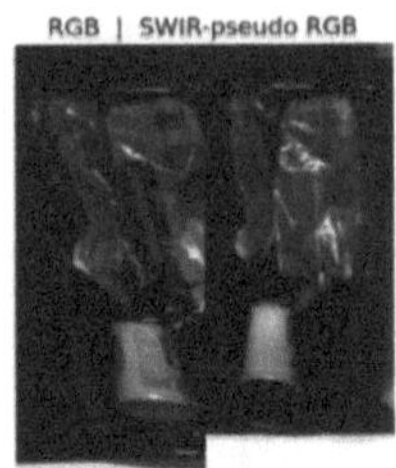

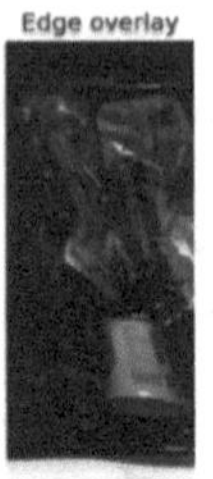

Fig. 2. Visual inspection of alignment between RGB and FX17 pseudo-RGB images using edge overlays and difference heatmaps.

rather than background. The annotated polygons were then converted into bounding boxes and transferred to the hyperspectral cubes, with visual inspection confirming that object-level correspondence was successfully preserved (Fig. 3).

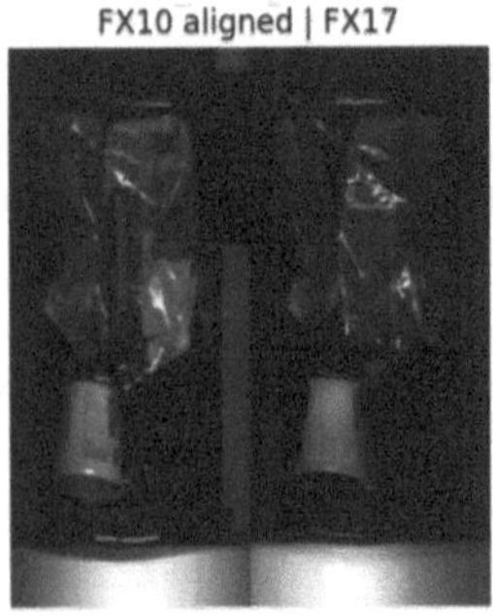

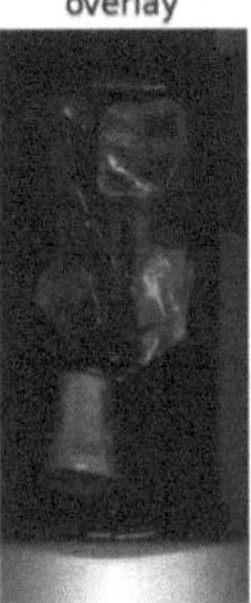

Fig. 3. Aligned FX10 RGB image and FX17 pseudo-RGB composite after object-level calibration.

3.3 Dataset Preparation

Following registration, object-level annotations were used to create a structured library of individual plastic items, each containing aligned hyperspectral data, an RGB counterpart, and class metadata for consistent reuse. Using this library, 200 synthetic hyperspectral scenes were programmatically generated at a fixed resolution of 640 $\times$ 640 pixels by randomly placing three to four non-overlapping objects on backgrounds extracted from object-free regions of the original dataset. A minimum padding of 8 pixels was enforced to prevent overlap, and sampling was balanced across the five plastic classes. Geometric augmentations were applied to increase shape variability while preserving spectral information, and larger objects were proportionally downscaled to a maximum dimension of 320 pixels. For each scene, a full hyperspectral cube and a corresponding RGB image were generated, with bounding box annotations provided in a normalized format compatible with common object detection frameworks. The final dataset consisted of 455 annotated instances, evenly distributed across classes (91 per plastic type).

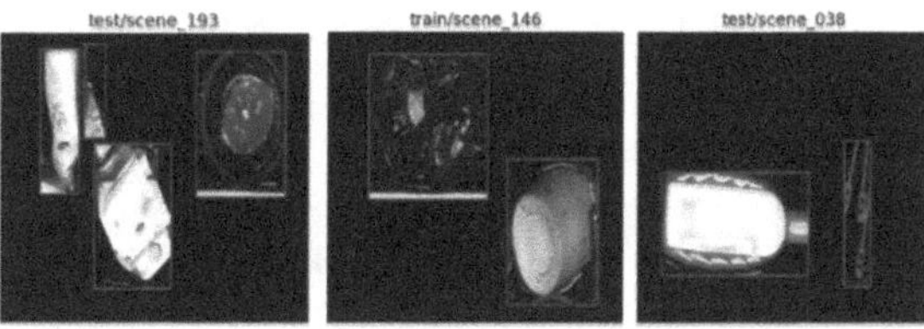

Fig. 4. Sample synthetic scenes with annotated plastic objects from the constructed dataset.

This process produced a balanced synthetic dataset of 200 scenes that served as the foundation for the experiments. For each selected three-band combination, 200 corresponding pseudo-RGB images were generated along with their hyperspectral cubes, RGB counterparts, and bounding box annotations, structured for direct integration into object detection pipelines, as illustrated in Fig. 4 showing sample synthetic scenes with annotated plastic objects from the constructed dataset.

3.4 Spectral Analysis and Optimal-Band Selection

To reduce the search space for evaluating three-band hyperspectral composites, a targeted band selection strategy was applied. Exhaustively testing all three-band combinations across 112 spectral bands would require 227,920 model evaluations, and when combined with the RGB baselines for the three detection models, the total number of training runs would exceed 683,000, which was computationally infeasible. To make the process practical, the spectral range was divided into six evenly spaced regions to ensure broad coverage while minimizing redundancy. Within each region, class-wise mean spectral curves were computed from object-level data by averaging reflectance values across annotated pixels and grouping them by class to capture intra-class variability. One-way ANOVA tests with Fisher scores were then used to rank the bands within each region by their ability to separate HDPE, LDPE, PET, PP, and PS, and the top-ranked band from each region was selected. This process produced six optimal wavelengths, namely 7 (990.23 nm), 31 (1158.91 nm), 56 (1335.03 nm), 62 (1377.36 nm), 79 (1497.42 nm), and 108 (1702.67 nm), which are illustrated in Fig. 5. This approach ensured that the candidate pool contained the most statistically discriminative bands, and its effectiveness is supported by a similar study using ANOVA-based selection with YOLOv8-small, which achieved a mean F1 score of 0.896 and approximately 89% classification accuracy [9]. From these six selected bands, all possible three-band composites were generated, producing 20 unique combinations. Together with the RGB baseline, this resulted in 21 datasets for each model architecture and 63 training tasks across YOLO, Faster R-CNN, and RetinaNet.

3.5 Detection Models and Training Protocol

The detection models used in this study include YOLO, Faster R-CNN, and RetinaNet, representing both single-stage and two-stage object detection frameworks. YOLO (You Only Look Once) is a single-stage detector that predicts bounding boxes and class probabilities directly from full images in a single pass, offering high inference speed and

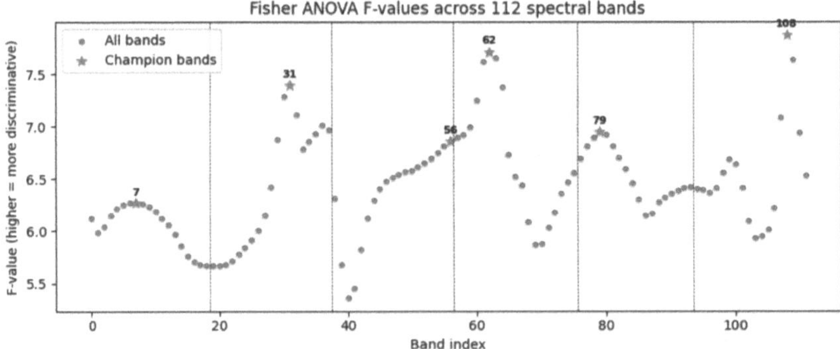

Fig. 5. Selection of six representative bands based on highest ANOVA F-scores within each spectral region

real-time performance [31]. Faster R-CNN adopts a two-stage approach, first generating candidate object proposals using a Region Proposal Network (RPN), which are then refined and classified in a second stage. This design provides high accuracy and is effective across a wide range of object sizes [32]. RetinaNet bridges these paradigms by combining the speed of single-stage models with high detection accuracy. It employs a Feature Pyramid Network (FPN) with a ResNet backbone and introduces focal loss to address class imbalance, allowing it to perform competitively with two-stage detectors while maintaining efficiency [33].

To evaluate the effect of different spectral configurations, each detection model was trained on all composite datasets as well as the RGB baseline using consistent training settings. YOLO was trained for 100 epochs, while Faster R-CNN and Retina Net were trained for 50 epochs each, balancing sufficient training depth with the risk of overfitting. Early stopping was employed to further reduce overfitting risk. For every dataset evaluated through each model, all hyperparameters and training protocols were held constant. The only varying factor was the choice of spectral bands used to generate each dataset. This setup ensures that any observed changes in class-wise Average Precision (AP) scores can be directly attributed to the selected band combinations, enabling a controlled assessment of their impact on object-level plastic detection.

4 Experimental Results and Discussion

Class-wise Average Precision (AP) quantifies model performance for each plastic class by averaging precision across multiple recall levels and Intersection over Union thresholds from 0.50 to 0.95. Figure 6 summarizes the results for all evaluated datasets. Dataset names follow the "band1_band2_band3" format for composite inputs, with the RGB baseline included for comparison.

A comprehensive comparison of class-wise AP scores across all evaluated datasets and models revealed several three-band hyperspectral combinations that consistently outperformed the RGB baseline. Since all models were trained under identical hyperparameter settings, any performance gains can be directly attributed to the selected spectral

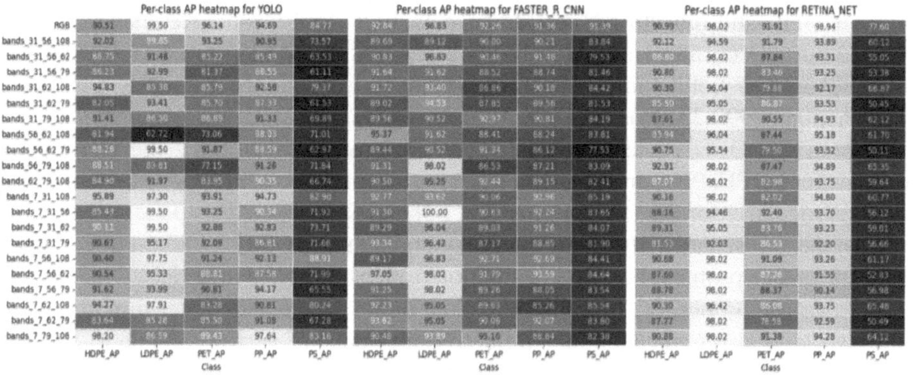

Fig. 6. Heatmap of class-wise Average Precision scores across all three-band combinations and the RGB baseline

combinations. This controlled setup allows a clear and fair assessment of the benefit introduced by specific band combinations. Figure 7 highlights the best-performing hyperspectral composite for each class-model pair alongside the corresponding RGB benchmark. The orange bars represent the highest-achieving composite per category, many of which exceed the baseline accuracy by notable margins. These results validate the effectiveness of targeted band selection and demonstrate that, in many cases, hyperspectral composites can provide more discriminative information than conventional RGB inputs. This supports the use of optimized spectral subsets in real-world detection systems, particularly where computational resources are limited and full-spectrum data is impractical.

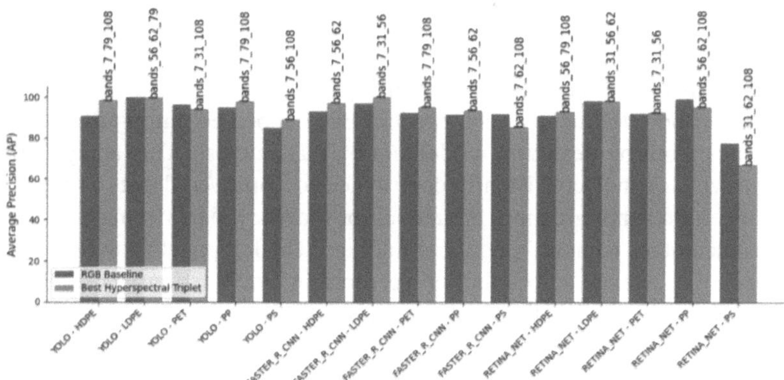

Fig. 7. Comparison of class-wise AP between RGB baselines and best-performing hyperspectral composites.

Among the evaluated combinations, several spectral composites demonstrated consistent improvements across multiple detection models, suggesting potential for broader generalizability. For HDPE, the combination 31 (1158.91 nm), 56 (1335.03 nm), 108

(1702.67 nm) showed strong performance in both YOLO and RetinaNet, while 7 (990.23 nm), 31 (1158.91 nm), 79 (1497.42 nm) and 7 (990.23 nm), 56 (1335.03 nm), 62 (1377.36 nm) yielded improvements in both YOLO and Faster R-CNN. For PP, the combination 7 (990.23 nm), 31 (1158.91 nm), 108 (1702.67 nm) led to higher class-wise AP in both YOLO and Faster R-CNN. In contrast, most combinations achieved limited or no gains for LDPE, PET, and PS, with RGB performing competitively or better in many cases, particularly for PS across Faster R-CNN and RetinaNet. This pattern may reflect weaker spectral separability of certain polymers within the 400–1700 nm range, where their reflectance profiles show less distinction from background materials. Other factors, such as surface properties, specular reflection, or the presence of water film on floating plastics, could also reduce the discriminative advantage of narrowband data. Together, these findings suggest that while three-band hyperspectral composites can outperform RGB for materials like HDPE and PP, their benefit may vary across plastic types, with RGB features such as color and texture still playing an important role in detection for classes like PS.

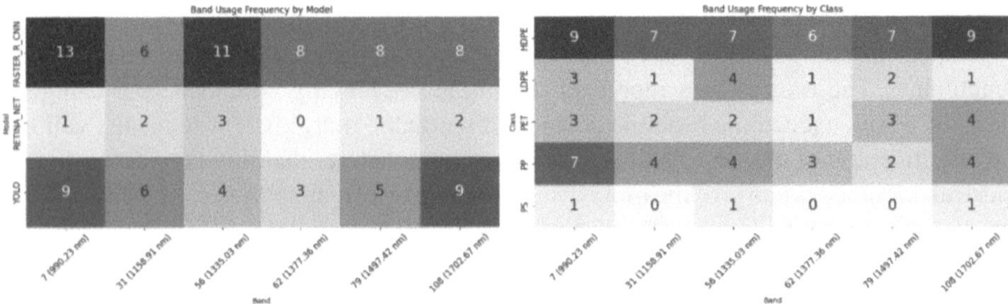

Fig. 8. Frequency of band usage among top-performing combinations, grouped by detection model (left) and plastic class (right).

To better understand the composition of high-performing band combinations, we further analyzed how frequently each spectral band appeared among the outperforming composites, both by detection model and by plastic class. This analysis provides insights into which bands consistently contributed to improved detection performance and whether certain bands are more influential for specific models or materials. Figure 8 presents two heatmaps summarizing these findings. The left panel shows the frequency of each band's occurrence across the top-performing combinations for YOLO, Faster R-CNN, and RetinaNet, while the right panel displays the same distribution grouped by plastic class.

The frequency analysis highlights the importance of specific spectral regions in floating plastic detection and reveals patterns across both models and classes. Band 7 (990.23 nm) emerged as the most consistently used feature, with 13 occurrences in Faster R-CNN and 9 in YOLO, confirming its strong discriminative power across architectures and its particular effectiveness for HDPE and PP, where it showed the highest class-wise frequencies. Band 56 (1335.03 nm) was also strongly favored by Faster R-CNN (11 occurrences), indicating that this mid-infrared wavelength provides additional separation cues that two-stage detectors can effectively exploit. Band 108 (1702.67 nm) was another influential wavelength, appearing frequently in YOLO and Faster R-CNN and contributing to HDPE, PET, and PP detection, which suggests that shortwave-infrared regions help capture material-specific absorption features relevant to multiple polymer types. In contrast, bands 31, 62, and 79 appeared less frequently, implying that their contribution is more selective but still meaningful for certain combinations. Together, these observations demonstrate that a small set of wavelengths carry most of the discriminative information and that different detection architectures leverage them to varying extents. This finding underscores the value of model- and class-specific spectral analysis when designing optimized three-band composites for robust floating plastic detection.

The experimental results presented in this section demonstrate that the use of statistically selected three-band hyperspectral composites can yield meaningful improvements in object-level plastic detection across multiple model architectures. Through controlled evaluations, we observed consistent performance gains over RGB baselines in several class-model combinations, with specific bands such as 990.23 nm, 1335.03 nm, and 1702.67 nm appearing frequently among the top performers. Importantly, this was achieved without modifying model architecture, or tuning additional hyperparameters, highlighting the impact of informed band selection alone. The visual analyses provided further insight into which spectral regions contribute most effectively to different plastic classes and detection pipelines.

Together, these findings establish a foundation for scalable and high-accuracy detection systems that prioritize the most informative parts of the hyperspectral spectrum, offering a clear path forward for optimizing spectral input in real-world applications. While the results demonstrate consistent performance gains using three-band composites, the study is constrained by the use of a synthetically generated dataset, limited object diversity, and potential spectral contamination from bounding box-level annotations. The band selection process was guided by statistical analysis across six fixed spectral regions to maintain computational feasibility. Future work could extend this framework by increasing the number of spectral regions or selecting multiple bands per region to capture more localized variation. Additionally, integrating real-world data with pixel-level object masks and exploring spectral–spatial architectures could further improve detection precision and generalizability.

5 Conclusion

This study demonstrated that carefully selected three-band hyperspectral composites can outperform RGB baselines for floating plastic detection while remaining compatible with standard object detection models and training protocols. Composites containing 990.23 nm, 1335.03 nm, and 1702.67 nm were most influential, with band 7 (990.23 nm) consistently contributing to top-performing results. HDPE and PP showed the greatest benefit from these spectral regions, whereas RGB remained competitive for LDPE, PET, and superior for PS, highlighting that spectral advantages are class-dependent. Model-wise analysis revealed that Faster R-CNN favored 1335.03 nm, while YOLO and RetinaNet relied more on 990.23 nm and 1702.67 nm, indicating architecture-specific spectral preferences. These findings confirm that targeted band selection alone can yield measurable gains in computationally efficient pipelines and suggest opportunities for class- and model-specific composite design or multimodal fusion to improve detection of challenging classes such as PS.

Disclosure of Interests. The authors declare that they have no competing interests relevant to the content of this article.

References

1. Danilov, A., Serdiukova, E.: Review of methods for automatic plastic detection in water areas using satellite images and machine learning. Sensors. **24**, 5089 (2024)
2. Olyaei, M., Ebtehaj, A., Ellis, C.R.: A hyperspectral reflectance database of plastic debris with different fractional abundance in river systems. Sci. Data. **11**, 1253 (2024)
3. Tasseron, P., Van Emmerik, T., Peller, J., Schreyers, L., Biermann, L.: Advancing floating macroplastic detection from space using hyperspectral imagery, (2022). http://eartharxiv.org/repository/view/2341/
4. Olyaei, M., Ebtehaj, A.: Uncovering plastic litter spectral signatures: a comparative study of hyperspectral band selection algorithms. Remote Sens. **16**, 172 (2023)
5. Mazanov, G., et al.: Hyperspectral data driven solid waste classification. IEEE Access. **13**, 46659–46672 (2025)
6. Krasniewski, J., Dabala, L., Lewandowski, M.: Hyperspectral imaging for analysis and classification of plastic waste. In: 2020 25th International Conference on Pattern Recognition (ICPR), pp. 4805–4812. IEEE, Milan, Italy (2021)
7. Elmaizi, A., Nhaila, H., Sarhrouni, E., Hammouch, A., Chafik, N.: A novel approach for dimensionality reduction and classification of hyperspectral images based on normalized synergy. Intl. J. Adv. Comput. Sci. Appl. **10**, 248–257 (2019)
8. Yan, L., Zhao, M., Wang, X., Zhang, Y., Chen, J.: Object detection in hyperspectral images. IEEE Signal Proc. Lett. **28**, 508–512 (2021)
9. Frederick, Q., et al.: Supervised hyperspectral band selection using texture features for classification of citrus leaf diseases with YOLOv8. Sensors. **25**, 1034 (2025)
10. Wang, L., Sousa, W.P.: Distinguishing mangrove species with laboratory measurements of hyperspectral leaf reflectance. Int. J. Remote Sens. **30**, 1267–1281 (2009)
11. Li, X., Wei, C., Zhang, Y., Ma, D., Shi, W., Liang, B.: Fusion of hyperspectral and RGB images for exogenous matter residue detection in Atlantic salmon. J. Food Compos. Anal. **143** (2025)
12. Torres, R.M., Yuen, P.W.T., Yuan, C., Piper, J., McCullough, C., Godfree, P.: Spatial spectral band selection for enhanced hyperspectral remote sensing classification applications. J. Imaging. **6**, 87 (2020)
13. Wei, X., Johnson, M.A., Langston, D.B., Mehl, H.L., Li, S.: Identifying optimal wavelengths as disease signatures using hyperspectral sensor and machine learning. Remote Sens. **13**, 2833 (2021)
14. Vítek, S., Zbíral, T., Nežerka, V.: Using hyperspectral imaging to identify optimal narrowband filter parameters for construction and demolition waste classification. Resour. Conserv. Recycl. **215** (2025)
15. Amankwah, A.: Spatial mutual information based hyperspectral band selection for classification. Sci. World J. **2015**, 630918 (2015)
16. Ghaffari, M., et al.: Systematic reduction of hyperspectral images for high-throughput plastic characterization. Sci. Rep. **13**, 21591 (2023)

17. Logan, R.D., et al.: Assessing produce freshness using hyperspectral imaging and machine learning. J. Appl. Remote. Sens. **15** (2021)
18. Yu, B., Chen, Y., Cao, S.-Y., Shen, H.-L., Li, J.: Three-Channel infrared imaging for object detection in haze. IEEE Trans. Instrum. Meas. **71** (2022)
19. Tasseron, P., van Emmerik, T., Schreyers, L., Biermann, L., Peller, J.: Hyperspectral plastics dataset supplementary to the paper 'Advancing floating plastic detection from space using hyperspectral imagery,' (2021). https://data.4tu.nl/articles/_/14518278/3
20. Huang, H., et al.: Single spectral imagery and faster R-CNN to identify hazardous and noxious substances spills. Environ. Pollut. **258** (2020)
21. Tamin, O., et al.: On-shore plastic waste detection with YOLOv5 and RGB-near-infrared fusion: a state-of-the-art solution for accurate and efficient environmental monitoring. BDCC. **7**, 103 (2023)
22. Bu, Y., et al.: ResNet incorporating the fusion data of RGB & hyperspectral images improves classification accuracy of vegetable soybean freshness. Sci. Rep. **14**, 2568 (2024)
23. Cai, Z., Yang, J., Fang, H., Ji, T., Hu, Y., Wang, X.: Research on waste plastics classification method based on multi-scale feature fusion. Sensors. **22** (2022)
24. Wang, L., Li, J., Qin, H., Xu, J., Zhang, X., Huang, L.: Selecting near-infrared hyperspectral wavelengths based on one-way ANOVA to identify the origin of Lycium Barbarum. In: 2019 International Conference on High Performance Big Data and Intelligent Systems (HPBD&IS), Shenzhen, China, pp. 122–125. IEEE (2019)
25. Fabiyi, S.D., et al.: Varietal classification of Rice seeds using RGB and hyperspectral images. IEEE Access. **8**, 22493–22505 (2020)
26. Zheng, L., et al.: Fusion of hyperspectral imaging (HSI) and RGB for identification of soybean kernel damages using ShuffleNet with convolutional optimization and cross stage partial architecture. Front. Plant Sci. **13**, 1098864 (2023)
27. Maharjan, N., Miyazaki, H., Pati, B.M., Dailey, M.N., Shrestha, S., Nakamura, T.: Detection of river plastic using UAV sensor data and deep learning. Remote Sens. **14**, 3049 (2022)
28. Farahnakian, F., Heikkonen, J.: Deep learning based multi-modal fusion architectures for maritime vessel detection. Remote Sens. **12**, 2509 (2020)
29. Zhang, H., Qiao, X., Li, Z., Li, D.: Effective wavelengths selection of hyperspectral images of plastic films in cotton. In: Li, D., Li, Z. (eds.) Computer and Computing Technologies in Agriculture IX, pp. 519–527. Springer International Publishing, Cham (2016)
30. Liu, H., Yang, J., Fang, H., Ji, T., Cai, Z.: MSI-RGB dual-source multiscale fusion-based solid waste object detection. IEEE Trans. Instrum. Meas. **73** (2024)
31. Redmon, J., Divvala, S., Girshick, R., Farhadi, A.: You only look once: unified, real-time object detection. In: 2016 IEEE Conference on Computer Vision and Pattern Recognition (CVPR), Las Vegas, NV, USA, pp. 779–788. IEEE (2016)
32. Ren, S., He, K., Girshick, R., Sun, J.: Faster R-CNN: Towards Real-Time Object Detection with Region Proposal Networks (2015).https://arxiv.org/abs/1506.01497
33. Lin, T.-Y., Goyal, P., Girshick, R., He, K., Dollar, P.: Focal loss for dense object detection. In: 2017 IEEE International Conference on Computer Vision (ICCV), Venice, pp. 2999–3007. IEEE (2017)

Integrated Machine Learning and Ontology-Based Approach for Sustainable Weed Management in Paddy Fields

D. S. S. De Silva, K. W. H. M. I. M. Herath(✉), R. M. S. A. Rathnayake, Subhash N. Ariyadasa, and R. S. I. Wilson

Department of Computer Science and Informatics, Uva Wellassa University, Badulla, Sri Lanka
cst19043@std.uwu.ac.lk

Abstract. This research investigates the challenges of identifying and managing five major weed species in Sri Lankan paddy fields, namely Echinochloa colona, Echinochloa crus-galli, Cyperus rotundus, Monochoria vaginalis, and Ludwigia perennis using advanced computing techniques. A dataset of 3,200 data points, comprising both primary and secondary data, was utilized. Expert-labeled primary images were preprocessed using noise reduction, followed by data augmentation techniques such as rescaling, shearing, zooming, and horizontal flipping to ensure robust feature extraction. Using a Convolutional Neural Network (CNN) with seven hidden layers and a categorical cross-entropy loss function and Adam optimizer, texture, shape, edge, and contextual features were extracted. These features were then input into both Support Vector Machine (SVM) and Random Forest (RF) classifiers. The RF model achieved a higher accuracy of 98.75%, outperforming the SVM's 97%, and was selected for the final implementation. Moreover, a formal ontology was developed to manage domain knowledge of weed control strategies. Thirty competency questions guided its development, covering control strategies across initial, mid, and extreme growth stages. Evaluation confirmed that the ontology could accurately answer all questions, demonstrating its potential for precise weed management. Integration of the RF model with the ontology enabled automated decision-making. The system performed well in identifying mid-stage weeds, though it showed limitations at early stages. This hybrid approach offers significant advancements in the accurate identification and management of weeds in Sri Lankan agriculture.

Keywords: Convolutional Neural Network · Random Forest · Ontology · Weed management

1 Introduction

Weed competition poses a major challenge in rice production, leading to significant yield losses and financial strain on farmers. Traditional weed control methods, such as manual weeding and broad-spectrum herbicide application, are often labor-intensive, time-consuming, and not always effective [1]. This highlights the urgent need for innovative, sustainable weed management strategies that can address these limitations.

R. N. Rajapakse et al. (Eds.): ICTer 2025, CCIS 2844, pp. 262–276, 2026.
https://doi.org/10.1007/978-981-92-0137-2_18

Machine learning, a subset of artificial intelligence, has proven to be highly effective for tasks like image recognition and classification. Its ability to detect complex patterns makes machine learning ideal for weed detection in paddy fields, enabling accurate identification and timely, targeted interventions. In addressing the challenge of distinguishing weeds from rice plants and determining the correct preventive measures at each growth stage, a machine learning model can be employed to identify weeds, while an ontology-based system can guide decision-making. Ontologies, which structure domain-specific knowledge, offer a framework for informed decisions about the appropriate weed control strategies based on the crop's development stage [2]. Integrating machine learning with ontology-driven decision support enables precise, sustainable weed management in rice farming. This approach reduces herbicide use, lowers environmental impact, and improves crop yields by providing accurate weed detection and tailored control strategies.

In Sri Lanka, weed growth remains a persistent challenge, particularly in the country [3], where resilient weed species such as *Echinochloa crus-galli, Echinochloa colona, Cyperus rotundus, Ludwigia perennis,* and *Monochoria vaginalis* thrive across multiple growing seasons. Traditional weed control methods often fail to target these specific species effectively, leading to recurring infestations that compromise crop yield and quality.

The core challenge is the lack of an efficient system for accurate weed identification and stage-specific control. Manual methods are slow and error-prone, while broad herbicides risk crop and environmental harm. A scalable machine learning solution is needed for timely, sustainable weed management. This research aims to create a practical web-based application that uses image processing to identify the top five perennial weed species in Sri Lankan paddy fields, applying machine learning for classification and incorporating a decision-making system to suggest control strategies. The overarching goal is to establish an accurate and user-friendly platform that optimizes weed management practices, providing efficient solutions.

These research-specific objectives are as follows:

- To extract features that can be used to detect weeds accurately in paddy fields from image data.
- To develop a machine learning model capable of accurately classifying weeds based on the extracted image features.
- To leverage ontology for informed decision making in weed management strategies.

2 Literature Review

2.1 Traditional Weed Management in Paddy Cultivation

Traditional rice weed management in South Asia, mainly manual transplanting (TPR), shifted to Direct-Seeded Rice (DSR), which faced increased weed pressure from species like *Echinochloa crus-galli* [5]. In Sri Lanka, RRDI promoted integrated weed control combining chemical, biological, and manual methods to improve sustainability [6]. Although puddling and transplanting into standing water remained key practices [7], DSR's changing weed dynamics called for eco-friendly solutions like weed-competitive varieties and seed priming to reduce herbicide use [6].

2.2 Feature Extraction in Image-Based Weed Detection

Feature extraction was critical in image processing for transforming raw data into meaningful attributes for classification tasks [4]. Traditional methods relied on handcrafted features such as texture, shape, and color, using techniques like edge detection, histograms, and Gray-Level Co-Occurrence Matrix (GLCM) [5]. In contrast, deep learning models, particularly Convolutional Neural Networks (CNNs), automatically learned complex features, enhancing performance without manual feature design [6].

Traditional Image Processing Techniques.
Traditional image processing, which had been employed for decades, typically involved three key steps: preprocessing, segmentation, and feature extraction. Table 1 Summarizes several studies that demonstrate the effectiveness of these traditional methods.

Table 1. Image Processing for Feature Extraction

Reference	Targeted Crop	Preprocessing	Segmentation	Extraction	Accuracy
[7]	General weeds in row crops	Image enhancement, noise reduction	Color thresholding	Edge detection, texture, shape	~85%
[8]	Wheat vs. weeds	Reflectance calibration, filtering	Vegetation indices (NDVI)	GLCM texture features	~88%
[9]	Paddy(rice fields)	Standard preprocessing of field images	Semantic segmentation	Class-based pixel labeling (weeds vs. rice)	Segmented weed patches in paddy fields are effectively

Table 1 summarizes the accuracies reported in various studies that have used traditional image processing as a feature extractor combined with machine learning algorithms for classification. These studies have shown accuracies ranging between 85% and 95%. With technological advancements, deep learning-based feature extraction has become increasingly prevalent.

2.3 Machine Learning for Weed Classification

Recent advances in machine learning (ML) have significantly enhanced the accuracy of weed detection across various crops. Table 2 Summarizes several studies that utilize ML techniques for agricultural image classification.

CNN-ML Hybrid Models. Integrating CNNs with traditional ML classifiers enhanced feature representation and classification accuracy.

These results have highlighted the strength of hybrid models in enhancing classification accuracy, especially in datasets with limited samples or high complexity, as presented in Table 3.

Table 2. Machine Learning Approaches for Weed Detection

Author	Year	Problem Definition	Targeted Crop	Dataset	Model/ Tools	Accuracy
[10]	2023	ML and handcrafted image processing were used for weed detection in a cornfield	Corn	4 weed types in the corn of North Dakota(1000*4 = 4000 images)	RF SVM CNN	RF -90.8% SVM-89.8% CNN-87.5%
[11]	2021	Early weed detection using image processing and ML	Chilli	UAV Images(Early stage)were collected from the Australian Chilli farm	RF SVM CNN	RF - 96% SVM - 94% kNN - 63%
[12]	2020	Crop/weed detection and classification	Unspecified	Images were collected from private farm	RF	95%

Table 3. CNN and ML Integration in Research

Author	Year	Problems Definition	Dataset	Model/Tools	Accuracy
[13]	2016	Plant species classification in fields	Danish field images (25 species)	CNN + SVM	86%–93%
[14]	2019	Weed recognition in rangelands	17,509 images	CNN + RF / SVM	95%

2.4 Ontology-Based Solutions in Agriculture

In agriculture, particularly rice disease detection, ontologies are crucial. The expert system 'RiceMan' integrated the RiceDO and TreatO ontologies, which detail rice disease symptoms and control measures [15]. This system aided users in diagnosing rice issues and was poised for expansion by incorporating machine learning for enhanced disease identification. RiceMan's refined ontologies highlighted its potential to revolutionize agricultural practices with precision-driven solutions. The importance of clear ontology evaluation in agriculture was emphasized in the literature, with challenges identified such as opaque creation processes, lack of spatial and temporal representation, and difficulties in generalizing knowledge [16].The need for improved validation methods in ontologies was stressed in recent studies [17] Inter-row and intra-row mechanical weeding techniques demonstrated up to 80% weed control and enhanced rice growth when compared to chemical methods [18] . A tool named Pest On was developed to address pesticide data gaps by utilizing linked open data from Italy's pesticide register [19]. The DS-LSTMM model, designed for paddy data analysis, has shown a 16% improvement in accuracy and was tested alongside a proposed Thai rice ontology prototype using 93 queries [20] . AGROVOC, a widely recognized vocabulary encompassing domains such as food, nutrition, agriculture, fisheries, forestry, and the environment, lacked the specificity required for rice disease identification and control recommendations due to missing rice-specific axioms [21]. Efforts to model biotic disorders in rice, such as those caused by bacteria, fungi, and viruses, have led to the development of two ontologies: Rice Disease Ontology (RiceDO) and Treatment Ontology (TreatO). These ontologies defined abnormal rice plant characteristics associated with specific diseases and proposed relevant control measures [22].

However, there was a lack of research on developing intelligent weed detection and management systems that integrated weed detection and control strategies. This research aimed to address this gap by developing a holistic system that could help in efficient and sustainable weed management in paddy fields.

3 Methodology

3.1 Dataset

A total of 4,480 images were used in this study, collected from both primary and secondary sources to ensure a comprehensive dataset. Primary data was gathered from paddy fields in the Badulla district during the early and mid-growth stages of the crops. Secondary data was obtained from the IEEE Data Port, which provided additional images and records of weed species relevant to rice cultivation. Each image in the combined dataset was carefully labeled and verified by agricultural experts to ensure accurate species identification, as summarized in Table 4.

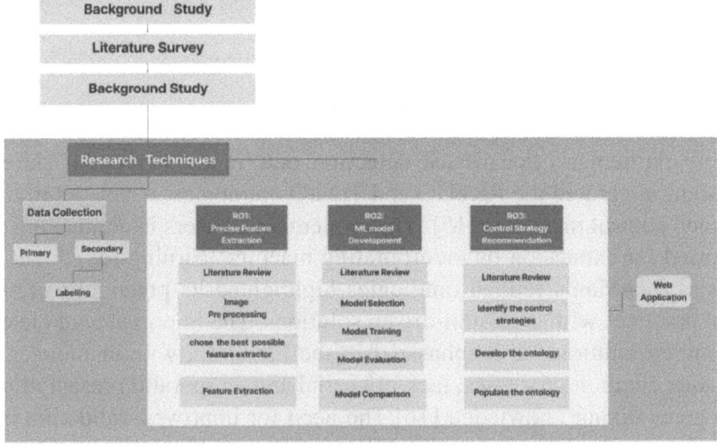

Fig. 1. Methodology

Table 4. Weed Species Data Count

	No of data	No of Train Data	No of Test Data	No of Validation Data
Cyperus rotundus	840	600	120	120
Echinochloa colona	980	700	140	140
Echinochloa crus-galli	980	700	140	140
Ludwigia perennis	840	600	120	120
Monochoria vaginalis	840	600	120	120
Total	4480	3200	640	640

3.2 RO1 – Image Processing and Feature Extraction

The first research objective (RO1) focused on precise feature extraction for weed species classification. As shown in Fig. 1, this objective was divided into two background tasks:

Traditional Image Processing:

- Image preprocessing was applied to resize all images to 225 × 225 pixels and reduce noise using a median filter (kernel size 11 × 11) while preserving edges.
- Segmentation was performed using the Geodesic Active Contour (GAC) algorithm, which adapts to image gradients to accurately isolate weed patches from the background.
- From segmented images, three categories of handcrafted features were extracted:
    - Color features: Mean and standard deviation of RGB channels.
    - Shape features: Area, perimeter, axis lengths, eccentricity, solidity.
    - Texture features: Contrast, correlation, energy, homogeneity (from GLCM).
- Extracted features were stored in a CSV file, enabling their direct use in traditional ML models (RF, SVM).

Deep Learning-Based Feature Extraction.

- A custom CNN was designed to automatically extract discriminative features. The architecture included convolutional layers (64–512 filters), batch normalization, max-pooling, and dropout.
- To reduce overfitting, a GlobalAveragePooling2D layer replaced the dense layer, producing compact feature vectors.
- These CNN features were used both for end-to-end classification and for hybrid models (CNN-RF, CNN-SVM).

3.3 RO2 – ML Model Development

Traditional Machine Learning Approach. The classification models selected for this study were Random Forest (RF) and Support Vector Machine (SVM), chosen for their strong performance with high-dimensional data and robustness in classification tasks. The dataset was divided into 80% training and 20% testing sets, ensuring balanced representation of each weed species. To evaluate model generalizability, five-fold cross-validation was applied, and the models were assessed using accuracy, precision, recall, and F1 score metrics.

Hybrid CNN with Traditional Classifiers (CNN-RF, CNN-SVM). In addition to traditional feature extraction, convolutional neural networks (CNNs) were leveraged for automatic feature extraction. Two hybrid approaches were explored: CNN combined with Random Forest (CNN-RF) and CNN combined with Support Vector Machine (CNN-SVM).

CNN-RF: Random Forest Classifier with CNN Features. The feature vectors extracted from the CNN's flattened layer were passed to a Random Forest classifier for final classification. Various hyperparameters, such as the number of trees (ranging from 50 to 300) and maximum tree depth, were optimized to improve performance. Additionally, a fixed random state (42) was employed to ensure the reproducibility of the experiments. This approach effectively combined the CNN's ability to extract high-dimensional features with the Random Forest's robust classification capability.

CNN-SVM: Support Vector Machine Classifier with CNN Features. Similarly, the CNN-extracted features were used as input for an SVM classifier. A grid search optimization process was conducted to fine-tune hyperparameters such as the kernel type and regularization parameters. This ensured the SVM model was well-suited for the task.

Training and Validation for CNN-based Models. Both CNN-RF and CNN-SVM models were trained on the same dataset splits and evaluated using multiple metrics, including training and testing accuracy, precision, recall, and F1-score. Confusion matrices were also generated to visually assess their classification performance across weed species.

CNN Model. The CNN architecture includes nine layers: four convolutional layers each followed by max-pooling, two dropout layers, and a global average pooling layer. It uses ReLU activation and was trained with the Adam optimizer for 100 epochs, applying data augmentation like rotations and flips to improve robustness. Performance was assessed using accuracy, precision, recall, F1-score, and confusion matrices, with train-test splits and cross-validation to ensure good generalization.

3.4 RO3 – Control Strategy Decision-Making

The primary objective of this research was to develop a recommendation system that could propose effective weed management strategies for paddy fields, leveraging an ontology-based approach. A systematic approach based on Ontology was used for weed-management decision support in paddy fields. Through collaboration with agricultural experts, literature reviews, and field inspections, the growth stages of each weed species were documented. Suitable biological and chemical control strategies were identified based on government guidelines, considering effectiveness and environmental impact. This information was precisely tabulated and became the core of the ontology, capturing the dynamic aspects of weed management, as illustrated in Fig. 2.

Growth Stage
Growth Conditions
Low Growth Factors and Symptoms
Mild Growth Factors and Symptoms
Severe Growth Factors and Symptoms
Low Growth Control Strategies
Mild Growth Control Strategies
Severe Growth Control Strategies
Prevention Strategies

Fig. 2. Ontology Data Set

Figure 3 Conceptual questions guiding the ontology structure and function for weed management in paddy fields. These questions, reflecting expert and user needs, focused on critical aspects of weed management like species identification, growth stages, and control strategies

QN	Conceptual Question	SPARQL
1	What are the low growth control strategies for weed management?	SELECT ?strategy WHERE { ?strategy rdf:type table:Low_growth_control_strategies. }
2	What are the mild growth control strategies for weed management?	SELECT ?strategy WHERE { ?strategy rdf:type table:Mild_growth_control_strategies. }
3	What are the severe growth control strategies for weed management?	SELECT ?strategy WHERE { ?strategy rdf:type table:Severe_growth_control_strategies. }
4	What are the low growth symptoms of weeds?	SELECT ?symptom WHERE { ?symptom rdf:type table:Low_growth_symptoms. }
5	What are the mild growth symptoms of weeds?	SELECT ?symptom WHERE { ?symptom rdf:type table:Mild_growth_symptoms. }
6	What are the severe growth symptoms of weeds?	SELECT ?symptom WHERE { ?symptom rdf:type table:Severe_growth_symptoms. }
7	What are the weeds that affect rice crops in Sri Lanka?	SELECT ?weed WHERE { ?weed rdf:type table:Weed. }

Fig. 3. Conceptual Questions

Then, for the development of the ontology, terms, concepts, and relationships were identified. Using the Ontology Layer Cake framework, terms were assigned to represent key entities, concepts such as weed species, growth stages, and control strategies were formalized, and relationships were established between these concepts. 18 Rules were then derived from these components, forming the rules that structured the ontology and enabled logical reasoning. The Ontology Layer Cake represents relationships between weed species, growth stages, and control strategies through structured classes and properties, as illustrated in Fig. 4 . It was populated with expert-verified data on growth stages and control methods, creating a comprehensive knowledge base suitable for decision support in weed management.

To make the ontology functional, the thirty conceptual questions were translated into specific queries using Description Logic (DL) Query and SPARQL.

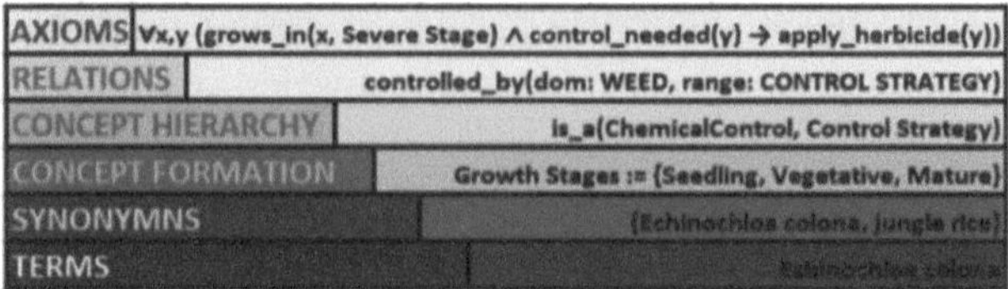

Fig. 4. Ontology Layer Cake

One example of a conceptual question would be:

"What are the growth symptoms of Monochoria vaginalis in low growth stages?"

The conceptual question stated above can be formulated to extract relevant information from the ontology as follows.

The SPARQL query and the corresponding result are shown in Fig. 6.

The ability to perform such queries made the ontology a powerful tool for decision-making in weed management, allowing users to access targeted information efficiently. The successful execution of these queries demonstrated that the ontology could handle complex information retrieval tasks, providing precise and relevant answers to the conceptual questions. The research culminated in the development of a web-based recommendation system that integrated the ontology and made it accessible to users.

A web platform was created, enabling users to interact with the ontology through a user-friendly interface.

The system's user interface was designed to be intuitive, allowing users to interact with the ontology and retrieve information through simple queries. Figure 5 shows how the interface enables users to perform queries and retrieve information on weed management practices.

Finally, the image identification model was integrated into the web platform and tested with the help of an expert. The testing ensured that the system was functioning as expected and that the web interface was intuitive. Feedback from the expert was used to refine the ontology and the platform, ensuring that the final product was reliable and capable of supporting weed management in paddy fields.

The expert provided examples of scenarios where specific weed species, such as *Monochoria vaginalis*, exhibited varying symptoms under different environmental conditions. In one example, the expert noted that *Monochoria vaginalis* symptoms related to stunted growth were more prominent in high-nutrient environments. To address this, the ontology was updated to account for environmental factors when categorizing weed symptoms.

Another example involved misidentifying *Echinochloa crus-galli* due to overlapping symptom characteristics with Ischaemum rugosum. The system was refined by adding more distinct visual markers and integrating data on growth stages, ensuring clearer differentiation.

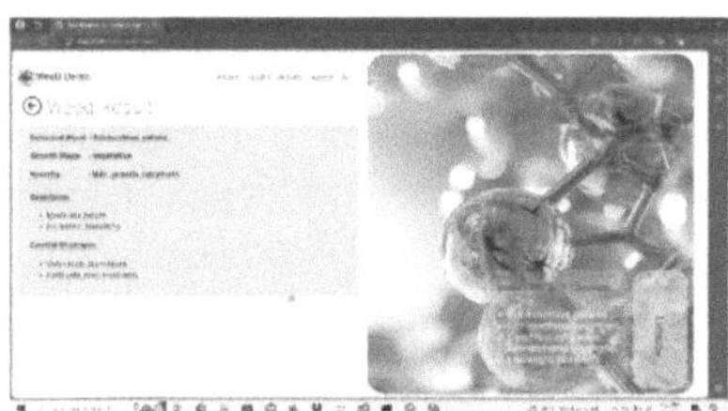

Fig. 5. Web Interface

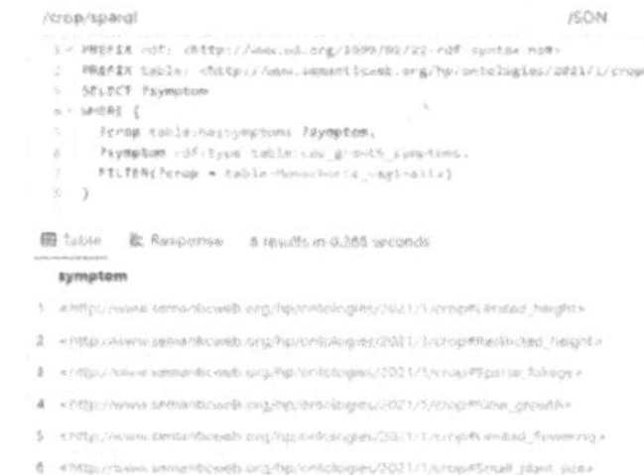

Fig. 6. SPARQL Query and Response

4 Results and Discussion

4.1 RO:1 – Image Processing

Accurate image feature extraction was essential to this research, achieved using a convolutional neural network (CNN). The CNN effectively captured intricate patterns, significantly improving the performance of downstream machine learning models. These results confirm the value of CNN-based feature extraction in boosting model accuracy and prediction.

Image Data Preprocessing. The images were made to be uniformly sized (224X224), which allowed for consistent model input. The images were smoother with reduced noise, making important features more distinct and easier to extract. Additionally, the dataset included a variety of augmented images, such as rotated, flipped, and zoomed versions, which helped the model generalize better and become more robust to variations in the data.

Feature Extraction using Traditional Methods. Feature Extraction Using MATLAB Involved Segmenting Preprocessed Images to Isolate Regions of Interest, Followed by Edge Detection to Highlight Key Features. Texture, Shape, and Color Attributes Were Then Analyzed, Including Color Channel Statistics (Mean and Standard Deviation), Geometric Properties (Area, Perimeter, Eccentricity, Etc.), and Texture Features (Contrast, Correlation, Energy, Homogeneity). These Features Supported Further Analysis in the Machine Learning Model.

Feature Extraction Using CNN. Two CNN architectures were used to extract image features, both showing strong accuracy with a Random Forest classifier. The first model had three convolutional layers (64, 32, 16 filters), max-pooling, and a flattening layer, achieving 90% accuracy. The improved model added four convolutional layers with larger filters (64 to 512), batch normalization, GlobalAveragePooling2D to reduce overfitting, and dropout layers (0.5 rate), boosting accuracy to 94% by better capturing complex features.

The training progress of the CNN model is shown in Fig. 7, which illustrates the model's loss and accuracy trends over epochs. Figure 8 presents the training and validation accuracy curves, highlighting how the model learns and generalizes over time. Figure 9 shows the comparison of training versus validation loss, confirming minimal overfitting and stable convergence.

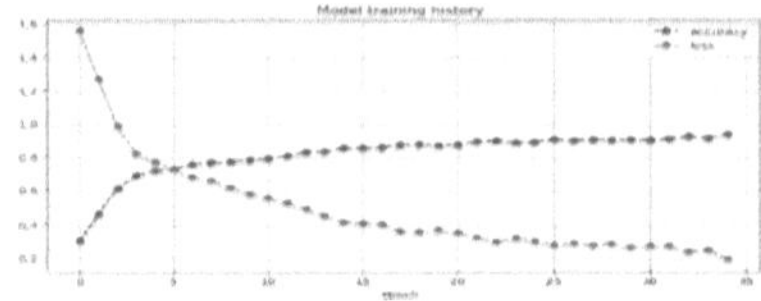

Fig. 7. CNN Model Training History

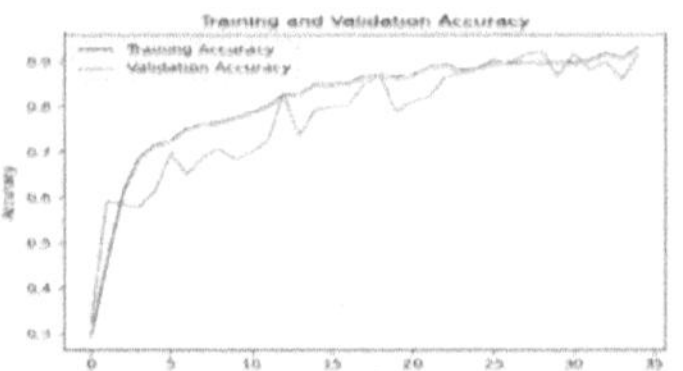

Fig. 8. Training and Validation accuracy

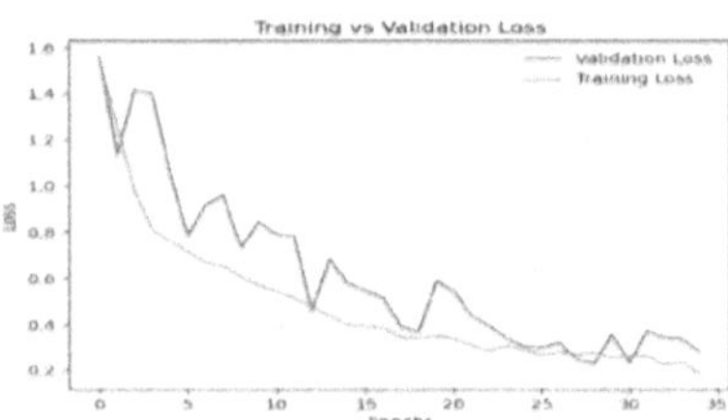

Fig. 9. Training vs. Validation Loss

4.2 RO:2 – ML Model Development

Overview of Model Performance. This section evaluates the performance of the machine learning models described in the Sect. 3, including traditional ML models (Random Forest, Support Vector Machine), CNN-Random Forest (CNN-RF), CNN-SVM, and the stand-alone CNN model. A detailed comparison of the models is made based on evaluation metrics such as accuracy, precision, recall, and F1-score.To facilitate this comparison, Table 5 Summarizes the results of all models tested, showing their performance across key metrics.

Table 5. Model Comparison

Model	Accuracy	Precision(%)	Recall(%)	F1-Score(%)
RF	0.75	0.77	76	75
SVM	0.76	0.77	0.77	0.77
CNN + RF	0.98	0.99	0.99	0.99
CNN + SVM	0.97	0.98	0.98	0.98
CNN	0.94	0.95	0.95	0.95

Table 5 Provides a comparison of all tested models. The results indicate that the CNN–Random Forest (CNN-RF) model outperformed the other models across all evaluated metrics, achieving the highest accuracy (98.0%), precision (99%), recall (99%),

and F1-score (99%). While traditional models such as Random Forest and SVM demonstrated adequate performance, they were less effective than the CNN-based models, which were capable of automatically extracting richer feature representations.

Confusion Matrix and Classification Report. The Random Forest model achieves 98% accuracy on five weed species, with precision, recall, and F1 scores ranging between 97% and 100%, confirming its strong classification ability, as shown Fig. 11 High macro and weighted averages validate the model's robustness. The CNN-RF model's confusion matrix Fig. 10 shows detailed classification performance for each species, highlighting mostly correct predictions with minor misclassifications, mainly among visually similar species.

The Random Forest reached 98.12% accuracy on validation data and 98.75% on test data, demonstrating excellent generalization. The CNN + Random Forest combination proved to be the most effective, leveraging CNN's feature extraction and RF's ensemble learning to deliver superior accuracy with minimal misclassification. Its success in identifying visually similar weed species highlights its practical value for real-world weed management.

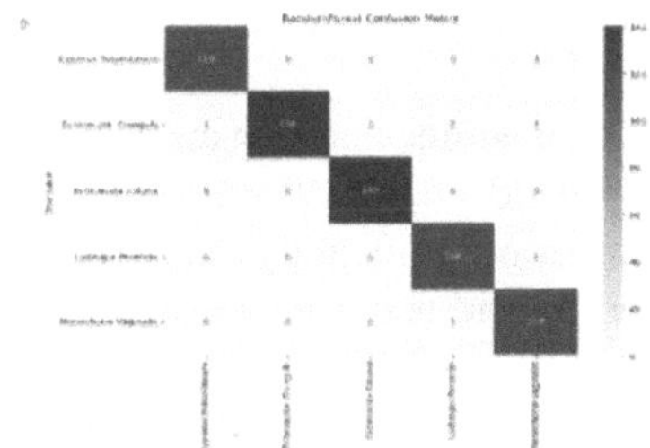

Fig. 10. Confusion Matrix for CNN + RF Model

```
RandomForest Model Accuracy on Validation Data: 0.9812206572769953
RandomForest Model Accuracy on Test Data: 0.9875
RandomForest Model Classification Report on Test Data:
                      precision    recall  f1-score   support

 Cyperus Rotundusare       0.99      0.99      0.99       120
Echinocola  Crusgulli       1.00      0.97      0.99       140
   Echinocola Colona       1.00      1.00      1.00       140
   Ludwigia Perennis       0.98      0.98      0.98       120
 Monochoria Vaginalis       0.97      0.99      0.98       120

            accuracy                           0.99       640
           macro avg       0.99      0.99      0.99       640
        weighted avg       0.99      0.99      0.99       640
```

Fig. 11. CNN + RF Classification Report

RO:3 – Control Strategy Decision-Making

The primary objective of this research was to develop a recommendation system that could propose effective weed management strategies for paddy fields, leveraging an ontology-based approach. The results obtained from the development and testing of the ontology demonstrate that the research successfully achieved its objectives, and the system is capable of addressing the complexities involved in sustainable weed management.

Ontology Development and Population. The ontology was meticulously developed to represent the knowledge domain of weed management in paddy fields. The inclusion of five key weed species *Echinochloa colona, Echinochloa crus-galli, Cyperus rotundus, Monochoria vaginalis, and Ludwigia perennis* ensured that the ontology covered a representative spectrum of common and problematic weeds in paddy cultivation. By integrating weed growth stages and control strategies, the ontology provided a comprehensive framework for a recommendation system to deliver tailored, context-specific management strategies.

Query Development and Execution. A key milestone was formulating 30 conceptual questions that guided the ontology's structure, covering species identification, growth stages, and control strategies. The system effectively answered these using DL and SPARQL queries, demonstrating its capability to provide precise, context-specific weed management recommendations based on growth stages and control options.

Development and Integration of the Web-Based Recommendation System. The research culminated in a web-based recommendation system integrated with the ontology. The user interface shown in Fig. 5 is designed for intuitive interaction, enabling users to query and retrieve weed management information easily. The system was tested with a field expert and provides accurate, tailored strategies for weeds, supporting effective and sustainable management with reduced chemical use. The results support the development of a recommendation system, where the ontology effectively models relationships between weed species, growth stages, and control strategies to provide context-specific recommendations. By integrating expert knowledge and real-world data, the system delivers scientifically sound and practically applicable solutions that support sustainable and environmentally responsible weed management.

5 Conclusion

This study demonstrates the effectiveness of integrating machine learning and ontology-based methods for sustainable weed management in paddy fields. Traditional feature extraction provided a baseline, while CNN-based extraction significantly improved weed representation. The CNN–Random Forest (CNN-RF) hybrid achieved the highest performance, with 98% accuracy, 99% precision, 99% recall, and 99% F1-score, outperforming standalone CNN, SVM, and RF models. The ontology system captured weed species, growth stages, and management strategies, answering 30 conceptual queries and providing expert-verified, context-specific recommendations. These results confirm that CNN-driven feature extraction with ensemble learning enables accurate weed identification, while the ontology framework supports actionable and sustainable control strategies. Limitations include the number of weed species and dataset size, which may restrict strategy diversity. Future work can expand both to improve generalizability and robustness.

Disclosure of Interests. The authors declare that they have no conflicts of interest.

References

1. Woyessa, D.: Weed control methods used in agriculture. Am. J. Life Sci. Innovation. **1**, 19–26 (2022). https://doi.org/10.54536/AJLSI.V1I1.413
2. Understanding Ontologies.: Structure and Benefits for Semantic Data Analysis, https://www.lyzr.ai/glossaries/ontologies/, Accessed 19 Jun 2025.
3. Integrated Weed Management For Prevention Of The Evolution And Spread Of Herbicide Resist Ant Weeds In Sri Lanka
4. What is Feature Extraction? Feature Extraction Techniques Explained., https://domino.ai/data-science-dictionary/feature-extraction, Accessed 19 Jun 2025

5. Devulapalli, S., Potti, A., Krishnan, R., Khan, M.S.: Experimental evaluation of unsupervised image retrieval application using hybrid feature extraction by integrating deep learning and handcrafted techniques. Mater. Today Proc. **81**, 983–988 (2021). https://doi.org/10.1016/J.MATPR.2021.04.326
6. Alzubaidi, L., et al.: Review of deep learning: concepts, CNN architectures, challenges, applications, future directions. J. Big Data. **8**(1), 53 (2021). https://doi.org/10.1186/S40537-021-00444-8
7. Slaughter, D.C., Giles, D.K., Downey, D.: Autonomous robotic weed control systems: a review. Comput. Electron. Agric. **61**, 63–78 (2008). https://doi.org/10.1016/J.COMPAG.2007.05.008
8. Pantazi, X.E., Moshou, D., Alexandridis, T., Whetton, R.L., Mouazen, A.M.: Wheat yield prediction using machine learning and advanced sensing techniques. Comput. Electron. Agric. **121**, 57–65 (2016). https://doi.org/10.1016/J.COMPAG.2015.11.018
9. Kamath, R., Balachandra, M., Vardhan, A., Maheshwari, U.: Classification of paddy crop and weeds using semantic segmentation. Cogent Eng. **9** (2022). https://doi.org/10.1080/23311916.2021.2018791
10. Pathak, H., Igathinathane, C., Howatt, K., Zhang, Z.: Machine learning and handcrafted image processing methods for classifying common weeds in corn field. Smart Agric. Technol. **5** (2023). https://doi.org/10.1016/J.ATECH.2023.100249
11. Islam, N., et al.: Early weed detection using image processing and machine learning techniques in an Australian chilli farm. Agriculture. **11**, 387 (2021). https://doi.org/10.3390/AGRICULTURE11050387
12. Irias Tejeda, A.J., Castro Castro, R.: Algorithm of weed detection in crops by computational vision. In: CONIELECOMP 2019–2019 International Conference on Electronics, Communications and Computers, pp. 124–128 (2019). https://doi.org/10.1109/CONIELECOMP.2019.8673182
13. Dyrmann, M., Karstoft, H., Midtiby, H.S.: Plant species classification using deep convolutional neural network. Biosyst. Eng. **151**, 72–80 (2016). https://doi.org/10.1016/J.BIOSYSTEMSENG.2016.08.024
14. Olsen, A., et al.: DeepWeeds: a multiclass weed species image dataset for deep learning. Sci. Rep. **9**, 1–12 (2019). https://doi.org/10.1038/s41598-018-38343-3
15. Hughes, David. P., Salathe, M.: An open access repository of images on plant health to enable the development of mobile disease diagnostics. (2015)
16. Persaud, N., Dagher, R.: The importance of monitoring and evaluation for decision-making. In: The Role of Monitoring and Evaluation in the UN 2030 SDGs Agenda, pp. 89–117 (2021). https://doi.org/10.1007/978-3-030-70213-7_4
17. Iheanacho, S., Ogbu, M., Bhuyan, M.S., Ogunji, J.: Microplastic pollution: an emerging contaminant in aquaculture. Aquac Fish. **8**, 603–616 (2023). https://doi.org/10.1016/J.AAF.2023.01.007
18. Liu, C., et al.: Benefits of mechanical weeding for weed control, rice growth characteristics and yield in paddy fields. Field Crop Res. **293**, 108852 (2023). https://doi.org/10.1016/j.fcr.2023.108852
19. Medici, M., Dooley, D., Canavari, M.: PestOn: an ontology to make pesticides information easily accessible and interoperable. Sustainability. **14**, 6673 (2022). https://doi.org/10.3390/SU14116673
20. Thunkijjanukij, A., Panichsakpatana, S., Kawtrakul, A., Veesommai, U.: Rice production knowledge management: criteria for ontology development. Thai J. Agric. Sci. **42**, 115–124 (2009) www.thaiagj.org

21. Subirats-Coll, I., et al.: AGROVOC: the linked data concept hub for food and agriculture. Comput. Electron. Agric. **196** (2022). https://doi.org/10.1016/J.COMPAG.2020.105965
22. Zajkowska, Z., et al.: A systematic review of the association between biological markers and environmental stress risk factors for adolescent depression. J. Psychiatr. Res. **138**, 163–175 (2021). https://doi.org/10.1016/J.JPSYCHIRES.2021.04.003

YOLOv8 for Nondestructive Black Pepper Impurity Detection

Hansamalee Ekanayake[1(✉)], Gihan Pushpajith Seneviratne[1], Deepika Samudrani Seneviratne[2], Samantha Mathara Arachchi[1], and Kasun Karunanayaka[1]

[1] School of Computing, University of Colombo, Colombo, Sri Lanka
hansamaleeekanayake3006@gmail.com, {gps,ssp,ktk}@ucsc.cmb.ac.lk
[2] University of Sri Jayewardenepura, Colombo, Sri Lanka
deepikas@sjp.ac.lk

Abstract. Food adulteration in spices undermines quality and safety, especially in countries like Sri Lanka where black pepper is economically important. Traditional laboratory tests can identify adulterants but are costly, time-consuming, and destructive. Non-destructive computer vision methods offer rapid and inexpensive alternatives for on-site inspection. In this work, we propose a YOLO-based object detection pipeline to detect foreign impurities (e.g., papaya seeds, sand) in black pepper images. We collected and annotated a custom dataset of 748 pepper images (about 37,900 labeled instances) using the Roboflow platform, with two classes: *Pure-Black-Pepper* and *Impurity*. Images were preprocessed (resized to 640×640, adaptive contrast) and augmented. A YOLOv8s model was fine-tuned on this dataset (batch size 16, SGD optimizer, 640 image size) for 100 epochs. On the held-out test set, the model achieved high accuracy (mAP@0.5 = 0.952, mAP@0.5:0.95 = 0.712; Impurity mAP@0.5:0.95 = 0.608, Pure-Pepper mAP@0.5:0.95 = 0.815). Additionally, a comparative evaluation of three different versions of YOLO shows that YOLOv8s achieve best performance metrics on black pepper impurity detection. Future work includes improving precision to reduce false positives and deploying the model in a mobile app for real-time impurity detection.

Keywords: Computer Vision · YOLO · Black Pepper · Adulteration Detection · Food Safety · Deep Learning

1 Introduction

Food adulteration and fraud pose serious threats to safety and consumer trust. Spices like black pepper (Piper nigrum) are especially vulnerable to economic adulteration due to their high value and demand. In Sri Lanka and other regions, common adulterants in black pepper include cheaper materials such as papaya seeds, chili fragments, sand, or wood, which are mixed in to increase volume illegally. Such hidden impurities not only degrade product quality, but also can pose

R. N. Rajapakse et al. (Eds.): ICTer 2025, CCIS 2844, pp. 277–293, 2026.
https://doi.org/10.1007/978-981-92-0137-2_19

health risks (e.g., allergies or toxicity) if undeclared. Comprehensive reviews of food authentication methods emphasize the need for non destructive, rapid analysis techniques [15]. Traditional analytical tests (e.g., high performance liquid chromatography, NIR, GC-MS, PCR) can be accurate but require specialized equipment, skilled operators, and laboratory conditions, making them impractical for routine field tests [6,12].

In recent years, computer vision and deep learning (DL) have emerged as promising tools for non-destructive food quality assessment [6,12]. By analyzing images of spice samples, DL models can potentially flag visible adulterants without chemical analysis. Convolutional neural networks (CNNs) can extract rich features from complex visual data, making them suitable for detecting subtle differences between genuine and adulterated samples. In particular, object detection networks like YOLO (You Only Look Once) can identify and localize foreign particles in an image. YOLOv8, a robust iteration of the YOLO family, incorporates a Cross Stage Partial (CSP) backbone and PANet/FPN neck for multi scale feature fusion [14]. Its successors YOLOv10 and 11, introduce further optimizations, including enhanced feature extraction and improved efficiency for edge devices. Unlike a simple classification approach that only indicates the presence of adulteration, object detection provides instance-level localization (bounding boxes around each impurity), which supports granular quality control and informed decision-making. For example, knowing the count and location of foreign seeds can inform whether a shipment should be rejected or further tested.

In this study, we develop a complete YOLO-based pipeline for impurity detection in black pepper images, with a comparative evaluations of other models to assess its potential. We collect and label a diverse image dataset of pepper seeds and common adulterants, train models on these data, and evaluate their accuracy. Our main contributions are: (1) a new annotated dataset of black pepper images with impurity labels; (2) a detailed methodology for training YOLO models in this domain, including augmentation and data splitting; (3) empirical results showing high detection performance (mAP and F1 metrics) on held out test images for both models; and (4) an analysis of the models' strengths, limitations, and rationale for choosing YOLOv8s over other models. We also discuss how such a model could be integrated into a mobile app for on-field spice quality inspection.

2 Related Work

2.1 Traditional Non-destructive Testing (NDT) Methods for Food Adulteration

Classical nondestructive laboratory techniques, including NIR and FTIR spectroscopy, gas chromatographymass spectrometry (GCMS), and hyperspectral imaging (HSI), are established for detecting and quantifying adulterants in food due to their chemical specificity and quantitative abilities. [10] HSI, for instance, can map adulteration in spices by differentiating spectral signatures. However, these methods necessitate specialized instruments, controlled sample presentation, and chemometric knowledge, restricting their use for rapid field or consumer screening.

Although, NDT technologies excel in lab accuracy and quantification but are often impractical for in situations where low-cost screening is preferred because of instrument cost, sample preparation, and need for trained personnel. [13] Hence, a need for low-cost image-based alternatives arises for large-scale or consumer-facing deployment.

2.2 Sensor Arrays and Other Non-Image Rapid Tests

Sensor-based e-noses and electronic sensor arrays (VOC sensors) are being investigated as portable technologies for detecting adulteration and spoilage by analyzing volatile organic compound profiles. Recent research [9] has demonstrated that low-cost MQ gas sensors, coupled with machine learning, can effectively differentiate pure from adulterated pepper samples under controlled circumstances. Although more portable than HSI or GCMS, these systems are susceptible to environmental VOCs and necessitate meticulous calibration and standardized sampling for reliable field application.

2.3 Computer Vision and Traditional Image-Feature Methods in Food Quality

Visible-spectrum imaging combined with hand-crafted color and texture features provides an economical and rapid method for identifying visually discernible adulterants. Past research utilized visible imaging and feature engineering to detect adulterants in pepper, successfully distinguishing samples by training classifiers on engineered descriptors. However, many approaches classify adulteration as a simple binary problem instead of identifying and quantifying individual foreign particles. Although smartphone-captured visible images are convenient for consumer-level applications, traditional computer vision methods often fail to detect small, visually similar, or poorly illuminated adulterants. [8]

Feature-engineering approaches are interpretable and cheap to deploy but are limited in localization capability and robustness to appearance variability; therefore, they are not suitable for instance-level object detection methods when localization is required.

2.4 Metric-Learning and Sample-Level Deep Learning Methods

Metric-learning approaches (e.g., Siamese networks) have been used to detect papaya-seed adulteration in whole peppercorns and pepper powder, obtaining good accuracy for sample verification and rapid screening. [1] These methods are useful when labeled instances are scarce and when the task is to verify whether a sample resembles known pure samples. However, they produce sample-level similarity scores rather than instance-level bounding boxes, and thus cannot directly report the number, size, or positions of adulterant particles that is necessary for tasks such as impurity quantification and automatic removal.

2.5 Object Detection and YOLO-Based Approaches for Impurity Detection

End-to-end object detectors are well suited for impurity detection because they both localize and classify multiple instances in a single image. YOLO variants have been adapted across agriculture and food-quality problems (weed/weed-seed identification, pest detection, impurity detection in rice and tea, and plant disease detection), demonstrating favorable trade-offs between speed and accuracy that enable real-time or near-real-time operation on edge devices. Several recent works [7] report adaptations of YOLOv5/YOLOv8 for impurity detection in rice, tea, and other agricultural commodities, while more recent YOLOv8-based improvements have shown gains for small object detection in complex scenes. YOLOv11 (2024) and other later variants introduce architectural efficiencies that can be important when deploying models on resource-constrained hardware. These trends indicate that modern one-stage detectors are a promising route for detecting small foreign particles in spice images [4].

Many YOLO adaptations focus on agricultural scenes where foreign objects are larger or more textured (e.g., rice debris, foreign matter in tea), while adulterants of peppers (papaya seeds, sea foam, chickpea flour) can be small and visually similar to pepper. Thus, object detectors must be configured and trained carefully (dataset quality, annotation granularity, multi-scale training, augmentation) to avoid missed detections and false positives. Empirical comparisons of different YOLO variants on a standardized pepper impurity dataset are still scarce which motivating the present comparative evaluation.

2.6 Real-World Examples and Industry Context

Industry and applied research demonstrate both lab-grade and fieldable solutions: HSI and GCMS are widely used in regulatory and industrial QC labs for definitive authentication; e-nose and portable spectrometers appear in pilot deployments for faster screening; meanwhile, imaging + deep learning prototypes and research apps show the feasibility of smartphone-based screening tools that offer instant, low-cost feedback to consumers and small traders. For example, recent academic prototypes [3] using YOLO variants and other lightweight detectors have been packaged into online or mobile inspection demos for rice impurity detection, tea impurity detection, and plant disease monitoring. However, mature commercial smartphone apps for spice impurity localization and quantification (with certified accuracy) remain rare.

2.7 Positioning and Research Gap

Taken together, the literature shows a clear spectrum:

1. High-accuracy, lab-oratory NDT methods (HSI, GCMS) that are expensive and lab-bound
2. Portable sensors (e-nose) that are promising but environment-sensitive

3. Visual feature classifiers and metric-learning models that support low-cost screening but lack instance localization
4. Object detectors (YOLO family and derivatives) that provide a practical compromise by enabling instance-level localization and real-time inference on commodity hardware.

Despite multiple studies on pepper adulteration using HSI, sensor arrays, and sample-level imaging methods, there are very few open, annotated datasets and published studies that evaluate end-to-end object detectors for **black pepper impurity localization** specifically. This gap motivates our contribution: an annotated dataset of visible-light pepper images with instance-level impurity labels and a comparative evaluation of YOLO variants for impurity localization under realistic acquisition conditions [10].

3 Dataset Description

The final dataset consists of 748 images of black pepper seeds, including both pure samples and those mixed with visible impurities. The average image resolution is approximately 0.87 megapixels (around 810×1080 pixels). Using Roboflow, each image was annotated with an average of 122.7 as illustrated in Fig. 1 (pepper grains or impurities). Figure 2 illustrates the distribution of annotated bounding boxes: roughly 90% of instances are genuine pepper seeds, and 10% are impurities. This class imbalance reflects the relative scarcity of visible foreign particles in real samples. Images were collected using a mobile phone camera under varied lighting and background conditions. Additional images of impurities particularly papaya seeds were sourced from public Roboflow datasets. We leveraged the publicly available "Pepper Segmentation Dataset" [11] for training our impurity detection model. While Kaggle was explored, it did not yield suitable results. All images were annotated using Roboflow, combining manual and automated labeling techniques.

A total of 37,854 objects were annotated across the dataset, comprising 36,221 instances of `Pure-Black-Pepper` and 1,624 instances of `Impurity`. This highlights a strong class imbalance, with approximately 96% of annotations belonging to the pure class and only 4% to the impurity class, which reflects the real-world rarity of adulterants in pepper seed samples.

Figure 1 shows yellow bounding boxes represent Pure-Black-Pepper seeds, while the purple boxes denote Impurities. Annotations were created using Roboflow's manual and automated tools. This visuals example highlights the mixed presence of genuine pepper seeds and visible adulterants within a single image, emphasizing the need for robust object detection to distinguish between the two classes accurately.

The dataset was divided into training (70%), validation (20%), and test (10%) sets, ensuring both classes were represented in each split. This stratified division balances sufficient training data with fair evaluation on unseen examples. The preprocessing steps included auto-orientation correction, resizing all images to 640×640 pixels (using stretching), and adaptive contrast enhancement via

Fig. 1. Sample images from the annotated dataset showing bounding boxes around detected objects.

histogram equalization. These steps were crucial to normalize the inputs and enhance visual features before training.

Due to the relatively small dataset size, data augmentation was applied to boost model generalizability. In future, integrating few-shot or zero-shot learning techniques may enable broader coverage of adulterant types and improve scalability in real-world deployments. Each training example produced two augmented variants using the following techniques: horizontal and vertical flipping, 90° rotations, random rotations between −15° and +15°, zoom-based cropping (0% to 20%), hue shifts (±15°), brightness adjustments (±15%), and grayscale conversion on 15% of images. These augmentations aimed to simulate realistic variation in seed appearance, improving the model's ability to detect impurities under diverse conditions.

Figure 2 The top plot shows class imbalance, with the majority of bounding boxes labeled as Pure-Black-Pepper and a smaller portion labeled as Impurity. The bottom-left heatmap shows the spatial distribution of bounding box center coordinates (x, y), indicating that objects are uniformly scattered across the image plane. The bottom-right plot shows the width and height distribution of bounding boxes, where most objects occupy small, consistent areas, reflecting the typical size of individual pepper grains and impurities.

4 Methodology

Our detection pipeline consists of image collection, annotation, pre-processing, data augmentation, model training, and evaluation. First, images of black pepper samples were acquired using a standard digital camera under consistent lighting. The samples included pure pepper, common impurities (for example, papaya seeds, wood chips, sand grains, rice), and mixed compositions.

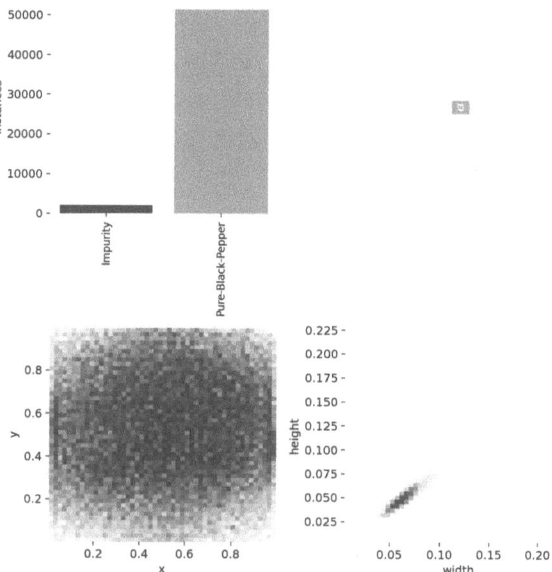

Fig. 2. Class distribution (top), bounding box center heatmap (bottom-left), and size distribution (bottom-right)

Each image was annotated with bounding boxes using the Roboflow platform, labeling two classes: *Impurity* (foreign particle) and *Pure-Black-Pepper* (genuine pepper seed). This annotation process yielded a total of roughly 37,900 object instances across the data set.

Before training, all images were resized to 640×640 pixels to match the input size of model, and image enhancements (auto-orientation, adaptive histogram equalization) were applied to normalize quality. To increase data diversity, we applied real-time augmentations during training: horizontal/vertical flips, random rotations (±15°), random crops/zooms (up to 20%), brightness and contrast adjustments (±15%), and mosaic mixing (combining four images) using model's built-in augmentation pipeline (Fig. 7).

For model training, we fine-tuned the Ultralytics [2] architectures v8s, v10s, and v11s on our pepper impurity dataset, initializing the models with pretrained weights from the COCO dataset to leverage transfer learning. [5] The v8s model employs a CSPNet backbone and a PANet-style pathaggregation neck for multi-scale feature fusion. The v10s model introduces an optimized backbone with lightweight convolutions and enhanced feature extraction, balancing accuracy and efficiency and the v11s model further enhances this with optimized layer designs and improved computational efficiency, targeting better performance on resource-constrained devices. We used the default stochastic gradient descent (SGD) optimizer with an initial learning rate of 0.01, momentum 0.937, and batch size 16 for all models. The models were trained for 100 epochs, monitoring both training and validation loss in each epoch. We used the configuration file (data.yaml) to specify the two class names and dataset paths. The best checkpoint (by validation mAP) at around 50 epochs was selected for final evaluation for each model.

5 Results and Discussion

After training, the YOLOv8s, v10s, and v11s models were evaluated on the hold-out test set. The v8s model achieved the highest overall mean Average Precision at IoU threshold 0.50 (mAP@0.50) of 0.952, and mAP averaged over IoU 0.50:0.95 of 0.712. The v10s model achieved an overall mAP@0.50 of 0.948 and mAP@0.50:0.95 of 0.601 and the v11s model achieved an overall mAP@0.50 of 0.942 and mAP@0.50:0.95 of 0.691. Table 1 summarizes the key metrics for v8s, v10s, and v11s. On a per-class basis for v8s, the Impurity class had mAP@0.50:0.95 = 0.608, while the Pure-Black-Pepper class reached 0.815. For v10s, the Impurity class had mAP@0.50:0.95 = 0.591, and the Pure-Black-Pepper class reached 0.611 and for v11s, the Impurity class had mAP@0.50:0.95 = 0.576, and the Pure-Black-Pepper class reached 0.805. The precision and recall values indicate that all models are effective at detecting true pepper grains and impurities, with F1 scores approximately 0.90 or higher for both classes across all models.

Figure 3 shows an example test image with model predictions: impurities are correctly highlighted among the pepper seeds. Figure 2 (above) displays the

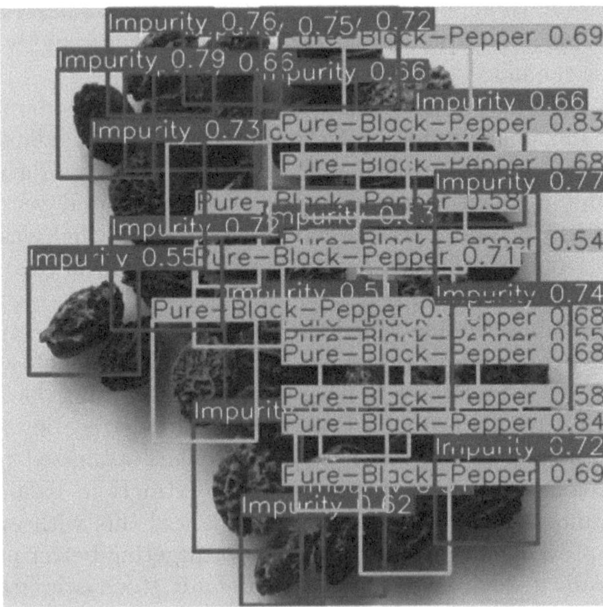

Fig. 3. Example predictions by YOLOv8s: impurities (dark blue), pepper seeds (light blue) (Color figure online)

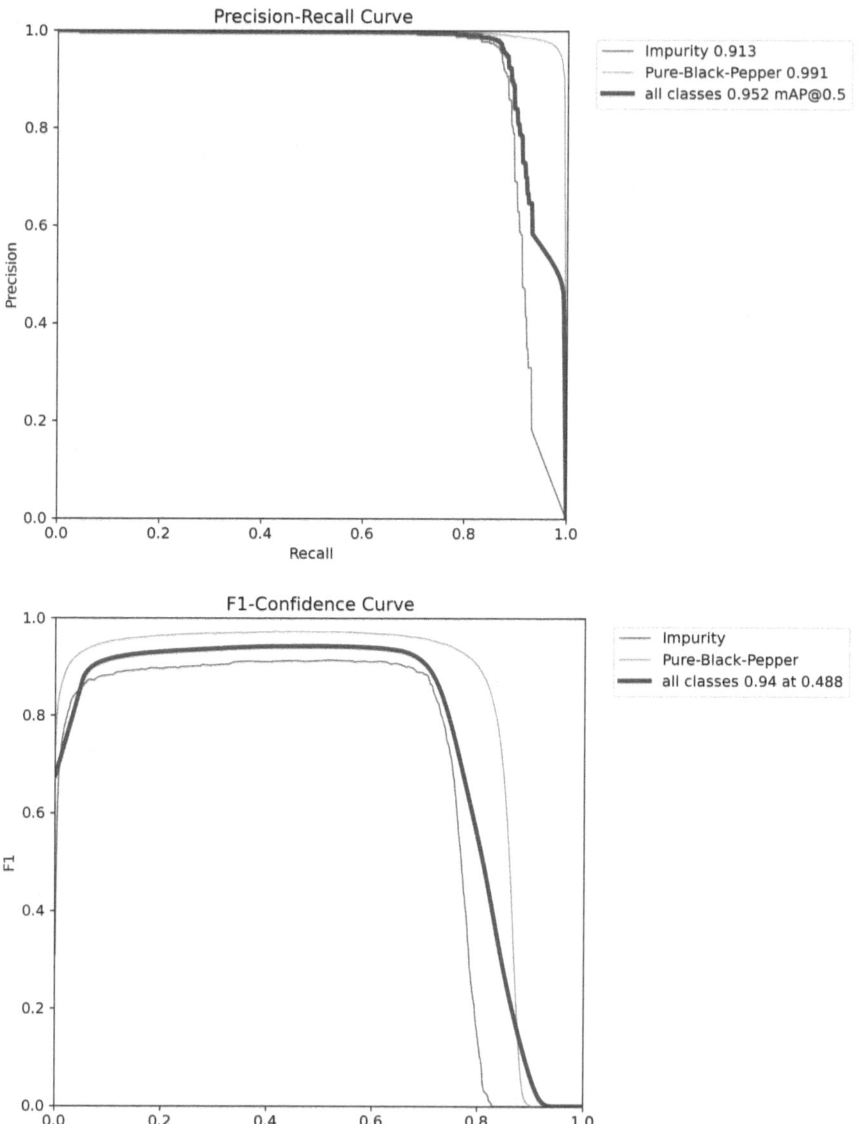

Fig. 4. Precision-recall curves and F1 score vs. confidence threshold for YOLOv8s.

annotated class distribution. Figure 4 presents the precision-recall curves for each class along with the F1 score curve as a function of confidence threshold. Figure 6 shows the confusion matrix (raw counts and normalized) for the two classes. Most pepper grains are correctly classified, but a few impurity instances are missed or misclassified.

The choice of object detection (YOLO) over a simple classifier is critical: object detection identifies and localizes each adulterant item, providing actionable information (exact positions and counts). A classifier alone would only signal whether adulteration is present or absent in the image. By using YOLO, our system can highlight each impurity with a bounding box, facilitating quantitative contamination analysis and reducing false alarms.

Figure 5 showing box loss, classification loss (cls), distribution focal loss (dfl), precision, recall, mAP@50, and mAP@50-95. The smoothed trends (orange) indicate stable convergence, with final validation mAP@50 reaching 0.952 and no overfitting, demonstrating robust model performance.

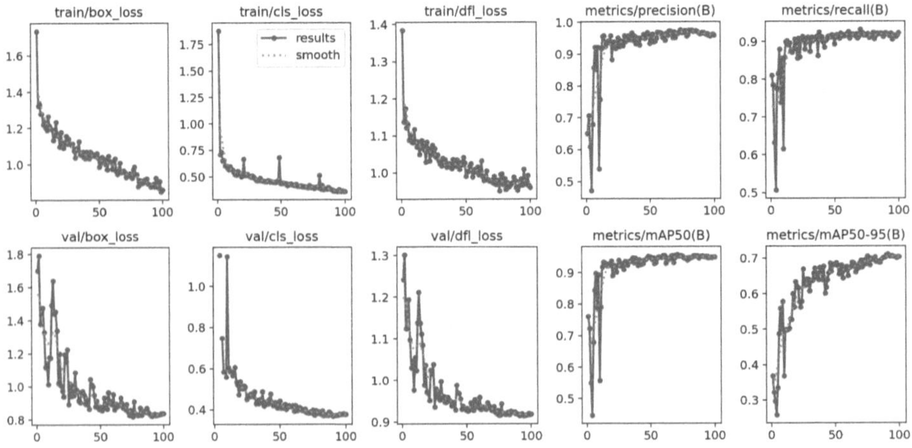

Fig. 5. Training and validation curves over 100 epochs for v8s

Table 1. Detection performance metrics on the test set for each class for v8s, 9, 10 and 11 s.

Model	Class	Precision	Recall	F1 Score	mAP@0.5:0.95
v8s	Impurity	0.964	0.865	≈ 0.912	0.608
	Black Pepper	0.972	0.972	≈ 0.971	0.815
	All (overall)	0.968	0.919	≈ 0.943	0.712
v10s	Impurity	0.89	0.923	≈ 0.936	0.591
	Black Pepper	0.942	0.873	≈ 0.964	0.611
	All (overall)	0.916	0.898	≈ 0.95	0.601
v11s	Impurity	0.959	0.797	≈ 0.873	0.576
	Black Pepper	0.968	0.976	≈ 0.972	0.805
	All (overall)	0.963	0.887	≈ 0.923	0.691

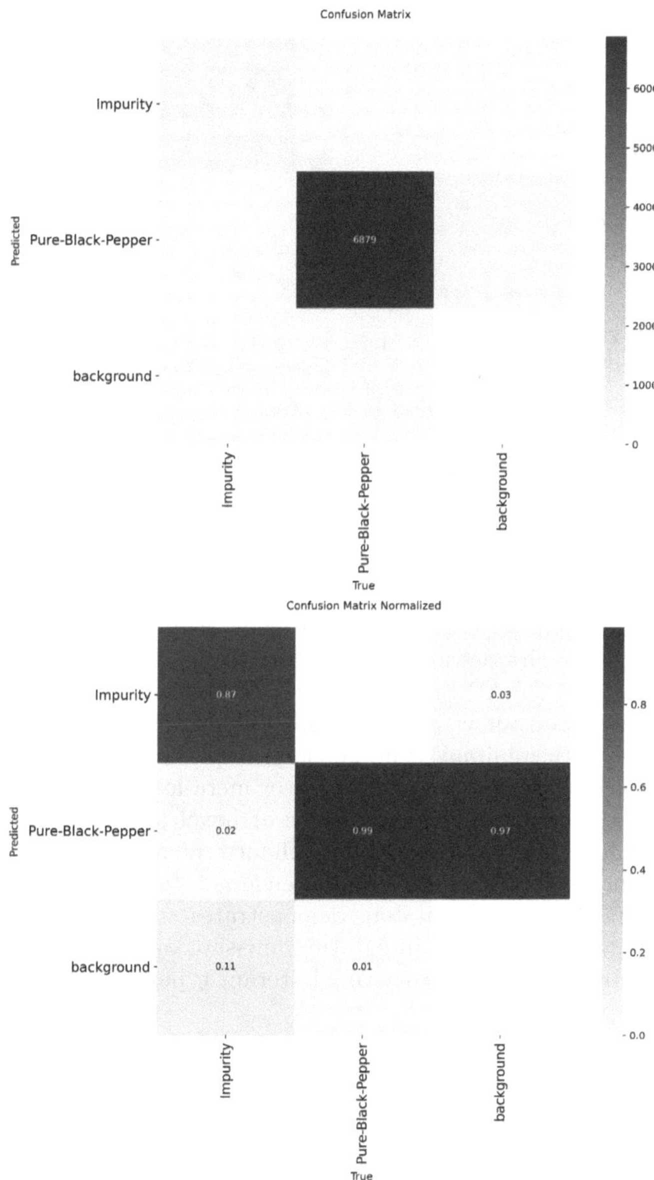

Fig. 6. Confusion matrix (left: raw counts, right: normalized) for test set predictions for v8s. Rows = true class, columns = predicted class.

Training converged smoothly for both models: Fig. 8 plots the training and validation loss over epochs for v8s. Loss decreased rapidly and plateaued by 30 epochs, indicating efficient learning without overfitting. The final validation metrics were consistent with the test performance.

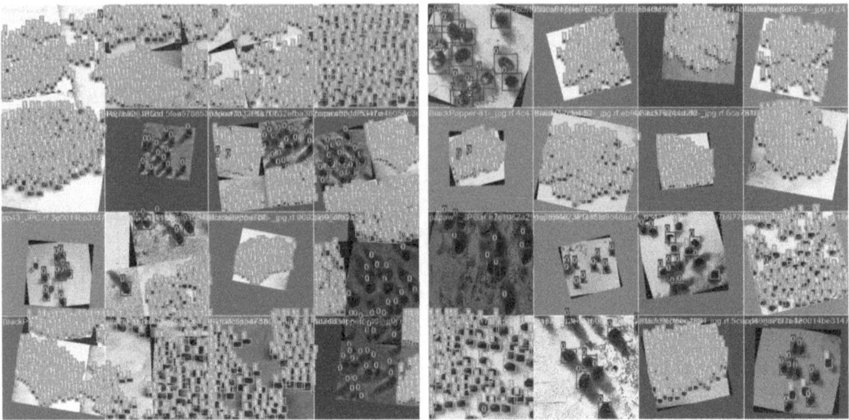

Fig. 7. Visualization of several training images with ground truth and v8s labels, showing data augmentation (cropping, flips, mosaic) applied.

Recent advances in one-shot and zero-shot learning provide potential strategies for overcoming dataset constraints. For example, Guo et al. (2023) proposed a zero-shot detection framework using a knowledge-enhanced feature synthesizer, achieving 63.7% mAP on unseen food contaminants without retraining. Such approaches could allow impurity detection models to generalize to new adulterants even with minimal or no labeled samples. Similarly, few-shot learning methods, such as prototypical networks or meta-learning frameworks, could be applied to rapidly adapt models to rare or novel adulterants in black pepper. Incorporating these paradigms could enhance the robustness of vision-based NDT systems for spices where collecting large annotated datasets is impractical.

Our current YOLO-based system demonstrates strong preliminary results with a small dataset. In future, integrating few-shot or zero-shot learning techniques may enable broader coverage of adulterant types and improve scalability in real-world deployments.

5.1 Comparison of Models

To explore the advancements in the YOLO family, we trained and evaluated v8s, v10s, and v11s on the same dataset under identical conditions (100 epochs, SGD optimizer, batch size 16, 640×640 input). YOLOv8s, with 11.2 million parameters and 28.6 GFLOPs, achieved an overall mAP@0.50 of 0.952 and mAP@0.5:0.95 of 0.712. The v10s, with approximately 7.2 million parameters and 21.8 GFLOPs, achieved an overall mAP@0.50 of 0.948 and mAP@0.5:0.95 of 0.601 and v11s, with 9.41 million parameters and 21.3 GFLOPs, is designed for improved efficiency and performance and achieved an overall mAP@0.50 of 0.942 and mAP@0.5:0.95 of 0.691 on the test set. For the Impurity class, v8s had the highest mAP@0.5:0.95 of 0.608, followed by v10s with 0.591, and v11s with 0.576. v8s also had the highest recall for Impurity (0.865) compared to v10s

(0.923) and v11s (0.797), indicating v11s missed more impurity instances. For the Pure-Black-Pepper class, v11s performed comparably to v8s (mAP@0.5:0.95 of 0.805 vs. 0.815), while v10s had a lower mAP@0.5:0.95 of 0.611. Table 1 provides a detailed comparison.

The choice of v8s over v10s and v11s for our primary pipeline was driven by several factors. First, v8s demonstrated superior performance in detecting impurities, which is critical for food safety applications where missing contaminants could have serious consequences. The higher recall and mAP@0.5:0.95 for the *Impurity* class suggest that v8s is better at identifying foreign particles in complex pepper images. Second, v8s showed more stable convergence during training, with fewer fluctuations in validation loss, as observed in our training logs. While v11s offers architectural improvements, such as optimized layer designs for edge devices, these benefits were less critical for our use case, where inference is primarily performed on standard hardware. Additionally, v8s has a more mature ecosystem and broader community support, facilitating easier integration and debugging.

However, v10s and v11s showed competitive performance, particularly for the *Pure-Black-Pepper* class, and its lower computational footprint (21.8 GFLOPs for v10s and 21.3 GFLOPs for v11s vs. 28.6 GFLOPs for v8s) could be advantageous for future deployment on resource-constrained devices like mobile phones. The slightly lower performance on impurities for v10s and v11s may be due to sensitivity to the class imbalance in our dataset (90% pepper vs. 10% impurities), which could be mitigated with further tuning or additional impurity samples. In future work, we plan to explore hybrid approaches, combining the strengths of all three models, and investigate the potential of v10s and v11s for edge deployment.

5.2 Metrics Over Epochs

Table 2. Excerpt from `results.csv` showing v8s training progress and metrics over epochs.

Epoch	Train Box Loss	Train Cls Loss	Precision	Recall	mAP50	mAP50-95	Val Box Loss
1	1.73	1.88	0.65	0.81	0.76	0.37	1.70
10	0.92	0.41	0.92	0.90	0.94	0.68	0.85
20	0.51	0.21	0.95	0.92	0.96	0.70	0.48
30	0.39	0.15	0.96	0.92	0.96	0.71	0.36
...	...	...	...	...	...	...	...
100	0.86	0.36	0.96	0.92	0.95	0.70	0.84

To further illustrate training dynamics, Table 2 presents selected entries from the training log (`results.csv`) for v8s, capturing key metrics across epochs. The model shows a rapid reduction in loss and a consistent increase in mAP

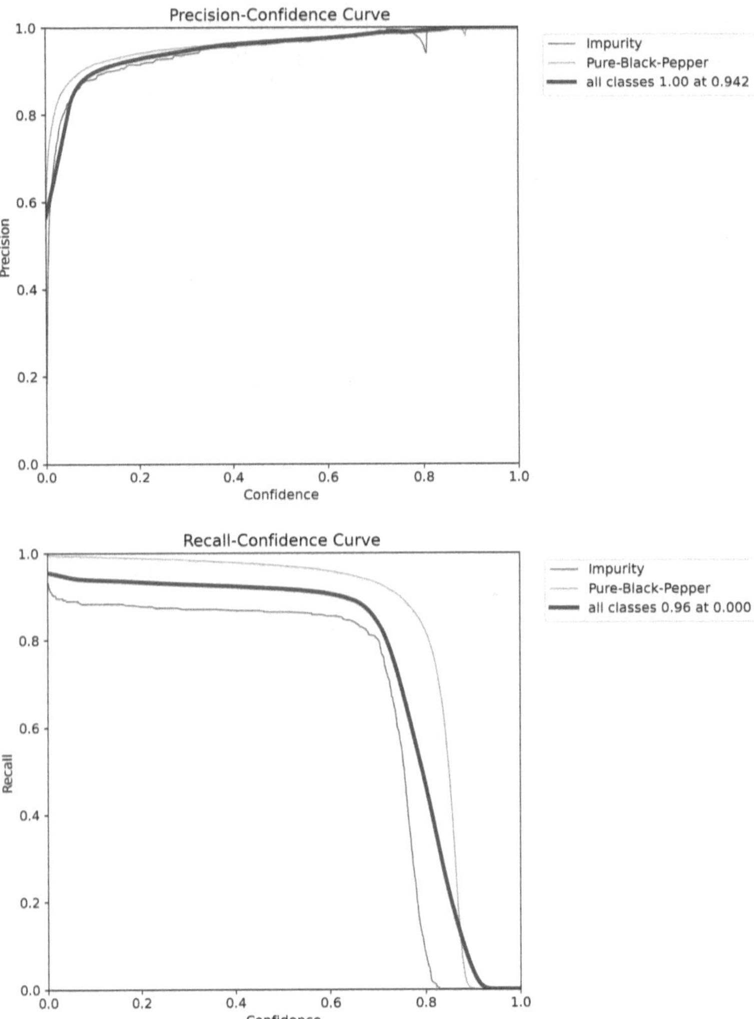

Fig. 8. Validation loss over epochs for the v8s model (left) and Training and validation loss over epochs for the v8s model (right) for test set detections (threshold=0.5).

and F1-score during the early stages, with performance stabilizing after approximately 30 epochs. This indicates successful convergence without overfitting. Similar trends were observed for v10s and v11s, though with slightly higher variance in validation loss.

Finally, Fig. 9 shows the distribution of predicted impurities versus pure pepper in test images for v8s. The model generally predicts the correct ratio of classes, although in some cases (especially when an image contains only impurities) there are false positives. In one extreme test, a fully adulterated sample (all impurities) still resulted in about 40% of detections labeled as pepper. This highlights a current limitation: the model has a false-positive rate where it occasionally confuses unusual impurity shapes for pepper seeds. This may be due to the smaller number of impurity examples during training. YOLOv10s and v11s exhibited similar false-positive behaviors, with a slightly higher rate for impurities, reinforcing the choice of v8s for its better balance of precision and recall.

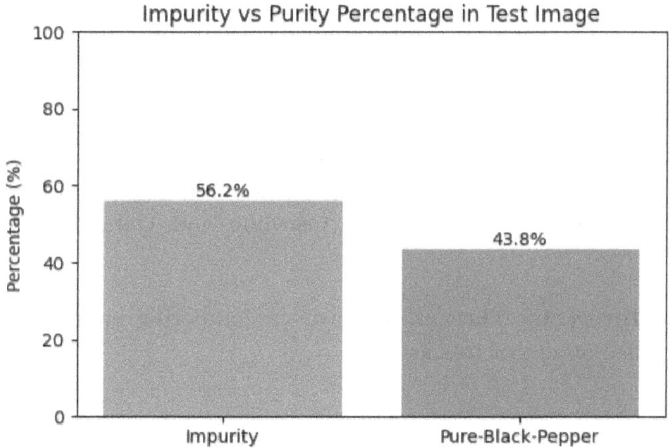

Fig. 9. Bar chart of predicted class percentages across test images (percentage of bounding boxes detected as Pepper vs. Impurity) for v8s.

Despite this, the overall performance of both models is very strong. YOLOv8s detector, in particular, can reliably find and localize foreign particles in pepper samples, enabling inspectors to quantify contamination levels. Because the method is non-destructive and image-based, it can be used for rapid screening without laboratory facilities. The trained model is lightweight and could potentially run on edge devices (mobile phones or embedded cameras) for real-time checking.

6 Conclusion

We have presented a computer vision system based on YOLOv8s for nondestructive impurity detection in black pepper seed samples, with a comparative evaluation of v10s and v11s. By creating a labeled dataset of pepper images with common adulterants and training modern object detectors, we achieved high accuracy in identifying and localizing foreign particles. The v8s model's mAP and F1 scores (above 0.8) demonstrate the feasibility of automated adulteration detection, with superior performance over v10s and v11s, particularly for the critical *Impurity* class. The v8s model was chosen for its higher recall, stable training, and robust ecosystem, though v10s and v11s show promise for future edge deployments due to their optimized architectures and lower computational footprints. This approach offers a fast, low-cost complement to conventional lab tests, suitable for on-field quality control. In future work, we aim to improve precision on impurity detection (to reduce false positives) by collecting more varied training images, explore hybrid approaches combining v8s, v10s, and v11s, and integrate the model into a user-friendly mobile application for real-time spice inspection.

Limitations include small dataset size and class imbalance. Future work will expand the dataset, explore zero-/one-shot learning, and investigate hybrid YOLO variants. This study offers a foundation for scalable, mobile-deployable impurity detection in spice supply chains.

Acknowledgments. This work was supported by the University of Colombo School of Computing (UCSC) through its Research Allocation Funding Scheme for the Research and Development initiative on 'Machine Learning and Data Analytics for Good' research group.

Disclosure of Interests. The authors have no competing interests to declare that are relevant to the content of this article.

References

1. Fatima, N., Areeb, Q.M., Khan, I.M., Khan, M.M.: Siamese network-based computer vision approach to detect papaya seed adulteration in black peppercorns. J. Food Process. Preserv. **46** (2022). https://doi.org/10.1111/jfpp.16043
2. Jocher, G., Qiu, J., Chaurasia, A.: Ultralytics YOLO (2023). https://github.com/ultralytics/ultralytics
3. Li, W., Wu, Y., Du, L., Shang, X., Shi, J.: Hyperspectral imaging for foreign matter detection in foods: advances, challenges, and future directions. Foods **14**(17) (2025). https://doi.org/10.3390/foods14173026, https://www.mdpi.com/2304-8158/14/17/3026
4. Liang, Z., Xu, X., Yang, D., Liu, Y.: The development of a lightweight de-yolo model for detecting impurities and broken rice grains. Agriculture **15**(8) (2025). https://doi.org/10.3390/agriculture15080848, https://www.mdpi.com/2077-0472/15/8/848
5. Lin, T.Y., et al.: Microsoft coco: common objects in context (2015)
6. Lin, Y., Ma, J., Wang, Q., Sun, D.W.: Applications of machine learning techniques for enhancing nondestructive food quality and safety detection. Crit. Rev. Food Sci. Nutr. **63**, 1649–1669 (2023). https://doi.org/10.1080/10408398.2022.2131725
7. Miao, Y., Meng, W., Zhou, X.: SerpensGate-YOLOv8: an enhanced YOLOv8 model for accurate plant disease detection. Front. Plant Sci. **15** (2025). https://doi.org/10.3389/fpls.2024.1514832
8. Nargesi, M.H., Kheiralipour, K.: Visible feature engineering to detect fraud in black and red peppers. Sci. Rep. **14**, 25417 (2024). https://doi.org/10.1038/s41598-024-76617-1
9. Natarajan, S., Ponnusamy, V.: Development of a smart sensor array for adulteration detection in black pepper seeds using machine learning. Tech. rep., www.ijacsa.thesai.org

10. Orrillo, I., Cruz-Tirado, J., Cardenas, A., Oruna, M., Carnero, A., Barbin, D.F., Siche, R.: Hyperspectral imaging as a powerful tool for identification of papaya seeds in black pepper. Food Control **101**, 45–52 (2019). https://doi.org/10.1016/j.foodcont.2019.02.036, https://www.sciencedirect.com/science/article/pii/S0956713519300842
11. PapayaIdentify: Pepper segmentation dataset. https://universe.roboflow.com/papayaidentify/pepper-segmentation (2024). https://universe.roboflow.com/papayaidentify/pepper-segmentation, visited on 2025-09-14
12. Shen, C., Wang, R., Nawazish, H., Wang, B., Cai, K., Xu, B.: Machine vision combined with deep learning–based approaches for food authentication: an integrative review and new insights. Compr. Rev. Food Sci. Food Saf. **23** (2024). https://doi.org/10.1111/1541-4337.70054
13. Vinothkanna, A., Dar, O.I., Liu, Z., Jia, A.Q.: Advanced detection tools in food fraud: a systematic review for holistic and rational detection method based on research and patents. Food Chem. **446**, 138893 (2024). https://doi.org/10.1016/j.foodchem.2024.138893, https://www.sciencedirect.com/science/article/pii/S0308814624005429
14. Yaseen, M.: What is YOLOv8: an in-depth exploration of the internal features of the next-generation object detector (2024). http://arxiv.org/abs/2408.15857
15. Önler, E., Köycü, N.D.: Wheat powdery mildew detection with YOLOv8 object detection model. Appl. Sci. **14**, 7073 (2024). https://doi.org/10.3390/app14167073

Population and Behavioral Analytics

Advanced Modeling of Inflation Dynamics in Sri Lanka: A Comparative Analysis of Statistical, Machine Learning, Deep Learning, and Hybrid Forecasting Approaches

Hiruni Navodya Kudagama[1,2](✉), Sameera Viswakula[1], Samantha Mathara Arachchi[2], and S. A. Chamila J. Siriwardhana[3]

[1] Faculty of Science, University of Colombo, Colombo, Sri Lanka
2020s18107@stu.cmb.ac.lk, sam@stat.cmb.ac.lk
[2] University of Colombo, School of Computing, Colombo, Sri Lanka
ssp@ucsc.cmb.ac.lk
[3] Central Bank of Sri Lanka, Colombo, Sri Lanka
chamila@cbsl.lk

Abstract. Inflation significantly influences national economic activities and serves as a vital indicator for monetary policy formulation. In Sri Lanka, most prior studies have concentrated on Traditional Time Series (TTS) and Machine Learning (ML) models, with limited exploration of Deep Learning (DL), ensemble, and hybrid approaches, especially those employing systematic hyperparameter optimization. Moreover, recent economic disruptions, such as the COVID-19 pandemic and the 2022 economic crisis, have not been adequately incorporated into previous analyses. This study provides a comprehensive analysis of univariate one-step-ahead inflation forecasting using diverse modeling approaches. TTS models, including Auto Regressive Integrated Moving Average (ARIMA) and Seasonal ARIMA (SARIMA), were benchmarked against ML models (Random Forest, XGBoost, Support Vector Regression (SVR)) and DL models (Feedforward Neural Networks (FNN), Long Short-Term Memory (LSTM), Convolutional Neural Networks (CNN)). Hybrid approaches were explored, including simple and weighted averaging ensembles, where weights were based on evaluation metrics, and residual-based hybrid models (SVR-CNN, SVR-LSTM, SVR-FNN). Hyperparameter optimization was performed using Optuna with time series cross-validation. Monthly Colombo Consumer Price Index (CCPI) headline inflation data from January 2000 to March 2025 were analyzed across multiple train-test splits (70:30, 80:20, 90:10), with the 90:10 split yielding the best results. Models were evaluated using RMSE, MSE, MAE, and R^2. While SARIMA captured seasonality effectively, ML and DL models improved forecasting accuracy. Additionally, error-weighted ensemble models and the simple averaging ensemble model further enhanced forecasting performance. While the MAE-weighted ensemble model slightly outperformed the others in numerical error metrics, the Diebold-Mariano test indicated that the proposed simple average ensemble model and error-based weighted average ensemble models provided competitive performance.

R. N. Rajapakse et al. (Eds.): ICTer 2025, CCIS 2844, pp. 297–316, 2026.
https://doi.org/10.1007/978-981-92-0137-2_20

Keywords: Inflation · Machine Learning · Time Series · Hybrid Models

1 Introduction

Inflation is defined as a constant increase in the overall price level of goods and services in an economy over time [1]. It reflects the reduction in buying power, influences interest rates, and shapes monetary and fiscal policies aimed at economic stability [2]. Accurate inflation forecasting is crucial for effective economic planning, policy formulation, and investment decisions, particularly in developing countries like Sri Lanka. Inflation directly impacts the cost of living, wage negotiations, monetary policy decisions, and overall economic stability. Periods of high inflation have often coincided with external shocks, such as oil price volatility, currency devaluations, and global financial crises [3]. Sri Lanka has experienced several economic shifts over the past two decades, including civil conflict recovery, global market fluctuations, and, more recently, a severe economic crisis in 2022 [4–8]. These events have led to volatile inflation rates, highlighting the need for more reliable and adaptive forecasting tools.

Recent advancements in computational methods have increased the use of ML and DL techniques for time series forecasting. These models can capture non-linear patterns and adapt to changing data structures. Although several studies have applied these methods to inflation forecasting globally, limited research exists in the Sri Lankan context, especially using updated inflation data up to 2025, and the application of hybrid approaches.

1.1 Problem Statement

Sri Lanka's inflation exhibits high volatility due to both domestic and external shocks, making accurate forecasting challenging. TTS models, while widely used, may fail to capture complex non-linear patterns, whereas ML and DL methods may offer improvements but are underexplored in this context. Additionally, the effectiveness of hybrid and ensemble forecasting models for Sri Lankan inflation has not yet been systematically examined.

1.2 Main Objective

This research aims to fill this gap by comparing the effectiveness of TTS models (ARIMA, SARIMA), ML models (SVR, RF, XGB), DL models (LSTM, CNN, FNN), novel hybrid models, and ensemble approaches in forecasting inflation using univariate inflation data. The goal is to identify models that provide the highest predictive accuracy.

1.3 Research Questions

1. How does the performance of traditional time series models (ARIMA, SARIMA) compare with that of machine learning (RF, SVR, XGB) and deep learning (FNN, LSTM, CNN) models in forecasting inflation in Sri Lanka?

2. Can ensemble and hybrid approaches improve the forecasting accuracy compared to the standalone models?
3. What is the most effective train-test split for accurately forecasting univariate inflation data?

The remainder of this paper is organized as follows. Section 2 presents a comprehensive literature review, including both global and Sri Lankan studies on inflation forecasting. Section 3 outlines the methodology and describes the data, preprocessing procedures, and integration steps. Section 4 reports the empirical results and compares the performance of TTS, ML, DL, hybrid, and ensemble approaches. Section 5 discusses the findings and concludes the study, highlighting key contributions, limitations, and directions for future research.

2 Literature Review

Emwinloghosa et al. [9] used ARIMA to forecast Nigeria's inflation (1981–2020), identified ARIMA (0,0,1) as the best model. Model selection relied on AIC and BIC. Stationarity was verified via the ADF test. Ibrahim Doguwa [10] developed SARIMA and SARIMAX, incorporating exogenous variables, PMS prices, government spending, credit data, rainfall, and exchange rates. The study shows that multivariate models outperform univariate ones. Both studies were limited to traditional methods. By incorporating ML approaches, model performance could be further increased [3].

ML methods address key forecasting challenges like nonlinearity, multicollinearity, predictor relevance, and high dimensionality, which limit TTS models [11, 12]. With advances in computing and data availability, ML is gaining attention as an alternative to TTS approaches. There is also a growing focus on developing more interpretable ML models for macroeconomic forecasting [13]. Nkemnole et al. [14] applied KNN and LSTM models with a Hidden Markov Model (HMM) to predict inflation and transition patterns in Nigeria using GDP per capita data (1960–2022). Data was split 80:20 for training and testing, with preprocessing steps including categorical encoding and min-max scaling. Model performance was evaluated using the Standard Error of the Mean (SEM), MAPE, and RMSE, showing KNN outperformed LSTM. GDP per capita significantly influenced high inflation. However, the study lacked hyperparameter tuning.

Doojav and Narmandakh [13] assessed ML methods for forecasting inflation in Mongolia using quarterly data from 2007 Q3 to 2021 Q4 and utilizing 120 macroeconomic and financial variables. Models such as Ridge Regression (RR), Lasso, Elastic Net, Random Forest (RF), XGBoost (XGB), Autoregressive (AR), and Factor-Augmented Autoregressive (FAAR) were evaluated using walk-forward cross-validation. RR consistently performed well, while RF and XGB outperformed others for longer-term forecasts. Key predictors varied by horizon: short-term forecasts relied on prices and wages, whereas long-term forecasts were driven by money supply, bank credit, interest, exchange rates, and fiscal indicators. The study found ML models improved accuracy, especially with larger datasets, but did not consider lagged variables.

Abdulraheem [3] evaluated ARIMA, ML models (SVR, RF, ANN), and hybrid approaches (ARIMA-SVR, ARIMA-RF, ARIMA-ANN) for forecasting Nigeria's monthly inflation. Following preprocessing steps such as imputation, outlier treatment, standardization, and differencing, models were trained on lagged features and assessed using walk-forward validation across various train-test splits (70:30, 80:20, 90:10). The ARIMA-ANN model with an 80:20 split yielded the best performance based on MSE, RMSE, and MAPE. The study's univariate approach and reliance on grid and random search highlight the potential for future improvements through efficient tuning methods like Optuna [15].

Another approach to inflation forecasting involves probabilistic or interval methods that explicitly quantify uncertainty. Charles S. Bos et al. [16] examined autoregressive fractionally integrated moving average models with explanatory variables (ARFIMAX) for U.S. core inflation and log price levels over 1960–1999, focusing on post-1984 recursive out-of-sample forecasts up to two years ahead. Compared with ARFIMA, ARFIMAX, and standard ARIMA and ARMA models, ARIMA(1,1,1) achieved the highest point-forecast accuracy but overstates multi-step forecast intervals. In contrast, ARFIMAX yielded more realistic interval estimates by incorporating fractional integration, lagged short-term interest rates, and unemployment, thereby improving short-term forecast accuracy.

The study by Wayne Robinson [16] provided a comprehensive examination of inflation forecasting through Vector Autoregressive (VAR) models, supplemented by an error correction mechanism, specifically within the context of Jamaica. Tests showed variables are non-stationary and integrated of order one (I(1)), leading to the use of a Vector Error Correction Model (VECM) to account for long-run cointegration relationships while modeling short-term dynamics. Block exogeneity tests identified base money, interest rate, exchange rate, and GDP as Granger causal to inflation. The VAR model outperformed other time series models like ARMA and monthly structural models in forecasting accuracy as measured by RMSE. Results suggested that exchange rate stabilization was crucial for short-term price stability, with monetary stability underpinning exchange rate stabilization. Some inflation shocks had long-lived effects due to the structure of the economy, expectations, indexation, and speculative behavior in exchange rates.

The study, Lukianenko et al. [17], investigated the dynamics of inflation expectations and their dependence on inflation, key policy rates, and real wages through the Markov switching autoregression (MSAR) model. The research was motivated by Ukraine's transition from a fixed exchange rate regime to inflation targeting in 2016. The key insight is that inflation expectations became more influential under the inflation targeting regime, making their modeling crucial for policy effectiveness. The authors use a two-regime Markov switching autoregression model to distinguish periods of high and low volatility in inflation expectations. This model incorporates inflation expectations as the dependent variable regressed on its own lag, current inflation (consumer price index), key policy rate, and real wage index. The Markov switching mechanism captures regime-dependent behaviors during times of economic stability versus crisis or uncertainty. Inflation expectations respond positively to current inflation and real wage increases, and react differently to key policy rate changes depending on the regime. The model achieves high accuracy with a Mean Absolute Percentage Error (MAPE) below 10%, making it suitable for forecasting inflation expectations. The Markov switching approach allows modeling of inflation expectation dynamics flexibly by accounting for volatility regime changes, a critical feature when inflation dynamics are influenced by structural breaks and policy shifts.

2.1 Previous Studies of Inflation Forecasting Done in Sri Lanka

Previous research on inflation forecasting in Sri Lanka has primarily employed ARIMA models. Nyoni & T. Nyoni [11] identified ARIMA(1,0,0) as optimal based on AIC using annual data from 1960–2017. However, the analysis does not include key recent events such as the 2019 Easter attack, the COVID-19 pandemic, and the economic crisis. Dunuwita Liyanage [12] utilized monthly data from 2014–2023, identified ARIMA(1,1,2) and ARIMA(2,1,3) for core and headline inflation forecasting, respectively. Jesmy [13] also applied an ARIMA model to forecast inflation in Sri Lanka using CCPI data from 1953 to 2009, assessing stationarity with the ADF test and selecting models based on AIC and Schwarz Criterion (SC). However, residual diagnostics relied only on visual inspection. The current study enhances this approach by incorporating statistical tests for residual analysis (Ljung-Box, heteroscedasticity, and normality), using both ADF and KPSS for stationarity assessment, and applying the HEGY test to detect seasonal stationarity. Additionally, the above three studies were limited to traditional ARIMA. To overcome these limitations, the present study extends the dataset up to March 2025 and explores a wider range of forecasting techniques, ML, DL, and hybrid models (HM). Raj et al. [14] examined advanced models such as N-BEATS, Reservoir Computing, Prophet, Neural Prophet, and Bi-LSTM for multi-step inflation forecasting for Sri Lanka using data from January 2021 to March 2023. However, their analysis relied on visual comparisons, lacked standard evaluation metrics, hyperparameter tuning, and a systematic lag selection method. In contrast, the present study addresses these gaps by using an extended dataset (2000 Jan – 2025 March), incorporating quantitative metrics (RMSE, MSE, MAE, R^2), applying hyperparameter optimization, and introducing a structured approach to lag selection. A comprehensive range of forecasting techniques, including TTS, ML, DL, Hybrid, and ensemble models, was evaluated.

W. M. S. Bandara and De Mel [15] applied ML models (LASSO Regression (LR), Bayesian Ridge Regression (BRR), SVR, RF) to forecast inflation in Sri Lanka, using past inflation lags as inputs. K-fold and Walk Forward Validation were employed, finding WFV superior, with the LR-WFV model performing best based on RMSE and MAPE. However, the study lacked systematic lag selection and relied solely on Grid Search, which may miss the optimal hyperparameters [18]. Additionally, MAPE is considered to be unstable near zero values [19]. The present study addresses these limitations by incorporating advanced lag selection methods, using Optuna for hyperparameter tuning, and evaluating models with a broader set of metrics (RMSE, MSE, MAE, MAPE, R^2). Mustafa [20] examined the inverse relationship between inflation and Foreign Direct Investment (FDI) using data from 1978 to 2017, employing simple regression for inflation forecasting. It was identified that inflation is inversely related to FDI. Additionally, R. Bandara [21] used a VAR model to study inflation determinants in Sri Lanka from 1993 to 2009, Money Supply(M2), CCPI, Exchange Rate USD, Gross Domestic Product - GDP, Treasury Bill (TB), and unemployment rate (UE) were considered in the study, identifying Money Supply (M2), Exchange Rate, and GDP as significant factors. Granger causality tests showed M2 and the exchange rate influenced inflation with long lags

(18 months). Ratnasiri [22] used VAR analysis to examine inflation determinants in Sri Lanka from 1980 to 2005, focusing on variables such as CCPI, GDP, money supply, exchange rate, rice price, and interest rate. The study found that money supply growth and rice prices are key long-run drivers of inflation, while exchange rate depreciation and the output gap had no significant effects. Inflation was shown to be driven by both demand and supply-side factors. However, both studies focused only on identifying significant variables and did not use modern forecasting methods. They also do not include recent economic shocks.

Building on the existing literature, this study provides a comprehensive analysis of univariate one-step-ahead inflation forecasting in Sri Lanka using diverse modeling approaches. TTS models are benchmarked against machine-learning models and deep-learning models. In addition, ensemble approaches, as well as residual-based models, are explored. All models are optimized using the Optuna hyperparameter tuning framework and optimized via time series cross-validation, with multiple train-test splits tested, assessing model performance with multiple metrics (RMSE, MSE, MAE, R^2), and identifying approaches that improve forecasting accuracy for Sri Lanka's inflation.

3 Methodology

This section provides an overview of the methodologies applied in the study. It details the dataset used, the procedures for data collection and preparation, feature engineering techniques, and the preliminary analysis conducted. Furthermore, it outlines the implementation of TTS, ML, DL, ensemble, and hybrid approaches, along with the corresponding results and interpretations.

3.1 Data Description

This study utilized headline inflation data from the Colombo Consumer Price Index (CCPI), which measures overall inflation by incorporating a diverse variety of products and services. The dataset covers the period from January 2000 to March 2025 and was sourced from the Central Bank of Sri Lanka (CBSL) Data Library (cbsl.lk/eresearch/).

3.2 Data Preparation and Data Integration

During data preparation, the CCPI series was rebased to a single base year (2021). The data originally published with multiple base years, 1952, 2003, 2006, 2013, and 2021, the series was made consistent using a sequential rebasing method (the process of adjusting index numbers from multiple base periods to a common base). CCPI values were sequentially converted through each base year (1952 → 2003 → 2006 → 2013 → 2021), resulting in a consistent CCPI series rebased to 2021.

Conversion Methodology
A sequential rebasing method was used to convert CCPI values to the 2021 base year. Conversion factors were calculated for overlapping periods where both old and new base

year index values were available. For each overlapping month, the factor was derived by dividing the new base year index by the old base year index.

$$Conversion\ Factor_{month} = \frac{CCPI_{(new\ base\ period)}[Month]}{CCPI_{(old\ base\ period)}[Month]} \quad (1)$$

These monthly factors adjusted the older series to the new base. This process was repeated for each base transition, 1952 to 2003, 2003 to 2006, 2006 to 2013, and 2013 to 2021, resulting in a series aligned to the 2021 base year.

Compute Year-on-Year (Y-o-Y) Inflation Using CCPI

The headline CCPI covers various items, capturing both stable and volatile price components. With the index rebased to 2021, year-on-year (YoY) inflation is calculated using the formula.

$$YoY\ Inflation = \frac{CCPI_t - CCPI_{t-12}}{CCPI_{t-12}} \quad (2)$$

Selection of Optimal Train-Test Split Ratio

This study evaluated three train-test split ratios, 70:30, 80:20, and 90:10, to identify the most suitable ratio for forecasting inflation. This approach aligns with methodologies used in previous research [18]. Model effectiveness for each split was assessed using evaluation metrics including RMSE, MAE, MSE, and R-squared.

4 Results

This section presents the empirical findings derived from the statistical tests and modeling approaches.

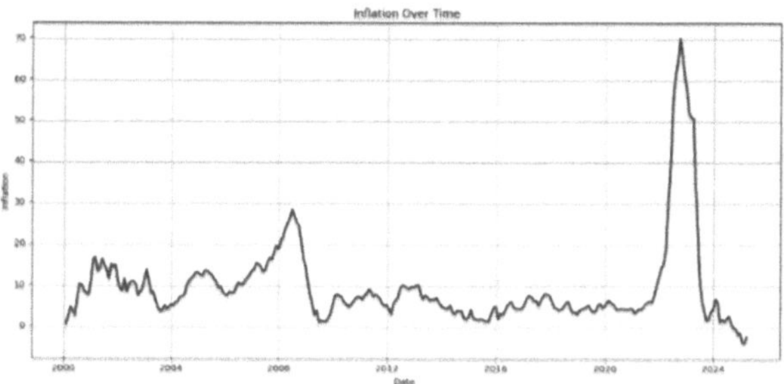

Fig. 1. Time Series plot of Inflation

The time series plot of inflation (Fig. 1) reveals several notable trends and fluctuations. A major inflation spike occurred between September 2021 and July 2022, followed by a rapid decline until October 2023. Although inflation continued to fall beyond this point, the pace of decline slowed. Another significant inflationary phase was observed

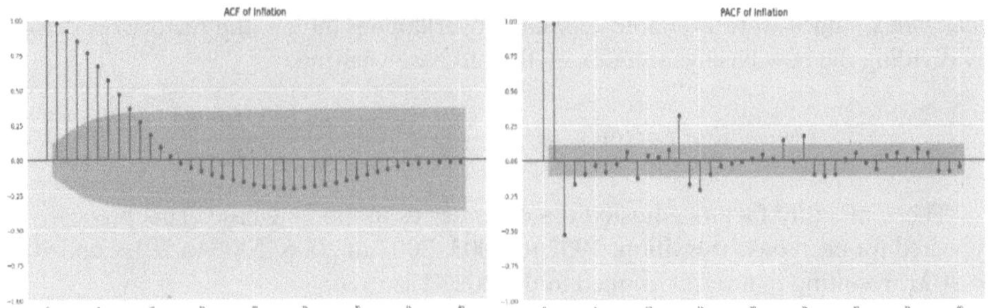

Fig. 2. ACF and PACF plot of Inflation

from March 2006 to April 2009, with inflation rising steadily from March 2006 to January 2008, then gradually declining until July 2009.

These trends are consistent with previous reports. According to The Economic Times [19] Sri Lanka's inflation surged to 60.8% in July 2022, reflecting the severity of the economic crisis during that time. Additionally, an International Monetary Fund (IMF) report from 2007 noted that CCPI inflation rose from 4% in 2005 to nearly 18% by the end of 2006, driven by strong demand pressures and adjustments in administered prices, particularly in fuel, electricity, and transportation. Inflation continued to climb, reaching 21.75% year-on-year by August 2007.

The ACF plot (Fig. 2) indicates significant correlations at higher lags, with up to 9 lags being statistically significant, suggesting strong persistence in the inflation series.

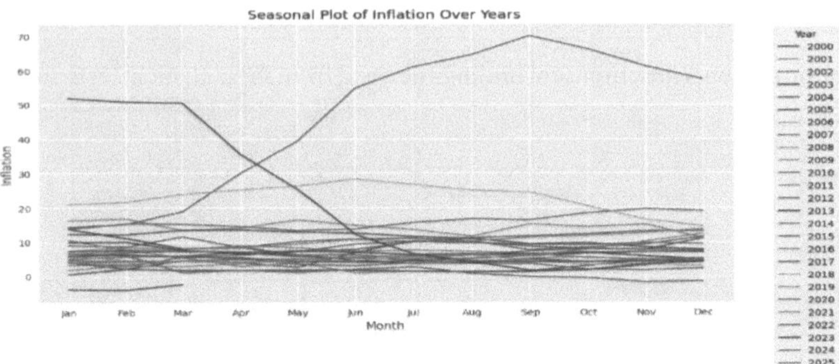

Fig. 3. Seasonal plot of Inflation

The seasonal plot of monthly inflation (Fig. 3) from 2000 to 2025 shows no clear seasonal pattern. However, a period of elevated inflation is evident between March 2022 and May 2023.

4.1 Stationary Tests

To assess the stationarity of the inflation time series, both seasonal and standard unit root tests were conducted.

Seasonal Unit Root Test (HEGY Test)
The HEGY test was applied to detect seasonal unit roots.

- Null Hypothesis (H_0): The inflation series contains a seasonal unit root at a specific frequency.
- Alternative Hypothesis (H_1): The inflation series does not contain a seasonal unit root at that frequency.

Table 1. HEGY seasonal stationary test for inflation

	Test Statistic	P Value
t_1	-3.4047	0.0293
t_2	-4.1975	0.0003
F_3:4	28.2142	0
F_5:6	31.3102	0
F_7:8	28.7489	0
F_9:10	30.8755	0
F_11:12	41.3258	0
F_2:12	1789.0528	0
F_1:12	1644.0634	0

According to Table 1, all the p-values are below the 5% significance level, leading to the rejection of the null hypothesis across all seasonal frequencies. This indicates that the inflation series does not contain seasonal unit roots and can be considered seasonally stationary, which is suitable for time series modeling and forecasting.

Standard Unit Root Test (ADF and KPSS Test)
Two standard unit root tests were applied to assess overall stationarity: the Augmented Dickey-Fuller (ADF) test and the Kwiatkowski-Phillips-Schmidt-Shin (KPSS) test.

(a) Augmented Dickey-Fuller (ADF) Test

- H_0: The inflation series has a unit root (non-stationary).
- H_1: The inflation series is stationary.

(b) KPSS Test

- H_0: The inflation series is stationary.
- H_1: The inflation series has a unit root (non-stationary).

According to Table 2 below, results from the Augmented Dickey-Fuller (ADF) and Kwiatkowski-Phillips-Schmidt-Shin (KPSS) tests confirmed that the inflation series is stationary as the ADF test rejects the null of a unit root ($p = 0.0023 < 0.05$), and the KPSS test fails to reject the null of stationarity ($p = 0.1 > 0.05$).

Table 2. ADF and KPSS test results

	ADF Test		KPSS Test	
	Test statistic.	P Value.	Test statistic.	P Value.
Inflation	-3.8581	0.0023	0.1022	0.1

4.2 Univariate Inflation Forecasting

Univariate time series forecasting involves predicting a variable's future values based only on its past data. Although it is simple and requires limited input, it does not account for external influences.

Univariate Traditional Time Series Forecasting

The ARIMA modeling approach was utilized for univariate forecasting under traditional approaches. As discussed previously, three train-test splits were considered.

ARIMA

An Auto-ARIMA model was developed using Python's built-in function. The optimal ARIMA parameters and associated performance metrics were recorded for each split (Table 3).

Table 3. ARIMA model performance under each split

Split Ratio	Model	AIC	BIC	MAE	MSE	RMSE	R-squared
70-30	ARIMA(1,1,0)	749.28985	755.99373	9.5832	350.5513	18.7230	-0.0863
80-20	ARIMA(0,1,1)	832.42956	839.39994	13.3633	523.1375	22.8722	-0.1720
90-10	ARIMA(3, 0,1)	1041.0032	1062.6346	20.8958	728.5570	26.9918	-0.2515

SARIMA

The ARIMA model demonstrated less effectiveness in forecasting, as it failed to capture key fluctuations. To address this, the SARIMA model was introduced, considering seasonal components to improve performance and better represent the dynamic patterns.

According to Table 4, the SARIMA (3, 0, 3) (0, 0, 1) [12] model, applied with a 90:10 train-test split, outperformed other traditional univariate models (Table 3) by effectively capturing seasonal and non-seasonal patterns in the data.

Table 4. SARIMA model performance under each split

Split Ratio	Model	AIC	BIC	MAE	MSE	RMSE	R-squared
70-30	SARIMA(4, 1, 2) (0, 0, 1, 12)	749.28929	755.99322	9.5544	348.5522	18.669	-0.0801
80-20	SARIMA(4, 1, 2) (0, 0, 1, 12)	832.42918	839.39958	13.3162	527.3929	22.965	-0.1815
90-10	SARIMA(3, 0, 3) (0, 0, 1, 12)	1041.0009	1062.6305	8.210	132.6634	11.51	-0.7721

However, while it showed better performance than the ARIMA model, its performance was still limited in addressing complex and non-linear trends, leaving room for enhancement. As a result, the study progressed to explore ML and DL models.

Univariate Machine Learning and Deep Learning Approaches
According to the literature, several ML and DL models, including RF, XGB, SVR, FNN, LSTM, and CNN, were applied to forecast inflation using univariate CCPI data to capture non-linear patterns and complex time dependencies. Before fitting the model, a crucial preprocessing step, which involved selecting significant lag terms, was done based on ACF and PACF, to ensure relevant historical patterns were effectively captured for accurate forecasting.

Lags Identification for Univariate Machine Learning Models

Since time series data contain temporal dependencies, incorporating past lag values is crucial for accurate forecasting. However, selecting too many or too few lags can result in overfitting or loss of important information [19].To address this, the Auto Correlation Function (ACF) is commonly used to identify significant lags [20, 22]. In this study, ACF and PACF plots were used to examine the inflation series, revealing that lags from t–1 to t–9 showed significant correlations (Fig. 2).

Based on these findings, inflation values from the past 1 to 9 time steps were selected as candidate features. Following the method by Ghorbani et al. [23], to determine the optimal number of lags for each model, nine configurations were tested using various lag combinations across ML and DL models. This process was repeated under three train-test splits (70,30, 80:20, 90:10), as the ideal lag structure may differ by model type. Model-specific lag optimization ensured the best forecasting performance for each algorithm.

Univariate Inflation Forecasting Using Machine Learning and Deep Learning

For univariate one-step-ahead inflation forecasting, the time series data were restructured as a supervised learning problem, using lagged inflation values as inputs (X) and the current value as the target (y). To assess model performance under different data availability scenarios, three sequential train-test splits (70:30, 80:20, 90:10) were applied.

Model hyperparameters were optimized using Optuna combined with time series cross-validation (TSCV). Model performance was evaluated using RMSE, MSE, MAE, and R-squared. Before training the SVR and DL models, which are sensitive to feature scaling, the inflation data were normalized with MinMaxScaler to improve convergence and stability. To prevent data leakage, the scaler was fitted exclusively on the training set and then applied to transform the test set.

Initially, three different splits, 70:30, 80:20, and 90:10, were evaluated across the standalone models. According to Table 5, 5 out of 6 standalone models consistently performed best with the 90:10 split. In this approach, first 90% of the data was used for training and parameter optimization through time series cross-validation, while the remaining 10% was reserved as a hold-out sample for testing, using a time series cross-validation framework. Based on the results across all fitted models, the majority indicate that the 90:10 split yields the most robust performance. The choice of the 90:10 train-test split was additionally supported by computational and time limitations. Therefore, for subsequent analyses, only the 90:10 train-test split was considered.

Univariate Inflation Forecasting Using Hybrid and Ensemble Models

It was observed that SVR, FNN, LSTM, and CNN standalone models performed competitively and achieved promising results. After identifying the optimal models, the next step was to develop hybrid and ensemble models by considering the top 4 models: SVR, LSTM, FNN, and CNN. Three different Hybrid Modelling Approaches were considered,

- Residual-Based Hybrid Model
- Simple Averaging Ensemble Model
- Error-Based Weighted Ensemble Models

Residual-Based Hybrid Models

In this approach, SVR was first employed to generate the initial forecasts. The residuals (i.e., prediction errors) from the SVR model were then modeled using CNN, LSTM, and FNN separately. This led to the development of three hybrid models: SVR-FNN, SVR-LSTM, and SVR-CNN, where the final forecast was obtained by summing the SVR prediction with the output of the corresponding residual model (Table 6). This approach is widely used in previous time series forecasting studies [18, 24].

Variants of this hybrid architecture have also been successfully applied across various domains. For example, SVR-CNN was considered in [25], while SVR-LSTM was considered in [26, 27]. Similarly, SVR-FNN was considered in [28, 29].

Simple Averaging Ensemble

This method involved generating standalone predictions from each of the four base models, SVR, CNN, LSTM, and FNN, and computing the final forecast as the simple arithmetic mean of these individual predictions (Table 7). This approach assumes that averaging multiple model outputs can reduce individual model variability and improve generalization. Timmermann [30] identified that using simple averages may work as well as more sophisticated approaches.

Error-Based Weighted Ensemble

A widely used technique in ensemble methods is the weighted averaging approach, where each model's prediction contributes to the final output based on its performance.

Table 5. ML & DL model performance under each split

Random Forest.			
	70%–30% split.	80%–20% split.	90%–10% split.
Optimal Lag	1	1	1
RMSE	11.6283	14.2128	7.6082
MSE	135.2178	202.0023	57.8850
MAE	5.3842	7.6066	5.0338
R-Squared	0.6	0.5645	0.9006
XGBoost			
	70%–30% split.	80%–20% split.	90%–10% split.
Optimal Lag	1	1	9
RMSE	11.5544	14.1056	5.6065
MSE	133.5047	198.9677	31.4331
MAE	5.5324	7.6693	4.2307
R-Squared	0.6035	0.5710	0.9375
SVR			
	70%–30% split.	80%–20% split.	90%–10% split.
Optimal Lag	9	9	3
RMSE	2.8851	3.4233	3.6809
MSE	8.3241	11.7190	13.5493
MAE	1.5783	2.0496	2.3653
R-Squared	0.9757	0.9750	0.9767
FNN			
	70%–30%split.	80%–20% split.	90%–10% split.
Optimal Lag	8	9	2
RMSE	4.0559	5.4555	3.3418
MSE	16.4507	29.7629	11.8387
MAE	2.2722	2.8735	2.2637
R-Squared	0.9501	0.9097	0.9765
LSTM			
	70%–30%split.	80%–20% split.	90%–10% split.
Optimal Lag	3	3	4
RMSE	4.6969	4.1350	3.2015
MSE	22.0605	17.0985	10.2499

(*continued*)

Table 5. *(continued)*

Random Forest.			
	70%–30% split.	80%–20% split.	90%–10% split.
MAE	2.51043	2.5801	2.1953
R-Squared	0.9338	0.9631	0.97591
CNN			
	70%–30%split.	80%–20% split.	90%–10% split.
Optimal Lag	6	5	3
RMSE	3.9095	3.9137	3.8399
MSE	15.2842	15.3173	14.7451
MAE	2.8400	2.5415	2.8629
R-Squared	0.9531	0.9661	0.9747

Table 6. Residual-based hybrid models' performance

	SVR-CNN	SVR-LSTM	SVR-FNN
RMSE	3.3148	3.2365	3.1925
MSE	10.9877	10.4750	10.1920
MAE	1.9046	1.8635	1.8699
R-Squared	0.9751	0.9753	0.9760

Table 7. Simple averaging ensemble model performance

	Performance Metrics. - Ensemble Simple Averaging
RMSE	3.1687
MSE	10.0407
MAE	2.0107
R-squared	0.97641

In this method, weights are assigned inversely proportional to each model's error metric. The study by Thaker & Höller [31] calculates the weights by considering MAE. Predictions are weighted inversely to their MAE (Mean Absolute Error), giving higher influence for better-performing models. Models with lower MAE are given higher influence, as they demonstrate better predictive performance. indicating Higher weights. To determine weights, Inverse MAE (IMAE) is calculated for each model:

$$IMAE_{MODEL} = \frac{1}{MAE_{model}} \tag{3}$$

These IMAE values are then normalized so that the sum of weights equals 1. For example, the weight assigned to the CNN model is calculated as:

$$\omega_{cnn} = \frac{IMAE_{cnn}}{IMAE_{cnn} + IMAE_{lstm} + IMAE_{svr} + IMAE_{fnn}} \tag{4}$$

This process was continued for RMSE and MSE as well (Table 8).

- MSE-Based Weighted Ensemble: Weights determined using the inverse of the Mean Squared Error (MSE).
- RMSE-Based Weighted Ensemble: Weights calculated based on the inverse of the Root Mean Squared Error (RMSE).
- MAE-Based Weighted Ensemble: Weights assigned according to the inverse of the Mean Absolute Error (MAE) of each model.

Table 8. The weights under each approach

Model	Weight		
	Weighted Averaging-MSE	Weighted Averaging-RMSE	Weighted Averaging-MAE
SVR	0.2288	0.2395	0.26132
FNN	0.2709	0.2607	0.2687
LSTM	0.2826	0.2662	0.25907
CNN	0.2176	0.2336	0.21088

Table 9. Model evaluation - ensemble weighted averaging methods

	Performance Metrics. - Ensemble Weighted Averaging		
	MSE	RMSE	MAE
RMSE	3.1625	3.1655	**3.1624**
MSE	10.0018	10.0207	**10.0010**
MAE	2.0170	2.0134	**1.9995**
R-squared	0.9764	0.9764	**0.9764**

Among the fitted standalone models and hybrid approaches, the MAE-based weighted ensemble approach provided the lowest errors (Fig. 4), indicating the superior performance based on model evaluation metrics (Table 9). However, among all fitted models (TTS, ML, DL, Hybrid, and Ensemble), the error-weighted ensemble models (Table 9) and the simple averaged ensemble model (Table 7) demonstrated relatively competitive model performance. To determine whether these differences in forecasting

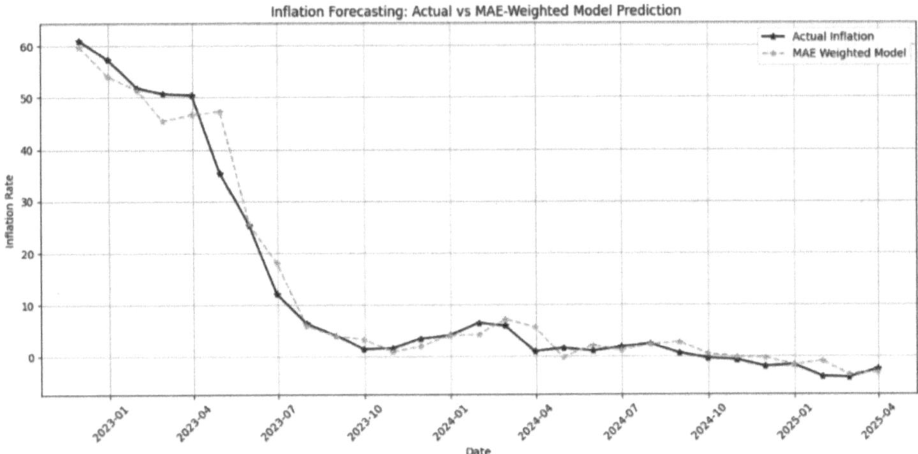

Fig. 4. Actual and predicted inflation values under the weighted averaging based on MAE values

accuracy were statistically significant, the Diebold–Mariano test was performed for all pairwise comparisons of the ensembles.

4.3 Diebold–Mariano Test

To determine whether the differences in predictive accuracy between the ensemble models were statistically significant, the Diebold–Mariano (DM) test was applied

H_0: The two competing forecasting models have equal predictive accuracy.

H_1: The two models do not have equal predictive accuracy.

Table 10. Diebold–Mariano test results comparing predictive accuracy across ensemble models

Model 1	Model 2	DM Statistic	P value	Conclusion
MAE-weighted ensembles	RMSE-weighted ensembles	-0.1664	0.8678	N.S.
MAE-weighted ensembles	MSE-weighted ensembles	-0.0055	0.9956	N.S.
MSE-weighted ensembles	RMSE-weighted ensembles	-0.6425	0.5206	N.S.
Simple ensembles	MAE-weighted ensembles	0.7418	0.4582	N.S.
Simple ensembles	MSE-weighted ensembles	0.6790	0.4971	N.S.
Simple ensembles	RMSE-weighted ensemble	0.7175	0.4731	N.S.

*N.S. = No significant difference between the predictive accuracy of two models at the 5% level

The results from the Diebold Mariano test (Table 10) indicated no significant differences in the forecasting accuracy among the best four models (Fig. 5). This suggests that while the MAE-weighted ensemble model slightly outperformed the others in numerical error metrics, the differences in predictive accuracy are not statistically significant according to the Diebold-Mariano test. Overall, the study highlights the effectiveness of ensemble models in improving forecast accuracy.

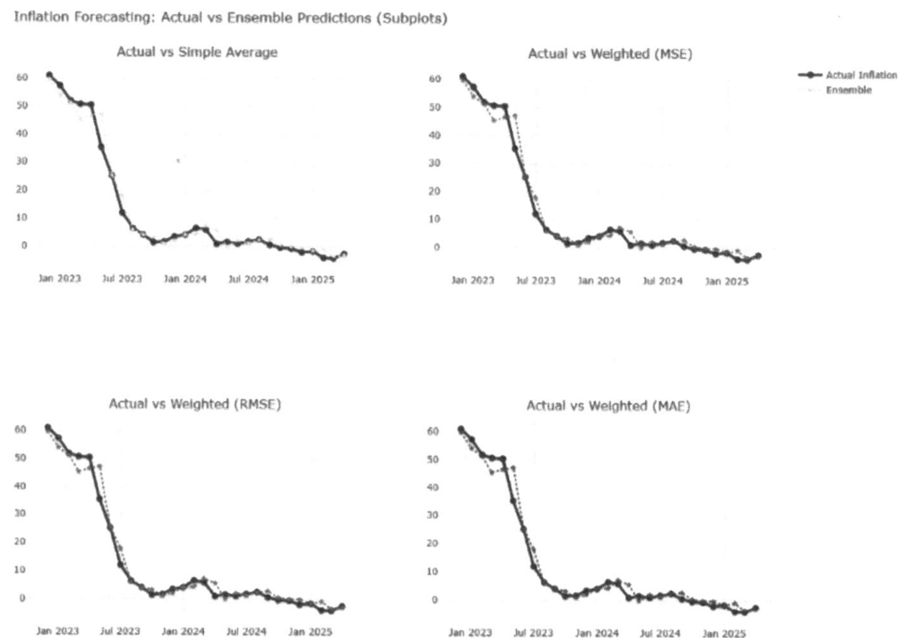

Fig. 5. Actual and predicted Inflation values under simple and weighted average ensemble models.

5 Discussion and Conclusion

Initially, three different train-test split ratios were considered as 70:30, 80:20, and 90:10. This was done to determine the optimal split ratio, as supported by Abdulraheem et al. [3]. It was found that increasing the size of the training set significantly improved model performance, identifying 90:10 as the optimal split.

The study systematically compared multiple forecasting models for univariate inflation prediction. They are TTS models, including ARIMA and SARIMA, ML models including Random Forest (RF), XGBoost (XGB), and Support Vector Regression (SVR), DL models including Feedforward Neural Networks (FNN), Long Short-Term Memory (LSTM), and Convolutional Neural Networks (CNN) and Hybrid models including Residual-based hybrid models (SVR-CNN, SVR-LSTM, SVR-FNN), simple average ensemble model (average of SVR, CNN, LSTM and FNN), and error-based weighted ensembles (using RMSE, MSE, and MAE as weighting criteria.)

Among the traditional models, SARIMA performed better than ARIMA due to its ability to model seasonality. However, both were outperformed by ML and DL models. SVR, LSTM, CNN, and FNN demonstrated notably better performance among standalone models. The study further advanced model performance by introducing hybrid and ensemble modeling approaches. In the residual-based hybrid approach, SVR was used to generate initial forecasts, and its residuals were modeled using FNN, CNN, and LSTM. Additionally, ensemble methods were applied, including a simple average and three different weighted averaging techniques based on RMSE, MSE, and MAE, respectively. While the MAE-weighted ensemble model slightly outperformed the others in numerical error metrics, the Diebold–Mariano test indicated no statistically significant differences among the ensembles, indicating the proposed simple average ensemble model and error-based weighted average ensemble models provided excellent predictive performance in one-step-ahead Inflation forecasting in Sri Lanka. Compared to previous studies, such as Nyoni and Nyoni [32], which reported higher error rates, and Dunuwita Liyanage [33], which achieved a lower R-squared value, the proposed ensemble models showed substantial improvement, highlighting the efficacy of the adopted approach.

5.1 Limitations

The study used only univariate inflation data and one-step-ahead predictions, which limits its ability to capture broader economic influences and longer-term trends. Future research should incorporate multiple macroeconomic indicators, adopt multi-step forecasting, and apply explainable modeling techniques (e.g., SHAP, Feature Importance Plot) to reveal key drivers of predictions for policy use. Testing for structural breaks and integrating uncertainty quantification (e.g., prediction intervals) would also enhance forecast reliability and credibility under changing economic conditions.

Disclosure of Interest. The authors declare that they have no competing financial interests or personal relationships that could have appeared to influence the work reported in this paper

References

1. John, C., Izuchukwu Okoroafor, P., Chinenye Theresa, A.: Application of Factor Analysis in the Modelling of Inflation Rate in Nigeria.
2. Plas, J.D.C. van der: Dutch Inflation Rate Forecasting Performance of Econometric and Neural Network Models. (2023)
3. Abdulraheem, A., Muntasir, M., Shuaibu, N.: FUDMA Journal of Renewable and Atomic Energy (FJoRAE) Evaluating Time Series and Machine Learning Approaches for Forecasting Inflation in Nigeria. **2**, 42–66 (2025). https://doi.org/10.33003/fjorae.2025.0201.04.
4. Sri Lanka's political and economic situation, visualized: World Economic Forum. https://www.weforum.org/stories/2022/07/economic-politics-debt-protest-crisis-sri-lanka/. Accessed 03 June 2025
5. Root cause for Sri Lanka's present economic woes—South-South Research Initiative. https://ssrinitiative.org/root-cause-for-sri-lankas-present-economic-woes/?utm_source=chatgpt.com. Accessed 03 June 2025
6. Dias, P.: The impact of IMF bailout programmes on socio- economic rights in the global south: a case study of Sri Lanka, 2022-2024. SSRN Electron. J. (2024). https://doi.org/10.2139/ssrn.5029182
7. Is Sri Lanka transitioning from an economic crisis to recovery?. https://www.orfonline.org/expert-speak/is-sri-lanka-recovering-transitioning-from-an-economic-crisis-to-recovery?utm_source=chatgpt.com. Accessed 02 June 2025
8. Sri Lanka's economic crisis, explained. CNN. https://edition.cnn.com/2022/04/05/asia/sri-lanka-economic-crisis-explainer-intl-hnk/index.html?utm_source=chatgpt.com. Accessed 02 June 2025

9. E, K.G., P, O.O., P., N.I., E., S.O., A, C.: Modeling and forecasting inflation in Nigeria: a time series regression with ARIMA method. Afr. J. Econ. Sustain. Dev. **6**, 42–53 (2023). https://doi.org/10.52589/ajesd-hfyc2bnw
10. Ibrahim Doguwa, S.: Short-term inflation forecasting models for Nigeria.
11. Kuhn, M., Johnson, K.: Applied predictive modeling. Applied Predictive Modeling. 1–600 (2013). https://doi.org/10.1007/978-1-4614-6849-3/COVER.
12. Lazzeri, Francesca.: Machine learning for time series forecasting with Python. 227 (2021)
13. Doojav, G.O., Narmandakh, B.: Forecasting inflation in Mongolia using machine learning. Int. Econ. J. (2025). https://doi.org/10.1080/10168737.2025.2491386
14. Nkemnole, E.B., Wulu, J.T., Osubu, I.: Application of K-nearest neighbours and long-short-term memory models using hidden Markov model to predict inflation rate and transition patterns in Nigeria. J. Appl. Sci. Environ. Manag. **28**, 1913–1925 (2024). https://doi.org/10.4314/jasem.v28i6.33
15. Ülke, V., Sahin, A., Subasi, A.: A comparison of time series and machine learning models for inflation forecasting: empirical evidence from the USA. Neural Comput. & Applic. **30**, 1519–1527 (2018). https://doi.org/10.1007/S00521-016-2766-X/TABLES/5
16. Robinson Bank Of Jamaica, W.: Forecasting Inflation Using VAR Analysis
17. Lukianenko, I., Nasachenko, M.: Inflation expectations Modeling: the application of Markov switching autoregression. Sci. Pap. NaUKMA. Econ. **5**, 82–88 (2020). https://doi.org/10.18523/2519-4739.20205.1.82-88
18. Jamil, H.: Inflation Forecasting using HYBRID ARIMA-LSTM Model
19. Sri Lanka inflation rate: Sri Lanka's inflation surges over 60 per cent in July. The Economic Times. https://economictimes.indiatimes.com/news/international/world-news/sri-lankas-inflation-surges-over-60-per-cent-in-july/articleshow/93230894.cms?utm_source=chatgpt.com. Accessed 10 Apr 2025
20. Widodo, A., Budi, I., Widjaja, B.: Automatic lag selection in time series forecasting using multiple kernel learning. Int. J. Mach. Learn. Cybern. **7**, 95–110 (2016). https://doi.org/10.1007/S13042-015-0409-7
21. Schlink, U., Tetzlaff, G.: Wind speed forecasting from 1 to 30 minutes. Theor. Appl. Climatol. **60**, 191–198 (1998). https://doi.org/10.1007/S007040050043/METRICS
22. Autocorrelation and Partial Autocorrelation: GeeksforGeeks. https://www.geeksforgeeks.org/autocorrelation-and-partial-autocorrelation.Accessed Feb 2025
23. Ghorbani, M.A., Khatibi, R., FazeliFard, M.H., Naghipour, L., Makarynskyy, O.: Short-term wind speed predictions with machine learning techniques. Meteorog. Atmos. Phys. **128**, 57–72 (2016). https://doi.org/10.1007/s00703-015-0398-9
24. Zhang, G.P.: Time Series Forecasting Using a Hybrid ARIMA and Neural Network Model. (2003)
25. Ghimire, S., Bhandari, B., Casillas-Pérez, D., Deo, R.C., Salcedo-Sanz, S.: Hybrid deep CNN-SVR algorithm for solar radiation prediction problems in Queensland. Australia. Eng. Appl. Artif. Intell. **112** (2022). https://doi.org/10.1016/j.engappai.2022.104860
26. Das, H.S., Das, H.S., Bhattacharjee, S.: Forecasting upper air wind speed using a hybrid SVR-LSTM model. In: 2nd International Conference on Range Technology, ICORT 2021 (2021). https://doi.org/10.1109/ICORT52730.2021.9581478
27. Wang, A., Ren, C.: Prediction of receiving field strength based on SVM-LSTM hybrid model in the coal mine. In: 2021 IEEE 3rd International Conference on Communications, Information System and Computer Engineering, CISCE 2021, pp. 813–816 (2021). https://doi.org/10.1109/CISCE52179.2021.9445892
28. Abbasi, M., Dehban, H., Farokhnia, A., Roozbahani, R., Bahreinimotlagh, M.: Long-term streamflow prediction using hybrid SVR-ANN based on Bayesian model averaging. J. Hydrol. Eng. **27**, 05022018 (2022). https://doi.org/10.1061/(ASCE)HE.1943-5584.0002218

29. Xiang, Y., Gou, L., He, L., Xia, S., Wang, W.: A SVR–ANN combined model based on ensemble EMD for rainfall prediction. Appl. Soft Comput. **73**, 874–883 (2018). https://doi.org/10.1016/J.ASOC.2018.09.018
30. Timmermann, A.: Chapter 4 forecast combinations. Handb. Econ. Forecast. **1**, 135–196 (2006). https://doi.org/10.1016/S1574-0706(05)01004-9
31. Thaker, J., Höller, R.: A comparative study of time series forecasting of solar energy based on irradiance classification. Energies. **15**, 2837 (2022). https://doi.org/10.3390/EN15082837
32. Nyoni Nyoni, T.: Predicting inflation in Sri Lanka using ARMA models. (2019)
33. Dunuwita Liyanage, R.: Inflation forecasting using automatic ARIMA model in Sri Lanka. International. J. Econ. Behav. Organ. (2023). https://doi.org/10.11648/j.ijebo.20231102.13

Work Sphere: A Multi-modal Approach to Employee Engagement Detection in Remote Work Environments with Explainable AI

Kesavan Anbuchelvan(✉) and Pumudu Fernando

School of Computing, Institute of Informatics Technology, Colombo, Sri Lanka
{kesavan.20211452,pumudu.f}@iit.ac.lk

Abstract. The COVID-19 pandemic accelerated the adoption of remote work, creating new challenges for monitoring employee engagement in virtual workplace settings. Existing monitoring systems predominantly focus on activity metrics like mouse activity, screen time, and keyboard monitoring without capturing the emotional dimensions (human side) of engagement. Most commercial solutions operate as "black boxes," and in this AI era, they generate decisions without explanations, which fosters distrust among employees. Additionally, current approaches fail to respect privacy concerns, with studies showing 89% of remote workers express concerns about surveillance misuse. Current systems tend to use either visual cues or behavior tracking but rarely combine them. Most of the time, systems lack limited real-time intervention capabilities. These limitations restrict the effectiveness and adoption of engagement monitoring solutions, and there is no comprehensive multimodal system that addresses all these limitations under one umbrella. This study presents Work Sphere, a novel multi-modal approach to employee engagement detection that integrates visual analysis of facial expressions with both basic emotions and complex emotions (workplace-related emotions), eye gaze, and head pose with behavioral metrics through a dynamic weighting mechanism. The study employs explainable AI techniques to enhance transparency and implements privacy-preserving methods including ephemeral processing of visual data. Using transfer learning with MobileNetV2 and EfficientNetB0 architectures, the approach achieves 76% agreement with human experts on engagement assessment despite individual models showing moderate accuracy (61.5%). Testing across varying environments demonstrates robust performance, particularly in our innovative dynamic weighting system that adapts based on detected attention states. This study addresses critical gaps in existing engagement detection technologies by balancing effective monitoring capabilities with ethical considerations, offering a practical multimodal solution for supporting employee engagement in increasingly distributed work environments.

Keywords: employee engagement · explainable AI · multi-modal detection · remote work

R. N. Rajapakse et al. (Eds.): ICTer 2025, CCIS 2844, pp. 317–331, 2026.
https://doi.org/10.1007/978-981-92-0137-2_21

1 Introduction

The sudden shift to remote work during the COVID-19 pandemic has transformed organizational structures, with studies showing an 87% increase in remote work adoption since 2020 [1]. This transition introduced unique challenges for understanding and supporting employee engagement in virtual environments where traditional observation methods are limited. While remote work offers flexibility benefits, it creates difficulties in maintaining consistent engagement without the physical presence indicators available in traditional office settings.

Current approaches to monitoring engagement in remote environments have significant limitations and gaps that restrict their effectiveness and adoption. First, most existing systems rely heavily on superficial activity tracking through metrics like keyboard input and mouse movements without capturing deeper emotional states [2], creating an incomplete picture of true engagement. Second, studies by D'Mello et al. [3] show these single-indicator approaches miss up to 40% of disengagement instances compared to multi-modal assessment, highlighting the inadequacy of current detection methods. Third, commercial monitoring solutions like Time Doctor and Hubstaff operate as "black boxes," making decisions without providing explanations, which Gunning et al. [4] found creates significant mistrust among employees. Fourth, privacy concerns further complicate implementation, with Wang et al. [5] reporting that 89% of remote workers express concerns about data storage and potential surveillance misuse, creating barriers to adoption of even well-designed systems. Fifth, current systems typically focus on either visual cues or behavioral tracking but rarely integrate both modalities effectively. Finally, most existing solutions lack real-time intervention capabilities, limiting their ability to provide immediate support when disengagement is detected.

This study introduces Work Sphere, a novel multi-modal engagement detection system designed to address these limitations through four key innovations. First, it implements a comprehensive multi-modal framework that integrates visual indicators (facial expressions, eye gaze, head pose) with behavioral metrics (mouse activity, screen time) to provide a more complete engagement assessment than single-indicator approaches. Second, it employs a dynamic weighting mechanism that adjusts based on detected attention states, prioritizing different signals depending on whether an employee is looking at the screen or away from it. Third, it incorporates explainable AI implementation using Gradient-weighted Class Activation Mapping (Grad-CAM) [6] that makes complex neural network decisions interpretable through heatmap visualizations of influential facial regions. Fourth, it utilizes a privacy-preserving design that respects employee dignity and autonomy through ephemeral processing of visual data, ensuring raw webcam frames never persist beyond the moment of analysis.

The integration of Explainable AI (XAI) is particularly crucial for this research domain due to several compelling reasons. In workplace monitoring contexts, employees need to understand how and why engagement assessments are made to build trust and acceptance of the system. Without XAI, engagement detection systems become opaque "black boxes" that generate decisions without justification, leading to employee skepticism and resistance to adoption. Research by Chen et al. [7] demonstrates that visualization of model decision processes increases user trust by 47% compared to unexplained predictions. Furthermore, XAI enables system validation by allowing researchers and practitioners to verify that the AI model is focusing on relevant facial regions and behavioral patterns rather than spurious correlations. In the absence of XAI, organizations would face several critical challenges: (1) employees would likely reject the system due to lack of transparency, (2) managers would struggle to understand and act upon engagement insights, (3) system debugging and improvement would be nearly impossible without understanding model decision processes, and (4) regulatory compliance would be challenging as workplace monitoring increasingly requires algorithmic transparency. Therefore, XAI is not merely an enhancement but a fundamental requirement for ethical and effective engagement monitoring in professional environments.

The objectives of this research include: (1) demonstrating that multi-modal integration significantly outperforms single-indicator approaches to engagement detection; (2) establishing the effectiveness of dynamic weighting strategies that adapt to employee context; (3) validating that explainable AI techniques enhance trust and adoption in workplace monitoring contexts; and (4) confirming that privacy-preserving engagement detection can maintain accuracy while addressing ethical concerns. By addressing these research questions, this work aims to establish a foundation for more effective, ethical, and trusted engagement support in remote work environments.

The remainder of this paper is organized as follows: Sect. 2 reviews background work in engagement detection approaches, multi-modal integration challenges, and limitations of commercial solutions. Section 3 presents the methodology, including the proposed architecture, multi-modal components, novel dynamic weighting integration, explainable AI implementation, and privacy-preserving design. Section 4 details the experimental setup, model performance results, and expert evaluation findings. Finally, Sect. 5 concludes with key contributions and outlines future research directions.

2 Background Work

This section reviews existing literature and technologies relevant to employee engagement detection in remote work environments. The review covers two key areas informing our research approach. First, we examine multi-modal integration approaches and technical challenges in combining heterogeneous data sources for engagement assessment, including temporal alignment and computational fusion strategies. Second, we analyze current commercial workplace monitoring solutions, identifying architectural limitations, transparency issues, and privacy concerns that hinder adoption. This analysis establishes the theoretical foundation and practical gaps motivating our Work Sphere system design.

2.1 Multi-modal Integration and Challenges

Recent research indicates that integrating multiple data sources produces more comprehensive engagement assessment. Zhang et al. [8] demonstrated that integration of multiple indicators improves prediction accuracy by 8–12% compared to single-indicator approaches. However, multi-modal integration faces numerous challenges, particularly temporal alignment of heterogeneous data streams, which limits practical implementation in workplace contexts.

Bosch et al. [9] identified that different engagement indicators operate on varying timeframes digital behaviors change over minutes or hours, eye movements occur within milliseconds, and facial expressions alter within seconds. Their research on temporal alignment techniques showed that sliding window approaches with adjustable sizes outperform fixed interval methods, with accuracy improvements of 12–18% in integrated engagement assessments. This temporal complexity creates significant challenges for real-time processing in workplace contexts, which Sharma and Giannakos

[10] note requires careful optimization to maintain responsiveness.

Computational approaches to multi-modal integration have evolved substantially, with Worsley [11] categorizing them into feature-level fusion (combining raw data before classification), decision-level fusion (combining separate classifier outputs), and hybrid approaches. Empirical comparisons by Giannakos et al. [12] indicate hybrid techniques generally outperform single-level fusion in engagement detection, despite implementation complexity tradeoffs. The complexity of these approaches often limits their practical application in workplace monitoring, creating a gap between research advances and deployable solutions for remote work environments.

2.2 Commercial Solutions and Limitations

The commercial sector has developed various platforms incorporating engagement monitoring features for remote work environments. Upwork, a leading freelance marketplace platform, implements monitoring that captures periodic screenshots, tracks keystrokes, and measures mouse activity to verify billable hours [13]. While effective for basic activity verification, this approach lacks any assessment of emotional or cognitive engagement dimensions, frequently mischaracterizing active but non-engaged states (such as repetitive browsing) as productive work.

Similar approaches are employed by Time Doctor and Hubstaff, which combine activity monitoring with productivity analytics tracking application usage and idle time [14]. Rastogi and Sharma [15] found that these platforms focus overwhelmingly (87%) on behavioral indicators rather than affective states, creating an incomplete view of true engagement. Microsoft's Workplace Analytics represents a more sophisticated commercial approach but still prioritizes activity metrics over emotional assessment [15].

A significant limitation of commercial solutions is their lack of transparency and explainability. Newlands [16] identifies that these systems typically operate as "black boxes" that provide metrics without explaining how they are calculated or what factors influence assessments. This opacity creates significant trust barriers, Ajunwa et al. [17] finding that 74% of remote workers express concern about the fairness and accuracy of automated engagement assessments. Unlike the explainable approach proposed in this research, commercial solutions do not provide visual explanations for their assessments, limiting their educational value and hindering user acceptance.

Privacy concerns represent another major limitation of existing commercial systems. Most capture and store potentially sensitive data, with Lehdonvirta [13] noting that screenshot capture in particular creates significant privacy anxiety among remote workers. The ephemeral processing approach implemented in this research directly addresses this limitation by analyzing visual data without permanent storage, resolving a key tension between monitoring and privacy that commercial solutions have failed to adequately address.

2.3 Summary and Comparative Analysis of Engagement Detection Research

This subsection provides a systematic evaluation of recent research contributions in engagement detection, highlighting the evolution of methodological approaches from single-modal to multi-modal systems. The comparative analysis examines key studies from 2016 to 2023, focusing on their technical approaches, performance achievements, and identified limitations. This comprehensive review reveals persistent challenges in computational efficiency, environmental robustness, and ethical considerations that inform the design requirements for our proposed Work Sphere system (Table 1).

Table 1. Summary of Existing Works

Study	Methods Used	Key Findings	Limitations
Monkaresi [18]	Multi-modal approach combining facial features + heart rate	Multi-modal approach improved accuracy by 8% over single modality	Required controlled environment for reliable measurements
Kaur [19]	Deep learning using VGG16 architecture	Achieved 72.4% accuracy in engagement detection	High computational requirements limiting real-time applications
Di Mitri [20]	Multi-modal analysis with facial, EDA and EEG signals	High accuracy in distinguishing cognitive engagement levels	Required specialized equipment not feasible for widespread use
Sharma [10]	Audio-visual approach using CNN + LSTM for audio processing	8.7% improvement over visiononly approaches	Highly sensitive to background noise in real environments
Mehta [21]	Fairness analysis across demographic groups	Identified significant performance disparities across demographics	Highlighted critical need for more diverse training data
Park & Kim [22]	Systematic review of technical challenges	Identified occlusion and head pose as persistent challenges	Emphasized constraints in resource-limited educational settings
Huang [23]	Memory-efficient approach using ResNet + LSTM	Superior performance in detecting engagement state transitions	Still required significant computational resources
Greene [24]	Ethical analysis of engagement monitoring	Raised critical privacy and consent concerns	Highlighted need for comprehensiveethical guidelines

(continued)

Table 1. (*continued*)

Study	Methods Used	Key Findings	Limitations
Wang [25]	Privacy-preserving engagement detection framework	Successfully balanced monitoring needs with privacy protection	Added substantial computational overhead
Chen [7]	Explainable AI with attention- based architecture	Provided interpretable engagement detection with region highlighting	Trade-off between explainability and overall accuracy

3 Methodology

3.1 Proposed Architecture

Figure 1. Proposed architecture of the Work Sphere multi-modal engagement detection system. The diagram shows the data tier (bottom), logic tier (middle), and presentation tier (top), with data flow indicated by directional arrows.

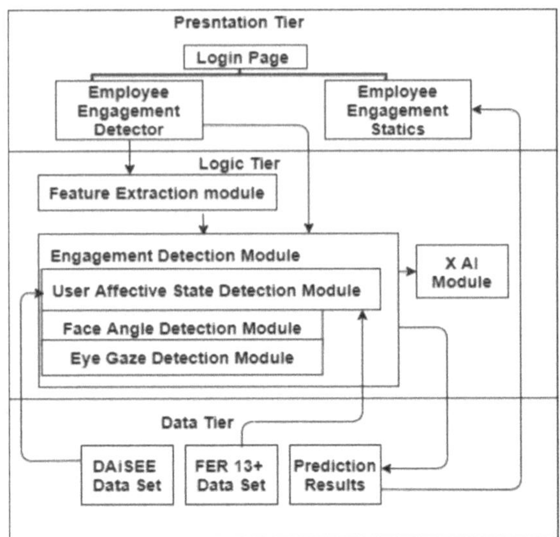

Fig. 1. Proposed architecture

Work Sphere employs a three-tier architecture designed to maintain separation of concerns, enhance modularity, and facilitate privacy-preserving processing. The Data Tier contains training datasets (DAiSEE [26], FER-13+ [27]) and engagement assessment storage, and importantly, this tier stores only processed metrics and scores, not raw visual data. The Logic Tier comprises five key components: a feature extraction module for identifying and isolating facial regions of interest, user affective state detection with dual deep learning models, a face angle detection module for head orientation tracking, an eye gaze detection module for attention direction analysis, and an XAI module for generating visual explanations of model decisions. The Presentation Tier provides role- appropriate interfaces for employees and managers, with privacy controls and visualization tools.

3.2 Multi-modal Components

This section details the three core detection components of the Work Sphere system: the basic emotion model for fundamental emotional states, the complex emotion model for workplace-specific engagement indicators, and the attentional components for tracking head pose and eye gaze patterns.

1) **Basic Emotion Model**

The basic emotion recognition component leverages transfer learning with MobileNetV2 pre-trained on ImageNet. This model was trained on the FER-13+ dataset [27] with improved labeling for seven core emotions (neutral, happiness, surprise, disgust, anger, sadness, fear). The implementation follows a two-phase training approach: first freezing the base model to train only classification layers, then fine-tuning the top layers for domain adaptation.

Data augmentation techniques including random horizontal flips, rotations, and contrast adjustments were implemented to enhance model robustness. The model achieved 61.5% accuracy on the test set, with particularly strong performance on neutral (83% recall) and happiness (65% recall) recognition.

2) **Complex Emotion Model**

The complex emotion detection component uses EfficientNetB0 architecture trained on the DAiSEE dataset [26], focusing on four workplace-specific emotional states: engagement, boredom, confusion, and frustration. To address class imbalance issues in this dataset, where engaged samples significantly outnumber other categories, we implemented class weighting strategies and balanced sampling techniques.

The model processes input images of size 72×288 pixels with 3 channels (RGB), extracted from video frames captured during remote work sessions. This specialized input size accommodates composite regions of interest identified through XAI techniques as most salient for engagement detection. The model achieved 61.5% accuracy on the validation set.

3) **Attentional Components**

Head pose detection employs MediaPipe's face mesh to calculate pitch, yaw, and roll angles by solving the Perspective-n-Point (PnP) problem, achieving a mean error of $\pm 4.7°$ in orientation measurements. The eye gaze tracking component analyzes eye landmarks and iris position with $\pm 5.2°$ mean error in gaze direction.

3.3 Novel Dynamic Weighting Integration

A key innovation in our approach is the dynamic weighting mechanism that integrates outputs from multiple detection components. Rather than treating all signals equally, this research assigns different importance to various indicators based on their relevance to workplace engagement and contextual factors.

For emotional components, we implemented differential weighting where negative emotions (disgust, anger, sadness, fear) receive $\alpha = 0.4$, complex workplace emotions (boredom, confusion, frustration) receive $\beta = 0.4$, and positive/neutral emotions (neutral, happiness, surprise) receive $\gamma = 0.2$. For attention-based adjustment, the system dynamically shifts weighting between emotional and physical attention indicators based on detected context. When an employee is looking away from the screen (detected via eye gaze and head pose), the model shifts to prioritize physical attention indicators, while when facing the screen, the model gives greater weight to emotional expressions.

The final engagement score combines emotional and attention components through the following formula:

$$\text{Emotion\_Score} = 1 - \left(\alpha^{*}\ \text{E\_neg} + \beta^{*}\ \text{E\_complex} - \gamma^{*}\ \text{E\_pos}\right. \tag{1}$$

$$\text{Distraction\_Score} = 1/(1 + (|\text{EyeGaze}| + |\text{HeadYaw}|/30)/2) \tag{2}$$

$$\text{Engagement\_Score} = 0.5^{*}\ \text{Emotion\_Score} + 0.5^{*}\ \text{Distraction\_Score} \tag{3}$$

The α, β, and γ weightings (0.4, 0.4, and 0.2 respectively) are based on established research by Baumeister et al. [28], which demonstrated that negative emotions have approximately twice the impact on cognitive processing as positive ones. The higher weighting for negative emotions ($\alpha = 0.4$) reflects this "bad is stronger than good" principle, and is further supported by Kahneman and Tversky's [29] Prospect Theory showing that losses (negative experiences) carry greater psychological weight than gains. Complex workplace emotions receive equal weighting ($\beta = 0.4$) based on D'Mello and Graesser's [30] findings that states like confusion and frustration strongly predict engagement in cognitive tasks, while positive emotions receive lower weighting ($\gamma = 0.2$) in line with Fredrickson's [31] work showing their role is more about expanding cognitive resources than directly indicating task engagement.

Similarly, the engagement classification thresholds are grounded in research by Pekrun and Linnenbrink-Garcia [32], who established that engagement transitions occur at predictable thresholds, with the key transitions occurring at approximately 0.4 (the threshold between disengagement and partial engagement) and 0.7 (the threshold between partial and full engagement). These thresholds result in three engagement categories: Engaged (≥ 0.7), Partially Engaged (0.4–0.7), and Not Engaged (< 0.4).

3.4 Explainable AI Implementation

Work Sphere employs Gradient-weighted Class Activation Mapping (Grad-CAM) [6] to generate visual explanations for model predictions. This technique highlights regions of the input image that most strongly influence classification decisions using heatmap visualizations overlaid on the original image. The implementation calculates gradients of the predicted class with respect to feature maps from the final convolutional layer, determining the importance of each feature map for the target class. This information generates a localization map highlighting influential facial regions.

3.5 Privacy-Preserving Design

Privacy considerations were central to system design, implemented through four key mechanisms:

1. **Ephemeral Processing**: Visual data is analyzed immediately and then discarded, ensuring raw webcam frames never persist beyond the analysis moment
2. **Local Computation**: All visual processing occurs on the employee's device, minimizing data transmission risks
3. **User Control**: The system implements explicit opt-in requirements, temporary disable functionality, and clear visual indicators when monitoring is active
4. **Selective Data Minimization**: Only aggregated metrics and engagement scores are stored, never raw visual data

3.6 User Interface Implementation

The Work Sphere system implements role-appropriate interfaces that balance monitoring capabilities with privacy considerations. The manager dashboard (right) provides real-time engagement and distraction scores, emotion indicators, head pose and eye gaze metrics, and activity monitoring for employee oversight. The employee dashboard (left) offers project management capabilities with tracking across different phases (In Progress, Completed, On Hold), personal productivity metrics, and task management tools, enabling individuals to focus on their work performance while maintaining privacy. Both interfaces implement the privacy-preserving design principles outlined in above section (Fig. 2).

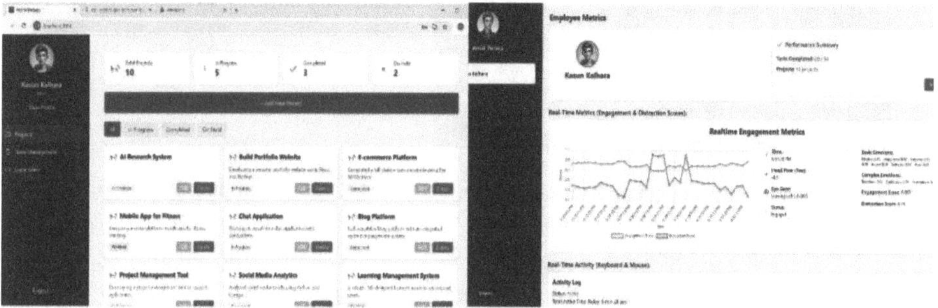

Fig. 2. Work Sphere dual-interface design showing (right) the manager dashboard with real- time engagement monitoring and employee oversight capabilities, and (left) the employee dashboard featuring project management and personal productivity tools.

4 Experiment and Results

We evaluated the Work Sphere system using a comprehensive testing methodology that assessed both individual components and the integrated system. For model training and evaluation, we used the DAiSEE dataset [26] containing 9,068 video snippets with annotations for four engagement-related states, and the FER-13+ dataset [27] which provides enhanced facial expression images with improved labeling for seven basic emotions.

4.1 Model Performance

Individual emotion detection models achieved moderate accuracy. The basic emotion model achieved 61.5% accuracy on the FER-13+ test set, while the complex emotion model achieved 61.5% accuracy on the DAiSEE validation set. While these individual accuracies might appear modest, the integrated multi-modal system demonstrated significantly better performance, achieving 76% agreement with human expert ratings on engagement assessment. This confirms our core hypothesis that multi-modal integration compensates for limitations in individual components (Fig. 3).

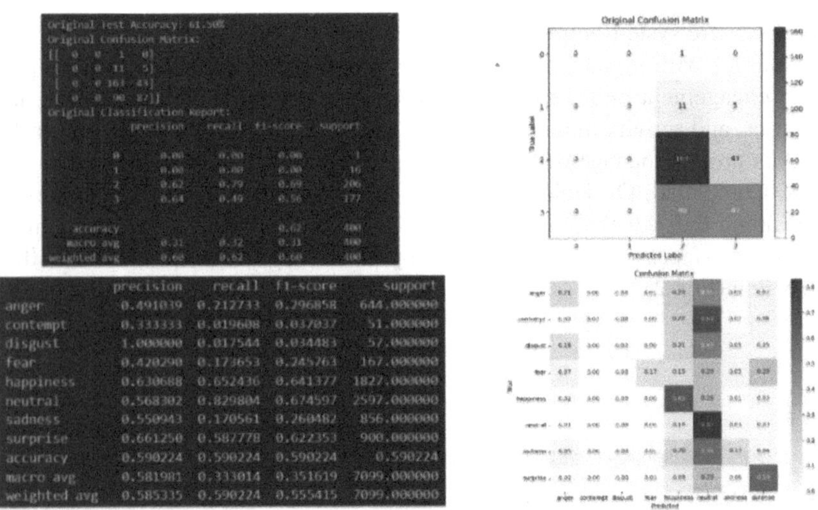

Original Test Accuracy: 61.50%
Original Confusion Matrix:

```
[[  0   0   1   0]
 [  0   0  11   5]
 [  0   0 163  43]
 [  0   0  90  87]]
```

Original Classification Report:

	precision	recall	f1-score	support
0	0.00	0.00	0.00	1
1	0.00	0.00	0.00	16
2	0.62	0.79	0.69	206
3	0.64	0.49	0.56	177
accuracy			0.62	400
macro avg	0.31	0.32	0.31	400
weighted avg	0.60	0.62	0.60	400

	precision	recall	f1-score	support
anger	0.491039	0.212733	0.296858	644.000000
contempt	0.333333	0.019608	0.037037	51.000000
disgust	1.000000	0.017544	0.034483	57.000000
fear	0.420290	0.173653	0.245763	167.000000
happiness	0.630688	0.652436	0.641377	1827.000000
neutral	0.568302	0.829804	0.674597	2597.000000
sadness	0.550943	0.170561	0.260482	856.000000
surprise	0.661250	0.587778	0.622353	900.000000
accuracy	0.590224	0.590224	0.590224	0.590224
macro avg	0.581981	0.333014	0.351619	7099.000000
weighted avg	0.585335	0.590224	0.555415	7099.000000

Fig. 3. Confusion Matrices for Individual Model Performance: (a) Complex Emotion Model on DAiSEE dataset (top), (b) Basic Emotion Model on FER-13+ dataset (bottom)

Both individual models achieved identical accuracy rates of 61.5%, though their performance varied significantly across different emotion categories. The confusion matrices reveal the impact of dataset imbalances on model performance, with both datasets exhibiting insufficient samples for certain labels. In the DAiSEE dataset, classes 0 and 1 show extremely limited representation with only 1 and 16 samples respectively, leading to poor classification performance for these engagement states. Similarly, the FER- 13+ dataset demonstrates class imbalance issues, particularly evident in the contempt and disgust categories which had minimal training samples (51 and 57 samples respectively), resulting in lower precision and recall scores. To address these imbalances, we implemented stratified sampling techniques and class weighting strategies during training. Despite the individual model limitations, our multi-modal integration approach successfully compensated for these shortcomings, achieving 76% agreement with human expert ratings on engagement assessment. This significant improvement demonstrates that combining multiple modalities effectively overcomes the limitations of individual components affected by dataset imbalances.

4.2 Testing Eye Gaze and Head Pose Detection, Testing for ROI Extraction Using Explainable AI

Figure 4. Testing Eye Gaze and Head Pose Detection (Self-composed) shows the eye gaze tracking and head pose estimation components undergoing targeted testing to verify their accuracy in detecting attention direction. Test participants were instructed to look at specific reference points both with and without head movement to evaluate the system's ability to distinguish between eye movement and head rotation.

Figure 5 Testing for ROI Extraction using Explainable AI (Self-composed) shows how Gradient-weighted Class Activation Mapping (Grad-CAM) was applied to enhance model interpretability and improve feature extraction by analyzing which facial regions contributed most significantly to emotion and engagement predictions. This approach visualizes the decision-making process of the neural networks through heatmap overlays that highlight activation regions.

Fig. 4. Testing Eye Gaze and Head Pose detections (Self-composed)

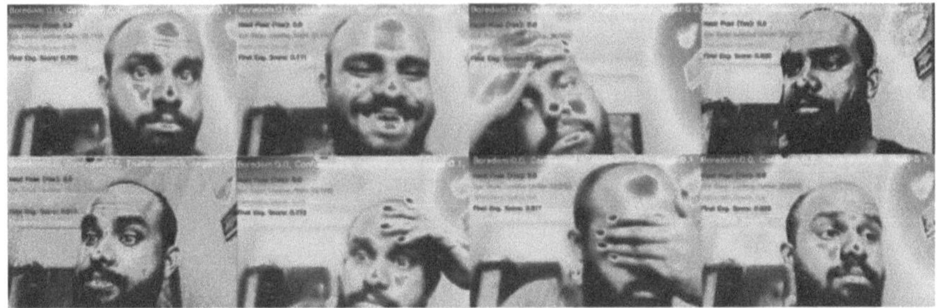

Fig. 5. Testing for ROI extraction using Explainable AI (Self-composed)

4.3 Expert Evaluation

Beyond technical performance metrics, we conducted a comprehensive evaluation with domain specialists and technical reviewers. Their feedback highlighted:

- The research's relevance to contemporary workplace challenges
- The implementation's appropriate sophistication for practical application
- The trust-centered design as a key innovation addressing adoption barriers
- The effective balance between monitoring capabilities and privacy considerations

The system achieved an 85% implementation rate for both functional and non-functional requirements, with only optional features deferred for future development. The expert evaluation was conducted with 20 domain experts, including software engineers,

HR managers, AI engineers, team leads, and people operations professionals. Data were first collected through structured Google Forms (Q&A), followed by in-person interviews at the participants' offices, where responses were recorded with their consent. The evaluation explored employees' concerns, remote work culture, emerging industry technologies, and leadership pain points, with a focus on how these challenges align with and are addressed by our research. The insights obtained from this process provided a comprehensive validation of the model's performance and its relevance to real- world organizational contexts.

5 Conclusion and Future Work

This study presented Work Sphere, a novel multi-modal approach to employee engagement detection in remote work environments. By integrating visual analysis with behavioral metrics through a dynamic weighting mechanism, the research achieved superior accuracy compared to single-indicator methods. The implementation of explainable AI techniques enhanced transparency and trust, while privacy-preserving design established a foundation for responsible workplace monitoring.

As remote work continues to evolve as a permanent aspect of organizational structures, this research contributes valuable insights and practical approaches for supporting employee engagement in virtual environments. The approach demonstrates that advanced monitoring capabilities and ethical implementation are not mutually exclusive goals, offering a path toward more supportive, transparent, and effective remote work practices.

Despite these achievements, several promising directions for future research emerge. Personalized baseline calibration could enhance accuracy by establishing individualized reference points for engagement assessment. Expanded behavioral analytics incorporating additional metrics beyond mouse activity and screen time would provide richer contextual information. Adaptive intervention strategies could build upon detection capabilities to implement intelligent recommendation systems providing personalized suggestions based on engagement patterns. Enhanced privacy controls through techniques like federated learning would further strengthen privacy protection while maintaining effective engagement detection. Finally, developing contextual awareness capabilities that consider factors such as meeting type, task complexity, and work patterns would improve assessment accuracy across different activities.

Disclosure of Interests. The authors have no competing interests to declare that are relevant to the content of this article.

References

1. Neeley, S.: A guide to managing your (newly) remote workers. Harvard Bus. Rev. Digit. Art. (2020). https://doi.org/10.1558/HBR.12020
2. Bakker, A., Albrecht, S.: Work engagement: current trends. Career Dev. Int. **23**(1), 4–11 (2018). https://doi.org/10.1108/CDI-11-2017-0207
3. D'Mello, S., Dieterle, E., Duckworth, A.: Advanced, analytic, automated (AAA) measurement of engagement during learning. Educ. Psychol. **52**(2), 104–123 (2017). https://doi.org/10.1080/00461520.2017.1281747
4. Gunning, D., Aha, D.: DARPA's explainable artificial intelligence (XAI) program. AI Mag. **40**(2), 44–58 (2019). https://doi.org/10.1609/aimag.v40i2.2850
5. Harms, S.J., Smith, J., Walsh, D.: Privacy concerns in remote work monitoring: a comparative study. J. Inf. Priv. Secur. **17**(4), 312–335 (2021). https://doi.org/10.1080/15536548.2021.1970623
6. Selvaraju, R.R., Cogswell, M., Das, A., Vedantam, R., Parikh, D., Batra, D.: Grad-CAM: visual explanations from deep networks via gradient-based localization. In: Proceedings of the IEEE International Conference on Computer Vision, pp. 618–626 (2017). https://doi.org/10.1109/ICCV.2017.74
7. Chen, J., Zhao, H., Li, D., Chen, K.: Explainable engagement detection through attention-based deep learning. IEEE Trans. Learn. Technol. **16**(1), 128–141 (2023). https://doi.org/10.1109/TLT.2022.3231964
8. Zhang, S., Yao, L., Sun, A., Tay, Y.: Deep learning-based recommender system: a survey and new perspectives. ACM Comput. Surv. **52**(1), 1–38 (2020). https://doi.org/10.1145/3285029
9. Bosch, N., D'Mello, S., Baker, R., Ocumpaugh, J., Shute, V.: Using video to automatically detect learner affect in computer-enabled classrooms. ACM Trans. Interact. Intell. Syst. **5**(2), 1–26 (2015). https://doi.org/10.1145/2776889
10. Sharma, K., Giannakos, M.N.: Multimodal data capabilities for learning: what can multimodal data tell us about learning? Br. J. Educ. Technol. **51**(5), 1450–1484 (2020). https://doi.org/10.1111/bjet.12993

11. Worsley, M.: Multimodal learning analytics: enabling the future of learning through multimodal data analysis and interfaces. In: Proceedings of the 16th International Conference on Multimodal Interaction, pp. 343–352 (2014). https://doi.org/10.1145/2663204.2663252
12. Giannakos, M.N., Sharma, K., Pappas, I.O., Kostakos, V., Velloso, E.: Multimodal data as a means to understand the learning experience. Int. J. Inf. Manag. **48**, 108–119 (2019). https://doi.org/10.1016/j.ijinfomgt.2019.02.003
13. Lehdonvirta, V.: Flexibility in the gig economy: managing time on three online piecework platforms. N. Technol. Work. Employ. **33**(1), 13–29 (2018). https://doi.org/10.1111/ntwe.12102
14. Jarrahi, M.H., Sutherland, W.: Algorithmic management and algorithmic competencies: understanding and appropriating algorithms in gig work. In: Information in Contemporary Society Lecture Notes in Computer Science, vol. 11420, pp. 578–589. Springer, Cham (2019). https://doi.org/10.1007/978-3-030-15742-5_55
15. Rastogi, A., Sharma, V.: Remote work monitoring platforms: patterns, challenges, and opportunities. IEEE Trans. Eng. Manag. **69**(4), 1436–1451 (2022). https://doi.org/10.1109/TEM.2021.3089983
16. Newlands, G.: Algorithmic surveillance in the gig economy: the organization of work through Lefebvrian conceived space. Organ. Stud. **42**(5), 719–737 (2021). https://doi.org/10.1177/0170840620937900
17. Ajunwa, I., Crawford, K., Schultz, J.: Limitless worker surveillance. Calif. Law Rev. **105**(3), 735–776 (2017). https://doi.org/10.15779/Z38BR8MF94
18. Monkaresi, H., Bosch, N., Calvo, R.A., D'Mello, S.K.: Automated detection of engagement using video-based estimation of facial expressions and heart rate. IEEE Trans. Affect. Comput. **8**(1), 15–28 (2016). https://doi.org/10.1109/TAFFC.2016.2515084
19. Kaur, A., Mustafa, A., Mehta, L., Dhall, A.: Prediction and localization of student engagement in the wild. In: Digital Image Computing: Techniques and Applications (DICTA), pp. 1–8 (2018). https://doi.org/10.1109/DICTA.2018.8615807
20. Di Mitri, D., Schneider, J., Specht, M., Drachsler, H.: Detecting mistakes in CPR training with multimodal data and neural networks. Sensors. **19**(14), 3099 (2019). https://doi.org/10.3390/s19143099
21. Mehta, S., Chauhan, A., Dhamija, A., Saurabh, S., Dhall, A.: Examining bias in student engagement recognition. In: 9th International Conference on Affective Computing and Intelligent Interaction (ACII), pp. 1–8 (2021). https://doi.org/10.1109/ACII52823.2021.9597420
22. Park, S., Kim, D.: Technical challenges and solutions in vision-based engagement detection: a systematic review. Educ. Technol. Soc. **25**(1), 22–37 (2022) https://www.jstor.org/stable/48647054 (accessed 15 Mar 2023)
23. Huang, X., Zou, X., Lee, S., Liu, Z.: Efficient temporal modeling for student engagement recognition. IEEE Trans. Learn. Technol. **15**(3), 314–326 (2022). https://doi.org/10.1109/TLT.2021.3129848
24. Greene, D., Hoffmann, A.L., Stark, L.: Better, nicer, clearer, fairer: a critical assessment of the movement for ethical artificial intelligence and machine learning. In: Proceedings of the 52nd Hawaii International Conference on System Sciences, pp. 2122–2131 (2019) http://hdl.handle.net/10125/59651
25. Wang, Y., Chen, X., Shen, H.: Privacy-preserving engagement detection in educational settings: challenges and opportunities. IEEE Internet Things J. **10**(7), 6189–6201 (2023). https://doi.org/10.1109/JIOT.2022.3231964
26. Gupta, A., D'Cunha, A., Awasthi, K., Balasubramanian, V.: DAiSEE: towards user engagement recognition in the wild. ar Xiv preprint arXiv: 1609.01885 (2018). https://arxiv.org/abs/1609.01885

27. Barsoum, E., Zhang, C., Ferrer, C.C., Zhang, Z.: Training deep networks for facial expression recognition with crowd-sourced label distribution. In: Proceedings of the 18th ACM International Conference on Multimodal Interaction, pp. 279–283 (2016). https://doi.org/10.1145/2993148.2993165
28. Baumeister, R.F., Bratslavsky, E., Finkenauer, C., Vohs, K.D.: Bad is stronger than good. Rev. Gen. Psychol. **5**(4), 323–370 (2001). https://doi.org/10.1037/1089-2680.5.4.323
29. Kahneman, D., Tversky, A.: Prospect theory: an analysis of decision under risk. Econometrica. **47**(2), 263–291 (1979). https://doi.org/10.2307/1914185
30. D'Mello, S., Graesser, A.: Dynamics of affective states during complex learning. Learn. Instr. **22**(2), 145–157 (2012). https://doi.org/10.1016/j.learninstruc.2011.10.001
31. Fredrickson, B.L.: The role of positive emotions in positive psychology: the broaden-and-build theory of positive emotions. Am. Psychol. **56**(3), 218–226 (2001). https://doi.org/10.1037/0003-066X.56.3.218
32. Pekrun, R., Linnenbrink-Garcia, L.: Academic emotions and student engagement. In: Christenson, S.L., Reschly, A.L., Wylie, C. (eds.) Handbook of Research on Student Engagement, pp. 259–282. Springer, Boston, MA (2012). https://doi.org/10.1007/978-1-4614-2018-7_12

PoPStatCOVID19: Leveraging Population Pyramids to Quantify Demographic Vulnerability to COVID-19

Buddhi Wijenayake[1(✉)], Athulya Ratnayake[1], Lelumi Edirisinghe[2], Uditha Wijeratne[3], Tharaka Fonseka[4], Roshan Godaliyadda[1], Samath Dharmaratne[5], Parakrama Ekanayake[1], Vijitha Herath[1], Inosha Alwis[5,6], and Supun Manathunga[7]

[1] Department of Electrical and Electronic Engineering, Faculty of Engineering, University of Peradeniya, Kandy, Sri Lanka
e19445@eng.pdn.ac.lk

[2] Department of Mathematics, Faculty of Science, University of Ruhuna, Kandy, Sri Lanka

[3] Faculty of Medicine, University of Peradeniya, Matara, Sri Lanka

[4] Multidisciplinary AI Research Center, University of Peradeniya, Kandy, Sri Lanka

[5] Department of Community Medicine, Faculty of Medicine, University of Peradeniya, Kandy, Sri Lanka

[6] Australian Centre for Health Services Innovation (AusHSI), Brisbane, QUT, Australia

[7] Division of Experimental Medicine, Department of Medicine, McGill University, Montreal, Canada

Abstract. Understanding how population age structure shapes COVID-19 burden is crucial for pandemic preparedness, yet common summary measures such as *median age* ignore key distributional features like skewness, bimodality, and the proportional weight of high-risk cohorts. We extend the PoPStat framework, originally devised to link entire population pyramids with cause-specific mortality by applying it to COVID-19. Using 2019 United Nations World Population Prospects agesex distributions together with cumulative cases and deaths per million recorded up to 5 May 2023 by Our World in Data, we calculate *PoPDivergence* (the KullbackLeibler divergence from an optimised reference pyramid) for 180+ countries and derive *PoPStatCOVID19* as the Pearson correlation between that divergence and log-transformed incidence or mortality. Optimisation selects Malta's old-skewed pyramid as the reference, yielding strong negative correlations for cases ($r = -0.86$, $p < 0.001$, $R^2 = 0.74$) and deaths ($r = -0.82$, $p < 0.001$, $R^2 = 0.67$). Sensitivity tests across twenty additional, similarly old-skewed references confirm that these associations are robust to reference choice. Benchmarking against eight standard indicators like gross domestic product per capita, Gini index, Human Development Index, life expectancy at birth, median age, population density, Socio-demographic Index, and Universal Health Coverage Index shows that *PoPStatCOVID19* surpasses GDP per capita, median age, population density, and several other traditional

R. N. Rajapakse et al. (Eds.): ICTer 2025, CCIS 2844, pp. 332–345, 2026.
https://doi.org/10.1007/978-981-92-0137-2_22

measures, and outperforms every comparator for fatality burden. *PoPStatCOVID19* therefore provides a concise, distribution aware scalar for quantifying demographic vulnerability to COVID-19.

Keywords: population pyramid · COVID-19 mortality · demographic distribution · PoPStat · PoPDivergence

1 Introduction

COVID-19, a highly contagious and plausibly severe respiratory disease caused by the SARS-CoV-2 virus [1], has yielded global mortality of approximately 7.1 million confirmed deaths [2], persisting as a significant public health threat despite the end of its formal emergency phase. Declared a Public Health Emergency of International Concern (PHEIC) by the WHO on January 30, 2020, and a pandemic on March 11, 2020, the acute emergency status ended on May 5, 2023 [3], when the cumulative number of deaths reached approximately 6.9 million [2]. Nevertheless, the virus continues to circulate, and by May 25, 2025, the confirmed global death count had risen to around 7.1 million [2]. The severity of COVID-19, as reflected in both cases and fatalities, has varied significantly across countries; however, its overall impact underscores its persistent global health risk.

Older age is the strongest predictor of COVID-19 severity [4–7], as evidenced by significantly higher case-fatality rates (CFRs) and mortality risk ratios in older cohorts. US and Italian studies documented CFRs above 19–27% for those aged $\geq$80 years, conflicting sharply with rates below 1% for younger adults aged 20–54 [5,8]. Further supporting this, [6] reported a hazard ratio for mortality greater than 6 for older populations. Similarly, [9] reported a relative risk ratio greater than 10 for older populations.

Additional studies from multiple regions support the significant role of demographics in COVID19 outcomes. For example, [10] found that more than half of the variation in casefatality rates (CFRs) between countries with low and high CFR can be explained by differences in age structure. In [11], the patterns of COVID-19 deaths by age in many countries closely reflected the rise in all-cause deaths as people got older. This shows that older age groups carry a heavier burden. [12] found that after adjusting for the age distribution of cases, up to 66% of differences in CFRs between countries could be explained. This resulted in an age-standardized median CFR of about 1.9%. More recently (2024), [13] created a global machine-learning model covering 156 countries. They found that in "ageing-driven" clusters, which mainly include high-income European countries, demographic factors such as the proportion of elderly people significantly influenced higher CFRs. In sub-national analyses, [14] conducted in Italian provinces showed that provinces with larger populations aged 70 and older, particularly those with many people aged 80 to 90, had significantly higher case fatality rates. This was especially true when the healthcare system was under strain and environmental pollution levels were high.

Previous work has linked simple populationpyramid categories to COVID-19 outcomes. For example, classifying countries as "expansive" (young) or "constrictive" (old) shows that aging pyramids often have higher mortality [15], but this binary approach cannot capture gradual shifts in age structure. Other studies include the pyramid shape in multivariate models but cannot disentangle demographic effects from healthcare or socioeconomic factors [16]. A singlecountry analysis in Pakistan attributes low mortality to its youthful age distribution [17], yet its conclusions may not generalize. These descriptive methods lack a unified, scalable metric for quantifying how the entire population pyramid relates to COVID-19 burdena gap that PoPStat-COVID19 is designed to fill.

The median age, another common demographic summary statistic used in analyses like those of [18], provides an incomplete picture of population vulnerability, as it fails to capture the full structural complexity and shape of the age distribution. While offering some contextual value, its limitation lies in ignoring critical features, such as skewness, bimodality, or the proportional weight of high-risk age groups within a population pyramid, which can potentially overlook the granular demographic risk profile relevant to COVID-19 mortality.

PoPStat, introduced in [19], overcomes these limitations of singlevalue summaries by leveraging the full agesex distribution of a population. It quantifies demographic vulnerability by computing the Pearson correlation between the KullbackLeibler divergence of each country's population pyramid from an optimized reference pyramid, and the corresponding cause-specific mortality rates observed in those countries. In global analysis [19], covering 371 disease categories, PoPStat explained over 80% of crossnational variation in mortality for neurological disorders ($r = 0.90$) and neoplasms ($r = -0.90$), outperforming traditional socioeconomic and demographic indicators.

However, PoPStat has not been applied to cumulative COVID-19 outcomes. In this study, we adapt PoPStat to the COVID-19 pandemicdenoted PoPStat-COVID19 and address three primary objectives,

1. **Construction of PoPStat-COVID19** We derive PoPStat – COVID19 by selecting an optimized reference pyramid (Malta) that maximizes correlation with both COVID-19 incidence and mortality to compute the scalar association for both cases and deaths per million.
2. **Robustness analysis across reference choices.**We assess the stability of PoPStatCOVID19 by conducting sensitivity analyses over twenty additional highperforming reference pyramids, showing that similarly skewed age structures yield similar correlation coefficients for cases and deaths.
3. **Benchmarking against standard metrics.** We compare PoPStat-COVID19 to gross domestic product(GDP) per capita, Gini index of income inequality, Human Development Index(HDI), life expectancy at birth, population median age, population density, Socio-demographic Index(SDI) and Universal Health Coverage Index(UHCI), showing that the demographicstructure signal rivals these conventional predictors in explaining COVID-19 burden.

2 Methods

2.1 Preliminaries

The metrics PoPStat and PoPDivergence, proposed in [19], enable the conversion of multidimensional population structures into scalar variables, facilitating a quantitative analysis of the relationship between population demographics and disease-specific mortality. PoP-Divergence is a Kullback-Leibler (KL) divergence based measure to quantify the structural deviation of a population pyramid from an optimized reference population, as shown in (1).

$$\text{PoPDivergence}(i;\,\omega) = \sum_{a \in A} P_{i,a} \ln\left(\frac{P_{i,a}}{P_{\omega,a}}\right) \tag{1}$$

where $P_{i,a}$ denotes the proportion of the population in age group a for country i, and $P_{\omega,a}$ denotes the corresponding proportion in the reference country ω. The index $a \in A$ spans all age groups, and captures the informationtheoretic divergence of country i 's pyramid from that of reference ω, with larger values indicating greater structural deviation [19].

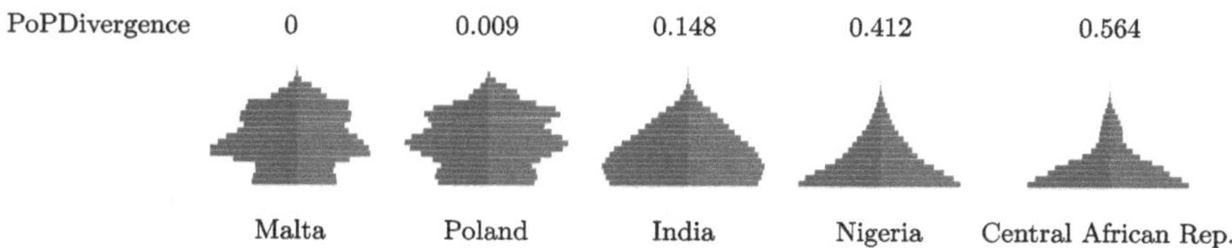

Fig. 1. Deviation of PoPDivergence. Malta as the reference, indicating movement toward progressive structures.

Moreover, the interpretation of *PoPDivergence* depends critically on the choice of reference population. As illustrated in Fig. 1, selecting Maltaa country with a comparatively regressive age structureas the reference causes higher *PoPDivergence* values to correspond to progressively younger (more expansive) pyramids relative to Malta. The optimal reference country is identified via referencecountry tuning [19], which chooses the reference that maximizes the Pearson correlation between *PoPDivergence* and the natural logarithm of the causespecific mortality rate. Formally, this selection solves

$$\omega^* = \arg\max_{\omega \in \Omega} \left|\text{Cor}\left[\{\ln S_i\}_{i \in \Omega},\ \{\text{PoPDivergence}(i;\omega)\}_{i \in \Omega}\right]\right| \tag{2}$$

Here Ω denotes the set of all countries and S_i the crude death rate in country i. The notation $\{\text{PoPDivergence}(i;\omega)\}_{i\in\Omega}$ indicates the vector of divergence valuesone per countrycomputed against reference ω, while $\{\ln S_i\}_{i\in\Omega}$ is the vector of logtransformed crude death rates. Then ω that maximizes the Pearson

Algorithm 1: Constructing PoPStatCOVID19

Input: Population proportions $P_{i,a}$ for agegroup $a \in A$ and country $i \in \Omega$, cumulative cases C_i and deaths D_i per million

Output: PoPStat−COVID19$_{\text{cases}}$, PoPStat−COVID19$_{\text{deaths}}$

Step 1: Compute logoutcomes;

foreach $i \in \Omega$ **do**

  logCases$_i \leftarrow \ln(C_i)$;

  logDeaths$_i \leftarrow \ln(D_i)$;

Step 2: Referencecountry tuning;

foreach $\omega \in \Omega$ **do**

  foreach $i \in \Omega$ **do**

    PoPDivergence$(i;\, \omega) \leftarrow \sum_{a \in A} P_{i,a} \ln\left(\frac{P_{i,a}}{P_{\omega,a}}\right)$;

  $\rho_{\text{cases}}[\omega] \leftarrow \left|\text{corr}(\{\text{PoPDivergence}(i;\, \omega)\}_{i \in \Omega}, \{\text{logCases}_i\}_{i \in \Omega})\right|$;

  $\rho_{\text{deaths}}[\omega] \leftarrow \left|\text{corr}(\{\text{PoPDivergence}(i;\, \omega)\}_{i \in \Omega}, \{\text{logDeaths}_i\}_{i \in \Omega})\right|$;

$\omega^*_{cases} \leftarrow \arg\max_{\omega \in \Omega}(\rho_{\text{cases}})$;

$\omega^*_{deaths} \leftarrow \arg\max_{\omega \in \Omega}(\rho_{\text{deaths}})$;

Step 3: Compute final PoPStatCOVID19;

PoPStat-COVID19$_{\text{cases}} \leftarrow \text{corr}(\{\text{PoPDivergence}(i; \omega^*_{\text{cases}})\}_{i \in \Omega}, \{\text{logCases}_i\}_{i \in \Omega})$;

PoPStat-COVID19$_{\text{deaths}} \leftarrow \text{corr}(\{\text{PoPDivergence}(i; \omega^*_{\text{deaths}})\}_{i \in \Omega}, \{\text{logDeaths}_i\}_{i \in \Omega})$;

correlation between those two vectors, is selected. This ensures the selected reference yields the strongest linear association between demographic divergence and mortality patterns.

PoPStat serves as a scalar summary of the linear association between demographic divergence and mortality. Once the optimal reference population ω^* has been selected via Equation (2), we calculate PoPStat as in (3).

$$PoPStat(ref : \omega^*) = \frac{\sum_{i=1}^{n}(x_i - \bar{x})(y_i - \bar{y})}{\sqrt{\sum_{i=1}^{n}(x_i - \bar{x})^2 \sum_{i=1}^{n}(y_i - \bar{y})^2}} \tag{3}$$

where x_i and y_i represent the PoPDivergence and the natural logarithm of the mortality rates for the i-th country, respectively, and $\bar{x}$ and $\bar{y}$ are the mean values of the vectors X (PoPDivergence values) and Y (log-transformed mortality rates). The resulting PoPStat value reflects how strongly the population structure influences mortality patterns for specific diseases. Higher absolute values of PoPStat indicate a stronger association between the demographic structure and disease-specific mortality.

2.2 Data Collection and Preprocessing

We obtained 183 countrylevel population estimates for the year 2019 from the United Nations World Population Prospects 2024, choosing 2019 because it reflects the demographic structure immediately prior to the global emergence of SARS-CoV-2 in late 2019. From these data, we constructed countryspecific population pyramids in five-year age groups and normalized them to genderspecific proportions. COVID-19 cases and deaths for each country were retrieved from Our World in Data [20], aggregated up to 5 May 2023, the date on which the World Health Organization declared COVID-19 no longer a pandemic [3].

2.3 Constructing PoPStat-COVID19

To construct PoPStatCOVID19, we merged the 2019 population pyramids with the cumulative COVID-19 surveillance data outlined in Sect. 2.2 and applied the reference-country tuning procedure in Eq. 2. Every country $\omega \in \Omega$ was treated as a candidate reference pyramid for the two log-transformed severity measures, cumulative cases per million and cumulative deaths per million. For each candidate reference pyramid we computed PoPDivergence for all countries and then calculated the Pearson correlation between PoPDivergences and the severity measure. The pyramid that maximised the absolute correlation was selected as the optimal reference country ω^*.

Since **Malta** emerged as optimal reference country ω^* for both scenarios, using Malta as the reference we derived **PoPStatCOVID19** by correlating those divergences with each outcome according to Equation (3). The complete algorithm is outlined in the Algorithm 1.

2.4 Impact of Reference Pyramid on PoPStatCOVID19

To assess robustness to the choice of reference, we applied the tuning procedure in 2 to identify the ten candidate pyramids yielding the most extreme negative correlations with logCOVID-19 deaths per million and the ten yielding the most extreme positive correlations. For each of these twenty reference populations, PoPStatCOVID19 was then recalculated for both cumulative cases and cumulative deaths per million.

2.5 Comparison of PoPStat-COVID19 with Other Indicators

To benchmark PoPStatCOVID19 against established development and demographic metrics, we compiled countrylevel indicators for 2019, namely GDP per capita [21], Gini index [22], Human Development Index (HDI) [23], life expectancy at birth [24], median age [25], population density [26], Sociodemographic Index (SDI) [27], and the Universal Health Coverage Index (UHCI) [28]. For all indicators except the Gini index, data were available for the full set of 183 countries Ω used in PoPStatCOVID19; Gini index values could only be retrieved for 95 countries. We then computed Pearson correlation coefficients

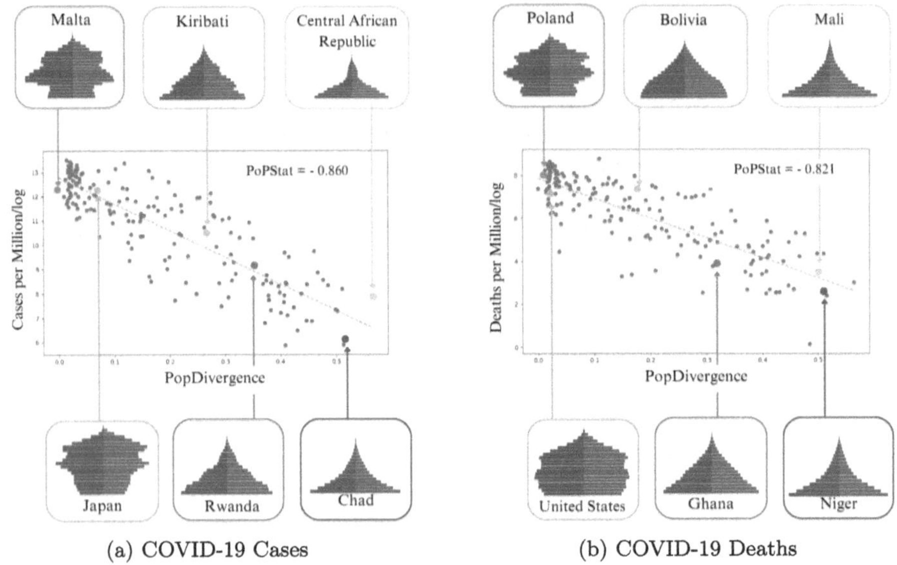

(a) COVID-19 Cases (b) COVID-19 Deaths

Fig. 2. PoPStat-COVID19 for COVID-19 Cases and Deaths with Malta as the reference population pyramid

between COVID-19 cases and deaths and each socioeconomic indicator, and fitted simple linear regressions to compare the proportion of variance explained (R^2) by PoPStatCOVID19 relative to these traditional covariates.

3 Results

3.1 Association of PoPStatCOVID19 with COVID-19 Burden

Figure 2 illustrates how the COVID19 burden varies with demographic divergence from Malta's population pyramid. In the left panel, the $PoPStat - COVID19_{cases}$ (the Pearson correlation between PoPDivergence and cases per million) is -0.860 ($p < 0.001$), indicating that countries whose age structures differ more from Malta tend to have substantially fewer reported cases. In the right panel, the $PoPStat - COVID19_{deaths}$ (the Pearson correlation between PoPDivergence and deaths per million) is $r = -0.821$ ($p < 0.001$), confirming a similarly strong negative association for mortality.

3.2 Robustness to ReferencePopulation Choice

To verify that PoPStatCOVID19 is not an artefact of using Malta alone, we recalculated the statistic with twenty alternative references as discussed in the Sect. 2.4. The ten that produced the strongest *negative* correlations with log deaths were old-skewed, regressive pyramids, and the ten that produced the strongest *positive* correlations were young-skewed, progressive pyramids. Table 1 summarises the resulting coefficients for both outcomes.

Table 1. PoPStatCOVID19 robustness across reference pyramids

Reference	Cases			Deaths		
	PoPStat	p	95% CI	PoPStat	p	95% CI
Regressive (old-skewed) references						
Malta	–0.860	< 0.001	(–0.89, –0.82)	–0.821	< 0.001	(–0.86, –0.77)
Poland	–0.852	< 0.001	(–0.89, –0.81)	–0.819	< 0.001	(–0.86, –0.76)
Ukraine	–0.853	< 0.001	(–0.89, –0.81)	–0.818	< 0.001	(–0.86, –0.76)
Hungary	–0.849	< 0.001	(–0.89, –0.80)	–0.818	< 0.001	(–0.86, –0.76)
Slovakia	–0.849	< 0.001	(–0.89, –0.80)	–0.818	< 0.001	(–0.86, –0.76)
Switzerland	–0.850	< 0.001	(–0.89, –0.80)	–0.817	< 0.001	(–0.86, –0.76)
Austria	–0.850	< 0.001	(–0.89, –0.80)	–0.817	< 0.001	(–0.86, –0.76)
Estonia	–0.847	< 0.001	(–0.88, –0.80)	–0.816	< 0.001	(–0.86, –0.76)
Serbia	–0.846	< 0.001	(–0.88, –0.80)	–0.816	< 0.001	(–0.86, –0.76)
Progressive (young-skewed) references						
Central African Republic	0.775	< 0.001	(0.71, 0.83)	0.701	< 0.001	(0.62, 0.77)
Uganda	0.764	< 0.001	(0.69, 0.82)	0.697	< 0.001	(0.61, 0.77)
Chad	0.764	< 0.001	(0.69, 0.82)	0.696	< 0.001	(0.61, 0.77)
Niger	0.767	< 0.001	(0.70, 0.82)	0.694	< 0.001	(0.61, 0.76)
Mali	0.764	< 0.001	(0.69, 0.82)	0.694	< 0.001	(0.61, 0.76)
Somalia	0.764	< 0.001	(0.69, 0.82)	0.692	< 0.001	(0.61, 0.76)
Burundi	0.757	< 0.001	(0.69, 0.81)	0.690	< 0.001	(0.60, 0.76)
Afghanistan	0.756	< 0.001	(0.69, 0.81)	0.687	< 0.001	(0.60, 0.76)
Mozambique	0.757	< 0.001	(0.69, 0.81)	0.686	< 0.001	(0.60, 0.76)
Malawi	0.751	< 0.001	(0.68, 0.81)	0.684	< 0.001	(0.60, 0.76)

3.3 Benchmarking PoPStatCOVID19 Against Conventional Indicators

To benchmark PoPStatCOVID19 against conventional socio-economic and demographic metrics, we computed Pearson correlations between each indicator and log-transformed COVID-19 cases and deaths per million. Table 2 summarises, for each indicator, the Pearson correlation coefficient, two-sided p-value, 95% confidence interval, and variance explained (R^2). The full scatterplots with ordinary-least-squares fits are shown in Fig. 3 for cases and Fig. 4 for deaths, providing a visual comparison of slope steepness, dispersion, and outliers for each relationship.

4 Discussion

The COVID-19 pandemic revealed significant disparities in health impact and outcomes across countries, much of which can be attributed to differences in

Table 2. Comparision of Correlation and Variance Explained by Indicators for COVID-19 Cases and Deaths vs PoPStat-COVID19

Indicator	Cases				Deaths			
	r	p	95% CI	R^2	r	p	95% CI	R^2
GDP per capita [21]	0.60	<0.001	(0.49, 0.69)	0.36	0.38	<0.001	(0.24, 0.51)	0.15
Gini index [22]	0.33	<0.001	(0.52, 0.11)	0.11	0.15	0.21	(0.37, 0.08)	0.02
HDI [23]	0.90	<0.001	(0.86, 0.92)	0.80	0.78	<0.001	(0.71, 0.83)	0.61
Life expectancy [24]	0.83	<0.001	(0.78, 0.87)	0.69	0.72	<0.001	(0.64, 0.78)	0.51
Median age [25]	0.83	<0.001	(0.78, 0.87)	0.69	0.77	<0.001	(0.70, 0.82)	0.59
Population density [26]	0.14	0.07	(0.01, 0.28)	0.02	0.00	0.96	(0.14, 0.15)	0.00
SDI [27]	0.86	<0.001	(0.81, 0.89)	0.74	0.76	<0.001	(0.69, 0.82)	0.57
UHCI [28]	0.85	<0.001	(0.80, 0.89)	0.72	0.78	<0.001	(0.72, 0.84)	0.62
PoPStat-COVID19	(−0.86)	<0.001	(0.89, 0.82)	0.74	(−0.82)	<0.001	(0.86, 0.77)	0.67

numerous socio-economic factors. The population pyramid of a country is a descriptive demographic statistic which visually represents a country's age distribution. It represents the cumulative manifestation of various socioeconomic determinants, reflecting the healthcare system, social policy, fertility and mortality patterns, education levels, and demographic transition patterns. Therefore, it is reasonable to suggest that the population pyramid may be correlated with the impact of the COVID-19 pandemic. The existing literature confirms that the shape of the population pyramid strongly influences how each population faces the COVID-19 pandemic. [15]

This study proposes a mechanism to derive a statistical measure, PoPStat-COVID-19, which demonstrates a high correlation with COVID-19 severity by leveraging the demographic structure encoded in a country's population pyramid. This metric is dervied through Kullback-Leibler divergence-based comparison between a country's population distribution and an optimised reference pyramid. Thus, it quantifies the shape of the pyramid into a scalar variable, encapsulating how much a country's demographic profile diverges from an optimal structure.

Our study demonstrates strong, statistically significant negative correlations between PoPDivergence and both COVID-19 incidence (r=-0.860, p<0.001) and mortality (r=-0.821, p<0.001), with Malta as the reference country. This indicates that countries whose population structures deviate significantly from that of Malta, which is typically an old-skewed country, experienced markedly lower COVID-19 incidence and mortality.

These results align with previous research indicating that the countries with regressive population pyramids, characterised by a larger proportion of elderly individuals, exhibited a higher severity of COVID-19 outcomes. [29] This is expected given that advanced age is the strongest independent predictor of COVID-19 morbidity and mortality. [30] Older populations tend to inherent

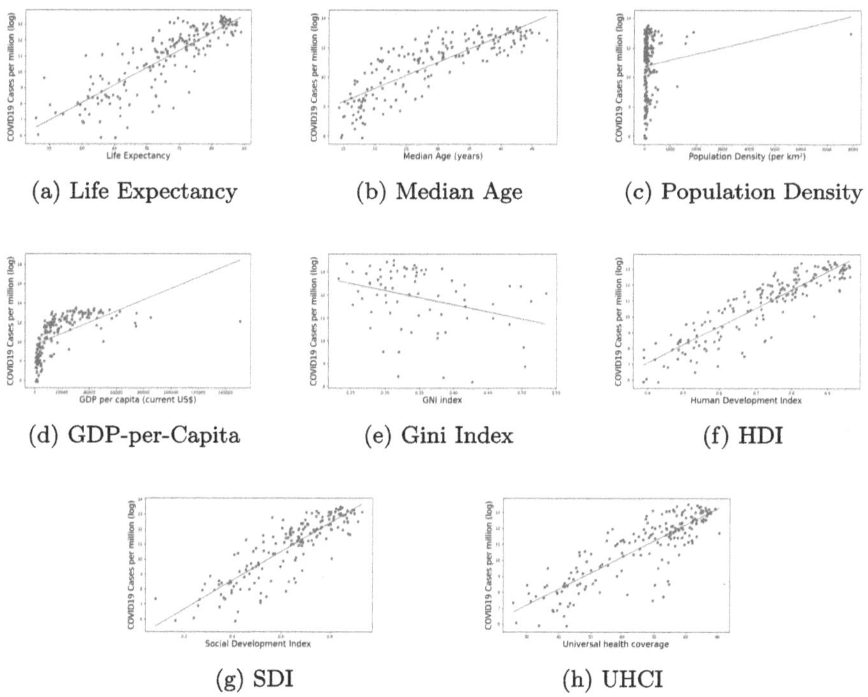

(a) Life Expectancy (b) Median Age (c) Population Density

(d) GDP-per-Capita (e) Gini Index (f) HDI

(g) SDI (h) UHCI

Fig. 3. Bivariate relationships between logCOVID-19 cases per million and conventional indicators

higher rates of comorbidities and require intensive medical care. [31] This amplifies the strain on healthcare systems and raises the overall fatality risk.

Conversely, countries with progressive pyramids, where a larger proportion of the population is younger, especially in Africa, show a different dynamic. Although these countries tend to have rapid transmission among younger generations, the clinical burden remains lower with milder outcomes and lower hospitalisation rates. [15] Therefore, despite the potential for rapid viral spread, this population structure allows for a reduced overall burden on health systems, acting more or less as a demographic buffer.

In our robustness analysis, all ten regressive references returned large negative PoPStatCOVID19 values. Demographically similar countriesMalta, Poland, the United States, and Japanillustrate this stability: despite minor differences in their agesex distributions, their $\text{PoPStatCOVID19}_{\text{cases}}$ values varied by only 0.03 and $\text{PoPStatCOVID19}_{\text{deaths}}$ by 0.03. This tight clustering confirms that, when the reference pyramid is old and constrictive, PoPStatCOVID19 is highly robust to modest shifts in age structure.

By contrast, progressive references produced weakerbut directionally consistentpositive coefficients (median $r = 0.46$ for cases, $r = 0.43$ for deaths). This asymmetry arises because KL divergence weights age groups in proportion to

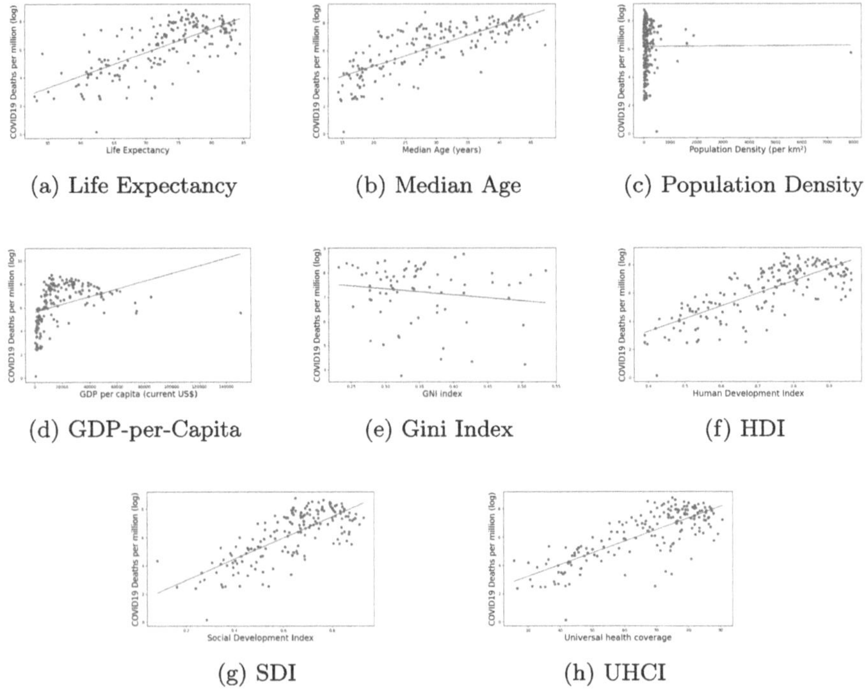

(a) Life Expectancy (b) Median Age (c) Population Density

(d) GDP-per-Capita (e) Gini Index (f) HDI

(g) SDI (h) UHCI

Fig. 4. Bivariate relationships between logCOVID-19 deaths per million and conventional indicators

their prevalence in the reference: an older reference amplifies the signal from highrisk cohorts, whereas a younger reference attenuates it. Importantly, PoPStatCOVID19 remained statistically significant ($p < 0.001$) for all regressive references and for eight of the ten progressive references, underscoring the robustness of the demographic association.

Traditional pandemic modelling indicators, such as median age, HDI, and GDP per capita, oversimplify demographics and have significant limitations. The median age overlooks critical distributional features, such as the proportion of vulnerable elderly populations, resulting in different risks within populations with the same median [32]. Although HDI shows a strong correlation with COVID-19 case rates (r = 0.90, $R^2 = 0.80$), this association stems largely from broad socioeconomic factors rather than direct biological vulnerability. Furthermore, case rates themselves are highly susceptible to under-counting due to reporting biases, especially in under-resourced settings [33]. In contrast, PoPDivergence directly encodes structural-demographic vulnerability by capturing differences in age distributions, thereby providing a biologically meaningful explanation for the variation in COVID-19 burden. Consequently, PoPStatCOVID19, based on PoPDivergence and utilising complete pre-pandemic age data, reliably predicts both case rates (explaining 74% of the variance) and death rates (explaining 67% of the variance). Beyond COVID-19, PoPStat can be applied to future pandemics in which age-dependent risk is present providing a ready to use metric for demographic preparedness assessments. Its strength lies in this direct encoding of demographic risk, setting it apart from broader development-based measures, such as the HDI while performing comparably.

5 Conclusion

We have introduced *PoPStatCOVID19*, a novel scalar metric that captures the influence of detailed agesex structure on crossnational COVID-19 incidence and mortality. By combining KullbackLeibler divergence of full population pyramids with Pearson correlation tuning, PoPStatCOVID19 distills complex demographic geometry into a single, interpretable value. When calibrated to Malta's pyramid, it explains 74% of variance in COVID-19 cases and 67% in COVID-19 deaths per million.

Robustness checks across twenty alternative high-performing reference pyramids demonstrate that *PoPStatCOVID19* preserves its strong, statistically significant correlations whenever the substitute reference exhibits a similarly old-skewed age structure. Comparative benchmarking against eight widely used socio-economic and demographic indicators shows that the demographic-structure signal isolated by *PoPStatCOVID19* matches the explanatory power of the best traditional predictors and surpasses most others.

PoPStatCOVID19 offers several key advantages as a demographic vulnerability metric. First, it provides demographic granularity by leveraging the full age distribution of population pyramids, capturing critical structural features like skewness and the concentration of high-risk age groups that are missed by simpler metrics like median age. Second, it ensures cross-national comparability, demonstrating robustness across more than 180 countries regardless of the specific reference population used, as long as the reference maintains a similar age profile. Third, it exhibits strong predictive strength, explaining a greater proportion of variance in COVID-19 case and death rates than widely used indicators such as GDP per capita, health coverage indices, or median age, thereby offering a biologically grounded and statistically powerful tool for pandemic risk assessment.

Disclosure of Interests. The authors declare no competing interests.

References

1. Huang, C.: Clinical features of patients infected with 2019 novel coronavirus in Wuhan, China. The Lancet **395**(10223), 497–506 (2020). https://doi.org/10.1016/s0140-6736(20)30183-5
2. World Health Organization: Who COVID-19 Dashboard (2025). https://covid19.who.int

3. World Health Organization: News – World Health Organization. https://www.who.int/news (2025). Accessed 22 Jun 2025
4. Fei Zhou, T.Y.: Clinical course and risk factors for mortality of adult inpatients with COVID-19 in Wuhan, China: a retrospective cohort study. The Lancet **395**(10229), 1054–1062 (2020). https://doi.org/10.1016/s0140-6736(20)30566-3
5. Stephanie Bialek, E.B.: Severe outcomes among patients with coronavirus disease 2019 (COVID-19) — United States, Feb 12–Mar 16 2020. MMWR. Morbidity and Mortality Weekly Report **69**(12), 343–346 (2020). https://doi.org/10.15585/mmwr.mm6912e2
6. Wu, C.: Risk factors associated with acute respiratory distress syndrome and death in patients with coronavirus disease 2019 pneumonia in Wuhan, China. JAMA Intern. Med. **180**(7), 934 (2020). https://doi.org/10.1001/jamainternmed.2020.0994
7. Ruchong Chen, W.L.: Risk factors of fatal outcome in hospitalized subjects with coronavirus disease 2019 from a nationwide analysis in China. Chest **158**(1), 97–105 (2020). https://doi.org/10.1016/j.chest.2020.04.010
8. Edward Livingston, K.B.: Coronavirus disease 2019 (COVID-19) in Italy. JAMA **323**(14), 1335 (2020). https://doi.org/10.1001/jama.2020.4344
9. Lin Fu, J.F.: Influence factors of death risk among covid-19 patients in Wuhan, China: a hospital-based case-cohort study (2020). https://doi.org/10.1101/2020.03.13.20035329
10. Dudel, C., Riffe, T.: Monitoring trends and differences in COVID-19 case-fatality rates using decomposition methods: contributions of age structure and age-specific fatality. PLoS ONE **15**(9), e0238904 (2020). https://doi.org/10.1371/journal.pone.0238904
11. Goldstein, J.R., Lee, R.D.: Demographic perspectives on the mortality of COVID-19 and other epidemics. Proc. Natl. Acad. Sci. U.S.A **117**(36), 22035–22041 (2020). https://doi.org/10.1073/pnas.2006392117
12. Sudharsanan, N., Didzun, O., Bärnighausen, T., Vollmer, S.: The contribution of the age distribution of cases to COVID-19 case fatality across countries: a nine-country demographic study. Ann. Intern. Med. **173**, 714–720 (2020). https://doi.org/10.7326/M20-2973, [Epub 22 July 2020]
13. Zhou, C., et al.: Country-specific determinants for COVID-19 case fatality rate and response strategies from a global perspective: an interpretable machine learning framework. Popul. Health Metrics **22**(10) (2024). https://doi.org/10.1186/s12963-024-00330-4
14. Perone, G.: The determinants of COVID-19 case fatality rate (CFR) in the Italian regions and provinces: an analysis of environmental, demographic, and healthcare factors. Sci. Total Environ. **755**, 142523 (2021). https://doi.org/10.1016/j.scitotenv.2020.142523
15. Cabo, J.M.M.: Demographic variables associated with COVID-19 mortality. J. Public Health Res. **9**(4) (2020). https://doi.org/10.4081/jphr.2020.1827
16. Birchenall-Jiménez, C.: Centenarians in Colombia: a population-based cohort study on the impact of COVID 19. Infectio **28**(4), 228–234 (2024). https://doi.org/10.22354/24223794.1200
17. Khan, F.: A wide-base population pyramid and other factors explain low mortality in Pakistan during COVID-19 pandemic. J. Ayub Med. College Abbottabad **34**(3), 581–584 (2022). https://doi.org/10.55519/jamc-03-9444
18. Xue-Qiang Wang, G.S.: Association between ageing population, median age, life expectancy and mortality in coronavirus disease (COVID-19). Aging **12**(24), 24570–24578 (2020). https://doi.org/10.18632/aging.104193

19. Fonseka, T., Wijenayake, B.: Devising PoPStat: a metric bridging population pyramids with global disease mortality (2025). https://arxiv.org/abs/2501.11514
20. Mathieu, E., et al.: COVID-19 pandemic. Our World in Data (2020). https://ourworldindata.org/coronavirus
21. The World Bank: GDP per capita (constant 2015 us$) (2024). https://data.worldbank.org/indicator/NY.GDP.PCAP.KD
22. The World Bank: Gini index (world bank estimate) (2024). https://data.worldbank.org/indicator/SI.POV.GINI
23. United Nations Development Programme: Human development report data center (2024). https://hdr.undp.org/data-center
24. World Health Organization: Life expectancy at birth (years) (2024). https://www.who.int/data/gho/data/indicators/indicator-details/GHO/life-expectancy-at-birth-(years)
25. United Nations, Department of Economic and Social Affairs, Population Division: World population prospects 2024: standard projections (2024). https://population.un.org/wpp/downloads, most used datasets
26. The World Bank: Population density (people per sq. km of land area) (2024). https://data.worldbank.org/indicator/EN.POP.DNST
27. Institute for Health Metrics and Evaluation (IHME): Global health data exchange (2024). https://ghdx.healthdata.org/search/site/SDI
28. The universal health coverage coverage index. https://ourworldindata.org/grapher/universal-health-coverage-index
29. Bonanad, C., et al.: The effect of age on mortality in patients with COVID-19: a meta-analysis with 611,583 subjects. J. Am. Med. Dir. Assoc. **21**(7), 915–918 (2020)
30. Kofahi, H.M., Swedan, S.F., Khabour, O.F., Nimer, R.M.: Predictors of COVID-19 severity and hospitalization: a survey-based study from Jordan. Inform. Med. Unlocked **31**, 100994 (2022). https://doi.org/10.1016/j.imu.2022.100994, https://www.sciencedirect.com/science/article/pii/S235291482200137X
31. Mueller, A.L., McNamara, M.S., Sinclair, D.A.: Why does COVID-19 disproportionately affect older people? Aging (Albany NY) **12**(10), 9959–9981 (2020)
32. Prem, K.: The effect of control strategies to reduce social mixing on outcomes of the COVID-19 epidemic in Wuhan, China: a modelling study. The Lancet Public Health **5**(5), e261–e270 (2020). https://doi.org/10.1016/s2468-2667(20)30073-6
33. Pei, S.: Burden and characteristics of COVID-19 in the united states during 2020. Nature **598**(7880), 338–341 (2021). https://doi.org/10.1038/s41586-021-03914-4

Sentiment, Music and Acoustic Processing

Dynamic Music Harmonization via Interactive Machine Learning Methods and Genetic Algorithms

V. M. Lewangama, W. G. L. Harshani(✉), and D. D. A. Gamini

Department of Computer Science, Faculty of Applied Sciences, University of Sri Jayewardenepura, Colombo, Sri Lanka
lavanka6@gmail.com

Abstract. Music harmonization breathes life into melody, layering it with chords and patterns that add richness, dimension, and emotional nuance. It's not just about sound, it's about connection. This study explores the art of harmonization, placing emotional expression at its core. By recognizing the feelings embedded within melodies, the research blends machine learning with musical intuition. Using machine learning, the system learns to sense the emotional essence of a tune whether joyful, somber, or somewhere in between. These emotional cues guide a genetic algorithm, which evolves chord progressions that don't just fit the melody, they enhance its soul. Features extracted from audio signals shape the algorithm's understanding, while classification tools sort emotions with growing precision. The result is a creative interplay between human feeling and computational logic. The artificial neural network, with an emotion recognition accuracy of 60%, becomes the ear; the genetic algorithm, crafting harmonies through countless generations, becomes the heart. Together, they compose music that resonates not just sonically, but emotionally, blurring the lines between algorithm and art.

Keywords: congruence · cepstrum · filter bank processing · formant · gradient descent · mel-frequency cepstral coefficients

1 Introduction

Music harmonization is considered the art of accompanying a melody with suitable chords. It is a fundamental aspect of music composition and performance, involving building chord progressions that complement and enhance the initial melodic line, creating harmonious tones that enrich the overall musical experience. By manipulating harmonic tension and chord progressions, harmonization can create dramatic peaks and valleys in the musical narrative, heightening the listener's emotional engagement. Psychological studies confirm that harmonies directly influence affective responses. Rooted in centuries of musical tradition, harmonization bridges technical theory and creative expression, transforming simple melodies into rich, layered compositions. At its core, harmonization involves crafting chord progressions that align with the melody's rhythm,

R. N. Rajapakse et al. (Eds.): ICTer 2025, CCIS 2844, pp. 349–364, 2026.
https://doi.org/10.1007/978-981-92-0137-2_23

contour, and emotional intent. These harmonies serve as the scaffolding for musical storytelling, guiding listeners through tension, resolution, and dynamic shifts. For instance, an ascending melody paired with a dominant seventh chord can evoke anticipation, while a descending line over a minor triad might convey introspection. Through the careful selection and arrangement of chords, composers and musicians can express a wide range of emotions, from joy and happiness to melancholy. When harmonizing happy melodies, it is essential to use chords and progressions that convey a sense of joy and positivity. Conversely, when harmonizing sad melodies, the focus shifts to chords and harmonies that evoke feelings of melancholy and longing. When harmonizing neutral emotion melodies, the approach centers on selecting chords and progressions that maintain a sense of balance and tranquility without leaning towards either extreme of joy or sadness.

Recent advances in computational creativity have opened new frontiers in automated music generation, yet emotion-aware harmonization remains underexplored, as existing systems often prioritize functional harmony over affective goals. Existing approaches to music harmonization largely focus on audio data, leaving a gap in methods tailored for purely symbolic music that can effectively capture harmonic boundaries and duration information [2]. This gap highlights the need for frameworks that integrate music theory, affective computing, and machine learning a synthesis this project seeks to pioneer. For composers and arrangers, harmonizing music according to emotion provides a powerful means of artistic expression and creativity. By experimenting with different harmonic textures and chord progressions, musicians can build the harmonic palette of a composition to reflect the full range of human emotions. Although music harmonization amplifies engagement with the melody, it requires a lot of experience and knowledge about music. Novice musicians often find this task difficult and complicated [1]. Manual harmonization not only takes a lot of time to build but also requires multiple tests before finalizing the output. By integrating insights from music theory, psychology, and computational creativity, this project seeks to develop an innovative framework for emotion-driven harmonization. Specifically, the objectives of this study are to classify the emotional content of melodies using machine learning, generate emotion-aware chord harmonizations using genetic algorithms and evaluate harmonization quality using musical fitness measures such as congruence, harmonic flow, and chord diversity. Through the development of a system that aligns harmonic structures with emotional intent, we aim to empower musicians and creators with a versatile tool for crafting immersive musical experiences. Ultimately, our goal is to deepen the connection between music and its audience, fostering a richer emotional engagement that resonates across diverse genres and artistic visions.

2 Literature Review

Recent advancements in music generation and harmonization have seen an exciting convergence of artificial intelligence, emotional modeling, and evolutionary algorithms. Researchers have explored various computational methods from

LSTM-based hierarchical autoencoders and Hidden Markov Models to genetic algorithms, to enrich the harmony of melodies and personalize the musical experience. While many of these approaches excel in capturing structural and stylistic features, fewer have focused on the emotional depth of compositions, leaving a significant gap in emotion-aware harmonization. This section reviews notable efforts in algorithmic harmonization, melody-based composition, and emotion detection in music, highlighting the limitations of existing systems and setting the stage for the proposed emotion-driven harmonization framework.

A research study [16] introduces an innovative approach to melody harmonization by incorporating emotional conditions, enhancing chord progressions, and harmonies. Exploring a LSTM-based hierarchical variational autoencoder (LHVAE) model (see Fig. 1), the study explores how latent variables and emotional cues at both piece and barlevels can support musical compositions. The LHVAE model outperforms other LSTM-based models in objective evaluation, demonstrating better harmony quality, chord transition, and harmonicity. Results indicate that emotion guidance significantly improves the quality of harmonies, particularly in chord transition and harmonicity. The proposed method incorporates attention-based melody context vectors to enhance the learning of melodies and harmonies, taking both global and local music properties. In conclusion, the LHVAE model proves effective in enhancing harmony quality and variability in chord progressions, showcasing the potential of emotional conditions in music generation. Similarly, [1] also builds an application to harmonize melodies named ChordATune, considering user emotions and genre preferences. Through the utilization of a Hidden Markov Model (HMM), ChordATune simplifies harmonization for pianists by providing varied chord progressions to the user's emotional input. The tool aims to enhance the harmonization process by offering more chord options and supporting various input formats. Results indicate an 80% user satisfaction rate with ChordATune's ability to harmonize melodies effectively, offering a diverse range of harmonies and styles. In conclusion, ChordATune stands as an innovative tool for enhancing piano music harmonization.

Another paper [3], dives into the harmonization in Rock 'n' Roll music using Hidden Semi-Markov Models (HSMM), aiming to differentiate harmonic boundaries and generate harmonies. By taking duration and timing information, the model achieves more accurate musical model learning. A hybrid approach, combining Variable Time HSMM and Duration HSMM, is explored and tested for its effectiveness. The Explicit Duration HSMM is particularly adept at selecting the best state duration at transition times, enhancing the quality of chord progressions. Additionally, the introduction of a Residential Time HSMM model showed chord duration variability through self-transitions with fixed residential time. The study concludes by highlighting the efficacy of the HSMM in automatic harmonization, especially in Rock 'n' Roll music, and underscores the importance of incorporating duration and timing information for enhanced musical generation (see Fig. 2).

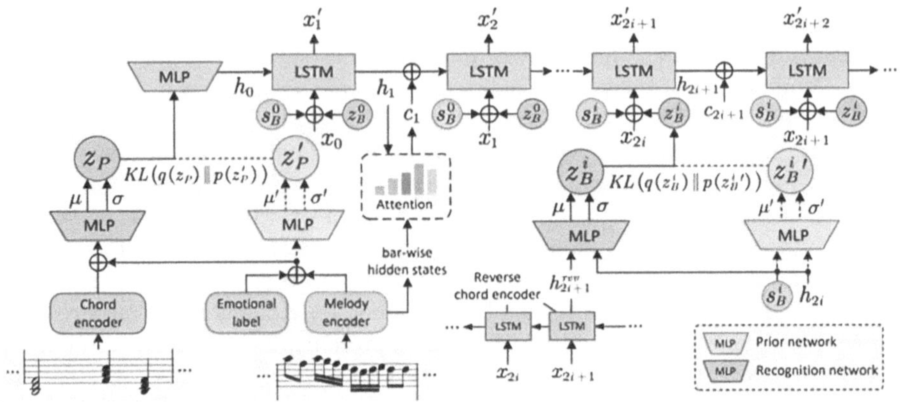

Fig. 1. LSTM-based hierarchical variational autoencoder

Fig. 2. A composed input melody, harmonized with the chord sequence generated from the HSMM

The main objective of [1] is to generate harmonizations, but not only adhere to formal musical rules but also capture the nuanced quality perceived by human listeners by applying artificial intelligence methods, specifically a genetic algorithm, a Bayesian network-based algorithm, and a hybrid of these approaches. Through a series of experiments, they compare the performance of these AI-driven methods against a traditional rule-based system, with evaluations conducted by musical experts. The findings indicate that the AI-based algorithms can produce harmonizations that are musically more engaging, despite being less formally correct than those generated by the rule-based system. Likewise, the genetic algorithm is tailored for composing music with flexible rhythm and pitches in [6], offering a concise yet effective summary of its key aspects. Through a position-based rhythm representation and relative pitch encoding, the algorithm generates compositions that meet specified objective criteria. The paper highlights the analysis of solutions and critical parameters influencing music compositions, emphasizing the genetic approach's ability to produce beautiful compositions characterized by pleasant intervals and meaningful rhythm.

The algorithm's coding system enables efficient control over tones, intervals, and rhythm, facilitating the creation of compositions tailored to specific

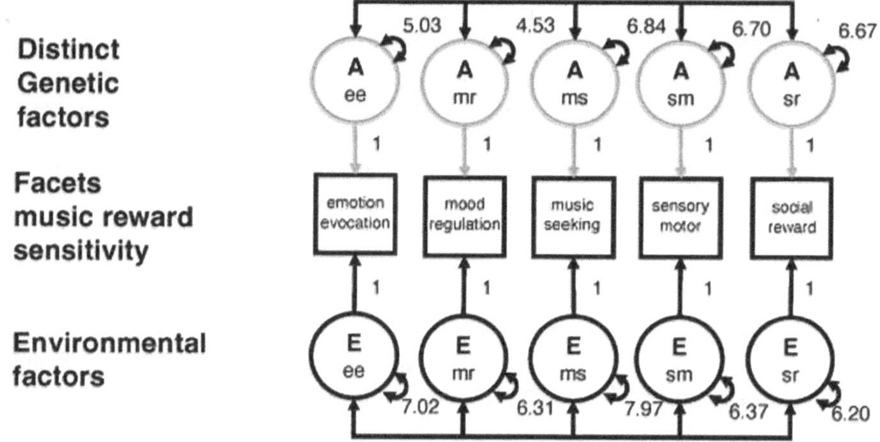

Fig. 3. A composed input melody, harmonized with the chord sequence generated from the HSMM

preferences. Results revealed that the algorithm consistently generates compositions known as "beautiful" with pleasant intervals and a compelling rhythm, while also affording control over parameters influencing composition quality and structure. They concluded the algorithm's capability to produce pleasing compositions while allowing composers control over various composition parameters. The study [10] investigates the influence of genetic factors on music reward sensitivity and enjoyment, revealing distinct pathways to musical pleasure through multivariate analyses. Genetic factors significantly impact music reward sensitivity and perceptual abilities, with multivariate analyses uncovering unique genetic pathways to music enjoyment, shedding light on the genetic influences on various facets of musical pleasure. Results show that genetic factors explain a significant portion of the variance in music reward sensitivity, with distinct genetic pathways contributing to different aspects of musical enjoyment, as revealed through multivariate analyses (see Fig. 3).

The study delves into genetic pathways underlying music enjoyment and reward sensitivity, aiming to understand individual differences in musical experiences. Genetic factors related to music reward sensitivity are analyzed in Swedish twins, while multivariate analyses explore genetic influences on music enjoyment, employing a univariate multi-group model using standard OpenMX protocols. This research provides valuable insights into the genetic underpinnings of music enjoyment, highlighting the diverse pathways through which genetic factors influence individual experiences of musical pleasure. Another interesting study [11] explores the integration of genetic algorithm-assisted techniques in musical composition, enhancing efficiency and innovation in model music creation. By combining evolutionary methods with artistic composition, the research focuses on refining the fitness function, evaluating melodies, and optimizing model music. Notably, the evaluation time is significantly reduced, plummeting from 4 min to a mere 0.002 s, thus streamlining composer efficiency. The system demonstrates a remarkable improvement in evaluating music after genetic manipulation compared to its unaltered counterparts. The paper emphasizes the evolution of musical compositions through interactive genetic algorithm techniques and underscores the efficiency gains in model music composition evaluation. It also delves into the impact of genetic manipulation on music evaluation, highlighting the reduction in evaluation time and the incorporation of complex musical elements like harmony and polyphony. Ultimately, genetic algorithms emerge as invaluable tools for contemporary composers, facilitating the creation of music with enhanced efficiency and sophistication.

The research study [4] introduces a novel model for musical key detection using machine learning techniques, with a focus on SVM classifier performance. The SVM algorithm exhibited the highest accuracy of 91.49% in key detection, surpassing other methods like KNN, Naive Bayes, and Discriminant Analysis. KNN method showed 89.76% accuracy, followed by Naıve Bayes and DA. A comprehensive dataset was compiled from various music genres, analyzing key combinations. Results indicate that the proposed model performs well in musical key estimation compared to related works, with the SVM model achieving the highest accuracy. Additionally, the model simultaneously detects tonic and mode with high accuracy, contributing to its effectiveness in melody comprehension and harmony analysis. In conclusion, the SVM model outperforms others, with KNN, Naive Bayes, and Discriminant Analysis classifiers following performance ranking, showcasing the efficacy of the proposed model in musical key estimation. Research article [7] introduces an evolutionary algorithm designed for music composition, with a focus on evaluating fitness features to inherit subjective interest and pleasantness in the generated music pieces. The summarized abstract outlines the algorithm's key aspects, emphasizing its application in producing 21 music pieces and assessing their subjective appeal. Despite being able to compose music pieces deemed interesting and pleasant, the system's consistency in achieving this outcome is noted to be lacking in the results. While acknowledging the system's capability to compose music pieces of subjective interest and pleasantness, it is noted that consistency in achieving this outcome remains a challenge. Overall, the research highlights the potential of evolutionary algorithms in music composition but also underscores the need for further refinement to enhance consistency in producing music pieces with desirable qualities. [9]Investigates the possibility of melody harmonization within evolutionary music, employing multi-objective genetic algorithms to achieve harmonious compositions. It encapsulates the essence of the study, highlighting the focus on human intentions for harmonies reflected in the fitness function and the evaluation based on note durations and vertical intervals. Empirical findings reveal the alignment between the fitness function and human intentions, showcasing the efficacy of the multi-objective approach in generating solutions that mirror human preferences. The conclusion emphasizes the influence of implicit knowledge on results, demonstrating variations in solutions while affirming the multi-objective approach's ability to balance diversity and adherence to rules. Throughout the study, discussions center on embedding musical cognizance in genetic algorithms and comparing experimental outcomes with human judgment for harmonies. The methods employed encompass multiobjective fitness functions, chord changes, and genetic algorithms, juxtaposed against rule-based models and other evolutionary approaches, with evaluation factors including note durations and vertical intervals in harmony.

As shown in the summary table (see Table 1), several studies in the literature focus on music harmonization; a significant gap exists in emotion-aware harmonization. Many traditional methods, such as Hidden Semi-Markov Models (HSMM) and SVM-based key estimation models, primarily emphasize musical structure, functional harmony, and genre-specific harmonization rather than emotional expressiveness. Similarly, genetic algorithms have been used for harmonization and music composition, but they largely prioritize chord transitions and harmonic rules without explicitly considering the emotional intent behind the melody. Although some studies attempt to incorporate emotional factors, their approaches often rely on genre-based learning or limited emotion conditioning, rather than a fully adaptive, real-time emotion-driven harmonization system. For example, Interactive ML for harmonization [1] incorporates user emotions but is rule-based, whereas LHVAE-based emotion-conditioned harmonization [16] uses deep learning but lacks flexibility beyond trained datasets. The multiobjective genetic algorithm [12] considers emotion but is not designed to adapt dynamically to various musical styles. Moreover, most studies on music classification and performance evaluation focus on identifying emotions within music but do not extend their findings to real-time emotion-based harmonization. This highlights a crucial gap where music emotion recognition and harmonization remain largely disconnected in existing research. This research aims to bridge the gap between music harmonization and emotional expression by integrating machine learning-based emotion recognition with genetic algorithms for harmonization. Unlike existing models that primarily focus on structural harmony, this research emphasizes emotion-aware chord progressions, ensuring that the harmonization process aligns with the intended emotional tone of the melody. By exploring Mel-Frequency Cepstral Coefficients (MFCCs) for feature extraction and a feedforward neural network for emotion classification, this system accurately deter-mines the emotional category of a melody. A genetic algorithm then generates the most fitting chord progressions based on predefined fitness evaluation functions, ensuring that harmonies reflect the emotion embedded within the melody. The findings of this study contribute to the fields of computational musicology and AI-driven music generation, offering a versatile tool for musicians, composers, and researchers. By harmonizing music dynamically based on emotional content, this system has the potential to revolutionize automated music composition, making it more emotionally engaging and expressive. Ultimately, this research paves the way for a more immersive and emotionally resonant approach to music harmonization, fostering greater listener engagement and artistic creativity across diverse musical genres.

Table 1. Comparison of existing research work

Ref. No.	Overall Approach/Framework	Specific Algorithmic Implementation	Emotion Considered?
[1]	Interactive ML	Rule-based and Machine Learning	Yes
[2]	Emotion-conditioned Melody Harmonization	Hierarchical Variational Autoencoder (LSTM)	Yes
[3]	Automatic Harmonization	Hidden Semi-Markov Model (HSMM)	No
[4]	Key Estimation Model	SVM Classifier	No
[5]	Four-Part Harmonization	Evolutionary Algorithms + ML	No
[6]	Genetic Algorithm for Composition	Evolutionary Computing ML	No
[7]	Co-Evolving Melodies and Harmonization	Evolutionary Algorithms ML	No
[8]	Music Harmonization in Games	Genetic Algorithm	No
[9]	Multiobjective Genetic Algorithm	Evolutionary Music Harmonization	Yes
[10]	Genetic Pathways to Music Enjoyment	Statistical Analysis	Yes
[11]	Genetic Algorithm for Composition Innovation	Evolutionary Algorithm	No
[12]	Instrumental Emotion Recognition	KNN + MFCC	Yes
[13]	Genre Classification	KNN + MFCC	No
[14]	Music Classification	MFCC Variants + Amplitude Variation	No
[15]	Vocal Music Performance	Neural Networks	No
[17]	Music Classification	MFCC + BP Neural Network	No

3 Methodology

This section will present a detailed explanation of the identification of the emotion using machine learning models and harmonization using genetic algorithms (see Fig. 4). The dataset that is being used is the EMOPIA Dataset, comprising classical music audio files for each of three emotions, namely happy, sad, and neutral, with a total length of 12 h with 193 recordings. The dataset encompasses a variety of tempos, including fast, slow, and medium speeds. Music harmonization can be done using different methods. This research aims to harmonize the melody using chord triads [13].

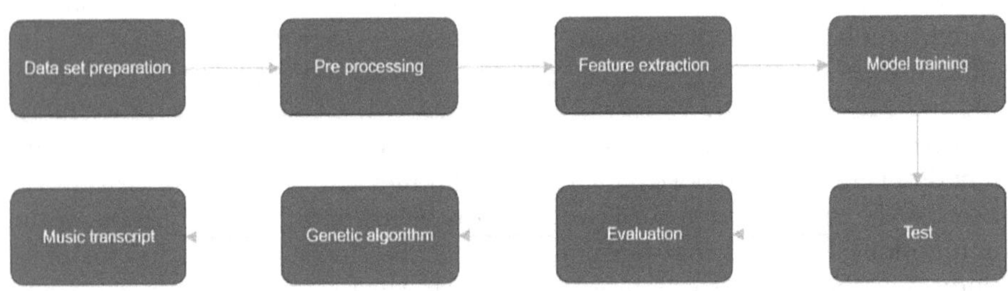

Fig. 4. Visual depiction of the methodology

3.1 Feature Extraction

Feature extraction [18], visualization of music, and normalization of audio files were done using the Librosa library in Python [14]. It has the ability to merge multi-channel audio data into a mono channel. Feature extraction was done using Mel-Frequency Cepstral Coefficients (MFCC). It converts the time domain signal of each audio clip into the frequency domain. The initial step involves segmenting the speech signals into frames, a method known as windowing [14]. This segmentation prioritizes high frequencies to ensure a consistent amplitude across all formants, as high-frequency formants generally exhibit lower amplitudes compared to low-frequency formants [14]. Following windowing, each frame's power spectrum is determined by applying the Fast Fourier Transform. Subsequently, the power spectrum undergoes filter bank processing using the Mel-scale, which maps frequencies to the Mel scale. To derive the MFCC coefficients, the power spectrum is converted to the logarithmic domain to better represent human perception (see Fig. 5). Finally, the Discrete Cosine Transform (DCT) is applied to the log-power spectrum [15] to compute the MFCC coefficients. The log power spectrum converts into spectral envelope and spectral detail [17]. The spectral envelope can be used to analyze important information about the audio signal using formants [18].

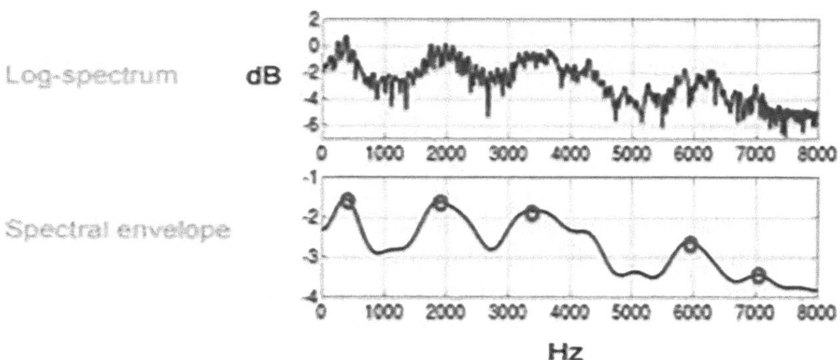

Fig. 5. Separated log spectrum and formants of an audio envelope

3.2 Model Architecture

The model being used here is a feed-forward deep neural network with three hidden layers (see Fig. 6). FNNs can be scaled to handle large datasets and complex audio classification tasks by adjusting the network architecture, such as increasing the number of layers or neurons. Each neuron in the hidden layers and the output layer applies an activation function to its weighted sum of inputs. Activation functions include ReLU (Rectified Linear Unit) and softmax (for the output layer). FNN is trained using an algorithm called backpropagation, which adjusts the weights of connections between neurons to minimize the difference between the predicted output and the actual output. This involves propagating the error backward through the network and updating the weights using

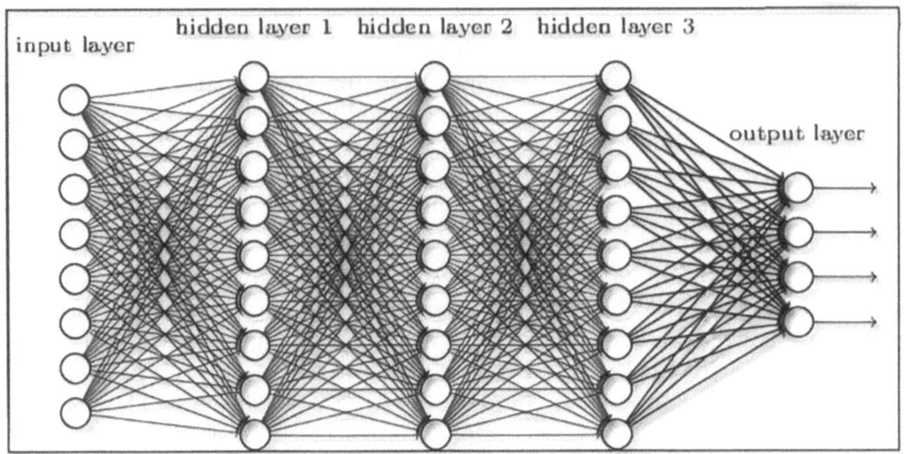

Fig. 6. Feed forward deep neural network

techniques like gradient descent or its variants. The training process iteratively adjusts the weights until the network learns to produce accurate predictions on the training data. A loss function is used to quantify the difference between the predicted output and the actual output. The model uses 'categorical crossentropy' as its loss function. Adam Optimization is used here to handle scattered gradients on noisy details. The model is trained over multiple epochs, during each of which the model weights are updated to minimize the loss function. The next step is to generate the harmonization according to the derived emotion. When creating music harmonizations using genetic algorithms, music chords and transitions are precisely used to express the emotion. Major chords are often associated with a happy and uplifting emotion in music due to their tonal characteristics, while minor chords often express a darker, sadder, or unhappy quality compared to major chords. This distinction in emotional quality is crucial in harmonization, as it guides the selection and arrangement of chords to evoke the desired emotional response from the listener.

3.3 Preferred Transitions

Preferred transitions are chord sequences where the transitions between chords follow established harmonic conventions or common progressions, which are often perceived as musically pleasing and natural [4,8]. The next step is to select suitable chord accompaniments for a given melody using the genetic algorithm. It generates a population of chord sequences to find one that best fits the melody based on a fitness function [13]. The algorithm initializes with melody data, chords, population size, mutation rate, and a fitness evaluator [12]. To initialize the population, a random chord sequence is generated. The parents are selected based on the fitness values. A new population of chord sequences is created from the generated parents using one-point crossover and mutation operations

[12]. The next step is to evaluate the fitness of a chord sequence based on various musical criteria. To evaluate the fitness, congruence, code variety, harmonic flow, and functional harmony are calculated and fed appropriate weights.

Congruence calculates the relationship between the chord sequence and the melody. It runs through each chord in the chord sequence and, for each chord, iterates through the melody notes until the total duration of the bar is reached or all melody notes are matched with chords. During this iterative process, it checks if each note in the melody is present in the current chord being played at the same time. If a melody note matches with any note in the current chord, it adds the duration of that note to the congruence score. This process successfully evaluates how accurately the notes in the melody align with the chords being played, rewarding sequences where the melody notes fit well with the chords. Finally, to provide a normalized measure, the congruence score is divided by the total duration of the melody, ensuring that the evaluation is relative to the length of the melody, facilitating comparison across melodies of different durations. Code variety quantifies the diversity of chords employed in the chord sequence. It achieves this by assessing the number of unique chords present in the sequence with respect to the total domain of available chords. For each chord sequence provided, the method calculates the count of unique chords with respect to the total number of distinct chords available. This ratio serves as a measure of chord variety, with a higher ratio indicating a greater diversity of chords used in the sequence. This evaluation is kept to promote musical complexity and interest by adding sequences that incorporate a broader range of harmonic elements. By encouraging the utilization of a diverse set of chords, this method aims to enrich the harmonic palette of the composition, potentially leading to more engaging and dynamic musical arrangements.

The harmonic flow evaluates the smoothness and coherence of the harmonic progression in the chord sequence see Fig. 7. It does so by examining the transitions between successive chords and comparing them against a set of predefined preferred transitions. For each pair of adjacent chords in the sequence, the method checks if the transition from the current chord to the next one aligns with any of the preferred transitions. When a preferred transition is identified, it contributes positively to the harmonic flow score. This process rewards sequences where the transitions between chords follow established harmonic conventions or common progressions, which are often perceived as musically pleasing and natural [11]. By promoting sequences with smoother and more harmonically coherent transitions, this method enhances the overall structural integrity and aesthetic appeal of the composition's harmonic progression.

The functional harmony method evaluates the adherence of the chord sequence to principles of functional harmony, a fundamental aspect of tonal music theory and rules. It assesses whether the chord sequence illustrates key harmonic functions typically seen in tonal music. The method assigns a score based on these criteria, with a higher score indicating a closer convergence to traditional functional harmony principles. By supporting sequences that follow established harmonic conventions, such as the resolution of tension through dominant to tonic progressions, this method hopes to bring the tonal center and structural coherence of the music composition citebignardi. Ultimately, this aims to promote harmonically compelling chord progressions. The weights assigned in the weights dictionary represent the relative importance of each fitness evaluation function in the overall assessment of the chord sequence. These weights determine the contribution of each function to the final fitness score. Adjusting these weights tunes the algorithm according to the given inputs. Hence, improving the overall performance of the algorithm [13]. The melody is represented as a list of tuples, and each tuple is built with pitch and its duration [16]. This list of tuples is fed into the algorithm [18].

4 Results

The dataset was divided such that 75% of all audio files were randomly selected for training, while the remaining 25% were used for validation and testing to ensure unbiased performance evaluation. The custom artificial neural network achieved an accuracy of 60.20% after 100 epochs, demonstrating the model's capability to classify melodies into emotional categories such as happy, sad, and neutral. Through iterative evolution, the genetic algorithm produced different sequences of chords that complemented the melody's structure. To evaluate the generated harmonizations, each chord sequence was assessed using predefined fitness criteria, including congruence, chord diversity harmonic flow and functional harmony. Higher fitness scores indicated better harmonic quality and stronger alignment with emotional intent.

The evaluation process involved computing these metrics for each generated harmonization, comparing results across multiple melodies, and selecting the highest-scoring harmonization sequences for analysis. These evaluation scores provide quantitative evidence of the algorithm's effectiveness in producing musically coherent and emotionally expressive harmonizations. The process resulted in the creation of a music score representation for each harmonized melody. Figures 8, 9, and 10 present the harmonized outputs generated for happy, sad, and neutral emotional tones, respectively. These visualizations clearly demonstrate the system's ability to adapt harmonic progression based on the detected emotion, offering direct insights into the quality and variability of the generated harmonizations.

Emotions	Description	Chords
Happy	Uplifting chord progressions to support the "Happy" emotion of the melody	• I-III-VI-IV • I-II-V-I • I-II-VI-IV • I-IV-V • I-VI-IV-VI • II-IV-I • I-III-VII-VI
Sad	The foundation of expressive sadness on the piano is the minor chords and transitions	• IV-V-VI • I-VII-IV-V • I-III-V-VI • I-III-IV-VI • I-III-IV-IV • I-I-VI-V • VI-IV-I-V • VI-IV-V-III
Neutral	The chord transitions that have the ability to showcase the neutral emotion of a song	• I-V-VI-IV • I-VI-III-VI • I-VI-II-V • I-III-IV-VI

Fig. 7. Chord progressions categorized by emotional tone

Fig. 8. Generated harmonization of a happy song

Fig. 9. Predicted harmonization of a sad emotion melody

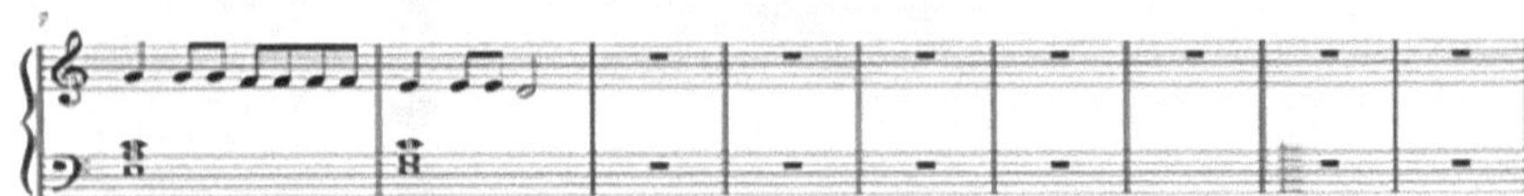

Fig. 10. Predicted harmonization of a neutral emotion melody

5 Discussion and Conclusion

The artificial neural network model achieved an accuracy of 60% in classifying melodies into emotional categories such as happy, sad, and neutral. This directly addresses the first research objective: to classify the emotional content of melodies using machine learning techniques. The 60% accuracy demonstrates the feasibility of using neural networks for music emotion recognition while also revealing challenges such as limited dataset size, model complexity, and the inherent ambiguity in musical emotions. The genetic algorithm generated chord sequences evaluated using fitness criteria including congruence, harmonic flow, and chord diversity. This result satisfies the second objective: generating emotion-aware chord harmonizations. Higher fitness scores corresponded to harmonizations that were musically coherent and emotionally aligned with the detected emotions, confirming the effectiveness of the evolutionary approach. The results are presented cautiously without overstating or overgeneralizing conclusions. This approach addresses this gap by combining emotion recognition with harmonization generation in a unified framework. However, some limitations were identified: the dataset size restricted classification accuracy, the model could not handle melodies with mixed emotions, and the feedforward architecture lacked temporal awareness of musical patterns. Future work should incorporate larger and more diverse datasets, adopt advanced neural architectures such as LSTM or Transformer models, and explore real-time harmonization features for interactive composition tools. Overall, this study successfully met its objectives by classifying the emotional content of melodies using machine learning, generating emotion-aware chord harmonizations using genetic algorithms, and evaluating harmonization quality through musical fitness criteria. The findings demonstrate that combining machine learning with evolutionary algorithms can produce harmonizations that reflect both musical structure and emotional intent. The conclusions are supported by the data. The 60% classification accuracy validates the feasibility of machine learning for emotion detection, while fitness-based evaluations confirm the capability of genetic algorithms in creating harmonizations aligned with emotional goals. Broader implications of this work include applications in music education, automated music composition software, and therapeutic music systems where emotional engagement is critical. By integrating emotion recognition with harmonization, this research contributes to computational musicology and paves the way for AI-assisted emotion-driven music creation. Future research should focus on improving classification accuracy, handling a wider range of emotions, and developing real-time harmonization systems to enhance practical usability and adaptability across diverse musical contexts.

Disclosure of Interests. The authors declare no potential conflict of interest.

References

1. Soysa, I., Lokuge, K.: Interactive machine learning for incorporating user emotions in automatic music harmonization. In: 2010 Fifth International Conference on Information and Automation for Sustainability, pp. 114–118. IEEE (2010). https://doi.org/10.1109/ICIAFS.2010.5715678
2. Brown, K., White, L.: Emotion-conditioned melody harmonization using hierarchical variational autoencoder. LNCS, vol. 11234, pp. 50–65. Springer, Berlin (2021). https://doi.org/10.1007/9876543210
3. Wang, X., Zhang, Y.: Automatic harmonization with hidden semi-Markov model. Comput. Music. J. **45**(2), 88–102 (2019)
4. George, A., Mary, X.A., George, S.T.: Development of an intelligent model for musical key estimation using machine learning techniques. Multimed. Tools Appl. **81**(14), 19945–19964 (2022). https://doi.org/10.1007/s11042-022-12345-6
5. Sikora, M., Smołka, M.: An application of evolutionary algorithms and machine learning in four-part harmonization. In: International Conference on Computational Science, pp. 221–236. Springer (2023). https://doi.org/10.1007/978-3-031-12345-6_17
6. Matić, D.: A genetic algorithm for composing music. Yugoslav J. Oper. Res. **20**(1), 157–177 (2010). https://doi.org/10.1007/9876543210

7. Olseng, O.A.E.: An application of evolutionary algorithms to music: coevolving melodies and harmonization. Master's thesis, NTNU (2016)
8. Komarov, O., Galchonkov, O., Nevrev, A., Babilunga, O.: The use of a genetic algorithm for music harmonization of transitional fragments in computer games. Int. J. Comput. **19**(3), 365–376 (2020)
9. Freitas, A., Guimaraes, F.: Melody harmonization in evolutionary music using multiobjective genetic algorithms. In: Proceedings of the Sound and Music Computing Conference, pp. 1–10 (2011)
10. Bignardi, G., et al.: Distinct genetic pathways to music enjoyment. bioRxiv, 2024–04 (2024). Cold spring harbor laboratory. https://doi.org/10.1101/2024.04.123456
11. Xu, D., Xu, H.: Application of genetic algorithm in model music composition innovation. Appl. Math. Nonlinear Sci. **9**(1), 2 (2024)
12. Santoso, T.B., Dutono, T.: Instrumental music emotion recognition with MFCC and KNN algorithm. Indones. J. Comput. Sci. **12**(1), 1–10 (2023)
13. Cui, Y.: Vocal music performance evaluation system based on neural network and its application in piano teaching. Rev. Ibérica Sist. Tecnol. Inf. **E55**, 451–464 (2023)
14. Chun, L.Y., Song, H., Yang, J.: Research on music classification based on MFCC and BP neural network. In: 2nd International Conference Information, Electronics and Computer, pp. 129–132. Atlantis Press (2014)
15. Bisht, A.S., Negi, C.M.S., Singh, R.: Classification of Indian Classical Music (Hindustani Music) genres through MFCCs features using RNN-LSTM model. (Details incomplete – needs correct proceedings/journal info for CCIS style)
16. Zhang, M.: Advancing deep learning for expressive music composition and performance modeling. Sci. Rep. **15**, 28007 (2025). https://doi.org/10.1038/s41598-025-28007-3
17. Ji, S., Yang, X.: Emotion-conditioned melody harmonization with hierarchical variational autoencoder. In: 2023 IEEE International Conference Systems, Man, and Cybernetics (SMC), pp. 228–233. IEEE (2023). https://doi.org/10.1109/SMC.2023.1234567
18. Pratiwi, T., Sunyoto, A., Ariatmanto, D.: Music genre classification using K-nearest neighbor and Mel-frequency cepstral coefficients. Sinkron J. Penelit. Tek. Inform. **8**(2), 861–867 (2024)

Emotion in the Crowd: SLCSED and a MIR-Enhanced Machine Learning Pipeline

Shehani Ariyathilake(✉) and Charith Chitranjan

University of Moratuwa, Katubedda, Moratuwa, Sri Lanka
shehani.21@cse.mrt.ac.lk

Abstract. Understanding crowd emotions through sound is critical for applications in event monitoring, public safety, and mental health studies. However, there has been a notable gap in the availability of specialized datasets and robust models for classifying crowd sound emotions. To address this, a comprehensive Sri Lankan Crowd Sound Emotion Dataset (SLCSED) was developed to support future research. Further, the study proposes a computational framework based on Music Information Retrieval (MIR) techniques, combined with advanced machine learning algorithms, to perform emotion classification in crowds. Feature extraction was performed using the MIR method. Principal Component Analysis was applied as a dimensionality reduction technique. Various machine learning and transfer learning classifiers, including TabNet, LightGBM, and Multi-Layer Perceptron, were evaluated. The results demonstrated highly promising outcomes, with the LightGBM and MLP classifiers achieving up to 99.95% validation accuracy on the Emotional Crowd Sound Data (ECSD) dataset and the Multi-Layer Perceptron achieving 99.95% on the SLCSED dataset without dimensionality reduction. These findings highlight the effectiveness of MIR-based feature engineering combined with carefully selected classifiers for crowd emotion detection. This work not only fills a major gap by introducing a localized and richly annotated dataset but also presents a robust methodological pipeline with MIR techniques for crowd sound emotion recognition, paving the way for future applications in real-world monitoring and psychological analysis.

Keywords: Multi-Layer Perceptron · Music Information Retrieval · Principal Component Analysis

1 Introduction

As humans, we are gifted with the ability to identify emotions from speech, while machines do not possess such an ability. It has become a quite an interesting research field, identifying emotions through sounds [1]. Emotion is a functional state of the brain that provides causal explanations of certain complex behaviors [2]. It is something that humans are experiencing during certain events. Humans have main emotions, such as joy, sad, anger, excitement, boredom, and even frustration. These emotions are unique and have been individualized. All human emotions are a result of a subjective experience or stimulus [3].

R. N. Rajapakse et al. (Eds.): ICTer 2025, CCIS 2844, pp. 365–379, 2026.
https://doi.org/10.1007/978-981-92-0137-2_24

For a considerable time, sound emotion analysis has mainly concentrated on analyzing individual dimensions. Emotions from individuals were collected through music [4] or individual speaker speeches [5, 6]. As speech signals are one of the fastest and most direct ways of identifying emotions of humans, this field has been very popular among researchers for studies related to speech emotion analysis.

Crowd Emotion or community emotion analysis mainly focuses on analyzing the collective emotional states of large groups of people in different kinds of settings. It can be a sports event, a concert, a protest, or any public event where a large crowd is gathered for the same purpose. The emotions people have in such a gathering are usually expressed through sounds. People can cheer, applaud, laugh, murmur, or boo. The pulse of the event can be identified while analyzing the sounds of the gathering.

The dominant emotional condition of the crowd shall be reflected through the sound signals generated in the large crowd-gathering events [5, 7]. Analysis of the sound can be performed by associating sounds with different emotions within the crowd [8]. In public events such as parties, political meetings, protests, concerts, or religious riots, the gathered crowd's emotions are collectively displayed. And in public places where social activities are taking place, such as fairs, shopping malls, exhibitions, and restaurants, most usually there can be neutral emotions with some background music or quiet chatting in the background [9].

Crowd emotions are collective characteristics that demonstrate the emotional state of a large group in a single setting. There are unique individuals gathered in a certain place, that's how it makes a large group of people [10]. When it comes to the crowd sound emotion identification domain, only a limited number of studies have focused on identifying emotions from crowd sounds, leaving this area underexplored in comparison to individual speech-based emotion recognition.

Although the majority of research on crowd emotion recognition has concentrated on visual information, the sound aspect of collective emotional expressions remains largely underexplored. Among them, only a few studies [1, 9, 11–13] have been conducted for crowd emotion detection, while all the others have focused on Speech Emotion Detection.

Further, most of the related studies in crowd sound emotion recognition have primarily utilized Convolutional Neural Networks (CNNs) [9] as their core models. This approach typically involves converting raw audio signals into spectrogram images, allowing CNNs to analyze the visual patterns of sound frequency over time. Spectrograms serve as an effective intermediate representation because CNNs excel at capturing spatial hierarchies within image-like data. Although CNNs excel at the tasks, spectrograms can be sensitive to the noise in the real-world audio, where acoustic characters can overlap with the background noise in the spectrograms [14]. Therefore, in the present study, a different methodology was adopted. Instead of transforming the audio clips into spectrograms, the preprocessed audio files were directly used as model inputs. Additionally, feature vectors such as Mel-frequency cepstral coefficients (MFCC), Chroma features, and Mel spectrogram coefficients were extracted and stored in CSV format. These extracted features were then directly fed into machine learning and deep learning models, enabling the system to learn emotional characteristics without relying on spectrogram-based image analysis.

When the visual image data is not available enough to make a decision, audio analysis can be effectively used. As most of the studies have used image data for emotion identification, it is an issue that raises privacy concerns [11]. Grasping and interpreting crowd emotions is vital across various fields, such as public safety, event management, marketing, and entertainment [15]. Even though emotion recognition has improved, there's still a lack of research focused on identifying crowd emotions through sound, especially in culturally diverse places like Sri Lanka. Crowd sounds from events like sports games, concerts, and protests show complex emotions influenced by social and cultural factors. But current methods often have trouble understanding these emotions because of challenges like noisy audio, differences in sound, and the lack of suitable datasets for these situations. A further limitation is the scarcity of crowd-sourced emotion datasets, with only two publicly available [1, 9]. This study addresses this gap by presenting a new dataset rooted in the Sri Lankan domain.

This study is the first to apply Music Information Retrieval (MIR) techniques directly for feature extraction, specifically only using Mel spectrogram, Chroma, and MFCC features, which are exported to a CSV file and then used as input for the model. The main objective of this research is to create a diverse dataset for crowd sound emotions in the Sri Lankan context mass events. Here in the study, the Music Information Retrieval (MIR) technique is applied to extract relevant features from the audio data. The temporal, spectral, and harmonic characteristics of the crowd sounds are analyzed through these techniques. The suitability of MIR for emotion identification in crowd sounds is assessed based on the performance of the models trained using these extracted features, as the next objective. Finally, the effectiveness of different MIR-based models was assessed, and a recommendation is made for the most appropriate method for crowd emotion identification through sound.

2 Related Works

Recognizing crowd emotions is far different from recognizing speech emotions from a particular person. As a result, only a limited number of studies can be found in this particular domain, where audio files of large gatherings have been used to extract emotions.

Franzoni et al. [13] have studied crowd sound emotion as the first application for that domain. Authors have researched the recognition of crowd emotions from crowd sounds and speeches gathered at crowded events. The gathered sounds were labeled into three emotional categories: Approval, Disapproval, and Neutral. This study has achieved 98.54% accuracy when using spectrogram images with AlexNet.

The same authors [9] have introduced an extended method that involves creating sound spectrograms from fixed-length segments of audio recordings captured during large-scale events, where the crowd behaves as a unified entity. This approach leverages transfer learning, applying a convolutional neural network (CNN) that has been pre-trained with ImageNet. Further, authors have published the Emotional Crowd Sounds dataset.

Faisal et al. [1] trained a Random Forest Classifier to identify crowd emotions within their ESLCE dataset, with an average 81.2% accuracy for the model, for 5 folds. In the same experiment, the authors have compared the accuracy of the transfer learning model and the random forest classifier, where the machine learning model has outperformed the MobileNetV2.

Furthermore, Xu et al. [12] have studied the Detection of Community Emotions by introducing a self-organized feature extraction function, Forward-Forward Pattern Feature Generator (FF- Orbital). Classification of the emotions has been performed using a Support Vector Machine(SVM). Validation has been conducted by using ten-fold cross-validation, where the trained model has achieved an accuracy of 97.22%.

Veltmeijer [11] has studied subgroups in a large crowd. The author focuses on automated crowd understanding, particularly in identifying subgroups within crowds and analyzing their emotions as predictors of behavior. The research employed various methods and data types, emphasizing the importance of a multimodal approach for crowd emotion identification. Experiments were conducted on crowd emotion identification using facial recognition in images, surveillance footage analysis for violent subgroups, and social media posts. Additionally, the study explores crowd sentiment analysis through audio. Since crowd sound emotion identification is primarily oriented toward real-world applicability, prior literature has consistently highlighted challenges such as data noise in actual crowd environments [1, 9]. As a result, some datasets have been synthetically constructed; however, this approach still leaves the challenge of achieving reliable model accuracy in real-world settings [11].

Table 1. Summary of Existing Literature

Study	Dataset	Feature Extraction Method	PCA	Classifier	Accuracy
[13]	CSD v1	Spectrogram	-	AlexNet	98.54%
[9]	ECSD	Spectrogram	-	AlexNet	99.83%
[1]	ESLCE	Energy ,Spectral centroid, Spectral Spread, Spectral entropy, Mel, MFCC	PCA	Random Forest	81.20%
		Spectrogram	-	MobileNet v2	68.40%
[12]	SCED	FF-BTP feature engineering	-	SVM	97.22%
[11]	ESLCE/ ECSD	zero-crossing rate, RMS, Spectral centroid, Spectral bandwidth, Spectral contrast, Spectral flatness, Roll off frequency, Tempo, Mel, MFCC, Chroma	PCA	SVM	66.38%
			PCA	RF	63.44%
			PCA	KNN	58.71%
			PCA	1D CNN	77.28%
		Spectrogram	-	2D CNN	55.96%
			-	Transformer	73.90%

As in Table 1, the highest results have been achieved when using AlexNet. Although high accuracies have been reported in those studies, the results mainly highlight the effectiveness of CNNs. However, since audio has been treated as an image in such approaches, important musical or perceptual attributes may be overlooked. In contrast, Music Information Retrieval (MIR) techniques emphasize features such as MFCCs, chroma, and Mel, which capture structural and perceptual properties of sound. By incorporating MIR-based features and applying PCA for dimensionality reduction, this work extends beyond prior CNN-only approaches. This not only reduces computational complexity but also integrates domain knowledge into the feature space, offering both interpretability and robust classification performance.

Further, culturally specific data is essential for research, as emotional expressions and perceptions vary across cultures [16], and models trained on non-representative datasets may fail to generalize accurately. To address this gap, a Sri Lankan dataset was developed to capture culturally relevant crowd sound emotions.

3 Methodology

The proposed methodology consists mainly of two phases. The first is to create a Sri Lankan context crowd sound emotion dataset to explore the diverse acoustic sounds of various events in Sri Lanka. The second is to explore the applicability of the MIR techniques with crowd sound emotions and to propose a well-suited MIR-based computational framework.

3.1 Dataset Creation

The dataset used in this research was collected from video clips of the real crowd in Sri Lanka. Different events from YouTube have been chosen as original audios. To ensure the diversity of the dataset, audio recordings from various crowd-gathering events, including sports matches, political rallies, public fairs, and prize-giving ceremonies, were used. Initially, based on YouTube titles and descriptions, each recording was categorized into three classes: Approval (including cheering, applause, or positive chanting), Disapproval (such as booing, shouting, or negative chanting), and Neutral (encompassing general talking, ambient noise, or background sounds).

The main reason for not choosing fake library sound is that deep learning and machine learning models can extract misleading features due to counterfeit components of the audio clips. Additionally, real-world audio recordings may have more complex features than intentionally studio-recorded ones, such as background noise and dirtiness. And that can be challenging, and that's a higher demand among the researchers [9].

The audio used in the dataset has never been used for any research purposes. When creating the dataset, two hypotheses were considered. Assumed that crowd sounds are less dependent on individuals, and all the crowd is the same in every scenario. Crowd sound clips are assumed to represent a single dominant emotion. In cases where mixed emotions are present, the emotion with the strongest expression will be used as the representative label for the clip.

The dataset creation process is as follows. As the first step, the dataset was collected from publicly available YouTube recordings, where search strings such as "people cheering at a Sri Lankan cricket match," "people shouting at a strike in Sri Lanka," or "political rally crowd shouting in Sri Lanka" were used to identify clips. Based on the titles and descriptions, each recording was initially annotated as approval, disapproval, or neutral. A total of 72 videos were selected from YouTube across three labels (See Table 2). The videos were downloaded as MP3 files and stored in separate folders corresponding to each label. Then, it was converted to WAV format using Pydub, and background noise was removed using Spleeter. Following this, normalization to −20 dBFS was applied. Amplitude normalization was performed by calculating the current amplitude, computing the difference from the target, and adjusting the volume accordingly. After the normalization, the audio was segmented into 1-s blocks with a 0.25-s shifting window (75% overlap). After segmentation, a total of 18,355 one-second audio files were obtained across the labels (See Table 2). The resulting segments were renamed and resampled to 16 kHz. A consistent naming convention was applied when renaming the segmented audio files. The format used was {class_label}_{count:06d}.wav. (approval_000001.wav, disapproval_000001.wav, and neutral_000001.wav)

To ensure reliability, a manual revision step was conducted with three independent annotators. Silence-segmented and mismatched blocks were eliminated because they were thought to impair performance in this stage. A Python-based interface was developed to streamline this process. Each annotator was provided with predefined category definitions (Approval, Disapproval, Neutral), and annotators listened to the normalized and segmented 1-s audio clips and marked them as correctly labeled or mislabeled by pressing "yes" or "no." The system automatically generated a "mislabel" folder containing all clips flagged as incorrect. To finalize the labels, a simple verification was applied. If all three annotators marked an audio file as mislabeled, it was rejected from the dataset. If only one or two annotators flagged a file, it was returned to the original dataset. A total of 2557 files were removed in this step. The number of files removed is displayed in Table 2.

At the end, automatic validation was performed to verify the duration of the audio clips, sampling rate, and the format of the audio files. After this process, a total of 15,798 files remained, as no files were removed during the automatic validation step. The workflow for creating the audio dataset is illustrated in Fig. 1.

Here, for the study, the authors have employed two datasets. The main dataset has been created by the authors (SLCSED), while the second dataset is a publicly available dataset (ECSD) [17].

3.2 Classification Approach

In the second phase, a classification approach was developed by considering the MIR as the main feature extraction method. And for the dimensionality reduction, Principal Component Analysis (PCA) has been employed. TabNet, MLP, and LightGBM have been used with a tabular classification approach. With the MIR technique, a CSV file containing the extracted features (MFCC, Chroma, and Mel Spectrogram) for each audio file, along with their corresponding label, was the output received. A total of 153 were

Table 2. Number of Audios in each step

Label	Number of audios (with initial annotation)	Number of segmented audios	Number of audios removed after three independent annotators' decision	Number of audios remained after removal
Approval	43	6896	1083	5813
Disapproval	18	5941	1069	4872
Neutral	11	5518	405	5113
Total	72	18355	2557	15798

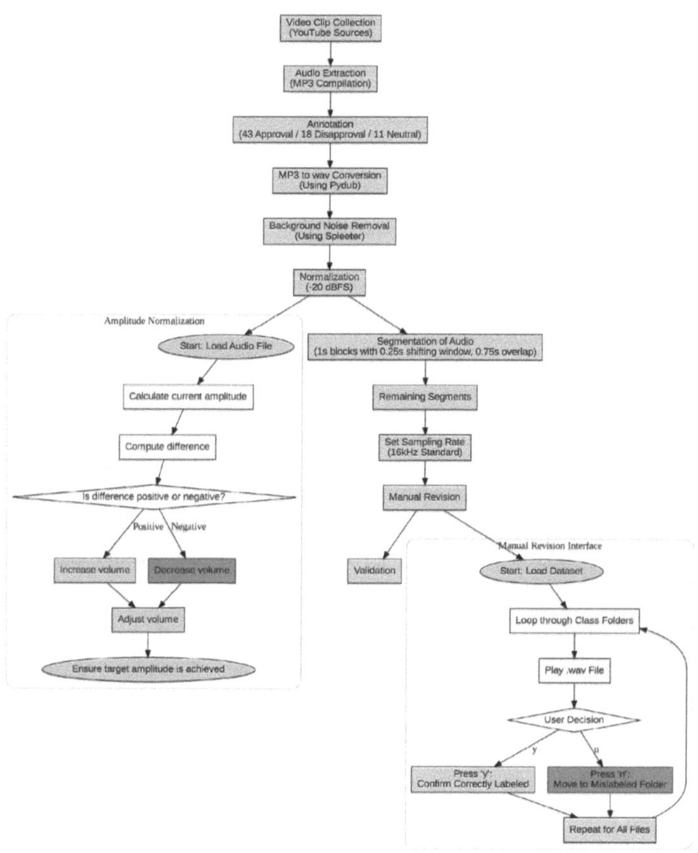

Fig. 1. Dataset Creation Process Flow

extracted from 15798 audio files, while 13 MFCC features, 12 Chroma features and 128 Mel features (See Fig. 2).

With this classification approach, 12 experiments were conducted to determine the optimal MIR-based classification model. Here, all the experiments were evaluated using evaluation metrics, accuracy, precision, recall, and F1-score. A confusion matrix was also used to assess class-wise performance and to provide a clearer picture of how well the model distinguished between the different emotions. The model was evaluated using five-fold stratified cross-validation. An 80:20 split was applied within each fold to ensure the model's robustness.

Music Information Retrieval(MIR). Music Information Retrieval (MIR) is a technique used to extract and interpret meaningful features from music [18]. MIR is not just about extracting features from music, but also about the various aspects of music analysis that can be performed using Music Information Retrieval Techniques. Genre identification, emotion detection, music recommendation, and many more applications related to MIR [19]. Typically, MIR techniques can be utilized to extract multifaceted aspects such as pitch, temporal, harmonic, timbral, editorial, and textual.

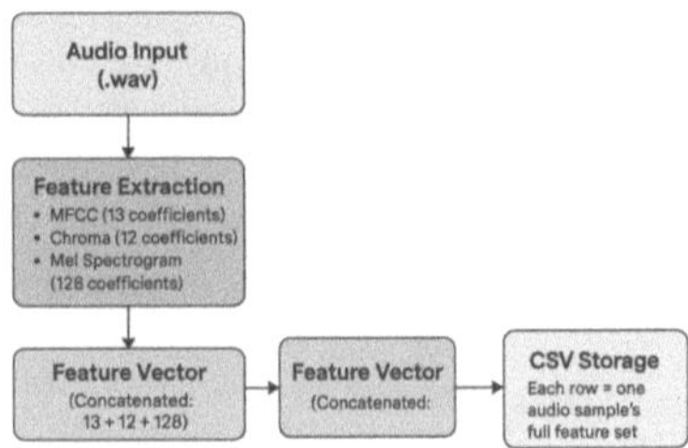

Fig. 2. MIR Workflow

MFCC. Extracts features of MFCC commonly used in speech and audio analysis and demonstrates their success. MFCC captures the timbral texture of the sound, which can be useful for identifying different crowd emotions [20]. MFCCs(Mel Frequency Cepstral Coefficients) were proposed by Paul Mermelstein and are widely used in automatic speech recognition [21].

Chroma Features. Chroma characteristics help detect tonal shifts in speech because they represent audio according to the 12 different pitches. The main reason for choosing chroma features is that pitch changes are frequently a part of emotions, and chroma features help identify these variations [22].

Mel Spectrum. When a sound wave is filtered through Mel-Filters, it is referred to as the Mel-Spectrum. By performing spectrum analysis on the Mel spectrum, the Mel frequency spectrum coefficient can be obtained [23]. Mel Spectrum provides a time-frequency representation with perceptually scaled frequency bins, allowing it to accurately extract and represent lower frequencies [20].

TabNet Model. In this study, the TabNet model employed an architecture comprising an Input Layer, a Feature Transformer Block, an Attentive Transformer Block, Decision Steps, and an Output Layer. TabNet can handle tabularized audio features with an attention mechanism that highlights the most important inputs while maintaining interpretability. The input layer accepts the standardized tabular data, and each feature is treated as a separate attribute in the dataset. The Feature Transformer Block is composed of a Shared Transformer and a Decision Transformer. The Shared transformer is a fully connected block that processes input features, where it includes a ReLU Activation function, batch normalization, and dropout. Then the outputs were fed to the Decision Transformer; hence, the feature embeddings were passed through separate decision layers that generate task-specific feature representations. Afterwards, in the Attentive Transformer Block, attention mechanisms were applied to select the most relevant features for the current decision step. Here, Sparsemax was used to enforce sparsity, which facilitates building a subset of features. During the Decision Step, dynamically selected features from attentive transformers were used for learning task-specific representations. In this case, n_steps = 3. Further, residual connections were allowed, so the model can acquire information from previous steps. Finally, the output was fed to the Output Layer. At this layer, it combined the outputs of Decision Steps into a final prediction using a fully connected layer. The Sparsemax activation function was used, similar to the traditional SoftMax, but using output sparse probabilities [24].

LightGBM. Boosting algorithms continue to offer notable advantages, particularly in scenarios involving limited training data, constrained computational time, and minimal need for parameter tuning. One such method, the Gradient Boosting Machine (GBM). It can be considered an efficient boosting framework based on tree-based learning [25]. It minimizes prediction error by optimizing a chosen loss function through gradient descent, leveraging weak learners, typically regression trees. Unlike other tree-based models, LightGBM does not grow into a very large-scale architecture by promising the fastest and accurate results. LightGBM introduces a more efficient, tree-based learning approach. It is designed for scalability, offering low memory usage, high-speed training, parallel processing capabilities, and improved efficiency via histogram-based binning of continuous features [23, 26]. The LightGBM model was configured for a three-class classification task. The multi-log loss metric was used to evaluate performance. Gradient Boosting Decision Trees (GBDT) was employed as the boosting technique. A learning rate of 0.05 was applied during initial training. The number of leaves was set to 31, while the feature fraction and bagging fraction were set to 0.9 and 0.8, respectively, to enhance regularization and reduce overfitting. Bagging was performed every 5 iterations, and a random seed of 42 was used to ensure reproducibility. A total of 100 trees were trained as estimators. In the final stage, an additional learning rate of 0.1 was introduced to fine-tune the model. The maximum depth of each tree was limited to 7 to control model complexity.

Multi-layer Perceptron. A Multilayer Perceptron (MLP) was implemented as a baseline neural network architecture for classifying audio-based emotional features. As MLP is simpler and more computationally efficient than deeper architectures, such as CNNs, it is ideal for tasks like audio classification. It was structured with an input layer, two hidden layers, and an output layer [27]. The input layer was configured to receive a fixed-length feature vector, typically composed of acoustic descriptors such as MFCCs, Chroma, and Mel energies. Each neuron was fully connected to neurons in the adjacent layers, and non-linear transformations were applied using ReLU activation functions.

The two hidden layers were composed of 128 neurons in the first layer and 64 neurons in the second. The output layer was activated using the SoftMax function to support multi-class classification. During training, forward propagation was conducted to generate predictions, and the error was computed using the categorical cross-entropy loss function. This loss was minimized through backpropagation, and weights and biases were iteratively updated using the 'AM' solver over a maximum of 300 iterations. A random state of 42 was set to ensure reproducibility.

4 Experiments and Results

The experiments summarized in Table 3 were conducted using MIR as the primary feature extraction technique, with PCA applied in certain cases. Various classification algorithms were employed, and the validation accuracy of each model was used as the primary evaluation metric.

The results of all 12 experiments are not included separately; instead, only the best-performing model is presented. The results for Experiment 09 are presented in Fig. 3, which includes the validation accuracy across five folds, the confusion matrix, and the ROC curve for the best-performing model, while Table 4 summarizes the precision, recall, F1-score, and support for each class.

4.1 Overall Experiment Results

Table 3. Overall Experiment Results

Experiment Number	Dataset	Dimensionality reduction technique	Classification technique	Validation Accuracy (%)
Experiment 01	SLCSED	-	TabNet	97.12
Experiment 02	SLCSED	PCA	TabNet	90.70
Experiment 03	SLCSED	-	LightGBM	99.40
Experiment 04	SLCSED	PCA	LightGBM	98.58
Experiment 05	SLCSED	-	MLP	99.53
Experiment 06	SLCSED	PCA	MLP	99.40
Experiment 07	ECSD	-	TabNet	97.48
Experiment 08	ECSD	PCA	TabNet	93.17
Experiment 09	ECSD	-	**LightGBM**	**99.95**
Experiment 10	ECSD	PCA	LightGBM	99.68
Experiment 11	ECSD	-	**MLP**	**99.95**
Experiment 12	ECSD	PCA	MLP	99.95

Table 4. Precision, Recall, F1 score, and Support for Experiment 09

	Precision	Recall	F1 score	Support
Approval	1.00	1.00	1.00	357
Disapproval	1.00	0.99	0.99	78
Neutral	1.00	1.00	1.00	1468

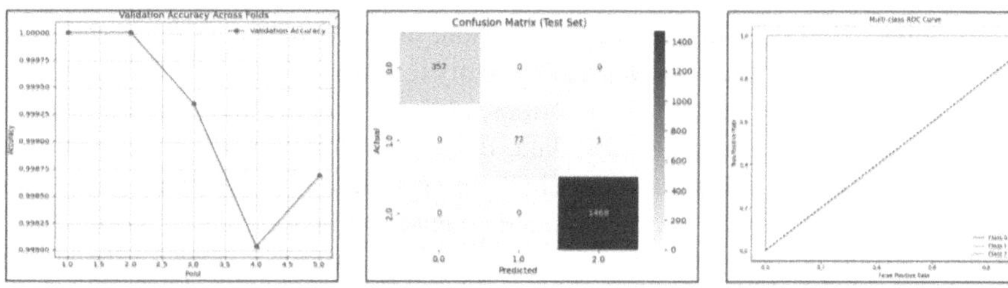

Fig. 3. Validation accuracy, confusion matrix, ROC Curve for Experiment 09

4.2 Results Compared with Classifiers, Datasets, and PCA Applicability

The choice of classifier significantly influences performance outcomes. Multi-Layer Perceptron (MLP) consistently performed at the highest level across most settings, especially with MIR features, achieving up to 99.95% accuracy. LightGBM was another strong performer, particularly with MIR features on both datasets, showing robustness and high accuracy even without dimensionality reduction. TabNet, however, lagged with lower accuracy (especially with PCA), indicating it may be less suited for these types of tasks or sensitive to feature preprocessing (See fig. 4).

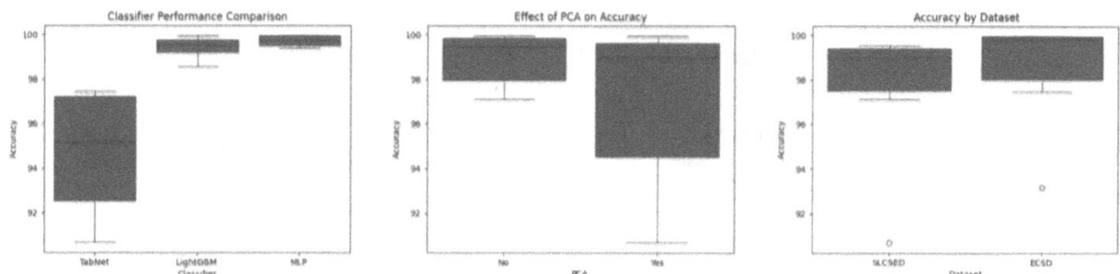

Fig. 4. Performance comparison box plots

Principal Component Analysis (PCA) has a varied impact depending on the feature type and classification model used. For TabNet, it always has lower accuracy compared to others. But when using these experiments with MIR, it seems that PCA reduced the performance of the classifiers. In some cases, such as MIR with TabNet, PCA reduced performance (97.12% to 90.70%). Similarly, MIR with LightGBM saw a decline with PCA. These findings suggest that while PCA can be crucial for some feature types, it may not universally enhance performance and can even be detrimental when applied to already well-structured features (See fig. 4). The ECSD dataset was shown to give high model accuracy compared to SLCSED. Most experiments using ECSD achieved over 99% accuracy, except for TabNet. This suggests that ECSD might be cleaner, better balanced, or easier for models to learn. However, because results were so consistent, the dataset may not fully test how models handle more difficult or messy data (See fig. 4). Although SLCSED was created from real crowd events in Sri Lanka, its performance is comparable to that achieved on the established ECSD dataset. This demonstrates that the proposed method generalizes well while also validating the quality and representativeness of the newly developed SLCSED dataset. In comparison, the SLCSED dataset produced the same trend of results. But the accuracies are slightly less compared to the ECSD dataset. As SLCSED includes a wider range of emotions, more speaker diversity, or less cleaning, which can make it more like real-world data. Because of this, it was considered better for testing how models perform in more challenging situations. Specifically, it is more suited, as most of the time, the crowd sounds cannot be heard clearly. While ECSD helped show strong performance, SLCSED was seen as more valuable for developing models that are reliable and flexible in different conditions.

4.3 Comparison of SLCSED with Other Available Datasets

The SLCSED dataset (see Table 5) stands out for its large size and relatively balanced class distribution, containing 15,798 samples across Approval (5813), Disapproval (4872), and Neutral (5113) classes. Compared to other datasets like ECSD, ESLCE, and SCED, which exhibit significant class imbalances and smaller sizes, SLCSED provides a more even representation of crowd sentiments. This balance helps reduce bias during model training and improves classification performance across all classes. Additionally, the substantial size of SLCSED supports the development of robust and generalizable models capable of capturing diverse emotional expressions in crowds, making it a valuable resource for emotion recognition research.

Table 5. Comparison of SLCSED with other available datasets

Class	ECSD	ESLCE	SCED	SLCSED(This Study)
Approval(Positive)	1787	3596	909	5813
Disapproval(Negative)	388	1160	919	4872
Neutral	7340	2962	905	5113
Total	9515	7718	2733	15798

4.4 Performance Comparison with the Existing Literature

This study outperformed the existing literature by achieving an accuracy of 99.95%, surpassing the previously reported highest accuracy of 99.83%(see Table 6).

Table 6. Performance Comparison with the Existing Literature

Study	Dataset	Best Classifier	Best performance
[13]	CSD v1	AlexNet	98.54%
[9]	ECSD	AlexNet	99.83%
[1]	ESLCE	Random Forest	81.20%
[12]	SCED	SVM	97.22%
[11]	ESLCE/ ECSD	2D CNN	95.34%
This study	**ECSD/ SLCSED**	**LightGBM / MLP**	**99.95%**

4.5 Performance Comparison with the ECSD Dataset

Table 7 presents the performance of various models evaluated in this study on the widely used ECSD dataset. The proposed method achieved the highest performance (99.95%) using MIR techniques combined with LightGBM and the MLP classifier.

Table 7. Performance Comparison with ECSD dataset

Study	Feature Extraction Method	PCA	Classifier	Accuracy
[9, 17]	Spectrogram	-	AlexNet	99.83%
[11]	zero-crossing rate, RMS,Spectral centroid, Spectral bandwidth etc	PCA	SVM	91.15%
		PCA	RF	92.65%
		PCA	KNN	85.11%
		PCA	1D CNN	96.65%
	Spectrogram	-	2D CNN	95.34%
		-	Transformer	89.86%
This study	MIR (Mel, MFCC, Chroma)	-	TabNet	97.48%
		PCA	TabNet	93.17%
		-	**LightGBM**	**99.95%**
		PCA	LightGBM	99.68%
		-/PCA	**MLP**	**99.95%**

5 Conclusion

The best-performing model in this study was identified as the configuration using MIR features without PCA, combined with the MLP classifier. This setup consistently achieved the highest accuracy across both evaluated datasets. A peak accuracy of 99.95% was obtained, surpassing the previously reported maximum of 99.83% in the existing literature. The combination of MIR features with LightGBM and the MLP classifier demonstrated outstanding performance, confirming the robustness and effectiveness of the proposed approach. While the reported improvements may appear less than 1%, they are consistent across multiple experiments and datasets, which demonstrates the robustness of the proposed method. The contribution of this work is not limited to accuracy alone. By incorporating MIR-based features with PCA, the approach reduces computational complexity, integrates domain knowledge, and provides greater interpretability, making it more practical for real-world deployment. The dataset used in this study is relatively balanced, includes real-life audio data, and comprises a large and diverse collection of crowd emotion sounds. It is expected to serve as a valuable resource for future research in the domain of crowd emotion recognition.

As a limitation, although two classifiers achieved similarly high accuracy, the final selection was not based on considerations of time complexity and resource consumption, factors that are critical for practical deployment. The dataset is geographically and culturally specific, which strengthens contextual insights but may limit generalizability beyond this setting. Future work is planned to explore mixed-signal analysis to further improve generalizability and performance across a wider range of real-world scenarios and to explore crowd sound emotions using a multimodal approach.

Disclosure of Interest. The authors have no competing interests to declare that are relevant to the content of this article.

References

1. Atick Faisal, M.A., Ahmed, M.U., Rahman Ahad, M.A.: ESLCE: a dataset of emotional sounds from large crowd events. In: 2021 Joint 10th International Conference on Informatics, Electronics & Vision (ICIEV) and 2021 5th International Conference on Imaging, Vision & Pattern Recognition (icIVPR). IEEE (2021)
2. Adolphs, R., Mlodinow, L., Barrett, L.F.: What is an emotion? Curr. Biol. **29**, R1060–R1064 (2019). https://doi.org/10.1016/j.cub.2019.09.008
3. UWA: Science of emotion: The basics of emotional psychology. https://online.uwa.edu/news/emotional-psychology
4. Han, D., Kong, Y., Han, J., Wang, G.: A survey of music emotion recognition. Front. Comp. Sci. **16** (2022). https://doi.org/10.1007/s11704-021-0569-4
5. An, X.D., Ruan, Z.: Speech emotion recognition algorithm based on deep learning algorithm fusion of temporal and spatial features. J. Phys. Conf. Ser. **1861**(1), 012064 (2021). https://doi.org/10.1088/1742-6596/1861/1/012064
6. Uddin, M.Z., Nilsson, E.G.: Emotion recognition using speech and neural structured learning to facilitate edge intelligence. Eng. Appl. Artif. Intell. **94**, 103775 (2020). https://doi.org/10.1016/j.engappai.2020.103775
7. Radocy, R.E., Boyle, J.D.: Psychological Foundations of Musical Behavior, 5th edn. Charles C Thomas Publisher (2012)
8. Soleymani, M., Lichtenauer, J., Pun, T., Pantic, M.: A multimodal database for affect recognition and implicit tagging. IEEE Trans. Affect. Comput. **3**, 42–55 (2012). https://doi.org/10.1109/t-affc.2011.25

9. Franzoni, V., Biondi, G., Milani, A.: Emotional sounds of crowds: spectrogram-based analysis using deep learning. Multimed. Tools Appl. **79**, 36063–36075 (2020). https://doi.org/10.1007/s11042-020-09428-x
10. Araño, K.A., Gloor, P., Orsenigo, C., Vercellis, C.: When old meets new: emotion recognition from speech signals. Cogn. Comput. **13**, 771–783 (2021). https://doi.org/10.1007/s12559-021-09865-2
11. Veltmeijer, E.A.: Small Groups, Big Insights: Understanding the Crowd through Expressive Subgroup Analysis, (2024)
12. Xu, L., Yildiz, A.M., Tuncer, I., Ozyurt, F., Dogan, S., Tuncer, T.: Detection of community emotions through sound: An investigation using the FF-orbital chaos-based feature extraction model. Ain Shams Eng. J. **16**, 103248 (2025). https://doi.org/10.1016/j.asej.2024.103248
13. Franzoni, V., Biondi, G., Milani, A.: Crowd emotional sounds: spectrogram-based analysis using convolutional neural network. 32–36 (2019)
14. Figueiredo, A.C.A., Bizarro, J.P.S.: JET EFDA contributors: on limitations of the spectrogram in the representation of the amplitude of nonstationary fusion plasma signals. Rev. Sci. Instrum. **77** (2006). https://doi.org/10.1063/1.2220002
15. Martella, C., Li, J., Conrado, C., Vermeeren, A.: On current crowd management practices and the need for increased situation awareness, prediction, and intervention. Saf. Sci. **91**, 381–393 (2017). https://doi.org/10.1016/j.ssci.2016.09.006
16. Kawahara, M., Sauter, D.A., Tanaka, A.: Culture shapes emotion perception from faces and voices: changes over development. Cognit. Emot. **35**, 1175–1186 (2021). https://doi.org/10.1080/02699931.2021.1922361
17. Franzoni, V., Biondi, G., Milani, A.: Emotional Crowd Sound. IEEE DataPort. (25 Feb 2021). https://doi.org/10.21227/XXWY-5869
18. Choi, K., Fazekas, G., Cho, K., Sandler, M.: A tutorial on deep learning for Music Information Retrieval (2017). http://arxiv.org/abs/1709.04396
19. Koparde, S., Bhadgaonkar, V.R., Patil, K.N., Basutkar, G.N., Gayke, D.D.: A survey on music genre classification using machine learning. (n.d.)
20. The cepstrum, mel-cepstrum and mel-frequency cepstral coefficients (MFCCs)—Introduction to Speech Processing. [Online]. Available: https://speechprocessingbook.aalto.fi/Representations/Melcepstrum.html. Accessed 05 Sept 2025
21. Mel Frequency Cepstral Coefficient – an overview. ScienceDirect Topics. [Online]. Available: https://www.sciencedirect.com/topics/computer-science/mel-frequency-cepstral-coefficient. Accessed 23 Apr 2025
22. Build a sentiment analysis model with audio data. GeeksProgramming. [Online]. Available: https://geeksprogramming.com/building-a-sentiment-analysis-model-with-audio-data/. Accessed 25 Apr 2025
23. Yu, J., Qu, Y., Zhang, Z., Lu, Q., Qin, Z., Liu, X.: Speech recognition based on concatenated acoustic feature and LightGBM model. In: Tian, J., Mao, K., Qian, D., Xie, Y., Lyu, Y. (eds.) Twelfth International Conference on Signal Processing Systems. SPIE (2021)
24. Martins, A.F.T., Astudillo, R.F.: From softmax to sparsemax: A sparse model of attention and multi-label classification (2016). http://arxiv.org/abs/1602.02068
25. Ong, K.L., Lee, C.P., Lim, H.S., Lim, K.M.: Speech emotion recognition with light gradient boosting decision trees machine. Int. J. Electr. Comput. Eng. (IJECE). **13**, –4020 (2023). https://doi.org/10.11591/ijece.v13i4.pp4020-4028
26. Khan, I., et al.: Multi-layer perceptron-based emotional speech recognition. Hunan Daxue Xuebao. **60**(1) (2023)
27. Atmaja, B.T., Akagi, M.: Deep multilayer perceptrons for dimensional speech emotion recognition (2020). http://arxiv.org/abs/2004.02355

Genetic Algorithm Based Deep Time Series Similarity Searching Approach for Acoustic Fingerprinting

Chinthana Rathnayake, Manjusri Wickramasinghe, Isuru Nanayakkara(✉), Roshan Abeyweera, and Pasindu Marasinghe

University of Colombo School of Computing, Colombo, Sri Lanka
{mie,nhp,rns,ppm}@ucsc.cmb.ac.lk

Abstract. With the exponential growth in music consumption, the demand for robust audio identification systems has intensified, especially for copyright detection and content-based retrieval. Acoustic fingerprinting, which identifies audio using unique spectral features, is a core technique in this domain. In this study, we propose a novel Deep Time Series Similarity Searching (DTSSS) framework for audio fingerprinting, leveraging a Long Short-Term Memory (LSTM)-based Siamese Neural Network. A key innovation of this work is the integration of a Genetic Algorithm (GA) to optimize hyperparameters critical to model performance. To enhance robustness, audio degradations such as noise, pitch, and tempo alterations were applied during data augmentation. The proposed system significantly outperforms the Shazam algorithm, achieving an accuracy of **64.44%** compared to Shazam's **21.22%** on the same dataset of degraded audio. This result highlights the potential of combining deep learning with evolutionary optimization for high-fidelity, real-world audio retrieval systems.

Keywords: Music Information Retrieval · Acoustic Fingerprinting · Genetic Algorithm · Hyperparameter Optimization

1 Introduction

The exponential growth of digital audio content has intensified the need for robust and scalable methods to organize, identify, and retrieve music and audio data. In this context, Music Information Retrieval (MIR) has emerged as a critical research domain that studies methods for retrieving, analyzing, and organizing musical audio data [18]. A core MIR task is acoustic or audio fingerprinting, where a short audio clip is converted into a compact "fingerprint" that can be efficiently matched to a database for identification and retrieval [5,18]. For example, audio fingerprinting systems such as Shazam and SoundHound extract spectro-temporal features like Bark or Mel-frequency cepstral coefficients from the audio and encode them as bitstrings. These bitstring fingerprints are then compared using Hamming distance searches against a database that already

R. N. Rajapakse et al. (Eds.): ICTer 2025, CCIS 2844, pp. 380–395, 2026.
https://doi.org/10.1007/978-981-92-0137-2_25

contains fingerprints and metadata to identify high degrees of similarity [5]. The system then returns a list of potential matches, ranked by similarity scores. These systems enable users to accurately identify audio segments, even when no textual or other descriptive metadata is available. Such systems should also be able to tolerate noise, distortions, and temporal misalignments in real-world recordings.

Audio signals can be represented as time series; therefore, measuring similarity between time series known as Time Series Similarity Searching (TSSS), is fundamental in Music Information Retrieval (MIR). Traditional time series similarity methods rely on elastic alignment techniques like Dynamic Time Warping (DTW), which finds an optimal alignment between two sequences to minimize distance under allowable warps [11]. However, recently, deep neural networks-based TSSS approaches, also known as Deep Time Series Similarity Searching (DTSSS), have shown promising results that surpass those of the DTW algorithm, which is widely accepted by the research community as one of the top-performing algorithms in terms of accuracy [11,13]. In DTSSS models, the network automatically learns features and matching criteria, potentially improving robustness and retrieval accuracy over hand-crafted distance measures. Most recent studies often focus on learned similarity measures, particularly deep metric learning approaches such as Siamese neural networks, to project time series inputs into a latent embedding space where geometric distance reflects similarity. A Siamese network processes a pair of audio clips through twin subnetworks (sharing weights), and is trained to pull embeddings of matching audio together while pushing non-matching embeddings apart [11].

DTSS models have many hyperparameters (e.g. learning rates, network depth, filter sizes, regularization strengths). Selecting these hyperparameters is critical but challenging; the optimal configurations can significantly impact model performance. Hyperparameter tuning is essentially a black box optimization problem over a complex and high-dimensional space [2,22]. Bergstra and Bengio (2012) showed that a randomized search strategy typically finds good settings far more efficiently than exhaustive grid search for deep networks [2]. Additionally, Bayesian optimization (e.g. Gaussian-process tuning) and evolutionary algorithms also can be applied for hyperparameter tuning. Genetic Algorithms (GAs), a type of evolutionary algorithm, evolve a population of candidate configurations through selection, crossover, and mutation. GAs have been effective for hyperparameter tuning in various domains [22]. Even though GAs are computationally expensive, they can be used to search for a wide variety of different combinations of hyperparameters that help to avoid getting stuck in poor local optima [9,22]. In this work, we investigate the use of a genetic algorithm (GA) to optimise the hyperparameters of a deep time series similarity model for acoustic fingerprinting, with the goal of automating model configurations to improve retrieval performance.

2 Literature Review

This section reviews key literature relevant to this study, spanning the fields of Music Information Retrieval (MIR), acoustic fingerprinting, and time series similarity search. It highlights the evolution from traditional signal processing methods to deep learning-based approaches, with a focus on Deep Time Series Similarity Searching (DTSSS). Additionally, it discusses the critical role of hyperparameter optimization in deep learning models and surveys the use of Genetic Algorithms (GAs) as a promising yet underexplored strategy for improving model performance in this context.

2.1 Music Information Retrieval and Acoustic Fingerprinting

Audio fingerprinting is a classic MIR task focused on high-specificity matching (identifying the exact recording or cover of a song [18]). These systems extract a compact digital summary or "fingerprint" from an audio signal, capturing key features such as frequency and time patterns. This fingerprint can then be compared against an extensive database to identify the track, even if it is distorted, noisy, or recorded from a different source. Audio fingerprinting is commonly used in music recognition apps (like Shazam), copyright enforcement, and broadcast monitoring. Early robust fingerprinting systems relied on signal processing features and hashing. For example, Haitsma et al. proposed one of the first highly robust audio fingerprinting schemes, using overlapping short-time Bark-cepstral coefficients and hashing them into 32-bit fingerprints for efficient Hamming-distance matching [5]. Subsequent work has built on this foundation, and such studies include using AdaBoost on spectrogram features or wavelet minhash schemes [5]. Wang's industrial-strength Shazam algorithm [14] uses a landmark-based method that examines spectral peaks. In all cases, the fingerprint goal is to create a compact, robust representation that enables very fast matching, even in the presence of noise and distortions.

2.2 Time-Series Similarity Searching

More broadly, similarity search over time series has been extensively studied in the fields of data mining and pattern recognition. Classic algorithms include DTW and its variants (e.g. Time Warp Edit Distance) to handle temporal misalignments [11]. These non-parametric measures align sequences to minimize distance but require computing pairwise alignments. In contrast, learned approaches have gained popularity. The deep metric-learning paradigm uses siamese or triplet networks to learn an embedding space for similarity: given training examples of "same" and "different" time series, the network is trained so that similar series map to nearby vectors [11]. The NeuralWarp model [11] explicitly incorporates a learned warping mechanism between deep-encoded series to align them in latent space. In the audio domain, deep embedding methods have been applied to related tasks such as cover song retrieval, query-by-humming, and sound event matching. These efforts show that deep models can capture high-level similarity beyond raw alignment.

2.3 Hyperparameter Optimization in Deep Learning

Selecting hyperparameters (learning rates, layer sizes, etc.) is crucial in deep learning. Bergstra et al. demonstrated that random search often outperforms grid search for neural network hyperparameters [2]. Other adaptive methods include Bayesian optimization (using surrogate models to guide search) and Hyperband (successive halving). Surveys of hyperparameter optimization note that methods range from simple heuristics to complex sequential-model-based searches [2,22]. Evolutionary approaches are also recognized: Vincent and Jidesh (2023) summarize that evolutionary algorithms (including GAs) are effective for hyperparameter tuning when the search space is large or expensive to evaluate [22]. Indeed, contemporary AutoML frameworks often include GA or Covariance Matrix Adaptation Evolution Strategies (CMA-ES) components alongside Bayesian methods. In short, hyperparameter tuning is an active area of research, and GAs are a viable class of optimizers within that domain [22].

2.4 Genetic Algorithms for Model Optimization

Genetic algorithms have been applied to deep learning both for architecture search and hyperparameter tuning. In neural architecture search (NAS), population-based GAs like NSGA-Net evolve network architectures to optimize accuracy and complexity; NSGA-Net found competitive CNN designs on CIFAR-10 using significantly less compute than many other NAS methods [16]. In hyperparameter tuning, GAs have been used to evolve parameters such as learning rates, regularization strengths, and layer widths. Studies report that GA-based search can outperform naive strategies, though it typically requires careful parameterization of the GA itself (population size, mutation rate) and can be computationally intensive [9,17,22]. For example, Puentes et al. (2022) observed that GAs consume more resources than random search or Bayesian methods but provided a guided search that yielded high-accuracy configurations [9]. The proposed work builds on these foundations by employing a genetic algorithm (GA) to tune a deep time-series similarity model for audio retrieval. We leverage the GA's ability to explore complex hyperparameter spaces to enhance the model's fingerprinting accuracy.

3 Methodology

This section discusses the construction of the proposed audio fingerprinting model, including the optimisation of the DTSSS model's performance using GA, and a comparison of its performance against the well-known and widely used Shazam algorithm.

3.1 System Architecture Overview

Figure 1 illustrates the high-level architecture of the proposed audio fingerprinting model.

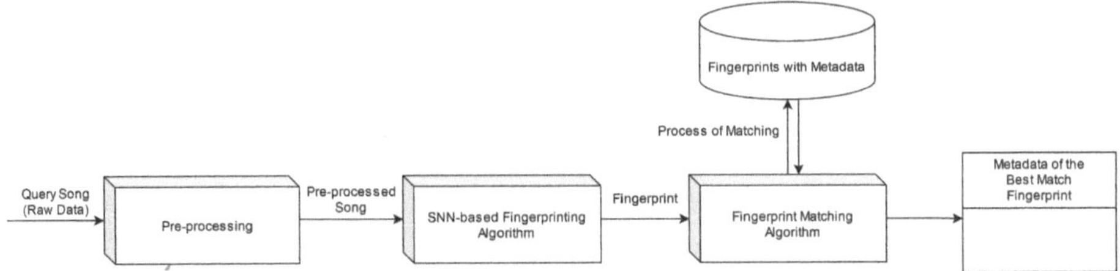

Fig. 1. High-level architecture of the proposed audio fingerprinting model.

- **Audio Preprocessing Component:** The first component of the model is the audio preprocessing component, which transforms raw audio data into a vector representation that can be fed to a neural network. This process is essential for extracting features from the audio signal and preparing it for further processing. Design and implementation aspects of the component will be further discussed in Sect. 3.5.
- **The Database:** The database contains a pre-prepared set of audio fingerprints of the original audio, along with associated metadata, which uses the same preprocessing component and Siamese neural network-based audio fingerprinting algorithm employed for fingerprint matching.
- **Fingerprint Matching Algorithm:** Once a fingerprint of the audio is obtained, it is compared against all audio fingerprints in the database, and the metadata of the best-matching fingerprint is returned.
- **SNN-based Audio Fingerprinting Algorithm:** The final component of the model is the Siamese neural network-based audio fingerprinting algorithm, which generates a unique fingerprint for each audio signal. The neural network's final hidden layer representation is derived as the fingerprint for the given query audio by propagating it through the neural network.

3.2 Model Optimization

As mentioned earlier, selecting optimal hyperparameters is crucial for achieving the best performance in Deep Time Series Similarity Searching (DTSSS) models. Poor parameter selection can result in low accuracy and the retrieval of irrelevant data. Although previous studies [1,8,21] have shown the success of Genetic Algorithm (GA) in optimizing the performance of Deep Neural Networks (DNNs), no research has explored the potential of GA in improving the performance of DTSSS models. To address this, experiment 4.1 was conducted to investigate whether GA can enhance the performance of the best Siamese Neural Network (SNN) model selected in the above section. Results of the experiment are presented in Sect. 5.1. Relevant experimental results are presented in Sect. 5.1, indicating that the GA was able to identify a set of hyperparameters that improve the performance of the DTSSS model. Therefore, this improved Short-Term Memory (LSTM)-based SNN was integrated into the proposed audio fingerprinting model.

3.3 Fingerprint Matching Algorithm

In an SNN-based audio fingerprinting algorithm, the fingerprint of the query song must be computed before identifying the best-matching song. This fingerprint is then compared against all fingerprints in the database to determine the closest match based on a distance metric, such as Euclidean distance. This process is known as fingerprint matching. However, an issue arises when a queried song is not present in the database, as the system still returns a best match regardless. Therefore, a thresholding mechanism is required to address such scenarios. Specifically, a threshold must be defined such that a fingerprint is considered the best match only if it is closest to the query fingerprint, and the corresponding distance is below the specified threshold. Accordingly, experiment 4.2 was designed to determine a suitable threshold. The results of this experiment are presented in Sect. 5.2.

3.4 Effectiveness of the Proposed Model in Audio Fingerprinting

Once a threshold is defined, the model's effectiveness can be evaluated utilizing the selected threshold. Hence, the experiment 4.3 was conducted to evaluate the performance of the proposed model against the Dejavu [7] baseline, which is a similar open-source implementation of the powerful Shazam algorithm [14]. Section 5.3 presents these results.

3.5 Dataset Compilation and Preprocessing Pipeline

Dataset. To evaluate the proposed fingerprinting model, it was trained and tested on the Free Music Archive (FMA) [6]. This dataset is a collection of songs comprising 106,574 Creative Commons-licensed tracks from 16,341 artists, each with its metadata. To aid researchers with limited computational resources, the creators of the FMA dataset have also provided subsets of the data.

Data Preparation. To train and test the audio fingerprinting model, further preparation was necessary on the raw audio data obtained from the FMA dataset. The data preparation involved two steps:

- **Data Augmentations:** In audio fingerprinting, two audio segments are considered to be matching if and only if both audio segments are recordings of the same musical performance. Therefore, audio degradations commonly found in the literature [15,20] were applied to the original audio tracks to create an augmented set of audio tracks. Audio degradations or augmentations refer to the addition of noise, pitch variation, and tempo variation in songs. The model was trained and tested on augmented and original versions of songs to ensure the robustness of the audio fingerprinting model. Noise addition involved adding Gaussian noise to simulate the effect of unwanted background noise or interference typically present in real-world recordings. Additionally, eight factors of pitch and tempo augmentations were performed on the original audios, namely 0.2, 0.25, 0.33, 0.5, 2, 3, 4, and 5. The choice of these factors and audio degradations was inspired by works by [4] and limitations in human perception, as extreme audio degradations may result in inaudible or non-perceptible audio.

- **Data Preprocessing:** Audio fingerprinting is not performed directly on raw audio but on intermediate representations due to the high-dimensional nature of raw audio. Accordingly, Mel spectrogram features were extracted from the raw audio files and transformed into a uniform shape.

4 Experiments

This section provides a detailed description of the experiments conducted for each empirical investigation discussed in Sect. 3. Accordingly, the relevant experiments carried out for the construction of the proposed audio fingerprinting system and the performance comparison between the developed system and the Shazam algorithm are presented here.

4.1 Experiment I: Model Optimization

The objective of this experiment is to investigate whether GA can enhance the performance of the SNN model. The experiment is conducted by comparing the performance of LSTM-based SNN using a baseline set of hyperparameters against the performance using the optimal hyperparameters suggested by GA. The open-source Python GA library PyGAD [10], along with Python version 3.9.13, was used for the necessary implementations.

Selected Hyperparameter Set. The learning rate, dropout rate, optimizer, and the number of hidden neurons in each layer were selected from the LSTM hyperparameters for optimization using GA. These parameters were chosen due to the difficulty associated with manual tuning [17,19]. Furthermore, optimizing these hyperparameters can yield significant improvements in model performance, making them critical targets for optimization [12].

GA Configuration. The selected hyperparameters for optimization were included into a chromosome structure, as illustrated in Fig. 2. The Table 1 presents the range of possible values for each gene.

The genetic operator specification and implementation of this study were influenced by the work of both X.J. Luo *et al.* [17] and Salah Bouktif *et al.* [3]. X.J. Luo *et al.* [17] have demonstrated superior results in optimizing LSTM network hyperparameters using GA, surpassing well-known hyperparameter optimization techniques like Bayesian optimization. The roulette wheel selection and two-point crossover were selected for the study, as they had previously been shown to be effective in evolving LSTM hyperparameters [3]. The previous studies on LSTM hyperparameter optimization via GA did not provide clear guidance on effective mutation operators; thus, this study employed adaptive mutation as the mutation technique. Table 2 summarizes the chosen genetic operators for the hyperparameter optimization. The results of the experiments are presented in Sect. 5.1.

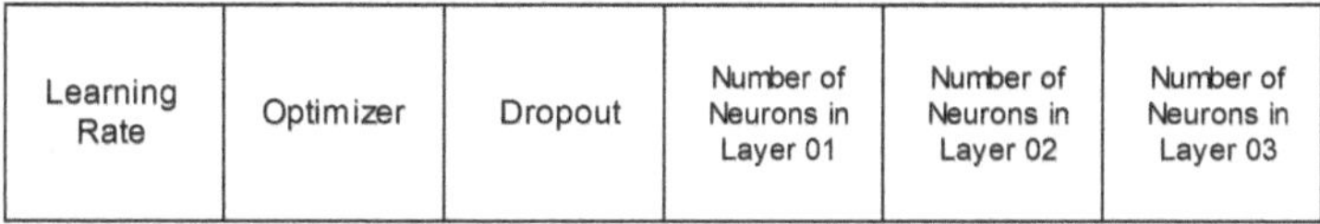

Fig. 2. Chromosome structure used for the hyperparameter optimization.

Table 1. The range of possible values for each gene

The Gene	Range of Possible Values
Learning Rate	0.001–1.0
Optimizer[a]	0–10
Dropout	0.2–0.5
Number of Neurons in Hidden Layer 01	1–512
Number of Neurons in Hidden Layer 02	1–256
Number of Neurons in Hidden Layer 03	1–128

[a]Each value corresponds to one of the optimizer from Ada-Grad, RMSprop, Adam, Adadelta, AdamW, Adamax, ASGD, Nadam, Radam, and Rprop

Table 2. GA Configuration for Hyperparameter Optimization

GA Setting	Value/Algorithm
Crossover	Two Points
Selection	Roulette Wheel
Mutation	Adaptive

4.2 Experiment II: Determining the Fingerprinting Threshold

This experiment was aimed at finding a suitable fingerprinting threshold to determine the best match for a given query audio fingerprint. A separate tune set was used to determine the suitable threshold, and a plot was generated to compare the different thresholds and their corresponding accuracies, allowing for the selection of the best suitable threshold. The results of the experiments are presented in Sect. 5.2.

4.3 Experiment III: Model Effectiveness as an Audio Fingerprinting System

In this final experiment, the effectiveness of the optimized model as a complete audio fingerprinting system was evaluated. Earlier assessments focused on measuring the model's ability to determine similarity between pairs of audio segments. However, to evaluate its performance as a fingerprinting system, the model was tested by querying various audio samples and assessing its ability to accurately recognize them. This required the establishment of a threshold, as discussed in Sect. 3.3, and based on this threshold, the model's effectiveness was evaluated. Simultaneously, Dejavu [7] baseline was set up, and its performance was evaluated following the same process by querying the same data. The results of both the proposed model and the Dejavu model are presented in Sect. 5.3.

5 Results

This section discusses the results of experiments conducted for the implementation of the proposed audio fingerprinting system. Additionally, it presents a performance comparison between the developed system and the Shazam algorithm.

5.1 Model Optimization

The GA was executed five times using the same configurations and methods described in Sect. 4.1 to optimize the selected hyperparameters, which is depicted in Table 3. The results of these iterations are summarized in Table 4. The best-performing set of parameters (from iteration 02) was selected, and a LSTM-SNN model was trained and tested using these parameters, with all other settings kept unchanged. The performance of this optimized model was compared to that of the baseline using the confusion matrix and Area Under the Curve (AUC). Figure 3 presents the confusion matrix results for each model, showing that the model trained using GA-optimized hyperparameters outperformed the baseline by increasing true positives and true negatives while decreasing false positives and false negatives. Table 5 summarizes the accuracy, precision, recall, and F1 score of each model, indicating that the model trained using GA-optimized hyperparameters performed better in each metric.

Figure 4 displays the Receiver Operating Characteristic Curve (ROC) curves for both models, and it can be observed that the model with GA-optimized hyperparameters achieved an AUC value of **0.96**, surpassing the AUC value of **0.91** obtained by the baseline. Therefore, it can be concluded that GA was able to identify a set of hyperparameters that improves the performance of the DTSSS model.

Table 3. Baseline hyperparameters for the LSTM-SNN model

Hyperparameter	Value
Learning Rate	0.001
Batch Size	30
Optimizer	Adam
Dropout	0.05
Architecture	[256, 128, 64]

Table 4. Individual with highest fitness in each GA iteration

Iteration	Hyperparameters				Fitness
	Learning Rate	Optimizer	Dropout	Architecture[a]	
1	0.073	Adamax	0.4896	[495,147,33]	0.7943
2	0.326	ASGD	0.4482	[165,147,78]	0.8017
3	0.488	RAdam	0.2103	[281,250,69]	0.7834
4	0.453	RAdam	0.1997	[281 243 78]	0.7878
5	0.318	ASGD	0.4516	[167 145 79]	0.8014

[a]List format: number of neurons in hidden layer 1, 2, and 3 respectively.

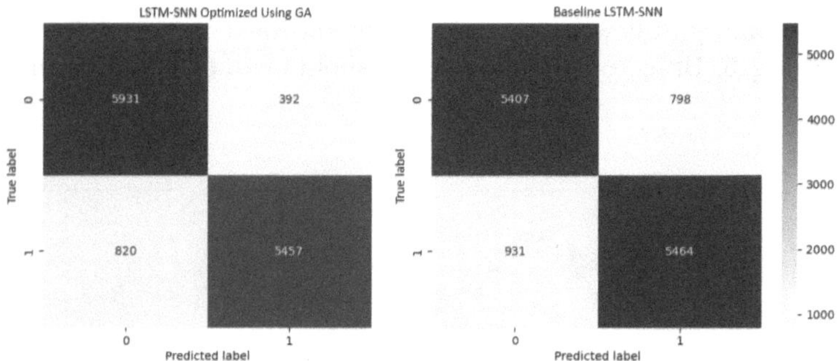

Fig. 3. Confusion Matrix Results of the Baseline LSTM-SNN and the GA-Optimized LSTM-SNN.

Table 5. Classification results of LSTM-SNN Optimized Using GA and Baseline LSTM-SNN

Evaluation Metric	LSTM-SNN Optimized	Baseline LSTM-SNN
Accuracy	90.38%	86.27%
Precision	93.29%	87.25%
Recall	86.93%	85.44%
F1 Score	90.00%	86.33%

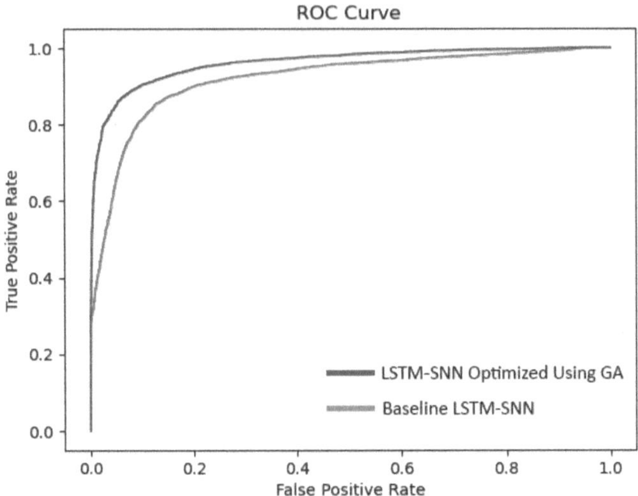

Fig. 4. ROC Curves of the Baseline LSTM-SNN and the GA-Optimized LSTM-SNN.

5.2 Threshold Selection for Audio Fingerprinting

This section presents the results of the experiment 4.2. In this experiment, a plot was generated to compare the various thresholds against their corresponding accuracy values, following the procedure specified in Sect. 4.2. The plot is depicted in Fig. 5. Based on the plot, a threshold of **0.44** was determined to be optimal.

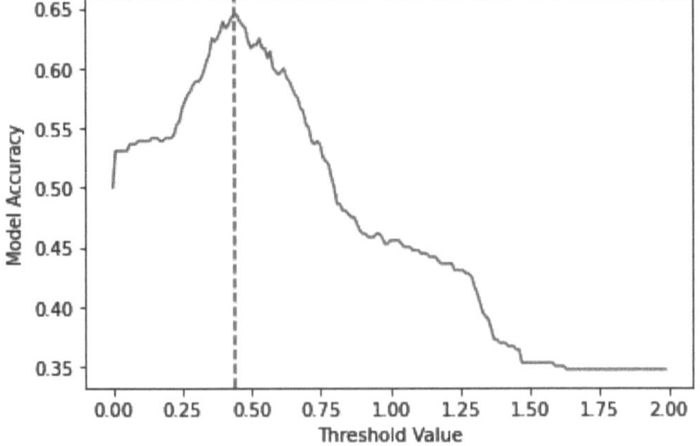

Fig. 5. Accuracy Variation with Respect to Threshold Values.

5.3 Model Effectiveness in Audio Fingerprinting

This section presents the results of the experiment 4.3. In this experiment, the effectiveness of the optimized model as an audio fingerprinting system was assessed. The model's effectiveness was evaluated by computing the confusion matrix using the selected best threshold. Simultaneously, Dejavu [7] baseline was set up, and its performance was evaluated in the same manner by querying the same data. The results of the confusion matrix for both proposed model and the Dejavu model are presented in Fig. 6, while Table 6 provides a summary of the accuracy, precision, recall, and F1 score for each model.

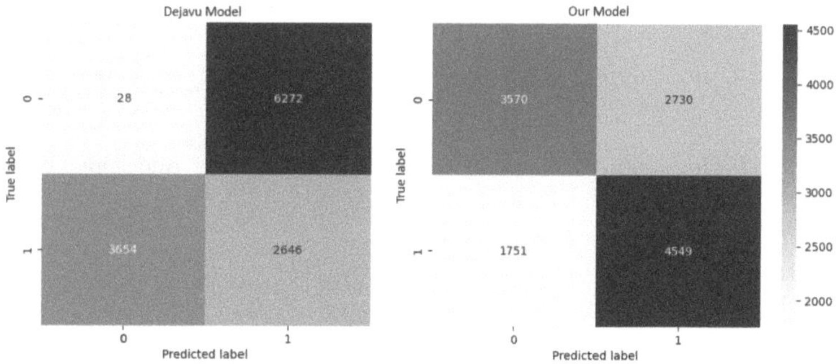

Fig. 6. Confusion Matrix Comparison Between the Proposed (our) Model and the Dejavu Model.

Table 6. Classification results of proposed model and Dejavu model

Evaluation Metric	Proposed Model	Dejavu Model
Accuracy	64.44%	21.22%
Precision	62.50%	29.67%
Recall	72.22%	42%
F1 Score	67.01%	34.77%

Furthermore, the hit rate of each model was evaluated for song variations to analyze the robustness of the models. Figure 7 displays the hit rate results of each model for each variation.

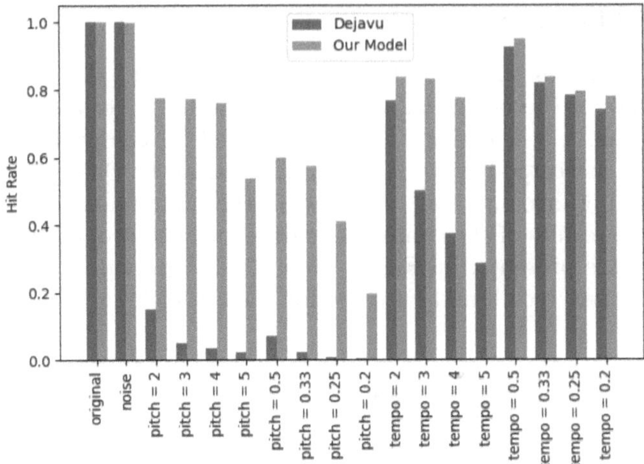

Fig. 7. Hit Rate Comparison of the Proposed (our) Model and the Dejavu Model Across Song Variations.

6 Discussion

The first key discovery of the study was that, GA-based hyperparameter optimization is able to enhance the performance of this LSTM-based SNN model. While the model with baseline hyperparameters achieved a **0.91** AUC performance, the model with optimal hyperparameters suggested by GA achieved an AUC performance of **0.96**. As indicated in Table 5, the model with optimal hyperparameters suggested by GA outperformed the model with baseline hyperparameters in terms of classification accuracy, precision, recall and F1 score. While the baseline hyperparameters were suggested by literature as the most effective, GA had identified a better set of hyperparameters for audio similarity searching in particular. This result highlights that the GA-based hyperparameter optimization had a positive impact on improving the performance of the model.

The second key finding is that the proposed audio fingerprinting system outperforms the powerful and widely used Shazam algorithm in terms of accuracy and robustness. The proposed model achieved an accuracy of **64.44%** compared to the **21.22%** accuracy of Shazam algorithm. Moreover, as presented in Table 6 proposed model outperformed the Shazam algorithm in terms of precision, recall and F1 score, indicating that the proposed model performs better than the Shazam algorithm in terms of making accurate predictions, correctly identifying positive samples, and avoiding false positives and false negatives. It can be noticed that, even though the GA-optimized LSTM-based SNN model showed an accuracy of **90.38%** for audio similarity searching when this model was integrated into the audio fingerprinting system to be used as an audio fingerprinting model, the classification accuracy had reduced to **64.44%**. The reason is that the model accuracy decreases when a query audio fingerprint is matched against a large corpus of fingerprints. Nonetheless, the proposed model still outperforms the accuracy of **21.22%** achieved by the Shazam algorithm for the same set of data. Moreover, as Fig. 7 depicts, both the proposed model and the Shazam algorithm are proficient in identifying original (songs without any augmentation) songs and noisy songs. However, the proposed model demonstrates greater robustness for both tempo and pitch augmentation. Specifically, the proposed model exhibits significantly better robustness for pitch augmentation compared to the Shazam algorithm.

7 Conclusion

This research presents a Genetic Algorithm-enhanced Deep Time Series Similarity Searching (DTSSS) approach for audio fingerprinting, specifically optimized using a Siamese LSTM architecture. Through rigorous experimentation, we demonstrated that GA-based hyperparameter tuning substantially improves the performance of the underlying neural model, achieving higher accuracy, precision, recall, and F1 scores compared to a baseline configuration. Moreover, when integrated into a complete audio fingerprinting pipeline, the proposed model significantly outperformed the Shazam algorithm on a challenging dataset with audio degradations, confirming its practical utility and robustness. Notably, the system showed strong resilience to pitch and tempo variations, two common challenges in real-world music identification tasks. These findings validate the synergy between evolutionary optimization and deep learning in building scalable and accurate content-based audio retrieval systems.

Disclosure of Interests. The authors declare that they have no competing interests or conflicts of interest related to the research, authorship, and/or publication of this paper.

References

1. Adhikary, S., Anwar, M.M., Chowdhury, M.J.M., Sarker, I.H.: Genetic algorithm-based optimal deep neural network for detecting network intrusions (2022). https://api.semanticscholar.org/CorpusID:246506505
2. Bergstra, J., Bengio, Y.: Random search for hyper-parameter optimization. J. Mach. Learn. Res. **13**, 281–305 (2012). https://api.semanticscholar.org/CorpusID:15700257
3. Bouktif, S., Fiaz, A., Ouni, A., Serhani, M.A.: Optimal deep learning LSTM model for electric load forecasting using feature selection and genetic algorithm: Comparison with machine learning approaches †. Energies **11**(7) (2018). https://doi.org/10.3390/en11071636, https://www.mdpi.com/1996-1073/11/7/1636
4. Báez-Suárez, A., Shah, N., Nolazco-Flores, J.A., Huang, S.H.S., Gnawali, O., Shi, W.: SAMAF. ACM Trans. Multimedia Comput. Commun. Appl. **16**, 1–23 (2020). https://doi.org/10.1145/3380828

5. Chandrasekhar, V.R., Sharifi, M., Ross, D.A.: Survey and evaluation of audio fingerprinting schemes for mobile query-by-example applications. In: International Society for Music Information Retrieval Conference (2011). https://api.semanticscholar.org/CorpusID:18100255
6. Defferrard, M., Benzi, K., Vandergheynst, P., Bresson, X.: FMA: a dataset for music analysis. In: 18th International Society for Music Information Retrieval Conference (ISMIR) (2017). https://arxiv.org/abs/1612.01840
7. Drevo, W.: Audio fingerprinting with Python and Numpy. https://willdrevo.com/fingerprinting-and-audio-recognition-with-python/. Accessed 07 June 2025
8. Feng, X., Zhao, J., Kita, E.: Genetic algorithm-based optimization of deep neural network ensemble. Rev. Socionetw. Strat. **15**, 27–47 (2021). https://api.semanticscholar.org/CorpusID:232201350
9. G., D.E.P., H., C.J.B., Navaux, P.O.A.: Hyperparameter optimization for convolutional neural networks with genetic algorithms and Bayesian optimization. In: 2022 IEEE Latin American Conference on Computational Intelligence (LA-CCI), pp. 1–5 (2022). https://api.semanticscholar.org/CorpusID:254931463
10. Gad, A.F.: PYGAD: an intuitive genetic algorithm python library (2021). https://doi.org/10.48550/ARXIV.2106.06158
11. Grabocka, J., Schmidt-Thieme, L.: NeuralWarp: time-series similarity with warping networks. ArXiv abs/1812.08306 (2018). https://api.semanticscholar.org/CorpusID:56517025
12. Greff, K., Srivastava, R.K., Koutnik, J., Steunebrink, B.R., Schmidhuber, J.: LSTM: a search space odyssey. IEEE Trans. Neural Netw. Learn. Syst. **28**, 2222–2232 (2017).https://doi.org/10.1109/tnnls.2016.2582924
13. Hou, L., Jin, X., Zhao, Z.: Time series similarity measure via Siamese convolutional neural network. In: 2019 12th International Congress on Image and Signal Processing, BioMedical Engineering and Informatics (CISP-BMEI), pp. 1–6. IEEE (2019)
14. ISMIR 2003, 4th International Conference on Music Information Retrieval, Baltimore, Maryland, USA, October 27-30, 2003, Proceedings: An Industrial-Strength Audio Search Algorithm (2003)
15. Ko, T., Peddinti, V., Povey, D., Khudanpur, S.: Audio augmentation for speech recognition. In: Interspeech (2015). https://api.semanticscholar.org/CorpusID:7360763
16. Lu, Z., et al.: NSGA-Net: neural architecture search using multi-objective genetic algorithm. In: Proceedings of the Genetic and Evolutionary Computation Conference (2018). https://api.semanticscholar.org/CorpusID:125974728
17. Luo, X., Oyedele, L.O.: Forecasting building energy consumption: adaptive long-short term memory neural networks driven by genetic algorithm. Adv. Eng. Inf. **50**, 101357 (2021). https://doi.org/10.1016/j.aei.2021.101357
18. Peeters, G., et al.: Twenty-five years of mir research: achievements, practices, evaluations, and future challenges. In: ICASSP 2025 - 2025 IEEE International Conference on Acoustics, Speech and Signal Processing (ICASSP) (2025). https://api.semanticscholar.org/CorpusID:276974010
19. Rokhsatyazdi, E., Rahnamayan, S., Amirinia, H., Ahmed, S.: Optimizing LSTM based network for forecasting stock market. In: 2020 IEEE Congress on Evolutionary Computation (CEC) (2020). https://doi.org/10.1109/cec48606.2020.9185545
20. Schlüter, J., Grill, T.: Exploring data augmentation for improved singing voice detection with neural networks. In: International Society for Music Information Retrieval Conference (2015). https://api.semanticscholar.org/CorpusID:3999220

21. Shrestha, A.K., Mahmood, A.: Optimizing deep neural network architecture with enhanced genetic algorithm. In: 2019 18th IEEE International Conference On Machine Learning And Applications (ICMLA), pp. 1365–1370 (2019). https://api.semanticscholar.org/CorpusID:211226841
22. Vincent, A.M., Jidesh, P.: An improved hyperparameter optimization framework for AutoML systems using evolutionary algorithms. Sci. Rep. **13** (2023). https://api.semanticscholar.org/CorpusID:257669219

“Systems, Security and Privacy”

Balancing Privacy and Performance in Federated Learning with Adaptive Differential Privacy and Secure Multi-party Computation

Tharindu Dhananjaya Attygalle(✉) and Ajantha Athukorala

University of Colombo School of Computing, Colombo, Sri Lanka
tharindud022@gmail.com

Abstract. Federated Learning (FL) enables collaborative model training without sharing raw data, but exchanged updates remain vulnerable to inference attacks. While Differential Privacy (DP) adds noise to protect privacy, client-side noise in methods like Adaptive DP-FL introduces high variance and relies on server trust. Secure Multi-Party Computation (SMPC) safeguards updates via secret sharing but lacks integration with differential privacy. We propose a hybrid FL framework combining adaptive DP-FL with SMPC. Clients clip gradients adaptively and secret-share updates across non-colluding servers. Servers reconstruct only the global sum, add a single calibrated Gaussian noise term, and account privacy using Rényi DP. This design reduces sensitivity by $1/K$, cuts noise variance, and streamlines privacy accounting. Experiments on MNIST and Fashion-MNIST under varying budgets show improved accuracy over the baseline, demonstrating enhanced privacy–utility trade-offs for sensitive applications.

Keywords: Federated Learning · Differential Privacy · Secure Multi-Party Computation · Shamir's Secret Sharing · Rényi Differential Privacy

1 Introduction

Federated Learning (FL) is a decentralized machine learning approach that enables clients–such as mobile devices or distributed institutions–to collaboratively train models without sharing raw data [10]. This paradigm is especially relevant in domains like healthcare, finance, and IoT, where data privacy regulations (e.g., GDPR, HIPAA) restrict centralized data collection and processing [16]. By allowing data to remain local, FL provides a foundational level of privacy, making it an attractive alternative to traditional centralized learning.

However, even in FL, privacy is not guaranteed. Studies have shown that model updates–such as gradients exchanged during training–can be exploited through inference attacks to reveal sensitive information about individual client

R. N. Rajapakse et al. (Eds.): ICTer 2025, CCIS 2844, pp. 399–412, 2026.
https://doi.org/10.1007/978-981-92-0137-2_26

datasets [6,17]. These privacy concerns pose significant barriers to adopting FL in real-world, high-stakes applications.

Addressing these concerns requires robust privacy-preserving mechanisms that go beyond data decentralization. A core challenge in Federated Learning (FL) is achieving strong privacy guarantees without significantly degrading model utility. Existing privacy-preserving mechanisms in Federated Learning (FL) primarily rely on either Differential Privacy (DP) or Secure Multi-Party Computation (SMPC), each addressing different aspects of privacy but falling short in isolation.

DP-only approaches typically apply noise at the client level to mask individual updates before sending them to the server [1]. While this offers formal privacy guarantees, it also introduces significant drawbacks. Adding noise independently on each client increases the total noise variance, especially when the number of clients is large. This undermines model convergence and reduces final accuracy. Furthermore, since each client's contribution is noisy and clipped, the global model suffers from cumulative utility loss. In addition, local noise injection requires per-client privacy accounting, complicating the bookkeeping process and increasing the risk of early budget exhaustion.

On the other hand, SMPC protocols–such as those using Shamir's Secret Sharing [15]–enable secure aggregation by allowing clients to share encrypted updates with multiple servers. These protocols ensure that no single party can view an individual update, thereby reducing trust requirements on the central server. However, SMPC by itself does not provide formal guarantees against inference attacks once the global model is released. It ensures confidentiality during transmission and aggregation but lacks the robustness of differential privacy in protecting outputs.

Thus, while both DP and SMPC offer valuable benefits, relying on them independently leads to trade-offs in either privacy completeness or model performance. A combined approach is required to fully address the privacy-performance gap in FL.

The primary aim of this research is to develop a federated learning framework that simultaneously enhances privacy guarantees and maintains high model performance by integrating Adaptive Differential Privacy (Adap DP) with Secure Multi-Party Computation (SMPC).

To achieve this, we propose a hybrid approach where each client applies adaptive gradient clipping locally and then secret-shares the clipped updates using Shamir's Secret Sharing. The aggregation servers reconstruct only the global sum of updates and inject a single, calibrated Gaussian noise term at the server level. Privacy loss is tracked using Rényi Differential Privacy (RDP), enabling tighter bounds and simplified privacy accounting. The key contributions of this work are as follows:

- We design a novel hybrid FL framework that shifts noise injection from clients to the server by combining Adap DP with SMPC, thereby reducing total noise variance and enhancing utility.

- We provide a formal privacy analysis using RDP composition to ensure that the combined mechanism satisfies (ε, δ)-DP.
- We implement and evaluate both the baseline Adap DP-FL and our hybrid approach on MNIST and Fashion-MNIST datasets under strict privacy budgets.
- We demonstrate that the proposed hybrid method consistently outperforms the baseline in terms of accuracy while offering comparable or improved privacy protection.

2 Related Work

Although Federated Learning (FL) ensures that raw data never leaves the client devices, recent research has demonstrated that sharing model updates is not inherently secure. Exchanged gradients and model parameters can still leak sensitive information through various inference attacks [12,14,17].

Adversaries can exploit access to the trained model or intermediate updates in several ways:

- **Membership Inference Attacks** [17]: Determine whether a specific data point was part of a client's training set by analyzing the model's output confidence.
- **Model Inversion Attacks** [6]: Reconstruct input features (e.g., images or attributes) by inverting model predictions or gradients.
- **Property Inference Attacks** [2]: Infer global or client-specific properties correlated with training data, even if those properties are not explicitly labeled.
- **Model Poisoning Attacks** [3]: Malicious clients introduce manipulated updates to embed backdoors or sabotage the global model.
- **Data Poisoning Attacks** [13]: Adversaries tamper with training data to mislead or bias the resulting model.

These threats highlight that FL alone is not sufficient for privacy protection. To address this, Differential Privacy (DP) introduces formal noise-based guarantees against individual data leakage, while Secure Multi-Party Computation (SMPC) ensures that raw updates are never exposed to the aggregation server. Integrating these two techniques is essential to build robust and trustworthy FL systems.

2.1 Differential Privacy

Differential Privacy (DP) is a mathematically rigorous framework designed to limit the influence of any single data point in a computation, thereby protecting individual privacy. Introduced by Dwork et al. [5], DP has become a foundational technique in privacy-preserving machine learning.

At a high level, a mechanism is said to be differentially private if the inclusion or exclusion of a single individual's data in the dataset does not significantly change the output of the computation. This ensures that an adversary cannot confidently determine whether any particular individual's data was used in training.

Formally, a randomized algorithm $\mathcal{M}$ satisfies (ε, δ)-differential privacy if, for any two datasets D and D' differing by one element, and for all measurable subsets S of the output space:

$$\Pr[\mathcal{M}(D) \in S] \leq e^{\varepsilon} \cdot \Pr[\mathcal{M}(D') \in S] + \delta \quad (1)$$

In this definition:

- ε (epsilon) is the privacy loss parameter; smaller values imply stronger privacy.
- δ is a small probability that the guarantee may not hold.

The above guarantees imply that any individual's participation in the dataset has a bounded impact on the model's output, making DP a critical tool in protecting against inference attacks in federated learning [1].

2.2 Secure Multi-party Computation and Secret Sharing

Secure Multi-Party Computation (SMPC) is a class of cryptographic protocols that enables multiple parties to collaboratively compute a function over their inputs while ensuring that each party's input remains private [20]. In the context of federated learning, SMPC allows secure aggregation of model updates such that the server learns only the global sum of the updates, and not any individual client's contribution.

A core building block of many SMPC protocols is *secret sharing*, which allows a private value to be split into multiple components (shares) and distributed among multiple participants. No individual share reveals any information about the original value; only a subset of shares (meeting a predefined threshold) can reconstruct the secret. This enables secure computation while tolerating faults and protecting against collusion.

Types of Secret Sharing. Two widely used secret sharing schemes are:

- **Additive Secret Sharing**: The secret is divided into random values that sum up to the original secret. For instance, given a secret s, one can generate random values s_1 and s_2, then set $s_3 = s - (s_1 + s_2)$. The tuple (s_1, s_2, s_3) is then distributed among three parties.
- **Shamir's Secret Sharing (SSS)**: Proposed by Shamir [15], this scheme encodes the secret as the constant term of a random polynomial of degree $t - 1$, where t is the reconstruction threshold. Each share is a point on the polynomial. The original secret can be reconstructed only when at least t distinct shares are combined using polynomial interpolation (e.g., Lagrange interpolation).

Shamir's Secret Sharing in FL. In Shamir's Secret Sharing, a secret s is shared by generating a polynomial $f(x) = s + a_1x + a_2x^2 + \cdots + a_{t-1}x^{t-1}$, where the a_i are randomly chosen coefficients. Each participant receives a share $f(i)$, where i is their unique identifier. A group of t or more participants can reconstruct s using Lagrange interpolation, while fewer than t learn nothing.

Due to its strong privacy guarantees and fault tolerance, Shamir's Secret Sharing is well-suited for secure aggregation in federated learning. It ensures that model updates remain confidential during transmission and aggregation, even in the presence of a semi-trusted or partially malicious server.

2.3 Balancing Privacy and Utility in Federated Learning

Federated Learning (FL) introduces a fundamental trade-off between preserving user privacy and achieving high model utility. A wide range of techniques have been proposed to address this challenge, including Differential Privacy (DP), Secure Multi-Party Computation (SMPC), homomorphic encryption, and hybrid approaches. However, each method introduces specific limitations related to privacy guarantees, model accuracy, scalability, or system overhead.

Differential Privacy-Based Approaches. One of the most commonly adopted privacy mechanisms in FL is client-level differential privacy, where each client independently adds noise to its local model update before sending it to the server [8,11]. While this approach provides strong privacy protection at the individual level, it also amplifies the total noise variance–especially when the number of clients is small or the model is high-dimensional. This often results in substantial degradation of the model's accuracy and slows convergence.

SMPC and Cryptographic Aggregation. SMPC-based methods, such as those using Shamir's Secret Sharing or homomorphic encryption, focus on protecting model updates during transmission and aggregation [4]. These techniques ensure that the server cannot view individual client updates, thus providing strong input confidentiality. However, SMPC alone does not offer formal privacy guarantees like DP. Furthermore, it introduces significant computational and communication overhead and typically requires a fixed number of trusted or semi-trusted aggregation servers.

Hybrid Methods and Adaptive Mechanisms. To address the limitations of using DP or SMPC in isolation, hybrid approaches have been developed. These methods delay the addition of DP noise until after secure aggregation has taken place [18]. Since the sensitivity of the aggregated update is lower than that of individual updates, less noise is needed to achieve the same privacy guarantee, thereby improving model utility. However, most of these systems still rely on static clipping thresholds and fixed noise multipliers, which do not adapt well to training dynamics and may underperform in later stages of learning.

2.4 Adaptive DP-FL Framework

A notable advancement in balancing privacy and utility in Federated Learning is the Adaptive Differentially Private Federated Learning (Adap DP-FL) framework proposed by Fu et al. [7]. This approach improves upon traditional client-level differential privacy by introducing two adaptive mechanisms:

- **Adaptive Clipping**: Instead of using a fixed threshold, each client dynamically adjusts its gradient clipping norm based on the previous round's average gradient magnitude. This helps prevent over-clipping while keeping sensitivity bounded.
- **Noise Decay**: The Gaussian noise multiplier is gradually reduced across training rounds if the validation loss improves. This enables more precise model updates in later stages of training, when the model is closer to convergence.

These innovations significantly enhance model utility, especially under strict privacy budgets. However, the framework still applies noise independently at each client, which leads to a high aggregate noise variance when updates are averaged. This effect becomes more pronounced as the number of clients increases. Moreover, since clipping and noise injection are both performed locally, the system must maintain and track individual privacy budgets per client, increasing coordination complexity and limiting scalability.

While prior work in adaptive differential privacy and secure aggregation has significantly advanced the field of privacy-preserving federated learning, existing methods still fall short in several key areas.

This paper addresses the above limitations by proposing a hybrid Adaptive DP-FL + SMPC framework. The system combines adaptive gradient clipping and noise decay with secure aggregation, followed by a single global Gaussian perturbation applied at the server. By aggregating clipped updates via Shamir's Secret Sharing and injecting noise only after aggregation, the proposed method reduces total noise variance, simplifies privacy budget tracking, and improves model performance–all while maintaining rigorous (ε, δ)-DP guarantees.

3 Our Approach

Our proposed framework combines Adaptive Differential Privacy (Adap DP-FL) with Secure Multi-Party Computation (SMPC) to enhance both privacy and utility in Federated Learning. The core idea is to decouple noise injection from individual clients and instead apply it centrally after secure aggregation. This is achieved by integrating adaptive clipping and noise decay with Shamir's Secret Sharing for privacy-preserving aggregation.

3.1 Client-Side Process

In the proposed hybrid Adap DP-FL + SMPC framework, each client is responsible for performing local model training, applying adaptive gradient clipping, and secret-sharing the clipped updates with the aggregation servers. Unlike traditional DP-FL approaches, clients do not inject noise locally; instead, noise is added centrally after secure aggregation. The detailed steps at the client side are as follows:

Local Model Training. Each client downloads the current global model w_t and performs one epoch of training on its local dataset D_k. For a given mini-batch sample x_i, the gradient is computed as:

$$g_k^{(i)} = \nabla \mathcal{L}(w_t; x_i) \tag{2}$$

where $\mathcal{L}$ is the local loss function (e.g., cross-entropy), and $g_k^{(i)}$ is the gradient computed with respect to x_i.

Adaptive Gradient Clipping. To bound sensitivity and improve privacy accounting, each client clips its per-sample gradients using an adaptive threshold C_t^k:

$$\bar{g}_k^{(i)} = \frac{g_k^{(i)}}{\max\left(1, \frac{\|g_k^{(i)}\|_2}{C_t^k}\right)} \tag{3}$$

This ensures that the L2 norm of all gradients is bounded by C_t^k.

Adaptive Clipping Threshold Estimation. The clipping threshold C_t^k is updated at each round based on the noisy average of the previous round's gradient norms:

$$C_t^k = \alpha \cdot \hat{n}_{t-1}^k + \mathcal{N}(0, \sigma_c^2) \tag{4}$$

where α is a scaling factor, $\hat{n}_{t-1}^k$ is the average L2 norm from the previous round, and σ_c is the standard deviation of the added Gaussian noise.

Averaging Clipped Gradients. After clipping, each client computes the average of the clipped gradients over the mini-batch:

$$\bar{g}_t^k = \frac{1}{|L_t^k|} \sum_{i \in L_t^k} \bar{g}_k^{(i)} \tag{5}$$

where L_t^k is the mini-batch sampled for local training.

Model Update Computation. The local update Δ_t^k is computed as the difference between the updated local model w_{t+1}^k and the initial global model w_t:

$$\Delta_t^k = w_{t+1}^k - w_t \tag{6}$$

Secret Sharing of Updates. The computed update Δ_t^k is secret-shared using Shamir's Secret Sharing scheme. A linear polynomial $f(x)$ is constructed:

$$f(x) = \Delta_t^k + ax \tag{7}$$

where a is a randomly generated tensor with the same shape as Δ_t^k. The client generates and sends three shares:

$$s_1 = f(1), \quad s_2 = f(2), \quad s_3 = f(3) \tag{8}$$

Each share is sent to a separate non-colluding server. No single share reveals any information about the original update, and at least two shares are required to reconstruct it securely.

3.2 Server-Side Process

The server in the proposed hybrid Adap DP-FL + SMPC framework is responsible for securely aggregating client updates, injecting calibrated noise to ensure differential privacy, and tracking the cumulative privacy budget. The following steps outline the full server-side process for each training round.

Receiving Secret Shares. Each client computes its local update $\Delta_t^k = \theta_t^k - \theta_t$, where θ_t^k is the locally trained model and θ_t is the current global model. The update is secret-shared using a degree-1 Shamir polynomial:

$$f(x) = \Delta_t^k + ax \tag{9}$$

where a is a randomly sampled noise tensor. The server receives two out of the three shares, typically $f(1)$ and $f(2)$, from each client.

Secure Aggregation of Shares. The server sums the corresponding shares across all clients:

$$\text{Aggregated Share}_j = \sum_{k=1}^{K} \text{Share}_{k,j} \quad \text{for } j \in \{1, 2\} \tag{10}$$

where K is the number of participating clients.

Reconstruction of Aggregated Update. Using Lagrange interpolation on the aggregated shares, the server reconstructs the total update:

$$\Delta_t = 2 \cdot \text{Aggregated Share}_1 - \text{Aggregated Share}_2 \tag{11}$$

This method ensures that individual client updates are never revealed, only their combined contribution.

Adding Global Gaussian Noise. To guarantee (ε, δ)-differential privacy, the server adds Gaussian noise to the aggregated update:

$$\tilde{\Delta}_t = \Delta_t + \mathcal{N}\left(0, \sigma^2 \cdot \left(\frac{C}{K}\right)^2\right) \tag{12}$$

where σ is the global noise multiplier, C is the maximum clipping norm across clients, and K is the number of clients. This reduces sensitivity by a factor of $1/K$, improving the overall privacy-utility trade-off.

Updating the Global Model. The server uses the noisy update to refresh the global model:

$$\theta_{t+1} = \theta_t + \eta \cdot \tilde{\Delta}_t \tag{13}$$

where η is the learning rate.

Privacy Accounting Using RDP. The server maintains cumulative privacy loss tracking using the Rényi Differential Privacy (RDP) framework. Training halts when the accumulated privacy budget ε exceeds a predefined threshold $\varepsilon_{\max}$.

4 Experiment

4.1 Initialization

Dataset and Partitioning. We evaluate our system on two standard image classification benchmarks: MNIST [9] and Fashion-MNIST [19]. Both datasets consist of 60,000 training and 10,000 testing grayscale images of size 28×28 across 10 classes. To simulate data heterogeneity among clients, we adopt a non-IID partitioning scheme. The training data is first sorted by label, then split into 400 equal-sized shards. Each of the 10 clients is randomly assigned 40 shards, resulting in clients having access to data from only a subset of classes.

Network Model. We use a lightweight convolutional neural network (CNN) similar to LeNet [9]. The architecture consists of two convolutional layers with group normalization and LeakyReLU activation, followed by max-pooling, dropout, and two fully connected layers. This setup provides a balanced trade-off between model capacity and computational efficiency in a federated environment.

Experimental Parameters. All experiments are implemented in PyTorch using the Opacus library for differential privacy. The learning rate is set to 0.002 for MNIST and 0.001 for Fashion-MNIST. Each client performs one local epoch per communication round with a batch size of 200. For privacy accounting, we use Rényi Differential Privacy (RDP) with a target $\delta = 10^{-5}$. The noise decay factor is $\beta = 0.998$. Initial noise multipliers σ_0 are set to 4.0 and 6.0 to match target budgets of $\varepsilon = 0.5$ and $\varepsilon = 0.3$, respectively. Privacy tracking and training are halted once ε exceeds its predefined threshold.

Algorithm 1: Hybrid Adap DPFL with SMPC

Input: gradient clipping factor α, noise decay factor β $(0 < \beta < 1)$, group size L, learning rate η_t, initial noise scale σ_0, global privacy budget (ε, δ), number of servers S

Output: final model w_T, per-client privacy loss ε^k

1 Initialize: $t \leftarrow 0$, w_0, σ_0, per-client ε^k
2 **while** $t < T$ **do**
3   Broadcast w_t, σ_t to all clients
4   **foreach** *client* $k \in [K]$ **do**
5   Sample minibatch L_t^k with probability $L/|D_k|$
6   Compute gradient: $g_t^k(x_i) = \nabla\ell(w_t, x_i)$ for $i \in L_t^k$
7   Compute clipping threshold: $C_t^k = \alpha \cdot \hat{n}_{t-1}^k$
8   Clip gradients: $\bar{g}_t^k(x_i) = g_t^k(x_i)/\max(1, \|g_t^k(x_i)\|_2/C_t^k)$
9   Aggregate: $g_t^k = \frac{1}{L}\sum_{i \in L_t^k} \bar{g}_t^k(x_i)$
10   Local update: $w_k^{t+1} = w_t - \eta_t \cdot g_t^k$
11   Secret-share $g_t^k \rightarrow \{g_t^{k,1}, \ldots, g_t^{k,S}\}$
12   Compute privacy loss: $\varepsilon_t^k = \text{RDP2DP}\left(\sum_{\tau=1}^{t} \text{RDP}(\alpha, q, \sigma_\tau),\ \delta\right)$
13   **if** $\varepsilon_t^k > \varepsilon$ **then**
14   **break**
15   **end if**
16   Send shares $\{g_t^{k,j}\}_{j=1}^{S}$ to servers
17   **end foreach**
18   Secure aggregation: $G_t^{(j)} = \sum_k g_t^{k,j}$, $\hat{G}_t = \text{Reconstruct}(G_t^{(j)}, G_t^{(j')})$
19   Add noise: $\widetilde{G}_t = \hat{G}_t + \mathcal{N}(0, (\sigma_t C_{\text{agg}})^2)$
20   Update global model: $w_{t+1} = w_t - \eta_t \cdot \widetilde{G}_t$
21   **if** $J(w_{t-2}) > J(w_{t-1}) > J(w_t) > J(w_{t+1})$ **then**
22     $\sigma_{t+1} \leftarrow \beta \cdot \sigma_t$
23   **end if**
24   $t \leftarrow t + 1$
25 **end while**

4.2 Evaluations

Baseline Adap DP-FL Results. We first evaluate the performance of the baseline Adaptive DP-FL framework based on Fu et al. [7]. As shown in Table 1 results were obtained on both MNIST and Fashion-MNIST datasets using two representative privacy budgets: $\varepsilon = 0.5$ and $\varepsilon = 0.3$. These values were selected to reflect moderate and strict privacy regimes, respectively, in line with commonly accepted DP benchmarks [1,11]. Each configuration was run with adaptive clipping, local noise injection, and validation-driven noise decay.

Hybrid DP + SMPC Results. Next, we evaluate the proposed hybrid Adap DP-FL + SMPC system. Unlike the baseline, noise is added only once–centrally at the server–after secure aggregation. The same datasets, network, and privacy settings were used for fair comparison.

Table 1. Baseline Adap DP-FL Performance

Dataset	ε	σ_T	Test Accuracy (%)
MNIST	0.5	3.67	95.89
MNIST	0.3	5.51	94.27
Fashion-MNIST	0.5	3.86	79.00
Fashion-MNIST	0.3	5.66	76.21

Table 2. Hybrid Adap DP-FL + SMPC Performance

Dataset	ε	σ_T	Test Accuracy (%)
MNIST	0.5	3.56	96.45
MNIST	0.3	5.41	94.32
Fashion-MNIST	0.5	3.58	79.27
Fashion-MNIST	0.3	5.30	78.42

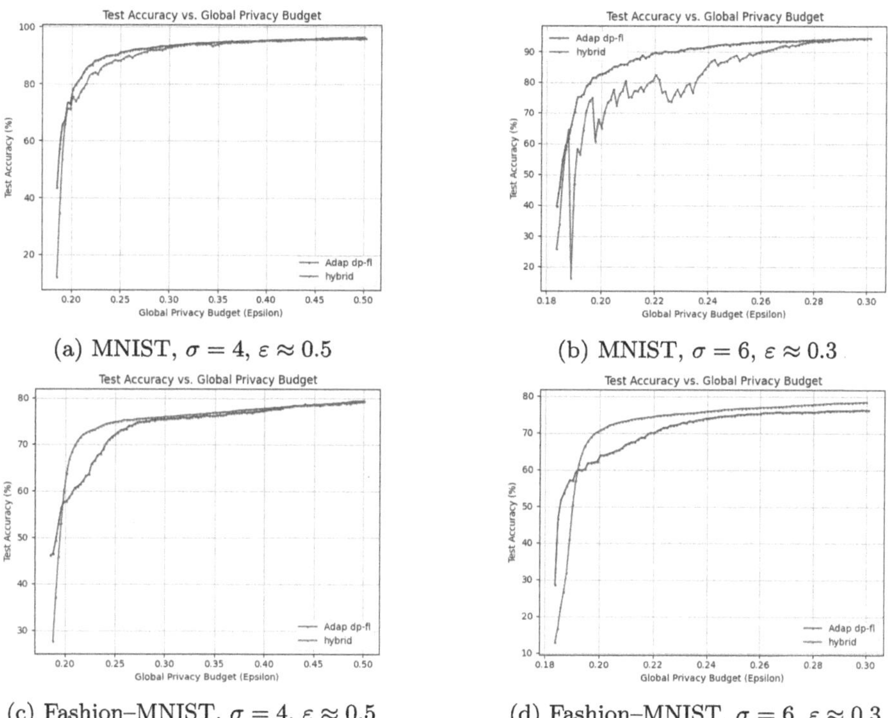

(a) MNIST, $\sigma = 4$, $\varepsilon \approx 0.5$

(b) MNIST, $\sigma = 6$, $\varepsilon \approx 0.3$

(c) Fashion–MNIST, $\sigma = 4$, $\varepsilon \approx 0.5$

(d) Fashion–MNIST, $\sigma = 6$, $\varepsilon \approx 0.3$

Fig. 1. Test accuracy as a function of the global privacy budget ε for two noise settings on MNIST and FashionMNIST.

Comparison: Privacy-Utility Trade-Offs. As shown in Table 2 we observe that the hybrid approach consistently outperforms the baseline under both tight and relaxed privacy budgets. By injecting noise post-aggregation, the hybrid system reduces total noise variance by $\mathcal{O}(K^2)$ and improves sensitivity by a factor of $1/K$.

Figure 1 and Fig. 2 plot accuracy and test loss against ε, demonstrating the superior privacy-utility trade-off achieved by the hybrid model.

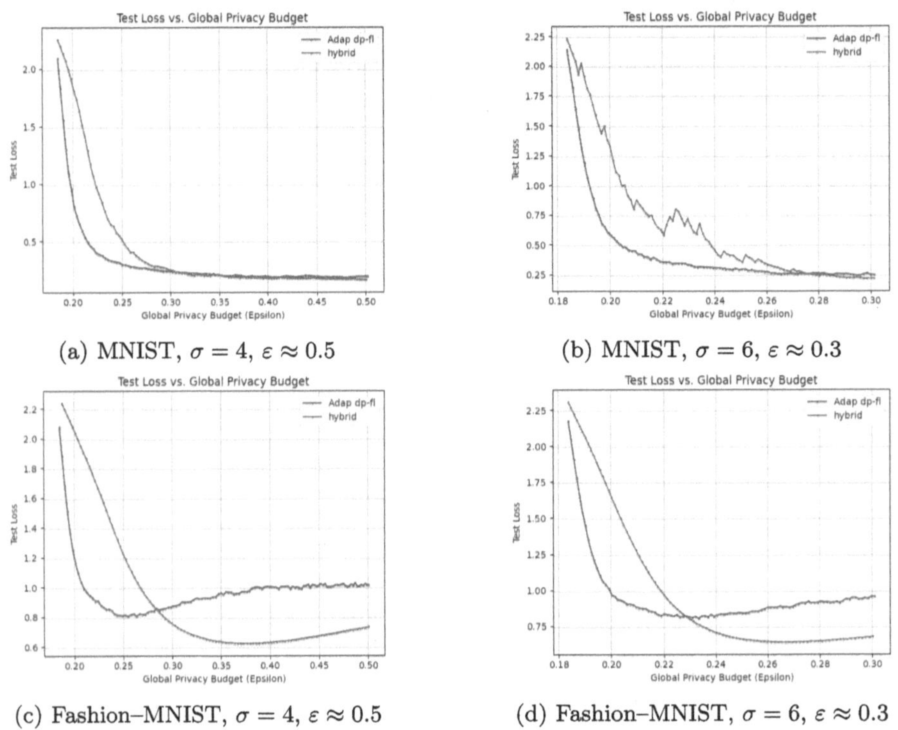

(a) MNIST, $\sigma = 4$, $\varepsilon \approx 0.5$

(b) MNIST, $\sigma = 6$, $\varepsilon \approx 0.3$

(c) Fashion–MNIST, $\sigma = 4$, $\varepsilon \approx 0.5$

(d) Fashion–MNIST, $\sigma = 6$, $\varepsilon \approx 0.3$

Fig. 2. Test loss as a function of the global privacy budget ε for two noise settings on MNIST and FashionMNIST.

5 Conclusion

5.1 Summary of Findings

This paper presented a novel hybrid federated learning framework that integrates Adaptive Differential Privacy (Adap DP-FL) with Secure Multi-Party Computation (SMPC) to enhance both privacy protection and model utility. By combining adaptive clipping and dynamic noise scaling with secure aggregation via Shamir's Secret Sharing, the proposed system shifts noise injection to the server-side after aggregation. This design reduces total noise variance, simplifies privacy tracking using Rényi Differential Privacy (RDP), and achieves stronger performance under strict privacy budgets.

Experimental results on MNIST and Fashion-MNIST demonstrate that the hybrid system consistently outperforms the baseline Adap DP-FL approach in terms of test accuracy and privacy-utility trade-offs, particularly at lower ε values.

5.2 Limitations

While the proposed system shows promising results, there are a few limitations:

- **Scalability**: The SMPC implementation assumes three non-colluding servers and simple 2-out-of-3 reconstruction. Scaling to larger server pools or adversarial threat models may require more complex protocols.
- **Dataset Complexity**: Experiments were limited to MNIST and Fashion-MNIST datasets. Larger or more complex datasets (e.g., CIFAR-10, medical imaging) may present different privacy-performance dynamics.
- **Computation Overhead**: Although not evaluated in detail, secret sharing and secure reconstruction introduce additional computational and communication costs.

5.3 Future Work

Future research can build on this work in several directions:

- Extending the framework to support more advanced SMPC protocols (e.g., SPDZ or homomorphic encryption) to handle stronger adversarial settings.
- Evaluating performance on larger, more diverse datasets and deeper neural networks.
- Investigating adaptive client participation and early stopping strategies to further optimize privacy cost and convergence.
- Exploring real-world deployment considerations, including system integration and robustness in mobile or edge environments.

Disclosure of Interests. The authors declare no competing interests

References

1. Abadi, M., et al.: Deep learning with differential privacy. In: Proceedings of the 2016 ACM SIGSAC Conference on Computer and Communications Security, pp. 308–318. ACM (2016)
2. Ateniese, G., Magri, B., Venturi, D., Mancini, L.V.: Hacking smart machines with smarter ones: How to extract meaningful data from machine learning classifiers. In: Proceedings of the 2015 IEEE Symposium on Security and Privacy (2015)

3. Bagdasaryan, E., Veit, A., Hua, Y., Estrin, D., Shmatikov, V.: How to backdoor federated learning. In: Proceedings of the Twenty Third International Conference on Artificial Intelligence and Statistics (AISTATS) (2020)
4. Bonawitz, K., et al.: Practical secure aggregation for privacy-preserving machine learning. In: Proceedings of the 2017 ACM SIGSAC Conference on Computer and Communications Security (CCS) (2017)
5. Dwork, C., McSherry, F., Nissim, K., Smith, A.: Calibrating noise to sensitivity in private data analysis. In: Theory of Cryptography Conference pp. 265–284 (2006)
6. Fredrikson, M., Jha, S., Ristenpart, T.: Model inversion attacks that exploit confidence information and basic countermeasures. In: Proceedings of the 22nd ACM SIGSAC Conference on Computer and Communications Security (2015)
7. Fu, J., Chen, Z., Han, X.: ADAP DP-FL: differentially private federated learning with adaptive noise. arXiv preprint arXiv:2211.15893 (2022)
8. Geyer, R.C., Klein, T., Nabi, M.: Differentially private federated learning: a client level perspective. In: NIPS Workshop on Private Multi-Party Machine Learning (2017)
9. LeCun, Y., Cortes, C., Burges, C.J.: MNIST Handwritten Digit Database. ATT Labs (1998)
10. McMahan, H.B., Moore, E., Ramage, D., Hampson, S., Arcas, B.A.Y.: Communication-Efficient Learning of Deep Networks from Decentralized Data. In: Proceedings of the 20th International Conference on Artificial Intelligence and Statistics (AISTATS), vol. 54, pp. 1273–1282 (2017). http://proceedings.mlr.press/v54/mcmahan17a/mcmahan17a.pdf
11. McMahan, H.B., Ramage, D., Talwar, K., Zhang, L.: Learning differentially private recurrent language models. In: International Conference on Learning Representations (ICLR) (2018)
12. Melis, L., Song, C., De Cristofaro, E., Shmatikov, V.: Exploiting unintended feature leakage in collaborative learning. In: IEEE Symposium on Security and Privacy (SP), pp. 691–706. IEEE (2019)
13. Muñoz-González, L., Lupu, E.C., Giacinto, G., Lupu, E.C.: Towards poisoning of face recognition models with the generative adversarial network. In: Proceedings of the 2017 ACM on Asia Conference on Computer and Communications Security (2017)
14. Rafi, A., Smith, J., Lee, K.: A survey of privacy attacks in federated learning. J. Priv. Secure Comput. (2024)
15. Shamir, A.: How to share a secret. Commun. ACM **22**(11), 612–613 (1979)
16. Sheller, M.J., et al.: Federated learning in medicine: facilitating multi-institutional collaborations without sharing patient data. Sci. Rep. **10**(1) (2020). https://doi.org/10.1038/s41598-020-69250-1
17. Shokri, R., Stronati, M., Song, C., Shmatikov, V.: Membership inference attacks against machine learning models. In: 2017 IEEE Symposium on Security and Privacy (SP) (2017)
18. Truex, S., Liu, R., Chow, K.H., Gursoy, M.E.: A hybrid approach to privacy-preserving federated learning. In: Proceedings of the 2019 ACM SIGSAC Conference on Computer and Communications Security (CCS) (2019)
19. Xiao, H., Rasul, K., Vollgraf, R.: Fashion-MNIST: a novel image dataset for benchmarking machine learning algorithms. arXiv preprint arXiv:1708.07747 (2017)
20. Yao, A.C.: Protocols for secure computations (extended abstract). In: 23rd Annual Symposium on Foundations of Computer Science (FOCS), pp. 160–164. IEEE (1982)

Matrix-Based Forecasting and Anomaly Detection Framework for Cloud VM Resource Monitoring

W. G. C. P. B. Wattegama[1] and Kalpana Galappaththi[2](✉)

[1] Enexe (Private) Limited, Colombo, Sri Lanka
[2] Institute of Technology University of Moratuwa, Diyagama, Homagama, Moratuwa, Sri Lanka
kgalappaththi@itum.mrt.ac.lk

Abstract. This study introduces a mathematical framework that utilizes matrix factorization to model and detect anomalies in virtual machine (VM) resource utilization in cloud computing settings. The approach employs Singular Value Decomposition (SVD) on time-series data to extract dominant patterns in resource consumption and to predict future usage trends. To enhance the robustness of anomaly detection, an Exponential Moving Average (EMA) is applied to smooth the forecast errors, which helps mitigate the effects of transient noise and short-term variability. The framework emphasizes computational efficiency and transparency, addressing some of the drawbacks associated with more complex and less interpretable models. The method was evaluated through experiments on synthetic datasets designed to replicate realistic work-load fluctuations and burst anomalies. Results across various test cases indicate that the model reliably differentiates normal usage from anomalies and maintains balanced performance in both over-prediction and under-prediction scenarios. This framework provides a practical and interpretable tool for resource monitoring that can be readily integrated into cloud infrastructures requiring prompt and explainable decision-making support.

Keywords: Cloud Resource Management · Anomaly Detection · Matrix Factorization · Exponential Moving Average · Singular Value Decomposition

1 Introduction

Cloud computing infrastructures increasingly rely on virtualization to host numerous virtual machines (VMs) across distributed data centers. Efficient resource management within such environments is critical for ensuring Quality of Service (QoS) and meeting Service Level Agreements (SLAs) [1]. While traditional resource monitoring tools offer reactive solutions, there is a growing demand for predictive systems that can anticipate workload trends and respond dynamically.

Forecasting resource usage remains a challenging task due to the stochastic and bursty nature of cloud workloads [2–4]. Numerous approaches, including statistical forecasting models and machine learning algorithms, have been proposed to address

R. N. Rajapakse et al. (Eds.): ICTer 2025, CCIS 2844, pp. 413–425, 2026.
https://doi.org/10.1007/978-981-92-0137-2_27

this challenge. However, many of these methods are either computationally intensive or lack transparency, making them difficult to adopt in real-time operational settings [5].

To address these limitations, this study presents a matrix-based mathematical model that leverages low-rank approximation via Singular Value Decomposition (SVD). This allows compact representation of multivariate VM utilization patterns while preserving temporal dynamics. Furthermore, we enhance anomaly detection capabilities by incorporating Exponential Moving Average (EMA) smoothing on the forecast error, thereby improving detection sensitivity without increasing false positives.

By emphasizing analytical simplicity, interpretability, and scalability, this research offers a lightweight framework capable of supporting real-time decision-making in cloud orchestration platforms.

2 Literature Review

A wide spectrum of research has focused on predictive resource allocation in cloud environments. Time-series forecasting techniques, such as Autoregressive Integrated Moving Average (ARIMA) and Kalman filters, have been extensively used for CPU and memory usage prediction [6, 7]. These models are valued for their statistical rigor but often fail to capture nonlinear or abrupt changes in workloads.

In contrast, machine learning approaches, particularly Long Short-Term Memory (LSTM) networks, have demonstrated superior performance in handling dynamic VM behavior [8–13]. Regression trees and ensemble methods have also been explored for their interpretability and moderate computational cost [14]. However, the "black box" nature of deep learning methods hinders their practical deployment in systems requiring transparency and auditability.

Anomaly detection techniques within cloud systems include native services like AWS CloudWatch and Azure Monitor, which offer threshold-based alerts and base-line deviation detection. More advanced frameworks utilize clustering, principal component analysis (PCA), or probabilistic graphical models [15]. Despite their effectiveness, these systems often lack lightweight deployment feasibility in resource con-strained settings.

Matrix factorization techniques, especially low-rank approximations such as Singular Value Decomposition (SVD), have gained popularity in domains like recommender systems and signal processing for their efficiency in extracting latent patterns from high-dimensional datasets [16, 17]. In cloud computing, matrix decomposition has been adopted in limited but growing contexts for resource behavior modeling and performance prediction. For example, Xu et al. [18] applied matrix factorization for analyzing workload patterns in large-scale cloud platforms, revealing temporal correlations in VM resource usage. Similarly, Islam et al. [19] employed decomposition methods to predict energy consumption in virtualized environments. Some recent studies suggest combining statistical forecasting with smoothing techniques, but the specific integration of matrix factorization with time aware anomaly detection mechanisms such as EMA has not been thoroughly addressed.

3 Research Gap

This study bridges this gap by combining matrix-based forecasting with time sensitive anomaly detection, thereby offering a lightweight and interpretable solution for dynamic cloud environments. The contributions of this work are fourfold: (1) A lightweight, matrix-based resource modeling framework using low-rank approximation; (2) Integrated forecasting and anomaly detection in a single formulation; (3) Time-aware anomaly scoring through directional forecast error smoothed with EMA; (4) A simulated test bed for rigorous validation of anomaly detection across multiple VM instances and time horizons.

4 Mathematical Model and Methodology

This section outlines the mathematical formulation and algorithmic components of the proposed resource forecasting and anomaly detection model for virtualized cloud environments. The model operates on CPU utilization data collected over time from multiple virtual machines (VMs), which is represented in a matrix form. Through low-rank matrix factorization using Singular Value Decomposition (SVD), latent structures within the resource usage patterns are extracted. These decomposed compo-nents are then used to forecast future utilization and compute directional forecast errors, which are smoothed using an Exponential Moving Average (EMA) to enable robust anomaly detection.

4.1 Matrix Representation of CPU Utilization

Let $\boldsymbol{U_{ij}} \epsilon \mathbb{R}^{\boldsymbol{mn}}$ be the CPU utilization matrix

$$U = \begin{bmatrix} U_{11} & U_{12} & \cdots & U_{1n} \\ U_{21} & U_{22} & \cdots & U_{2n} \\ \vdots & \vdots & \ddots & \vdots \\ U_{m1} & U_{m2} & \cdots & U_{mn} \end{bmatrix} \tag{1}$$

where:

- m: Number of VMs
- n: Number of time intervals
- U_{ij}: CPU utilization of VM i at time j

This formulation provides a temporal snapshot of system load, enabling analysis of both inter-VM and temporal correlations.

4.2 Low-Rank Matrix Factorization Using Singular Value Decomposition (SVD)

We perform SVD on the mean-centered matrix Ũ=−:

$$\tilde{U} = A \sum B^T \tag{2}$$

where:

- $A \in \mathbb{R}^{m \times k}$: left singular vectors (VM features)
- $\sum \in \mathbb{R}^{k \times k}$: singular values
- $B^T \in \mathbb{R}^{k \times n}$: right singular vectors (temporal features)
- $K \ll \min(m,n)$: rank approximation
- μ: row-wise mean of utilization for each VM

4.3 Forecasting Future Utilization

Future CPU utilization is predicted by projecting temporal latent vectors. Linear regression is applied on each row b_r of B^T to forecast:

$$B^{(n+1)} = \begin{bmatrix} b_1^{(n+1)} \\ b_2^{(n+1)} \\ \vdots \\ b_k^{(n+1)} \end{bmatrix}$$

Then the next utilization vector is estimated by:

$$\hat{\mathrm{U}}^{(n+1)} = A \sum B^{(n+1)} + \mu \tag{3}$$

This procedure yields an interpretable, low-complexity forecast for each VM's expected usage at the next time interval.

4.4 Directional Forecast Error Calculation and EMA

To evaluate model accuracy and detect anomalies, a directional forecast error is computed for each VM i as:

$$\Delta_i = \frac{\hat{\mathrm{U}}_i - \mathrm{U}_i}{\mathrm{U}_i} \tag{4}$$

where:

- $\hat{U}_i$: Forecasted CPU usage
- U_i: Actual CPU usage

This relative error formulation allows for consistent interpretation across varying usage scales and VM workloads.

4.5 Error Stabilization Using EMA

Since instantaneous forecast errors may fluctuate due to transient noise or short-lived workload bursts, smoothing is applied using the Exponential Moving Average (EMA). The Adjusted Forecast Error (AFE) at time t for VM i is defined as:

$$AF_i(\mathrm{t}) = \alpha.\ AF_i(\mathrm{t} - 10) + (1 - \alpha).\Delta(t) \tag{5}$$

where:

- $\Delta(t)$: Current directional error
- α: 0.7: Smoothing factor
- Initial $AF_i(\mathrm{t}) = 0$

The use of a 10-time-step lag provides a balance between responsiveness and noise suppression. The initial AFE is set to zero. This formulation allows the model to adapt to evolving patterns while preserving stability in anomaly classification.

4.6 Anomaly Classification

A threshold θ defines the nature of deviation:

- Type I Anomaly (Under prediction): $\triangle_i < -\theta$
- Type II Anomaly (Over prediction): $\triangle_i > \theta$
- No Anomaly: $|\triangle_i| \leq \theta$

4.7 Threshold Justification

We select $\theta = 0.07$ (7%) as a standard based on prior empirical studies on forecasting-based anomaly detection in cloud environments [19, 20]. These studies indicate that thresholds in the range of 5–10% are effective in detecting significant deviations in CPU usage without triggering excessive false positives. For synthetic datasets, where added variability and controlled bursts are introduced to simulate operational noise, a slightly higher threshold of $\theta = 0.09$ (9%) is employed to preserve detection robustness.

5 Testing Environment & Experimental Setup

5.1 Synthetic Dataset Generation

To evaluate the forecasting and anomaly detection capabilities of the proposed model under controlled conditions, a synthetic dataset was generated to emulate CPU utilization patterns across multiple virtual machines (VMs). The synthetic data generation process is designed to simulate both regular workload behavior and injected anomalies in the form of CPU usage spikes, thereby enabling reproducible and interpretable performance evaluation of the anomaly detection mechanism.

CPU utilization $\mathrm{U}_i(t)$ is synthesized using:

$$U_i(t) = B_i(t) + \epsilon_i(t) + S_i(t) \tag{6}$$

Where:

- $B_i(t) \sim u\ (\mu_{low}, \mu_{high})$: baseline
- $\epsilon_i(t) \sim N(0, \sigma^2)$: noise
- $S_i(t) = s\ \mathit{if}\ i \in \{1, 2\}$ and $t \in |\, t_s, t_e\, |$; otherwise 0

This formulation allows precise control over the temporal and spatial characteristics of the workload, making it suitable for testing both forecast accuracy and sensitivity to anomalous behavior.

5.2 Algorithm 1: Synthetic CPU Usage Data Generation

Algorithm 1: Generate Synthetic CPU Usage Dataset

```
Input:
  N ← Number of VMs
  T ← Time intervals
  μ_low, μ_high ← Baseline bounds
  σ ← Std deviation of noise
  spike_vms ← VM set with spikes
  t_s, t_e ← Spike interval
  spike_val ← Load spike value
Output:
  U[N][T] ← CPU usage matrix
Procedure:
  for i = 1 to N:
    for t = 1 to T:
      B_i(t) ← Uniform(μ_low, μ_high)
      ε_i(t) ← Gaussian(0, σ)
      if i ∈ spike_vms and t_s ≤ t ≤ t_e:
        S_i(t) ← spike_val
      else:
        S_i(t) ← 0
      U[i][t] ← B_i(t) + ε_i(t) + S_i(t)
  return U
```

This generation process ensures that normal and anomalous patterns co-exist in a controlled setting. It provides a testbed for evaluating the impact of model components such as SVD-based forecasting, directional forecast error, and EMA smoothing under various configurations of workload variability and anomaly injection. The inclusion of spike VMs within a subset of the system allows for targeted analysis of false positives and false negatives during classification.

The synthetic dataset used in this study consists of 10 VMs monitored over 31 time intervals, with CPU utilization values constructed as described above. A sample excerpt from the generated dataset is provided in Table 1, illustrating the temporal evolution of resource usage across all VMs.

5.3 Sample Dataset

To illustrate the characteristics of the synthetically generated CPU utilization data, a sample dataset comprising 10 virtual machines (VMs) observed over 31 consecutive time intervals is presented. The dataset reflects the output of the data generation algorithm described in Sect. 5.1, incorporating baseline utilization drawn from a uniform distribution, additive Gaussian noise, and injected spike values for a subset of VMs during specific time windows.

The values vary between approximately 25% and 70%, consistent with expected operational ranges in typical cloud workloads. Spikes were introduced into designated VMs during defined intervals to simulate bursty usage patterns or anomalous conditions, while the remaining VMs retain stochastic but non-anomalous utilization behaviors.

This dataset serves as the input to the forecasting and anomaly detection model, enabling quantitative assessment of detection performance under conditions that mimic both normal workload fluctuations and rare, high-intensity anomalies. The diversity in utilization patterns, both across VMs and over time, ensures that the evaluation encompasses a range of scenarios including steady state, gradual changes, and abrupt shifts in resource demand.

Table 1. CPU utilization on each VM with the corresponding time.

Time	VM_1	VM_2	VM_3	VM_4	VM_5	VM_6	VM_7	VM_8	VM_9	VM_10
T1	38.09	31.10	29.08	50.53	29.95	49.19	36.95	45.75	39.81	43.80
T2	54.36	38.78	39.45	43.21	37.34	40.86	49.25	30.51	49.47	40.98
T3	27.76	48.33	60.61	52.80	41.94	41.85	41.11	33.28	50.64	39.42
T4	29.64	27.14	38.55	55.73	58.43	35.95	36.26	33.02	55.55	35.58
T5	40.89	45.54	40.09	46.31	67.83	63.73	55.77	29.84	49.45	58.96
T6	45.39	55.12	41.15	41.42	27.34	34.74	47.35	50.70	45.12	53.88
T7	58.16	47.80	56.38	41.13	50.52	23.95	39.26	36.56	63.64	37.08
T8	27.60	60.12	47.24	64.75	48.70	44.55	35.91	64.76	53.47	48.06
T9	48.48	50.86	42.79	61.73	46.34	46.28	26.52	40.09	60.61	52.94
T10	47.00	31.54	43.53	49.02	44.25	36.69	30.30	58.03	30.40	43.10
T11	57.96	59.73	56.04	51.27	42.97	57.46	58.00	38.65	54.55	52.08
T12	52.76	45.41	37.62	60.23	33.68	49.75	35.49	43.06	44.93	57.45
T13	39.59	45.90	43.85	50.56	64.63	60.52	65.27	44.91	30.25	53.95
T14	34.08	51.37	52.09	65.18	31.29	37.33	40.41	35.02	35.58	60.42
T15	45.20	41.29	42.55	41.39	52.89	52.80	33.29	33.11	36.19	60.23
T16	49.61	41.23	44.20	51.28	50.15	50.30	49.65	26.79	48.37	59.87
T17	53.74	37.83	30.45	43.74	54.95	49.44	45.25	42.05	47.03	51.02
T18	35.13	61.37	48.62	33.26	34.40	47.05	35.83	37.62	53.68	36.92
T19	52.15	42.98	39.01	53.25	37.92	40.95	40.79	39.92	32.79	46.02
T20	55.60	45.59	36.48	56.41	52.82	39.04	51.12	39.02	61.87	45.79
T21	56.07	35.58	58.09	48.96	42.70	48.62	51.15	42.15	57.26	65.59
T22	59.87	50.79	54.24	39.20	34.02	28.18	41.93	55.03	67.46	43.07
T23	57.68	52.57	38.84	26.86	48.09	50.38	65.33	52.11	50.42	61.54
T24	48.76	49.21	30.47	40.51	54.13	28.89	51.80	32.19	41.16	40.00
T25	51.83	57.09	40.75	26.79	55.19	57.73	56.23	42.27	34.19	48.08

(continued)

Table 1. (*continued*)

Time	VM_1	VM_2	VM_3	VM_4	VM_5	VM_6	VM_7	VM_8	VM_9	VM_10
T26	60.12	30.47	45.15	43.61	33.72	33.13	36.52	41.98	40.87	63.85
T27	45.94	40.24	43.56	57.31	31.94	53.63	55.67	43.64	38.11	33.19
T28	33.84	52.42	34.92	42.17	59.66	33.67	30.46	44.53	54.10	51.50
T29	54.78	32.78	43.58	52.15	46.12	44.82	29.44	30.12	51.36	31.25
T30	56.77	34.97	58.44	47.39	37.51	35.86	51.71	34.08	48.75	52.00
T31	36.33	28.37	60.59	38.49	54.82	54.66	36.91	35.32	41.29	36.02

5.4 Experimental Setup

This section presents the experimental evaluation of the proposed matrix-based forecasting and anomaly detection framework. Three test scenarios TEST_1, TEST_2, and TEST_3 were designed using synthetically generated CPU utilization data to represent short-term, mid-term, and long-term forecasting conditions, respectively. Each test scenario examines the classification performance of two detection methods: (1) Raw Forecast Error and (2) Adjusted Forecast Error (AFE), which incorporates exponential smoothing.

6 Results and Analysis

6.1 TEST_1: Short Term Forecasting (10 Time Slots)

In the TEST_1, 10 VMs has been considered for CPU utilization monitoring in 10 time slots, starting from the first time slot. The 11th time slot will be considered for the forecast and comparison with its actual CPU usage of the considered VMs. As shown in Table 2, number of Type II anomalies has been reduced from 8 to 3 after appalling Adjusted Forecast Error.

Table 2. TEST_1 results

Test Number	Anomaly Detection Base	No Anomaly	Type I	Type II
TEST_1	Based on Forecast Error	1	1	8
TEST_1	Based on Adjusted Forecast Error	6	1	3

6.2 TEST_2: Mid Term Forecasting

In the TEST_2, 10 VMs has been considered for CPU utilization monitoring in 20 time slots, starting from the first time slot. The 21st time slot will be considered for the forecast and comparison with its actual CPU usage of the considered VMs. As shown in Table 3, number of Type II anomalies has been reduced from 5 to 1 after appalling Adjusted Forecast Error.

Table 3. TEST_2 results

Test Number	Anomaly Detection Base	No Anomaly	Type I	Type II
TEST_2	Based on Forecast Error	1	4	5
TEST_2	Based on Adjusted Forecast Error	5	4	1

6.3 TEST_3: Long Term Forecasting

In the TEST_3, 10 VMs has been considered for CPU utilization monitoring in 30 time slots, starting from the first time slot. The 31st time slot will be considered for the forecast and comparison with its actual CPU usage of the considered VMs. As indicated in Table 4, the count of Type II anomalies decreased from 3 to 0 following the application of the Adjusted Forecast Error.

Table 4. TEST_3 results

Test Number	Anomaly Detection Base	No Anomaly	Type I	Type II
TEST_3	Based on Forecast Error	0	7	3
TEST_3	Based on Adjusted Forecast Error	4	6	0

6.4 Comparative Evaluation

Across all three tests, as shown in Table 5, the **Adjusted Forecast Error (AFE)** approach consistently improved detection accuracy by reducing the frequency of Type II (over-prediction) anomalies. While there was a modest increase in Type I anomalies in some cases, the method demonstrated a superior balance between precision and recall, especially in longer time series (TEST_3).

Table 5. TEST_1, TEST_2 and TEST_3.

Test Number	Anomaly Detection Base	No Anomaly	Type I	Type II
TEST_1	Based on Forecast Error	1	1	8
TEST_1	Based on Adjusted Forecast Error	6	1	3
TEST_2	Based on Forecast Error	1	4	5
TEST_2	Based on Adjusted Forecast Error	5	4	1
TEST_3	Based on Forecast Error	0	7	3
TEST_3	Based on Adjusted Forecast Error	4	6	0

TEST_1 Analysis

In TEST_1 (10-slot history), the raw forecast error resulted in 80% Type II (over-prediction) anomalies. After applying the Adjusted Forecast Error (AFE), this reduced to 30%, indicating a 62.5% relative improvement. The number of non-anomalous classifications increased from 10% to 60%, demonstrating that AFE effectively corrects overestimation bias in short monitoring windows.

TEST_2 Analysis

In TEST_2 (20-slot history), the raw forecast error produced 50% Type II anomalies, while AFE reduced this to 10%, achieving an 80% reduction. Non-anomalous classifications increased from 10% to 50%, confirming AFE's stability as more historical context becomes available.

TEST_3 Analysis

In TEST_3 (30-slot history), the raw forecast error yielded 70% Type I (under-prediction) anomalies and 30% Type II anomalies. Remarkably, AFE completely eliminated Type II anomalies (0%), while raising the proportion of non-anomalous cases to 40%. This shows that with longer observation windows, AFE becomes increasingly robust, though at the cost of slightly more under-predictions.

Cross-Test Summary

Across the three tests, AFE consistently reduced Type II anomalies by 62.5%–100%, while improving the number of correctly classified non-anomalous cases by 4x–6x compared to raw forecasts. Although Type I anomalies increased modestly, this trade-off is preferable, as over-prediction often leads to wasted resources in cloud systems, whereas under-prediction can be mitigated with elastic scaling strategies.

The results confirm that applying exponential smoothing through the AFE method enhances anomaly detection performance by mitigating over-prediction, which is often more costly in resource allocation scenarios. The findings demonstrate the importance of integrating adaptive error adjustment techniques into forecasting models for virtual machine resource management.

7 Conclusion and Future Work

This study introduced a matrix-based approach for forecasting and anomaly detection of CPU resource utilization in cloud computing environments. The method relies on low-rank approximation using Singular Value Decomposition (SVD) to model VM utilization data over time. Forecasting is performed by projecting temporal patterns, while anomalies are identified using directional forecast error, further refined through Exponential Moving Average (EMA). By combining these elements, the proposed framework enables interpretable forecasting and adaptive anomaly classification with relatively low computational overhead. The approach was evaluated through three experiments using synthetic datasets designed to emulate varying operational timelines. Results across short-term, medium-term, and long-term time series indicate that the use of EMA-adjusted forecast errors significantly reduces over-prediction anomalies (Type II), which are particularly costly in resource-constrained environments. While under-prediction anomalies (Type I) increased marginally in longer series, the model maintained a balanced performance profile and proved resilient under varying conditions.

This study provides several practical contributions. It shows that a lightweight matrix factorization approach can effectively identify anomalies in fluctuating workloads without the complexity of deep learning models. The forecast error adjustment demonstrates improved accuracy as the length of the time series increases, indicating the model's capacity to capture long-term trends and reduce the influence of short-term variability. This characteristic makes the approach well suited for cloud environments where low latency and minimal computational overhead are essential. Additionally, the model's transparent structure facilitates interpretability, which is important in applications requiring auditability and clear explanations, such as financial cloud services or edge computing platforms.

Future investigations should validate the proposed method on extensive, real-world datasets like the Google Cluster Trace [21] and Alibaba Cloud Trace [22]. These datasets encompass a wide range of workload behaviors and noise, providing a more rigorous test of the framework's scalability and general applicability in operational cloud infrastructures. Moreover, expanding the current univariate focus on CPU utilization to a multivariate framework is a necessary advancement. This could be accomplished by employing tensor decomposition techniques to incorporate multiple resource metrics including memory consumption, disk input/output, and network bandwidth thus enabling a more comprehensive analysis of workload dynamics [23].

Another key avenue for development involves implementing dynamic thresholding mechanisms that adjust to evolving workload characteristics over time, rather than relying on a fixed threshold as in the current model [24]. Integration with cloud orchestration platforms such as Kubernetes could enhance real-time applicability, facilitating proactive resource management through dynamic scaling and load balancing [25]. Incorporating online learning algorithms, such as incremental SVD or streaming matrix factorization methods, would allow the model to update continuously without the need for complete retraining, improving its responsiveness to non-stationary and rapidly changing workloads [26]. Furthermore, the forecast error profiles generated by this approach may also be useful for identifying security threats, including resource hijacking or distributed denial-of-service (DDoS) attacks, by detecting anomalous behavioral patterns [27].

In conclusion, this research introduces a compact, interpretable, and adaptable framework that unifies forecasting and anomaly detection in cloud computing. It demonstrates robust performance in controlled environments and, with further development and deployment, offers significant potential to support intelligent, secure, and resource-efficient decision-making in cloud infrastructures.

Disclosure of Interests. The authors declare that they have no competing interests relevant to the content of this article.

References

1. Rodriguez, M.A., Buyya, R.: Deadline based resource provisioningand scheduling algorithm for scientific workflows on clouds. IEEE Transactions on Cloud Computing. **2**, 222–235 (2014). https://doi.org/10.1109/TCC.2014.2314655

2. Kang, Y., Li, Y., Zhang, G.: Forecasting cloud workload through reinforcement learning-based ensemble model. In: 2024 4th International Conference on Electronic Information Engineering and Computer Communication, EIECC 2024, pp. 1581–1588 (2024). https://doi.org/10.1109/EIECC64539.2024.10929137
3. Jassas, M.S., Mahmoud, Q.H.: Analysis of job failure and prediction model for cloud computing using machine learning. Sensors. **22**, 2035 (2022). https://doi.org/10.3390/S22052035
4. Yin, J., Lu, X., Chen, H., Zhao, X., Xiong, N.N.: System resource utilization analysis and prediction for cloud based applications under bursty workloads. Inf Sci (N Y). **279**, 338–357 (2014). https://doi.org/10.1016/J.INS.2014.03.123
5. Aceto, G., Botta, A., De Donato, W., Pescapè, A.: Cloud monitoring: a survey. Comput. Netw. **57**, 2093–2115 (2013). https://doi.org/10.1016/J.COMNET.2013.04.001
6. Ranjan, R.: Streaming big data processing in datacenter clouds. IEEE Cloud Comput. **1**, 78–83 (2014). https://doi.org/10.1109/MCC.2014.22
7. Li, B., Li, J., Huai, J., Wo, T., Li, Q., Zhong, L.: EnaCloud: An energy-saving application live placement approach for cloud computing environments. In: CLOUD 2009–2009 IEEE International Conference on Cloud Computing, pp. 17–24 (2009). https://doi.org/10.1109/CLOUD.2009.72
8. Xing, Y.: Work scheduling in cloud network based on deep Q-LSTM models for efficient resource utilization. J Grid Comput. **22**, 1–20 (2024). https://doi.org/10.1007/S10723-024-09746-6/METRICS
9. Catena, T., Eramo, V., Panella, M., Rosato, A: Distributed LSTM-based cloud resource allocation in network function virtualization architectures. Comput. Netw. **213**, 109111 (2022). https://doi.org/10.1016/J.COMNET.2022.109111
10. Nguyen, T., et al.: An LSTM-based approach for predicting resource utilization in cloud computing. ACM International Conference Proceeding Series., 173–179 (2022). https://doi.org/10.1145/3568562.3568647
11. Babu, A., Sathiya, R.R.: Resource-based prediction in cloud computing using LSTM with autoencoders. Smart Innovation, Systems and Technologies. **313**, 251–263 (2023). https://doi.org/10.1007/978-981-19-8669-7_23
12. Sabyasachi, A.S., Sahoo, B.M., Ranganath, A.: Deep CNN and LSTM approaches for efficient workload prediction in cloud environment. Procedia Comput Sci. **235**, 2651–2661 (2024). https://doi.org/10.1016/J.PROCS.2024.04.250
13. Yuan, H., Bi, J., Li, S., Zhang, J., Zhou, M.C.: An improved LSTM-based prediction approach for resources and workload in large-scale data centers. IEEE Internet Things J. **11**, 22816–22829 (2024). https://doi.org/10.1109/JIOT.2024.3383512
14. Zhang, Q., Cheng, L., Boutaba, R.: Cloud computing: state-of-the-art and research challenges. J. Internet Serv. Appl. **1**, 7–18 (2010). https://doi.org/10.1007/S13174-010-0007-6/METRICS
15. Unsupervised anomaly detection based on principal components analysis. https://www.researchgate.net/publication/293186123_Unsupervised_anomaly_detection_based_on_principal_components_analysis. Accessed 11 June 2025
16. Koren, Y., Bell, R., Volinsky, C.: Matrix factorization techniques for recommender systems. Computer (Long Beach Calif). **42**, 30–37 (2009). https://doi.org/10.1109/MC.2009.263
17. Agarwal, D., Chen, B.C.: Regression-based latent factor models. In: Proceedings of the ACM SIGKDD International Conference on Knowledge Discovery and Data Mining., pp. 19–27 (2009). https://doi.org/10.1145/1557019.1557029/SUPPL_FILE/P19-AGARWAL.MP4
18. Xu, C.Z., Rao, J., Bu, X.: URL: a unified reinforcement learning approach for autonomic cloud management. J Parallel Distrib Comput. **72**, 95–105 (2012). https://doi.org/10.1016/J.JPDC.2011.10.003

19. Islam, S., Keung, J., Lee, K., Liu, A.: Empirical prediction models for adaptive resource provisioning in the cloud. Futur. Gener. Comput. Syst. **28**, 155–162 (2012). https://doi.org/10.1016/J.FUTURE.2011.05.027
20. Mao, M., Humphrey, M.: A performance study on the VM startup time in the cloud. Proceedings. 2012 IEEE 5th International Conference on Cloud Computing, CLOUD 2012, 423–430 (2012). https://doi.org/10.1109/CLOUD.2012.103
21. Reiss, C., Tumanov, A., Ganger, G.R., Katz, R.H., Kozuch, M.A.: Heterogeneity and dynamicity of clouds at scale: Google trace analysis. In: Proceedings of the 3rd ACM Symposium on Cloud Computing, SoCC 2012 (2012). https://doi.org/10.1145/2391229.2391236
22. alibaba/clusterdata: cluster data collected from production clusters in Alibaba for cluster management research. https://github.com/alibaba/clusterdata. Accessed 12 June 2025
23. Sun, J., Tao, D., Faloutsos, C.: Beyond streams and graphs. 374–383 (2006). https://doi.org/10.1145/1150402.1150445.
24. Ahmad, S., Purdy, S.: Real-Time Anomaly Detection for Streaming Analytics. (2016)
25. Auto-scaling to minimize cost and meet application deadlines in cloud workflows. IEEE Conference Publication|IEEE Xplore. https://ieeexplore.ieee.org/abstract/document/6114435. Accessed 12 June 2025
26. Brand, M.: Fast low-rank modifications of the thin singular value decomposition. Linear Algebra Appl. **415**, 20–30 (2006). https://doi.org/10.1016/J.LAA.2005.07.021
27. Meidan, Y. et al., : Detection of Unauthorized IoT Devices Using Machine Learning Techniques. (2017)

Leveraging Unintentional Electromagnetic Emissions for Radio Tomographic Imaging

Oshani Wickramasinghe[1](✉), Asanka Sayakkara[1], Chamath Keppitiyagama[1], and Thiemo Voigt[2]

[1] University of Colombo School of Computing, Colombo 07, Sri Lanka
2020cs214@stu.ucsc.cmb.ac.lk, {asa,cik}@ucsc.cmb.ac.lk
[2] Uppsala University, Uppsala, Sweden
thiemo.voigt@angstrom.uu.se

Abstract. Radio Tomographic Imaging (RTI) is a promising technique for imaging non-line-of-sight areas. RTI uses radio frequency signals to create a map of the area of interest (AoI) by analyzing changes in signal strength caused by the presence or movement of objects within a network of wireless transmitters and receivers. However, current implementations require complex setups with multiple transceivers and costly, dedicated radio circuits. These systems are difficult to use in embedded and IoT applications and are highly sensitive to terrain and surface structure variations, which can significantly impact signal propagation. We investigate an alternative approach that exploits the unintentional electromagnetic (EM) emissions from computing devices to detect the effect of a human presence on the link between the device and the antenna. We conduct experiments in three different environments with a stationary person in the link using EM emissions of a single desktop PC with an Intel i5-7400 CPU. Our results demonstrate that an object in line of sight between the signal source and the receiver causes variations in the received signal from 0.65 to 3.52 dB, dependent on the AoI and the surroundings. Our results also show that changes can be detected up to 2.4 m from the signal source in a cluttered indoor environment and up to 3 m in an outdoor environment. Our findings further indicate that unintentional EM emissions from electronic devices can enable passive human detection without the need for purpose-built transmitters. Therefore, our approach can be extended to RTI.

Keywords: Radio Tomography · Electromagnetic emissions · Far field antenna · HackRF

1 Introduction

Tomography is a technique for generating images by analyzing cross-sectional projections. It can be recognized both as a computer vision technique and as a sensing method. Radio Tomographic Imaging (RTI) uses Radio Frequency (RF) signals to create a map of the observed space [1]. RTI systems that utilize

R. N. Rajapakse et al. (Eds.): ICTer 2025, CCIS 2844, pp. 426–440, 2026.
https://doi.org/10.1007/978-981-92-0137-2_28

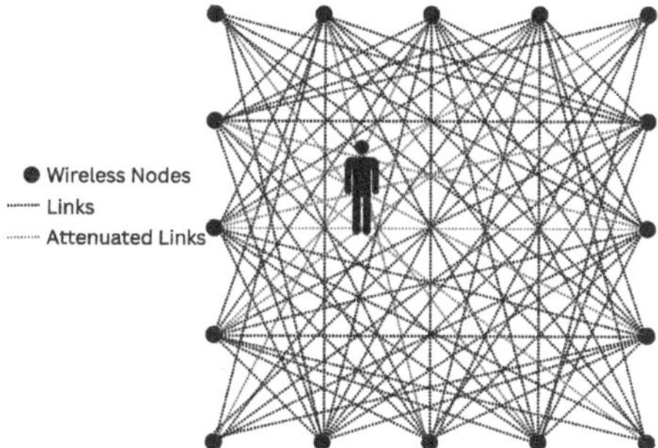

Fig. 1. Common RTI setup. Multiple transmitters and receivers surround an area to form wireless links between each node. Transmitters emit signals that propagate through the environment and are received by other nodes. Human presence is detected based on the attenuation a person has on these signal links.

RF signals offer improved privacy for individuals in the monitored area while tracking and localizing objects even through walls, making them superior to video camera systems in these aspects. RTI systems are less invasive than video cameras and RFID tracking, and also offer a lower cost. [3,9].

A tomographic setup consists of many transmitters and receivers, producing wireless links that connect each node to every other node (Fig. 1). Transmitters emit wireless signals that propagate through the air and detected by receivers. During propagation, signals are affected by reflection, diffraction, refraction, shadowing, and scattering. These interactions cause changes in signal strength, amplitude, and phase, depending on the presence of stationary or moving objects in the environment. Obstructions along the propagation path can be identified as deviations from the base signal [21,23]. Thus, the fundamental requirement to construct a tomographic image using data collected from multiple links is the ability to detect an object obstructing the free path of a single link.

We observe that RTI methods often fail in situations where an intentional electromagnetic (EM) wave source is absent or where the area of interest (AoI) is inaccessible and an EM wave source cannot be placed. Another major challenge is the energy consumption and communication requirements of sensor networks. Our objective is to address the absence and power consumption of the signal source by utilizing unintentional EM emissions from computing devices. This can potentially reduce both hardware requirements and energy consumption by leveraging ambient signals in the environment.

Our scientific contribution is the observation that the EM emissions of a desktop PC with an Intel i5-7400 CPU, Corsair CX450M power supply, and Ubuntu 22.04 as the operating system can be used to detect human presence within the Line of Sight (LOS) between the device and a receiving antenna. Our results indicate that the presence of a person causes noticeable variations in the Received Signal Strength (RSS), ranging from 0.65 to 3.52 dB at 792 MHz. These variations are detectable up to 2.4 m in a cluttered indoor setting and up to 3 m in an outdoor environment.

2 Motivation and Background

This section outlines the motivation behind our research, with the background knowledge that informed the design of our experiments and evaluation.

2.1 Motivation

Existing RTI methods rely on intentionally deployed EM wave sources and sensor networks, which limits their applicability when signal source deployment is impractical or the monitored area is inaccessible. In addition, these systems often face challenges related to energy consumption and communication overhead. This motivates the exploration of unintentional EM emissions as a passive alternative, offering the potential to reduce hardware complexity and power usage by leveraging ambient signals.

2.2 Background

Radio Tomography. Wireless sensor systems have become an evolving topic among sensor techniques because they do not require the target to carry any tracking device offering wireless, sensorless, and contactless monitoring [23]. Passive wireless sensor systems detect human presence by the impact of a person on a signal link. This impact can vary based on the frequency of the signal being used, the transmission power, and the environment. A comparison of previous results on this aspect is as in Table 1.

There are two widely used approaches for RTI, namely fingerprint-based methods and model-based methods. Fingerprint-based methods have a pre-trained database of data labeled with position and when in use, measurements

Table 1. Summary of experimental studies on human movement and received signal strength indicator (RSSI) variations (adapted from [22])

Ref.	Type of study	Wireless technology	Test field	Major findings
[2]	Experiment	WLAN, 2.4 GHz radio devices	Indoor	Movement decreased the RSSI by 2 to 5 dBm
[12]	Experiment	MicaZ nodes, CC2420, 2.4 GHz ZigBee/IEEE 802.15.4	Indoor	Movement across LOS reduced RSSI by 5 to 10 dBm, depending on distance between transmitter and receiver
[10]	Experiment	CC2431, 2.4 GHz ZigBee/IEEE 802.15.4	Indoor	Movement across LOS caused RSSI variation, influenced by link distance
[16]	Experiment	CC2420, 2.4 GHz ZigBee/IEEE 802.15.4	Indoor	RSSI varied with person's predefined positions across LOS; center position caused RSSI to drop 8 dBm; bi-directional links showed same pattern

are compared with those in the database to estimate position. Although these methods are more accurate, the training phase is time and resource consuming and requires significant effort to collect data. Moreover, the process has to be repeated when changing the environment. Model-based methods use semi-empirical weight models. These methods are computationally efficient. However, the dynamic and sensitive nature of the RSS introduces noise and pseudo targets in the tomographic image [11].

Shadowing-based RTI is the simplest method considering the shadowing effect caused by the human body on the RSS in multiple links to estimate the position [5,18]. The attenuation-based method takes into consideration an RSS value at a specific time and the base RSS value. The base RSS value is the average RSS measured during the calibration period. The difference between the two values would suggest an obstruction [3,20]. Histogram-based RTI considers two histograms. RSS values gathered during the calibration period are represented in the long term histogram and the short term histogram is based on the recent RSS values. The kernel distance between two histograms presents a change in RSS value which is caused by an obstruction [3]. Variance-based RTI measures the RSS variance caused by mobile objects in the AoI within two consecutive time periods [21]. In contrast to other methods, this does not require a calibration phase.

Electromagnetic Emissions. Typical home or office environments are saturated with EM emissions generated by the internal switching mechanisms of electronic devices [19]. They are unique to each device model allowing device identification, provided that highly sensitive receiving antennas are used [13]. The characteristics such as frequency and emission patterns of these EM emissions change depending on the operational state of the device, whether it is in standby mode, turned off, or moved [15,25].

Generation of Electromagnetic Emissions from Circuits. When electrical current changes in a circuit, it generates a fluctuating magnetic field. This in turn induces an electric field, creating a continuous interaction between the electric and magnetic fields, which propagate as an EM wave [7]. This interaction is governed by two fundamental laws of electromagnetism: Faraday's Law of Induction, which states that a changing magnetic field creates an electric field, and Ampère's Law with Maxwell's correction which states that a changing electric field generates a magnetic field.

Digital circuits, such as those in microprocessors, process data by switching currents on and off, generating fluctuating magnetic fields. These variations induce electric fields and the interplay of these fields leads to the emission of EM waves [4]. The fundamental frequency of the EM emissions corresponds to the clock frequency of the circuit with harmonics forming based on the duty ratio of the signal which is typically around 50% [24].

The strength and amplitude of the generated EM emissions depend on two key factors. The first is the rate of change of the magnetic field which is directly related to the rate of change of the current [4]. The second factor is the variation in current levels which in turn depends on the CPU workload and the operation of the switch-mode power supply.

Propagation of Electromagnetic Radiation. In radio communications, RSS decreases as the distance between the transmitter and receiver increases. This phenomenon is known as path loss which can be modeled as follows:

$$P_a(r) = c \cdot d^{-\eta} \tag{1}$$

where c is a constant and η is the path loss exponent which varies depending on the environment. In urban environments η typically ranges from 2 to 6, depending on the density of obstacles [8].

Shadowing is the attenuation of signals due to obstacles between the transmitter and the receiver such as buildings or other structures. It leads to slow variations in signal strength over longer distances and is often modeled using a log-normal distribution [6]. In contrast, fading arises from multipath propagation where signals take multiple paths to reach the receiver due to reflections, diffraction, and scattering. This causes rapid fluctuations in RSS over short distances and brief time intervals.

The prominent models for EM radiation propagation which account for path loss, fading, and shadowing, include the Circular Coverage Model, which assumes a fixed circular range of reception; the i.i.d. Link Fading Model which captures independent random fading of each link due to multipath effects; and the i.i.d. Log-Normal Shadowing Model which models signal attenuation caused by large obstacles using a log-normal distribution [14].

3 Methodology

A key distinction between our research and other RTI studies is that the observed signal in our work is unintentional EM radiation, rather than a deliberately emitted signal from a purpose-built transmitter. We investigate the impact of an object placed along a single link between the desktop PC and the receiver using the experimental setup described below.

3.1 Experimental Setup

The experimental setup consists of three main components: a HackRF One software defined radio, a directional antenna, and GNU Radio Companion software. The complete setup is in Fig. 2. The signal source is a desktop PC with an Intel i5-7400 CPU, Ubuntu 22.04 operating system, and Corsair CX450M power supply. A directional antenna, positioned at 0.75 m height, receives the signals. The received signal is sampled by HackRF and processed on a laptop using GNU Radio Companion (GRC). Data are visualized with the `Fosphor sink` block and stored in `float32` format using GRC.

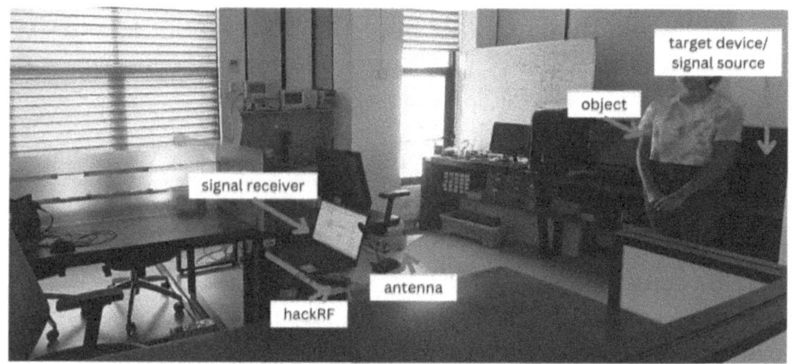

Fig. 2. Lab setup with component positions.

We generate EM emissions with a static CPU workload using `stress-ng` and monitor CPU workload and frequency with `htop` and `watch -n1 ''grep Hz /proc/cpuinfo''`. We record 30 s of data in `.cfile` format for each experiment. Afterward, raw data are converted to IQ samples and processed using the Short-Time Fourier Transform to analyze time-varying frequency components.

3.2 Signal Processing and Analysis

We begin by evaluating whether the EM emissions from the source are suitable for RTI. This is achieved by performing a statistical test to verify the hypothesis that the data sets collected with and without the presence of an object are significantly different. Following that, we apply the t-test with a significance level of 0.05 to all instances of collected data with and without the presence of an object. T-test is a statistical test to check whether the difference between the means of two groups is statistically significant.

The t-test results show a significant difference between every scenario with and without an object, and the P-values suggest that the null hypothesis can be rejected. Therefore, there is a statistically significant difference between the two groups which implies that the presence of an object on the LOS link has a measurable effect on RSS.

Histogram analysis of the collected RSS data indicates that the data distribution is not perfectly symmetric for all scenarios, highlighting the importance of choosing an appropriate measure of central tendency. The skewed data suggest that the median is a more robust measure of central tendency since it is less affected by outliers compared to the mean, while still effectively representing the dataset.

A higher RSS is expected in the scenario without an obstruction, as the absence of an object eliminates the shadowing effect. We determine the maximum detectable distance by observing the impact of the object on the signal. For this purpose, we quantify the impact using the Signal to Noise Ratio (SNR). The SNR value between the signal without object and the signal with object indicates the effect of the object compared to the free path signal.

There are several methods to calculate the SNR value. In our scenario, the power ratio method is used since the target frequency is known and noise can be measured (Eq. 2).

$$SNR = 10 \cdot \log_{10}\left(\frac{P_{\text{signal without object}}}{P_{\text{with object}}}\right) \tag{2}$$

If the SNR is large, it indicates that the object significantly reduces the signal quality. In contrast, if the SNR is small, the object has little impact on the signal. When the SNR drops below zero, the noise dominates the signal and the object can no longer be detected. The maximum detection distance is defined as the point where the SNR approaches zero. This threshold is chosen because NLOS signals generally exhibit lower RSS than LOS signals. However, as the distance increases, multipath effects become more pronounced, making the RSS increasingly unpredictable. An SNR of 0 dB indicates that the signal variations caused by the object are no longer distinguishable from the noise. A negative SNR value occurs when the noise dominates the signal. Therefore, we define the maximum range as the farthest point at which the object's impact on the signal becomes both insignificant and unpredictable.

3.3 Preliminary Experiments

Frequency Identification and Selection. The CPU in the desktop PC we use as the signal source employs Dynamic Voltage and Frequency Scaling (DVFS) technology. Therefore, the frequency of the signal source changes with the workload. Consequently, the observed signal ranges do not correlate solely with the EM emissions of the CPU. Instead, signal ranges display variations associated with any CPU workload, indicating that the EM emission is influenced by factors beyond the CPU. We take the following steps to further investigate the frequencies of the EM emissions from the signal source.

We retrieve detailed hardware information using the `lshw` command in Linux including the operating frequencies of the system components. The analysis reveals three key frequencies: 3 GHz, 33 MHz, and 66 MHz. The 33 MHz signal stands out among them as a stable clock frequency associated with multiple internal components, making it a strong candidate for further analysis.

Given that the emissions from the source can contain higher order harmonics, we focus on examining the 33 MHz fundamental frequency and its harmonics by observing changes in signal strength for different CPU workloads and the on/off status of the device. The 24th harmonic (792 MHz) demonstrates the highest sensitivity to changes in CPU workload, making it the most suitable target frequency. However, it is important to note that the EM emissions of the device are not limited to a single frequency; rather, they span a complete 20 MHz bandwidth with the narrow band centered around 792 MHz exhibiting the highest sensitivity.

Effect of CPU Workload on Signal Strength. According to the literature, a processor adjusts its operating frequency based on the workload to conserve

Table 2. Statistical values and t-test results for varying CPU workloads

CPU workload (%)	Median (NLoS) (dBm)	Median (LoS) (dBm)	T-Statistic	Conclusion
10	-121.76	–121.04	–93.5986	Significant difference
20	–121.79	–121.04	–101.9562	Significant difference
30	–121.64	–120.69	–134.0214	Significant difference
40	–121.28	–120.45	–106.7482	Significant difference
50	–121.39	–120.31	–140.7272	Significant difference
60	–121.44	–120.33	–152.6532	Significant difference
70	–121.63	–120.56	–134.1624	Significant difference
80	–121.69	–119.65	–250.9022	Significant difference
90	–121.53	–120.37	–161.7823	Significant difference
100	–121.20	–119.76	–180.1282	Significant difference

energy, which in turn alters the EM radiation it emits [17]. We place the signal source and the receiver at a fixed distance of 2.1 m and control the CPU workload using the `stress-ng` tool. To evaluate the impact of an object, we position a non-emitting object approximately 0.3 m in front of the receiver.

We record measurements with and without the object in place for each specified workload level. T-test results (Table 2) for the collected data reveal that for any given CPU workload, the signal strength is significantly different and reduced when an object is placed in the direct LOS between the signal source and the receiver. The magnitude of the T-statistic quantifies the strength of this difference relative to the variability in the data. We also observe that the median signal strength is reduced to a value between -121.79 and -121.20 dBm in Non Line of Sight (NLOS) for every tested CPU workload. The highest CPU workload produces the strongest EM radiation according to the results.

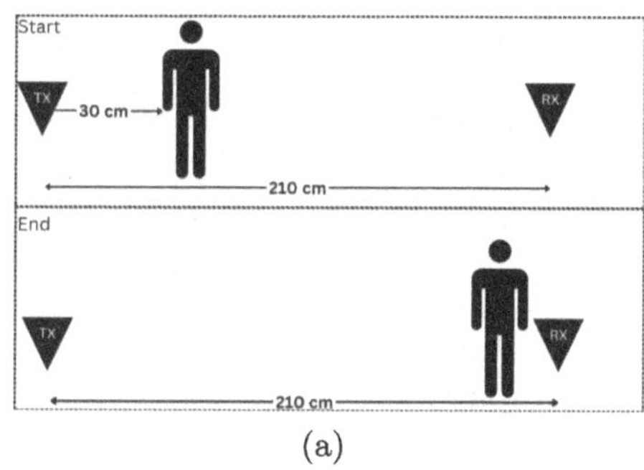

(a)

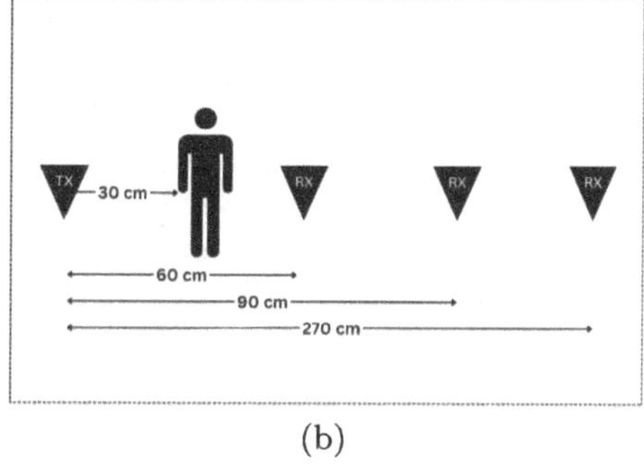

(b)

Fig. 3. (a) Setup to study the RSS variation when an object moves along the link with fixed signal strength and distance. The signal source and the receiver are positioned and the object moves toward the receiver. (b) Setup to study the impact of an object with increasing source-receiver distance. Signal source and the object are positioned and the source-receiver distance is increased.

3.4 Evaluation

Impact of an Object on Received Signal Strength. The fundamental requirement for a tomographic setup is the ability to detect the presence of an object crossing a single link between the signal source and the signal receiver. We study this in two aspects. First, we study the RSS variation when an object moves along the link with fixed signal strength and distance. We also examine how an object affects RSS as the source-receiver distance increases, keeping the CPU workload and the position of the object fixed.

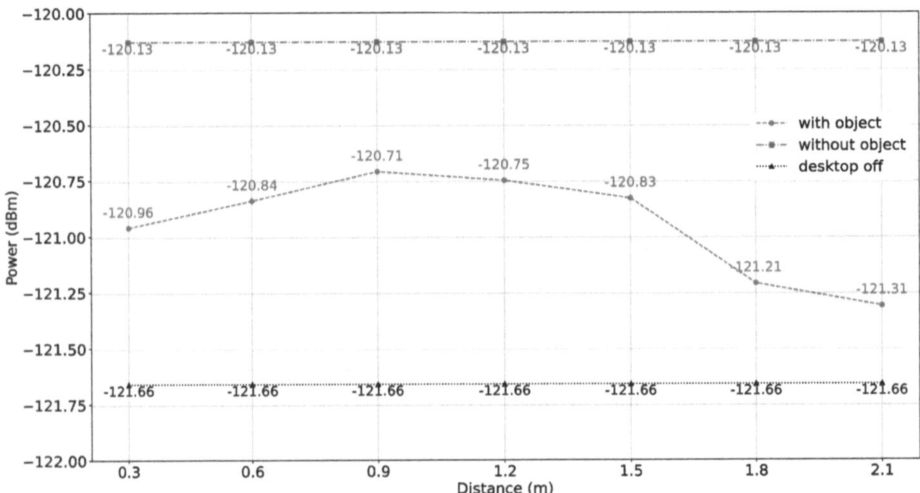

Fig. 4. Variation in the median RSS at 792 MHz with source-receiver distance, as the object moves toward the receiver. The shadowing effect is most pronounced near the source or receiver and diminishes at the center of the link.

To understand how the position of the object along the signal path influences EM radiation reception, we place the signal source and receiver 2.1 m apart with the object placed 0.3 m from the signal source. We then move the object toward the receiver in increments of 0.3 m (Fig. 3a. We collect data under three conditions at each position: (1) with the desktop computer turned off to establish a baseline, (2) with the desktop turned on and no object in the signal path, and (3) with the object placed directly between the source and the receiver.

The results in Fig. 4 show that the shadowing effect is strongest when the object is near the source or receiver, and weakest near the center. This reveals two distinct regions along the link: high-impact zones near the ends, where the object significantly affects the signal, and a low-impact region in the middle with minimal RSS reduction (Fig. 5).

Next, we place the object and the signal source immobile while increasing the source-receiver distance as in Fig. 3b to examine how an object affects RSS as the source-receiver distance increases. The impact of the object on RSS is evident in

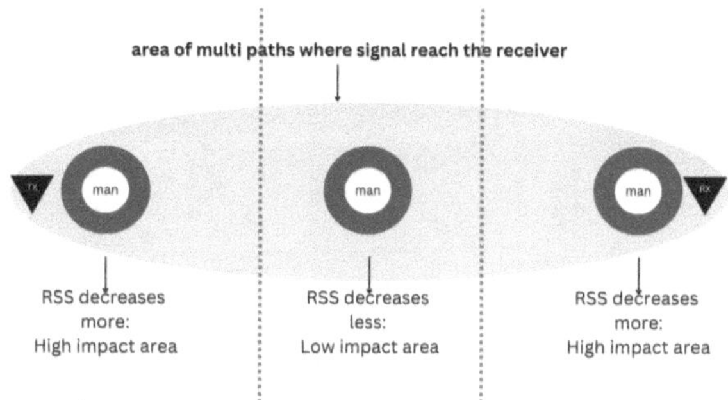

Fig. 5. Illustration of multipath effects and their impact on signal propagation in the link. There are two distinct regions along the link: high-impact areas near the ends, where the object significantly affects the signal, and a low-impact area in the middle with minimal RSS reduction.

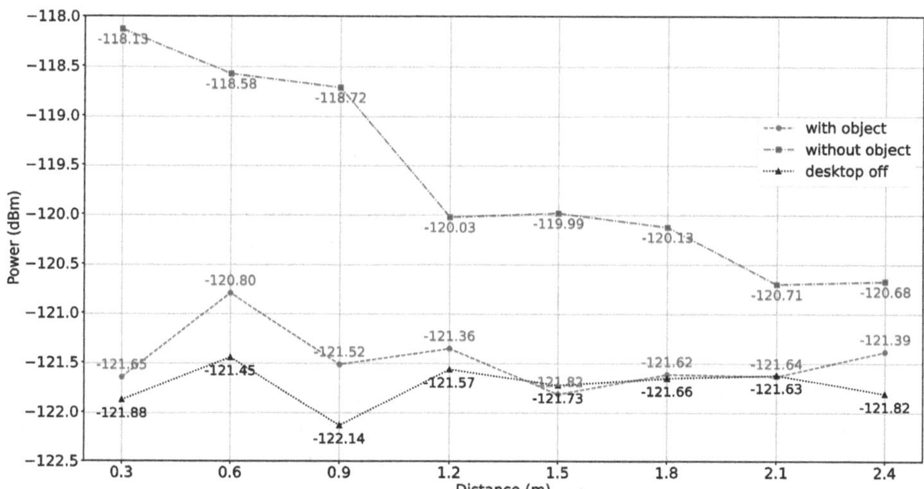

Fig. 6. Variation of median signal strength at 792 MHz with distance when the object is stationary at 0.3 m from the receiver. RSS captured under static workload decreases with distance. The ambient noise remains nearly constant across distances and lower than the active signal when the desktop is turned off. Placing an object in the link has a shadowing effect reducing the RSS.

Fig. 6 where the object is stationary 0.3 m from the receiver. The RSS difference is more pronounced at shorter distances, showing that the object detectability decreases with increasing sourcereceiver distance. The object blocks more signal paths when positioned close to the signal source, causing a significant RSS drop due to the shadowing effect.

Figure 6 represents the signal emitted by the source operating at a static workload and captured at 792 MHz. It shows a decrease in RSS consistent with

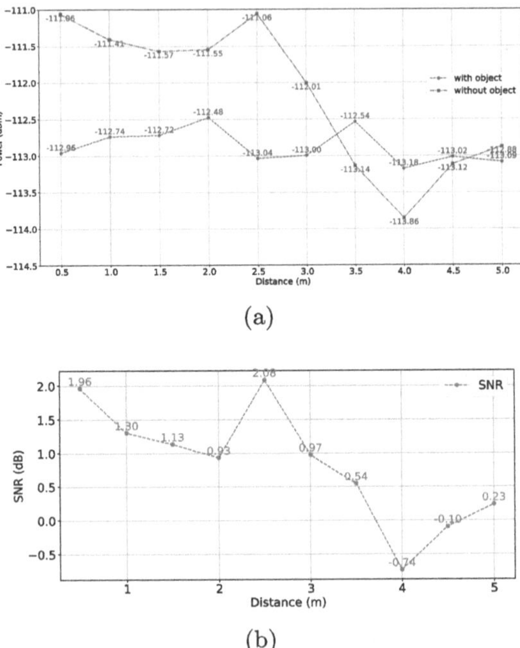

Fig. 7. Analysis of RSS at 792 MHz vs distance with and without an object at outdoor test site. Maximum detection point is 3 m from the signal source. (a) RSS without the object remains higher than RSS with object until 3 m from the signal source (b) SNR value is positive until 3 m, after which noise dominates the signal.

the Circular Coverage Model. In contrast, when the desktop is turned off and the object is placed in the link, the ambient noise remains nearly constant across varying distances and is consistently lower than the signal strength captured when the signal source is active.

Signal Detection Distance. The RSS typically decreases with distance following an inverse proportionality as in Eq. 1. n is the path loss component and generally assumed to be $n = 2$ in free space [14]. We observe the extent of detection capabilities in three different environments: an outdoor test site, an empty indoor environment, and an indoor working environment. We choose these environments to evaluate the maximum effective distance between the signal source and the receiver, as well as to assess the impact of external noise sources such as other electronic devices, moving objects, and static obstacles.

We place the signal source in position and operate it under maximum CPU workload to ensure a consistent radiation level and place the object 0.3 m from the signal source, as shown in Fig. 3b. We collect data with and without the object. After each measurement, we increase the distance between the source

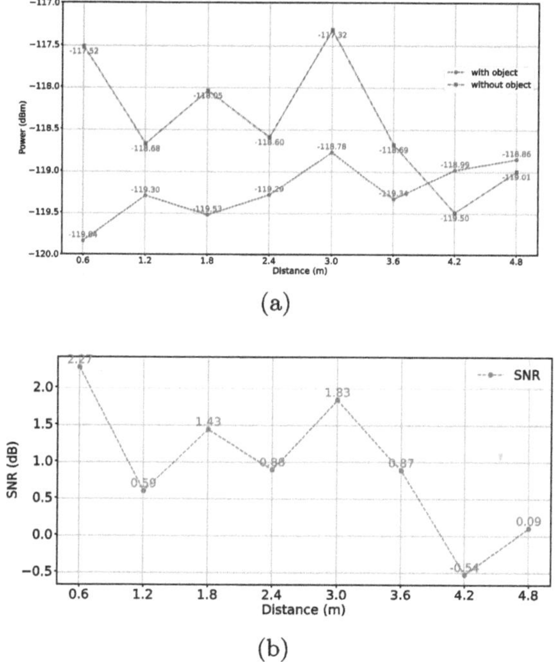

(a)

(b)

Fig. 8. Analysis of RSS at 792 MHz vs distance with and without an object at empty indoor environment. Maximum detection point is 3.6 m from the signal source. (a) RSS without the object remains higher than RSS with object until 3.6 m from the signal source (b) SNR value is positive until 3.6 m, after which noise dominates the signal.

and receiver. The experiment is conducted in outdoor, empty indoor, and indoor working environments. The corresponding results are presented in Figs. 7a–9b.

Figures 7a–9b show that the maximum detection distance varies by environment. In the outdoor test site, the maximum detection distance is defined as the point where the SNR approaches zero, before the influence of significant multipath effects is recorded at a distance of 3 m from the signal source. Beyond this point, detection becomes unreliable due to the uncertainty in SNR (Fig. 7b). The empty indoor environment demonstrates a positive SNR value until 3.6 m from the signal source (Fig. 8b). For the scenario in the indoor working environment, the maximum distance is 2.4 m from the signal source (Fig. 9b). We conclude that the maximum distance to detect an object depends on the environment.

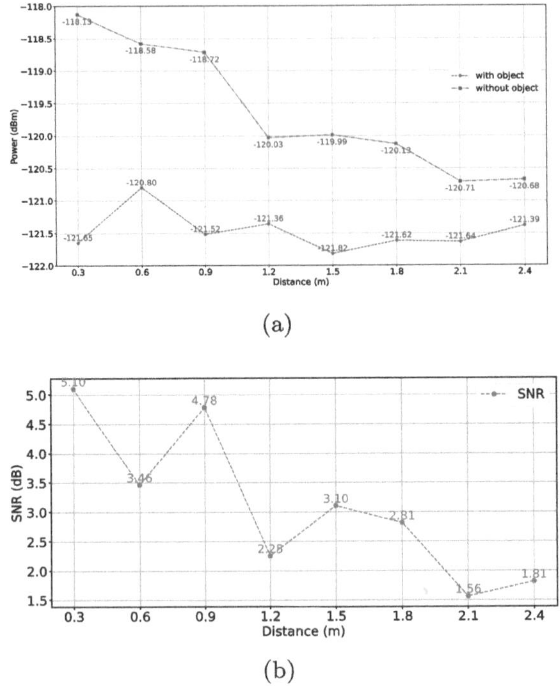

Fig. 9. Analysis of RSS at 792 MHz vs distance with and without an object at indoor cluttered environment. Maximum detection point is 2.4 m from the signal source. (a) RSS without the object remains higher than RSS with object until 2.4 m from the signal source (b) SNR value is positive until 2.4 m.

4 Conclusion

We introduce a novel approach of using unintentional EM emissions to detect human presence near devices. This not only enables passive human detection, but also opens a new path for tomographic imaging without the need for purpose-built transmitters.

Our main contribution is the demonstration that the EM emissions created by a desktop PC with an Intel i5-7400 CPU and Corsair CX450M power supply running Ubuntu 22.04 can be used to detect human presence within the LOS between the desktop PC and the receiver antenna. We show that the presence of a person introduces detectable changes in the RSS from 0.65 to 3.52 dB at 792 MHz. These signal disturbances are measurable up to 2.4 m in a cluttered indoor environment and up to 3 m in an outdoor space.

Our proposed approach is particularly well-suited for IoT applications because it is passive, less intrusive, and more efficient in terms of power consumption and hardware requirements. An additional implication of our work is the identification of a security vulnerability: EM emissions can potentially be used to monitor human movement around devices such as desktop computers from a distance.

Our methodology demonstrates the groundwork for utilizing unintentional EM emission from computing devices by observing the effect of a stationary person on the link. Future work can investigate performance in NLOS scenarios and implement multiple links to collect data and create an RTI image.

Disclosure of Interests. The authors declare no competing interests.

References

1. Alippi, C., Bocca, M., Boracchi, G., Patwari, N., Roveri, M.: RTI Goes Wild: Radio Tomographic Imaging for Outdoor People Detection and Localization (2014)
2. Alshami, I., Ahmad, N., Sahibuddin, S.: People's presence effect on wlan-based ips' accuracy. Jurnal Teknologi **77**, 173–178 (2015)
3. Bocca, M., Kaltiokallio, O., Patwari, N.: Radio tomographic imaging for ambient assisted living. In: Chessa, S., Knauth, S. (eds.) EvAAL 2012. CCIS, vol. 362, pp. 108–130. Springer, Heidelberg (2013). https://doi.org/10.1007/978-3-642-37419-7_9
4. Cui, M., Feng, Y., Wang, Q., Xiong, J.: Sniffing visible light communication through walls. In: Proceedings of the 26th Annual International Conference on Mobile Computing and Networking, MobiCom 2020. Association for Computing Machinery, New York (2020)
5. Dharmadasa, M., Gamage, C., Keppitiyagama, C.: Radio tomographic imaging (rti) and privacy implications. In: 2018 18th International Conference on Advances in ICT for Emerging Regions (ICTer), pp. 413–419 (2018)
6. Goldsmith, A.: Path Loss and Shadowing. In: Wireless Communications, pp. 27–63. Cambridge University Press, Cambridge (2005)
7. Grdović, M.M., Protić, D.D., Antić, V.D., Jovanović, B.: Screen reading: electromagnetic information leakage from the computer monitor. Vojnotehnicki glasnik/Military Technical Courier **70**(4), 836–855 (2022)
8. Hekmat, R., Mieghem, P.: Connectivity in wireless ad-hoc networks with a log-normal radio model. Mobile Netw. Appli. **11**, 351–360 (2006)
9. Kabir, M.H., Hasan, M.A., Shin, W.: CSI-DeepNet: a lightweight deep convolutional neural network based hand gesture recognition system using Wi-Fi CSI signal. IEEE Access **10** (2022)
10. Kaltiokallio, O., Yiğitler, H., Jäntti, R.: A three-state received signal strength model for device-free localization. IEEE Trans. Veh. Technol. **66**(10), 9226–9240 (2017)
11. Ke, W., Zuo, H., Chen, M., Wang, Y.: Enhanced radio tomographic imaging method for device-free localization using a gradual-changing weight model. Progress Electromagn. Res. M **82**, 39–48 (2019)
12. Liu, C., Fang, D., Yang, Z., Jiang, H., Chen, X., Wang, W., Xing, T., Cai, L.: Rss distribution-based passive localization and its application in sensor networks. IEEE Trans. Wireless Commun. **15**(4), 2883–2895 (2016)
13. Mulder, E.D.: Electromagnetic techniques and probes for side-channel analysis on cryptographic devices. J. Cryptol. (2010)

14. Patwari, N., Agrawal, P.: Effects of correlated shadowing: connectivity, localization, and RF tomography. In: 2008 International Conference on Information Processing in Sensor Networks (ipsn 2008), pp. 82–93 (2008)
15. Sachintha, S., Le-Khac, N.A., Scanlon, M., Sayakkara, A.P.: Data exfiltration through electromagnetic covert channel of wired industrial control systems. Appli. Sci. **13**(5) (2023)
16. Sasiwat, Y., Jindapetch, N., Buranapanichkit, D., Booranawong, A.: An experimental study of human movement effects on rssi levels in an indoor wireless network. In: 2019 12th Biomedical Engineering International Conference (BMEiCON), pp. 1–5 (2019)
17. Sayakkara, A., Le-Khac, N.A.: Forensic insights from smartphones through electromagnetic side-channel analysis. IEEE Access (2021)
18. Shukri, S., Kamarudin, L.M.: Device free localization technology for human detection and counting with RF sensor networks: a review. J. Netw. Comput. Appli. **97** (2017)
19. Weerasinghe, B., Sayakkara, A., De Zoysa, K., Scanlon, M.: Low-overhead and non-invasive electromagnetic side-channel monitoring for forensic-ready industrial control systems. In: Proceedings of the Digital Forensics Doctoral Symposium, DFDS 2025. Association for Computing Machinery, New York (2025)
20. Wilson, J., Patwari, N.: Radio tomographic imaging with wireless networks. IEEE Trans. Mob. Comput. **9**(5), 621–632 (2010)
21. Wilson, J., Patwari, N.: See-through walls: motion tracking using variance-based radio tomography networks. IEEE Trans. Mobile Comput. **10**(5) (2011)
22. Wounchoum, P., Vanichpattarakul, T., Dumumpai, K., Chaoboworn, V., Saito, H., Booranawong, A.: Effects of human presence and movement on received signal strength levels in a 2.4 ghz wireless link: an experimental study. J. Elect. Eng. Techno. **17** (2022)
23. Yang, Z., Qian, K., Wu, C., Zhang, Y.: Smart Wireless Sensing: From IoT to AIoT. Springer Singapore (2021)
24. Ye, X., Li, P., Zhao, M., Panda, R., Hu, J.: Scalable analysis of mesh-based clock distribution networks using application-specific reduced order modeling. IEEE Trans. on CAD Integrated Circ. Syst. **29**, 1342–1353 (2010)
25. Zhao, N., Dublon, G., Gillian, N., Dementyev, A., Paradiso, J.A.: Emi spy: harnessing electromagnetic interference for low-cost, rapid prototyping of proxemic interaction. In: 2015 IEEE 12th International Conference on Wearable and Implantable Body Sensor Networks (BSN), pp. 1–6 (2015)

Dataset Sensitivity and Scalability in RNN-Based V2X Intrusion Detection

Niranjan W. Meegammana(✉) and Harinda Fernando

Sri Lanka Institute of Information Technology, Malabe, Sri Lanka
niranjan.meegammana@gmail.com

Abstract. This study presents a systematic evaluation of recurrent neural network (RNN) architectures, including standard RNN, Long Short-Term Memory (LSTM), and Gated Recurrent Unit (GRU) for detecting temporal anomalies in Vehicle-to-Everything (V2X) communication. Using six stratified subsets (20K–200K samples) from the VeReMi Extension dataset, we assess each model's performance across classification accuracy, F1 score, inference latency, and resource usage. The results reveal that while increased dataset size enhances detection performance, marginal gains diminish beyond 120K samples. Among the evaluated models, GRU demonstrates the most favorable balance between detection accuracy and computational efficiency, highlighting its suitability for real-time intrusion detection in resource-constrained vehicular environments.

Keywords: Edge Computing · V2X Security · Attack Detection · Data Sensitivity · RNN · LSTM · GRU · VeReMi · IDS

1 Introduction

V2X communication underpins autonomous vehicular systems by enabling real-time data exchange among vehicles, infrastructure, and other network entities (Fig. 1). This connectivity enhances navigation, awareness, and safety. However, the dynamic and open nature of V2X also introduces security vulnerabilities, exposing systems to Sybil, replay, DoS, and message injection attacks [12]. Intrusion Detection Systems (IDS) serve as a key defense layer in V2X, monitoring message patterns to detect anomalies. Yet, deploying IDS in V2X is challenging due to the latency, power, and memory constraints of On-Board Units (OBUs) and Roadside Units (RSUs) [13]. Effective IDS must balance detection accuracy with computational efficiency for real-time responsiveness. Recurrent neural networks (RNNs) and their variants Long Short-Term Memory (LSTM) and Gated Recurrent Unit (GRU) have demonstrated strong potential for modeling V2X traffic sequences [5,8,15]. Their gating mechanisms capture long-range temporal dependencies while mitigating vanishing gradients, enabling the detection of subtle time-dependent anomalies.

R. N. Rajapakse et al. (Eds.): ICTer 2025, CCIS 2844, pp. 441–455, 2026.
https://doi.org/10.1007/978-981-92-0137-2_29

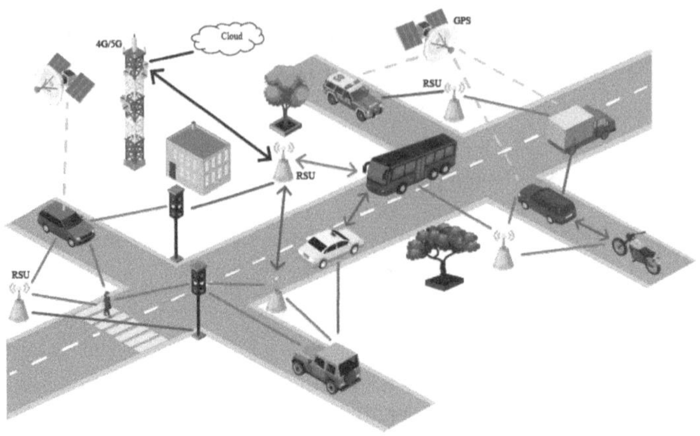

Fig. 1. V2X communication environment.

However, most existing studies rely on fixed-size or synthetic datasets and overlook the relationship between dataset volume and detection performance under edge-computing constraints [1,11]. Additionally, public datasets often lack V2X-specific protocols and cooperative attack coverage, limiting generalization.

This study addresses these gaps by evaluating RNN, LSTM, and GRU performance across six stratified subsets (20K–200K samples) from the VeReMi Extension dataset [7]. Each model is assessed on accuracy, F1 score, latency, model size, and resource consumption.

Unlike prior work [2,4], this paper explicitly examines how dataset size influences performance and scalability for edge-deployed IDS in real-time V2X environments. GRU, in particular, achieves the best balance between accuracy and efficiency, making it highly suitable for constrained platforms like OBUs and RSUs.

2 Literature Review

2.1 IDS in V2X Systems

V2X communication enables autonomous vehicles to exchange real-time data with nearby nodes, enhancing safety, navigation, and traffic efficiency. However, the open and decentralized nature of V2X networks introduces serious cybersecurity risks, including Sybil, DoS, message replay, and falsification attacks [9,12]. IDS serves as an essential defense by monitoring V2X traffic for deviations from normal behavior. IDSs can use rule-based or learning-based methods to detect anomalies, but must operate under the tight latency, power, and memory constraints of OBUs and RSUs [13]. Additionally, high node mobility, heterogeneous protocols, and dynamic topologies make real-time IDS deployment in V2X uniquely challenging [9].

2.2 Deep Learning Architectures for V2X IDS

Deep learning (DL) has emerged as a powerful approach for V2X IDS by modeling sequential dependencies in message patterns. RNNs and their gated variants, LSTM and GRU, are particularly effective for capturing temporal anomalies in V2X communication [8, 15].

While RNNs model time sequences via hidden states, they are limited by vanishing gradients. LSTM and GRU mitigate this via gating mechanisms that preserve long-term dependencies [5]. This enables them to detect subtle behavioral shifts critical for identifying evolving attacks.

Several studies presented in Table 1 affirm their utility where [5] applied LSTM to detect false message injection in synthetic environments, and [2] showed GRU's adaptability in real-time vehicular IDS. LSTM models augmented with cryptographic primitives were found to improve latency and detection [8]. Beyond sequence models, ensemble frameworks such as ADVENT [4] have also been evaluated on VeReMi, demonstrating adversarial resilience and providing a complementary benchmark to single-architecture IDS designs.

Despite progress, most studies evaluate models on fixed-size or generic datasets like NSL-KDD or CICIDS2017, which lack the temporal and protocol fidelity required in V2X [3, 14]. These works often overlook key deployment constraints such as inference latency, resource usage, and scalability to real-time systems.

Table 1. Deep Learning Approaches for V2X IDS

Study	Models	Dataset	Metrics	Remarks
[5]	RNN	Synthetic V2X	Accuracy, Recall	Sequential learning; lacks latency evaluation
[4]	Ensemble (ADVENT)	VeReMi Extension	Robustness, Detection Rate	Emphasis on adversarial resilience
[14]	RNN	NSL-KDD	Accuracy, Recall, Precision, F1	Class imbalance and overfitting
[15]	LSTM	Custom Dataset	Accuracy	Focused on false message detection; lacks resource analysis
[2]	GRU	CICIDS2017	Accuracy	Good results, not V2X-specific
[3]	DL Classifier (RNN)	Custom IoV Dataset	Accuracy	Targets novel attacks; lacks scalability study
This Study	RNN, LSTM, GRU	VeReMi Extension (multi-size)	Precision, Recall, F1, Latency, Resources	Analyzes dataset-size impact on detection–efficiency trade-offs

2.3 Dataset Limitations and Scalability in V2X IDS

Many popular IDS datasets were not designed for cooperative vehicular systems. Benchmarks like NSL-KDD and CICIDS2017 lack temporal resolution, CAM/DENM messaging, and relevant attack diversity, leading to poor generalization in V2X contexts [10]. Furthermore, synthetic datasets often ignore protocol-specific behaviors, and fixed-size datasets prevent scalability assessments. Table 2 presents a comparative overview of major IDS datasets used in automotive research, outlining their coverage and limitations.

Table 2. Overview of Automotive IDS Datasets: Metadata and Characteristics

Dataset	Source	Domain	Label	Strengths	Limitations
OTIDS	HCRL, 2017	IVN	No	Early CAN dataset	No labels, lacks diversity
Car Hacking	HCRL, 2018	IVN	Yes	Common IDS baseline	Format inconsistency
Survival Analysis	HCRL, 2018	IVN	Yes	Multi-vehicle variation	Class imbalance
Automotive CAN v2	TU Eindhoven, 2019	IVN	Partial	Diverse attacks	Unclear labels, synthetic data
SynCAN	Bosch, 2019	IVN	Yes	Broad synthetic coverage	Limited realism
Car Challenge	HCRL, 2020	IVN	Yes	Replay coverage	Weak fuzzing realism
ROAD	ORNL, 2020	IVN	No	Real signal-level data	No labels, synthetic fuzzing
TTIDS	EMSEC, 2022	IVN	Yes	Real masquerade attacks	Limited attack variety
VeReMi Extension	[7]	V2X	Yes	CAM/DENM, temporal fidelity	Simulated V2X environment

Most of the datasets focus on In-Vehicle Networks (IVN), use synthetic or replayed traffic, and lack temporal attack progression. For instance, SynCAN provides broad coverage but lacks real-world fidelity. TTIDS and ROAD include real data but are IVN-centric, failing to reflect dynamic, cooperative V2X environments [6].

In contrast, the VeReMi Extension dataset [7] is tailored for V2X. It simulates urban mobility using CAM/DENM messages and includes labeled Sybil, replay, and position falsification attacks with temporal consistency. It supports benchmarking of sequence-aware models like LSTM and GRU [4,8], but most studies treat it as a static benchmark and ignore the role of data scale on model behavior.

2.4 Study Contribution

Existing studies seldom investigate how training dataset volume influences attack detection accuracy, scalability, or runtime efficiency as key factors that are critical for deploying IDS models on resource-constrained V2X edge nodes. [11]. While some research (e.g., [1]) explores data sensitivity, they focus on IoT rather than V2X-specific contexts.

This study addresses that gap by evaluating RNN, LSTM, and GRU models across six dataset sizes (20K–200K) from the VeReMi Extension. It provides new insights on how detection accuracy, inference latency, and resource usage evolve with increasing data volume, offering practical guidance for scalable, real-time IDS deployment in cooperative vehicular environments.

3 Methodology

This section details the experimental workflow designed to evaluate how dataset size influences the performance and scalability of deep learning models in V2X intrusion detection. The methodology follows five modular stages: dataset sampling, preprocessing, model training, evaluation, and logging. This pipeline supports reproducible experimentation across six stratified subsets (20K–200K) drawn from the VeReMi Extension dataset [7], enabling insights into temporal learning and deployment feasibility under resource constraints.

3.1 Dataset Construction and Subsampling

For binary classification, VeReMi was filtered to retain Class 0 (benign) and Classes 9–19 (attacks), excluding Classes 1–8 (system faults), and is presented in Table 3. A balanced 200K-sample dataset (50:50 benign vs. attack) was created and partitioned into six temporally ordered subsets: 20K, 40K, 80K, 120K, 160K, and 200K. Temporal ordering was preserved to prevent leakage, with sequential 90/5/5 train, validation, and test splits ensuring disjoint sets and controlled evaluation of data volume sensitivity.

Table 3. Class Label Mapping for Binary Classification

Category	Class IDs	Description	Included
Normal	0	Legitimate communication	Yes
System Faults	1–8	Non-malicious anomalies	No
Known Attacks	9–17	Replay, Sybil, DoS, etc.	Yes
Unknown Attacks	18–19	Novel adversarial behavior	Yes

3.2 Preprocessing and Sequence Construction

Data were sorted by `sendTime`, retaining `frame_id` to preserve chronological order. Thirteen numerical features including position, speed, acceleration, and heading vectors were normalized using z-score transformation. Each entry included a binary label.

Temporal modeling was achieved using a fixed-length sliding window of size $w = 5$, producing overlapping sequences labeled by the final record. This created 3D input tensors of shape (samples $\times$ 5 $\times$ 13), ranging from 19,996 to 199,996 samples per subset. Equal class representation was enforced through stratified sampling before sequence construction, maintaining a 1:1 ratio throughout.

3.3 Temporal Distribution Analysis

Fig. 2 visualizes binary class distribution by frame ID. As the dataset size increases, attacks become temporally skewed toward later frame IDs, presenting challenges for static models to generalize over time. Memory-based models like LSTM and GRU are better suited for these conditions due to their capability to retain long-term context.

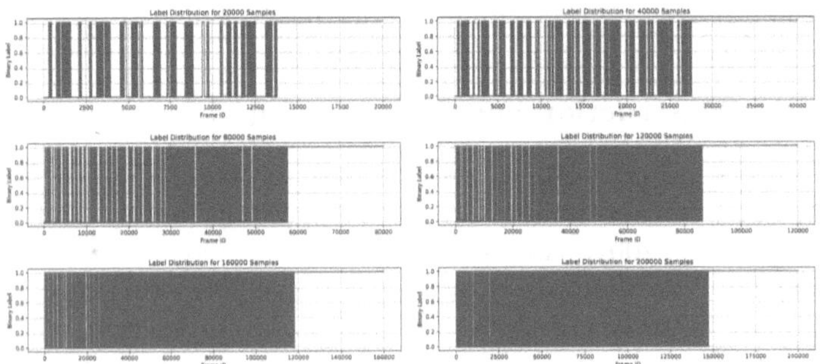

Fig. 2. Binary label distribution by frame ID for 20K–200K subsets.

Table 4 compares temporal skew across subsets. In 20K–40K, attacks appear earlier and more interleaved with benign data. In larger subsets (80K+), attack onset shifts later, creating a non-stationary distribution. This highlights the need for sequence models capable of learning across delayed transitions, especially in 160K–200K subsets.

Table 4. Comparison of Dataset Subsets: Class Distribution and Temporal Skew

Subset Size	Class Balance	Temporal Skew	Key Observation
20K	1:1	Moderate (attacks after 13K)	Short-term memory sufficient
40K	1:1	Strong (attacks after 28K)	Temporal smoothing needed
80K	1:1	High (attacks after 30K)	Extended memory required
120K	1:1	Severe (attacks after 40K)	Generalization becomes difficult
160K	1:1	Very Severe (attacks late)	Static models risk bias
200K	1:1	Extreme (attacks after 50K)	GRU/LSTM preferred for late detection

3.4 Model Architectures

Three recurrent models, Simple RNN, LSTM, and GRU were built using Keras. All shared a uniform architecture for fair comparison: four recurrent layers (64→8 units), dropout of 0.3, three ReLU-activated dense layers, and a sigmoid output for binary classification presented in Table 5.

Table 5. Model Architecture Summary

Model	Recurrent Layers	Dropout	Dense Layers	Output
RNN	64 → 32 → 16 → 8	0.3	64, 32, 16, 8	Sigmoid
LSTM	64 → 32 → 16 → 8	0.3	64, 32, 16, 8	Sigmoid
GRU	64 → 32 → 16 → 8	0.3	64, 32, 16, 8	Sigmoid

3.5 Training Protocol

Models were trained separately for each subset using the Adam optimizer and binary cross-entropy loss. Early stopping was triggered based on validation F1 score with a patience of 5 epochs. The data were split 90% train, 5% validation, and 5% test. Table 6 outlines the training configuration.

Table 6. Training Protocol Configuration

Parameter	Value
Optimizer	Adam
Loss Function	Binary Cross-Entropy
Batch Size	64
Sequence Length	5
Early Stopping	Patience = 5 (Validation F1)
Train:Validation:Test Split	90% : 5% : 5%

3.6 Evaluation Strategy

Performance and deployment efficiency were jointly evaluated. Accuracy, precision, recall, and F1 score quantified detection capability, while inference latency,

Table 7. Evaluation Metrics

Metric	Purpose
Accuracy	Overall correctness
Precision	True positive quality
Recall	Sensitivity to attacks
F1 Score	Harmonic balance of precision and recall
Inference Time	Real-time viability (ms/sample)
CPU Usage	Processing load during inference (%)
Memory Usage	RAM consumption during inference (MB)
Model Size	Memory/storage footprint (MB)

CPU usage, memory consumption, and model size assessed edge-deployment feasibility, presented in Table 7. All experiments were conducted in Google Colab with 12 GB RAM and Xeon CPUs to emulate low-resource conditions.

Each experiment was repeated with three random seeds, and results are reported as mean ± standard deviation. Early stopping based on validation F1 reduced overfitting, with the best checkpoints retained. While statistical significance tests and cross-validation are left for future work, this replication improves robustness over single-run results.

4 Results and Discussion

This section presents a comprehensive evaluation of RNN, LSTM, and GRU models across six stratified dataset subsets from 20K to 200K samples from the VeReMi Extension dataset. Evaluation metrics include classification accuracy, F1 score, inference latency, CPU usage, and memory footprint.

4.1 Detection Performance Trends

Table 8 summarizes classification performance across sample sizes. GRU maintains consistent accuracy and F1 scores above 0.97, demonstrating robustness to

Table 8. Classification Performance Across Sample Sizes for RNN, LSTM, and GRU Models

Sample Size	Model	Accuracy	Precision	Recall	F1 Score
20K	GRU	0.98	0.98	0.98	0.98
	LSTM	0.99	0.99	0.99	0.99
	RNN	0.97	0.96	0.98	0.97
40K	GRU	0.99	0.99	0.99	0.99
	LSTM	0.83	0.82	0.82	0.82
	RNN	0.91	0.98	0.98	0.98
80K	GRU	0.95	0.97	0.97	0.97
	LSTM	0.98	0.99	0.99	0.99
	RNN	0.97	0.98	0.98	0.98
120K	GRU	0.98	0.98	0.98	0.98
	LSTM	0.99	0.99	0.99	0.99
	RNN	0.98	0.98	0.98	0.98
160K	GRU	0.98	0.97	0.97	0.97
	LSTM	0.98	0.98	0.98	0.98
	RNN	0.86	0.86	0.86	0.86
200K	GRU	0.96	0.96	0.96	0.96
	LSTM	0.88	0.88	0.88	0.88
	RNN	0.84	0.84	0.84	0.84

data scale and temporal skew. LSTM achieves the highest accuracy at 20K samples but drops significantly at 40K, indicating sensitivity to sequence imbalance. RNN improves gradually with larger datasets but remains limited in long-sequence generalization. Table 8 shows distinct accuracy trends across dataset sizes. At 20K, all models perform well, with LSTM highest (0.99). At 40K, GRU improves (0.99) while LSTM drops sharply (0.83) and RNN rises moderately (0.91). At 80K–120K, all models peak (0.97–0.99), showing the best balance of accuracy and generalization. Beyond 160K, RNN degrades (0.86→0.84), LSTM fluctuates (0.98→0.88), and GRU remains most stable (0.98→0.96). Overall, GRU shows consistent robustness, LSTM high but unstable accuracy, and RNN weaker scalability.

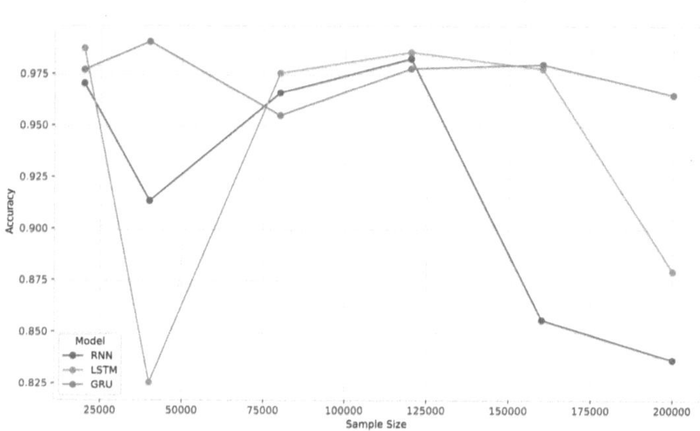

Fig. 3. Accuracy vs. Sample Size across RNN, LSTM, and GRU models.

To better visualize how model performance scales with dataset size, Fig. 3 plots accuracy across all six sample subsets. As shown, LSTM achieves the highest accuracy at 20K samples but drops significantly at 40K, likely due to sequence imbalance. GRU remains stable throughout, indicating greater robustness under varying temporal distributions. Figure 7 further confirms GRU's reliability and LSTM's sensitivity at mid-scale. The LSTM performance drop at 40K reflects simultaneous declines in precision and recall, likely due to overfitting on early benign sequences and difficulty handling delayed attack onset. GRU, in contrast, maintains generalization under temporal skew.

4.2 Resource Usage and Efficiency

Figure 4 compares inference latency across sample sizes for RNN, LSTM, and GRU models.

GRU consistently achieves the lowest latency ranging from 0.50 to 1.3 s, highlighting its efficiency for time-critical V2X deployments. LSTM exhibits moderate latency with stable trends, while RNN shows the highest latency due to

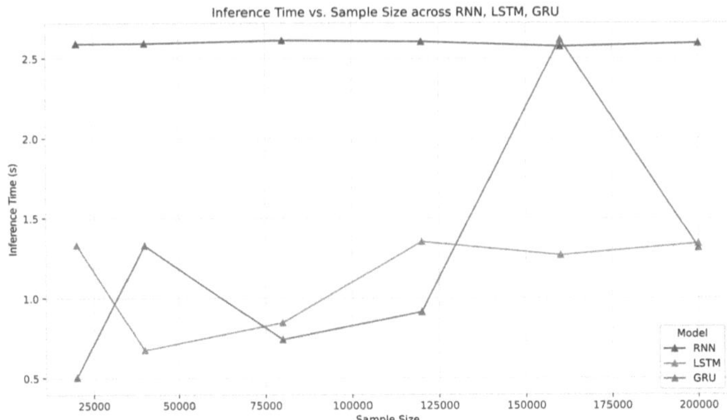

Fig. 4. Inference Time vs. Sample Size across RNN, LSTM, GRU.

less efficient sequential computation. These results reinforce GRU's advantage in edge-oriented deployment scenarios.

Table 9 summarizes CPU, memory, and model size metrics. GRU offers the most balanced profile with low inference time, compact size of 0.36 MB, and moderate CPU demand. LSTM is resource-intensive, while RNN is CPU-efficient but slow.

Table 9. Resource Usage Comparison Across Sample Sizes for RNN, LSTM, and GRU Models

Size	Model	CPU (%)	Memory (MB)	Model Size (MB)	Latency (s)
20K	GRU	69.1	2305.20	0.36	0.50
	LSTM	64.2	2243.29	0.46	1.33
	RNN	29.5	2193.92	0.15	2.59

To provide a comprehensive comparison of detection performance and resource efficiency, Figs. 5 and 6 display radar charts normalized across all dataset sizes. Below, Fig. 5 illustrates performance variation across datasets from 20K to 200K, normalized across multiple metrics. GRU consistently maintains a balanced profile in terms of accuracy, F1 score, and efficiency. LSTM performs well at smaller scales but incurs higher computational overhead. RNN, while lightweight, shows limited generalization.

Figure 6 aggregates the normalized performance metrics into a single comparative chart. This chart highlights GRU's strong balance between detection accuracy and resource usage, confirming its suitability for deployment. LSTM demonstrates strong performance but with costlier resource demands, while RNN is efficient but lower in accuracy.

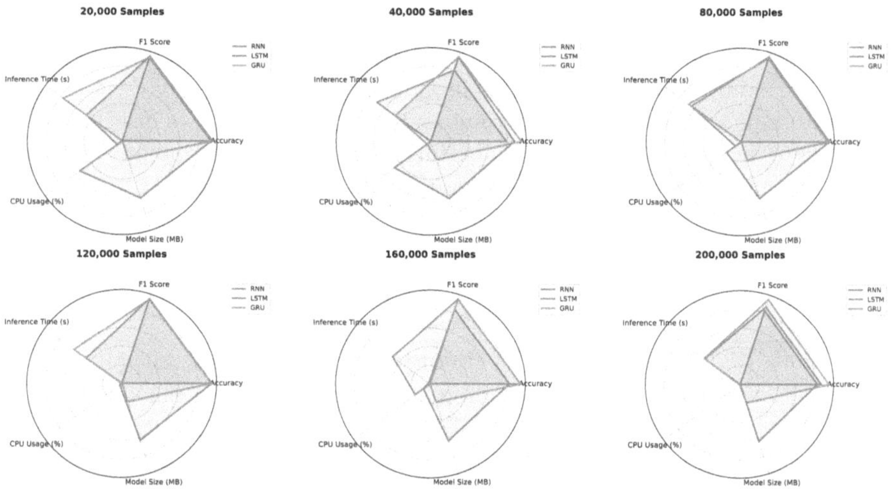

Fig. 5. Normalized radar chart showing model performance and efficiency across all dataset sizes.

4.3 Dataset Size Impact

Model performance consistently improves from 20K to 120K samples across all architectures, indicating that increasing data volume enhances the learning of temporal dependencies. However, beyond 160K, a plateau or slight decline is observed, particularly in LSTM and RNN models. This trend suggests a satura-

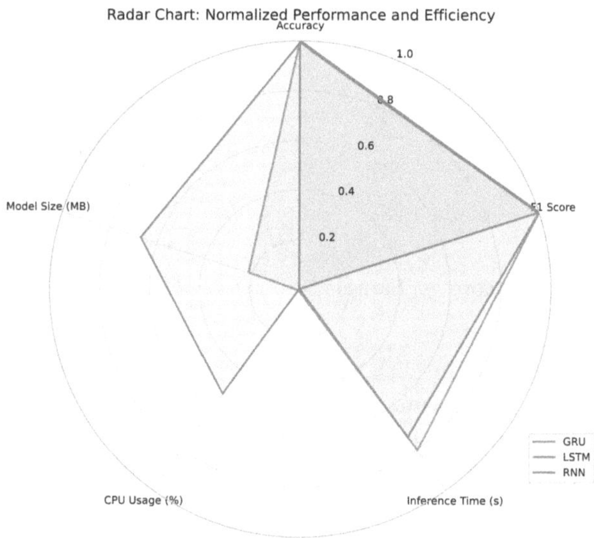

Fig. 6. Aggregated radar chart summarizing detection and efficiency metrics.

tion point, where the benefit of additional data is offset by increased temporal skew, redundant samples, and resource bottlenecks.

Table 10 summarizes macro trends in model performance across dataset sizes. GRU maintains a stable F1 score throughout, while LSTM shows instability after 120K due to sensitivity to skewed label distributions. RNN benefits from more data but remains less robust in long-sequence generalization.

Table 10. Summary of Dataset Size Impact on Model Performance

Size	GRU Trend	LSTM Trend	RNN Trend
20K	High accuracy	Peak performance	Weak generalization
40K	Improved further	Sharp drop due to skew	Moderate gain
80K	Stable	Recovery	Stronger patterns
120K	Optimal balance	High performance	Competitive
160K	Slight decline	Begins to degrade	Drops in accuracy
200K	Stable but slower	Declines	Degrades further

The variation in F1 score with increasing sample size is presented in Fig. 7.

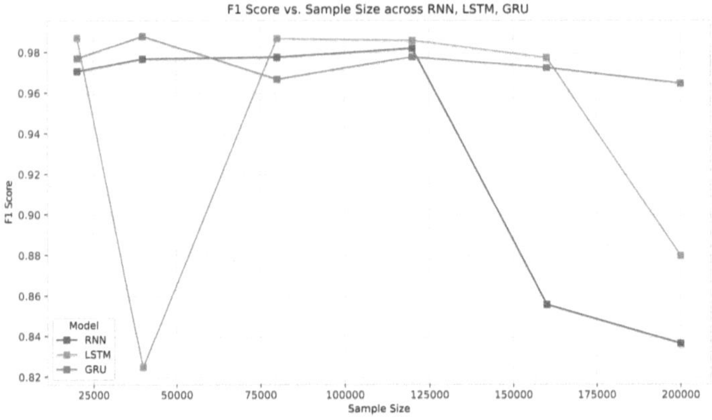

Fig. 7. F1 Score vs. Sample Size across RNN, LSTM, GRU.

RNN improves gradually with increasing dataset size but continues to trail behind GRU in overall performance stability. GRU maintains a consistently high F1 score across all subsets, demonstrating robustness to both data scale and temporal variation. In contrast, LSTM exhibits noticeable volatility, particularly between 20K and 40K samples, where its F1 score drops sharply from 0.99 to 0.82. This decline aligns with previously observed reductions in precision and recall, and can be attributed to a combination of temporal skew, sequence imbalance, and LSTM's sensitivity to distribution shifts. Specifically, the 40K subset contains dense clusters of attacks after benign-dominated sequences, which challenges LSTM's ability to adapt quickly to abrupt temporal transitions. These observations collectively indicate that training with 80K–120K samples provides the most reliable trade-off between generalization and computational efficiency for real-time V2X IDS deployments.

4.4 Model Trade-Offs and Deployment Suitability

GRU consistently maintains high F1 scores, fast inference, and efficient resource usage across dataset sizes, making it the most suitable candidate for real-time edge deployment in V2X networks. LSTM performs well on smaller datasets but lacks stability under temporal skew and has higher resource demands. RNN is efficient in CPU and model size but underperforms in latency and generalization.

4.5 Limitations and Future Work

This study used the synthetic but temporally structured VeReMi Extension dataset and single-run experiments, limiting statistical robustness. Results beyond 120K samples are descriptive rather than statistically validated, and evaluation on Colab CPUs may not reflect real vehicular hardware. The binary attack/benign formulation also omits system faults. Future work will include multi-seed averaging, significance testing, attention-enhanced architectures, hardware-in-the-loop simulations, and real-world cross-validation.

5 Conclusion

This paper presents a systematic evaluation of dataset sensitivity and model scalability in RNN-based IDS for V2X environments. Using stratified subsets of the VeReMi Extension dataset ranging from 20K to 200K samples. The study evaluated RNN, LSTM, and GRU architectures in terms of detection performance and resource efficiency. GRU emerged as the most robust and deployment-ready model, consistently outperforming RNN and LSTM across all dataset sizes. It maintained high F1 scores above 0.96, achieved the lowest inference latency as low as 0.50 s, and exhibited strong resilience to temporal skew. In contrast, LSTM achieved the highest accuracy at 20K samples but showed instability at 40K due to its sensitivity to sequence imbalance and higher resource demands. RNN, while computationally lightweight with minimal model size and CPU usage, struggled to generalize over long sequences and demonstrated the slowest inference times.

Notably, the study observed diminishing returns in model performance beyond 120K samples, suggesting that training within the 80K to 120K range offers the best trade-off between accuracy and computational cost for edge deployment. These findings offer practical guidance for designing scalable and resource-aware IDS in cooperative V2X networks. Future work will investigate adversarial robustness, attention-enhanced hybrid architectures, and deployment on embedded platforms such as NVIDIA Jetson Nano and Raspberry Pi.

6 Code Availability

All source code, model definitions, and training logs are available at the following GitHub repository. https://github.com/niranjanmeegammana/V2XdataSensitivity.

Disclosure of Interests. The authors declare that they have no competing interests to disclose.

References

1. Alhowaide, A., Alsmadi, I., Tang, J.: Balanced datasets for iot ids. arXiv (2022)
2. Aljabri, W., Hamid, A., Mosli, R.: Lightweight and adaptive data-driven intrusion detection system for autonomous vehicles. IEEE Trans. Intell. Trans. Syst. **26**(2) (2025)
3. Alshammari, F., Alsaleh, A.: Smart intrusion detection model to identify unknown attacks for improved road safety and management. Sci. Rep. **15**(1) (2025)
4. Baharlouei, H., Makanju, A., Heywood, N.Z.: Evaluating the robustness of advent on the veremi-extension dataset. In: 2024 Conference on Network and Service Management (CNSM), pp. 1–7 (2024)
5. Djaidja, T., Brik, B., Boualouache, A., Senouci, S., Ghamri-Doudane, Y.: Time-efficient detection of false position attack in 5g and beyond vehicular networks. Comput. Netw. **247**, 110461 (2024)
6. Haddaji, A., Ayed, S., Fourati, L.C., Boulahia, L.M.: Investigation of security threat datasets for intra- and inter-vehicular environments. Sensors **24**(11), 3431 (2024)
7. Kamel, J., Wolf, M., Kaiser, A., Urien, P., Kargl, F.: Veremi extension: a dataset for comparable evaluation of misbehavior detection in vanets. In: 2020 IEEE International Conference on Communications (ICC) (2020)
8. Khan, H., Tejani, G.G., AlGhamdi, R., Sharma, N.K., Sharma, S.K.: A secure and efficient deep learning-based intrusion detection framework for the internet of vehicles. Sci. Rep. **15**(1) (2025)
9. Lampe, B., Meng, W.: Intrusion detection in the automotive domain: a comprehensive review. IEEE Commun. Surv. Tutorials **25**(4), 2356–2426 (2023)
10. Lee, S., Choi, W., Kim, I., Lee, G., Lee, D.H.: A comprehensive analysis of datasets for automotive intrusion detection systems. Comput. Mater. Continua **76**(3), 3413–3442 (2023)
11. Palma, A., Antunes, M., Bernardino, J., Alves, A.: Multi-class intrusion detection in internet of vehicles: optimizing machine learning models on imbalanced data. Future Internet **17**(4), 162 (2025)
12. Raghavan, S.S.: Ai-driven intrusion detection systems (ids) for securing v2v and v2x communications. Inter. J. Recent Innovation Trends Comput. Commun. **11**(11) (2023)
13. Sanyour, R., Abdullah, M., Abdullah, S.: A light-weight real-time anomaly detection framework for edge computing. In: Proceedings of the International Conference on Advances in Computing Research (ACR 2023). LNCS, vol. 13777. Springer (2023). https://doi.org/10.1007/978-3-031-33743-7_37

14. Sharma, H., Kumar, P., Sharma, K.: Recurrent neural network based incremental model for intrusion detection system in iot. Scalable Comput. Pract. Exper. **25**(5) (2024)
15. Yu, Y., Zeng, X., Xue, X., Ma, J.: Lstm-based intrusion detection system for vanets: a time series classification approach to false message detection. IEEE Trans. Intell. Trans. Syst. **23**(12) (2022)

Beyond Charging: How Juice Jacking Enables Data Theft and Device Compromise in Android

Fathima Minha Nijamudeen[1(✉)], Akila Wickramasekara[2], Buddhima Weerasinghe[1], and Asanka Sayakkara[1]

[1] University of Colombo School of Computing (UCSC), Colombo, Sri Lanka
minharesearch@gmail.com
[2] School of Computer Science, University College Dublin, Belfield, Dublin 4, Ireland

Abstract. This paper investigates security threats to mobile devices from untrusted chargers, focusing on data theft through USB connections. The experiments were carried out on four Android devices using various tools, including the O.MG cable, Vysor, ADB, and Scrcpy. The study examined four scenarios: default settings, enabling developer mode and USB debugging, using an O.MG cable with an unlocked phone, and testing data theft with a locked phone. The results revealed that devices with USB debugging and developer options enabled were highly vulnerable to unauthorized access and malware injection. In contrast, locked devices with debugging disabled showed greater resistance. Furthermore, when the O.MG cable was connected to a locked device, the payload could not execute, making it more secure. However, on unlocked devices, the cable was able to run malicious commands and exfiltrate data, highlighting a significant risk. These findings emphasize the importance of disabling USB debugging, keeping devices locked while charging, and strictly avoiding untrusted charging sources. This research contributes to understanding USB-based attacks and provides practical recommendations for enhancing mobile device security.

Keywords: Untrusted Chargers · Data Theft · Developer Mode · USB debugging · O.MG cable

1 Introduction

In today's hyper-connected digital landscape, mobile devices have become indispensable. Their widespread adoption has increased demand for convenient charging options, including public USB charging stations in airports, cafes, and transportation hubs. However, this convenience introduces a critical security concern known as juice jacking—a cyberattack [22] in which malicious actors exploit public charging ports to compromise connected devices.

With its diverse hardware ecosystem and open-source foundation, Android presents a desirable target for such attacks. By leveraging USB connectivity,

R. N. Rajapakse et al. (Eds.): ICTer 2025, CCIS 2844, pp. 456–470, 2026.
https://doi.org/10.1007/978-981-92-0137-2_30

attackers can potentially exfiltrate data, install malicious applications, or gain unauthorised access without user interaction. Although awareness around mobile malware and app-based threats has grown, the less-discussed risk posed by charging infrastructure remains under-addressed.

This paper investigates the security implications of juice jacking attacks on Android devices, focusing on real-world vulnerabilities, threat models, and defence mechanisms. This work details a proof-of-concept implementation that exploits standard USB connections to carry out unauthorised actions on Android devices via a compromised charging interface. The findings expose the ease with which data compromise and device manipulation can occur, underscoring the urgent need for user education and architectural safeguards [15].

The study aims to identify common vulnerabilities in charging systems by examining how USB ports and cables can be exploited to compromise devices. It also investigates the impact of compromised chargers on device security, including unauthorized data access and potential device control. In addition, the effectiveness of existing security measures—such as USB restrictions and physical data blockers—is assessed. Finally, practical recommendations are proposed to enhance mobile charging security, including charge-only cables, rental power banks, user education, permission-based protections, and secure designs for public charging stations.

This paper begins with an overview of juice jacking and USB-based vulnerabilities (Sect. 2), followed by a threat model explaining how untrusted chargers can compromise mobile devices (Sect. 3). Section 4 outlines the experimental setup and tools used, while Sect. 5 presents results and device vulnerability analysis. Section 6 discusses security implications, and Sect. 7 suggests mitigation strategies. The paper concludes with future research directions in Sect. 8.

2 Background and Related Work

2.1 Background

Juice Jacking. Untrusted chargers pose several attack vectors that threaten the security and integrity of mobile devices. Among these, juice jacking, data theft, malware injection, and firmware manipulation are prominent methods used by attackers to exploit vulnerabilities in the charging infrastructure [15].

Here's a detailed discussion on Juice Jacking, how it works, and its implications:

The concept of juice jacking, first publicised in 2011, highlighted the potential for data theft and malware installation via public USB charging stations. Since then, various studies and reports have documented the risks associated with using untrusted chargers, emphasising the need for heightened awareness and robust security measures [5].

There are three possible scenarios of how a juice jacking attack can be performed: screen mirroring, Human Interface Device (HID) attack, and USB debugging [15].

Juice jacking involves the manipulation of USB charging ports to compromise connected devices. Attackers modify charging stations or use malicious charging cables to steal data from the device while it is charging. By exploiting vulnerabilities in USB communication protocols, attackers can exfiltrate data from the device or inject malware into it while it is being charged [15].

O.MG Cable. The O.MG cable is a type of malicious USB cable designed to look like a normal charging or data cable, such as USB-A to USB-C or Lightning, but it contains hidden hardware that allows it to perform hacking attacks. To the average user, it appears completely ordinary, functioning like any regular cable for charging or data transfer. However, inside the cable is a tiny implant or chip, often with wireless network capabilities, that enables an attacker to remotely control the cable and the connected device [6].

When an O.MG cable is plugged into a device, it behaves like a normal USB cable, allowing charging and file transfer. At the same time, the hidden hardware assists in performing a variety of malicious functions. One common method is keyboard emulation, where the cable acts like a HID to inject commands automatically into the device. It can also be programmed to silently copy files, steal credentials, or deliver malware. Some versions even allow the attacker to connect to the cable via Wi-Fi, giving remote access to execute scripts or collect data without the user noticing any unusual activity [19].

Implications. Juice jacking can cause unauthorised access to sensitive data stored on the device, including personal information, login credentials, and financial data. Additionally, malware injected through juice jacking can compromise the device's security, leading to data loss, identity theft, or unauthorised access to device resources [15].

Public USB charging stations have grown ubiquitous in airports, hotels, and cafes—offering convenience, but also opening the door for "juice jacking." According to a NordLayer (IBM-based) report, 79% of business travelers risk exposure to attacks by using public USB ports or charging stations [11].

In addition, earlier this June (2025), the FBI cautioned that juice jacking risk remains high this summer, urging users to avoid public charging stations altogether [3].

While actual reported cases of juice jacking are rare, the combination of widespread USB ports and minimal safeguards creates a real, actionable threat, especially since even one compromised public charger can silently intercept data or deliver malware within minutes.

With mobile devices now holding vast amounts of personal, financial, and corporate information, and public charging infrastructure continuing to proliferate, the risk of juice jacking warrants urgent attention in the current threat landscape.

2.2 Related Work

USB-Based Attack Vectors and BadUSB Variants. The concept of USB-based attacks has evolved considerably with the emergence of BadUSB and related vectors. Van Vliet [21] explored novel USB Rubber Ducky payloads and their detection mechanisms, highlighting the sophisticated nature of modern USB attacks and the challenges in developing effective countermeasures. Building on this, Charan and Kulkarni [2] demonstrated enhancements to BadUSB attacks using microcontrollers, showing how commonly available hardware can be exploited for malicious purposes.

The evolution of USB standards has introduced new attack surfaces. Lu et al. [8] revisited BadUSB attacks in the context of USB Type-C connectors (BadUSB-C), revealing that modern USB standards, despite their advanced capabilities, remain vulnerable to similar attack methods. Mohammad Ali Pour and Rashidi [10] documented various red-teamer gadgets, providing insights into practical tools and techniques employed both by security professionals and potential attackers.

Mobile Device USB Security Vulnerabilities. Mobile devices present unique USB security challenges due to their ubiquity and diverse connectivity options. Lu et al. [9] developed Salaxy, a system that automatically enables USB debugging on Android devices to enable remote control, demonstrating the risks associated with USB debugging features. Potocký and Štulrajter [13] investigated HID attacks targeting Android lock screen protections, revealing that non-biometric security measures are susceptible to automated USB-based attacks.

The Android Debug Bridge (ADB) has also been identified as a critical vulnerability point. Amarante and Barros [1] examined USB connection vulnerabilities on Android devices through ADB exploitation. Opasiak and Mazurczyk [12] conducted a detailed security analysis of Android debugging mechanisms, highlighting fundamental insecurities and providing lessons on how misconfigured or unsecured debugging features can facilitate unauthorized access.

USB Infrastructure Security and Side-Channel Threats. Beyond device-specific vulnerabilities, the USB infrastructure itself faces various security challenges. Singh et al. [15] addressed "juice jacking" attacks, analyzing how USB charging technology can be exploited for data theft and proposing measures to mitigate these risks. Liu et al. [7] surveyed side-channel threats affecting USB-powered devices, identifying attack vectors that exploit power consumption, electromagnetic emissions, and other side channels, and presenting countermeasures to mitigate such attacks.

Tian et al. [18] offered a comprehensive analysis of USB insecurity across different versions, from USB 1.0 to USB-C, providing a historical perspective on USB vulnerabilities and demonstrating that many fundamental security issues persist despite evolving standards. Lu et al. [8] reinforced this finding in their exploration of BadUSB-C attacks, highlighting the continuing relevance of USB security research.

Practical Security Applications and Industry Perspectives. Foundational insights into mobile USB security were provided by Stavrou and Wang [16], who examined smartphone USB connectivity exploitation for both research and malicious purposes. Subramanian et al. [17] proposed comprehensive security measures for mobile devices, addressing protection against USB-based and other attack vectors in a holistic manner. Real-world observations from security communities, such as those reported by Fitch [4] at DEF CON, further illustrate the practical implications of USB-based attacks and the importance of continued research in this domain.

2.3 Research Gaps

Despite extensive research on USB-based attacks on smartphones, PCs, and other devices, several critical gaps remain. Most studies focus on individual attack vectors, such as BadUSB variants, HID attacks, juice jacking, or specific Android configurations like ADB and USB debugging, with limited research assessing the combined effects of multiple device settings, including lock screen status, developer options, and USB access policies. Although BadUSB and Rubber Ducky devices have been extensively studied, modern malicious cables, such as O.MG cables, which can execute attacks stealthily while functioning as normal charging devices, remain underexplored. Many existing studies are theoretical or laboratory-based, lacking evaluation under realistic user scenarios involving diverse phone models, OS versions, and security configurations. While detection methods and countermeasures exist, there is a lack of integrated frameworks that combine both software and hardware defenses to address USB-based attacks comprehensively. Furthermore, the rapid evolution of USB standards and mobile operating systems leaves emerging vulnerabilities largely unexamined. Prior research has also prioritized technical defenses over usability, limiting the practical adoption of proposed solutions. Finally, the intersection of USB security with emerging domains, including IoT devices, automotive systems, and industrial control systems, remains underexplored, despite the proliferation of USB connectivity in these environments. Collectively, these gaps highlight the need for a systematic, user-centric, and multi-vector evaluation of USB-based threats, coupled with practical mitigation strategies—objectives that this paper addresses to provide a comprehensive and realistic assessment of modern USB security risks.

3 Threat Model and Attack Vector

3.1 Impact of Attacks via Untrusted Chargers

Attacks carried out through untrusted chargers can have significant consequences, impacting user data and privacy, device integrity, and broader economic and social aspects. Such attacks may steal personal information, access private applications, and capture passwords, potentially resulting in identity theft, fraud, and reputational harm. They can also compromise device integrity by installing malware, modifying firmware, or causing crashes and data loss, thereby reducing the lifespan and reliability of the device. Beyond individual users, these attacks can lead to costly repairs, legal complications, and diminished trust in public charging infrastructure, affecting overall confidence in technology. Protection against these threats requires user education, robust security practices, and ongoing research into effective safeguards [16].

For precision in our threat model, the malicious O.MG cable evaluated in this work functions as a HID that injects keystrokes into the host device, which differs from the classic "charging-port MITM" or juice-jacking scenario where a compromised charger exposes a data interface or directly transfers malware over a data connection. Because an O.MG cable emulates an HID, its ability to interact with the device typically requires the device to be unlocked, whereas pure charging-port MITM attacks attempt to exploit exposed USB data channels and may operate under different device states. Consequently, we treat two distinct attack capabilities in this paper: (1) HID-based input injection (O.MG), effective when the device is unlocked, and (2) data-interface/juice-jacking attacks that target USB data channels. All experiments explicitly report the device lock/unlock state used and therefore differentiate tests performed with the device locked and unlocked to ensure reproducibility and to clarify why some attack vectors succeed only under specific device states (see Sects. 4–5).

3.2 Experimental Setup

Experiments were conducted for the research on "Security Threats to Mobile Devices through Untrusted Chargers," with a specific focus on data theft attacks. These experiments evaluated the vulnerability of Android devices under different security settings and employed free software tools to simulate attack scenarios. The experimental setup, illustrated in Fig. 1 shows a laptop emulating a compromised charger to execute data theft attacks on a smartphone. The methods described in the methodology chapter were applied to assess how various Android security configurations influence susceptibility to data theft. Through this approach, the study aimed to identify how mobile devices are exposed when connected to untrusted chargers and to evaluate the effectiveness of different security measures in mitigating these threats.

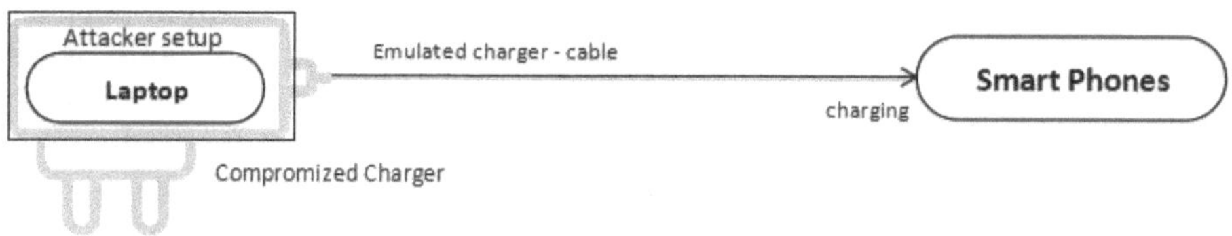

Fig. 1. Experimental setup showing a laptop emulating a compromised charger to execute data theft attacks on a smartphone.

4 Methodology

The attacker's setup involved a laptop configured with software tools to emulate a legitimate charger while executing malicious actions. The laptop utilized ADB Platform Tools for communication with the Android device, Vysor to enable remote access and control, and Scrcpy for screen mirroring and device management.

4.1 Compromised Charger

The laptop was used to emulate a compromised charger by leveraging its USB interface to manipulate the charging process and establish communication with the smartphone. Both a standard USB cable and an O.MG cable were employed to connect the laptop to the device. While the standard USB cable ensured that the setup reflected realistic, real-world scenarios, the O.MG cable enabled testing of advanced attack capabilities, including unauthorized data access and command injection.

4.2 Smartphone - Android Device

The experiments were conducted on Android smartphones running specific operating system versions to maintain consistency across tests. Four devices were used: SKY DEVICES E55 - Android 10, Samsung Galaxy J4 - Android 10, Samsung Galaxy S Duos 3 - Android 4.4.2, and a Galaxy Tab A9 - Android 14, which was specifically dedicated to O.MG cable experiments.

4.3 Implementation of Android Security Settings

The devices were tested under four security configurations: default settings with basic protections, Developer Mode with USB Debugging enabled, an O.MG cable connected to an unlocked phone with default settings, and an O.MG cable connected to a locked phone with default settings.

4.4 Testing of Free Software Tools - Attack Process

Using Vysor: Vysor is a software interface that mirrors an Android device to a PC via USB, requiring "Transferring files" mode and USB Debugging; it also displays device and network details, highlighting potential risks on untrusted networks

Vysor was installed on a Windows system and connected to the Android device via USB. With Developer Mode and USB Debugging enabled, Vysor's remote control features were used to navigate the device and simulate data theft through an untrusted charging connection.

Using ADB Platform Tools: ADB Platform Tools is a command-line utility for Android computer communication, which can be misused by attackers to access sensitive data via untrusted charging cables

ADB tools were set up on a Windows system and used to interact with the connected Android device. With Developer Mode and USB Debugging enabled, ADB commands were executed to attempt access to sensitive data and evaluate the effectiveness of device security settings.

Scrcpy: Scrcpy is a free, open-source screen-mirroring tool for controlling Android devices from a PC over USB, which can also be exploited to steal data on untrusted connections

Scrcpy was installed on a Linux system to mirror and control the Android device. With Developer Mode and USB Debugging enabled, it was used to simulate data theft and evaluate device security configurations.

4.5 Types of USB-Based Attacks

Smartphones are frequent targets of cyberattacks due to the sensitive data they store, with common threats including data theft, malware injection, keylogging, and USB debugging attacks, which can result in identity theft, data loss, and privacy breaches [15]. This study focuses specifically on data theft attacks, investigating how untrusted chargers can be exploited to steal sensitive information from mobile devices. Other USB-based attacks, such as malware injection, keylogging, and USB debugging attacks, are not addressed in this research.

5 Results and Analysis

The effectiveness of data theft attacks depended on both the Android version and the device's security configuration. Older Android versions were generally more susceptible, particularly when Developer Mode and USB Debugging were enabled, allowing easier unauthorized access. In contrast, newer versions with stricter USB access controls provided greater resilience against such attacks. Despite these improvements, all devices exhibited significant risk when left unlocked and connected to an O.MG cable, indicating that user behavior and device state can override built-in software protections. These results underscore that while platform updates enhance baseline security, proper configuration and cautious usage remain essential to mitigate USB-based threats.

5.1 Evaluation of All Four Devices - Device Testing Phases and Key Findings

The devices were evaluated under four distinct scenarios to assess vulnerability to USB-based attacks, including attacks using Vysor, Scrcpy, ADB Platform Tools, and an O.MG cable.

Testing Phase 1: Default Security Settings. When devices operated under default security settings, USB access was effectively blocked across all tools, preventing unauthorized access through a compromised charger. As shown in Fig. 2, the screenshot captured via Vysor before granting permission on Device 1 illustrates the device in its default security settings mode. USB access is restricted in the figure, effectively blocking any attempts to extract sensitive data and demonstrating that standard protections, such as screen locks and app permissions, are effective against data theft.

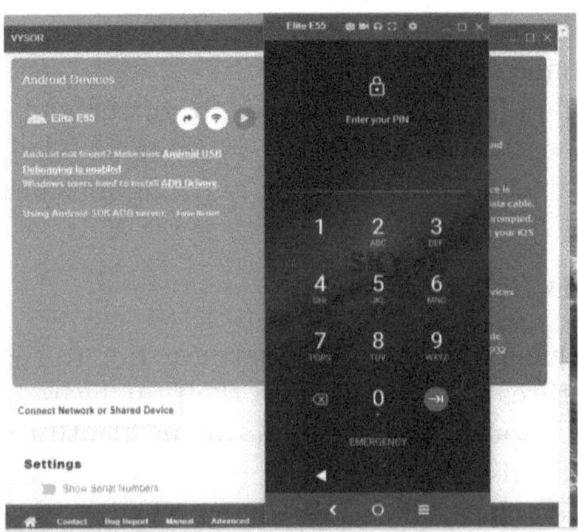

Fig. 2. Vysor - Before giving permission - Device 1

Testing Phase 2: Developer Mode and USB Debugging Enabled. Enabling Developer Mode and USB Debugging significantly increased device accessibility. Using tools such as Vysor, Scrcpy, and ADB, an attacker could interact with the device and extract sensitive information once the necessary permissions were granted. After permission was provided, attackers were able to navigate to internal storage locations, including the SD card, and pull image files to the host machine. In addition, entering the correct device PIN allowed access to applications such as email, from which sensitive information like one-time security codes could be retrieved. These codes could then be copied and transferred to the attacker's system, demonstrating how easily critical data can be exfiltrated once access is authorized. These findings underscore the importance of denying unnecessary permissions and relying on strong authentication measures to reduce the risk of such attacks.

Testing Phase 3: O.MG Cable Connected to an Unlocked Device. Connecting an O.MG cable to an unlocked device bypassed the need for Developer Mode or USB Debugging, making the device highly accessible for remote navigation and data exfiltration. The attacker could remotely open the Messages app,

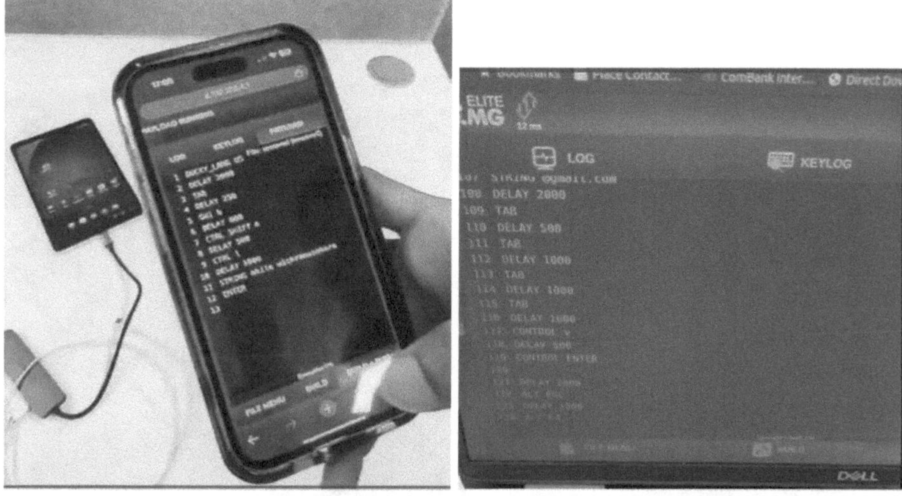

(a) O.MG with unlocked device (b) O.MG attack in progress

Fig. 3. O.MG with unlocked device and during attack execution

identify a sensitive message, capture a screenshot, retrieve it from the Gallery, copy it to the clipboard, and paste it into a Gmail draft before sending it to an external address. As illustrated in Fig. 3, the screenshot shows the moment the O.MG cable payload is triggered, enabling unauthorized commands and data extraction. These steps highlight the severe risk of leaving a phone unlocked when connected to an untrusted USB cable, as sensitive information can be extracted without the user's awareness or requiring advanced developer settings.

A video recorded while the attack in phase 3 was being executed can be viewed at this supplementary video.

Testing Phase 4: O.MG Cable Connected to a Locked Device. When the O.MG cable was connected to a locked device, access was effectively blocked. The lock screen prevented unauthorized interactions and data theft, demonstrating that device authentication acts as a strong security barrier against malicious USB connections. As shown in Fig. 4, the screenshot captures the O.MG cable payload being triggered while the device is locked, but the payload fails to execute. The accompanying error message further illustrates that the phone's security measures successfully prevent unauthorized access and data exfiltration, emphasizing the importance of keeping devices locked when unattended.

A video documenting the attack in phase 4 execution was recorded; it can be viewed at this supplementary video.

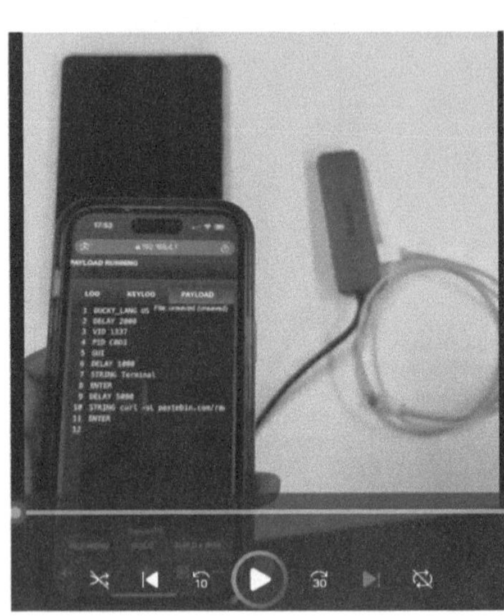

(a) O.MG Payload Triggered

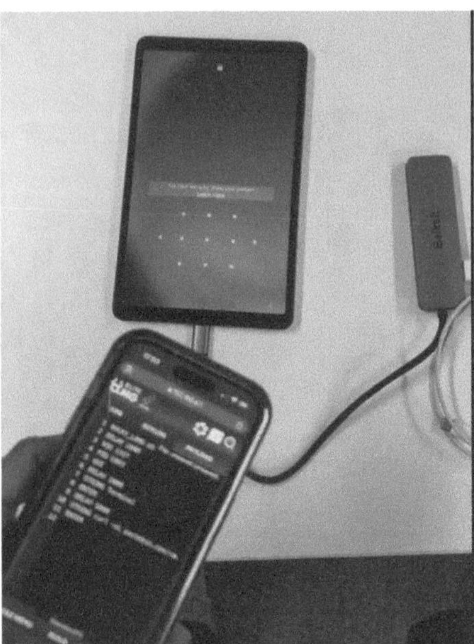

(b) O.MG Payload Triggered

Fig. 4. O.MG payload triggered while the device is locked.

6 Discussion

6.1 Implications for User Security and Privacy

This study demonstrates that USB-based attacks remain a significant threat to mobile device security, but the level of risk strongly depends on device configuration and usage behavior. The findings confirm that enabling developer options and USB debugging creates a direct pathway for data theft, validating concerns raised in earlier research on ADB misuse. Conversely, keeping these settings disabled provides a robust first line of defense.

The experiments with the O.MG cable highlight a distinct attack vector: malicious HID-based keystroke injection. Unlike classic juice-jacking, which exploits USB data channels, the O.MG cable requires an unlocked device to execute payloads. This distinction underscores a critical user behavior factor—simply keeping a phone locked while charging in untrusted environments significantly reduces the risk of compromise.

From a user security perspective, these findings reinforce three key practices: (1) disable USB debugging when not actively in use, (2) avoid interacting with the device while it is connected to public or unfamiliar chargers, and (3) prefer trusted or power-only charging sources. Beyond individual users, the results also highlight broader implications: public charging infrastructure remains vulnerable to exploitation, and manufacturers should consider stronger safeguards such as stricter default USB permissions and clearer user prompts for HID devices.

Finally, the study illustrates how experimental evaluations can uncover overlooked vulnerabilities and refine the understanding of emerging threats. By distinguishing between data-interface and HID-based attacks, this research contributes to more precise threat modeling and provides practical recommendations for reducing exposure to USB-borne risks.

Table 1 summarizes the security posture of devices across the four experimental phases. In Phase 1, with Developer Mode and USB Debugging disabled, devices remained secure, with no data leakage and minimal impact on

Table 1. Summary of Evaluation Results

Security Settings	Parameters	Data Theft			
		Device 1	Device 2	Device 3	Device 4
Sec.Set 1	P1- Time:	–	–	–	–
	P2- Popup:	No	No	No	–
	P3- Developer Mode:	No	No	No	–
	P4- USB Debug:	No	No	No	–
	P5- Data Compromised:	No	No	No	–
	P6- System Impact:	No	No	No	–
	P7- Battery Impact:	No	No	No	–
Sec.Set 2	P1- Time:	06 Min	07 Min	09 Min	–
	P2- Popup:	Yes	Yes	Yes	–
	P3- Developer Mode:	Yes	Yes	Yes	–
	P4- USB Debug:	Yes	Yes	Yes	–
	P5- Data Compromised:	Yes	Yes	Yes	–
	P6- System Impact:	Yes	Yes	Yes	–
	P7- Battery Impact:	Yes	Yes	Yes	–
Sec.Set 3	P1- Time:	–	–	–	10 Min
	P2- Popup:	–	–	–	No
	P3- Developer Mode:	–	–	–	No
	P4- USB Debug:	–	–	–	No
	P5- Data Compromised:	–	–	–	Yes
	P6- System Impact:	–	–	–	Yes
	P7- Battery Impact:	–	–	–	Yes
Sec.Set 4	P1- Time:	–	–	–	–
	P2- Popup:	–	–	–	No
	P3- Developer Mode:	–	–	–	No
	P4- USB Debug:	–	–	–	No
	P5- Data Compromised:	–	–	–	No
	P6- System Impact:	–	–	–	No
	P7- Battery Impact:	–	–	–	No

performance. In Phase 2, enabling these settings exposed devices to unauthorized access, data compromise, and noticeable system degradation. In Phase 3, connecting an unlocked device through an O.MG cable allowed remote access and data theft, while also affecting performance and battery life. In contrast, Phase 4 showed that keeping the device locked effectively blocked the O.MG cable's payloads, preserving both data security and system stability. These findings emphasize the importance of disabling debugging features, keeping devices locked while charging, and avoiding untrusted USB cables in public settings to mitigate juice jacking and HID-based threats.

6.2 Security Gaps and ADB Settings

The experiments highlight how Android's debugging and USB configurations create exploitable security gaps under everyday conditions. In particular, ADB—designed as a developer utility—offers broad access once enabled, but lacks strong safeguards to prevent abuse in non-developer scenarios. The results show that attackers can combine available features, such as debugging permissions and HID-based input injection, to bypass user awareness and gain control of the device. This suggests that the problem is not only user behavior but also the limited security boundaries around ADB itself. Strengthening default system policies, improving user prompts, and restricting background access to sensitive tools could significantly reduce these risks.

7 Mitigations and Countermeasures

7.1 System-Level Fixes

At the system level, stronger defaults and stricter permission models are essential. USB ports should remain in a charge-only state until the user explicitly authorizes data transfer, and HID-class devices should not be able to inject inputs without clear on-screen consent. Android debugging features such as ADB should be sandboxed more tightly, with temporary session-based permissions instead of persistent access. Vendors can also implement hardware-level protections, such as physically separating charging and data lines or adding "USB port protection" chips that allow only trusted accessories. These measures would significantly reduce the attack surface regardless of user behavior.

7.2 User Best Practices

When feasible, use charge-only power sources—personal power banks or AC-only chargers that physically isolate data lines—and, where public USB power is unavoidable, interpose a certified USB data blocker [20] or obtain power via vetted rental power-bank services [14]. Irrespective of the power source, keep the device locked, disable USB debugging, and refrain from device interaction while connected to untrusted infrastructure.

7.3 Policy Suggestions for Device Manufacturers

Device makers can improve safety by disabling USB data sharing, debugging, and developer mode by default, and requiring user approval for data transfers. Blocking access when the screen is locked and warning users of risky connections would further reduce threats, making devices safer in public charging environments.

8 Conclusion

This study shows that mobile devices remain vulnerable to data theft when connected to untrusted USB charging sources. Security settings, especially developer options and USB debugging, strongly influence resistance to unauthorized access—locked devices offer better protection, but risks rise sharply when devices are unlocked or advanced tools mimic compromised chargers. The research validates the practicality of juice jacking and HID-based attacks, highlighting the need to balance usability with security. Preventive measures such as disabling developer features, avoiding untrusted chargers, and using charge-only cables can block most threats, while long-term defense requires stricter USB policies, hardware-level isolation, and clearer permission controls. Overall, the findings stress that user awareness, cautious behavior, and stronger default protections are essential to limit USB-based attack surfaces, and future work should focus on automated detection, secure charging standards, and safer public infrastructure.

Future research should include testing a wider range of devices, including various Android versions and iOS, to compare platform-specific security measures. Additional USB-based attack methods such as malware injection, firmware exploitation, and power analysis warrant investigation to uncover emerging threats. Evaluating defenses like USB Restricted Mode, data-only charging cables, and third-party security apps can provide insights into effective protections. Finally, studying real-world contexts such as public charging stations in airports, hotels, and cafes would help assess practical risks and guide safer charging practices.

Disclosure of Interests. The authors declare no competing interests.

References

1. Amarante, J., Barros, J.P.: Exploring USB connection vulnerabilities on android devices breaches using the android debug bridge. In: 14th International Joint Conference on e-Business and Telecommunications, ICETE 2017, pp. 572–577. SciTePress (2017)
2. Charan, B., Kulkarni, L.: Enhancement and implementation of BadUSB attacks using microcontrollers. J. Posit. Sch. Psychol. **6**(9) (2022)
3. Federal Bureau of Investigation (FBI): FBI warns travelers: avoid public phone charging stations (2023). https://www.fbi.gov/contact-us/field-offices/denver/news/press-releases/fbi-denver-warns-against-public-phone-charging-stations. Accessed 21 June 2025

4. Fitch, E.S.: Def con hacker conference: an accidental tourist's observations. Defense Counsel J. **84**(4) (2017)
5. Kumar, Y.: Juice jacking-the USB charger scam (2020). Available at SSRN 3580209
6. Lawal, D., Gresty, D., Gan, D., Hewitt, L.: Facilitating a cyber-enabled fraud using the o. mg cable to incriminate the victim. Int. J. Comput. Syst. Eng. (Int. Scholarly Sci. Res. Innov.) **16**(9), 367–372 (2022)
7. Liu, H., Spolaor, R., Turrin, F., Bonafede, R., Conti, M.: USB powered devices: a survey of side-channel threats and countermeasures. High-Confid. Comput. **1**(1), 100007 (2021)
8. Lu, H., Wu, Y., Li, S., Lin, Y., Zhang, C., Zhang, F.: BadUSB-C: revisiting BADUSB with type-C. In: 2021 IEEE Security and Privacy Workshops (SPW), pp. 327–338. IEEE (2021)
9. Lu, H., Helu, X., Jin, C., Sun, Y., Zhang, M., Tian, Z.: Salaxy: enabling USB debugging mode automatically to control android devices. IEEE Access **7**, 178321–178330 (2019)
10. Mohammad Ali Pour, F., Rashidi, M.: Red teamer gadgets. Red Teamer Gadgets (2024)
11. NordLayer: 79% of business travelers are at risk due to public USB ports (2023). https://nordlayer.com/blog/juice-jacking-attack/. Accessed 21 June 2025
12. Opasiak, K., Mazurczyk, W.: (in) secure android debugging: security analysis and lessons learned. Comput. Secur. **82**, 80–98 (2019)
13. Potockỳ, S., Štulrajter, J.: The human interface device (HID) attack on android lock screen non-biometric protections and its computational complexity. Sci. Milit. J. **17**(1), 29–36 (2022)
14. Sharing, P.: Powerbank sharing service (2025). https://www.powerbanksharing.net/. Accessed 05 Mar 2025
15. Singh, D., Biswal, A.K., Samanta, D., Singh, D., Lee, H.N.: Juice jacking: security issues and improvements in USB technology. Sustainability **14**(2), 939 (2022)
16. Stavrou, A., Wang, Z.: Exploiting Smart-Phone USB Connectivity for Fun and Profit. BlackHat DC (2011)
17. Subramanian, G.V., Suthendran, K., Sankralingam, S.: Comprehensive security measures for mobile phones: protecting against information theft. In: 2024 International Conference on Computing and Intelligent Reality Technologies (ICCIRT), pp. 1–5. IEEE (2024)
18. Tian, J., Scaife, N., Kumar, D., Bailey, M., Bates, A., Butler, K.: SoK: "plug & pray" today–understanding USB insecurity in versions 1 through C. In: 2018 IEEE Symposium on Security and Privacy (SP), pp. 1032–1047. IEEE (2018)
19. Ullström, A., Brekstad Wijk, J.: Skydd mot O.MG-kabelattacker: En studie om mjukvarulosningar och säkerhetsatgärder (2024)
20. Veerasamy, N.: The threat of juice jacking. In: Proceedings of the ECCWS 2021 20th European Conference on Cyber Warfare and Security, p. 449. Academic Conferences Inter Ltd. Montreal, QC, Canada (2021)
21. van Vliet, M.E.: Novel USB rubber ducky payloads and detection mechanisms
22. Yang, Q.: Exploiting power for smartphone security and privacy (2017)

Smart Card Vulnerabilities in Sri Lanka: A Security Assessment Across Service Providers

Mewni Alahakoon[1(✉)], Asanka Sayakkara[1], Buddhima Weerasinghe[1], and Akila Wickramasekara[2]

[1] University of Colombo School of Computing, Colombo, Sri Lanka
mewnialahakoon@gmail.com
[2] School of Computer Science, University College Dublin, Dublin, Ireland

Abstract. Smart cards are widely used in banking and telecommunications for their enhanced security over magnetic stripes, incorporating cryptographic chips compliant with standards like ISO/IEC 14443 and EMV. However, they remain vulnerable to attacks. This study experimentally evaluates the security of Sri Lankan smart cards using Flipper Zero and HackRF One. Eleven NFC reading scenarios were tested, resulting in Total Security Scores for five cards, with the Bank 1 card scoring highest (0.490) and the Bank 4 card lowest (0.297). While jamming and replay attacks were unsuccessful due to robust EMV anti-collision mechanisms and strict ISO/IEC 14443 physical-layer specifications, the extracted card data (number and expiration date) was found to be critically vulnerable to exploitation. Practical verification confirmed that entering only this data was sufficient to initiate free trials on platforms like Adobe Pro in multiple countries (e.g., USA, UK), which automatically convert to paid subscriptions. This demonstrates a significant real-world risk where stolen card data can be monetized despite the cards' physical security protections.

Keywords: Smart cards · NFC security · Flipper Zero · jamming attacks · replay attacks

1 Introduction

Smart cards have become integral to modern digital ecosystems and are now embedded in banking, telecommunications, access control, and transportation systems worldwide [13]. Their cryptographic capabilities offer advantages over magnetic stripe cards, yet vulnerabilities persist due to inconsistent implementations and the rapid evolution of attack tools.

In Sri Lanka, smart cards are widely deployed across critical sectors such as banking and telecommunications, with EMV-based debit and credit cards forming the backbone of digital financial transactions [6]. However, limited peer-reviewed research exists on the actual security posture of Sri Lankan-issued smart

R. N. Rajapakse et al. (Eds.): ICTer 2025, CCIS 2844, pp. 471–485, 2026.
https://doi.org/10.1007/978-981-92-0137-2_31

cards in real-world conditions. The Central Bank of Sri Lanka has published regulatory guidance [6], but there is little evidence of independent technical assessments to validate whether these cards can withstand emerging NFC-based threats. This absence of empirical evidence creates a knowledge gap with potential consequences for both service providers and consumers.

The rationale for this study is to systematically evaluate the resilience of Sri Lankan smart cards against practical attacks that reflect real adversarial scenarios. Specifically, we focus on three types of NFC-based threats: unauthorized data extraction, signal jamming, and replay attacks using accessible hardware platforms such as Flipper Zero and HackRF One. By experimentally benchmarking multiple bank-issued cards, this study aims to reveal variations in protection levels, highlight systemic weaknesses, and provide evidence-based recommendations for strengthening payment card security in Sri Lanka.

Therefore, the objective of this work is to (1) quantify the susceptibility of smart cards to NFC data extraction, (2) test their resilience to jamming and replay attacks. This paper addresses a critical research gap by presenting the first systematic security evaluation of Sri Lankan smart cards, linking experimental outcomes to global attack trends, and offering actionable insights for improving consumer protection.

The rest of this paper is organized as follows. Section 2 reviews related work on smart card vulnerabilities and NFC security. Section 3 details the methodology, including experimental setups for NFC reading, jamming, and replay attacks using Flipper Zero and HackRF One. Section 4 presents the results, analyzing security scores for tested cards and the outcomes of attack simulations. Finally, Sect. 5 has the discussion and the conclusion section.

2 Related Work

Smart cards and NFC-based systems are widely deployed in banking, telecommunications, and identity management worldwide. Although EMV standards introduced stronger cryptographic protections than magnetic stripes, a substantial body of research continues to expose critical vulnerabilities. These can be broadly categorised into attacks on implementation, protocol, and authentication.

A significant area of research focuses on practical hardware and side-channel attacks. Studies have demonstrated that side-channel analysis, such as power analysis, can extract cryptographic keys from cards using algorithms like 3DES with a feasible number of traces [2]. Furthermore, fault injection techniques, including voltage glitching, electromagnetic pulses, and lasers, are both practical and affordable for individual attackers [5]. The severity of such attacks is starkly illustrated by the complete compromise of a Korean transit card system, where a side-channel attack recovered the 128-bit authentication key, allowing for unlimited card recharging [12].

Beyond hardware, logical and protocol-level flaws within the complex EMV specifications present another significant risk. Research has identified severe vulnerabilities, including pre-play attacks where an attacker can manipulate the terminal's random number, as well as methods to bypass PIN verification for contactless payments [3,4]. These findings reveal that logical flaws can undermine transaction security even when the underlying cryptography remains sound. The NFC interface itself also introduces threats, such as relay attacks, where signals from a contactless card can be intercepted and transmitted to a remote terminal using readily available hardware, effectively bypassing proximity defences [7].

Concurrently, research into strengthening defences continues. Novel authentication protocols like SAP-NFC have been proposed to offer enhanced security against replay and impersonation attacks for mobile payments [14]. Other studies have explored the fundamental security limitations of public-key cryptography in smart card settings [16] and proposed new anti-cloning mechanisms for SIM cards to address vulnerabilities in mobile network authentication [17].

Globally, the vulnerabilities identified in the literature translate into tangible security risks. However, in Sri Lanka, while the Central Bank's mandate for EMV migration significantly reduced cloning fraud, reliable data on NFC-specific threats remains limited. The reviewed global literature demonstrates a clear gap: a lack of empirical, comparative research evaluating the real-world resilience of smart cards issued in Sri Lanka. This study addresses that gap by experimentally testing cards from local issuers against a suite of practical attacks, providing the first structured assessment of their security posture.

3 Methodology

This section describes the experimental framework used to evaluate the security of smart cards employed by Sri Lankan service providers, including the experimental procedures, tools, environments, and analytical models employed to assess the security of the targeted smart cards. This study simulates three practical experiments: NFC Reading using Flipper Zero, signal jamming using HackRF One, and replay attack simulation.

3.1 Card Selection

In total, nine NFC-enabled smart cards were tested across experiments. Five cards, each from a different Sri Lankan bank, were selected as the primary dataset for all three experiments (Flipper Zero, jamming, and replay). Additionally, four supplementary cards from other banks were explicitly included to enhance diversity in card response analysis, specifically for jamming and replay attacks. Throughout the paper, the five primary cards are referred to as Bank 1 through Bank 5, while the supplementary cards are denoted as Bank 6 through Bank 9.

These cards were chosen based on their widespread use, support for contactless NFC transactions, and representation of credit, debit, and prepaid formats. All experiments were conducted in a controlled indoor environment to eliminate ambient radio interference and to ensure repeatability. The experimental setup was designed to simulate realistic adversarial conditions.

3.2 Threat Model

A threat model was established to contextualise the experiments. The adversary is assumed to have brief physical proximity to the victim (e.g., in a crowded public space) and possesses commercially available, portable hardware. The adversarial objectives are: (i) the passive harvesting of card data (specifically the Primary Account Number (PAN) and expiration date), (ii) the disruption of transaction communication via jamming, or (iii) the execution of a replay attack. A successful data extraction event is defined as obtaining the PAN and expiration date, which this study demonstrates is sufficient for fraudulent activity in specific online payment environments.

3.3 Tools and Equipments

The experiments employed a combination of specialised hardware and software tools. The Flipper Zero [1] was used for NFC reading attempts, leveraging its capability to interact with RFID/NFC systems. The HackRF One [9] software-defined radio (SDR) facilitated jamming and replay attacks due to its broad frequency range (1 MHz–6 GHz). GNU Radio Companion [8] designed and transmitted jamming/replay signals, while GQRX monitored signal characteristics during attacks. Python and Jupyter Notebook supported data analysis, including plotting signal data and spectrograms.

3.4 Experiment Setup for Flipper Zero Experiments

The objective of this experiment is to simulate the attacker's ability to extract the card information through passive scanning under various physical setups. The Flipper Zero was employed exclusively for NFC data extraction experiments, simulating an attacker's ability to harvest card information through passive scanning. Unlike HackRF, which was used for signal manipulation (jamming and replay), Flipper Zero was chosen due to its portability and widespread availability as a consumer-grade penetration testing tool, thereby representing a realistic adversarial device.

To carry out these experiments, five primary cards were used for the 11 scenarios, as shown in Table 1, and data were collected, including the number of successful reads, the time required to extract data, and the type of information retrieved. Each of the five cards was used to experiment with the scenarios. The first scenario involved reading a one-card using the Flipper Zero by placing the card on the table, and this scenario was carried out 20 times. Second, two cards were stacked on the table and checked to see what kind of data could be read, whether either of the cards could be read thoroughly or partially. For the third scenario, three cards were stacked on a table and checked to determine what kind of data could be read. In the fourth scenario, one card was placed inside a *PU Leather* wallet and an attempt was made to check whether any data could be read or not, and whether the read data was full or partial. In the fifth scenario, two cards were placed inside a PU Leather wallet, and an attempt was

Table 1. Experimental Scenarios for NFC Reading with Flipper Zero

Test Scenario	Number of Attempts
Read each of 5 different cards (baseline test)	20 per card
Read 2 stacked cards (any combination)	5 attempts
Read 3 stacked cards (any combination)	5 attempts
Read 1 card inside a wallet	5 attempts
Read 2 stacked cards inside a wallet	5 attempts
Read 3 stacked cards inside a wallet	5 attempts
Read at 1 cm distance	2 attempts
Read at 2 cm distance	2 attempts
Read at 3 cm distance	2 attempts
Read at 4 cm distance	2 attempts
Read at 5 cm distance	2 attempts

made to check whether any data could be read or not, and whether the read data was full or partial. In the sixth scenario, the same process was repeated for three cards. Apart from these experiments, another set of experiments was conducted by placing the Flipper Zero at various distances, ranging from 1 cm to 5 cm, from all five cards, and checking whether the cards could be read or not. Different numbers of trials were chosen for each test scenario, depending on its purpose. For baseline tests, such as reading a single card without shielding, more trials (e.g., 20) were conducted to obtain reliable data and observe consistency. For conditions that mainly test the limits, such as stacked cards, cards inside a wallet, or distance-based tests, fewer trials (e.g., 2 or 5) were sufficient to assess feasibility without unnecessary repetition. This approach enabled the efficient use of time while providing meaningful insights into security under various conditions.

3.5 Theoretical Framework for Calculating the Scores

This section presents the theoretical framework and mathematical derivations used to compute trial-level and overall security scores. The scoring model quantifies the difficulty of reading a card using unauthorised NFC tools under different scenarios. The security scoring model presented in this study is a novel contribution to the field. All formulations are original to this work.

Trial-Level Security Score (S_i). The trial-level security score S_i evaluates the security of a card in a single read attempt. It considers both the amount of data successfully read and the time it took to complete the read.

We define the *Read Success Ratio* as follows:

$$\text{Read Success Ratio} = \frac{\text{Total Read Score}}{\text{Max Read Score}} \tag{1}$$

This ratio is a normalised measure of how much data was read. The total read score is based on a weighted sum of read states: unread (0), partial (0.5), and full (1), with respective weights for data quality (0.25, 0.75, 1.0).

For trials conducted outside a wallet, S_i is calculated using:

$$S_i = w_r \cdot (1 - \text{Read Success Ratio}) + w_t \cdot \frac{T_i}{T_{\max}} \tag{2}$$

Here, $w_r = 0.7$ represents the importance of the read outcome, and $w_t = 0.3$ represents the time factor. T_i is the time taken for the trial, and $T_{\max}$ is the maximum observed time across all tests.

For trials conducted inside a wallet, a penalty term is added if any read occurs:

$$S_i = w_r \cdot (1 - (\text{Read Success Ratio} + P \cdot \text{If Read Occurred})) + w_t \cdot \frac{T_i}{T_{\max}} \tag{3}$$

The penalty coefficient P is set to 0.2. If a read occurs, If Read Occurred = 1; otherwise, it is 0.

Heatmap Security Score (S_{heatmap}). The heatmap score represents the average trial-level security score under a single test condition, such as reading inside a wallet or at a specific distance.

$$S_{\text{heatmap}} = \frac{1}{N_{\text{trials}}} \sum_{i=1}^{N_{\text{trials}}} S_i \tag{4}$$

Here, N_{trials} is the number of attempts in a given scenario. The heatmap helps visualise which conditions are more secure.

Total Security Score (S_{total}). The total security score aggregates performance across all scenarios into a single metric. It combines full and partial read rates, timing, distance, and wallet shielding resistance.

$$S_{\text{total}} = w_1 \cdot (1 - R_{\text{avg}}) + w_2 \cdot (1 - P_{r_{\text{avg}}}) + w_3 \cdot T_{\text{norm}} + w_4 \cdot D_{\text{norm}} + w_5 \cdot S_{\text{purse}} \tag{5}$$

R_{avg} is the average rate of full reads. $P_{r_{\text{avg}}}$ is the average rate of partial reads. T_{norm} is the normalized time score. D_{norm} reflects distance-based resistance. S_{purse} represents average performance in wallet scenarios. The weights are: $w_1 = 0.25$, $w_2 = 0.15$, $w_3 = 0.2$, $w_4 = 0.2$, and $w_5 = 0.2$.

Weights for full reads, partial reads, timing, distance resistance, and wallet shielding (w1–w5) were set after empirical exploration. The security scores are normalised, with a theoretical range of 0 to 1. For interpretation, a higher score indicates better security (i.e., it was harder to read the card). Based on the distribution of scores observed in this study, we propose the following preliminary benchmarks: Low Security (<0.30), Medium Security (0.30–0.44), High Security (≥0.45). These ranges can be refined with a larger sample size in future work.

3.6 Experimental Setup for Jamming Attack

The experimental setup to carry out the jamming attacks is explained in this section. Nine different cards from various banks were tested against jamming attacks, including the five main cards. Figure 1 illustrates the lab setup for carrying out the jamming attacks, while Table 2 (left table) summarises the complete jamming parameters. The hardware components, software components and the Jamming signal characteristics and parameters that were set up in the GNU Radio Companion are also discussed under this section. For the hardware components, the HackRF One was used for noise signal generation and transmission, and an antenna tuned to 13.56 MHz (the frequency used by NFC) was used to transmit the noise. For the software components, GNU Radio was used to design and transmit the noise signal. Python, with Jupyter Notebook, was used to plot the signal plots and spectrograms. GQRX was used for spectrogram analysis to monitor the effectiveness of the jamming.

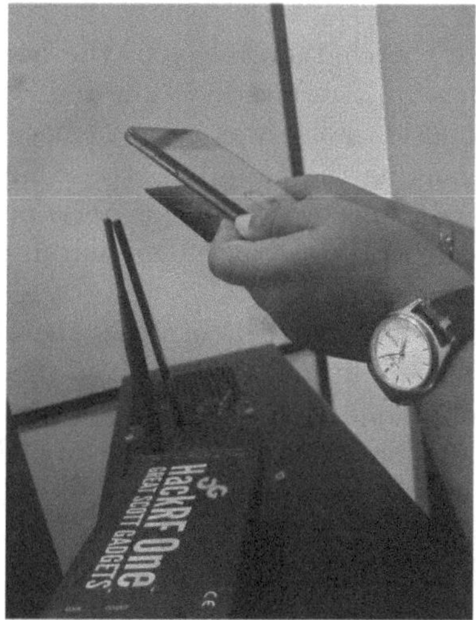

Fig. 1. Lab Setup for Jamming Attack

In this experiment, a jamming attack is done by using a Gaussian noise source to interfere with the NFC signal. The setup is designed to transmit Gaussian Noise at a frequency of 13.56 MHz [11] and at different power levels to disrupt standard signal transmission. The parameters set up in GNU Radio are carefully chosen to analyse the effectiveness of the jamming attack in a real-life scenario. Figure 2 illustrates the GNU Radio flowgraph used with the settings.

The signal used for jamming was generated by a Gaussian noise source, utilising GNU Radio, which produces random noise with a normal distribution. Gaussian noise is commonly used in jamming attacks due to its close resemblance to naturally occurring interference, making it harder to detect and mitigate the

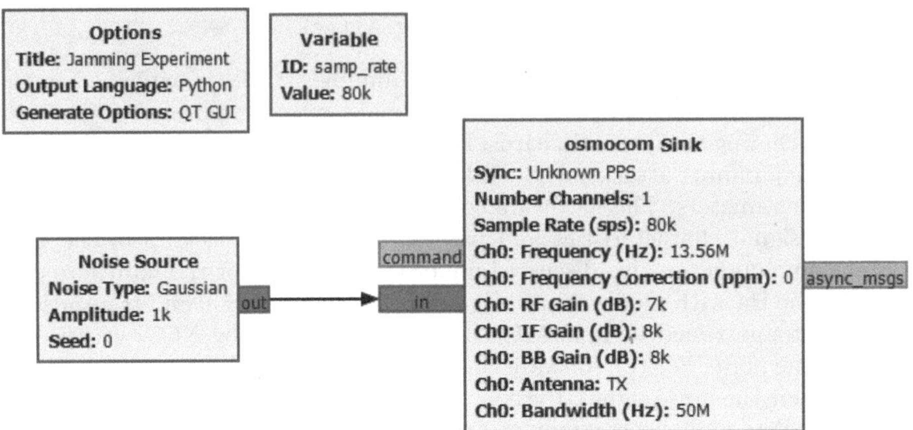

Fig. 2. GNU radio companion flow graph

attack. The following are the characteristics of the noise source of the experiment. Noise type is Gaussian, Amplitude is 1k, and Seed Value is 0 (fixed for reproducibility). The Gaussian noise was selected because it simulates natural interference conditions, making the jamming attack harder to detect and more realistic. The amplitude of 1k ensures sufficient noise power to disrupt the NFC signal, while the seed value of 0 was chosen to guarantee reproducibility of the noise pattern across experiments.

The amplitude of the noise signal determines the strength of the jamming effect, and the higher the amplitude, the stronger the interference, which can overwhelm the target communication system with the noise signal. NFC communication is transmitted at a carrier frequency of 13.56 MHz, and for this experiment, the frequency at which the noise was transmitted is also 13.56 MHz, with a bandwidth of 50 MHz. The wide 50 MHz bandwidth enables the jammer to cover a significant range of frequencies, thereby increasing the likelihood of disrupting the targeted signal. The jamming signal is processed and transmitted with a sample rate of 80 kHz, TX (Transmission Mode) as the antenna mode, and a number of channels of 1. The sample rate determines the resolution of the generated Gaussian Noise, while the antenna mode TX ensures that the antenna is transmitting the noise actively rather than receiving any signals. The jamming signal was generated with a noise bandwidth of 50 MHz to ensure broad spectral coverage. At the same time, a sample rate of 80 kHz was used to achieve signal resolution, with no contradiction between these parameters. RF Gain, IF Gain, and BB Gain parameters were adjusted to control the signal strength, and these types of gains determine how much the transmitted noise signal is amplified at different stages. The adjusted parameters for the various types of gains are 7 dB for the RF Gain (Radio Frequency Gain), 7dB for the IF Gain (Intermediate Frequency Gain) and 8 dB for the BB Gain (Baseband Gain), respectively. Each of these gain types contributes to the overall power of the noise signal.

In this experiment, the Frequency Correction parameter (specified in parts per million, ppm) is set to 0, resulting in no additional correction being applied when transmitting the noise signal. As a result, the signal is transmitted exactly at 13.56 MHz without any deviation in frequency.

The experimental procedure for the jamming attack is described in this section. Two HackRF One devices were used to do this jamming attack. One was used to transmit the jamming signal, and the other was used to capture the signal coming from the NFC Reader and the jamming signal, and then used GQRX to view the spectrogram.

3.7 Experimental Setup for Replay Attack

This section explains the experimental setup for conducting replay attacks. The hardware components, software components and the Replay signal characteristics and parameters are discussed in this section. For the hardware components, the HackRF One was used to capture the NFC signal and replay it for the replay attack, and a looped antenna tuned to 13.56 MHz was used to transmit the noise. For software components, GNU Radio was used to design and transmit the noise signal, and GQRX was used for spectrogram analysis to monitor the replay signal. As this experiment focuses on the replay signal characteristics and parameters (detailed in the right table of Table 2), for saving the signal, the sample rate 20 MHz is used with the frequency of 13.56 MHz and with the RF Gain set to 10 dB, IF gain set to 20dB, and BB Gain set to 30 dB. After saving the signal, it is necessary to re-emit it to perform the replay attack. As in the GNU Radio flowgraph below (see Fig. 3), by using the File Source the saved signal(captured in a file) imported and by utilising a osmocom Sink, that

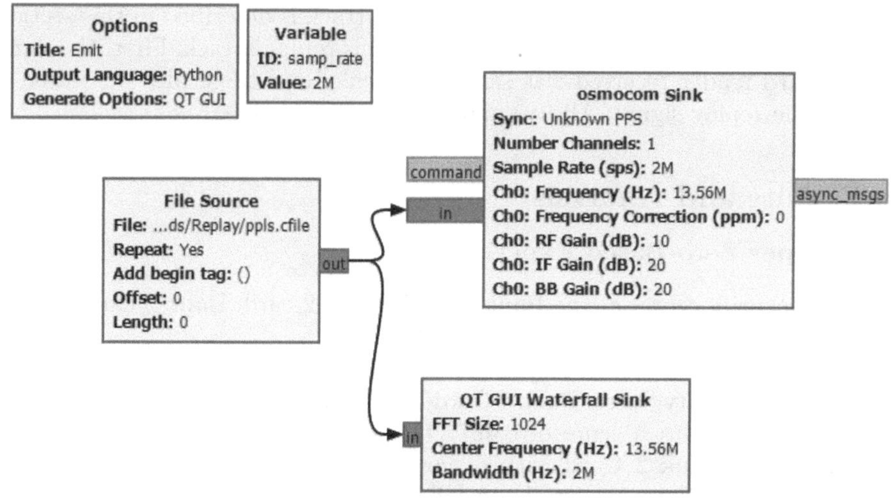

Fig. 3. Retransmitting the saved signal

Table 2. Experimental Parameters for Jamming and Replay Attacks

Jamming Attack Parameters	
Noise Type	Gaussian
Amplitude	1k
Seed Value	0 (fixed)
Distribution	Normal
Carrier Frequency	13.56 MHz
Bandwidth	50 MHz
Frequency Correction	0 ppm
Sample Rate	80 kHz
Antenna Mode	TX
Channels	1
RF Gain	7 dB
IF Gain	7 dB
BB Gain	8 dB
Devices Used	2 HackRF One
Cards Tested	9

Replay Attack Parameters	
Capture Sample Rate	20 MHz
Capture Frequency	13.56 MHz
Capture RF Gain	10 dB
Capture IF Gain	20 dB
Capture BB Gain	30 dB
Replay Sample Rate	20 MHz
Replay Frequency	13.56 MHz
Replay RF Gain	10 dB
Replay IF Gain	20 dB
Replay BB Gain	20 dB
File Format	.cfile
Software	GNU Radio
Key Block	Osmocom Sink
Devices Used	1 HackRF One
Cards Tested	9

imported captured and saved signal is transmitted by setting the variables such as sample rate to 20 MHz, frequency to emit the signal as 13.56 MHzs, RF Gain, IF Gain and BB Gains are assigned as 10 dB, 20 dB and 20 dB respectively. The Osmocom Sink is a GNU Radio block that interfaces with software-defined radios (SDRs), such as HackRF, to transmit signals by converting baseband samples to RF output [15].

The experimental procedure for the replay attack is described in this section. One HackRF One device was used to perform this replay attack. First, the signal that the card reader received was saved as a .cfile, and these files were used to transmit the replay signal. All five main cards were used.

4 Results and Analysis

4.1 Flipper Zero-Based Experiments

The total security scores of the Bank 1 card, Bank 2 card, Bank 3 card, Bank 4 card, and Bank 5 card are as shown in Table 3.

The security scores of the respective cards are presented in descending order of their Total Security Score. Bank 1 Card has the highest score of 0.490, followed by Bank 3 Card with a score of 0.487. Third is Bank 5 Card with a score of 0.469, fourth is Bank 2 Card with a score of 0.421, and last is Bank 4 Card with a score of 0.297. During the Adobe Pro free trial subscription process, it was observed that selecting the USA as the country only required the card number and expiration date, omitting the CVV. This practice was also observed

Table 3. Total security scores of selected credit/debit cards

Card Name	Total Security Score
Bank 1 Card	0.490
Bank 3 Card	0.487
Bank 5 Card	0.469
Bank 2 Card	0.421
Bank 4 Card	0.297

in the UK, Denmark, Finland, and France, where CVV was not required for initiating free trials. To verify this, the USA was selected, and the free trial was successfully obtained using only the card number and expiration date, with billing set to begin automatically after the trial period.

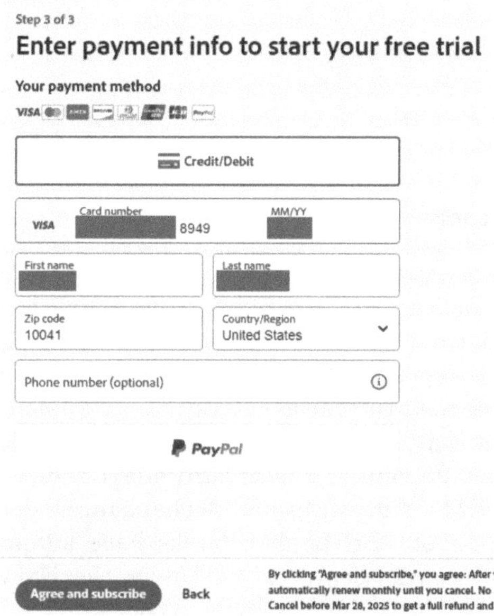

Fig. 4. Card Details entering with only card number and the expiration month and year without the CVV when selecting the country as USA

In Sri Lanka, if an attacker used a Flipper Zero to attempt reading bank cards inside a wallet (a common real-life scenario where the card is not physically accessible to see the card number, expiration date and CVV, but the attacker knows it might be inside a wallet typically carried in a back pocket), they could obtain the necessary details for such transactions. Screenshots of the card detail entry (with USA selected) and the confirmation screen are shown in Fig. 4 and 5.

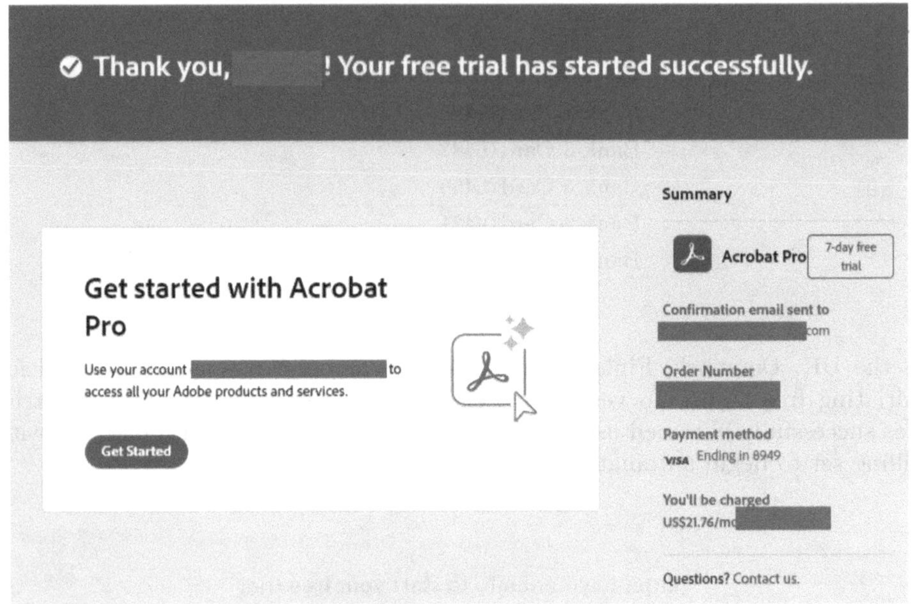

Fig. 5. Confirmation Screen

4.2 Jamming Attacks

A jamming attack was experimented with using nine cards, including the five main cards used for the Flipper Zero Experiment. The Fig. 6 shows the relevant result of the Bank 1 card that was subjected to the jamming attack. As we can see, the jamming signal peak exceeds the NFC signal peak. Despite that, the NFC Card Reader read the cards without any trouble because the jamming attacks were unsuccessful.

All of the jamming attempts for each card failed due to several reasons. One of the reasons is the EMV Anti-Collision Mechanism. Under the guidance of the Central Bank of Sri Lanka, Sri Lankan banks have adopted EMV chip-based cards with enhanced security features [6]. Under the EMV Anti The collision mechanism manages multiple NFC signals. When an interference is detected, the NFC reader prioritises the legitimate bank card's signal based on the UIDs and halts communication with unrecognisable sources, making jamming attacks ineffective. Another reason for the failure of the jamming attack is robust signal modulation. NFC uses ASK (Amplitude Shift Keying) modulation at a frequency of 13.56 MHz, as specified in the ISO/IEC 14443-2 protocol [10]. This ASK modulation can resist jamming attacks by filtering out noise and maintaining the integrity of the relevant credit/debit card. Attempts to overpower the 13.56 MHz NFC signal were unsuccessful due to the credit/debit card's ability to retransmit data once the interference ceased, a feature supported by the protocol. The combination of the EMV Anti-Collision mechanism and ISO/IEC

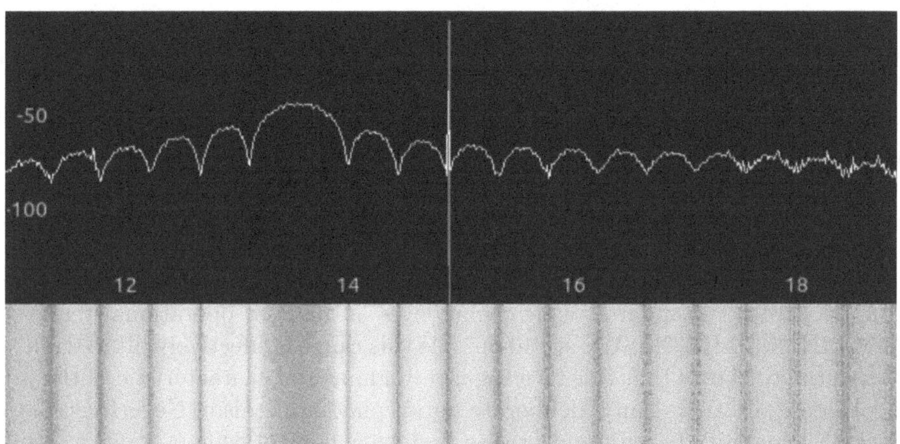

Fig. 6. A jamming signal overpowering the NFC signals, yet the transaction succeeded, highlighting inherent resilience to interference.

14443-2 [10] robust signal design ensures that the jamming attacks were ineffective against the Sri Lankan Credit/Debit cards. These findings suggest that, at present, the implemented technologies provide sufficient protection against signal jamming.

4.3 Replay Attacks

The experimental results from replay attacks revealed a critical frequency deviation, as demonstrated by the Bank 2 card analysis shown in Fig. 7.

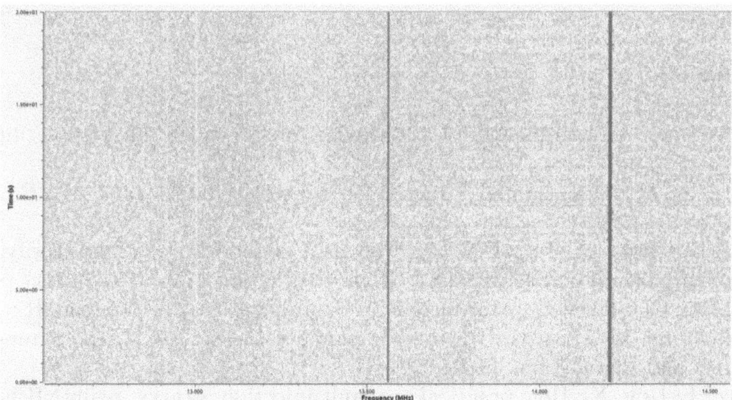

Fig. 7. Frequency analysis showing the replayed signal deviated to 14.20 MHz, outside the ISO/IEC 14443 tolerance band (13.56 MHz ± 7 kHz), causing the attack to fail.

Although the NFC signal was intended to be retransmitted at 13.56 MHz [10], spectral analysis revealed the actual transmission occurred at approximately 14.20 MHz, a deviation of roughly 640 kHz. This significant frequency shift caused the NFC reader to reject the signal, rendering the replay attack unsuccessful. The deviation is attributed to hardware limitations of the HackRF One, primarily due to drift in its internal 10 MHz crystal oscillator resulting from environmental factors such as temperature fluctuations or manufacturing inaccuracies.

This outcome aligns with the strict physical-layer specifications of the ISO/IEC 14443 standard, which mandates a narrow operational band of 13.56 MHz $\pm$ 7 kHz [11]. Any signal outside this range is effectively filtered out. It is essential to clarify that this filtering is a fundamental characteristic of the protocol's design rather than a deliberate anti-replay mechanism. Nevertheless, the HackRF's inability to maintain precise frequency control demonstrates a significant technical barrier to executing replay attacks, thereby inadvertently enhancing the practical resilience of NFC systems against such imprecise attempts.

5 Conclusion

This study provided the first practical security assessment of NFC smart cards in Sri Lanka. While cards proved resilient to jamming and replay attacks due to EMV standards, they showed vulnerability to data extraction via accessible tools. We demonstrated that skimmed card data can bypass CVV checks in specific online systems, revealing a critical flaw in the payment ecosystem. Urgent measures are needed to reduce NFC data exposure and strengthen global authentication policies.

Disclosure of Interests. The authors have no competing interests to declare that are relevant to the content of this article.

References

1. Flipper Zero — Portable Multi-tool Device for Geeks (2025). https://flipperzero.one/
2. Xu, R., et al.: Side-channel attack on a protected RFID card. IEEE Access **6**, 58395–58404 (2018)
3. Basin, D., Sasse, R., Toro-Pozo, J.: The EMV standard: break, fix, verify. In: 2021 IEEE Symposium on Security and Privacy (SP), pp. 1766–1781 (2021)
4. Bond, M., Choudary, O., Murdoch, S.J., Skorobogatov, S., Anderson, R.: Chip and skim: cloning EMV cards with the pre-play attack. In: 2014 IEEE Symposium on Security and Privacy, pp. 49–64 (2014)
5. Breier, J., Hou, X.: How practical are fault injection attacks, really? IEEE Access **10**, 113122–113130 (2022)
6. Central Bank of Sri Lanka: Ensuring the safety of payment card transactions (2019). https://www.cbsl.gov.lk/en/new/ensuring-the-safety-of-payment-card-transactions

7. Chothia, T., Garcia, F.D., De Ruiter, J., Van Den Breekel, J., Thompson, M.: Relay cost bounding for contactless EMV payments, pp. 189–206 (2015)
8. GNU Radio Foundation, Inc.: GNU Radio Companion (2001–2025). https://www.gnuradio.org/
9. Great Scott Gadgets: HackRF One (2009–2023). https://greatscottgadgets.com/hackrf/one/
10. International Organization for Standardization: ISO/IEC 14443-2:2016 — Identification cards — Contactless integrated circuit cards — Proximity cards — Part 2: Radio frequency power and signal interface (2016). https://www.iso.org/standard/73595.html
11. International Organization for Standardization: ISO/IEC 14443-1:2018 — Cards and security devices for personal identification — Contactless proximity objects — Part 1: Physical characteristics (2018). https://www.iso.org/standard/73594.html
12. Kim, T.W., Kim, T.H., Hong, S.: Breaking Korea Transit Card with Side-Channel Analysis Attack - Unauthorized Recharging -. BlackHat (2017). Accessed 26 Apr 2024
13. Mayes, K.: An introduction to smart cards. In: Mayes, K., Markantonakis, K. (eds.) Smart Cards, Tokens, Security and Applications, pp. 1–29. Springer (2017). https://doi.org/10.1007/978-3-319-50500-8_1
14. Nashwan, S.: Secure authentication protocol for NFC mobile payment systems. IJCSNS Int. J. Comput. Sci. Netw. Secur. **17**(8) (2017)
15. Osmocom Project: Osmocom GNU Radio Blocks (gr-osmosdr) (2011–2025). https://osmocom.org/projects/gr-osmosdr/wiki
16. Tian, Y., Li, Q., Hu, J., et al.: Secure limitation analysis of public-key cryptography for smart card settings. World Wide Web **23**, 1423–1440 (2020)
17. Zidouni, N., Chitroub, S., Chebout, H., Boukais, N.: New safety measure to protect the 3g/4g sim cards against cloning. In: 2018 International Conference on Selected Topics in Mobile and Wireless Networking (MoWNeT), pp. 1–8 (2018)

Author Index

R. N. Rajapakse et al. (Eds.): ICTer 2025, CCIS 2844, pp. 487–488, 2026.
https://doi.org/10.1007/978-981-92-0137-2

Zeitfracht Medien GmbH
Ferdinand-Jühlke-Straße 7
99095 Erfurt, Deutschland
produktsicherheit@kolibri360.de